World Political Patterns

Maps by WILLIS R. HEATH
University of Washington

LEWIS M. ALEXANDER

University of Rhode Island

World Political Patterns

Second Edition

RAND M^cNALLY & COMPANY - Chicago
JOHN MURRAY - London

Rand McNally Geography Series

Edward B. Espenshade, Jr., ADVISORY EDITOR

AAG Monograph Series
1. Hartshorne, *Perspective on the Nature of Geography*
2. Meinig, *On the Margins of the Good Earth*
3. Alexander, *Offshore Geography of Northwestern Europe*

Alexander, *World Political Patterns*, 2nd Edition
de Blij, *A Geography of Subsaharan Africa*
Espenshade, ed., *Goode's World Atlas*, 12th Edition
Espenshade, ed., *Rand McNally Regional Atlas*, 2nd Edition
Highsmith, Jensen, Rudd, *Conservation in the United States*
Murphey, *An Introduction to Geography*

THIS BOOK IS SET IN INTERTYPE BASKERVILLE
COMPOSITION, PRINTING, AND BINDING BY RAND McNALLY & COMPANY
BOOK DESIGN BY GORDON HARTSHORNE AND GEORGETTE ROUX

To Jacqueline

CONTENTS

LIST OF MAPS

LIST OF TABLES

PREFACE

● This book is the product of several years of teaching regional political geography, and it represents an attempt to analyze the complex pattern of political units throughout the world. On the global or continental scale consideration is given to such forces as nationalism, imperialism, and economic competition, as they influence the political control of territory. On a more restricted scale national and local aspects of the political pattern are studied. At all levels of observation primary emphasis is placed on the nature of political control in a given region, on the effect of control on non-political aspects of the landscape, and on the pressures which exist for change in the type and areal extent of this control. This approach has been selected with two objectives in mind. First, it offers an opportunty for the student to become acquainted with the existing pattern of political units on the earth's surface and with some of the territorial problems attendant upon this geographic distribution. Second, by means of generalizations and sample studies of particular situations, it enables him to gain insight into the basic principles of the field of political geography, thereby equipping him to analyze in more detail the conditions of sovereignty throughout the world and to understand future problems of territorial control as they may arise.

The task of analyzing the world political pattern is complicated, first, by the great number and variety of political units and, second, by the constantly changing nature of the pattern. In order to produce a concise book, suitable for teaching purposes, much material had to be sacrificed, but it is hoped that the lack of detail in many cases will be more than offset by the attempt at clearness of purpose and the adherence to a rigid definition of what the field of political geography encompasses. One of my principal reasons for writing this book was to answer those critics who claim that most college courses in political geography adhere to no clearly defined area of study, and that as a result world political geography has become virtually indistinguishable from the general field of world regional geography. As for the changing nature of the world political pattern, I can only hope to outline some of the basic forces now in operation and to suggest the types of changes in territorial control which are likely to occur in years to come.

The book is intended to serve two purposes: as an introduction to political geography and as a presentation of the geographic basis of international affairs. In any study of the political units of the world there are many elements of common interest to both fields, although the student of political geography approaches the material from the standpoint of the geography of political areas, while the student of international affairs is concerned primarily with the interactions which take place between States. It seems unnecessary to superimpose an artificial boundary through the area of study common to both disciplines. Since the purpose of this text is to consider the world distribution of political units, the relevancy of both political geography and international affairs is clearly acknowledged.

To my many colleagues who have helped with the preparation of this text I am deeply indebted. Among these special acknowledgement should be made to Dr. Arthur E. Moodie and Dr. W. A. Douglas Jackson for their many comments and suggestions; to Mrs. Wilma Fairchild, editor of *The Geographical Review,* and Miss Alice Taylor, editor of *Focus,* for generously permitting the reproduction of considerable material from their respective publications; to Dr. Harm de Blij for suggestions on the organization of the chapters on Africa; and to Professor Joseph E. Schwartzberg, Professor Laurence G. Wolf, Dr. Eric Fischer, and Dr. George W. Hoffman for detailed criticisms of material in the first edition of this text.

L. M. A.

1

THE NATURE OF POLITICAL GEOGRAPHY

● The world political pattern—that is, the distribution of political regions on a global scale—is a basic component of the field of political geography. A political region or area may be defined as a portion of the earth's surface throughout which a particular type or types of political phenomena take place. The term "political phenomena" is taken to include both "the features produced by political forces and the political ideas which generate those forces." Although the political geographer concentrates primarily on the study of features, he cannot ignore the ideas and attitudes which produced them, nor the effects of the features on current or future attitudes. The phenomena most frequently used in the delimitation of political regions involve political control over territory by a government. In terms of political control the land surface of the globe may be divided into many political regions, ranging in level of organization from national units down to counties, townships, and villages.

Political geography is the study of political regions as features of the earth's surface. The nature and extent of these regions is determined by variations of the political phenomena existing throughout the world. In some parts of the world political regions are relatively stable over long periods of time, while in other areas they may undergo frequent change, as in the Congo River basin, the Korean Peninsula, or eastern Europe. "In no small part, the ultimate goal of geography is to provide scientific description of the way in which the originally unorganized areas of the earth are organized into various kinds of functioning regions."[1] By studying political phe-

[1] Richard Hartshorne, "Political Geography in the Modern World," *Journal of Conflict Resolution,* IV (1960), 53.

nomena in their association with other features of the earth's surface, such as landforms, water bodies, or settlement patterns, political geographers are able to describe and analyze the diverse ways in which man organizes space for political purposes. Thus, for example, a political geographer might study a national political unit, such as Canada, representing as it does an organized political region within which an effective central government has been established with control over the entire area. A study might also be made of a political subdivision in Canada, such as the Province of Quebec, or one of its town or city municipalities. Systematic studies might be made of particular political phenomena, such as boundaries or capital cities as they exist over the earth's surface. But a geographer might also concentrate on some area of the earth's surface which is *not* politically organized, but which nevertheless is characterized by the existence of some political phenomena. River basins encompassing several countries, centers of separatist trends in Iran, the limits to Bulgaria's historic territorial ambitions—examples such as these illustrate the types of politically unorganized regions which may also be of interest to political geography. Some unorganized regions may in time become organized, as did the slaveholding areas of the American southeast for a period of years, or the Warsaw-Krakow-Poznan area of what eventually became Poland. The so-called Afro-Asian bloc in the United Nations represents one form of unorganized political region, as does French-speaking Canada, or the watershed of the Nile River, the control of which is an important consideration for the Egyptian government.

An illustration of the basic characteristics of an organized political region may be found in a typical county in the United States. The limits of the county are defined on the map by political boundaries. Administration over the area within these boundaries is carried on by the central government, located at the county seat. The county is divided and subdivided into other political regions—townships, cities, and villages (Figure 1). Within the boundaries of the county are natural features, such as climate, landforms, soils, and water resources. Here also are population features, including size and distribution as well as composition according to race, religion, and language. There are the economic features of agriculture, industry, and commerce. Finally, there are political features, reflecting political behavior; these include the boundaries, the county seat, and administrative subdivisions.

Although the county boundaries cannot actually be seen unless there are special markers, they nevertheless represent sharp lines of political control separating one county from its neighbors. Various aspects of county life, such as voting districts, school laws, and police jurisdiction, change immediately as one crosses the boundary. On the other hand, nonpolitical features, such as climate, soils, race, or economic activities, may change very gradually as one passes from one county to another. Indeed, the county may have had economic validity years ago at the time of its establishment

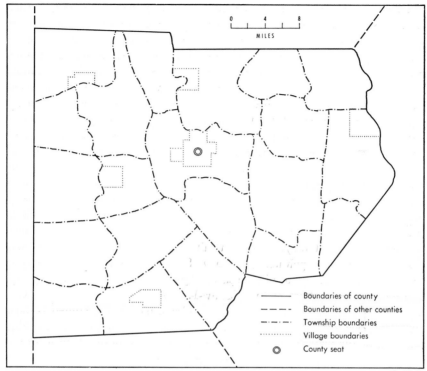

Figure 1. The County as a Political Region.

but, with the passage of time, have lost much of its economic significance as a separate political entity. Thus political boundaries may exist independently of physical or cultural boundaries, and the change represented by the existence of these political dividing lines is far more distinct than that of other boundaries.

Within the county—as in all organized political regions—there exist the following five basic elements:

1. **An expanse of territory delimited by boundaries.** The term "territory" is taken here to include not only size but also the various physical features associated with area. Any change in extent of territory means, of course, a change in the physical features of a region. The boundaries may be well marked, or they may be extremely obscure. The relations existing between neighboring political regions (particularly States) are frequently reflected in the conditions existing along their common boundaries.

2. **An effective administrative system.** The central administration should, ideally, exercise political control over all the area within the boundaries of the political region. Of considerable interest to political geographers

is the manner in which this control, and the laws associated with it, conform to the particular conditions of the political region. How does the government respond to the pressures of regional interest groups? Can it protect the area under its control from outside threats? Is it wholly or partially dependent on some outside administrative group?

3. A resident population. The inhabitants of a political region should be thought of in terms not only of total number, but of distribution, ethnic types, and of rates of increase or decrease. The values and skills of the population are also important factors because of their bearing on the ways in which the people utilize the physical resources of the area which they inhabit.

4. An economic structure. All political regions possess economic structures, which often influence strongly their political functioning. Internally, the economic structure is related both to the availability of resources and to the distribution and the values and skills of the population; externally, to the viability of the political region in terms of other regions.

5. A circulatory system. The movement of people, goods, and ideas both within the political region and across its boundaries to other regions is of great importance to its political functioning. Movement is one of the basic components of man's activities on the earth's surface, and the instabilities and change which this movement implies are factors which must constantly be taken into account when considering the nature of the political world.

A more detailed discussion of these five basic elements will be found in Chapters 3, 4, and 5. The interaction of these elements determines, to a large extent, the degree of viability of the political region, that is, its capacity to exist, both internally and externally, as an integral political unit.

In a study of political regions as features of the earth's surface several approaches are possible. In discussing these approaches we shall limit ourselves for the sake of convenience to the analysis of the national political unit, that is, the State.[2] One approach is to study the genesis and development of the State, how it came to its present structure and extent. This essentially historical approach is of interest primarily in terms of individual cases. A detailed analysis of Luxembourg, for example, would include an explanation of how the Grand Duchy developed as it did, and of the effects of this development on its present form. The danger from such generic studies is, first, that a student of political geography may eventually become bogged down in a mass of historical detail so that in time his work is indistinguishable from that of political historians, and, second, that from a study

[2] The term "State" is used here in referring to a national political region which has *de jure* (legal) independence, while a "state" is a component part of a federal State such as the United States of America. A "country" is any political unit on the national scale, regardless of whether it is dependent or independent. A "Nation-State" is a State in which there is not only independence but also a general sense of national cohesion among all or most of the inhabitants (see page 87 for discussion of "nation").

of individual cases he may be tempted to work out "principles" governing the development of States which presumably would hold true for all cases. Much has been written in the past of the "organic" State, and of the "laws" governing its growth, despite the fact that the historical development of each State is a unique occurrence about which it is extremely difficult to generalize. What "laws" exist in common, for example, in the development of Sweden and India, or of Cuba and Israel? The point here is that a basically historical study of States may contribute relatively little that is meaningful to the analysis of these regions as contemporary political features of the earth's surface.

A second approach is that of the regional geographer, who would consider the State in terms of its various geographic elements, such as size, shape, climate, resources, and population. Like the historical approach, this one tends to weigh down the political geographer with a mass of facts. Here again there is little purpose of study, except to describe the geography of a series of individual regions. A political geography which is but a regional description of States has little which is unique and meaningful to justify its existence as a separate branch of geography.

The third approach is a functional one, that is, the study of the State or other political region in terms of its internal and external operations. How does the region maintain itself internally as an integral political unit? What effects do nonpolitical forces such as climate, mountains, or the presence of diverse ethnic groups have on the political activities of the State, and what effect in turn do the political aspects have on such features as settlement patterns, resource use, or the development of road and rail nets? Externally, is the State a viable political unit with respect to other States? Is the government independent or under some form of dependency, are there unresolved territorial problems with neighbors, is the economy dependent upon that of another State? It is by emphasizing the element of function, rather than of genesis or structure, that one is able to correlate the significant features of the State in terms of one specific objective, namely, the manner in which it carries out the purposes for which it was constituted.

The functional approach to the study of political regions does not rule out the use of either the generic or "structural" elements of the region, providing they contribute to the over-all analysis of the functional pattern. Historical factors may at times be of great importance. "The emotional character of political thought holds communities and states to traditional patterns and practices long after their original connections with the natural environment have been forgotten. Sound political geography therefore must trace these relict forms and procedures to their source."[3] History may be as imperative to the understanding of regional differences *within* a State

---

[3] Derwent Whittlesey, *The Earth and the State: A Study of Political Geography* (New York: Henry Holt & Company, 1944), p. 591.

(as in the American South) as it is of the State itself. Israel's origins and development are essential to an awareness of its viability with respect to its neighbors, as are also the genesis of Pakistan and South Vietnam. But the historical element should be brought in not for its own sake, but in order to appreciate better the functional aspects of the region.

So far as nonpolitical features of a region's geography are concerned, their relationships with the functional aspects may work in one of two ways; either one may study the significance of the nonpolitical elements to the functioning of the region, or else analyze the effects of the existence of the political region on nonpolitical features of the environment. Since ancient times scholars have dealt with aspects of the former type of relationship— the effects of climate or location on the power of states, the divisive effects of mountain ranges on national unity, the advantages to a state of access to the sea.

Two points should be noted with regard to this type of "geographic" relationship. The first is that, while certain factors such as climate, mountains, or the possession of minerals may be of profound significance to the functioning of States, it is difficult to generalize as to exactly *what* effects the appearance of these features within a particular State's borders will have. Different peoples react differently to humid tropical or to arid climates, mountain ranges vary considerably in extent and form, and not all seacoasts are of equal value for ports or as springboards for territorial expansion. Thus "laws" or "principles" based on such politico-geographic relationships are frequently of little value. A second point is that the significance of these geographic features varies with time, even in a single area. Mountain ranges, deserts, and swamps tend to lose their barrier functions as a result of technological advances, the economic importance of boundaries may decline because of multilateral trade agreements, and the significance of certain resources changes with technical improvements. Here again it is often difficult to establish "principles" regarding the effects of geographic elements on the political activities of a State. Relationships which men like Aristotle, Ritter, and Ratzel once took as relatively simple and unvarying have turned out to be of the greatest complexity, and geography is no longer thought of as a science of relationships, but rather as the description and interpretation of areal differences on the earth's surface.

The effects of the existence of a political region on nonpolitical aspects of the environment have only recently attracted the interests of geographers. Derwent Whittlesey, in "The Impress of Effective Central Authority Upon the Landscape,"[4] was among the first of the geographers to discuss this relationship, and during the past quarter-century a number of other studies have been made dealing with this topic. Edward Ullman, for example,

---

[4] *Annals of the Association of American Geographers,* XXV (1935), 85–97.

analyzed the effects of the Rhode Island–Massachusetts boundary on settlement patterns and economic development in the general border area.[5] P. P. Karan has considered the consequences of boundaries on the allocation of waters in the American Southwest and the Indian subcontinent,[6] while Hartshorne has written of the effects in the Silesian area of the post-World War I partitioning of that industrial district.[7] In view of the constantly changing nature of the world political pattern, there exists a wide and fruitful area for study of the effects of political phenomena on the cultural geography of political regions.

It was noted earlier that the relationships between political and non-political aspects of the landscape will alter if the boundaries of a political region change. An important aspect of the work done by political geographers is that concerned with the nature and function of international or intranational boundaries, and of the causes for and effects of change in boundary location. Throughout much of the world international boundaries have never been carefully determined, and despite the reduction in boundary functions in certain areas such as western Europe, there appears to be little at present to indicate any radical decline in the number or complexity of boundary problems in the foreseeable future. This important aspect of the field is treated in detail in Chapter 4.

A political region does not operate *in vacuo*, but rather as part of a highly complex association of factors, which include both physical and cultural aspects of the territory involved and the ideas and opinions of the peoples inhabiting the territory. Stephen Jones has suggested a link-chain analogy connecting political ideas on the one hand with political areas (or regions) on the other.[8] The chain is as follows: Political Idea–Decision–Movement–Field–Political Area. Political ideas or attitudes may lead through discussion to decisions, both by individuals and groups. Decisions in turn involve movement in one way or another of men, goods, or ideas within a more or less definite area.

Movement creates a field of interaction of forces, a series of resulting conditions out of which a politically organized area may eventually develop. Movement may result in the growth of towns, in changes in types of economies, in wars and boundary revisions, in achievement for an area of autonomy, and ultimately perhaps of independence. This field of interaction may have a time as well as a space dimension, since movement in response to decisions may continue for many years. The Balfour Declaration of 1917

---

[5] "The Eastern Rhode Island–Massachusetts Boundary Zone," *The Geographical Review*, XXIX (1939), 291–302.
[6] "Dividing the Water: A Problem in Political Geography," *The Professional Geographer*, XIII (1961), 1–6.
[7] "Geographic and Political Boundaries in Upper Silesia," *Annals of the Association of American Geographers*, XXIII (1933), 194–228.
[8] "A Unified Field Theory of Political Geography," *Annals of the Association of American Geographers*, XLIV (1954), 111–24.

ushered in a thirty-year period of Jewish emigration to Palestine. The political area in this link-chain analogy corresponds with the political region as we have defined it earlier.

Movement along the idea-area chain may be in either direction. Flow from idea toward area is essentially a process of controlling or creating. The decision by a relatively few Americans to strike for independence from the British created movement which eventually led to the creation of the United States. Flow from area toward idea is more a process of conditioning. The new American government soon began conditioning movement, decisions, and even political ideas within the area which had become self-governing.

The idea-area chain is useful in analyzing both organized and unorganized political regions, that is, those with specific boundaries and an effective administrative system, and those which are characterized only by the presence of some political phenomena, such as the existence of an idea, or possibly of a decision. The "Holy Land" to which the Crusaders were directed was not an organized political area, but rather an area representing an objective for the Christian warriors. The idea-area chain also provides a link between political science, which handles problems of political ideas and decision-making, and political geography, concerned as it is with political areas or regions of the earth's surface. No one can hope to understand the functioning of a state or other political region without taking into account the prevailing ideas and attitudes of the peoples involved in its operations. An important problem here (and one which generally lies beyond the boundaries of geography) concerns the methods to be used in determing the nature and extent of popular attitudes toward political problems. How strong, for example, is the feeling for a separatist movement in northern Nigeria, or for the union of two or more of the territories of former French West Africa? These are questions of degree but they may be highly important in assessing the likelihood of territorial change in these areas. Karl Deutsch, among others, has written on nationalism and communication effectiveness[9] and has suggested a mathematical model for assessing rates of assimilation of one group into another. He discusses causes for the failure of the Germans in Bohemia to become assimilated within the Czech nation between World Wars I and II, and from this and other examples he derives guideposts for measuring the development of national consciousness. Theodore Herman's "Group Values Toward the National Space; the Case of China"[10] examines the basic values of one nation-group toward the control and utilization of its national space. In its development of tools and techniques for examining the functional aspects of States, political geography has begun making use of the research methods of the political scientist, the sociologist, and the social psychologist.

One persistent problem involves what is sometimes referred to as

---

[9] *Nationalism and Social Communication* (New York: John Wiley & Sons, 1953).
[10] *The Geographical Review*, XLIX (1959), 164–83.

"national behavior." What persons or groups are in decision-making positions? Who determines what course a State will follow, and on what do they base their actions? In examining this matter the Sprouts have written of *cognitive behaviorism* ("a person reacts to his mileu . . . as he perceives and interprets it in the light of past experiences") and they distinguish between the *psychological environment,* with reference to which an individual defines choices and makes decisions, and the *operational environment,* which sets limits to what can happen once a decision has been executed.[11] The psychological environment of Russia, with reference to which Hitler decided on attack in June, 1941, was different from the operational environment in which the invasion actually took place—with disastrous results for the Germans.

It follows from the discussions of the last few pages that political regions, particularly at the national level, are highly complex phenomena, and that political geographers still have much to learn concerning the processes by which these regions function. The physical and cultural geography of a region represents but one component in the determination of its functioning. History is another component, as are also the values and skills of the population and the forces originating from outside its boundaries which may influence the region's operations. How then can we handle this great variety of influences on an individual State?

The solution lies in the scale of observation employed. There are in the world today some 120 States in varying degrees of independence, as well as a dozen or so more which soon will achieve independence. To function successfully each of these units must (1) maintain its internal cohesion, (2) protect its territorial integrity, and (3) maintain its economic viability. These tasks it accomplishes singly or in regional associations with other States.

If we accept this threefold definition of the *minimum* requirements for successful functioning of a State, we have at least a yardstick against which to measure individual cases. It is true, of course, that in addition to these minimum requirements a State may be faced with other problems, such as the return of historic borderlands, resistance to internal Communism, or the retention of overseas holdings. Again it should be stressed that political regions are basically dynamic in nature, that people, goods, and ideas are constantly moving, and that with this movement may come changes in popular ideas and attitudes, in the economic-political systems and, ultimately, in the form and extent of political control over territory.

In discussing the study of political regions, one cannot ignore what might be termed "applied" political geography. Having analyzed the functional aspects of political regions, to what practical uses might the geographer put this information? The most obvious answers would seem to lie in

---

[11] Harold and Margaret Sprout, *Man-Milieu Relationship Hypothesis in the Context of International Politics* (Princeton: Princeton University Press, 1956).

/ the field of international relations: having studied political regions, particularly States, as functioning units, the geographer would have developed a sound background for an analysis of international events. This line of reasoning is valid as far as it goes. One major difficulty, however, is that emphasis is now on events, rather than geography, so that a careful analysis of the functioning of States may become tailored to fit the requirements of the international relations expert. Another problem is that history, political science, economics, and other nongeographic disciplines are also involved in a comprehensive study of international affairs.

2. A second possibility is the study of power politics, either from the point of view of one State's self-interest, or from a more objective standpoint of assessing relative power potentials. The term "geopolitics" has on occasion been used with reference to this combination of geography and world power, although in view of the many uses to which this word has been subjected over the past half-century it might seem advisable now to abandon it altogether as a working term. Studies of power potentials and of national strategy may seem on the surface to be relatively simple affairs; since the mid-1930's a whole cult of "armchair strategists" has emerged, equipped sometimes with little else than a newspaper, a globe, and boundless imagination. In truth, however, such analyses, to be meaningful, require the utmost background and care, and political geographers can at best suggest certain ingredients for the power expert or the strategist to utilize in developing his conclusions.

The political geographer may also at times be called upon to apply his specialized training and experience to situations directly involving territorial control. In the case of a specific boundary dispute he may render an opinion as to the most equitable decision possible, as American geographers did during the peace conference following World War I. He would also be able to contribute to studies relating to such matters as the relocation of political boundaries within a State, a shift in the location of the capital, and the partitioning of a particular country or uniting it with a neighboring State. Political geographers are frequently employed as intelligence analysts or as advisors on foreign policy, since they are trained to handle problems such as the viability of newly emerging States, or the chances for federation or division of political units. Even in situations where no disputes over territorial control are present, political geography has much to offer. The pattern of political regions in western Europe, for example, has a decided influence on local commerce and industry. Canal construction in Belgium and the Netherlands, shipping restrictions on the Rhine, or the movement of iron ore in the Luxembourg-Lorraine area are economic activities which can be understood thoroughly only after the pattern of political control in the area has been carefully studied.

The scale of observation of political regions may vary from sweeping analyses to "microgeographic" investigations. In the case of large areas, local differences are obscured and only broad generalizations can be drawn. On the other hand, local studies, such as those relating to specific boundary locations, may involve individual streets, houses, or plots of land. Generalizations on one scale of study may require modifications on another scale. For example, that the Andes Mountains form a good physical basis upon which to draw the boundary between Argentina and Chile is a valid generalization on a global scale; on a more local scale, however, various difficulties can be observed. The crest of the mountains and the drainage divide frequently do not coincide, the southern sector of the chain is low and the crests poorly marked, and there is the problem of control of passes through the mountains. Other "large-scale" politico-geographic studies might involve the allocation of water rights in a river system, voting patterns in a country, or the applicability of legal systems to a particular geographic environment. Whittlesey, among others, has considered this last problem and concluded: "Legal systems are images of the regions in which they function, sometimes faithful and sometimes distorted. Individual laws mirror the society and the habitat in which they are created. Because humanity occupies its habitat dynamically, laws tend to become outmoded. When this occurs, they are occasionally revoked, sometimes they are disregarded, usually they are given new meaning."[12] Of a purely political nature is the study of administrative subdivision within States, and of the manner in which they correspond to existing regional differences.

Contrasted with these are studies of an international character. At this level one is dealing with at least a portion of the over-all world political pattern. Since the State is itself a dynamic phenomenon, the world pattern, representing a great number and variety of States, is also dynamic and in many areas frequently changing. At the upper limits of the scale of observation one is confronted with problems of the world political pattern as a whole, and of the regional groupings which exist there. By way of introduction to the chapters which will follow, a brief discussion is given here of four basic trends in the world political pattern since the end of World War II.

1. The break-up of empires and establishment of independent states. The pre-World War II empires of Great Britain, France, the Netherlands, Belgium, the United States, Italy, and Japan have been reduced in size and population, and from these former colonial areas have emerged over 45 independent States—the great majority of them in Africa and Asia. This process of empire change is still going on. Over 900 million persons occupy areas affected by this trend.

2. The expansion of Communist control. Since the end of World War II the Soviet Union has expanded its boundaries and established a Moscow-oriented empire in eastern Europe. Mainland China has been communized and Communist regimes installed in North Korea and North Vietnam. Mon-

---

[12] *The Earth and the State,* p. 565.

golia is also a part of the Communist bloc. In Laos and along the northern borders of India Communist control is gradually expanding. Over 700 million people have come under Communist control since May, 1945.

3. The break-up or union of States. Some of the break-ups of States have been associated with independence, as evidenced by India-Pakistan and Israel; others have been more closely tied to Communist expansion (Korea, Vietnam, China, Germany). There have been relatively few unions of States, although mention should be made of the Eritrean-Ethiopian union, the joining of British and Italian Somaliland into the new Somali Republic, and the short-lived United Arab Republic, consisting of Egypt and Syria. The Federation of the Rhodesias and Nyasaland, the projected East African Federation (Tanganyika, Uganda, Kenya), and a new United Arab Republic are among possible association movements of the future.

4. The expansion of territorial control into previously unclaimed areas. This trend involves areas of the high seas and of the air space above States. In both cases national boundaries are slowly encroaching on what used to be considered areas free to the use of all people.

These four trends are intended merely as guides for the study of changes which have been taking place in the world political pattern. All four show signs of continuing operation, and the reader might do well to relate them to current territorial problems which exist at the time he reads this text.

Emphasis in this book will be placed primarily on problems of political control of territory at the national and international rather than local levels. In order to cover the entire world adequately in a few hundred pages of text, it was felt that "microgeographic" studies should for the most part be omitted, unless they contributed directly to an understanding of the world pattern of States. Basic forces in the current world political pattern will be dealt with not only in their relationship to specific areas but also as they illustrate fundamental principles of political geography. In this way attention may be given both to the regional treatment of political geography and to the systematic aspects of the field, which in turn may form the basis for more detailed investigations of political regions in more advanced courses in the field.

BIBLIOGRAPHY

GOTTMAN, JEAN. "Geography and International Relations," *World Politics,* III (1950), 153–73.

———. "The Political Partitioning of Our World: an Attempt at Analysis," *World Politics,* IV, No. 4 (July, 1952), 512–19.

A theoretical approach to the establishment of political control in an area.

HARTSHORNE, RICHARD. "The Functional Approach in Political Geography," *Annals of the Association of American Geographers,* XL (1950), 95–131.

A discussion of the manner in which political regions operate, both internally and externally.

———. "Political Geography," *American Geography: Inventory and Prospect.* P. E. JAMES and C. F. JONES (eds.). Syracuse: Syracuse University Press, 1954. Pp. 167–226.

The development and the conflicting concepts of political geography.

———. "Political Geography in the Modern World," *Journal of Conflict Resolution,* IV (1960), 52–67.

A concise treatment of the general principles of political geography.

———. "Recent Developments in Political Geography," *American Political Science Review,* XXIX (1935), 758–804, 943–66.

A detailed discussion of various concepts of political geography (up to 1935), including a thorough bibliography.

JONES, STEPHEN B. "A Unified Field Theory of Political Geography," *Annals of the Association of American Geographers,* XLIV (1954), 111–24.

A proposed outline which can be applied to various studies of political phenomena.

WHITTLESEY, DERWENT S. "The Impress of Effective Central Authority Upon the Landscape," *Annals of the Association of American Geographers,* XXV (1935), 85–97.

A concise study of the effects of political phenomena on the cultural landscape.

2

THE DEVELOPMENT OF POLITICAL GEOGRAPHY

● The study of political geography began more than 2,000 years ago, although only since the late nineteenth century has the subject been recognized as a separate discipline. Prior to this time what is now known as political geography was included in the broad field of human geography. Some of the relationships which past scholars found to exist between physical features and political behavior have survived down to the present time to be incorporated as basic principles of political geography. Other relationships have been found to be scientifically false and have been discarded. Aristotle, for example, noted that in regions of diverse topography a number of political areas instead of one tended to develop. The validity of this idea has been borne out by history. On the other hand, the direct influence which climate was once thought to have on the abilities of certain groups to govern others is no longer considered to be a true relationship.

A brief survey of the historical development of political geography will be presented here in order to provide a basis for considering recent concepts in the field. For purposes of classification, this survey will be divided into three phases: (1) the study of environmental relationships, (2) the study of national power, and (3) the study of political regions. Two points should be noted with respect to these politico-geographic concepts. The first is that they have kept pace with intellectual and technical developments. Thus Aristotle thought in terms of the city-state in a protected lowland, Ritter of the pre-eminence of Europe, and Mackinder of sea power versus land power on a global scale. Seversky's recent theory of air supremacy is a response to the development of a new medium for transportation and for warfare.

A second point is that the three-way division presented here of the history of political geography does not imply that as new approaches to the subject were developed the old ones were quickly abandoned. The environmental relationships which the Greek and Roman scholars propounded still found acceptance among many political geographers during the first few decades of the twentieth century. Likewise, variations of the "National Power" approach of the late nineteenth and early twentieth centuries are still evident in the writings of political geographers and persons in allied fields today. Attempts to catalogue the various theories in any branch of knowledge involve the risk of oversimplification, both as to content and to time. The following survey is offered merely as a device for better understanding the over-all field of political geography.

THE STUDY OF ENVIRONMENTAL RELATIONSHIPS

The diversity which exists among peoples and among countries throughout the world has long held the attention of scholars. These scholars sought not only to describe such diversity, but also to interpret it—and in their interpretations they sought correlation between cultural differences on the one hand and differences in physical phenomena, such as climate, soils, and landforms, on the other. Although the earliest writers turned their attentions primarily to the study of differences among peoples and groups, it was not long before political units were also being considered in terms of their form, their power potential, and their types of government. Ultimately the concept of relationships led to the combination of individuals, cultural groups, and political phenomena into one cosmic system, governed by the iron laws of nature. Within such a system man had little freedom of choice; his principal hope lay in understanding the laws of nature and in learning to utilize these laws for his own betterment.

Among the earliest of the Greek scholars to consider the effects of the physical environment on human development was the physician Hippocrates (460–376 B. C.), who found the inhabitants of warm, humid climates to be tall and handsome, although lazy and lacking in valor. Peoples of perpetually cold climates are also large, but lethargic, indolent, and not prolific, while those who live in lands of changing seasons (that is, Greece) are slender, well jointed, sturdy, as well as high-spirited and intelligent. Although most of the "environmentalist" scholars adhered to the best scientific traditions of their times, they tended toward ethnocentrism, and the results of their investigations generally favored the physical environments in which the scholars themselves lived. Aristotle (383–322 B. C.) wrote in his *Politics* (Book VII, Chapter 7):

> The peoples of cold countries generally, and particularly those of Europe, are full of spirit, but deficient in skill and intelligence;

and this is why they continue to remain comparatively free, but attain no political development and show no capacity for governing others. The peoples of Asia are endowed with skill and intelligence but are deficient in spirit: and this is why they continue to be peoples of subjects and slaves. The Greek stock, intermediate in geographical position, unites the qualities of both sets of peoples. It possesses both spirit and intelligence: the one quality makes it continue free; the other enables it to attain the highest political development, and to show a capacity for governing every other people—if only it could achieve political unity.[1]

Living in the city-state of Athens, Aristotle felt that a nation should be well protected by hills against possible attack and situated close to a good harbor in order to make use of overseas commerce. Through the wise utilization of physical resources, such a nation could become powerful and eventually expand its territory.

Other writers of ancient times also considered such environmental relationships. Lucretius (99–55 B. C.) wrote of the innate hostility of nature to man, claiming that nature is always ready to take advantage of man's weakness. Man must resist nature; thus unfavorable conditions often give rise to extraordinary fighting abilities. Strabo (63 B. C.–A. D. 24), a Greek scholar surveying the Roman Empire, concluded in his *Geography* that a large political unit required a strong central government with one ruling head in order to function properly. He also reasoned that because of its excellent location, climate, and resources, Italy was the logical place for this state to be situated.

During the Dark Ages philosophical efforts were concentrated largely on religious questions, and little was accomplished in the realm of geographic thought. Beginning in the sixteenth century, however, the study of relationships between physical and political phenomena was again pursued. Bodin (1530–96), particularly in his *Six livres de la république,* reasoned that national characteristics vary both with changes in climate and in topography. Peoples of cold climates, or those living in mountains, are strong, well disciplined, courageous. Since national character differs according to differing environments, so must the political structure of states; and the laws governing those states must be adjusted to conform with human character as molded by the environment. Here is the beginning of a comprehensive theory of determinism, in which man's physical nature, his temperament, talents, and will as well as the political systems which govern him are parts of the universal system of nature. Montesquieu (1689–1755), in his *De l'esprit des lois,* considered the effects of climate, topography, and

---

[1] Ernest Barker (trans.), *The Politics of Aristotle* (Oxford: Clarendon Press, 1946), p. 296. Reprinted by permission.

even of continents and islands on people, on laws, and on political systems. Cold climates are generally associated with political freedom, while warm climates lead to despotism and slavery. Plains regions favor large empires, while mountains and hills foster feelings of independence and a yearning for liberty. Island peoples can defend their freedom more effectively than those on the mainland, and therefore have a higher regard for liberty.

Through the works of all of these scholars runs the theme of regional differences—in national character, in the nature of states, and in the forms of government. Within the grand scheme of nature, man had little choice but to comply. The question of human will was a complex one. Bodin granted that human reason existed independent of the physical environment, but felt that nature determined man's will to resist its laws. Even Montesquieu, who held that man, through his historical development, gradually liberates himself from the iron bonds of nature, did not depart radically from the general philosophy that it is the physical environment which determines the nature of peoples and of their political institutions.

During the nineteenth century many of the environmentalist concepts of earlier scholars were brought together and systematically developed. In political geography much of the progress made at this time was due to the efforts of two Germans, Karl Ritter and Friederich Ratzel. Ritter (1779–1859) was, for many years, Professor of Geography at the University of Berlin. He developed the thesis that human cultures are organic entities within nature, and that these cultures are born, mature, and eventually die. Man and his institutions are a part of the cosmic oneness of the world. "The unity of the earth, the unity of the continents, the unity of every physical feature of the continents, and the building all up together in a perfect symmetry and mutual adaptation of parts, is the crowning thought of Geographical Science."[2]

Ritter, like many who had gone before him, found parallels between cultural and environmental conditions. He emphasized continents as the primary organs of the living globe. "Europe, the smallest of the continents, was destined to gain precedence over all the rest, Asia included," he wrote, for "Europe, limited in size and confined to the temperate zone, but most complex in its subdivisions . . . has been especially fitted for the reception of stranger races, and for the development of their energies and the advance of their culture."[3] By taking note of two sets of variables—the physical environment as it differs from place to place, and the developmental stage of each culture—Ritter was able to set up a more sophisticated body of theory than had the earlier environmentalists. By understanding the laws of nature, a strong culture might be able to foresee and guide the destinies of States.

---

[2] *Comparative Geography* (Philadelphia: J. B. Lippincott Company, 1864), p. 184.
[3] *Ibid.*, p. 200.

THE STUDY OF NATIONAL POWER

The second major approach to political geography—that of the geographic basis of national and international power—was developed largely by Ratzel (1844–1904), who became Professor of Geography at the University of Leipzig about twenty years after Ritter's death. Aristotle, Strabo, and other scholars had written of broad general relationships existing between environment and power, but it was for Ratzel and those who followed him to evolve a systematic classification of environmental influence on the power of States.

National Determinism

In his writings on political geography Ratzel was particularly interested in the growth of States. Building on Ritter's concept of organic cultures, he went on to describe the organic State, a living entity existing in space. Darwin had already written on the biological laws of natural selection, survival of the fittest, and the need a healthy species has for space in which to develop. From there it would follow that the State, an organic being, is involved in an endless struggle for space, or "living room" (*Lebensraum*). A youthful State, in a favorable physical environment, could expand its borders and become an extremely powerful political unit. Pursuing this line of reasoning, Ratzel worked out seven laws of the expansion of States:

1. The space of States grows with the growth of culture.
2. The growth of States follows other aspects of development, such as commerce, ideas, and missionary activity.
3. States grow through the amalgamation and absorption of smaller units.
4. The frontier is the peripheral organ of the State and reflects the growth, the strength, and the changes in the State.
5. In the process of growth the State seeks to include politically valuable areas, such as coast lines, river valleys, plains, and regions which are rich in resources.
6. The first impetus for territorial growth comes to a primitive State from beyond its borders, from a higher civilization.
7. The general trend toward amalgamation transmits the tendency for expansion from State to State and increases the tendency in the process of transmission (in other words, the process of amalgamation whets the appetite for greater expansion).

In fairness to Ratzel and to those who emulated his thoughts, it should be pointed out that what he sought were the basic laws of cultural development, and that his theories were consistent with the scientific concepts of his time. In 1897 Ratzel published *Politische Geographie,* the first book really to embody the principles of political geography as they had been developed up to that time. Throughout the book runs the theme that the land area of a State is the best indication of its political power, and that the people of a State should develop a "space conception," that is, an idea of the possible limits of territorial control. Youthful peoples, with a large space conception, are likely to press for expansion of their State's boundaries. The decay of a state, he concluded, is the result of a declining space conception. A frontier is not a line but a "shifting zone of assimilation"; rather than existing as a permanent feature of the landscape, it should be thought of as a temporary phenomenon which shifts in response to a State's requirements.

Ratzel's concepts of the growth of States were thought of as being applicable throughout the world, and in his writings he paid considerable attention to the United States as illustrative of his ideas. The State conceived of as a living organism represented something of a climax—a blending together of theories of earlier scholars. Differences in the nature of peoples and of cultures reflect differences in climate, landforms, soils, and other physical phenomena. The Nation-State represents the political expression of a particular culture. This State is part of an organic entity which includes also the geographic environment and the people who make it up. States, as well as cultures, experience youth, maturity, and old age, as civilizations in various parts of the world gradually undergo change.

A modification in the concept of the State as an organic being was offered by the Swedish writer Rudolf Kjellén (1864–1922). Kjellén advanced a step beyond Ratzel's thinking in that he envisioned the State not only as a living organism, but also as a conscious being equipped with moral-intellectual capacities. He agreed with Ratzel that the final objective of a State's development was the attainment of power; however, Kjellén held that in its quest for power the State need not follow the simple organic laws of territorial expansion. Instead it might employ modern cultural advances and techniques in the achievement of its desired goals. The final objective of a State's power development was "to acquire good natural frontiers externally, and harmonious unity internally."[4] Kjellén was the first writer to use the term "geopolitics," which he defined as the natural environment of the State. He believed that the power of maritime empires would eventually pass to land empires, and he forecast the ultimate emergence of a few giant States of the world.

Although Kjellén treated the State as an organic being with both a body and a soul, Ladis Kristof wrote, "one cannot but conclude that he speaks in metaphor. The individuals and the nation are to him more important than the state."[5] Kristof quoted Kjellén's conclusion that "the life

---

[4] Andrew Gyorgy, *Geopolitics: The New German Science* (Berkeley and Los Angeles: University of California Press, 1944), p. 166.
[5] "The Origins and Evolution of Geopolitics," *Journal of Conflict Resolution*, IV (1960), 22.

of the state is ultimately in the hands of the individuals," although even here there are strong determinist leanings. Kjellén played down morality and the rule of law, and instead laid great stress on contests of power. "Wars, expansion, and breaches of international law are . . . not due to some fatalistic and deterministic force standing outside men but to the will and self-preservation drive of men, nations, and their leaders."[6] To Kjellén's mind the forces impelling men and nations to act stemmed from more complex sources than were conceived of in Aristotle's time, but people and States were still largely the victims of forces beyond their control.

The French Possibilists

In contrast with the determinist doctrines of Ratzel, Kjellén, and their contemporaries were the possibilist theories of leading French geographers of the late nineteenth and early twentieth centuries, including Jean Brunhes, Jacques Ancel, Albert Demangeon, and Paul Vidal de la Blache. These writers held that the State is not an oragnic power-political entity, but rather a cultural and national unit whose activities are directed by the collective consciousness of its citizens. The physical environment, rather than exerting a determining influence on human activities, as Ratzel and Kjellén had claimed, actually presented the citizens with a number of possible choices for development, leaving them free to select which course the State should pursue. The writers rejected the principle of national existence as a fight for space, and pointed out that throughout history many small States had survived for long periods of time and contributed significantly to human culture. This humanist philosophy laid great stress on moral and spiritual forces, such as liberty and patriotism, but it failed to offer such concise explanations of national behavior as did the theories of the determinists, with their ready answers to the complex relationships of physical, cultural, and political forces.

The Rise of Geopolitics

These writers of the late nineteenth and early twentieth centuries were objective in approach. They dealt in abstractions, using the examples of specific countries as illustrations for their hypotheses. But in the years following World War I there emerged in Germany a new doctrine, based on the application of the concept of the organic State to the German nation. This doctrine was labelled "geopolitics" and was in its final analysis a shrewd manipulation of earlier theories in the interests of German nationalism. Its leading proponent was Karl Haushofer (1869–1946), a German geographer and soldier of the early twentieth century. Haushofer was sent by the Ger-

---

[6] Quoted in *ibid.*, p. 25.

man General Staff to Japan as a military observer in 1908, when he was a young army officer. From this visit he acquired a firsthand knowledge of the Far East and the Pacific Ocean. He taught geography at Munich prior to World War I, and during the war he rose to the rank of major general in the German army. Following the armistice, he returned to Munich to teach political geography and military science. In 1924 he helped to found the *Zeitschrift für Geopolitik*, a magazine devoted to the furthering of geopolitics.

Haushofer borrowed widely from other writers in forming his concepts. He agreed with Ratzel that the Pacific was a dominant power area, and he accepted the doctrine of the organic State and its need for space. Unlike Ratzel, however, he was an outspoken nationalist and continually applied his concepts to the needs of the German nation. With the rise of Hitler, Haushofer and his contemporaries at the Munich Institute for Geopolitics assumed an important role in German political and cultural life.[7] The institute engaged in the assemblage of a great storehouse of facts about the non-German world for use by government agencies; it took an active part in disseminating "geopolitical" dogma to the nation's educational institutions, and was responsible for the publication of maps and atlases for popular use in which, through clever cartography, German geopolitical doctrines were made to appear as scientific facts. The institute was also associated with the training of men entering the foreign service, and at least indirectly, it took part in the preparation for German territorial expansion.

Haushofer was intrigued with the potentialities of the Soviet Union and looked forward to the day when Germany would be in control of this vital area. He never advocated war with Russia, but rather concentrated on a "conquest by subversion," the first step of which was a German-Russian alliance. This alliance would be followed by a gradual German encroachment on Russia's military and economic systems. Haushofer was delighted with the signing of the Russo-German nonaggression pact in August, 1939; two years later, when Germany invaded the U.S.S.R., he had grave doubts about the outcome of the struggle.

With the collapse of Nazi Germany the elaborate system of *Geopolitik* also was abandoned. But two related items still deserve the attention of political geographers. The first involves the use of the term "geopolitics." Because of Nazi Germany's exploitation of the word, it was fallen into considerable disrepute. Since the end of World War II there have been suggestions, by both geographers and political scientists, for a revival of the

[7] For discussions of German geopolitics, see Andreas Dorpalen, *The World of General Haushofer* (New York: Farrar & Rinehart, 1942); Andrew Gyorgy, *Geopolitics: The New German Science* (Berkeley and Los Angeles: University of California Press, 1944); Robert Strausz-Hupé, *Geopolitics: The Struggle for Space and Power* (New York: G. P Putnam's Sons, 1942); Hans Weigert, *Generals and Geographers: The Twilight of Geopolitics* (New York: Oxford University Press, 1942); Derwent Whittlesey, *et al.*, *German Strategy of World Conquest* (New York: Farrar & Rinehart, 1942).

term to designate the "borderland" between geography and political science.[8] Among these is the suggestion that it be used to refer to "applied" political geography, that is, to the study of the political world from the viewpoint of national self-interest. It would seem, however, that "geopolitics" is a term which has already been much abused, and which might well be abandoned by both geographers and political scientists, except when used in its historic context.

A second point is that in the writings of Ratzel and Kjellén—as well as of those who preceded them—there are many provocative ideas and observations. As the memories of German expansionism recede with time, new propagandists may well emerge in various States of the world to "reassess" these determinist concepts and to relate them—as "scientific" principles—to their own particular area. The organic State, boundaries adjusted to satisfy national "requirements," life as a fight for space—slogans such as these are ever in readiness for national spokesmen to utilize in justifying territorial aggrandizement.

Global Relationships

The emphasis in political geography on national power led certain writers to broaden their scope of interests to include political patterns on a global scale. The growth of colonial empires during the nineteenth century focused attention on Africa and Asia and on the sea lanes which connect these continents with Europe and North America. In 1900 Ratzel published a book in which he conceived of the sea as the great unifying element in human culture. He wrote at length on the eventual struggle for world domination between continental and maritime peoples, and concluded that ultimate victory would go to the land-based power because of its superior resources. The Pacific was characterized as the "ocean of the future"; the nations bordering it would in time become world powers.

The role of the sea in human destiny was also treated by an American admiral, Alfred Thayer Mahan (1840–1914). Mahan emphasized the importance of maritime development in a State's history, and asserted that the most essential geographic factor of national power was not the number of square miles of land in a country but the length of its coast line and the character of the harbors. He was greatly impressed by the overseas expansion of Great Britain; the United States, he felt, should pay close attention to its own sea frontiers. Mahan advocated possession of the Hawaiian Islands, establishment of control in the Caribbean, and construction of a canal across Central America to link the Atlantic and Pacific oceans. Mahan's best-known work was *The Influence of Sea Power upon History, 1660–1783*. Throughout this and other writings runs the theme that future

---

[8] See particularly Kristof, *op. cit.*

world power rests on control of the seas. His books were read and appreciated by Theodore Roosevelt, himself an advocate of naval supremacy. During Roosevelt's administration many of Mahan's ideas were adopted as basic tenets of American foreign policy.

One of the best-known concepts of global power forces has been the Heartland theory of the British scholar Sir Halford Mackinder (1861–1947). In a paper entitled "The Geographical Pivot of History,"[9] read in London in 1904, Mackinder propounded the thesis that in the northern and interior portion of the Eurasian continent is an area inaccessible to sea power, which in time was capable of becoming the seat of a land power of overwhelming importance.

In 1919 and again in 1943 Mackinder restated his ideas,[10] and although the details of the pivot area or Heartland varied with later publications, the essential features of the Heartland concept were not greatly changed.

The physical basis of power in the Heartland lies in the protected interior lowlands of Eurasia, stretching from the Baltic–Black Sea isthmus 2,500 miles eastward to the Yenisey River, and from the Arctic Ocean south to the mountain barriers which extend from Turkey to Mongolia. Here lies an enormous plain of 4¼ million square miles with great potentialities in terms of natural resources. The state occupying this interior lowland would, according to Mackinder, be virtually invulnerable to attack except from the west. Its rivers drain to the Arctic or to inland bodies of water. Only through the Baltic and Black seas could hostile naval forces strike at the Heartland. It is secured from overland attack as a result of its protective ring of mountains and deserts and by the Arctic Ocean. Only in the west, between the Carpathian Mountains and the Baltic Sea, is there a direct lowland route into the Heartland.

Mackinder felt that the Heartland power could utilize its resources for the development of a strong agricultural-industrial economy. If some other strong power, such as Germany, were allied with the Heartland nation, they could then spread out over adjoining countries to the seacoasts of Eurasia, great fleets could be built challenging the sea power of Britain, Japan, and other "insular" states, and the "empire of the world" would then be in sight. Since the gateway to the Heartland lies in eastern Europe, and since the Heartland is a natural fortress capable of development and expansion, Mackinder formulated his famous hypothesis:

Who rules East Europe commands the Heartland:
Who rules the Heartland commands the World-Island:
Who rules the World-Island commands the World.

---

[9] *Geographical Journal*, XXIII (1904), 421–44.
[10] *Democratic Ideals and Reality: A Study in the Politics of Reconstruction* (New York: Henry Holt & Company, 1944); "The Round World and the Winning of the Peace," *Foreign Affairs*, XXI (1943), 595–606.

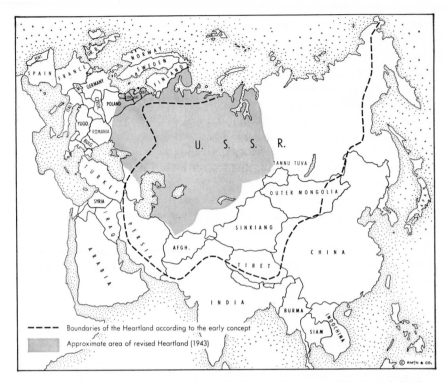

Figure 2. Mackinder's Heartland. (After Mackinder, *Democratic Ideals and Reality*. Used by permission of Holt, Rinehart and Winston, Inc., copyright 1919, 1942.)

Mackinder's Heartland concept was practically unnoticed by his contemporaries for many years, although during and since World War II there has been a considerable display of interest in his prophecy of the development of a strong Heartland power. Arthur Hall has commented,

> In 1904 and 1919 it appeared to Mackinder that Heartland dominance might be brought about only through a combination of Germany and Russia, or possibly through a conquest of the Heartland by Japan and China. It is difficult to see how the Heartland could have remained anything but a peripheral area for a long time if either of these two possibilities had come to pass, for the center of power would have been outside the Heartland, either to the west or to the east. Because of the fortunes of war the success of the Heartland power has exceeded even Mackinder's expectations. The center of power is not in some outside capital, such as Berlin, Tokyo, or Peking, but in Moscow, within the edge of the Heartland itself.[11]

---

[11] "Mackinder and the Course of Events," *Annals of the Association of American Geographers,* XLV (1955), 120.

The defeat of Germany and Japan in World War II and the weakening of China, Britain, and France created a situation in which the Soviet Union emerged as a dominant power. Yet Dr. Hall feels that the emergence of Russia does not substantiate Mackinder's prophecy. "The analysis by which the formula was derived was faulty in two respects; first, the area chosen as the most important seat of power had not in fact played a pivotal role in world history during a long period of time; and second, the existence of another heartland in Anglo-America was overlooked, and this heartland was capable of occupying as important a place in planetary affairs as the one in Eurasia."[12]

Nearly four decades after the first appearance of Mackinder's thesis, an American, Nicholas J. Spykman (1893–1943), countered with a "Rimland" theory, in which he postulated that control of Eurasia, and ultimately of the world, might more logically lie in the belt of nations surrounding the Heartland than in the Heartland itself. "Geography is the most fundamental factor in the foreign policy of states because it is the most permanent," he once wrote. "Ministers come and ministers go, even dictators die, but mountain ranges stand unperturbed."[13]

His most outstanding work from a geopolitical point of view was *The Geography of the Peace,* published in 1944, shortly after his death. Several basic ideas concerning geopolitical thought were outlined in this book. The first was that national power is the final determinant of security for a state. The only way to achieve lasting peace is through a collective security system, such as an armed League of Nations or by means of an international balance-of-power arrangement. His second idea was in line with Mackinder's thesis, namely, that control of the World-Island could enable a nation to achieve eventual world domination. Spykman approached the problem from the American point of view, and remarked that the Western Hemisphere is "surrounded" by the Eastern Hemisphere, including the Eurasian land mass and the continents of Africa and Australia. The area of the Eastern Hemisphere is two and a half times that of the Western, and its population is ten times as great. In terms of 1937 output, the Old World produced over two-thirds of the earth's coal and iron ore. Spykman's conclusion was that the Western Hemisphere could scarcely stand up against the Eastern in a prolonged global struggle; therefore one of the basic tenets of American foreign policy should be to prevent the consolidation of Eurasia under one power.

In his book Spykman considered Mackinder's analysis of global politics and concluded that there were several fallacies in the Englishman's reasoning. The most important of these to Spykman's mind was Mackinder's overemphasis of the Heartland's potentialities. The American writer pointed out that much of the area between Poland and the Yenisey River is waste-

---

[12] *Ibid.*, p. 125.
[13] Nicholas J. Spykman, *America's Strategy in World Politics: The United States and the Balance of Power* (New York: Harcourt, Brace & Company, 1942), p. 41.

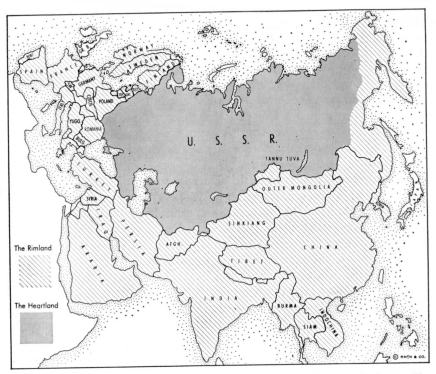

Figure 3. Spykman's Rimland. (After a map by J. McA. Smiley in Spykman, *The Geography of the Peace.* Used by permission of Harcourt, Brace & World, Inc., copyright 1944.)

land, and the real power potential of Eurasia lies not in the Heartland itself but in the belt of nations surrounding the Heartland. This belt Spykman called the "Rimland" (Figure 3). Within it are the majority of the world's population and much of its resources. History, he maintained, has never been a clear-cut struggle between land power and sea power, but rather a series of contests in which the Rimland has served as a buffer zone between the Heartland and the island empires of Britain and Japan. Spykman concluded that the geopolitical slogan of world power should read, "Who controls the Rimland rules Eurasia; who rules Eurasia controls the destinies of the world."[14]

Despite the apparent logic of the global predictions of Mahan, Mackinder and Spykman, considerable criticism has been leveled against them on the grounds that they are oversimplifications of history. Each great political analysis was written for a particular era; regardless of how valid

[14] Nicholas Spykman, *The Geography of the Peace* (New York: Harcourt, Brace & Company, 1944), p. 43.

the conclusions may have been at the time they were first announced, they could not apply over an indefinite period of time. Writing in the magazine *Foreign Affairs* in 1950, the British geographer W. Gordon East asserted that Mackinder's theory "contains generalizations and assumptions which scarcely withstand close analysis. In a world of rapid technological progress the geography of territory, since it is ever-changing, should be continually revalued."[15] Professor East was aware of similarities between Mackinder's Heartland idea and the present world power alignment, yet he maintained, "'It is surely both unwise and dangerous to accept as a predetermined end the prediction that world hegemony must, on certain assumptions, inevitably pass to the rulers of one specified portion of the earth."[16]

Even if we dismiss these world power theories as overgeneralizations, we still face a problem of correlating the manifold elements of national power on a global basis. "The problem of how to view the world in meaningful perspective is a fundamental challenge constantly confronting the geographer," Meinig has written, and he suggested retention of the terms "heartland" and "rimland," although the boundaries of these areas are somewhat different from those laid down by the earlier writers. "Mackinder and Spykman have given us fresh ideas as to how to view the world in meaningful perspective; their concepts of heartland and rimland are useful and important . . . if they are to become of maximum value, applicable beyond any momentary context of strategic patterns, those definitions must become specific in concept yet flexible in historical-spatial use." He concluded, "The basic geopolitical patterns of the world are inherently dynamic, changing day by day, often inscrutably, always complexly. It is essential that our images of the world reflect those changes and this demands generalized tools and concepts."[17]

In line with post-World War II technical developments, new global theories have been evolved which hold that air is now the medium in which ultimate power resides. One of the most noted proponents of this type of theory is Major Alexander de Seversky, whose book *Air Power: Key to Survival*[18] has been widely read and discussed. In Seversky's reasoning global power reaches its ultimate form. He described the bipolarization of power in North America and in Eurasia, and concluded that a great industrial nation should organize its military efforts toward the establishment of world-wide supremacy. Seversky holds no brief for small wars, as in Korea and Indochina, since they sap the strength of the United States without seriously affecting the basic strength of the Soviet Union. He feels that

---

[15] W. Gordon East, "How Strong is the Heartland?" *Foreign Affairs*, XXIX (1950), 80.
[16] *Ibid.*
[17] Donald Meinig, "Heartland and Rimland in Eurasian History," *The Western Political Quarterly*, IX (1956), 555, 568.
[18] New York: Simon & Schuster, 1950.

the great deterrent to Communist aggression should be the threat of massive air retaliation on so large a scale as to amount to virtual annihilation of the enemy. Under such conditions the United States has little need for military bases and alliances in the Eastern Hemisphere; rather it should confine itself to the defense of the Americas.

In summarizing the "National Power" approach to political geography we may note, first, the analysis of the State as a power organism and, second, the consideration of the world political pattern from the point of view of permanent or semipermanent power areas. There is nothing inherently wrong in these types of analysis, although the following three items should be noted concerning such power studies: (1) The analyst is tempted to view power phenomena from the viewpoint of his own State; therefore if findings are based on the principles of national self-interest, they should be recognized as such, and not advertised as universal truths. (2) In order for his findings to be both meaningful and objective, the analyst must have a thorough background in history, geography, military science, and other related disciplines; otherwise he will fall victim to half-truths which do not stand up under rigid testing. (3) Power analyses such as these can hardly be labelled "geography." In the sense that they point up regional differences they are "geographic" in nature, but if the end product is to assess national power in one form or another, such studies should be recognized as power analyses.

THE STUDY OF POLITICAL REGIONS

During the early years of the twentieth century not all the work done in the field of political geography was concerned with the different power aspects of the world. A trend was developing among geographers toward more detailed studies of specific politico-geographic problems. By 1920, for example, several excellent books had appeared in Britain on the subject of international frontiers. During the deliberations of Allied statesmen at the peace conference following World War I, political geographers were able to be of particular service. When the time came to redraw the political map of Europe, President Woodrow Wilson sought the advice of geographic specialists, among them Dr. Isaiah Bowman, then Director of the American Geographical Society. Several of the experts' recommendations were used by the American delegation as bases for discussions with representatives of other Allied nations, thereby demonstrating a practical application of the political geographer's training and experience to international affairs.

In 1921 Dr. Bowman published *The New World*, in which he discussed most of the politico-geographic problem areas then in existence throughout the world. Although much of its factual material is no longer pertinent, the book is recognized as one of the most important works to appear in the field of political geography. For the first time a geographer had compiled a volume in which the major problem areas of the time were assembled and analyzed, not only as individual studies, but also in their relationship to the over-all political pattern of the world. In this way emphasis was placed on the importance of regional studies within the framework of global political geography.

Since 1921 increased American participation in world affairs, together with advances in the theoretical aspects of political geography, has led to the appearance of many books, articles, and monographs in the field. A rough breakdown of these writings might be made under the following three headings: (1) theoretical aspects of political regions, (2) studies of political phenomena, and (3) studies of specific political areas.

Theoretical Aspects of Political Regions

Relatively little work has been done in developing a body of theory for political geography. Even as late as the mid-1930's Hartshorne was unable to find a clear basis for determining the purpose and scope of the field. On the eve of World War II Whittlesey wrote, "For me the differentiation of political phenomena from place to place over the earth is the essence of political geography,"[19] an approach which other recent writers have generally accepted. Hans Weigert feels that political geography "deals with the political organizations of men on the face of the globe."[20] Theodore Herman conceives of it as "the study of the organization and expression of political power on the surface of the earth,"[21] while Hartshorne has defined political geography as "the study of the variations of political phenomena from place to place in interconnection with variations in other features of the earth as the home of man."[22]

Geographers generally approach the study of the political world from the point of view of political phenomena of the earth's surface. The political scientist, on the other hand, concerned as he is primarily with political process, has found he must do more than develop generalizations independent of differences in given areas; these processes must be studied as they operate in particular areas. Thus the political area or region represents the organizational framework within which processes involving political power may be analyzed in terms of their interaction with the various features of the earth's surface. In this sense, then, the political region represents the starting point (a) from which other political features of the earth's surface, such as boundaries, capitals, or other administrative subdivisions, may be studied, and (b) from which to analyze the spatial characteristics of political proc-

---

[19] *The Earth and the State*, p. iii.
[20] *Principles of Political Geography* (New York: Appleton-Century-Crofts, 1957), p. 26.
[21] "Group Values Toward the National Space: The Case of China," *The Geographical Review*, XLIX (1959), 164.
[22] "Political Geography in the Modern World," p. 52.

esses, such as cohesion or disunity within states, expansion of national power, or the development of regional attitudes or voting characteristics.

Publications on the development and theory of political geography per se have been relatively scarce. In 1935 Hartshorne discussed developments in political geography up to that time and suggested a "morphological" approach to the study of political regions, based primarily on the physical and cultural characteristics of the State as a geographic area.[23]

In 1950 he reconsidered his position and came out in favor of a functional approach to the study of political regions with emphasis on the forces of unity and diversity within the state. "State areas are important," he wrote, " . . . in what the area as a whole means to its parts and to its relations as a whole with outside areas."[24] Seven years later, while still holding to the functional analysis of regions, he came out strongly for studies of the effects of political phenomena on nonpolitical aspects of the environment.[25]

Stephen Jones, in his analyses of political regions,[26] has described the link between political area on the one hand, and political ideas and decisions on the other (see page 7). He has written on national power from the point of view both of resources and of national strategy, or, as he put it, "the art of using power for the attainment of goals in competition."[27] He has also considered the ways in which man views the political world, and has suggested a global view of national power based both upon "Man Settling" and "Man Travelling" (see page 609). Jean Gottman has made a number of studies on the processes of organization of space into political regions.[28] "Linking sovereignty to the right to regional differentiation, to a freedom of ways of life, may perhaps help formulate a 'spatial' principle of sovereignty," he once wrote. "Sovereignty may well be the legal tool through which people attempt to preserve their right to differentiate themselves from their neighbors."[29]

David Neft has sought to work out a statistical method for determining the relative magnitude of influence of a particular country in some foreign area.[30] Basing his calculations on population and income potentials, he has developed interesting hypotheses on the "realm of influence" of the United States in Southeast Asia, and the implications these findings have for American foreign policy. It is studies such as these which have pointed the way

[23] "Recent Developments in Political Geography," *American Political Science Review*, XXIX (1935), 784–804, 943–66.
[24] "The Functional Approach in Political Geography," *Annals of the Association of American Geographers*, XL (1950), 128.
[25] "Political Geography in the Modern World."
[26] "A Unified Field Theory of Political Geography."
[27] "The Power Inventory and National Strategy," *World Politics*, VI (1954), 421–53.
[28] *La politique des états et leur geographie* (Paris: Armand Colin, 1952); "Geography and International Relations," *World Politics*, III (1950–51), 153–73; "The Political Partitioning of our World: An Attempt at Analysis," *ibid.*, IV (1952), 512–19.
[29] "Geography and International Relations," p. 172.
[30] "Macrogeography and the Realms of Influence in Asia," *Journal of Conflict Resolution*, V (1961), 254–74.

for the gradual development of a distinct and coherent body of politico-geographic knowledge. "In perhaps no other branch of geography," Hartshorne once complained, "has the attempt to teach others gone so far ahead of the pursuit of learning by the teachers."[31] In the dynamic political world of today only a beginning has been made to the investigation of the interactions existing between political processes on the one hand and the various features of the earth's surface on the other.

Studies of Individual Political Phenomena

In Chapter 1 the term "political phenomena" was defined as including both the features produced by political forces and the political ideas generating those forces. In terms of specific political features, there are numerous writings on such subjects as political boundaries, capitals, and related phenomena. The literature on boundaries is treated in detail in Chapter 4. Mention will be made here only of the books on boundaries by S. W. Boggs, Stephen Jones, and Vittorio Adami; the articles by Jones, Norman Pounds, Eric Fischer, Ladis Kristof, and Jan Broek; and the work on offshore boundaries by Boggs and Pearcy. Benjamin Thomas, Edward Ullman, and others have written of boundaries between individual states of the United States.[32]

Among the studies of other individual political features are those of Vaughan Cornish and O. H. K. Spate on capital cities, of G. W. S. Robinson on exclaves of the world, of Alexander Melamid on neutral territories, and of J. R. V. Prescott and John K. Wright on "electoral" geography, that is, the spatial distribution of election results.[33] To date little work has been

---

[31] "Political Geography," in P. E. James and C. F. Jones (eds.), *American Geography: Inventory and Prospect* (Syracuse: Syracuse University Press, 1954), p. 170.

[32] Boggs, *International Boundaries: A Study of Boundary Functions and Problems* (New York: Columbia University Press, 1940); Jones, *Boundary-Making: A Handbook for Statesmen, Treaty Editors and Boundary Commissioners* (New York: Columbia University Press, 1945); Adami, *National Frontiers in Relation to International Law*, trans. H. H. Behrens (London: Oxford University Press, 1927); Jones, "Boundary Concepts in the Setting of Time and Place," *Annals of the Association of American Geographers*, XLIX (1959), 241–55; Pounds, "The Origin of the Idea of Natural Frontiers in France," *Annals of the Association of American Geographers*, XLI (1951), 146–57, and "France and 'Les Limits Naturelles' from the Seventeenth to the Twentieth Centuries," *ibid.*, XLIV (1954), 51–62; Fischer, "On Boundaries," *World Politics*, I (1948–49), 196–222; Kristof, "The Nature of Frontiers and Boundaries," *Annals of the Association of American Geographers*, XLIX (1959), 269–82; Broek, "The Problem of 'Natural Frontiers,'" in Committee on International Relations, University of California, *Frontiers of the Future* (Berkeley and Los Angeles: University of California Press, 1941), pp. 3–20; Boggs, "National Claims in Adjacent Seas," *The Geographical Review*, XLI (1951), 185–210; Pearcy, "Geographical Aspects of the Law of the Sea," *Annals of the Association of American Geographers*, XLIX (1959), 1–24; Thomas, "Boundaries and Internal Problems of Idaho," *The Geographical Review*, XXXIX (1949), 99–109; Ullman, "The Eastern Rhode Island–Massachusetts Boundary Zone," *The Geographical Review*, XXIX (1939), 291–302.

[33] Cornish, *The Great Capitals, an Historical Geography* (London, Methuen & Company, 1926); Spate, "Factors in the Development of Capital Cities," *The Geographical Review*, XXXII (1942), 622–32; Robinson, "Exclaves," *Annals of the Association of American Geographers*, XLIX (1959), 283–96; Melamid, "The Economic Geography of Neutral Territories," *The Geographical Review*, XLV (1955), 359–74; Prescott, "The Function and Methods of Electoral Geography," *Annals of the Association of American Geographers*, XLIX (1959), 296–305; Wright, "Voting Habits in the United States," *The Geographical Review*, XXII (1932), 666–72.

done by geographers on such topics as differences in the administrative sub-divisions of various States, in the relationships between geography and the laws of nations, or in techniques of mapping the areal distribution of polit-ical interest groups within a country. The emphasis in a great many po-litico-geographic studies on boundaries and problems of territorial control has tended to obscure other important topics relating to the functioning of the political region.

Studies of Specific Political Areas

A majority of the publications in political geography have involved the description and analysis of specific areas. Only a few representative studies will be noted here.

Territorial problems have attracted much attention, as evidenced by Sarah Wambaugh's intensive study of the plebiscites following World War I, Sophia Saucerman's analysis of European territorial changes after 1918, and descriptions of individual regions, such as Kashmir, South Tyrol, and the Saarland. Keith Buchanan wrote on unity and diversity in northern Nigeria, while Spate considered the political effects of the partitioning of the Indian subcontinent. A. E. Moodie, Hartshorne, Robert Platt, and George Hoffman are among the scores of writers who have considered in-dividual problem areas relating to international boundaries.[34]

Some writers have sought to describe the factors of political individu-ality of certain regions, the phenomena which differentiate one region from another. Whittlesey's studies of Andorra's autonomy, Hoffman's work on Austria's survival as an independent unit, and James Johnson's writings on the distinctiveness of Northern Ireland are representative of this type of approach.[35]

The scale of study of political regions may be contracted in order to concentrate on specific features, or expanded to include a number of regions brought together in one political grouping, such as NATO, the Common

---

[34] Wambaugh, *Plebiscites Since the World War* (Washington: Carnegie Endowment for Inter-national Peace, 1933); Saucerman, *International Transfers of Territory in Europe* (Washington: U.S. Government Printing Office, 1937); Robert C. Mayfield, "A Geographic Study of the Kashmir Issue," *The Geographical Review*, XLV (1955), 181–97; Guido C. Weigend, "Effects of Boundary Changes in the South Tyrol," *The Geographical Review*, XL (1950), 364–76; Colbert C. Held, "The New Saarland," *The Geographical Review*, XLI (1951), 590–606; Buchanan, "The Northern Region of Nigeria: The Geographical Background of its Political Duality," *The Geographical Re-view*, XLIII (1953), 451–74; Spate, "The Partition of India and the Prospects of Pakistan," *The Geographical Review*, XXXVIII (1948), 5–30; Moodie, *The Italo-Yugoslav Boundary* (London: George Philip and Son, 1945); Hartshorne, "Geographic and Political Boundaries in Upper Silesia"; Platt, "Conflicting Territorial Claims in the Upper Amazon," in C. C. Colby (ed.), *Geographic Aspects of International Relations* (Chicago: University of Chicago Press, 1938); Hoffman, "The Netherlands Demands on Germany: A Post-War Problem in Political Geography," *Annals of the Association of American Geographers*, XLII (1952), 129–53.
[35] Whittlesey, "Andorra's Autonomy," *Journal of Modern History*, VI (1934), 147–55; Hoffman, "The Survival of an Independent Austria," *The Geographical Review*, XLI (1951), 606–22; John-son, "The Political Distinctiveness of Northern Ireland," *The Geographical Review*, LII (1962), 78–92.

Market, or the Warsaw Pact countries. Here again one may deal with the internal or external functioning of such organizations and their effects on nonpolitical aspects of the landscape, such as the movement of goods or of people across international borders. Included under this general heading would be studies of particular "power areas," such as Donald Meinig's "Heartland and Rimland in Eurasian History." It is, perhaps, unfortunate that more work has not been done in recent years by political geographers in this international phase of the field—not to seek out sweeping laws and relationships, but merely to identify trends in the changing pattern of States, and to analyze problems involved in the functioning of "superpolitical" units.

The various publications listed in the past several pages by no means exhaust the writing done in political geography, but they suggest the breadth of topics which have been considered during the past several decades. Again, it should be emphasized that so far as the political world is concerned, only a beginning has been made by geographers and others in allied fields in the process of description and analysis. Much remains to be learned of the various ways in which man organizes space for political purposes and of the effects of this political organization on the landscape of particular areas.

BIBLIOGRAPHY

BOWMAN, ISAIAH. "Geography *vs.* Geopolitics," *The Geographical Review,* XXXII (1942), 646–58.
A discussion of differences between the two fields.

———. *The New World.* Yonkers-on-Hudson: The World Book Company, 1921.
A basic text on political regions throughout the world.

DORPALEN, ANDREAS. *The World of General Haushofer: Geopolitics in Action.* New York: Farrar & Rinehart, 1942.
A well-documented history of German geopolitics.

GYORGY, ANDREW. *Geopolitics: The New German Science.* Berkeley and Los Angeles: University of California Press, 1944.
Extremely detailed account of German geopolitics.

HALL, ARTHUR R. "Mackinder and the Course of Events," *Annals of the Association of American Geographers,* XLV (1955), 109–26.
An excellent evaluation of Mackinder's thesis.

JONES, STEPHEN B. "Views of the Political World," *The Geographical Review,* XLV (1955), 309–26.

————. "Global Strategic Views," *The Geographical Review,* XLV (1955), 492–508.
A careful discussion of methods of analyzing the political world.

KISH, GEORGE. "Political Geography into Geopolitics: Recent Trends in Germany," *The Geographical Review,* XXXII (1942), 632–45.
A discussion of pre-World War II trends in geopolitics in Germany.

KRISTOF, LADIS K. "The Origins and Evolutions of Geopolitics," *Journal of Conflict Resolution,* IV (1960), 15–52.
An extremely valuable account of the field of geopolitics.

MACKINDER, SIR HALFORD J. "The Round World and the Winning of the Peace," *Foreign Affairs,* XXI (1943), 595–606
A restatement of Mackinder's theory of world power in the light of World War II developments.

RATZEL, FRIEDRICH. *Politische Geographie.* Munich: R. Oldenbourg Verlag, 1897.
A book of historical interest because of the early concepts of the field which it contains.

RITTER, KARL. *Comparative Geography.* Philadelphia: J. B. Lippincott Company, 1864.
A treatment of the early organic theory of cultures.

SAUCERMAN, SOPHIA. *International Transfers of Territory in Europe.* Washington: U.S. Government Printing Office, 1937.
An extremely detailed summary of territorial transfers in Europe following World War I.

SPYKMAN, NICHOLAS J. *The Geography of the Peace.* New York: Harcourt, Brace & Company, 1944.
Spykman's major concepts of national power.

STRAUSZ-HUPÉ, ROBERT. *Geopolitics: The Struggle for Space and Power.* New York: G. P. Putnam's Sons, 1942.
A general treatment of the principles of geopolitics.

WAMBAUGH, SARAH. *Plebiscites Since the World War, with a Collection of Official Documents.* Washington: Carnegie Endowment for International Peace, 1933.

The basic work on this subject.

WEIGERT, HANS W. *Generals and Geographers: The Twilight of Geopolitics.* New York: Oxford University Press, 1942.

Like the writings of Dorpalen and Strausz-Hupé, this is a contemporary book on the German geopolitics.

WHITTLESEY, DERWENT. *The Earth and the State: A Study of Political Geography.* New York: Henry Holt & Company, 1944.

A world regional text which contains a great many fundamental concepts of political geography.

3

THE STRUCTURE OF THE STATE
AS A POLITICO-GEOGRAPHIC UNIT

● The State is a basic component of the world political pattern. Each State is a unique phenomenon with respect, first, to the physical attributes of the territory which constitutes it, second, to the consequences to the area of man's occupance of this territory, and, third, to the relationships existing between this State and other political areas of the world. In terms of its functional aspects, that is, the manner in which it performs the tasks for which it was created, the State, as noted in Chapter 1, might be thought of as possessing the following five elements: (1) an expanse of territory delimited by boundaries, (2) an effective administrative system which controls the area, (3) a resident population, (4) an economic structure, and (5) a circulatory system of transportation and communication media. Obviously States differ markedly from one another in terms of the particular features they possess under each of these five headings. Some, like the United States and the U.S.S.R., are large in area and rich in resources, while other States are small and poorly endowed. Belgium has an effective central government, Laos does not; China's enormous population is perhaps its most distinguishing feature; Canada's population is ethnically divided, while Brazil's is distributed unevenly about the State with large stretches of empty area between groups.

AN EXPANSE OF TERRITORY DELIMITED BY BOUNDARIES

The entire land surface of the globe—with the exception of Antarctica —is divided into political regions. Some are dependent, some independent, yet each has a central gevernmental structure, and each is separated from its neighbors by political boundaries. The word "territory" implies not only areal extent but also the physical attributes which accrue to a region. The "boundaries" represent the outer limits of the territory within which the central government exercises political control. In the discussion which follows, this element of a State will be described in terms first of territory, then of boundaries.

The Physical Attributes of Territory

The physical attributes of territory include location, size, shape, climate, surface configuration, soils, vegetation and animal life, water features, and mineral resources. These physical attributes, alone and in association with one another, place limits on the types of activities man may carry on within a given area. Within broad limits man has a variety of choices from which to select the manner in which he will occupy his habitat; the presence of certain features may, of course, present him with unusual opportunities, as, for example, the oil resources of Kuwait, the fertile soils of the Ukraine, or the fisheries resources in the waters adjoining Iceland. Germany's coal deposits have aided that State's industrial development and the development of its military power potential. Panama's location at the isthmus connecting North and South America, Japan's island environment, and Greenland's inhospitable climate present other cases in which physical attributes have been of particular significance to the functioning of a political region.

1. Location is probably the most important single aspect of a State's physical make-up. Among the more important headings under which it may be considered are location with respect to latitude, to land and water bodies, to other States, and to natural resources outside the boundaries of the State itself.

In terms of latitude it is significant that no State lying wholly or primarily within the tropical or polar regions has succeeded as yet in modern times in developing into a strong, cohesive nation. The principal cause for this is climate, although in many areas the limiting influence of climate is due more to human preference than to inherent qualities of "good" or "bad" in the climate itself (see page 41). Another factor is the general location of coal resources between 40 and 60 degrees of latitude, thereby providing the base for industrialization of States within this zone. If atomic power can be successfully harnessed for industry, however, the coal-poor tropical lands of the world will have greater opportunity for national development than has been the case in the past.

Location with respect to water bodies is important because of the tempering effect they have on climate and of the opportunities the seas and oceans offer for commercial activities and for political and economic ex-

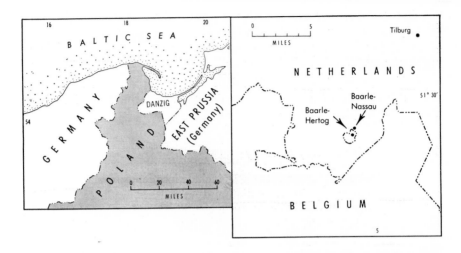

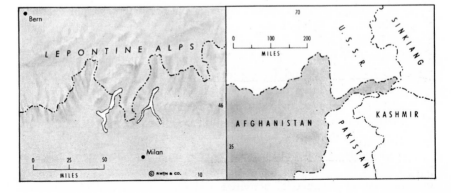

Figure 4. Extremes of Shape.

Poland's Corridor to the Baltic Sea, 1920–39.

Belgian Enclave in the Netherlands.

Dutch Bridgehead in Belgian Territory.

Swiss Glacis Extending South into Italy.

Projection of Afghanistan Between U.S.S.R. and Pakistan.

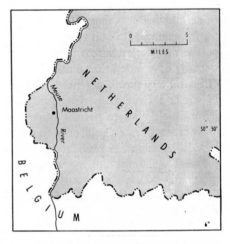

pansion. Britain's maritime location illustrates these advantages. Access to the sea is a prize many States have sought at various times (Figure 4). Some, such as the United States and France, have access to several seas; others, like Iraq and Belgium, have only limited coast lines; still others (Bolivia, Austria) have no borders whatever on the sea.

Proximity to land bodies, on the other hand, may entail climatic extremes, it may provide opportunities for trade and territorial expansion on the mainland, and it may also be a source of danger because of potential invasion and occupation by states located on the mainland. Japan may be taken to illustrate all three points. Cold air masses in winter move eastward from Asia to Japan; nearness to the mainland provided opportunity for Japanese territorial expansion there in the first four decades of the twentieth century; finally, proximity to the Asian land mass since World War II has carried with it the danger of attack on Japan from a continental power.

Location with respect to other States (vicinal location) is probably the most important of the three locational aspects. The boundaries which separate a State from its neighbors and the territorial disputes arising therefrom are of profound importance to the State's political development; the problems relating to invasion, defense, and economic dominance take on added significance. Thus, for example, Poland's territorial problems with its neighbors have been a major factor in that state's history as a national unit. Belgium—although its boundaries have remained fairly stable since 1839—has twice been the victim of German military aggression directed toward France. The history of territorial control in Korea has been strongly influenced by the peninsula's location with respect to Japan, China, and Russia.

2. Size is important to a State in terms of both defense and political control. The more area a State has in which to fall back before invading forces, the better are its chances for survival. The position of the Soviet Union during World War II is an example of trading "space for time" in the face of the enemy. Large size also permits dispersion of population and industries as targets for bombing; on the other hand, it also means longer borders to defend against ground and air attack. With respect to internal control, large size may be a disadvantage, for communications between the capital and faraway regions may be difficult to maintain, leading to the possible development of separatist movements in peripheral areas. For example, distance has historically been an important factor in the weakening of China's control over Sinkiang and Outer Mongolia.

3. Shape is also important for defense and internal control. A narrow country, no matter how great the area, is more difficult to defend than one which is compact. For internal political cohesion, a circular shape, with the capital in the center, would be advantageous, since distances from the capital to outlying areas are kept to a minimum.

Special concepts relative to shape are found in the *bridgehead,* the *glacis,* and the *projection* (Figure 4). An *enclave* is a portion of one country's territory that is completely surrounded by another country. In most situations the terms *enclave* and *exclave* are used interchangeably. West Berlin, for example, is an *enclave* within East Germany and an *exclave* of West Germany. "Exclaves," Robinson noted, "are not important phenomena in political geography. They are rare and mostly small. But their special status is of value in illustrating the relations of states in difficult geographical circumstances and in illuminating the importance of uninterrupted territory to present-day states."[1] Most exclaves are relics of historical political patterns, or of military compromises, such as the Hebrew University exclave in the Jordanian sector of Jerusalem. East Pakistan, almost entirely surrounded on its land borders by India, is too large to be considered an *exclave;* a better term for it might be *outlier.*

A *glacis* is an extension of territorial control of a country across a mountain divide. One of the most famous was that of the Austrians in South Tyrol, prior to World War I. The glacis extended south of the Brenner Pass, marking the crossing of the main crest of the Alps, and was inhabited largely by German-speaking people. Following World War I, Italy annexed the South Tyrol, but the problem of the German-speaking population has never been satisfactorily solved (see page 249).

Two other extremes of shape are the *projection* and the *bridgehead.* A *projection* is a long, narrow extension of territory separating two foreign countries from one another, such as the eastward projection of Afghanistan between the Soviet Union and what is now Pakistan. A *bridgehead* is an extension of territorial control by one State across a river. Few examples of bridgeheads are left in the world; one is the Dutch bridgehead across the Meuse River at Maastricht. Belgian ships using the Meuse pass into and out of Dutch territory at this point.

Several countries of the world, such as Chile and Norway, are extremely long and narrow, although there are few politically divisive forces in these countries resulting from shape. Panama, once a narrow northward extension of Colombian territory, became politically separated from Colombia early in the twentieth century, not because of shape, but because it included the most practical route for a transoceanic canal, and Colombia refused to sanction United States construction of such a canal. Pakistan has a noncontiguous shape and considerable political diversity between its two parts—a diversity existing largely because of the completely different physical and cultural environments (except for the dominant religion) in the two areas. The point here is that shape alone does not directly affect a State's political functioning. Afghanistan's eastward projection passes

---

[1] G. W. S. Robinson, "Exclaves," p 283.

through uninhabited territory. But shape *may* be of indirect importance through its effect on communications between a State and its outlying area (as in the case of West Berlin), because an unusual shape may result in a State's borders including areas which differ from the main body of the country (for example East Pakistan), or because a peripheral area may be the subject of territorial controversy and ultimate separation from the State (South Tyrol).

4. Climate, as it affects political development, may be difficult to assess, for it is often impossible to isolate the climatic influence from that of other physical and cultural forms. During past centuries there has been a spread of civilization from warmer to cooler climates, with a resultant strengthening of cultures in the cooler areas. Today the great world powers are located in the middle latitudes where there are seasonal variations of temperature.

Much has been written about a climatic "optimum" in the middle latitudes, but many of the conclusions stressed are debatable. The seasonal cold and the forests of the higher latitudes undoubtedly were effective obstacles to the northward spread of early civilizations from their subtropical locations. Toynbee wrote that "the challenge of the northern seasonal cold . . . evoked a new creative response in such as did not succumb to it."[2] Only with the development of new tools and techniques were the people of early civilizations able to overcome the challenge of the cold and the forests. Certainly Western civilization, as we know it today, had its roots in the Roman-Hellenic world, but was nourished and developed first in the forest clearings of northwestern Europe and later in the pioneer lands of the New World. The development of a particular civilization is associated with the economic, military, and political strength of its political units, especially in relation to the units of other civilizations.

When Western civilization spread outward from its center in northwestern and north central Europe, it became established for the most part in those places of the world that had humid, mid-latitude climates, similar to the climates left behind in Europe. Neither the humid tropics, the desert oases, the steppe grasslands, nor the northern lands held much attraction for settlement by the European peoples; to these areas they came primarily for exploitation rather than for permanent settlement. Even in the colonization of humid, mid-latitude climates the initial goals of the Europeans were essentially exploitative, but this period lasted a relatively short time. In such areas as Canada, Australia, the United States, and New Zealand exploitation eventually gave way to permanent settlement.

The present location of Western industrial societies throughout the world is thus more the result of human preference than of inherent limita-

[2] Arnold J. Toynbee, *A Study of History*, abridgement by D. C. Somervell (New York and London: Oxford University Press, 1947), p. 70.

tions of particular climates. The Europeans chose to transfer their culture to areas having mid-latitude climates; this culture, with its greater utilization of inanimate energy and its background of technical discoveries, has provided the basis for the development of the world's most powerful nations. During the past several decades there has been a process of diffusion—as opposed to the earlier displacement—of Western civilization into new areas in both the middle and low latitudes. The latter case—that is, the spread to subtropical areas of Western industrial cultures, and with it the potentialities for achievement of major-power status—refutes the theory of direct relationships between climate and the power position of nations.

In addition to climatic influences on the distribution of world power areas, there are relationships between climate and the political structure of individual States, particularly the effects of climatic diversity on forces of political unity and disunity. The pattern of climates within a State is related to population distribution. Regions of pronounced cold or aridity or humid, tropical climates are often sparsely populated, a factor contributing to the State's political complexity. Within each State is the *ecumene,* defined as "the most populous region of the state, particularly that part most closely knit by communication lines."[3] Frequently the capital city is located in, or close to, the ecumene, so that there is a concentration of economic and political power there. If population is concentrated in only a small portion of the national territory (as in China), much of the State's area may not be effectively organized, and in time parts of it may become separated from the capital's control. On the other hand, there may be two or more population centers in a State (as in Bolivia), separated by sparsely inhabited territory, resulting in the presence of strong centrifugal forces.

Climatic differences may also contribute to economic diversity in a State. The resultant conflict of interests may represent a strong centrifugal force, such as existed between North and South prior to the Civil War, where the South, because of its humid, subtropical climate, depended largely on a plantation economy and the use of slaves, while the North could not benefit from this type of economy. On the other hand, economic differences may contribute to national unity, as, for example, in Australia, where regional groups saw the advantages of combining into a single political unit.

5. Surface Configuration —that is, mountains, plateaus, hills, and plains—may be of great importance to a State's politico-geographic structure. Mountain peoples may enjoy some semblance of isolation with resulting independence (Afghanistan, Andorra), while people in lowland areas, such as the Ukrainians, may often be subject to foreign interference and thus have little opportunity for self-rule. The presence of mountain ranges along a

---

[3] Derwent Whittlesey, *The Earth and the State,* p. 597.

Figure 5. Diverse Topography. Peru also claims the territory from the present eastern boundary west to dotted line. See also Figure 30.

boundary can help to defend a State against attack from its neighbors and therefore preserve its independence. The Pyrenees between France and Spain and the Alps separating Italy from Austria are examples of mountain areas which have figured prominently in military campaigns between the adjoining states. Mountain areas may also serve as redoubts for guerrilla forces, as in Yugoslavia during World War II, after the war in northern Greece, and later for Castro's forces in Cuba. In all of these cases effective control by the central government was impossible in the rugged upland areas.

There are various situations in which surface configuration affects the internal unity of a State. Upland and lowland areas, like climate, influence population distribution and thus the location of a State's core area. The presence of mountain ranges may hamper communications between the capital and outlying regions, and as a consequence tend to weaken the State's political cohesion. Likewise, groups inhabiting upland areas may develop different attitudes and goals than those in lowland environments, again creating disruptive political forces within the State. Ecuador, with upland and lowland core areas (centered on Quito, in the mountains, and Guayaquil, on the coast), illustrates the conflict of interests resulting in part from a mountain and lowland environment within the State (Figure 5).

6. Soils and 7. Natural Vegetation and Animal Life may in themselves have little effect on the political life of States, although they may represent prizes over which territorial disputes and even warfare may develop. Timberland, at the end of World Wars I and II, formed one of the bases for claims by some of the Benelux countries to German territory. Similarly, the fertile soils of the Ukraine have represented one of the principal assets of this area over which so much disputed control has existed during past centuries. As special cases mention should be made of countries off whose shores are extremely valuable fisheries resources. Iceland, Norway, the Faeroe Islands, and Peru are examples of countries whose internal economy and external relations have on occasion been strongly affected by the biological life in and immediately adjacent to their territorial limits.

8. Water Features may be of considerable significance to a State. Rivers are frequently cohesive factors within a country, as are the Tigris and Euphrates in Iraq or the Magdalena in central Colombia. Lakes may have a similar role. Along the shores of Lake Malar was formed a political nucleus for the early development of southern Sweden, while a somewhat analogous situation with respect to Switzerland took place about Lake Lucerne. The sea represents a unifying element in island States, such as Japan, the Philippines, and Indonesia.

On the other hand, water bodies may divide areas rather than unite them. Rivers, such as the Rio Grande and the Amur, and lakes, such as Lake Erie and Lake Geneva, are often used to make international boundaries. Some boundary rivers may be of importance to the defense of a State, although in modern warfare such physical barriers are generally overrun rapidly, witness the rate of the Allied advance across the Rhine against Germany in the spring of 1945.

Water features may be important for transportation and trade, or for irrigation and hydroelectric power. The Volga River in the U.S.S.R. serves the three functions of transportation, power, and irrigation. For use as transportation, a river must have a relatively gentle gradient; moreover, to be truly effective, it must serve an economically valuable area and flow in the direction products are likely to move. The Amazon drains a basin which, to a great extent, is virtually uninhabited, while three major rivers of Soviet Siberia flow north to the Arctic Ocean. Frequently a river basin encompasses more than one country; rivers of the past have served as avenues for expansion of a State's holdings, such as occurred in Africa in the nineteenth century when the limits of several colonies were defined in terms of the basin areas of particular streams. One of the long-term ambitions of Egypt has been to control the lands occupying the basin of the Nile, a basin measuring some 1 million square miles in extent.[4]

9. Mineral Resources (including coal and petroleum) are significant not only as fundamental requirements of modern industrial society, but also because they may figure prominently in territorial disputes. Few States of the world possess more than a few of the major minerals needed for industrialization in sufficient quantities to be meaningful, and industrial States, such as the United States, Britain, and the Soviet Union, are keenly interested in less powerful areas (for example, Venezuela, Iran, and Bolivia) within whose boundaries are located valuable resources. To protect their access to these resources, the industrial States may at times establish various forms of "power spheres" over the weaker States.

---

[4] See Derwent Whittlesey, "Lands Athwart the Nile," *World Politics*, V (1953), 214–42.

The existence of valuable mineral resources in border areas may result in armed conflict between neighboring States. For example, discovery of nitrate deposits in the Atacama Desert of western South America led to the violent War of the Pacific (1879–84), involving Chile, Peru, and Bolivia, for possession of the area. Petroleum in Kuwait and the Buraimi Oasis of the southeastern Arabian Peninsula, nickel in northeastern Finland, and water power sites along the French-Italian border are other examples of these conditions.

This discussion of physical attributes does not imply that within each State all nine elements are of equal importance to matters relating to the area's functioning. Within each State all nine elements exist, to one degree or another, but in each State only one or two attributes may be of political significance. The classification given here, as well as the discussions which follow in this chapter, should be thought of as something of a check list to be used in analyzing a particular political region. By considering the significant elements one may gain considerable insight into the functioning of a particular State.

Boundaries

Boundaries are important components of a State since they limit the areas of territorial control. There are two principal classification systems for boundaries, one based on origin and one on cultural relationships. Both systems are presented here, since each, under certain conditions, can prove useful to an analysis of a political region.

A Generic Classification. The classification based on origin consists of four types of boundaries—physical, ethnic, historical, and geometric. Actually many boundaries represent combinations of two or more of these types.

1. PHYSICAL BOUNDARIES are those which follow some physical feature, such as a mountain range, river, seacoast, lake, or swamp (Figure 6). One of the chief advantages of physical boundaries is the relative ease of establishing their location, both on a map and in the field. Many of the boundaries which cross sparsely inhabited territory, as in South America or Africa, are of this type.

Numerous problems, however, arise in connection with physical boundaries if one examines them closely. In the case of rivers, should the boundary follow the middle of the channel? What then of fishing and navigation rights; maintenance of bridges, dams, and navigation channels; distribution of water for irrigation? What if the river frequently shifts its course during flood time? River valleys are often ethnic and economic units; to divide them politically may work hardship on the inhabitants. With mountain boundaries other problems are present. Should the boundary line follow the crest itself or the drainage divide? What State should control the

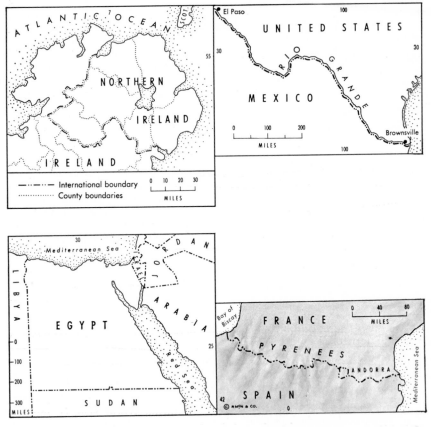

Figure 6. Types of Boundaries.

Historical Boundary.	Physical-Ethnic Boundary.
Geometric Boundary.	Physical Boundary.

passes? What of intermontane basins? Still other problems come up in the case of lakes and swamps. Each type of physical feature has its distinctive problems with respect to use as a political boundary.

Theoretically, the best type of physical boundary is the coast line of a sea or ocean, since only one State is generally involved in the determination and maintenance of the boundary. Even here, however, difficulties may arise. A foreign power may gain control of offshore islands—for example, Hong Kong and Macao off the China coast. Another problem is that of offshore limits of control. Since 1793 the United States has adhered to a three-mile limit of territorial sovereignty, although recently this distance has been affected by boundary claims of individual states (see page 144).

In the case of other countries the figure varies considerably, some (including the Soviet Union) claiming sovereignty up to 12 miles from shore and some up to 200 miles. Beyond these limits there are questions concerning the control of resources (particularly petroleum) which lie beneath the ocean floor, as well as of fishing rights in waters adjacent to a particular country.

2. ETHNIC BOUNDARIES separate peoples of differing cultural characteristics, based on such factors as language, religion, nationality, and race. (Figure 6). If accurately delimited,[5] they may be successful in reducing friction between States, for each political region would then contain its own particular ethnic group or groups. Unfortunately, ethnic boundaries are often extremely difficult to delimit, particularly if the various groups have inhabited a boundary area for many years and their patterns of settlement are closely intermingled. Following World War I many of the boundaries of central and eastern Europe were redrawn so as to separate dissimilar cultural groups wherever possible. Plebiscites were resorted to on several occasions in order to ascertain the desires of people in border areas. Despite the efforts of Allied statesmen at the Versailles Conference, 3,200,000 Germans, 700,000 Hungarians, and 80,000 Poles were included within Czechoslovakia; over 900,000 Germans were left within Poland's borders; 420,000 Albanians remained in Yugoslavia; and there were many parallel cases involving smaller numbers of peoples.

If they remain undisturbed for long periods of time, ethnic boundaries may come to achieve their primary purpose of reducing friction, for the peoples on both sides of the border will gradually adjust themselves to its presence. Such has been the case along the northern German-Dutch border. Demands by the Netherlands in 1945 for modifications of this border were justified on the basis of German aggression during World War II, but opposing this was the fact that the existing border had become a well-functioning division line. The peoples close to the border had come to accept it as a more or less permanent feature of the landscape; a new delimitation, many experts felt, would serve only to destroy a well-adjusted boundary situation and lead to future friction between the Dutch and the Germans.

Ethnic boundaries are sometimes based on physical features, and as such may be considered a combined ethnic-physical type. In the central Pyrenees between France and Spain, for example, the physical feature has served to divide cultural groups as well as States from one another. Actually there are few international boundaries which succeed completely in separating unlike cultural groups, unless considerable unoccupied area exists between population centers or there has been a mass deportation of minorities across the border.

3. HISTORICAL BOUNDARIES follow old political division lines, and as

---

[5] The term "delimit" refers to fixing the location of a boundary on a map. "Demarcate" means to locate a boundary line on the ground.

such may not coincide with either physical or ethnic patterns. The French-German boundary, for example, follows in part the historical boundaries of the duchy of Alsace; the border between Northern Ireland and the Republic of Ireland coincides with the boundaries of old counties (Figure 6). In both instances ethnic groups are divided from one another, although neither boundary coincided exactly with the dividing point between cultural groups. Thousands of Irish Catholics were left in Northern Ireland by the boundary location, while along the French-German border many persons on the French side speak German as their native tongue. Other examples of historical borders are those of Switzerland and some Latin American States. Many historic boundaries following old political division lines are, in reality, complex boundaries (see below), since they also are based on physical or cultural phenomena of the earth's surface.

4. GEOMETRIC BOUNDARIES normally follow a straight line, a meridian of longitude, or a parallel of latitude (Figure 6). Such boundaries exist primarily in regions of sparse population, as in Africa or the American Northwest, for if a considerable population is present in the boundary area, demands for modifications of the boundary are likely to be made to conform to ethnic or economic needs. The principal asset of geometric boundaries lies in the simplicity of their delimitation on a map and in the fact that they can be demarcated accurately by astronomical measurements. There also are certain unusual cases, such as circular county boundaries in Kentucky, or oblique line boundaries in Arizona and New Mexico, which are geometric in nature and have no relationship to the physical or cultural features of the area across which the boundary is drawn.

5. COMPLEX BOUNDARIES are those which combine two or more of the types mentioned above. Parts of the India-Pakistan boundary were both historical and ethnic in nature at the time of their delimitation; the Czech-German boundary, prior to September, 1938, was physical and ethnic. In a sense the straight baselines used along rugged coasts for measuring the breadth of the territorial sea are both physical and geometric in nature, for they connect points on offshore rocks and islands with one another, and with prominent points along the mainland.

We should also note what might be termed *compound* boundaries, that is, boundaries which for part of their course conform to one classification, and for part to another. The United States–Mexican border, for example, is both physical and geometric. Naturally the worth of any classification such as this is dependent upon its value in interpreting and assessing the complicated character of international boundaries throughout the world. For our purposes here, boundaries are important in terms of the roles they play in the functioning of the State. Thus it is well, when studying a particular boundary, to determine the manner in which it was originally delimited, but it may also be necessary to assess the nature of its contemporary role. For this reason a second classification of boundaries is also offered.

A Functional Classification. A functional classification of boundaries is based on cultural relationships, that is, it considers boundary characteristics with respect to human aspects of the landscape, such as patterns of settlement and land utilization, or the distribution of various population types. The three categories in this classification are *antecedent, superimposed,* and *consequent.*

Antecedent boundaries are those which predate the development of an area's cultural features, such as the arrangement of roads and villages or the pattern of economic activities. The United States–Canadian boundary west of Lake Superior is antecedent; so are many of the boundaries of Africa and Latin America.

In contrast with these are the boundaries which have been delimited after the development of an area has taken place. Such boundaries (sometimes termed *subsequent*) may cut across the cultural pattern of an area and thus are *superimposed*, or they may conform to the distribution of population or of ethnic or economic regions and thus are *consequent* in nature. The Israeli-Jordan border in the vicinity of Jerusalem is superimposed; the boundary between Norway and Sweden is consequent, since it has always effectively separated the peoples of the two States from one another because of the nature of the terrain. As in the case of generic boundaries, there may be cases where, from the functional point of view, the boundaries are compound.

The Significance of Boundaries to the State. Several aspects of boundaries should be noted in terms of their significance to the State. For one thing, their effectiveness often reflects relations between neighboring States. A boundary which has been delimited in the most "scientific" manner possible may still prove a source of friction, should there be general tension between the States involved. On the other hand, boundaries which by their manner of delimitation would seem to offer numerous sources for potential friction will actually cause few problems if the respective States maintain cordial relations with one another.

Not all boundaries are sharp lines of cultural delimitation. In many cases boundaries run through "border zones," that is, regions in which the peoples on both sides of the boundary are of similar ethnic character, and in which little attention is actually paid to the boundary's existence. Examples of this are the Pakistan-Afghan boundary, much of the boundary between China and Burma, or the boundary in North Africa between Algeria and Mauritania. Generally the boundaries in such areas have never been demarcated, except at important crossing points. As political regions in the future become increasingly organized (through more effective development of their circulation media), the number of such border zones is likely to diminish.

Boundaries in time come to have significant effects on the landscape of an area. Road and rail patterns become adjusted to the boundary, frequently crossing it only at specified points, and the patterns of towns, industries, services (such as electricity, transportation, education, and health) come to conform to the boundary's existence. If a boundary changes, many of these adjustments continue to remain as features of the landscape. Prior to World War I, for example, a railroad close to the German-Belgian boundary connected the German cities of Eupen and Malmédy (see Figure 37). Following the war the boundary was shifted eastward, bringing both cities within Belgian territory, although the railroad, for a part of its course between the two cities, continued to pass through Germany—a situation which still exists today, as a relic of a former adjustment to boundary location.

One of the greatest effects of boundaries on the landscape has been the existence of the "Iron Curtain" dividing Communist from non-Communist Europe. On the Communist side of this boundary buildings, trees, and other possible hiding places have been removed across a broad strip, and barbed wire, trenches, and guard towers have been erected. Finally, in Berlin, the Communists have erected the wall, separating East from West, as a permanent symbol of the city's partitioning.

The majority of the boundaries of the world have never been fully demarcated. In his book *Boundary-Making; A Handbook for Statesmen, Treaty Editors and Boundary Commissioners,* Stephen Jones describes many of the problems involved in actually locating the boundary in a particular area and marking out its course. "Many treaties leave, and all should leave, to the demarcators the final adjustment of the line to local needs and the realities of the terrain. These final adjustments may be of great importance to the smooth functioning of a boundary."[6] Unfortunately many of the boundaries which have appeared since World War II have either duplicated previous borders, regardless of the effectiveness of their functioning, or have represented power compromises of one kind or another (such as the "cease-fire" lines or the eastern and western boundaries of Poland).

Because of the roles they play, boundaries are of great importance to the functioning of a State. Attack against the State comes from across one or more of its boundaries, fugitives from justice may flee across the boundary, and military assistance may cross the boundary from a neighboring State. Any change in the areal extent of a State as a result of boundary changes affects the other various features which it possesses, such as resources, population, and transportation nets, and any such changes are thus of vital concern to the government of the State. There are no such things as "natural" boundaries, since the State itself is not a natural phenomenon, nor are boundaries inherently "good" or "bad." Each boundary, like the States which it separates, is unique; although certain generalizations may be made for the successful functioning of particular boundaries, in the final analysis

---

[6] P. 165.

each one must be studied as an individual case, with individual problems and potentials.

AN EFFECTIVE ADMINISTRATIVE SYSTEM

The form or structure of government by itself, that is, the division of functions among executive, legislative, and judicial branches, or whether it is democratic or totalitarian, is not focal to the concern of political geographers. These are matters for the political scientist. Political geography asks the question, Is there a central government exercising control over a certain portion of the earth's surface? Associated with this question are four topics: (1) the *type* of political control which is exercised over an area, (2) the *degree* of control, (3) the *form* of internal organization, and (4) the *effectiveness* of control processes.

Type of Political Control

The differences in type of political control are reflected, first, in the existence of both dependent and independent countries throughout the world, and, second, in the several variations of dependencies which have been developed. The present political pattern consists of over 120 independent States. "Independent" and "dependent" are, of course, relative terms. How "independent" for example, is North Vietnam of Chinese control, or Hungary of the Soviets? Any global classification of States will vary according to whether or not these terms are considered in their legal (*de jure*) sense, or in actual fact. Even within this division there are variations, since not all governments recognize the legal independence of such States as North Korea, North Vietnam, and Taiwan.

Despite the variety of political associations one State may have with another, there are certain broad categories of control which currently exist throughout the world. These are colonies, protectorates, trusteeship territories, international zones, and condominiums.

In a *colony* much of the political power is exercised by the mother country. It is presumed that the local inhabitants are not in a position to handle their own affairs except at local levels, and there is frequently little or no native representation on the governing bodies which make major decisions with regard to the colonial area. Nationals of the mother country often receive special privileges in the colony, and the economy of the region generally is geared for the benefit of the colonial power. Within the British and French empires there are also *dependencies* of the colonies, which are minor territorial areas governed by the colony's administration.

Colonial areas may receive varying degrees of self-government from the mother country. Southern Rhodesia has been a self-governing colony since 1923, and British Guiana has its own legislature and executive, independent of Britain; Iceland for 36 years was joined with Denmark in a "personal union," and Denmark assumed *de facto* control of Iceland's foreign policy. Iceland, in this case, was no longer a "colony" but was still in a form of colonial relationship with Denmark. Puerto Rico, which is officially designated as a "commonwealth," is a self-governing territory, whose defense and foreign affairs are handled by the United States.

The negligible dependent areas of the United States (with the exception of the Commonwealth of Puerto Rico) are termed "territories" and "possessions" rather than colonies. The degree of local autonomy varies among the several possessions, but in all of them the executive officers are appointed by the President of the United States, and many of the important affairs relating to the possession are handled in Washington.

A *protectorate* is a colonial area in which there is a local ruler, but in which defense, foreign affairs, and various other matters are in the hands of the mother country. A governor general, or other administrative officer appointed by the controlling state, wields considerable power over the protectorate, generally including the right of veto over any legislation passed by the local governing councils. Zanzibar and the British Solomon Islands are examples of protectorates, as are also Bechuanaland and the Tonga Islands.

Trusteeship territories are an outgrowth of the former League of Nations mandate system, set up in 1920, under which the colonial possessions of the defeated powers of World War I were apportioned among some of the victorious Allied states. The League undertook to guarantee certain civil liberties of the native populations, and annual reports on the administration of the territories were made to the international body by the mandate powers. If the situation in a given territory appeared to warrant it, there was a provision for an investigation by the League Mandates Commission, leading to a possible recall of the mandate and its reassignment to some other power. With the establishment of the United Nations in 1945, supervision over the former mandates passed to the United Nations Trusteeship Council. Accordingly, the former mandate powers (with the exception of Japan and the Republic of South Africa) became trusteeship powers, while the mandates themselves became trusteeship (or trust) territories (see also page 122). The Republic of South Africa has refused to transform Southwest Africa into a trust territory, and, in principle at least, continues to govern it as a mandate. In the years since World War II most of the former trust territories have become independent, or joined to some State, so that only the former Japanese islands in the Pacific north of the Equator, northeastern New Guinea, and the Pacific island of Nauru remain as trusteeship territories of the United Nations.

Perhaps the most difficult form of political relationship about which to generalize is that between the East European Communist states (excluding

Yugoslavia) and the Soviet Union, and between Communist China and its two neighbors North Korea and North Vietnam. The term "satellite" has frequently been used with respect to these smaller States, but obviously the degrees of political dependence vary, and in the absence of specific information on the types of relationships existing, it is dangerous to categorize the Communist bloc system with a single phrase. Soviet intervention in the East German uprising of 1953 and the Hungarian uprising three years later left no doubt as to the extent the U.S.S.R. is prepared to go to prevent "unfriendly" governments from coming to power in its East European sphere. On the other hand, Poland in 1956 installed a "liberal" Communist regime as a result of popular discontent, Albania has tended to orient its policies more toward those of Communist China than those of the Soviet Union, while Mongolia, located between the two giant Communist powers, has apparently become the "satellite" of neither one, and, without abandoning Communism, has been able to achieve at least some flexibility in its actions on both the national and international scenes.

Finally, there are special forms of territorial control, such as international areas, condominiums, occupation zones, and military bases. The concept of an *international area* was exemplified by the city of Tangier on the North African coast just west of the Strait of Gibraltar. Because of the port's strategic location, there were bitter disputes among European powers over control of the area, and an international commission was set up in 1925 to administer the city. The international status lasted until 1956, when Tangier was incorporated into the new state of Morocco. Another variety of international control was applied under the League of Nations between World Wars I and II, when League commissions were established to administer the Saar and the city of Danzig (now a part of Poland). Since the founding of the United Nations two proposals for international control have been suggested, one for Trieste and the other for Jerusalem, but neither proposal was put into operation.

Where two or more powers share control of an area, the resultant governmental structure is known as a *condominium.* The degree of control by each State may vary considerably. The Sudan—formerly the Anglo-Egyptian Sudan—was until 1955 the major condominium of the world; the New Hebrides Islands and Nauru Island in the Pacific are the only significant condominiums still in existence.[7]

Occupation zones are sectors of a state which remain occupied by foreign troops for a limited time following cessation of warfare. In 1945, for example, Germany and Austria were each temporarily divided into four

---

[7] The United Nations trusteeship over Nauru Island is held jointly by Britain, Australia, and New Zealand, but the area is actually administered by Australia. Canton and Enderbury islands in the central Pacific are condominiums of Britain and the United States. The two so-called Neutral Zones on the Arabian Peninsula also have a condominium status.

occupation zones. In these zones government was carried on by the occupying power, although it was understood that such control was to be for a short time only. In addition, Berlin and Vienna were set up as special four-power occupation areas. Japan, Korea, Trieste, and various States of Eastern Europe were also under military occupation for several years after World War II.

In a somewhat different category are the *military zones* and *bases* which one country may control within the boundaries of another. In Panama, for example, the United States has rights "in perpetuity" over a ten-mile-wide strip of territory through which passes the canal. The United States also has many military establishments on foreign soil; in each instance special agreements exist with regard to matters of sovereignty within the military area. Permission for the United States to operate these military establishments is granted voluntarily by sovereign States and may be withdrawn at any time if the foreign government so decides.

Degree of Control

The actual degree of control which central governments exercise over the territory within their States' boundaries varies widely from place to place. In some cases, such as remote areas of the Amazon basin, there exist groups of people who are untouched by the laws and requirements of the national government. Thus the capital exercises *de jure*, but not *de facto*, control over these areas.[8] More frequent, perhaps, are situations where the capital's authority over certain parts of the State may be effective only at certain times and under certain conditions. Invasion, or threat of invasion, for example, is a potent force for strengthening central authority within a state. Maps showing conditions of *de facto* political control by central governments throughout the world, although difficult to compile, might have more meaning than those showing the familiar *de jure* pattern of sovereignty.

Certain aspects of governmental control over a political region were described by Richard Hartshorne in an article entitled "The Functional Approach in Political Geography." He used the term "centripetal forces" to apply to those pressures which tend to unite regions together into a State. Among these forces is the state-idea, that is, the *raison d'être*, or reason for the State's existence as a separate political region. If the state-idea is weak initially—or if in time it should disappear—then the existence of the State as a political entity may be seriously threatened. Another centripetal force is the "concept of nation," " . . . a feeling of kinship, of

---

[8] The term *de jure* is defined as "by right, according to law." *De facto* means "actually existing, whether with or without right." These terms are important to any consideration of the realities of territorial control throughout the world.

belonging together."[9] This sense of belonging to a certain area on the part of its citizens may be an important element of a State's cohesiveness. Switzerland is cited as an example in which this concept of nation is strong, despite the existence of dissimilar languages and of other elements tending to divide the nation (see also page 217).

Against these forces are the "centrifugal forces" working to divide the political regions. Among these would be distance, the presence of physical features hindering communications between various sectors, the existence of ethnically diverse groups within a State, and regional differences in attitudes. Thus each political region has the two types of forces, the one working to unite and the other to divide.

The *raison d'être* and the concept of nation, if applied to various political regions, often provide clues to the cohesion of States and to the possibilities for future change in the political pattern. In Africa and southeast Asia, for example, the boundaries of many of the colonial areas were delimited during the nineteenth century, often with little reference to physical, ethnic, or historical considerations. Such *raison d'être* as existed for these areas was based largely on administrative efficiency. By the mid-twentieth century centrifugal forces within a number of these countries had become strong, and pressures existed for partitioning the political regions. In India and Palestine the approach of independence resulted in considerable weakening of the former state-idea. Economic and religious factors outweighed any concept of nation which might have been developed among the majority of the peoples in these areas, and political partitioning was the eventual outcome. On the other hand, Burma and the Sudan have retained their preindependence borders, despite the various differences which exist in both States. In each of these two areas the *raison d'être* is a complex one; among the contributing factors is the determination of the dominant political and economic groups in both Burma and the Sudan to prevent any break-up of their country, and the largely negative reason that many of the diverse peoples included in these States have little or no notion, as yet, of nationalism. Even though the borders remain intact, however, there is no common concept of nation throughout either of these States, with the result that powerful centrifugal forces still exist.

Capitals and Core Areas. The location and functioning of a State's capital and the position of the core area are important aspects of the degree of control exercised by the central government within a State. Each State forms originally about a particular nucleus, or *core area*. In time, however, the capital city may move away from the core area, or additional core areas of regions with separatist tendencies may develop; in either situation strong centrifugal forces may come into being. Brazil is an example in

---

[9] "The Functional Approach in Political Geography," p. 113.

which the core area moved away from the original nucleus along the north-east coast. Spain, on the other hand, represents a country in which there are two core areas, one centered at Madrid, the capital, and the other at Barcelona.

The capital city may remain at the original nucleus (London, Paris), it may shift to conform with the major population center, or it may be located away from both the original nucleus and the contemporary population centers. Canberra, Australia, for example, lies midway between the two great cities of Sydney and Melbourne, and Ottawa was chosen as a neutral position with respect to both English- and French-speaking Canada. In analyzing the location and functioning of a national capital, historical forces must be taken into account, for the role played by the capital city in the early years of a State may change considerably in later times. O. H. K. Spate[10] has classified capital cities into three types according to function: (1) as a unifying center in a federation, (2) as a link with external influences, and 3) as a "forward capital" close to an active frontier. Canberra represents a unifying center; London, in historical times, was a link with the Continent; while Berlin was once a "forward capital," facing the dynamic eastern frontier. Regardless of their original function, most capitals, if their location remains fixed, will in time become economic and population centers, with the result that their original functions may become obscured. Spate terms this "historical inertia" and compares it with "historical imitation," in which the seat of government may be moved to a former capital city for prestige purposes. For example, the Italians in the early 1870's located the capital of the modern Italian State at Rome, and the Chinese Communists, once they had overrun the country, moved the capital from Nanking back to Peking (Peiping).

Form of Internal Organization

The success a State achieves in maintaining political cohesion depends in part on its internal governmental system, that is, whether it is *unitary* or *federal*. The principal basis of distinction between these two is the nature of the authority which controls the territorial distribution of governmental powers. Under a unitary system the central government is the authority which decides on degrees of local self-government. It may determine the number and nature of self-governing political subdivisions and possesses the right to allocate governmental powers and responsibilities to these subdivisions. No sphere of local powers is guaranteed against expansion of central control. This does not mean there is no government at local and at provincial (or state) levels, mainly that this government exists at the discretion of the central authority.

---

[10] "Factors in the Development of Capital Cities."

Such a system exists in a great many States of the world, including Great Britain, France, Spain, Sweden, and a majority of the states of Latin America, Africa, and Asia. Its principal advantage is the flexibility in the distribution of control which is granted to the central government. In time of crisis, or of malfunction of provincial or local governments, the central authority can easily assume the necessary power to meet the particular needs. It can move effectively in cases of discrimination against minority groups in certain regions. On the other hand, there is the ever present danger of overcentralization, of inability by the central government to account for regional differences within the various parts of the State, and, with the removal of control from the immediate area, a tendency for citizens to lose interest in the rights and obligations of self-government.

Under the federal system autonomy for provinces or other subdivisions is protected by adequate constitutional arrangements. Both the central government and the local governments derive their powers ultimately from the constitution. There also must be provisions relating to amendments to the constitution such that neither the central nor the local governments has the exclusive right to change the constitution. The principal method for allocating authority is to define clearly the powers of the central government and to stipulate that all other powers are to be exercised by the governments of the political subdivisions. Federal systems exist in the United States, Canada, Australia, Switzerland, Brazil, Argentina, Mexico, Malaya, and Nigeria.

The two principal advantages of the federal system are, first, that it represents something of a protection against overcentralization of power in the national capital, and, second, that it provides for regional differences within a State. For the latter reason it is useful in large States. In many cases, however, it may be less effective than the unitary system, first, because the policies of the central government may only with difficulty be brought to bear in certain regions (witness the problems of the federal government of the United States in protecting the rights of Negroes in the Southeast) and, second, because the central body can do relatively little to remedy malfunction of government at the various local levels.

A third governmental system is the *confederation,* a weak union of States possessing central agencies for the discharge of certain functions. Under the Articles of Confederation the thirteen American states were for a time united in a confederation, as were the German states in the German Bund during the first part of the nineteenth century. States which have united in a confederation retain the right to withdraw if they so desire, and the central body has no power of enforcement of decisions which have been reached nor of raising funds for its own operation; these responsibilities reside with the several States, which may or may not discharge them effectively. Confederations would appear to represent a plausible arrangement for some of the newly independent States, particularly in Africa, which will permit each one to retain its sovereignty, while bringing to them the benefits of united action in such matters as trade, resource utilization, and possibly defense.[11]

The Effectiveness of Control Processes

In addition to type, degree, and internal organization of control is this fourth aspect, which is associated largely with internal politico-geographic situations. The effectiveness of a State's political and legal systems depends in part upon the adaptation of these systems to the physical and cultural environment. Laws relating to land ownership, or to mineral and fishing rights, for instance, should conform to the particular requirements of the political region in which they apply, otherwise unnecessary disputes may arise over the settlement of claims, resources may not be wisely used, and the cultural needs of the peoples involved will not be adequately served.

The transfer of political systems formulated in one type of environment to a totally different type may have significant effects of cultural adjustments to physical conditions. The techniques of boundary delimitation in Belgium, for example, obviously differ from those in the former Belgian Congo, the Arabian desert, or the Arctic wastes; so, too, do the respective laws relating to border functioning, voting, taxation, and many other problems. One of the important aspects of the spread of European culture to overseas areas since 1500 has been the gradual evolution of new techniques of political control to conform to new environmental conditions. Political geographers have only begun to analyze the complex relationships which exist between processes of political control and the physical and cultural environment. Nevertheless, such relationships represent important components of the over-all problem of governmental control of territory.

A RESIDENT POPULATION

Population factors of a political region are of great importance in a politico-geographic study. Size, distribution, and type of population are the three major aspects to consider.

The number of people resident within a national region is important not only in terms of a State's ability to provide for its own needs but also of its power potential. Certain States, such as Italy, Japan, the Netherlands, and Britain, are densely populated, particularly with respect to their arable

---

[11] The system of government in the Soviet Union is difficult to categorize. Under the constitution power is divided between the central government and the republics, implying a federation, yet each republic under the constitution is given the right to secede from the U.S.S.R., as well as to enter into direct relations with foreign states—indicative of a confederation. On the other hand, amendment of the constitution is in the hands of the central government, and the actual powers denied the central government (and thus falling to the individual republics) are of minor importance. The Soviets would seem, in fact, to have a unitary system of government.

land. Even with modern agricultural techniques, they are unable to raise sufficient food to feed their people and must build up exports or services to pay for the needed imports. The problems of "overcrowded" States are extremely complex; only a few aspects can be suggested here.

The normal method for obtaining exports in food-deficient countries is through industrial production. Industry provides employment for many of the people and will earn foreign credits. Along with production, however, must come markets for the manufactured goods. As more countries begin to industrialize, thereby producing goods to satisfy their own needs, markets become scarcer for the exports of densely populated States. At the present time some of the greatest potential markets in the world for industrial goods lie in the Communist countries; yet to send these countries the industrial goods they desire, such as machinery and locomotives, would increase their economic and military strength relative to the non-Communist world. On the other hand, failure of the industrialized non-Communist states to secure markets for their exports may lead to economic instability, unemployment, and inability to assume important roles in the anti-Communist movement.

In place of industrialization and exports a densely populated country may (1) increase domestic food sources, (2) build up an overseas empire which will assist it in economic development, (3) reduce its population through large-scale emigration, or (4) substantially lower its general standard of living. An increase in domestic food supplies to a magnitude sufficient to feed the entire population may be impossible due to limitations of the physical environment. Even a lesser expansion of food production may be economically impractical due to the availability of inexpensive food imports.

The other three alternatives have strong political connotations. The days of colonial empires are gradually disappearing, as the Dutch, the British, and the French have discovered. Areas for emigration are generally restricted by quotas, as in the United States, Canada, and Australia, or by undesirable physical features, such as are found in parts of Latin America and Africa. Further, emigration may weaken the population structure of a state, for the young and ambitious are often the ones to leave. Finally, no democratic government can operate for long on a policy of continued reduction in the standard of living; eventually the voters will turn it out of office.

The relationship between population size and national power potential involves education and technological skills, as well as the ability of the central government to organize the population for the service of the State. Education and technological skills enable the people to utilize effectively the national resources. An example of organization was evidenced in Germany prior to and during World War II. Here were 65 million persons, possessing considerable talent and skills, who were organized for the furtherance of national aims. Much of Germany's remarkable political and military power during those years must be attributed to the size and training of its population.

Allied with population size is the question of distribution, which is significant in terms of both internal unity and diversity, and of relations between one State and another. Many of the political effects of population distribution have already been alluded to. For instance, regions of dense population have a profound effect on the cohesive structure of a state; similarly, areas of sparsely inhabited land lying between populated areas may be conducive to powerful centrifugal forces. Large-scale population movements may result in a shifting of the major power centers of an area. On the international scene, boundaries through regions of low population density frequently cause less friction than those through more crowded areas. Populous areas located close to a potentially hostile neighbor may be detrimental to a State, for the capture of an area might seriously weaken the State's resistance. The location of Paris with respect to France's northeastern boundary is a case in point.

A third aspect of population—that of type—includes language, religion, nationality, and race. Differing language groups exist in Canada, Belgium, Czechoslovakia, and Yugoslavia, while religious cleavages are found in Canada, Yugoslavia, the Netherlands, Indonesia, and Northern Ireland. Dissimilar racial groups inhabit the Republic of South Africa, Malaya, and the United States.

The presence of more than one language or other such group within a State may seriously weaken its political unity, for the groups may seek to change the existing pattern of control. In some instances there is a movement by one group to separate the territory it inhabits from the control of the national government and set up an independent state, as the Karens attempted in Burma. At other times the various groups vie for control of the central government itself, as the Walloons and the Flemings have done in Belgium. Some groups retain ties of national loyalty with foreign powers rather than with the State in which they reside. Czechoslovakia, prior to the Munich crisis of 1938, had Germans, Hungarians, and Poles within its borders whose loyalties were primarily with their respective "homelands." Such a situation can be of great potential danger, for these groups may seek the political partitioning of the State and annexation of the areas they inhabit by an adjoining country. There are some cases in which little or no friction develops as a result of cultural complexity. The States of Latin America, for example, have few difficulties as a result of the intermixture of various racial groups within their borders.

Divisive forces within a State may arise as a result of class differences just as readily as from ethnic ones. Marx wrote of the inevitability of class struggle in a capitalist society, and in recent years, as certain classes, particularly economic, become increasingly integrated and self-conscious, the possibilities of interclass conflict have in many countries become stronger. Internal stability and the rule of the government are thus, in part, a function of the social structure and of the distribution of wealth within the State.

AN ECONOMIC STRUCTURE

In society economic strength is a basic criterion for military and political power. American industrial and agricultural output have been major factors in the Allied victories of World Wars I and II. Likewise, near-autarky, or economic self-sufficiency, enabled the Germans to resist Allied blockades on imports of strategic commodities in both conflicts. In time of peace economic domination of one country by another often carries with it measures of political influence as well. Nazi Germany's economic dominance over Romania, Hungary, and Bulgaria prior to World War II is an illustration of this occurrence.

The relationships which may exist between economic and political diversity within a State were mentioned on page 42. Differences in economic interests may foster strong centrifugal forces. On the other hand, diverse economic regions within a State may complement one another and serve to unite the area for interregional trade, thus leading to close political ties between groups. Under these conditions people in differing economic regions would find it more to their mutual advantage to remain together within one political unit than to separate into two or more States. In addition to Australia, both the United States and Canada may be cited as examples in which the desire for economic unity on the part of various groups was an important stimulus to political unification. Conversely, the partitioning of India demonstrates that the attracion of economic unity may be insufficient to hold a political unit together.

Another factor is that of economic exploitation by one State over another, a situation which may or may not be accompanied by political domination as well. In the development of the great part of the overseas empires of modern times political annexation was carried out subsequent to, or in conjunction with, economic expansion of the mother country over the colonial area. Even after a colonial country receives political independence (as in the case of Iraq), it may not in reality be truly sovereign unless it achieves a measure of economic freedom from its former mother country as well. Whittlesey in *The Earth and the State* considered at some length what he termed "the concept of the exploitable world." He pointed out a number of important correlations between the political and economic relationships between States. For instance, he wrote, "The real test of exploitability is economic subservience rather than political dependence. Cuba, politically independent, is exploitable, whereas British Canada is not."[12]

---

[12] P. 81.

Here, as in other situations, the relationships between economic and political control of territory may have many elements of interdependence with one another.

A CIRCULATORY SYSTEM

The final essential element of a State involves the accessibility of its various areas—and of the State itself—to people and to ideas. Movement is essential to the political organization of space and to the maintenance of this organization. The term circulation is used here to denote "the flow of peoples, armies, material goods, capital, messages, and ideas across the space open to men's activities."[13] The various media through which this flow is made possible form the "circulatory system" and include such factors as transportation systems, radio, and the press.

The increase in the facilities for communication, particularly since the beginning of the twentieth century, has, of course, greatly improved the effectiveness of circulatory systems throughout the world. One result of this has been stronger political organization of space. The number of people who still remain untouched by the authority of their country's government is steadily declining, so that in only a relatively few areas of the world is the *de facto* control of the central government completely ineffective. Another indication of this improved effectiveness is that even uninhabited Antarctica is becoming politically organized.

The effects of circulation within States are of two general types. On the one hand, it tends to unite the political area in that it permits the central authority to be carried more effectively to outlying regions; on the other hand, it can be a source of instability and change, inasmuch as it exposes many people to new ideas and new wants, with the result that they may become dissatisfied with the conditions of political organization that currently exist. As illustration, the increased effectiveness of Canada's circulatory system after the mid-nineteenth century prevented a possible partitioning of the country and the creation of a separate political entity in the far west. In contrast with this, an expanded circulatory system in the new Sudan State could signify an attempt to strengthen Khartoum's authority over the Negroid peoples who inhabit the southern forest lands. Some of these peoples, already distrustful of the Arab majority in the central and northern parts of the country, might seek a partitioning of the Sudan, particularly if the Arabs attempt to force their own culture on them.

Circulatory systems function on the international level as well. Foreign travel and the beaming of propaganda, or, conversely, the imposition of "iron curtains" and the jamming of radio programs, are aspects of circulation which often have strong political overtones. Again, the net effect may be

---

[13] Jean Gottman, "The Political Partitioning of our World: an Attempt at Analysis," p. 515.

toward either political cohesion or political diversity. Within each State and between it and other States is a complex series of circulation media, which, like the four elements covered earlier in this chapter, contribute to the basic structure of a political region.

The complex nature of territorial control throughout the world becomes evident when one considers all the possible variations which exist with respect to these five basic elements of a State. In a survey covering the entire globe only the most obvious features of each political region can be considered. Major power centers, significant changes in political status, territorial disputes which have (or once had) important international repercussions—items such as these represent the basic materials for a general study of world political geography. If time and interest permit, however, closer examination of any one of the various political regions of the world will reveal significant (if less earth-shaking) aspects of governmental control of territory, which could form the basis for rewarding research and analysis.

BIBLIOGRAPHY

BOWMAN, ISAIAH. "The Strategy of Territorial Decisions," *Foreign Affairs,* XXIV (1946), 177–95.

Some of the fundamental problems involved in territorial claims and adjustments.

EAST, W. GORDON, and MOODIE, A. E. (eds.). *The Changing World.* Yonkers-on-Hudson: World Book Company, 1956.

A detailed and valuable text in regional political geography.

HARTSHORNE, RICHARD. "The Politico-Geographic Pattern of the World," *The Annals,* CCXVIII (1941), 45–57.

A discussion, with map, of actual degrees of political control throughout the world, prior to World War II.

HAUSER, PHILIP M. *Population and World Politics.* Glencoe, Ill.: The Free Press, 1958.

Interesting assessments of world population problems.

MELAMID, ALEXANDER. "The Economic Geography of Neutral Territories," *The Geographical Review,* XLV (1955), 359–74.

A discussion of microterritorial political phenomena.

Pounds, Norman J. G. "A Free and Secure Access to the Sea," *Annals of the Association of American Geographers,* XLIX (1959), 256–69.
A discussion, with maps, of this difficult problem.

Robinson, G. W. S. "Exclaves," *Annals of the Association of American Geographers,* XLIX (1959), 283–96.
Like Melamid's article, a survey of territorial anomalies.

Van Valkenburg, Samuel and Stotz, Carl L. *Elements of Political Geography,* 2nd ed. New York: Prentice-Hall, 1954.
A text on politico-geographic phenomena.

Weigert, Hans W. (ed.). *Principles of Political Geography.* New York: Appleton-Century-Crofts, 1957.
A comprehensive survey of various politico-geographic phenomena, with contributions from leading experts.

4

THE CHANGING NATURE OF INTERNATIONAL BOUNDARIES

● An international boundary marks the outer limits of the area over which a government has sovereignty. The nature of the boundary depends in part on the criteria used for its delimitation, and in part on the characteristics of the area through which it passes. The manner in which it functions depends on three factors—its effectiveness (which in turn depends on the nature of the boundary), the role it is intended to serve, and the relationships existing between the areas which it separates. In theory a good boundary should serve to reduce friction between States as much as possible; in practice much of the friction existing between neighboring States has little or no relation to the boundaries which separate them.

International boundaries in recent years have been undergoing considerable change both in form and in function as a result of processes affecting the patterns of political control throughout the world. These processes are listed below. In this chapter brief discussions will be given of their general effects on contemporary international boundaries.

1. The rise of newly independent States has created new boundary pressures.

2. Increase of the circulation of people, ideas, and goods, together with ideological pressures, has led to the creation of regional groupings within which various boundary functions have been reduced.

3. About the borders of the Communist bloc of states ideological boundaries have developed. These boundaries frequently take on the nature of frontiers.

4. In order to reduce the possibilities of a major war, recourse has been made on several occasions to the use of an international force to maintain order along sensitive boundaries.

5. The political partitioning of previously unclaimed areas has led to increases in delimitation problems both in the marginal seas and in the air.

Mention should be made at the outset of four concepts relating to boundaries. The first are "natural" boundaries, that is, boundaries which conform to the laws of Nature. The concept of natural boundaries arose during the Age of Reason, with philosophers appealing to Nature (as they interpreted it) for guidance in boundary delimitation. Norman Pounds has quoted Gregoire on the annexation of Savoy in 1792: "Before considering whether you should, in accordance with the freely expressed wish of Savoie, incorporate it in the French Republic, you should consult the Law of Nature and see what it permits and requires in this respect."[1] The idea of a "natural" setting for the development of States is a well-worn theme which still retains a certain propaganda appeal. The Rhine, the Alps, and the Pyrenees are "natural" political limits, although the Caucasus, Europe's highest mountains, are not, since Soviet territory extends across them into Transcausasia. Obviously what is "natural" to the people of one State may not appear so to those of a neighboring area.

Second, there is the question of "organic" or "power-political" boundaries. These boundaries, as Ratzel suggested, conform to "changes of the state organism" and expand or contract as warranted by differentials in national power. One can easily think back to the United States in the nineteenth century, to Nazi Germany during the 1930's, or to Communist China of the 1950's. The fact that such boundary changes generally involve (or at least carry the threat of) armed conflict makes them particularly dangerous in a world faced with the threat of nuclear disaster.

As a third point, mention should be made of "contractual" boundaries, based on the principle that two countries agree on a line and adhere to it. Such boundaries presuppose general acceptance of the rule of international law, and conform rather closely to the views of the majority of the peoples of "mature" States of the world, such as the United States, Britain, and France. Change in political status (such as achievement of independence) may take place *within* the assigned boundaries, but change in boundary location should come about only through agreement between the interested States.

A variation of "contractual" boundaries would be "self-determination" boundaries, that is, boundaries which conform to the freely expressed wishes of national groups. Such boundaries are contractual only in that they

---

[1] "France and 'Les Limites Naturelles,' " p. 54.

represent agreement between the State or group of States delimiting the boundaries on the one hand, and the resident population of the areas affected on the other. Following World War I a number of boundary changes were carried out by the Allied Powers at the expense of Germany, Austria-Hungary, and Russia in the interests of self-determination. Again, many residents of "mature" States would support the principle of self-determination boundaries, providing they can be drawn without risking the danger of war.[2]

Finally, a distinction should be noted between boundaries and frontiers. "Frontiers," Ladis Kristof wrote, "are a characteristic of rudimentary sociopolitical relations; relations marked by rebelliousness, lawlessness, and/or absence of laws. The presence of boundaries is a sign that the political community has reached a relative degree of maturity and orderliness, a state of law abidance."[3] A boundary is a line, a separating factor, which is "inner-oriented," that is, "created and maintained by the will of the central government." A frontier is a zone of transition, an integrating factor, "representing forces which are neither fully assimilated to nor satisfied" with either one way of life or another, an outer-oriented phenomenon whose "main attention is directed toward the outlying areas which are both a source of danger and a coveted prize."[4] The American West of the nineteenth century, the historic borderlands of China, the Sudan of northeastern Africa have functioned as frontier zones. With increasing political and cultural organization of space, it might seem that the era of frontiers is passing, but actually this is far from the case, for there remain many examples of frontiers, both on land and in the sea and air.

BOUNDARIES ASSOCIATED WITH NEWLY INDEPENDENT STATES

Most boundaries of the States which have become independent since the end of World War II are historic in nature, that is, they were laid down by the mother country when the area was a colony and have been inherited by the new State. With respect to the character of African boundaries, R. J. Harrison Church has written:

> The key to understanding African boundaries is the speed with which they were defined. Most of them were decided between 1884 and 1919, and great lengths were agreed upon in each treaty.
> Once a European Power had secured as much territory as was then thought possible and desirable, boundary definition was

---

[2] The ideal time to delimit such boundaries is at the successful conclusion of a war, when (1) the damage to international peace has already been done, and (2) they will not be delimited at the expense of the victorious states. These boundaries may be "contractual" in the sense that the governments of the defeated states are forced to accept them.
[3] Ladis Kristof, "The Nature of Frontiers and Boundaries," p. 281.
[4] *Ibid.*, p. 271.

necessary, both for the development of the African possession and for the sake of peace in Europe. Many boundaries represent approximate limits of either military or political penetration in the past—*e.g.*, the northern Gold Coast boundary. Some are the results of compromise such as the northwestern boundary of Nigeria. Others follow an exchange, such as the northwestern Sierra Leone boundary.

Boundaries drawn on maps by European politicians bore little relation to the physical and even less to the social, economic, or political fabric of indigenous societies. Yet, of course, the rapid and intensive partition of Africa took place when little or no detailed knowledge was available of the terrain, peoples, and economy of the interior. Nevertheless, even if that knowledge had been available, the mood of the statesmen who partitioned Africa was not such as to suggest that they would have been willing to use it in their boundary deliberations.[5]

Under conditions such as these it is remarkable that the boundaries of the new African States have remained as stable as they have. True, there are disagreements. The Somali Republic, for example, questions its border with Ethiopia, and Morocco with Mauritania and Spanish Sahara. Discoveries of oil in the Sahara may well result in disagreements over the boundaries of such areas as Algeria, Libya, and Morocco. It is probable, barring important resource discoveries in border areas, that the attentions of the new States, at least for a few years to come, will be directed primarily toward problems of internal development; on the other hand, it is always tempting, particularly in time of crisis, for a government to divert its people's minds from immediate problems by concentrating on real or imagined difficulties with its neighbors. Certainly in Africa there are many cases in which valid arguments might be raised for the need for border revisions to conform more closely with cultural divisions between States.

What is true of Africa is, to a considerable extent, true of Asia as well. Here again boundaries of colonial possessions were often laid down with little regard for existing conditions in the areas through which they passed. In the case of some of the southern and eastern parts of the Arabian Peninsula political boundaries are still undetermined. The colonial boundaries of India and Burma have been challenged by Communist China and by Afghanistan. There is little question but that the rise of nationalism, particularly in Africa and Asia, has served to intensify boundary problems in these areas. Coupled with this have been the divisions of Korea, Vietnam, Kashmir, and Palestine and the development of what might be termed

---

[5] W. Gordon East and A. E. Moodie (eds.), *The Changing World* (Yonkers-on-Hudson: World Book Company, 1956), pp. 744–45. Reprinted by permission of Harcourt, Brace & World, Inc.

conditions of "permanent instability." In the space of a few years the world has come to live with this instability—a condition which represents neither agreement nor armed conflict, but rather a mutual decision to "agree to disagree." In Kashmir and along the Indian-Chinese and Arab-Israeli borders, this condition is in evidence. In years to come one might well expect an increase in the number of "permanent instabilities," particularly as the alternative to such instability, namely, war, becomes an increasingly impractical solution.

REDUCTIONS IN BOUNDARY FUNCTIONS

The emergence of various economic, military, and ideological blocs of States since World War II has resulted in various changes in the role of international boundaries. Some of the best illustrations of this may be found among the states of Western Europe.

The various border disputes engendered by World War I, the resurgence of German nationalism under Hitler, and the adjustments of World War II are related in detail in Chapter 10. The Saarland, Alsace-Lorraine, and the Benelux-German border are historic areas of dispute between Germany on the one hand and its western neighbors on the other. Yet despite these traditional antagonisms, the western borders of Germany are now not only unchallenged by the respective governments, but also have had their barrier functions reduced as a result of recent agreements. Because of the North Atlantic Treaty Organization (NATO), German soldiers now train across the border on French soil. Because of the Common Market the tariffs on the exchange of goods between Germany and its western neighbors are gradually being lowered, as are also barriers on the exchange of capital or of workers. Already studies are being carried out on the possibility of creating some sort of political federation of the Common Market States, in which case the border functions will be even further reduced. In the complex world of the present, national isolation is becoming increasingly difficult to maintain, and more and more governments are moving in the direction of regional alignments. The Warsaw Pact countries of East Europe, the economic unions among the States of what were once French West and French Equatorial Africa, the moves toward an economic union of the Central American States—examples such as these point up this trend toward international cooperation and a consequent de-emphasizing of the divisive effects of the boundaries.

Ultimately such cooperative efforts might lead to political unity, although in practice this trend is scarcely in evidence. The United Arab Republic, embracing Egypt and Syria, broke up after three years of operation, efforts on the part of the government of French Sudan (now Mali) to combine politically with its neighbors have been unsuccessful, and even as well-prepared a federation as that of the British West Indies islands foundered on the rocks of Jamaican nationalism. Thus, although specific boundary functions may be reduced, the world continues to be faced by a constantly growing number of individual States, each with its own borders and with its own specific border problems.

PRESSURES ALONG IDEOLOGICAL BOUNDARIES

The growth of the Communist bloc of states since World War II has been accompanied by the development of what might be termed ideological frontiers, separating this bloc from non-Communist states. These frontiers exist for the most part as completely closed systems—or, as non-Communist Westerners have referred to them, as "iron" or "bamboo" curtains. The degree to which they operate as barriers to circulation is apparently a response more to pressures from within than without the Communist orbit. The wall dividing Berlin, for example, was erected in order to prevent the escape of East Germans to West Berlin, rather than to shut out the West Germans from East Berlin.

Such an ideological frontier, with its ban on movement, and frequently with a cleared or "no-man's" zone adjoining it on the Communist side, is a very distinct feature of the landscape, as evidenced in Germany, Korea, and Vietnam. Here, where it is superimposed on formerly united political regions, the whole pattern of life in the border regions must be readjusted. Only in Berlin, prior to the summer of 1961, was the existence of an ideological boundary permitted without interference of the movement of persons across it. But since August, 1961, the closing off of the Communist bloc has become complete, and only a relatively few persons are permitted to cross in and out of the Communist area.

A second aspect of the ideological boundary is its development of what might be termed an "organic" quality. The boundaries of Communism are not looked upon as "contractual," except for limited periods of time. Communism is a dynamic ideology; thus the borders of the Communist world are also dynamic. To realize the truth of this one has but to think of conditions in northern Greece or northwestern Iran in the years immediately following World War II, or later of South Korea, North Vietnam, Laos, or the border between China and India. In all cases the Communists sought to expand their territory at the expense of the non-Communists. Indeed, the areas across the ideological border might be viewed from the Communist point of view as having the nature of a frontier—a zone of expansion of power, which ultimately may be brought within the Communist system.

It is easy to generalize on the "organic" boundaries of Communism; actually the problem is a very complex one. Since 1948 the boundaries of the Soviet Union and of its East European "sphere" have remained unchanged; in 1955 Soviet forces actually withdrew from eastern Austria, permitting that state freely to adopt a non-Communist ideology. Expansion of Communist control in Asia since World War II has been carried out largely through "liberation" wars, by "popular" moves for reunification, as in Korea, or through "reappraisal" of border agreements initially worked out with former colonial powers. In the case of liberation wars, local groups overtly or covertly receive military assistance from Communist states across the border. In January, 1961, Premier Khrushchev declared as justifiable such liberation wars against imperialists. In both southeast and southwest Asia are States adjoining or close to the ideological boundaries. Even though such States have been freed from the ties of colonialism, they still may be controlled by "imperialists." With shaky economies, unstable governments, and a lack of strong cohesive forces within their borders, such States may well become prey to Communist-inspired and Communist-led "liberation" wars, which, if successful, may result in the *de facto* extension outward of the ideological boundaries of the Communist bloc.

"INTERNATIONALIZED" BOUNDARIES

Since the end of World War II a special category of boundary has been created, that of boundaries delimited, and on occasion patrolled, by international agencies. The truce lines across Korea and Vietnam are examples of this type. Such boundaries have come about largely as a result of the general fear of the outbreak of a major war and the destruction which would follow. Regardless of the threats of thermonuclear explosion, military action within and between countries still takes place as a result both of the emergence of newly independent States and of the encroachments of international Communism. It would appear, therefore, that additional cases may develop in future years in which truces are arranged between warring factions, boundaries are delimited either on the basis of "cease-fire" or of compromise lines, and boundary violations are then guarded against by international forces.

BOUNDARIES IN OFFSHORE WATERS

The history of national claims to control of the waters adjacent to a country's coast is a long and complex one. By the end of the thirteenth century, for example, it had been established in Norwegian law that foreigners were not entitled to sail north of Bergen without a royal license, and King John of England in 1201 issued an ordinance requiring all ships at sea to lower their sails when so ordered by English war vessels. Up until the beginning of the eighteenth century many writers and political leaders adhered to the principal of *mare clausum,* that is, sovereignty may be extended over large areas of the sea—a policy followed at one time by Venice with regard to the Adriatic, and by Spain and Portugal in terms of the oceans of the world.[6]

The alternative to a policy of closed seas was the recognition of the rights of States to certain waters along their coasts. Grotius in 1605 had suggested that the sea could not be subjected to private ownership except in the case of gulfs and straits where customary international laws were not violated, or of enclosed parts of the sea, providing they were not large in comparison with the lands surrounding them. A century later Bynkershoek argued that effective control over marginal waters could be maintained only by shore-based fortifications—a policy which implied a series of protected zones of sovereignty along a coast. In contrast with this "cannon-shot" principle, however, was a growing acceptance of the concept of zones of fixed breadth along a country's coasts within which sovereignty might be maintained as regards fishing, neutrality, and other functions. Denmark in 1691 proclaimed a neutrality zone about its coasts equal in breadth to the range of vision, while the British in 1736 adopted the first of their "Hovering Acts" establishing a customs zone twelve miles in breadth along their coasts.

The fusion of the cannon-shot and fixed-distance principles is frequently credited to the Italian jurist Galiani, who in 1782 suggested that three miles be taken as the maximum range of cannon, that uniform belts of this distance be established over which a coastal State exercised sovereignty, and that neutrality belts should be taken as twice this distance. Eleven years later the United States adopted a provisional neutrality belt three miles in breadth, this, according to President Washington, being the smallest distance claimed by any nation for a neutrality belt. The American position gradually gained favor in Britain, and ultimately the three-mile principle began to spread to other countries as well. There was at the time little actual relationship between the three miles and the maximum range of cannon, since even as late as 1814 the maximum range was slightly over one mile.

With the recognition of the rights of countries to claim sovereignty over belts of water along their coasts have come delimitation problems, some of which are as yet unresolved. How should the boundaries of these belts be delimited? Should all States adopt three miles as the breadth of their territorial seas? Can additional zones of limited control be justified beyond territorial limits? Such questions have been debated by statesmen and lawyers for many years. The general consensus is that, if possible, a universal law of the sea applicable to all coasts should be worked out with regard to offshore claims. In 1930 the problem of offshore claims was brought up at an international conference held at The Hague, and the International

---

[6] By the Treaty of Tordesillas (1494) a demarcative line was drawn through the Atlantic Ocean defining the domains of Spain (to the west of the line) and of Portugal (to the east).

Law Commission, established by the United Nations in 1946, undertook as its first project the development of a proposed Law of the Sea. The results of its work were brought out ten years later, and in 1958 delegates from 86 states assembled at Geneva for the first Law of the Sea Conference to consider the work of the Law Commission. Many of its recommendations were accepted by a majority of the delegates at the conference.[7] In the sections which follow certain aspects of offshore control will be considered in the light of the work done before and during the First Geneva Conference on the Law of the Sea.

Problems of offshore control may involve one or more of the following five zones lying off a country's coast: (1) the zone of internal waters, (2) the territorial sea, (3) the contiguous zone, (4) the zone of "diffusion," and (5) the continental shelf. Internal waters comprise the harbors, bays, and rivers over which a State has unrestricted and uncontested sovereignty. It also includes those waters adjoining the coast, which under special circumstances, are on the landward side of the baseline used to measure the breadth of the territorial sea.

The territorial sea is that zone over which a State's sovereignty is limited only by the right of innocent passage through these waters by foreign vessels.[8] The right of innocent passage does not, however, extend to aircraft flying above territorial waters. In the contiguous zone, located beyond territorial limits, the coastal State may exercise control necessary to prevent infringements of customs, fiscal, sanitation, or immigration restriction within its territory. Except for the exercise of these preventive rights, the coastal State has no jurisdiction in the contiguous zone, and the waters in this zone are a part of the high seas over which no government has sovereignty. The outer limits of the contiguous zone are generally twelve miles from shore; if a coastal State claims its territorial sea to be twelve miles in breadth (as in the case, for example, of the Soviet Union), there is no additional contiguous zone seaward of the territorial waters.

Beyond the contiguous zone is an ill-defined area which might be termed the "zone of diffusion," in which various States have claimed unilateral rights in terms of fisheries control or of security. Peru, for example, claims a zone of exclusive fisheries out to 200 miles from its coasts, as do Chile, Ecuador, and Costa Rica. South Korea has attempted to ban foreign fishermen from an area which at some points extends out more than 100 miles from shore (see Figure 106). A 1946 Argentine declaration defines the sovereign power of the State as extending over all water lying about the adjacent continental shelf, an area which includes the Falkland Islands,

---

[7] See United Nations Conference on the Law of the Sea, Geneva, 24 February–27 April, 1958 (A/Conf. 13/38), Vol. II, *Plenary Meetings.*

[8] A coastal state has the right to suspend temporarily the innocent passage of foreign ships through its territorial waters, if such suspension is essential for the protection of its security.

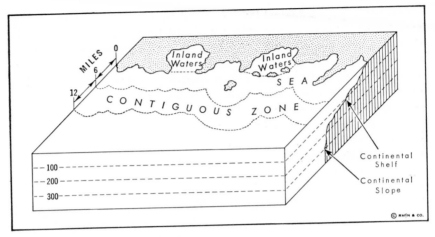

Figure 7. Block Diagram of Offshore Features.

280 miles from the mainland. In terms of security zones, perhaps the best-known was that established in 1939 by the foreign ministers of the American republics in the western Atlantic with a minimum breadth of about 300 miles. Within this zone all hostile actions by warships of the belligerent powers were prohibited in the interests of Western Hemisphere neutrality.

Zones of diffusion are not recognized by international law and can be maintained only through the power of the coastal State. In 1953, for example, a fishing vessel belonging to the Onassis fleet was apprehended 185 miles off the Peruvian coast and was subsequently fined $3 million for violating Peruvian sovereignty. The fine was eventually paid in order that the vessel might be released.

The continental shelf is that gradually dipping platform sloping away from the coast to a general depth of about 200 meters (656 feet). Beyond this outer edge the degree of slope increases markedly down to the ocean depths. On and above the shelf valuable fisheries resources, including various kinds of shellfish, are frequently concentrated, while beneath the surface of the shelf there may be petroleum, natural gas, and sulphur which are capable of recovery. In 1945 President Truman issued a proclamation that the natural resources of the continental shelf contiguous to the coasts of the United States were subject to United States jurisdiction and control, although the character of the high seas above the shelf (that is, the waters beyond territorial limits) was not affected by these claims. This principle was followed by the International Law Commission and at the Geneva Conference. Coastal States may exercise sovereign rights over the continental shelf[9] for the purpose of exploring and exploiting its natural resources. Control over the fisheries in the waters beyond territorial limits which cover the shelf is explicitly forbidden to the coastal State, except in the case of organisms which "at the harvestable state are either immobile on or under the sea bed, or are unable to move except in constant physical contact with the seabed or subsoil." Among such organisms are coral, sponges, oysters, mussels, and cockles.

The problem of delimiting boundaries for the various offshore zones is a complex one because of the great physical variety existing among the coast lines of the world. Some coast lines are smooth and unbroken, others include bays and river mouths, still others are fringed by offshore islands and rocks. Problems of boundary delimitation also arise in the case of drying banks and rocks (which are covered by water at high tide), of estuaries, such as the Gulf of St. Lawrence, and of roadsteads normally used for the loading and unloading of ships. Finally, there are cases of "historic" waters—that is, of coastal waters which have traditionally been claimed by the adjacent State as part of its territory; in such cases the waters are classed as internal waters of the State.

The first step in providing for these contingencies of boundary delimitations was to decide on the nature of the baseline separating internal from territorial waters. From this baseline the breadth of territorial and contiguous zones could be measured. For most coast lines the baseline selected was the high-tide line along the shore. In the case of bays, a straight baseline not more than ten miles in length has traditionally been drawn across the entrance of the bay at the first point where the distance from shore to shore is less than ten miles. If the waters enclosed by the baseline are as great or greater in extent than the area of a semicircle whose diameter equals the length of the closing line, then this line marks the outer limits of internal waters. If, on the other hand, the bay is a mere curvature of the coast, enclosing relatively little water area, the baseline continues to follow the low-water line of the shore (see Figure 8).

A belt of territorial water surrounds each island—defined at the 1958 Geneva Conference as "a naturally formed area of land, surrounded by water, which is above water at low tide." Low-tide elevations, that is, areas of land which are submerged at high tide, have no territorial belt of their own; if, however, they are located within a State's territorial sea, they may themselves be utilized as base points for the determination of the outer limits of that sea. If, for example, a country claiming a three-mile

---

[9] Defined at the 1958 Geneva Conference as "the seabed and subsoil of the submarine areas adjacent to the coast but outside the area of the territorial sea to a depth of 200 meters, or, beyond that limit, to where the depth of the superjacent waters admits of the exploitation of the natural resources."

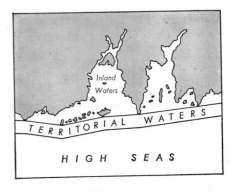

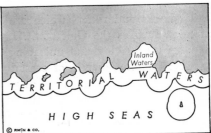

Figure 8. Arcs of Circles and Straight Baseline Boundaries.

territorial belt has a low-tide elevation located two miles off shore, the territorial sea at that point extends out to five miles from the shore.

The outermost permanent harbor works are taken as an integral part of a State's harbor system and are regarded as forming part of the coast in determining the breadth of the territorial sea. Likewise, roadsteads which are normally used for loading, unloading, and anchoring of ships, and which would otherwise be located wholly or in part outside the outer limits of a State's territorial sea, are considered by the Geneva Convention as included within territorial limits. In the case of rivers flowing directly into the sea, the baseline dividing internal from territorial waters lies across the river mouth between points on the low-tide lines of its banks.

Despite the careful attention given at the Geneva Conference to these various offshore features, there remains the problem of coasts which are deeply indented, or off which there is a fringe of offshore islands. In such cases the rule of straight baselines comes into play (see below).

Having determined the baseline from which the breadth of the territorial and contiguous zones are to be measured, there is then the necessity of determining the outer limits of these zones. Merely to reproduce the baseline three, six, or twelve miles offshore may lead to considerable complications along complex coasts; as an alternative process the "arcs of circles" principle is now generally adopted. According to this principle, a series of arcs of circles having radii equal to the breadth of the territorial sea are described from prominent points along the coast, and from offshore islands and rocks. These arcs are joined together in a continuous line marking the outer limits of the zones. Every point on this outer line is then within x miles of some point on the baseline, x being the breadth of the territorial or contiguous zone (see Figure 8).

The system of straight baselines consists of a series of straight lines connecting islands and offshore rocks with one another and with prominent points along the mainland. The principal advocate of straight baselines has been Norway, whose coast has an extremely rugged configuration. Norway's right to delimit straight baselines was upheld by the International Court of Justice in 1951 in the Anglo-Norwegian Fisheries Case, and at the 1958 Geneva Conference it was decided that a straight baseline regime might be used along coasts which are deeply indented or have a fringe of islands off shore in the immediate vicinity. No mathematical limitations were placed on the length of individual baselines, nor on the distance they might lie off shore; the only requirements are that they must conform to the general configuration of the coast, and that the sea areas enclosed by the

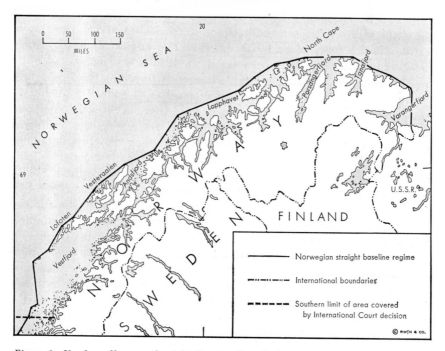

Figure 9. Northern Norway: Straight Baseline Boundaries.

lines must be sufficiently closely linked to the land domain to be subject to the regime of internal waters.

The outer territorial limits in the case of straight baselines are marked by a series of straight lines parallel to the baselines. Among the countries which have adopted straight baseline regimes are Iceland, Ireland (along the west and south coasts), and the Faeroe Islands. No provisions were made at the Geneva Conference for island groups or archipelagoes not immediately adjoining a mainland coast. Indonesia has connected its outermost islands with straight baselines beyond which it measures its territorial waters.

The boundary between territorial waters of adjacent states, or those facing one another across narrow straits, would, in the absence of other agreements, be a median line, every point of which is equidistant from the nearest points on the two coasts. The same principle pertains in the case of contiguous zones. No action was taken at the Geneva Conference on the question of historic waters, other than to refer the matter to the General Assembly of the United Nations. Thus, from the point of view of international law, the legal status of such water bodies as Hudson Bay or Peter the Great Bay, at the entrance to Vladivostok, is still uncertain, so far as a majority of the States of the world are concerned.

Two basic questions facing the delegates at the 1958 Law of the Sea Conference involved the breadth of the territorial sea and the legality of extraterritorial zones of exclusive fisheries. The origins of the three-mile territorial sea have already been noted. In 1930 it was found that of 37 reporting States, 22, or 59 per cent, favored a three-mile territorial belt. Thirty years later this percentage had dropped to 31 (out of a total of 70 reporting States). The United States, Japan, Australia, New Zealand, and several of the States of northwestern Europe are among the traditional champions of the three-mile limit, thereby permitting the greatest possible extent of the high seas. Norway, Sweden, and Finland are among the four-mile countries, Italy, Spain, and Greece claim six miles, while the U.S.S.R., Egypt, Indonesia, and Communist China maintain twelve-mile limits.

At the 1958 Law of the Sea Conference no compromise was possible on a universal breadth to the territorial sea, and two years later a second international conference was convened at Geneva primarily for the purpose of attempting to reach agreement on this problem. One of the major complexities with regard to territorial limits involved the status of commercial fishing. States such as Britain, Japan, and the United States maintain important distant-water fishing fleets which frequently work close to the territorial limits of other countries; at the same time these countries are generally not inconvenienced by foreigners fishing close to their own coasts.[10]

---

[10] French, Belgian, and German vessels appear at times close to Britain's territorial limits, particu-

Other states, however, such as Iceland, Norway, and Canada, off whose coasts there are rich fisheries resources, are desirous of protecting their coastal fisheries as much as possible against foreign exploitation. Local fishermen in small boats may have to compete with foreign trawlers just beyond territorial limits. Thus the principle of exclusive fisheries zones beyond territorial limits has been evolved. Under such an agreement a State might claim territorial limits out to three or four miles, beyond which is an exclusive fisheries zone to a distance of twelve miles from shore. The advantage of this over an outright extension of territorial limits to twelve miles is that freedom of navigation by all ships is permitted beyond four miles; in time of war, if the coastal state is neutral, it need only patrol waters out to four miles from the coasts to prevent infringements of its neutrality by belligerent ships. On the other hand, from the point of view of foreign fishermen, there is no difference between a twelve-mile territorial sea and a three-mile territorial belt beyond which is a nine-mile exclusive fisheries zone.

The situation is well illustrated in the case of Iceland. British and other foreign trawlers since the early part of the twentieth century have engaged in fishing in the waters beyond Iceland's three-mile territorial limits. The island of Iceland has few natural resources, and the great bulk of its foreign exchange has traditionally been earned through the export of fish and fish products. Most Icelandic fishermen operate from small boats and are keenly aware of seasonal or yearly fluctuations in the catch of cod, haddock, saithe, and other species taken from the waters about the island. Icelandic officials have long been concerned over the possibilities of over-fishing and of damage to inshore spawning and nursery grounds through dragging of the bottom by trawls.

In 1944 Iceland became completely freed from Denmark; for several years thereafter there was pressure on the Icelandic government for increased protection to local fishermen against foreign trawlers, and in 1952 a series of straight baselines were delimited about the island from which a four-mile exclusive fisheries zone was measured. Since the previous three-mile territorial belt had been measured from the low-water line along the coast, or from ten-mile closing lines in the fjords, these new regulations shut out foreign fishermen from a wide area of rich fishing grounds. The straight baseline system had been approved by the International Court of Justice in the Anglo-Norwegian Case, and the Icelandic government held it could show historic grounds for its four-mile territorial claim. Four years later, however, the government announced the extension of the exclusive fisheries limit out to twelve miles from the straight baselines, while retaining

larly off Scotland, when they compete with local fishermen for the catch. Japanese vessels come close to Alaska.

the four-mile territorial zone. The British refused to recognize this new extension and sent warships to Iceland to protect trawlers against seizure by the Icelanders in the four-to-twelve mile zone.

At the second Law of the Sea Conference a joint United States–Canadian proposal called for a maximum breadth of six miles for the territorial sea, with an exclusive fisheries zone between the territorial limits and the twelve-mile limit measured from the baseline from which the breadth of the territorial sea was reckoned. An additional feature was that states having "historic fishing rights" in the waters in question might continue to fish beyond territorial limits for an additional ten years.

The concept of historic rights is based on the traditional practice of certain States of fishing off another country's coasts. British fishermen, for example, have long worked the fishing grounds off Iceland, northern Norway, and the Faeroes, while Americans have traditionally fished off the Maritime Provinces of Canada. Suddenly to close these grounds to those countries whose fishing industries have long depended on these sources of supply would, according to the proponents of this concept, represent a serious economic loss. Either the countries having historic rights should be permitted to continue fishing these grounds (to the exclusion of all other foreigners who can claim no such rights), or there should be a transition period during which the foreign fishing fleets are permitted to adjust to their eventual exclusion from the grounds. The United States–Canadian proposal failed of adoption at the Geneva Conference, however, and no standardization of territorial limits has thus been possible.

As technological progress continues to be made in the utilization of the resources of the sea, and as States seek more and more to harvest the wealth of the sea, there is an ever increasing possibility that the boundaries of offshore zones will be moved seaward, thereby closing valuable areas of the high seas to the free use of all countries. Governments may lay claims to bays and coastal seas as being "historic waters" and thus capable of being closed off as internal.[11] Island States may close off all waters between the islands as internal or territorial, while the extensive fisheries claims made by Latin American States in the eastern Pacific may, if unchallenged, be emulated by governments in other parts of the world. Unless strong countermeasures can be devised, the "free seas" are in danger of gradually being divided up among coastal States.

BOUNDARIES IN SPACE

When the Soviets in 1957 launched their first Sputnik, they opened up a new era in boundary delimitation—that of boundaries in space. The

---

[11] Several years ago the Soviet Union closed off Peter the Great Bay as historic (and thus excluded to Japanese fishermen), while Iceland claims the waters of Faxafloi as historic, despite the fact that the island has been independent only since 1918.

Chicago International Air Treaty of 1944 recognizes that every State has complete and exclusive sovereignty over the air space above its territory, although the treaty offers no definition of the term "air space," nor does it mention the difference between air space and outer space. There is general legal agreement that national sovereignty ends at some point in space. Once this point has been determined, the question then still remains, What activities will be legal in the "free" space beyond national boundaries?

In 1958 the Legal Advisor of the United States State Department suggested that the term "air space" might possibly be defined to include the space in which there is an atmosphere, and that astronomically the earth's atmosphere might be said to extend as much as 10,000 miles above its surface. One of the leading experts on international law, however, has written:

> International law does not recognize any limit to a state's airspace. The airspace under sovereignty of the subjacent state goes up as far as an aircraft or ballon can go because, no matter how high, jettison of a bomb or anything else jeopardizes that state. Beyond airspace is outer space which is not under the sovereignty of any state. . . . Theorists have recognized the vital difference between aircraft that endanger the territory below because of the law of gravitation, and of missiles or satellites traveling at such a velocity that they do not endanger the territory below them at any moment. Outer space vehicles are not, at present, subject to practical control by the subjacent state. There appears to be a band more than 100 miles wide separating the space where there is sufficient air to support airplanes or balloons (certainly not more than 50 miles up) from outer space, where there is not enough air to impede the progress of satellites. . . . While a state from whose territory a missile or satellite is launched may be responsible for damage resulting from its landing anywhere, international law recognizes no trespass upon the state whose territory may be below it at any moment of its flight.[12]

The American Bar Association has recommended that it would be "premature" to attempt now to draft a comprehensive law governing space, since so little is known about its potential uses. The trend seems to be toward the establishment of an upper boundary of sovereignty somewhere below 100 miles—the approximate lowest altitude at which a satellite can orbit at least once around the earth. Above this point "spy" satellites can apparently move freely obtaining photographs of foreign countries.

---

[12] Quincy Wright, "Legal Aspects of the U-2 Incident," American Journal of International Law, LIV (1960), 847.

THE REALITY OF INTERNATIONAL BOUNDARIES

The political map of the world portrays a series of well-defined units, each bordered by land boundaries separating it from its neighbors or by water bodies. The only indication on this map that conditions are not as stable as portrayed may be the appearance of striped areas, labeled "in dispute," or of dashed lines showing the position of the boundaries still undetermined. Yet in fact the position of many boundaries of the world are far from settled, on land, in sea areas, and in space.

Fifty years ago Ellen Churchill Semple wrote, "Nature abhors fixed boundary lines and sudden transitions; all her forces combine against them. . . . If, by some cataclysm, sharp lines of demarcation are drawn she straightway begins to blur them by creating intermediate forms, and thus established the boundary zone which characterizes the inanimate and animate world."[13] Certainly in the sea and air portions of the globe the trend seems to be toward the creation of zones or frontiers of national sovereignty, despite the efforts of lawyers, statesmen, and geographers to clarify wherever possible the areal limits of control. Even on land the concept of a neatly partitioned political world is not valid for many areas. It may be that in parts of the world international boundaries may come to lose their significance and become merely internal administrative lines, but this is an advanced stage which generally occurs only after the boundary locations have been carefully determined. There exists quite a gap between this and the early stage in which boundary delimitations have not yet been fully carried out. It is within this gap that the principal danger of boundary controversy lies.

BIBLIOGRAPHY

ALEXANDER, LEWIS M. *Offshore Geography of Northwestern Europe.* Chicago: Rand McNally & Company, 1963.

A survey of offshore boundaries in this area.

BOGGS, S. WHITTEMORE. *International Boundaries: A Study of Boundary Functions and Problems.* New York: Columbia University Press, 1940.

A basic text on the nature and function of international boundaries.

———. "National Claims in Adjacent Seas," *The Geographical Review,* XLI (1950), 185–210.

A fully documented description of this problem as it existed at the time of publication.

[13] *Influences of Geographic Environment* (New York: Henry Holt & Company, 1911), p. 204.

"Boundary Concepts and Definitions." Geographic Report No. 1, April 28, 1961. Washington: Department of State, Office of the Geographer.
A careful description of boundary terminology.

Broek, Jan O. M. "The Problem of Natural Frontiers," in Committee on International Relations, University of California, *Frontiers of the Future*. Berkeley and Los Angeles: University of California Press, 1940. Pp. 3–20.
Description, with illustrations, of the concept of "natural" frontiers.

Dean, Arthur H. "Freedom of the Seas," *Foreign Affairs*, XXXVII (1958), 83–95.
Basic problems of political control of offshore waters.

Fawcett, Charles B. *Frontiers: A Study in Political Geography*. Oxford: Clarendon Press, 1918.
One of the early works on this subject. Many of the conclusions are still pertinent to current conditions.

Hall, H. Duncan. "Zones of the International Frontier," *The Geographical Review*, XXXVIII (1948), 615–25.
A detailed handling of certain problems of colonial administration.

Holdich, Thomas H. *Political Frontiers and Boundary Making*. London: Macmillan and Company, 1916.
Like Fawcett's book, this is one of the early classics on boundaries.

Jones, Stephen B. "Boundary Concepts in the Setting of Place and Time," *Annals of the Association of American Geographers*, XLIX (1959), 241–55.
A comprehensive and well-documented discussion of boundaries.

————. *Boundary-Making: A Handbook for Statesmen, Treaty Editors and Boundary Commissioners*. New York: Columbia University Press, 1945.
A detailed discussion of the techniques of boundary delimitation.

Kristof, Ladis K. O. "The Nature of Frontiers and Boundaries," *Annals of the Association of American Geographers*, XLIX (1959), 269–82.
An excellent treatment of the differences between frontiers and boundaries.

PEARCY, G. ETZEL, "Geographical Aspects of the Law of the Sea," *Annals of the Association of American Geographers,* XLIX (1959), 1–24.

A survey of the results of the 1958 Geneva Conference on the Law of the Sea, in terms of offshore boundaries.

QUIGG, PHILIP W. "Open Skies and Open Space," *Foreign Affairs,* XXXVII (1958), 95–107.

A general discussion of sovereignty in space.

5

THE STATE AS A VIABLE POLITICAL UNIT

● Any national political unit has three basic functions to perform. It must
maintain its internal cohesion, its economic consistency, and its territorial
security. Its success in these three areas determines whether or not it is
actually a viable political unit, that is, one which is capable of functioning
for a sustained period of time as an independent agent among the family
of nations. Among the over forty political units which have become independent since the end of World War II, there exist quite a number of
cases in which this test of viability might reveal serious weaknesses in the
structure of the political unit. In dividing their overseas territories into
political subdivisions, the Western colonial powers were frequently uncon-
cerned with the question of whether or not, if these subdivisions became
independent, they could exist for long as separate national units. Yet
in time the pressures for self-rule did indeed result in independence. Most
of the larger and more populous of the Western colonial territories are now
free; often they have been divided into two or more States, as occurred in
India, Indochina, and French West and French Equatorial Africa. Now
many of the smaller units are moving toward self-rule, either as single
units or in federation with other States. Each of these new political units
faces the problem of economic and political viability. In this chapter the
three criteria of viability will be considered in detail.

THE MAINTENANCE OF INTERNAL COHESION

The strongest of the centripetal forces holding a State together is the
state-idea, that is, "the concept or idea justifying the existence of this particular state incorporating these particular regions; the state must have a

raison d'être—reason for existing."[1] Israel is an example of a State with a strong *raison d'être;* one might, on the other hand, question the *raison d'être* of the proposed independent Federation of Rhodesia and Nyasaland— what reason would these three regions have for existing as one political entity? Economic strength might be one answer; common ideas and values might be another, although here one could ask what particular values the Africans of Nyasaland have with the whites of Southern Rhodesia? Austria-Hungary following World War I is often taken as an example of a political unit which no longer possessed a valid state-idea.

The importance of the economic factor in assessing the state-idea deserves emphasis. Indeed, a study of what might be termed "successful" state-ideas would reveal that in the great majority of cases there existed a strong economic *raison d'être.* The proposed West Indies Federation of British territories in the Caribbean had as its basis an economic justification; ultimately it foundered largely because of the unwillingness of a majority of the voters of Jamaica to assume economic responsibilities for the poorer islands lying between themselves and Trinidad. The pressures for statehood for Alaska and Hawaii were largely economic in nature, as were also the pressures of the German states in the later nineteenth century to come together into the German Empire. Yet many of the newly independent States of Asia and Africa have, as isolated units, very little economic *raison d'être.* Each one was governed as a separate colony by its mother country; thus, at time of independence, each one became a separate political unit. History and the administrative policies of the colonial powers are, in many cases, the primary force of the state-idea.

Certain conditions may, if present in a State, aid it in its achievement of "maturity." "A state is geopolitically *mature* when it has established a *raison d'être* that is so thoroughly accepted by the peoples of all of its different regions that they accept without question the inclusion of the regions as integral parts of the state-area."[2] One of these conditions involves communication (or circulation) media. Whittlesey suggested that a State should match the status of communications. Most large States, he held, do not possess adequate communication media and hence are "geopolitically immature." Admittedly the test of maturity cannot be measured quantitatively. Has India achieved maturity, inasmuch as various groups in the northeast apparently do not accept the state-idea? What of the Soviet Union, composed as it is of so many differing ethnic groups? A "valid" state-idea may, of course, be achievable by force as well as by persuasion, a process which may in time become evident in Mainland China.

Eventually the state-idea may result in consciousness on the part of

---

[1] Richard Hartshorne, "The Functional Approach in Political Geography," p. 110.
[2] Richard Hartshorne, "The Concepts of 'Raison d'Etre' and 'Maturity of States'" (abstract), *Annals of the Association of American Geographers,* XXX (1940), 59–60.

the inhabitants of a sense of loyalty to the State, of a feeling of "together-ness" with their fellow countrymen, of common understanding and of common values. They also feel a source of identification with a particular geographic area—an area they wish to organize as *their* State. In this way the concept of "nation" is developed.[3] Such a nation may not have the same boundaries as a particular State. It may predate the formation of a State (as in the case of Poland) or exist in only a portion of the State (as in Great Britain before the partitioning of Ireland). If, however, the area of the nation and State are codeterminous, as in the United States, the term "Nation-State" is frequently applied. In the Nation-State there is a much stronger centripetal force than was present when there was merely some economic, historical, or other justification for the existence of the State as a separate entity. But developing a concept of "nation" takes time and may easily be impeded by the existence within the State of two or more groups with diverse attitudes, by the physical separation of one part of the State from another (as in Pakistan), by competing economic interests within the State, or by other divisive forces. The concept of "nation" was not strong enough in the United States to prevent the outbreak of the Civil War, in India to prevent the partition of the subcon-tinent, or in nineteenth-century Sweden to prevent the ultimate independ-ence of Norway. In many of the newer countries this concept of "nation" is far from developed, and one of the critical politico-geographic questions of contemporary times is what ultimate territorial form some of the newly emerging States will assume.

The State is a dynamic phenomenon, both in terms of its mode of creation and of changes which take place in its nature. Each State, at least in modern times, has evolved from territory which was already politically organized, either as a dependent or independent area. Some territories are obviously more liable to change in political status than others, and the political geographer, viewing the world political pattern, should be con-tinually alert to the possibilities of such change, whether (as in a majority of cases) the pressures for change originate from *within* the political unit, or whether the change is largely the result of outside forces.

Hartshorne's "centrifugal" forces within a political unit tend toward change, toward a lessening of the power and control of the central govern-ment. The circulation of men, materials, and ideas is often an unsettling force, unless the movement is oriented toward the central authority.[4]

---

[3] Hartshorne defines a "nation" as "a group of people occupying a particular area who feel them-selves held together in terms of common acceptance of particular values that are of such prime importance to them that they demand that their area and the people should be organized in a distinct state, as the political agency by which those values may be preserved and furthered." "The Functional Approach in Political Geography," p. 114.

[4] Actually circulation may be a force both for unity and for diversity. Hartshorne has written that a state achieves maturity when the state-idea permeates the entire national area. The expansion of the state-idea is obviously a function of circulation. But increased circulation *within* a region may increase the people's awareness of their regional distinctiveness.

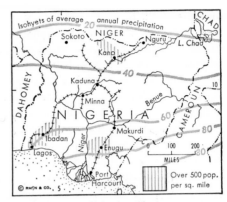

Figure 10. Nigeria.

Opposing the state-idea may be the growth of political self-awareness on the part of one or more groups within the national area. Karl Deutsch, in his study of the foundations of nationalism,[5] discussed trends of national assimilation and differentiation and possible means of measuring these trends statistically. He delimited nine population groups (based on whether or not they are "mobilized" for intensive communications and "assimilated" with respect to the national culture). For each of these groups there are various rates of change, depending on whether the groups are becoming more or less mobilized and more or less assimilated with the passage of time. Studies such as these, based on statistical data and population predictions, may provide valuable clues as to future trends toward change in the political status of particular areas.

The Case of Nigeria

The State of Nigeria illustrates several of the problems involved in maintaining internal cohesion. Not until 1914 were the various British colonies and protectorates in this part of Africa brought together to form the "colony and protectorate" of Nigeria (Figure 10). With an area of some 340,000 square miles and a population of over 35 million, Nigeria encompasses a number of physical regions, ranging from the hot, wet, mangrove-swamp forest along the southern coast to the grassland and semidesert of the extreme north. Between these the vegetation reflects the decreasing precipitation as one proceeds northward—tropical rainforest, inland from the mangrove swamps, giving way to semideciduous forest, and then to open woodland and savanna grassland. The Niger River and its tributaries form something of a unifying element for the country, although the waters of southwestern Nigeria drain directly to the Gulf of Guinea, while those of the northeast flow eastward to Lake Chad.

Four main tribal groups form the nucleus of the State, the Yoruba in the Western Region, centered on the cities of Lagos and Ibadan, the Ibo

---

[5] *Nationalism and Social Communication* (New York: John Wiley & Sons, 1953).

in the Eastern Region, with Enugu as their principal center, and the Hausa and Fulani in the Northern Region, with Kano as their major city. The nuclei of these four groups are separated from one another by considerable expanses of territory, occupied by lesser groups,[6] of whom there are over 250, speaking scores of different dialects. Religiously, the peoples of the north are predominantly Moslem, while both Christians and pagans are to be found in the eastern and western areas.

The major political subdivisions of Nigeria have followed its ethnic pattern. For over forty years the colony was administered by the British under a unitary system, but in 1954 it became a federation. Buchanan wrote, "Unfortunately, the original groupings of provinces, on which the present Regions are based, appears to have been governed largely by historical accident and administrative expediency rather than by cultural or geographic unity. Today not one of the Regions can be regarded as a coherent geographic unit. Each shows a distinct cultural and economic duality—a core area with a marked degree of ethnic homogeneity and a high level of economic development, with a peripheral area, thinly inhabited by a variety of minority peoples and often at a lower level of economic development."[7] In his study he portrayed the division of the Northern Region into the "Sudan Provinces" (including Kano) of the north with their higher population density and more advanced economic development, and the "Middle Provinces" to the south with fewer people and a more primitive economy. Supplementing this work is Prescott's article detailing problems of boundary delimitation between the Regions. Prescott pointed out that the internal boundaries of Nigeria originally had simple administrative functions and that their exact locations were never worked out. They have recently become the objects of extreme regional feeling, and he wrote, "their functions are becoming increasingly complex, so that they are touching upon many aspects of the individual's life. Moreover, the relations between the Regions have deteriorated since the substitution of national for colonial government."[8]

Clearly Nigeria's hope as an independent state is to weld together its three diverse regions into a cohesive national unit. Yet rail and road connections between these regions are generally meager, and parts of the northeastern and eastern portions of the state are, from the standpoint of communications, virtually beyond the effective national territory.[9] Lacking a

---

[6] See the map of tribal nuclei in J. R. V. Prescott, "Nigeria's Regional Boundary Problems," *The Geographical Review*, XLIX (1959), 487.

[7] Keith Buchanan, "The Northern Region of Nigeria: The Geographical Background of its Political Duality," pp. 451–52.

[8] Prescott, *op. cit.*, p. 487.

[9] The inclusion in 1961 of the northern portion of the former British trust territory of Cameroons within Nigeria did little to alleviate this condition, since only one all-season motor road crosses the area. Northern Cameroons has become a province within the Northern Region of Nigeria. In July, 1963, the inhabitants of Benin and Delta Provinces in the Western Region voted to form a fourth Region, the Midwest state, composed largely of members of the Edo tribe. Other tribes in Nigeria may soon desire greater autonomy.

strong history of unity, Nigeria faces extreme difficulties in evolving a sense of nationalism on the part of its people. Even its economic *raison d'être* is not strong. Much of the surplus production of the various areas is destined for foreign trade, although there is a certain amount of inter-regional exchange of goods, such as the movement southward of salt, cattle, skins, and cotton, and northward of palm oil, cotton, and groundnuts. This potential wealth might be more readily developed (and investment capital more readily obtained) if the State remained unified than if it were divided into separate States.

The Federation of Nigeria became independent in October, 1960. Experts had been concerned over the possible composition of its political parties, since 55 per cent of the total population came from the Northern Region, and if the parties split along regional lines this area might have a voting majority. In actual practice, however, the dominant parties of the Northern and Eastern regions have formed a loosely knit governing coalition for the country.

In assessing the forces of internal cohesion within a State, one must consider the possible attraction of areas lying beyond the national borders, such as the prewar attraction of Czech Sudetenland to Nazi Germany, or that of the Mexican province of Texas to the United States. Fortunately for Nigeria, there is little in the areas adjacent to its borders which would tend to act as an external centrifugal force; rather, the reverse might in time be true, namely that a dynamic Nigeria could act as an attracting force on regions of Dahomey, Niger, and Cameroons which border it.

THE NEED FOR ECONOMIC CONSISTENCY

Every State must, in the final analysis, have the capacity to finance the cost of its national operations. It must carry out certain responsibilities at the international level and provide for the needs of its inhabitants. Its ability to meet its economic obligations depends on two variables, its expenses and its sources of revenue.

For any State there are three principal categories of expenses. The first involves the general costs of government—executive, legislative, and judicial expenses, the postal service, law enforcement agencies, and so on. The distribution of these expenses between the central and local governments depends on the type of governmental system which has been established, but one way or another these costs must be borne. They are, in a relative sense, fixed expenses, or at least ones which tend to increase or decrease fairly slowly.

A second category covers what are largely the State's international obligations—defense, the cost of overseas territories, and contributions to the maintenance of international organizations. Such expenses are generally more flexible than those of the first category. Military forces may be reduced, overseas bases discontinued, and colonial areas set free, although the former mother country may, for a time, be obligated to meet certain expenses of the new States created from its colonial areas. Contributions to international organizations may be withheld, since, as in the case of the United Nations, there are no means of forcing member states to pay their assessed costs.

With respect to the third category, a State may assume considerable responsibilities regarding its citizens in terms of social welfare programs. Free medical care, unemployment insurance, federal care of the aged, these and similar projects may involve the government in expenses which it can ill afford to meet, unless additional sources of revenue may be found. Here again, the costs are flexible; a State may elect to engage in relatively few social welfare activities. On the other hand, the prevailing political theories in the State may dictate the inauguration of such programs in the face of extremely limited financial resources.

So far as revenue is concerned, the primary basis for a State's wealth lies in its productivity and the exchange of its goods, either within its own borders or as exports. The productivity of the United States did not drop appreciably at the time of the 1929 crash, but the exchange of its goods did. A State may produce but be unable to export. Following World War II a number of States, such as Britain and the Netherlands, embarked on national programs of increasing production and exports, while at the same time decreasing imports in order to bring about a favorable balance of trade. A government acquires revenue through the taxation of its inhabitants. If the government's need for revenue increases, presumably taxes may be raised, although if the level of productivity and of exchange of goods does not rise proportionately, a limit to the degree of taxation may in time be reached. After this the government must look to other sources for revenue— or else reduce its commitments.

Overseas territories may represent a source of wealth, as until recently was the case in the Belgian Congo. By and large, however, colonies are not generally revenue producers, but rather consumers, so far as the national government of the mother country is concerned. Another potential source of wealth is the income derived from foreign investments, or from services rendered by residents of the state to foreigners. Many countries, either through the government or through private citizens, have important investments in other areas. Among the types of services which may be rendered are shipping and air transportation, the accommodation of foreign and international tourists, insurance, and banking.

A final source of revenue may be through foreign-aid programs. From 1945 through 1962 the United States spent nearly 98 billion dollars in foreign aid, approximately 60 per cent of which was in the form of economic aid and the rest for military assistance. During this period the countries of

Europe received over 43 billion dollars, representing a substantial contribution to their national economies.

A primary economic responsibility of a State is to ensure that its population receives food, clothing, and other necessities. This ability to provide depends on a number of variables: the State's resource base and the availability of capital and technological skills to utilize this base; the possibility of obtaining needed goods from outside areas; the total population of the state; and the level of demand (or the "want scales") of the various segments of the population for these goods. Theoretically if the national government is unable to provide for the necessities of its population, (1) it will be replaced by another regime, or (2) the State may cease to exist as a separate independent unit.

The differentials in resource base between various political units were considered in Chapter 3. Some areas are unusually rich in known resources, whether these be agricultural, mineral, or both, while other areas are extremely poor. In contrast with the resource wealth of Nigeria, for example, is the lack of known resources in El Salvador, Somalia, Jordan, or the former French territory of Chad. Future exploration may, of course, uncover minerals or power fuels in previously barren areas, such as the recent discovery of oil in southeastern Algeria. Even if a State contains valuable resources, it may lack the capital or technical skills to develop them. In this case it may permit foreign groups to develop and market them (as in Venezuela or Kuwait) and derive revenue through royalties on the sales.

Much has been written on the so-called population-resource ratio in a given State. In 1798 Malthus had predicted that since the human animal tended to double his number in twenty-five years, the population of an area over a period of time would grow geometrically (1, 2, 4, 8, 16,), while the means of subsistence would grow arithmetically (1, 2, 3, 4, 5). In two centuries the population would be to the means of subsistence as 256 to 9, unless population growth were checked by wars, famine, disease, or moral restraint. Reduced to its simplest form, the question arises, Can a State feed, clothe, and provide the other basic necessities of life for its population either through its own productivity or through purchase from other countries?

No State in the world produces all of its own food, clothing, and other basic necessities (housing, transportation, medical supplies, armaments, and so on), but some could produce the great bulk of these necessities if forced to do so. Each State, by producing and selling surplus products over and above its own needs (or by acquiring revenue in some other manner), is in a position to purchase needed imports. The productivity of the State, both for the needs of its own population and for exports, depends on the resources available to it and on the stage of development of these resources by its population. The quantity of the available resources is, in a sense, finite. Climate, slope, and soil, for example, place definite limitations on the extent of land which the Soviets can, with profit, place in crops. New resources may, of course, be discovered within a State's borders, thereby increasing the resource base, but such possibilities cannot be calculated in determining existing resource potentials.

At the other side of the equation is population. Given a relatively fixed resource base, we might postulate that a marked increase in the population of a country results in greater pressures on its resources and, perhaps, in a general lowering of the standard of living of the population. There are, of course, many variables here. A proportion of the population may emigrate, an increase in export sales (particularly of manufactured goods) may bring in sufficient wealth to overcome the population increase, the boundaries may be expanded to acquire *Lebensraum*. But aside from these possibilities, the fact remains that beyond a certain level any marked increase in a State's population (whether from natural increase or from immigration) may have a negative effect on the standard of living of its people. At first there might be widespread unemployment, or at least poor job opportunities for most people. Later there may be real shortages of basic commodities; ultimately portions of the State may be threatened by mass starvation. Let us look briefly at some of the factors of world population.

In 1960 the total world population was increasing at a rate of approximately 46 million a year or 1.7 per cent annually. This rate is expected to increase so that by the year 2000 the total will have gone from less than 3 billion to over 6 billion, two-thirds of whom will be in Asia. China's projected population in 2000 will be 1.6 billion and India's 1 billion, while the Soviet Union and United States will have 370 million and 280 million, respectively. Looking at Communist China alone, for a moment, we may note that, because of ideological and other pressures, we have here a relatively isolated economic unit, which theoretically should be able to provide for the basic needs of its population. Yet each year the population of China increases by nearly 17 million. By the year 2000 the total will have risen by close to 1 billion as the rate of increase climbs. Long before this China's population will have far outdistanced its resources.

India, Japan, South Korea, Egypt, Jamaica—these and other countries face growing problems of population pressure. Yet it must also be remembered that, as communications increase, and as peoples become more aware of the world about them, their demands—for more food and clothing, better housing, medical care, and education—also tend to increase. Thus many parts of the world are faced not only with growing numbers of people, but also with greater "want scales" and greater levels of expectation. Ironically, it is frequently those countries which have recently experienced political change (with all the economic instability and loss of foreign capital this may entail) which face some of the gravest problems of population demand. For States such as these viability as a political unit is intimately tied with their degree of economic viability.

Because of these economic pressures many government and civilian leaders throughout the world are concerned with the choice of economic system to be followed in developing their State as rapidly as possible. They compare the economic growth rates of various countries and frequently look with admiration at statistics of the Soviet Union and of Communist China, particularly when compared with recent growth figures for the United States and Britain. In setting up a planned economy along the lines of the U.S.S.R., they may hope to profit from the advantages of the Soviet economic system, without embracing the Communist ideology; to this end they accept economic aid and advice from the Soviets. A great many persons have been sold on the efficacy of planned economies, despite the regimentation and, frequently, loss of individual liberties which such economies involve.

The Availability of Resources

The industrialized countries of the world—particularly the United States and Canada, western Europe, the Soviet Union, and Japan—must import a great many of their mineral and power needs from such areas as the Middle East, central Africa, South America, and southeast Asia. The United States, for example, depends on South America for important amounts of its petroleum, iron ore, copper, tin, bauxite, and industrial diamonds, while western Europe looks to the Middle East for the bulk of its petroleum and to central Africa for copper, diamonds, lead, zinc, and uranium. The need for industrial raw materials was one of the major factors behind Japan's drive toward southeast Asia immediately preceding its entry into World War II.

Any modern industrial State must constantly reassess the sources of supply of its industrial and power resources. The Suez crisis of 1956, and the resultant closing of the canal, shut off western Europe temporarily from its petroleum supplies from the Middle East. The Allied blockade of Germany in World War II created a shortage of aviation gasoline in that country which apparently affected its air operations during the closing months of the war. When its sources of tin in Malaya and Indonesia were cut off early in World War II, the United States was forced to depend almost entirely on imports from Bolivia, and political conditions in that country were watched closely in Washington lest there be some interruption in supply. In the regional chapters which follow other examples of resource dependence such as these will be considered.

One of the early manifestations of the Cold War was the move by the

United States and other non-Communist countries to impose an embargo on the export of strategic items, such as copper, cobalt, and tin, to the Soviet Union. This move gained momentum after the outbreak of the Korean War in 1950. The Soviet Union, however, is apparently well endowed with most industrial resources except tin, and with rapid strides in the development of these resources the Russians have become largely independent of imports of mineral and power resources. They have, on the other hand, begun exporting petroleum to non-Communist countries, generally at prices below those of the Western producers.

Economic Blocs

A final point in this discussion of economics concerns the postwar development of economic blocs, in which tariffs are reduced between member states and a common tariff regime is adopted toward trade from nonmembers. Both the United States and the Soviet Union owe their economic growth in part to their enormous home market and to the lack of restrictions on trade throughout the national area.

The most important of the economic blocs has been the European Economic Community, or Common Market, inaugurated on January 1, 1958. This community includes France, West Germany, Italy, the Netherlands, Belgium, and Luxembourg, with a combined population in 1960 of 170 million (as compared with 212 million for the U.S.S.R. and 182 million for the United States). Within the Common Market tariffs are gradually to be reduced on the movement of goods between member states until some time after 1970, when complete freedom of trade is envisioned within the area. Restrictions on the movement of capital and of labor are also being reduced, and common policies on agriculture, transportation, and fisheries are being formulated (for details of the Common Market see page 272). A less well-defined economic system has been worked out for the Communist countries of East Europe (with the exception of Yugoslavia). Known as the Council for Mutual Economic Aid, it provides for coordinating bilateral trade agreements and long-range development plans. An economic union has long been in the planning stage for the countries of Central America, and, in theory at least, the former French territories of French West and French Equatorial Africa are united in economic groups.

In 1960 a European Free Trade Association was established with seven members—Britain, Norway, Sweden, Switzerland, Portugal, Denmark, and Austria. Finland became an associate member in 1961. This association (sometimes termed the "Outer Seven") is looser in structure than the Common Market. It seeks to create a free-trade area by 1970 through removal of trade barriers between the member states, but permits agricultural subsidies to be retained by the various governments. Unlike the Common Market, it does not envision the opening of the doors to the free movement of labor between states. By 1961 the British government had begun serious talks with officials of the Common Market with a view toward British membership in that body—a move, which, if successfully concluded, would spell the end of the EFTA.

THE MAINTENANCE OF TERRITORIAL SECURITY

A State may be faced by threats to its territorial security through either one of two moves, a desire by one of its neighbors to alter the common border at the State's expense without otherwise impinging on its independence, or by complete conquest of the State. In either case the State's capacity to resist demands depends largely on its power position relative to that of the country which is threatening it.

Stephen Jones has written that any estimate of national power has two related aspects, resources and national strategy. "Power" he has defined as "that which permits participation in the making of decisions" and "strategy" as "the art of using power for the attainment of goals in competition." A resource is to him "anything a nation has, can obtain, or can conjure up to support its strategy."[10]

Much has been written about the power inventory of a State, that is, the resources it has available for use in connection with its strategy. Klaus Knorr, considering the war potential of nations, put these resources in the category of "economic capacity," which is but one of the three determinants of military power, the other two being the will to fight and administrative capacity.[11] Obviously these last two elements are extremely difficult to measure, particularly in terms of comparing the war potential of one State with that of another. Resources must be thought of not only with respect to the different types available, but also to quantity, quality, vulnerability, accessibility (How long will it be before they can actually be used?), rates of depletion, and cost to the country of their exploitation. Only when a complete inventory has been prepared of the actual availability of resources for crises of both short and long duration can a State's leaders estimate the conditions under which they may plan their strategy, including the moves they might make in the face of aggressive acts by the enemy. Obviously an alliance with a powerful neighbor is one of the best forms of resource a State can have to support its strategy; so, too, would be the destruction of an alliance involving an adversary and one or more of *its* friends.

States in the past have been called upon to defend their frontiers against forcible change by their neighbors, or to assert their rights in disputed areas. Throughout much of the world today such actions are no longer feasible. If

---

[10] "The Power Inventory and National Strategy."
[11] *The War Potential of Nations* (Princeton: Princeton University Press, 1956).

one country threatens the territory of another, military action is frequently not limited to this border area, but leads to the complete defeat of one country. The country which is threatened may, of course, elect not to fight, and instead peaceably hand over the disputed area, as occurred in 1938 when the Czechs permitted the Germans to occupy the Sudetenland. Hungary and Poland also availed themselves at that time of the opportunity of annexing portions of Czechoslovakia, and within a few months the entire Czech State had been occupied by Germany. Bolivia and Paraguay, on the other hand, fought to the point of exhaustion over control of the Chaco area lying between them.

A State may not only be forced to guard its own borders, but also those of its overseas territories. Britain, France, the United States, and Belgium are among those countries which, in past years, have used their possessions as training grounds for their military forces, whether the actions be against the Moros in the Philippines, the Arabs in the Sahara, or the tribesmen along India's North-West Frontier. Even today Britain retains mobile forces to send on short notice to Kuwait, British Guiana, or other areas as the occasion demands.

The image of a State's forces drawn up along a hostile border is still a valid one in many parts of the world, despite the threats of nuclear holocausts should war break out. In Pakistan, Israel, South Korea, and Berlin the troops are in readiness against violation of the borders, as they have also been in Tunisia, eastern Turkey, and northern India. But a state assessing its defensive position against a potential enemy may have to consider the possibilities of conquest by subversion as well as by massed armies. Where are the enemy troops in South Vietnam, where were they in Greece in 1948, or, for many months prior to Dienbienphu, in North Vietnam? Governments may now face civil wars within their borders, the rebels ostensibly under the leadership of dissident citizens, but frequently supplied and advised by professionals from across the borders. Guerrilla bands attack the government's troops, terrorize rural areas, and, by destroying production, carry on a war of economic attrition. Howitzers, four-jet bombers, and massive tanks may be able to do little in these situations unless and until a final pitched battle is waged. When faced with campaigns of this sort (or, as the Communists term them, "wars of national liberation") government leaders must re-evaluate their power inventory and their strategy in far different terms than would be the case if there were an overt border violation.

THE TIME FACTOR IN A STATE'S VIABILITY

The three criteria laid down for a State's viability are by no means constant for any given political unit. One could, as an intellectual exercise, assign quantitative measures to each of these criteria, calculate an "index of viability" for each State, and then map variations in this index throughout the world. But regardless of the procedure used to set up these measurements, a reappraisal several years later would reveal many changes in the index distribution. Consider, for example, over a ten-year period, the positions of Communist China, of West Germany, of Israel, of Indonesia, and of the Soviet Union, so far as the viability test is concerned. What of the former Belgian Congo, or of Laos, or of Cuba? Even without quantitative measurements, however, there is opportunity to assess the degree of viability of any particular State, and from this, to look at trends in its external and internal developments.

BIBLIOGRAPHY

BARNETT, HAROLD J. "The Changing Relation of Natural Resources to National Security," *Economic Geography,* XXXIV (1958), 189–202.
Resources and defense in the Space Age.

BIDWELL, PERCY W. "Raw Materials and National Policy," *Foreign Affairs,* XXXVII (1958), 144–56.
Thoughts on United States policies with respect to access to raw materials.

JONES, STEPHEN B. "The Power Inventory and National Strategy," *World Politics,* VI (1954), 421–53.
Thought-provoking ideas on the bases of national power.

"Major Political Entities of the World." Geographic Report No. 2 (Revised), March 7, 1962. Washington: Department of State, Office of the Geographer.
Descriptions, with statistics, of the countries of the world.

PRESCOTT, J. R. V. "The Function and Methods of Electoral Geography," *Annals of the Association of American Geographers,* XLIX (1959), 296–305.
A discussion of an interesting branch of political geography.

6

THE DECLINE OF WESTERN COLONIALISM

● In the years since World War I the pattern of colonialism throughout the world has been radically changed. Many of the formerly dependent areas have achieved self-rule; other States, once independent, have passed under foreign domination. The empires of Britain, France, the Netherlands, Belgium, Japan, and several other countries have been substantially reduced in size and population, while the Soviet Union and China have emerged as centers of new colonial systems, in which the status of dependence is masked by such terms as "democracies" and "people's republics." These various changes in sovereignty have had far-reaching effects on the dependent or formerly dependent areas, on the mother countries, and on the general pattern of power areas existing throughout the world.

The history of empire development since the mid-fifteenth century has been associated largely with the maritime States of Europe. From these States explorers and traders went out to other continents and island areas, claiming these territories in the name of their homeland countries. The political partitioning of the non-European world was a long and complicated process, accompanied by a great number of territorial disputes, purchases and exchanges, and colonial wars. In the shifting patterns of control Spain and Portugal emerged as the early dominant powers, to be followed first by the Netherlands and then by France and Britain. Other European States also entered the race for colonies. By the end of the nineteenth century practically all of the land area of the globe had been politically partitioned, with a large portion passing under the sovereignty of the European States. In addition the United States and Japan had begun acquiring overseas holdings.

The classic pattern of colonialism has been one in which an area whose rate of cultural and economic development has been relatively slow is controlled politically by a more highly developed people. The colonial area is generally separated geographically from its mother country; the dependent area often supplies agricultural and industrial raw materials to the mother country and serves both as a reserve of manpower for labor and (at times) military forces, and as a market for goods from the mother country. It may also function militarily as an area for the establishment of bases or as a springboard for further territorial acquisitions. Citizens of the mother country who live in, or deal with, the colonial area generally do so on a basis of legal and economic superiority.

Three types of questions arise as to the nature of colonial areas. The first is, given the cultural and economic inferiority of the dependent areas, is it natural to assume that in time they may develop to the point where they are prepared for independence? Such development would imply that the mother country has taken active steps to improve economic and educational conditions in its colonies and to prepare the leaders of the indigenous, or "native," groups for assumption of the responsibilities of self-rule. Is it logical to assume that in time no areas of the world will remain as colonies of another State? If so, what forms will they assume with independence—particularly islands and island groups or small colonies incapable of sustaining themselves as individual States?

A second question is one largely of semantics. Can colonial territories exist within the borders of a particular State, or in territories adjacent to it? How about the Moslem republics of the Soviet Union, the proposed native areas of the Republic of South Africa, or some of the Indian territories in the United States and Canada? Is Tannu Tuva in effect a colony of the U.S.S.R., Tibet a colony of Mainland China? A *de jure* confederation of units may, in reality, represent the existence of one area in a colonial type of relationship to another. Turning to adjacent areas, we might consider the colonial status of the East European "satellites" to the Soviet Union, or of North Vietnam to Communist China, or of Southwest Africa to the Republic of South Africa.

A third consideration involves the problem of dominance by one State of another's economy, even though politically both are independent of one another. Whittlesey, as noted earlier, has written that the real test of exploitability is economic subservience rather than political dependence. How "independent" of Britain is the Irish Republic, when the British normally account for three-fifths of Ireland's foreign trade, or Panama of the United States since over 90 per cent of its exports go to the United States? Here, as in other situations, the relationships between economic and political control of territory may have many elements of interdependence with one another.

The political partitioning of the land surface of the globe was virtually completed at the end of the nineteenth century, by which time all of the continent of Africa had been placed either under local or foreign control. Only Antarctica and a few remote oceanic islands remained unclaimed. The islands have since been annexed by various States, while Antarctica now enjoys a special political status in which all territorial claims have for a time been renounced (see page 204). By 1900 the major colonial powers were Britain, France, the Netherlands, Belgium, Portugal, Spain, Turkey, and Germany. The United States had recently acquired territory from Spain and Japan from China, while the Italians were gradually expanding their holdings in the Mediterranean–East Africa area.

During the first four and a half decades of the twentieth century there was considerable reshuffling of colonial possessions among the major powers, but relatively little change in the total area of colonial holdings, with the exception of six British dominions which in 1931 achieved complete independence. These dominions—Canada, Australia, New Zealand, Ireland, South Africa, anrd Newfoundland—were peopled largely by Europeans, and their attitudes and political institutions conformed fairly closely to those in Britain itself. At the end of World War I the empires of Germany and of Turkey were apportioned among other powers in the form of League of Nations mandates, but by the mid-1930's practically none of these countries had yet advanced from dependent to independent status. At that time the colonial areas of the world covered 14 million square miles, with a combined population of 760 million, or over one-third of the world's total.

In the years immediately preceding World War II both Japan and Italy expanded their colonial holdings, but at the end of the war these countries were completely stripped of their overseas territories. Thus by 1945 the United States, Britain, France, the Netherlands, Belgium, Portugal, and Spain remained as the principal Western colonial powers of the world. Since that time there has been a steady reduction in the size of these countries' overseas holdings. At the same time both the Soviet Union and Mainland China have emerged as important colonial powers, although their territories are for the most part adjacent to and included within their boundaries, and the relationships between the two Communist powers and their "dependencies" are not of the traditional mother country–colony variety. In the discussion which follows consideration will be limited to the Western colonial powers.

Overseas territories may serve as sites for bases or as springboards for further territorial expansion, as sources for raw materials, and as areas for investment or marketing of the mother country's products. They may also be potential regions for emigration from the homeland, and the local inhabitants may provide cheap labor or be available for service in the armed forces. Gibraltar, Guam, and Aden have strategic military locations. Eritrea

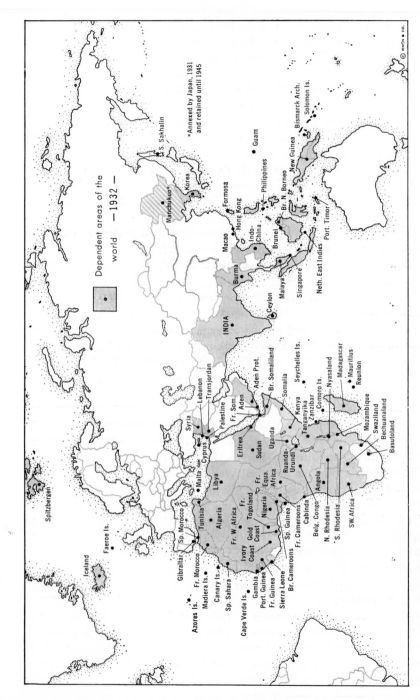

Figure 11. Dependent Areas of the World, 1932.

was used by the Italians in the conquest of Ethiopia; Nigeria, Malaya, and the former Belgian Congo are rich in mineral and agricultural resources, and, during their years of dependent status, served to enrich their respective mother countries.

Naturally the assets and liabilities of overseas territories to the mother country may vary widely with changing political conditions. The Netherlands East Indies was once of great economic value to the Netherlands, while Indochina was of key importance to France. Yet in time both of these areas came to represent liabilities because of great costs involved in combating local struggles for independence. Territories which have attained independence may continue to be of economic and military value to the former mother country because of investment and market opportunities and of the availability of sites for military bases. Iraq, Egypt, and the Republic of South Africa represent areas in which Britain retained important economic and military influence after the achievement of self-rule; in all three countries, however, this influence has declined considerably since the end of World War II.

In terms of colonial policies Britain and the United States have taken the lead in promoting self-rule among their possessions, or in granting local representation on governing councils in areas where complete self-rule is still far in the future. Both France and the Netherlands have inaugurated somewhat nebulous "unions" in order to tie dependent areas more closely to the mother country. Portugal has adopted an *assimilado* policy, under which a colonial subject may become "civilized" or assimilated, that is, acquire education and adopt a European way of life. Belgium denied the vote to both white and nonwhite inhabitants of its territories, until such time as the nonwhites were prepared to take part in the administration of these areas. Spain continues, as it has in the past, to administer its colonies with little or no native representation.

The contrast between the colonial policies of Britain, on the one hand, and those of France (and to a lesser extent of Portugal, Belgium, Spain, and the Netherlands), on the other, points up a fundamental difference in political thinking. Whittlesey contrasted the two major colonial systems in Africa by describing "Indirect Rule," practiced by the British, as " . . . government which leaves the African political structure untouched, except for supervision by British political officers, organized not to supersede the indigenous government, but to parallel and supplement it," and "Direct Rule," practiced by the French, as " . . . exerted through a governor and his subordinates . . . All responsible officials directly engaged in administering government are Europeans, except the men immediately in control of the smallest units . . . in order to integrate the colonies with the home country in the fullest possible degree."[1] In the system of direct rule local

---

[1] Derwent Whittlesey, *The Earth and the State*, p. 379. Reprinted by permission of Holt, Rinehart and Winston, Inc., copyright 1944.

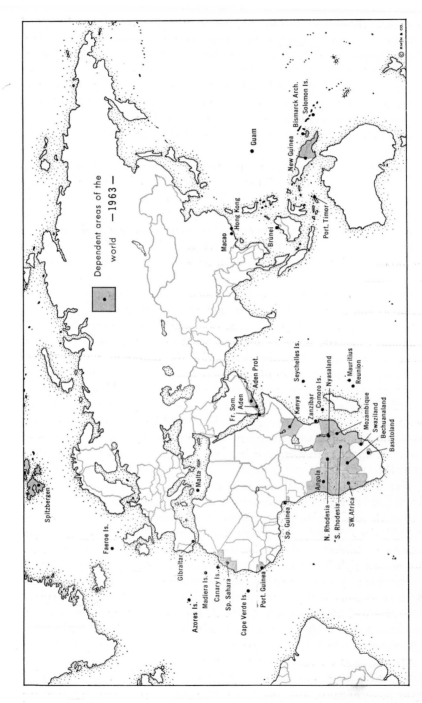

Figure 12. Dependent Areas of the World, 1962.

peoples are indoctrinated with the language and customs of the mother country, and there is a tendency to disrupt tribal organizations. The process of detribalization may work much hardship on the colonial peoples, for at some state of "Europeanization" they give up fundamental elements of their former culture, and yet as colonials do not receive the full economic and political benefits of the European way of life. The United States followed a general policy of indirect rule in the Philippines, but one of more direct rule in Alaska, Hawaii, and Puerto Rico, leading to the assimilation of these areas into the United States.

Partly as a result of empire losses since the end of World War II, the power position of the western European colonial States has declined relative to other parts of the world, particularly Anglo-America, the Soviet Union, southern Asia, and North Africa. Since these colonial States are members of various Western military alliances, this declining power position is important to the Cold War. Not only have several of the European States been forced to adjust their economies in recent years as a result of losses of colonial markets, investments, and sources for raw materials, but also, in the military and political sense, their leaders can no longer speak for the large areas and populations formerly under their control.

United action on the part of non-Communist countries in the face of Communist expansion is one of the most significant aspects of the changing colonial pattern. The difficulties confronting the European States with respect to Communist pressures differ widely from the difficulties which exist in southern Asia or Africa, where new States, having achieved independence from the Europeans, are struggling with local problems of national development. These different problems have been well recognized by Communist political leaders, who often pursue one type of policy in dealing with the Europeans and another type with dependent or recently independent countries.

The degree of political and military unity existing between the European nations and their former possessions varies from place to place. Some States, such as Canada, Australia, and New Zealand, have continued to maintain close ties with their former mother country, but many others, as, for example, Indonesia, Cambodia, and Burma, have not. An additional factor of disunity in former imperial areas is the international tensions which have developed between newly independent States over such matters as control of territory and treatment of minority groups. The India-Pakistan and Israeli-Arab disputes are examples of this type. The rise of the so-called Afro-Asian bloc of States—composed largely of former colonial territories— serves to complicate further the position of the non-Communist world. Finally, at the United Nations and other international forums, the former colonial territories—with their recent memories of colonialism—have frequently been at odds with the very European states which have banded

together through NATO and other organizations to oppose the spread of
Communist power. The net effect has been to accentuate the differences in
interests between States of the non-Communist world and to complicate
efforts to unite them in common action in the face of Communist moves,
such as the suppression of the Hungarian uprising or the violation of the
nuclear test ban agreement.

In the sections which follow the various Western colonial systems will
be considered in terms of the relationships existing between the mother country and its overseas possessions. More complete descriptions of the present
or former dependent states appear in the chapters on the regions in which
they are located.

GREAT BRITAIN AND THE COMMONWEALTH

In the early 1920's Great Britain was the seat of an empire in which the
overseas possessions measured 13,600,000 square miles in area (26 per cent
of the land area of the globe, excluding Antarctica), with a population of
460 million. By the middle of 1963 the overseas empire had been reduced to
approximately 1,327,000 square miles, containing about 27 million inhabitants, although it still ranked first in size and in population among the colonial systems of the world. Fifteen independent States have been created
from the British Empire of the 1920's, but most of these have continued
within the framework of the British Commonwealth.

A unique empire relationship has been evolved by Great Britain with
respect to its overseas possessions. As a result of wide differences in economic
and political conditions throughout the areas under British control, a Commonwealth arrangement was established in 1931, consisting of the United
Kingdom, the dominions and republics, the colonies, protectorates, and protected territories, and the territories under trusteeship. Of the overseas units,
the dominions and republics are self-governing, while the colonies, protectorates, protected territories, and trusteeships constitute what is left of
the British Empire. By August, 1963, there were fifteen independent members of the Commonwealth: Australia, Canada, Ceylon, Cyprus, Federation
of Malaya, Federation of Nigeria, Ghana (formerly Gold Coast), India,
Jamaica, New Zealand, Pakistan, Sierra Leone, Tanganyika, Trinidad and
Uganda. Taken together these independent members cover an area of over
9½ million square miles with a population in excess of 640 million.

The independent members of the British Commonwealth are equal in
status, in no way subordinate to one another in any aspect of their domestic
or external affairs, and united in common allegiance to the Crown. India,
Pakistan, Ghana, and Cyprus, as sovereign independent republics, recognize the Queen as symbolic head of the Commonwealth, but differ from the
other states in that the Queen is not titular head. Economic and cultural
ties also continue between Britain and the independent members, resulting

in mutual benefit for the various Commonwealth states. Once a year the heads of the independent Commonwealth members meet in London to discuss problems of mutual interest.

The British colonial possessions are located, for the most part, in three areas: central and southern Africa, the Caribbean basin (including the Guiana coast), and southeast Asia and the southern Pacific Ocean. Some of these possessions are of particular importance as military bases. Because of the low average income of most of the inhabitants of the colonies and protectorates, the market potential of many of these areas is still small. It is perhaps paradoxical that as the local peoples advance their economic status (thereby increasing the market potential), they also hasten their political independence from Britain.

The possessions still under British control are shown in Table 1. Pressures for change in political status are particular evident in Malta, Gambia, Zanzibar and Pemba, Kenya, the Federation of Rhodesia and Nyasaland, British Guiana, British Honduras, and the British West Indies. In all but the first of these the trend is toward independence. Many of the Maltese have desired inclusion with the United Kingdom. Should the various territories noted above become independent,[2] Britain's colonial empire would be reduced in size and in population by more than two-thirds.

Since 1921 a number of areas have become completely separated from Britain's imperial system. The Class A mandates, set up after World War I, eventually became independent, but not Commonwealth members. Iraq and Transjordan for a number of years continued to maintain military ties with the British, but the area of Palestine, after its partition, did not. Of the trusteeship territories (formerly Class C League of Nations mandates), Tanganyika has become independent, and the southern sector of British Cameroons has joined independent Cameroun (formerly a French possesison). British Togoland and northern British Cameroons have remained within the Commonwealth, since the former is now associated with Ghana and the latter with Nigeria. The Irish Republic became a sovereign independent area in 1949, completely free of Commonwealth connections except for continued membership in the sterling bloc. Egypt, Burma, Sudan, and the Republic of South Africa have likewise ended their political associations with the Commonwealth, thereby reflecting the strong desires for complete freedom of action by the governments of these areas.

The Significance of the Commonwealth to Britain

The economic value of the Commonwealth to Great Britain is not as great as it once was. During the nineteenth and early twentieth centuries the colonies served (1) as suppliers of raw materials, such as grains, tin,

[2] Malaysia (comprising Malaya, Singapore, Sarawak, and Sabah—former North Borneo) became independent in September, 1963. At that time Kenya and Zanzibar (including Pemba) were scheduled for independence in December, 1963, while Malta, Northern Rhodesia, Nyasaland, and Gambia were to become independent in 1964.

Table 1

OVERSEAS TERRITORIES OF THE WESTERN COLONIAL POWERS

	Area (Sq. mi.)	Population (1962 estimates)
The British Commonwealth of Nations	11,173,999	721,004,000
United Kingdom (Great Britain and Northern Ireland)	94,212	52,360,000
Self-governing Commonwealth countries	9,568,814	640,168,000
Australia	2,974,581	10,227,000
Canada	3,845,774	18,085,000
Ceylon	25,332	9,165,000
Cyprus	3,572	561,000
Federation of Malaya	50,598	6,815,000
Federation of Nigeria	350,291	35,297,000
Ghana	91,840	6,691,000
India	1,267,089	436,424,000
Jamaica	4,706	1,607,000
New Zealand	103,736	2,370,000
Pakistan	364,737	93,812,000
Sierra Leone	27,924	2,500,000
Tanganyika	362,674	9,233,000
Trinidad and Tobago	1,979	826,000
Uganda	93,981	6,524,000
British Possessions	1,327,207	26,597,000
Europe		
Channel Islands (Jersey, Guernsey, etc.) . . .	75	100,000
Isle of Man	221	56,000
Gibraltar	2	26,000
Malta	122	327,000
Asia		
Aden	80	138,000
Aden Protectorate (incl. Socotra)	105,000	660,000
Singapore (incl. Christmas Island)	289	1,634,000
North Borneo (incl. Labuan)	29,386	429,000
Brunei	2,226	80,000
Sarawak	47,069	744,000
Hong Kong	391	2,919,000
Africa		
Federation of Rhodesia and Nyasaland . . .	486,069	8,330,000
Southern Rhodesia	150,327	3,070,000
Northern Rhodesia	290,300	2,430,000
Nyasaland	48,442	2,830,000
Bechuanaland	275,000	297,000
Basutoland	11,716	642,000
Swaziland	6,705	237,000
Kenya	224,960	6,550,000
Zanzibar (incl. Pemba)	1,020	299,000
Gambia	4,003	326,000
Indian Ocean		
Mauritius	809	631,000
Seychelles	156	41,000
Maldive Islands	115	82,000

Table 1—*(Continued)*

OVERSEAS TERRITORIES OF THE WESTERN COLONIAL POWERS

	Area (Sq. mi.)	Population (1962 estimates)
Pacific Ocean		
Fiji	7,040	388,000
Gilbert and Ellice Islands (incl. Pheonix and Line Isls. and Ocean Isl.)	369	44,000
Pitcairn Island	2	146
New Hebrides (condominium with France). .	5,700	56,000
Canton and Enderbury Islands (condominium with United States; included in Gilbert and Ellice Islands colony)	27	300
Tonga	269	57,000
British Solomon Islands	11,500	115,000
Atlantic Ocean		
Bermuda	22	44,000
Falkland Islands (incl. South Georgia) . . .	6,068	3,000
St. Helena and dependencies	119	4,600
Middle America		
British Honduras	8,867	90,000
British Guiana	82,997	558,000
Bahamas	4,404	104,000
British West Indies	1,409	674,000
Barbados	166	232,000
Leeward Islands	423	130,000
Windward Islands	820	312,000
Australian Possessions (see Table 16)	183,563	1,861,000
New Zealand Possessions (see Table 16) . . .	203	25,000
The French Community	4,041,938	87,301,000
France (incl. Corsica)	213,009	45,730,000
Member States	3,767,974	40,209,000
Central African Republic	238,000	1,193,000
Republic of the Congo	132,000	795,000
Republic of Ivory Coast	123,000	3,115,000
Republic of Dahomey	43,800	2,003,000
Gabonese Republic	103,000	421,000
Republic of Upper Volta	106,000	4,004,000
Malagasy Republic (Madagascar)	227,950	5,184,000
Republic of Mali	460,500	4,307,000
Islamic Republic of Mauritania	416,100	727,000
Republic of Niger	494,600	2,803,000
Republic of Senegal	80,600	2,597,000
Republic of Chad	496.000	2,576,000
Algeria	846,124	10,484,000
Overseas Areas	60,955	1,362,000
Overseas Departments		
Martinique	425	267,000
Guadeloupe and dependencies	687	275,000

Table 1—(Continued)

OVERSEAS TERRITORIES OF THE WESTERN COLONIAL POWERS

	Area (Sq. mi.)	Population (1962 estimates)
French Guiana	35,000	32,000
Réunion	970	330,000
Overseas Territories		
French Somaliland	8,500	67,000
Comoro Islands	834	183,000
French Oceania	1,544	75,000
New Caledonia and dependencies	7,202	72,000
St. Pierre and Miquelon	93	5,000
Condominium		
New Hebrides (with Great Britain)	5,700	56,000
The Portuguese Empire	837,710	21,205,000
Portugal (incl. Azores and Madeira)	35,414	9,049,000
Overseas Provinces	802,296	12,156,000
Cape Verde Islands	1,557	170,000
Portuguese Guinea	13,948	570,000
Sao Tome and Principe	372	60,000
Angola	481,350	4,375,000
Mozambique	297,731	6,270,000
Macao	6	215,000
Portuguese Timor	7,332	496,000
The Spanish Empire	309,115	31,608,000
Spain (incl. Canary Islands)	194,988	31,168,000
Spanish Possessions	114,127	440,000
Spanish Guinea (Rio Muni, Fernando Po, and nearby islands)	10,831	213,000
Ifni	579	50,000
Spanish Sahara	102,703	24,000
Spanish Possessions in North Africa (incl. Ceuta and Melilla; and isls. of Alhucemas, Chafarinas, and Penon de Valez de la Govera)	14	153,000
The Netherlands Union	68,535	11,915,000
The Netherlands	13,025	11,417,000
Overseas Possessions	55,510	498,000
Surinam	55,144	302,000
Netherlands Antilles (Curaçao, Aruba, Bonaire, St. Eustatius, Saba, and southern part of St. Martin)	366	196,000
The Danish Empire	857,116	4,929,000
Denmark	16,576	4,563,000

Table 1—(Continued)

OVERSEAS TERRITORIES OF THE WESTERN COLONIAL POWERS

	Area (Sq. mi.)	Population (1962 estimates)
Danish Possessions	840,540	66,000
Greenland	840,000	31,000
Faeroe Islands	540	35,000
The Norwegian Empire	149,298	3,575,000
Norway	125,064	3,571,000
Norwegian Possessions	24,234	4,000
Spitsbergen (Svalbard)	23,979	(winter) 4,000
Jan Mayen Island	141	10
Bouvet Island	22	—
Peter I Island	92	—
The United States Empire	3,556,738	182,844,000
United States	3,552,197	180,299,000
United States Possessions	4,541	2,545,000
Puerto Rico	3,423	2,350,000
Virgin Islands	133	32,000
Guam	209	67,000
American Samoa	76	20,000
Pacific Islands (trusteeship territory)	700	76,000

rubber, diamonds, gold, sugar, cotton, and wool; (2) as markets for the mother country's industrial products; and (3) as areas for investment by British capital. In recent decades, however, the situation has changed. Such areas as Canada and Australia have advanced to the point where they can supply many of their required industrial items, and Canada is beginning to emerge as an exporter of finished industrial goods in competition with Britain. Markets for Britain's manufactured goods in India and Pakistan are also growing scarcer, due in part to the growing ability of these countries to supply their own needs. In 1920 Britain's trade with Commonwealth members amounted to 60 per cent by value of its foreign trade; by 1961 this figure had declined to 40 per cent, of which nearly seven-eighths was with the now-independent dominions and republics.

The Commonwealth is also important to Britain in terms of military and political activities, as well as for prestige purposes. During the past two world wars the Commonwealth has supplied large quantities of men and equipment for use against Britain's enemies, and in peacetime the British, through the use of certain Commonwealth areas, have been able to maintain a world-wide system of military bases. The British Crown still represents a symbol of allegiance for hundreds of millions of people, and London, as the seat of the Commonwealth, continues to be one of the great capital cities of the world.

Mention has already been made of the inevitability of centrifugal forces developing within such global political systems as the overseas possessions and associated countries of the European powers. Within the British Commonwealth such forces are represented by a number of different situations—the rise of "neutralism" in India and Ceylon, the racial problems in the Rhodesias and Kenya, the challenge of Arab nationalism to British power in the Middle East and Latin American nationalism to British control in portions of the Western Hemisphere. Despite these forces, however, the British Commonwealth remains a political entity of great size and population, a symbol of wise colonial policy which has effected the transformation of what was once the world's largest empire into what is now the world's largest political association of independent and dependent States.

THE FRENCH UNION

The French empire, like the British, has been undergoing major changes since the end of World War II. The strong nationalism in the overseas possessions and the weakened power position of France itself after defeat and occupation by the Germans resulted in the gradual decline of French power in southern Asia and in North Africa. Unlike the British, the French were unwilling to accede to demands by colonial peoples for complete independence, and instead sought to work out arrangements whereby certain overseas territories would become autonomous units while remaining under France's control. Such concessions to nationalist movements were not great enough to stem the rising tide of insurrection, however, and France was eventually forced to relinquish its political control both in Indochina and in North Africa.

Prior to World War II the political framework of the French empire was far less complex than that of the British Commonwealth, for there existed a relatively simple mother country–colony relationship between France and its possessions. Although Syria and Lebanon, former League of Nations mandates, became independent at the end of World War II, the remaining empire was at that time the largest in area in the world, measuring over 4 million square miles, with a population of some 80 million people. In 1946, in response to pressures for increased self-rule in some of the colonial areas, the Paris government established the French Union, consisting of Metropolitan France, Algeria, the overseas departments and territories, the trusteeship territories, the condominium of New Hebrides, and the associated states and protectorates.

Nowhere in the organizational framework of the French Union was there a provision for attainment of dominion status or of eventual independence. The Union's purpose was " . . . to enable each territory to develop freely along democratic lines, while remaining linked to France by common interests."[3] The concept of "linked by common interests" can obviously mean many things to many persons; even among French officials its definition apparently varied widely. It was partly because of the ambiguity of the political relationships that were envisioned between France and its overseas possessions at the time of the Union's establishment that so much local resentment developed against the French in Southeast Asia and in Africa.

In June, 1958, four years after the first defeat in Indochina, General de Gaulle proposed a new constitution for France under which overseas territories were offered the choice of retaining their current status, of becoming overseas departments, or of receiving independence as member States of the newly constituted French Community. Only French Guinea, among the overseas territories, voted against the constitution. In September, 1958, this area became the independent Republic of Guinea, completely free of French ties. Two years later the French trusteeships of Cameroon and Togoland became respectively the independent Republic of Cameroun and Republic of Togo. By the end of 1960 the former territories of French West Africa, French Equatorial Africa, and Madagascar had become independent States within the French Union. Madagascar was renamed the Malagasy Republic, and from French West and French Equatorial Africa eleven new States were created (see Table 1). All twelve became member states of the French Community. Within the Community there exists an economic, technical, and customs union of the former French Equatorial Africa (Central African Republic, Congo, Gabon, and Chad States), an *entente* of four former members of French West Africa (Ivory Coast, Dahomey, Upper Volta, Niger), and a West African customs union embracing Senegal, Mali, Ivory Coast, Dahomey, Upper Volta, Niger, and Mauritania.

The four overseas departments — Martinique, Guadeloupe, French Guiana, and Réunion—are considered integral parts of France and send representatives to the French National Assembly. French policy with respect to these areas, as well as to the overseas territories, has been one of assimilation, attempting to bring all inhabitants within the social, cultural, and political family of France. In view of the low cultural levels of many of the colonial peoples, the actual implementation of this policy has taken place only on a small scale.

In the former associated states of Cambodia, Laos, and Vietnam and in the protectorates of Tunisia and Morocco there was little interference with

---

[3] *The French Union*, French Information Service, 1949, p. 1.

local institutions. The inability of the French to come to an agreement with local leaders on the terms of the political status of the associated states and protectorates led to the gradual weakening of political ties between these areas and the mother country. By 1956 France had officially ended its rule in Morocco and Tunisia and in the States of Indochina. In a last effort to retain something of its influence in the two North African territories, the French government maintained it was still linked to Morocco and Tunisia by ties of "interdependence," although, as in former times, the actual nature of these ties was not clearly determined. In 1959 Tunisia ended its customs union with France, and two years later there were armed clashes in Tunisia over French reluctance to set a definite date for evacuation of its base at Bizerte. All French troops in Morocco had been withdrawn by the end of 1961.

Algeria, which was the home of nearly one million Frenchmen, was treated for years as a part of metropolitan France, and, like the overseas departments, sent representatives to the French National Assembly. Among the overseas possessions it was France's leading trade partner and the source of greatest investment; after 1957 it became an increasingly important source of petroleum and natural gas. But the seven-year-long struggle for Algerian independence ended in July, 1962, with Algeria's complete political separation from France. The prolonged warfare in Algeria helped to destroy any plans De Gaulle had for the creation of a French "power zone" in the western Mediterranean based on close cooperation between France and its former North African territories.

Assets and Liabilities of the Community

The importance of the French Community to France might be summed up in three terms—prestige, manpower, and commerce. Although the majority of the French people has never been particularly "colony conscious," the overseas possessions have always been a source of national pride. Countering this, however, have been certain liabilities, such as the long, slow retreat in Indochina and the rebellions in North Africa, which have harmed rather than enhanced France's prestige. Loss of political control in these two areas has, of course, affected their use as settlement areas for the French. In the first eight months of 1962, for example, nearly 500,000 French settlers in Algeria had fled to France.

The French have long looked to overseas possessions as sources for military manpower. Non-European troops have been important to the maintenance of French power throughout its world-wide empire. Since World War II, however, the overseas possessions have been more of a liability than an asset to France in this respect. The Indochina war cost the French army (including the Foreign Legion) 49,000 dead and necessitated the deployment of several French divisions to that area, some of which had to be withdrawn from western Europe, where they were intended for use with the North Atlantic Treaty Organization. The Algerian war resulted in the loss of another 15,000 men and the deployment of a maximum of 400,-000 troops to that area.

The Community is France's greatest trade partner, accounting for about one-quarter of France's imports and nearly 40 per cent of its exports. From the Community members come iron ore, phosphate, grain, wine, sugar, graphite, and, from Algeria, petroleum. Continued improvement in the standard of living of the peoples in dependent areas of the Community will mean greater markets for French exports, and increase the potential economic value of the overseas possessions to France. The French have also sought to retain close economic ties with many of their former dependencies in Africa (see Chapter 14) and thus continue to realize some of the benefits of the preindependence years.

THE PORTUGUESE EMPIRE

Portugal was the first State in Europe to develop an overseas empire. Early in the fifteenth century Portuguese expeditions began exploring the west coast of Africa in an effort to discover a sea route to India, and in subsequent years Portuguese colonies were established in Africa, Asia, and the East Indies. Brazil was Portugal's one possession in the Western Hemisphere. Many of these territories were eventually lost, but Portugal still retains a considerable colonial area for development. The decline of Portugal's empire after the middle of the sixteenth century was occasioned by a number of factors, including the gradual depletion of manpower in the nation as a result of prolonged military campaigns and the persecutions and expulsion of Jews, whose wealth and skills had formed an important base for Portugal's expansion. Other countries, with greater resources and manpower, supplanted Portugal as the seats of world empires.

Of the 802,000 square miles of Portugal's overseas territory, 99 per cent lies in Africa and off the African coast. Angola (with its northern exclave of Cabinda) and Mozambique are the two largest Portuguese territories. Others are Portuguese Guinea, located on Africa's west coast, the Cape Verde Islands, lying west of Dakar in the Atlantic Ocean, and the islands of Sao Tome and Principe in the Gulf of Guinea. In 1961 Portugal's enclaves in India were forcibly annexed by the Indian government, leaving only Macao on the coast of China and the Portuguese sector of the island of Timor as vestiges of the once-great Portuguese empire in eastern Asia.

Portugal has been more successful than other European States in retaining its overseas territories. The Portuguese constitution officially bars the cession of any of the overseas territories to foreign powers, and no programs have been set up for the establishment of independence. To counter the demands of its African peoples for increased economic and political opportunities, Portugal has inaugurated an *assimilado* policy, whereby a small proportion of the indigenous population in the colonies may be educated to Portuguese citizenship and thereby enjoy the privileges of the Europeans. Even before India's seizure of Goa and the other coastal enclaves, international pressure was mounting against Portugal because of its refusal to grant independence, particularly to its two large African possessions.

Portugal's historic alliance with Great Britain provided the protection of the British fleet and saved at least a part of the African possessions from annexation by other European powers. In recent years Portugal has also maintained close military relations with the United States. Portugal is a member of the North Atlantic Treaty Organization, its principal contribution being the granting of permission to the United States to build and maintain an air base in the Azores Islands.

Portugal's well-known overseas possession the Azores Islands lies a thousand miles west of Portugal itself and is an important air stop for transatlantic flights. The islands are administered as districts of Portugal. Likewise, the Madeira Islands, southwest of the Azores, are considered part of Portugal. The total population of Portugal's overseas possessions (excluding the Azores and Madeira) is about 12¼ million. Although the colonial peoples in Portugal's overseas possessions are generally at a low stage of cultural development, the empire ranks as Portugal's leading trade partner, accounting in 1959 for about 26 per cent by value of its foreign trade. Employment opportunities in Portugal are insufficient to satisfy the needs of the present population, and there has been pressure for emigration to the African colonies. If agricultural, mineral, and power resources in Portuguese Africa are further developed, and if internal stability and continuing colonial status can be maintained, the empire may in time prove to be an important asset to the people of Portugal.

THE SPANISH EMPIRE

Spain, whose empire ranks well down in size among those of the Western European states, was once the greatest maritime power of the Continent. In 1494 in the Treaty of Tordesillas Spain was awarded all newly discovered lands west of 50° west longitude; as a result Spain's colonial possessions were confined largely to the Western Hemisphere. The Philippines were the only major Spanish possession in the Far East. Spanish ships also sailed along the west coast of Africa, and this exploration led to the establishment of colonies to the south of Morocco and in the area of the Gulf of Guinea.

The defeat of the Spanish Armada by the British in 1588 spelled the end of Spain's dominance of the seas, but the nation continued to control many of its overseas possessions until the nineteenth century, when a majority of the Latin American states achieved independence. Later, as a result of the Spanish-American War, Spain was forced to withdraw completely from Latin America and from the Pacific. Thus since the beginning of the twentieth century Spain has had only its African possessions left to develop.

The tremendous energies expended by the State in colonial activities three and four centuries ago are no longer evident either in its domestic or its overseas activities. "Assimilation" and "monopoly" are terms which may best describe Spanish colonial policy. Both the Balearic and Canary islands are administered as an integral part of Spain. In other areas attempts have been made by both church and state to Christianize the inhabitants and instill in them something of Spanish culture. Non-Spanish commercial enterprises are discouraged from operating in the overseas territories, and there has been no attempt to prepare the local peoples for self-government.

In 1956 the Spanish government announced the ending of its protectorate over Spanish Morocco, and two years later Southern Morocco was also ceded to Morocco. The remaining territories—Spanish Sahara and Ifni and Spanish Guinea, together with three coastal enclaves in Morocco and three offshore islands—have a combined area of 114,000 square miles and a population of about 450,000. Spain's possessions are of relatively little economic value, however, and the Spanish people themselves are not particularly concerned with the country's colonial activities. Rio de Oro in Spanish West Africa is important as a base for fishing fleets, and Spanish Guinea exports agricultural products, such as cocoa and coffee.

THE NETHERLANDS EMPIRE

The Netherlands, like Spain, is an important colonial power of the past. In the early seventeenth century Holland built up a great overseas empire in the Western Hemisphere, Africa, and the Far East. Although the African and most of the Western Hemisphere possessions were eventually lost to other powers, Dutch holdings in the East Indies were retained through World War II; with the loss of the western portion of New Guinea in 1962, only a few possessions in Latin America still remain under Dutch control.

Prior to World War II the Dutch empire measured over 800,000 square miles and contained nearly 80 million persons. The wealth of the Netherlands East Indies was an important element of the nation's economy, for the colony served as an area for emigration, a market for exports, and a source of raw materials and investment opportunities. On the eve of World War II there were over 230,000 Dutch nationals living in the East Indies, and from that area came such valuable products as tin, petroleum, rubber, sugar, and quinine. The Dutch were leaders among the European powers in the art of colonial administration, partly as a result of their concern for health, education, and economic progress of the local peoples. The political policies of The Hague government were conservative, however, and there was little thought given to native self-rule other than that connected with local affairs. Thus the Netherlands' colonial policy, lying somewhere between the "autonomy" of the British and the "assimilation" of the French and Portuguese, contained some of the negative features of both systems. The Dutch made relatively few attempts to indoctrinate their colonial peoples with Dutch culture; rather, they respected local institutions and did what they could to protect them. On the other hand, the Dutch were unwilling to face the logical outcome of local economic and political progress, namely, that the people would in time reach a point where they would actively demand self-rule.

During World War II the Netherlands East Indies were occupied by the Japanese. Following the war Holland was unable to re-establish effective control over its possession. In 1949 the entire area, with the exception of western New Guinea, became independent (see also Chapter 15). For years the question of western New Guinea's status exacerbated relations between the Netherlands and Indonesia (see page 519). In August, 1962, the Dutch finally agreed to relinquish control of the area. As a result the Dutch overseas territories are now reduced to Surinam in northern South America and to the Netherlands Antilles, consisting of the Caribbean islands of Aruba, Bonaire, Curacao, Saba, St. Eustatius, and the southern half of St. Martin. Both Surinam and the Netherlands Antilles have local autonomy, with the Dutch retaining control of defense and foreign affairs.

THE DANISH EMPIRE

Danish control of overseas territories dates back to the late fourteenth century, when Iceland became a colony. Later colonization efforts led to the establishment of Danish territories in Greenland, the Faeroes, the West Indies, and Africa. The African possessions, acquired in the seventeenth century, were only held for a short time, but the other territories remained under Danish control down to the twentieth century. In 1917 the United States acquired possession of the Danish West Indies (now known as the Virgin Islands), and the following year Iceland became a sovereign State, joined in a personal union with Denmark.[4]

Greenland and the Faeroe Islands, Denmark's remaining overseas territories, measure 840,540 square miles in area. Both are important as sites for bases in the defense of the North Atlantic, but neither one is of great economic importance to Denmark, except for the fishing activities carried

---

[4] The establishment of Iceland in a commonwealth type of relationship with Denmark preceded similar British, French, American, and Dutch organizations by a number of years. In 1944 Iceland became completely independent of Danish political ties.

on by the local peoples. In 1953 Greenland was officially made an integral part of the Danish State, and the area's approximately 31,000 inhabitants were thus politically (if not culturally) assimilated within Denmark itself. The Faeroe Islands received local autonomy in 1948. The Faeroes are economically dependent upon Danish subsidies, and there is little pressure there, or in Greenland, for national independence.

THE UNITED STATES EMPIRE

The growth of the American overseas empire began in the 1850's, when tiny Howland, Baker, and Jarvis islands in the mid-Pacific were acquired because of their guano deposits, which were being exploited by United States companies. In 1867 the Midway Islands were also annexed, and in the same year the United States purchased Alaska from Russia for $7,200,000. Although at the time of the purchase the United States showed little interest in Alaska, the territory has since proved extremely valuable in terms of resources (gold, fish, furs, timber) and of strategic location. Five years later American Samoa was obtained as a naval base. In 1898, upon the petition of its government, Hawaii became a United States possession, and following the war with Spain (1898) Puerto Rico and the Philippines were also acquired. Construction of the Panama Canal in the early years of the twentieth century led to the granting by Panama in 1903 of a perpetual lease over the Canal Zone. In 1917 the Danish Virgin Islands, east of Puerto Rico, were purchased from Denmark to protect the eastern approaches to the canal. Thus by the end of World War I the American empire totalled nearly 700,000 square miles in area, placing it eighth in size among the empires of the world. With the exception of Alaska, virtually all the United States possessions were of particular naval significance, indicating the trend of thinking prevalent among statesmen during the years when the United States was taking its position among the leading political powers of the world.

Since 1920 three major developments have occurred in America's overseas territories. These are, first, the granting of independence to the Philippines in 1946, second, the acquisition of United Nations trusteeships over the former Japanese-mandated islands in the central and western Pacific following World War II, and, third, the granting of statehood to Alaska and Hawaii. As a result of these changes the empire of the United States now totals just under 4,000 square miles with a population of 2½ million.

The overseas possessions have never assumed as important a role in United States affairs as have, for example, the territories of Britain, France, and the Netherlands in those nations' activities. Political control of the Panama Canal Zone and of island areas in the Pacific affords the United States sites for military bases, while Puerto Rico is an important market and area for investments. Few Americans emigrate to the overseas territories; rather, thousands of territorial residents, particularly from Puerto Rico, come each year to reside in the United States, most of them in the hope of obtaining better employment than is possible on the island. Indeed, only recently has the United States really been faced by the problem of relatively large numbers of "colonial" persons emigrating to the mother country in search of low-paying jobs.

Control of the United States over its various overseas possessions is in a state of gradual change. Puerto Rico has become a commonwealth, rather than independent or a state of the United States. Some degree of internal autonomy may eventually be granted to American Samoa, particularly in view of the award of independence to Western Samoa by New Zealand in 1961. Pressure is periodically applied by Panama on the United States for evacuation, or at least some change in the political status, of the Canal Zone (see page 190). Generally speaking, however, the American empire represents a fairly stable political entity, both in size and in geographical distribution.

THE AUSTRALIAN AND NEW ZEALAND EMPIRES

Both Australia and New Zealand have colonial possessions in the Pacific. Australia controls southeast New Guinea (Papua), across the Torres Strait from the Australian mainland, and administers northeast New Guinea (Territory of New Guinea) and the islands to the northeast and east as a United Nations trusteeship territory. These areas are of little economic value, and because of the generally low cultural level of the indigenous inhabitants, the Australians have made few moves toward granting self-rule. Control of eastern New Guinea and the adjacent islands does, however, provide a defensive screen against potential attack from the north.

New Zealand's overseas territories include the Cook and Tokelau islands in the southern Pacific. New Zealand also controlled the trusteeship territory of Western Samoa, but in 1961 this area, with a population of just over 100,000, was granted independence. Neither the Cook nor the Tokelau islands are of much commercial value, and there is little pressure there for independence from New Zealand's control.

OTHER EMPIRES

Norway, Belgium, and the Republic of South Africa are three other States which have been noted for their colonial holdings. Norway in 1925 was granted sovereignty over the group of islands in the Arctic Ocean collectively called Spitsbergen (or Svalbard), with the provision that they be permanently demilitarized and that certain other powers be granted economic rights there. The chief resource of Spitsbergen is coal, some of which is exported to Norway (the nation has practically no domestic coal supplies) and some to the Soviet Union. The Norwegians also control Jan Mayen Island (uninhabited except for Norwegian meteorological personnel), located between northern Norway and the coast of Greenland, tiny Bouvet Island in the South Atlantic, and Peter I Island in the Antarctic Ocean. Norway's maritime interests are reflected in the fact that all of her overseas possessions are insular. The territories have a total area of 24,000 square miles and a population of less than 3,500 persons.

Belgium's history of colonial control dates back only to the late nineteenth century. The country's independence was not achieved until the 1830's, and in the decades which followed Belgium's leaders devoted their energies to building up their country's economic level, giving little attention to the acquisition of colonial areas. In 1878, however, Belgium's King Leopold I sent the noted explorer Henry Morton Stanley into the Congo River basin to supervise the establishment of Belgian outposts and to explore the area more fully. At the Berlin Conference of 1884–85 Leopold was declared sovereign of the Congo Free State, and for over twenty years he controlled the region as his own private estate. Not until 1908 did the Belgian government assume responsibility for the large tropical area.

At the end of World War I Belgium was awarded a League of Nations mandate over Ruanda-Urundi, a former German possession adjoining the Belgian Congo in central Africa. In 1960 the Belgian government, in response to strong nationalist pressures, ended its control over the Belgian Congo (see Chapter 15), and two years later Ruanda-Urundi was split into the two independent States of Rwanda and Burundi. Thus Belgium has ceased to be a colonial power.

The Republic of South Africa, is, in effect, a colonial power, although its territory adjoins the mother country. South Africa was granted a mandate over German Southwest Africa, an area of over 300,000 square miles, following World War I, and over forty years later the Republic refuses to consider any plans for independence for Southwest Africa (see page 454). Italy and Japan, two former colonial powers, were stripped of their overseas holdings following World War II. Italy in 1950 received a ten-year United Nations trusteeship over former Italian Somaliland, but this trusteeship has now been terminated.

Trends in Western Colonialism

The decline of colonialism has, since the end of World War II, been one of the major trends in the world political pattern. In Africa, Kenya, the Federation of Rhodesia and Nyasaland, Southwest Africa, and the two

Portuguese territories of Angola and Mozambique are the principal dependent areas which still remain. Other important areas of the world are the three Guianas, British Honduras, eastern New Guinea, and the territories of northern Borneo. Taken together the remaining dependent areas have a combined population of some 30 million.

It is interesting to note that the elaborate trusteeship machinery set up by the United Nations has little material with which to work except for the former Japanese mandated islands in the Pacific (now administered by the United States), northeast New Guinea, and Nauru Island in the Pacific (under the combined control of Great Britain, Australia, and New Zealand). Thus the era of international inspection of colonial holdings has almost disappeared. Regardless of differing stages of cultural or economic development, a great part of the tropical and subtropical work has become (or will soon become) politically free.

The successful achievement of independence by so many peoples and political regions raises a number of difficult questions so far as future conditions are concerned. Some of these will be considered briefly here.

1. Will the newly independent States retain the territorial form they had at the time of independence? In practically every case the boundaries of these new States were laid down by the former colonial powers in the interests of administrative efficiency (or of compromise between conflicting interests). In the new era of nationalism there may be pressures by one State or another to relocate borders. There may be moves to divide existing States into two or more parts, or, conversely, to unite two or more States into some larger political unit. Such potential changes could involve friction and possible warfare.

2. Can the new States achieve economic viability? Some of the former colonies have great natural wealth; others are poor in resources. There are great differences in pressures of population among these States, as well as in training and education of the inhabitants and of availability of capital. Along with independence frequently come greater demands by the people of a State for material goods and an increase in the level of expectations. Yet attainment of self-rule is frequently followed by a withdrawal of foreign capital, through fear of violence or of instability of the government.

3. What ideologies will ultimately be adopted by a new State? Although the States which have achieved independence since World War II were colonies of the European nations or of the United States, it does not necessarily follow that they will adhere to the political and social traditions of these areas. Political leaders in the new States have often been educated in Europe or the United States (and frequently imprisoned by the mother country for insurrectionist activities), but in an effort to achieve economic and social goals as rapidly as possible, these leaders, or those who succeed them, may turn to Communism, or a socialist type of dictatorship. Com-

munist propagandists promise rapid economic advancement ("look at the economic growth rates of the U.S.S.R."), while dictatorships are held to be more efficient than democracies.

4. How will the new States react toward international crisis? The stereotyped leader of a newly independent State is (*a*) suspicious of everything "Western" because of his country's recent colonialism; (*b*) impressed with the Soviet Union because of its stand against colonialism and its recent economic growth rate; (*c*) desirous of world peace, and thus susceptible to unrealistic peace proposals; (*d*) concerned above all with the development of his own State, and thus willing to accept aid from whatever source, while at the same time reluctant to support international action which does not immediately concern his own people. Although such a description, in its entirety, does not fit all, or even a majority, of the leaders of newly independent States, there is sufficient truth in it to illustrate some of the difficulties encountered at the United Nations and elsewhere in the soliciting of support in time of international emergencies, such as those in Israel, the Congo, or Laos.

Perhaps the greatest difficulty of all experienced by leaders of many of the new States is in recognizing and assessing what might be called the "new colonialism" of the mid-twentieth century—that of the Communist States, particularly the Soviet Union and Mainland China. The Soviet Union, since the start of World War II, has incorporated within its borders the former independent states of Latvia, Lithuania, Estonia, and Tannu Tuva, as well as portions of Finland, Poland, Czechoslovakia, and Romania. It has set up Moscow-oriented regimes in Poland, Czechoslovakia, Hungary, Bulgaria, Romania, Albania, and East Germany. Communist China has extended its sway over Tibet and North Vietnam, and from North Vietnam Communist forces are threatening Laos and South Vietnam. The Soviet Union also moved into North Korea in the closing days of World War II and from there launched an attack on South Korea in 1950.

This new colonialism differs in several respects from the traditional variety. The "colonial" territories are for the most part contiguous to the mother country rather than separated from it by expanses of ocean. There are no official acknowledgements of the colonial ties (although, following the Hungarian uprising of 1956, the Soviet Union complained that the United Nations had no business investigating a crisis "within the Socialist camp"). The freedom of action of leaders of the so-called satellites varies considerably. Ulbricht of East Germany is virtually unable to move without instructions from Moscow, while Hoxha of Albania has engaged in vituperative exchanges with Khrushchev and is apparently moving closer ideologically to Peking. There are no guidelines to follow on the way to "independence" under this new form of colonialism. The wall in Berlin, the truce line in Korea, and the disputed border along the Himalayas symbolize the territorial limits of the new empires, about which so few operational details are in fact known, and toward which so many responsible persons are unwilling to look objectively.

BIBLIOGRAPHY

BOWMAN, ISAIAH. "Population Outlets in Overseas Territories," in *Geographic Aspects of Internal Relations*. C. C. COLBY (ed). Chicago: University of Chicago Press, 1938.

Dated, but nonetheless valuable, discussion of the problem.

CARRINGTON, C. E. "Decolonization: the Last Stages," *International Affairs*, XXXVIII (1962), 29–41.

An interesting discussion of a passing trend.

EASTON, STUART C. *The Twilight of European Colonialism*. London: Methuen & Company, 1961.

Causes and effects of the ending of Western colonialism.

HALL, H. DUNCAN. *Mandates, Dependencies and Trusteeships*. Washington: Carnegie Endowment for International Peace, 1948.

A detailed handling of certain problems of colonial administration.

"Newly Independent States." Geographic Report No. 3 (Revised), April 2, 1962. Washington: Department of State, Office of the Geographer.

A frequently revised listing of new States, with statistics.

WRIGHT, QUINCY. *Mandates Under the League of Nations*. Chicago: University of Chicago Press, 1930.

Although much of the material is out of date, this is an important book to any understanding of the mandate system.

7

THE UNITED STATES

● The United States is a unique politico-geographic phenomenon—unique because of its location and resource potential, unique because of the course of its political and economic development, and unique because of the current problems of adjustment to changing world conditions which it faces. Through the years of its existence as an independent political unit it has (with one notable exception) satisfied the three criteria for viability, that is, the maintenance of internal cohesion, of economic consistency, and of territorial security. The State has not lost a war, nor has its territory been invaded during the past century and a half. As the greatest economic and military power on earth following World War II, it was forced, albeit reluctantly, into a position of leadership in world affairs, a position which has resulted in the focusing of world attention on some of the traditional problems of internal development within the United States. The days of "splendid isolation" have disappeared, to be replaced first by the brief era of undisputed supremacy, and more recently by a time of questioning and reappraisal in the face both of the growing power of the Soviet Union, Communist China, and the European Common Market, and of new complexities in the ideological struggle with Communism. As a political region the United States might be considered in terms of the five basic elements listed in Chapter 3; as a world power phenomenon it will be considered instead under the three categories of uniqueness noted at the beginning of the chapter.

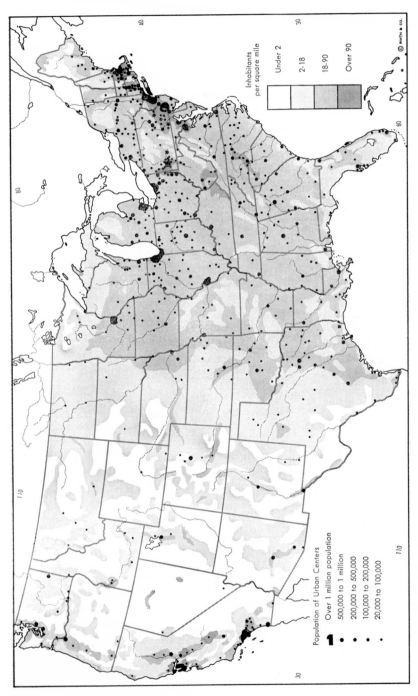

Figure 13. The United States.

LOCATION AND RESOURCE POTENTIAL

Location has been one of the dominant influences in the development of the United States. The protection afforded by three thousand miles of ocean, the mid-latitude climates, and the vicinal location with respect to the rest of the Western Hemisphere have all contributed in many ways to the United States' power position. Although the barrier effect of the Atlantic has been diminishing since the advent of the Air Age, the presence of this water body, together with that of the Pacific Ocean and of the Arctic region, still represents an element of protection for Anglo-America from potential enemies in Eurasia. Location on two oceans means that the United States has long sea frontiers to defend, but it has facilitated the State's maritime development and the establishment of overseas contacts with the other parts of the world.

Because of the mid-latitude location of the United States there are no areas of arctic climate, except for some of the high mountain regions, and the only tropical climate is in southernmost Florida. Thus Europeans were attracted to the country for settlement as far back as the early seventeenth century. Another climatic advantage of the United States is that there is a sufficiently wide variety of climates within its borders to permit many types of crops to be grown. On the other hand, the major climatic disadvantage is the fact that much of the western portion is arid, or semiarid, a limiting factor on the nation's agricultural potential.

An additional locational advantage is that neither Canada nor Mexico represents a potential rival to United States power, nor do any other of the States of the Western Hemisphere, either alone or in alliance with one another. The dominance of the United States in its hemisphere is an asset which has frequently been noted by writers living in the Eastern Hemisphere, where national power is more diverse. The dominance is largely the result of the size of the population of the United States, of the development by the population of the State's agricultural, mineral, and power resources, and of the political and cultural conditions existing within the United States under which this development was made possible. Both Canada and Brazil are of commensurate size, but climate and lack of good agricultural land have kept their populations well below the United States level. The remaining areas of Latin America have been politically divided into States so much smaller in size and population than the United States that they in no way compete with it in terms of national power.

The land area of the United States totals 3,552,197 square miles, placing it fourth in size among the countries of the world, behind the Soviet Union, Communist China, and Canada. The State's size has been sufficiently great to permit considerable expansion of settlement and to offer the possibilities of a wide variety of natural resources within the borders. In terms of internal control distance represents a strong centrifugal force which has been over-come to a considerable extent by the development of an extensive circulatory system throughout the country.

Surface configuration in the United States is significant primarily in terms of the economy. The upland areas are important for water power and for timber; some of the mountains and hills are also rich in minerals and power fuels. Upland regions, however, often limit the agricultural potential of particular areas as a result of slope, of soil types, or of their effects on temperature and precipitation. In terms of internal political cohesion, surface configuration is important primarily because of its effect on population distribution. This, in turn, has influenced the distribution of political power within the United States, but its effect on national unity has been minimized with the development of modern communication media. Mountain groups may have certain cultural differences from the majority of the population, but here again there are no powerful centrifugal forces when measured on the national scale. Surface configuration also has little effect on the structure and functioning of the international borders. For only 175 miles, between Maine and Quebec, does a portion of the United States boundary follow a landform—in this case an upland area, which is a northern extension of the White Mountains. Mountains, however, have provided the bases for the delimitation of some state borders, as between Idaho and Montana and North Carolina and Tennessee.

Soils and natural vegetation contribute to the resource base of the United States, although in both cases human use—or misuse—has tended to lessen their value. Most of the virgin forests of the country have dis-appeared, and the United States is now dependent on Canada for much of its wood requirements. The destruction of the forests has resulted in serious soil erosion; the tremendous quantities of alluvium which are carried downstream each year by the Mississippi River and its tributaries are in part the result of deforestation in the upper Mississippi basin. The plowing up of natural grasslands in the semiarid parts of the United States has contributed to the great dust storms in that area, which have further depleted the natural resource base. Here then are two physical assets whose potential value has declined considerably within the past two centuries.

With regard to minerals and power resources, the United States is self-sufficient in many items, such as coal, copper, petroleum, iron ore, molyb-denum, and sulphur, although the gradual depletion of domestic sources of petroleum and iron ore is forcing the Americans to look to other areas for supplies. The United States, however, is almost completely dependent on foreign sources for chromite, nickel, tin, manganese, platinum, asbestos, quartz crystals, and industrial diamonds; it is also partially dependent on foreign areas for over a dozen other items, including cobalt, lead, zinc, and tungsten. Of the mineral shortages Canada and Mexico together make up much of the deficiencies in nickel, asbestos, lead, and zinc, and Canada is becoming increasingly important as a source of iron ore. The State has a large water power potential which is not completely utilized. Further developments on such rivers as the Niagara, the Colorado, and the Columbia will increase considerably the national hydroelectric power output.

Water features are a final physical asset. In terms of transportation the Mississippi and its tributaries (notably the Ohio, the Tennessee, and the Missouri) and the Great Lakes comprise two of the most valuable inland water systems of the world. Canalization, dredging, and the development of the St. Lawrence Seaway, connecting the Great Lakes with the Atlantic, are engineering improvements which have greatly enhanced the value of these waterways to the United States. The factor of hydroelectric power has already been mentioned. In addition, some of the water bodies have also been useful for irrigation and for water supplies to industrial areas.

Type, Size, and Distribution of Population

The population of the United States is an important aspect of its resource potential, representing as it does a complex mixture of cultural groups. Only one element, the 350,000 Indians, are descendants of the original inhabitants of the country. Generally speaking, the various groups composing the white population have become well assimilated. Little attention is normally paid to differences among Protestant, Catholic, or Jew, among descendants of particular European stocks, or between recent immigrants and those whose forefathers have been in the United States for many decades. Difficulties, however, do arise in connection with the nonwhite population—Negroes, Indians, and Orientals—as well as with Latin American groups, such as Mexicans and Puerto Ricans. One of the major causes of discrimination against these groups is fear on the part of many American whites of a lowering of their social and economic levels, should full economic and political equality be granted to these lower-income groups. The proportions of this racial conflict are magnified in the United States because of the large number of nonwhites and of Mexicans and Puerto Ricans who reside within its borders.

The problem of minority groups tends to weaken the over-all structure of political cohesion. There are nearly 19 million Negroes in the United States, representing over 10 per cent of the total population. In some southern states the Negro population approaches that of the white, with resultant social, economic, and political repercussions (Figure 14). Twenty per cent of Alaska's population consists of Indians and Eskimos, while in Hawaii only 32 per cent of the people are white, the rest being Japanese, Filipino, Chinese, and others.

The problem of discrimination against the Negroes has represented

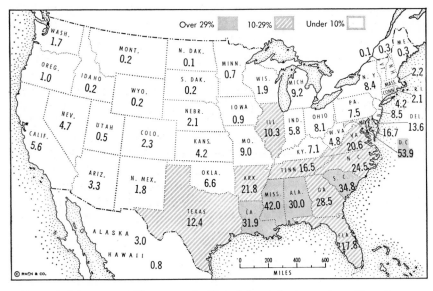

Figure 14. Percentage of Negroes in the United States by States, 1960. Note the correlation between the distribution of Negroes and the states of the Confederacy in the Civil War (Figure 21).

a major source of controversy between federal and state powers in the United States. In May, 1954, a decision of the Supreme Court of the United States outlawed segregation in the public schools of the United States; three years later United States troops were sent to Little Rock, Arkansas, to enforce a federal court's order for the integration of twelve Negro pupils into the public schools there. By 1961 only four southern states (Missisippi, Alabama, Georgia, and South Carolina) had refused to accept token integration. In Louisiana four Negro students attended mixed classes; in North Carolina, 50; in Arkansas, 100. Thus the southeastern states continue to resist the rulings of the federal government.

The difficulties of racial discrimination (involving also Negro voting rights, discussed on page 145) are complicated by the shifts which have been taking place in the distribution of the American Negro. John Fraser Hart[1] notes that in the twentieth century the Negro is becoming increasingly urbanized, largely as a result of migration from the rural South to metropolitan areas outside the South. To the urban areas of the Northeast have come migrants from the South Atlantic states; others from the Mississippi Delta, the state of Mississippi itself, and central Alabama moved to Detroit, Chicago, St. Louis, and other midwestern cities; still other Negroes from

[1] "The Changing Distribution of the American Negro," *Annals of the Association of American Geographers,* L (1960), 242–67.

Arkansas, northern Louisiana, and eastern Texas went to the West Coast cities. Within the South itself there has been considerable movement of Negroes from rural areas to the southern cities.[2]

The growth of the United States population from about 3 million at the time of independence to over 179 million in 1960 was occasioned not only by natural increase but also by large-scale immigration, particularly from Europe. Between 1860 and 1924 over 33 million persons immigrated to the United States. In the years of an expanding agricultural frontier and of growing industrialization, the United States could absorb a great number of foreigners to form a reservoir of cheap labor. By the beginning of the twentieth century, however, the era of unclaimed agricultural land was ending, and not long after this the industrial expansion of the country was also slowed due to the decline in domestic and foreign markets. In the face of widespread unemployment following World War I, the United States government promulgated an immigration law (1921) which limited immigration from Europe and certain other areas to 3 per cent of the population of each country resident within the United States at the time of the 1910 census. Quotas for most Asiatic countries had already been fixed by separate agreements, while immigration from other parts of the Western Hemisphere continued without numerical restrictions. In 1924 the quota was reduced from 3 to 2 per cent, where it now remains. Special provisions have at times been made for the admittance of refugees above the specific quota, such as those from Hungary after the 1956 uprising or from Communist China. In terms of the national population, however, these exceptions affect an extremely small number of people.

The existence of a large, relatively unified, population in the United States, with a high degree of education and training, is one of the important facets of the State's power potential. The rate of annual population increase in 1960 was approximately 1.5 per cent, or over 2.6 million persons. In the period of national prosperity which has followed the ending of World War II, the birth rate at no time has dropped below 2 per cent per year. Thus, unlike some of the States of western Europe, the United States has not yet approached the point of stability of national population total.

The distribution of population has been affected both by climate and by industrialization. Although the bulk of the people in the past has been concentrated east of the Mississippi, the geographic center of population has been moving steadily westward, so that in 1960 it was in southwestern Illinois. Between 1950 and 1960 three western states—Nevada, Arizona, and Alaska—reported population increases of more than 70 per cent; California's increase was over 40 per cent, while Florida, with the highest in the nation, had an increase of 76 per cent. Accompanying this shift away

---

[2] Between 1950 and 1960 the South lost 1,457,000 Negroes, while the Northeast gained 541,000, the North Central region 558,000, and the West 332,000.

from the Northeast has been the movement of people to urban areas, so that by 1960 70 per cent of the total population was classed as urban. These population changes, of course, influence the distribution of political power, as evidenced by the increase in membership from the Far West in the House of Representatives and the corresponding decrease in membership from the northeastern states. In 1960 California gained eight seats in the House of Representatives over its 1950 quota, and Florida gained four, while Pennsylvania lost three, and New York and Massachusetts each lost two.

POLITICAL AND ECONOMIC DEVELOPMENT

The original settlements by Europeans in what is now the United States were a series of isolated coastal communities along the Atlantic seaboard. To the north the French had established a ribbon of settlements along the St. Lawrence River, and in the south the Spanish had occupied parts of the Florida and Gulf coasts. Gradually the isolated coastal settlements from Maine southward expanded inland and toward one another; in time they evolved into the thirteen colonies which formed the basis of the United States.

The United States became independent in 1783. At that time its area was just over 800,000 square miles, but almost immediately the new country began to expand in a westward direction. Little resistance was encountered from other powers during this expansion. There was no political unit on

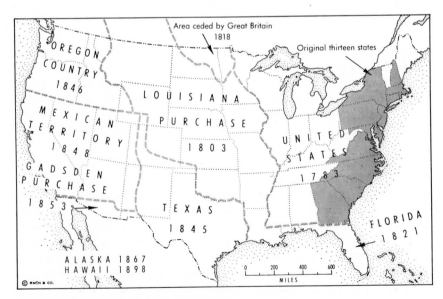

Figure 15. United States: Territorial Growth.

the west coast of sufficient strength to expand eastward through the Great Plains and challenge the supremacy of the eastern states. The center of power in Mexico lay nearly a thousand miles to the south of the United States' path of westward progress, while to the north in Canada energies were being devoted for the most part to problems of development of the eastern regions, rather than to interference with United States expansion to the west. Although territorial disputes with both the Mexicans and Canadians arose during the first half of the nineteenth century, they were eventually settled with few lasting ill effects. By 1853 the United States had reached its present size and shape (Figure 15), exclusive of Alaska and Hawaii. Because of the unusual conditions of admission surrounding these two non-contiguous states, separate descriptions are given here of each of them.

Alaska

Largest of the former outlying territories of the United States, Alaska has an area of 571,000 square miles and had a population in 1960 of 226,000. Purchased from Russia shortly after the end of the Civil War, it became a territory by act of Congress in 1912, with its own legislative assembly and with one nonvoting delegate elected biennially to the United States House of Representatives. Increased development of resources and the expansion of military facilities in the strategic area have been responsible for the trebling of the area's inhabitants since 1930. Accompanying this population increase were growing pressures for Alaska's admittance to the United States as a state, thereby granting its people voting representation in Congress.

Within Alaska important population concentrations are few and widely separated from one another. The southern part of the state—including the southeastern Panhandle—consists of a series of mountain ranges which tend to isolate the central lowland from the southern coast. The central region, drained by the Yukon, opens westward to the Bering Sea. North of this is the Brooks Range, and beyond it a broad plain which slopes northward to the Arctic Ocean.

The three areas of population concentration are (1) the southeast, including the Juneau-Skagway region, (2) the Seward-Anchorage district to the west along the southern coast, and (3) the Fairbanks region some two hundred miles north of Anchorage in the Yukon lowland. Included within the second district is the Matanuska Valley, one of the most promising agricultural regions in Alaska. The Alaskan capital, Juneau, is located in the southeast, and was one of the early towns. It is outranked in population by both Anchorage and Fairbanks. In years to come pressure may develop in Alaska for a shift of the capital to a more centrally located area.

Economy. Alaska's economy is based primarily upon the development of three resources—fish, fur, and minerals—of which fish (particularly salmon) represents about 70 per cent of the total income. Gold is the most important mineral produced, but the state is known to have extensive coal deposits, and there is the possibility of large-scale petroleum resources. The potential for water power development is very good, particularly in southern Alaska. In the southeast permission of the Canadian government would be necessary before large-scale power projects could be undertaken, for most of the essential water is on the Canadian side of the border. The Canadians, already involved in hydroelectric developments of their own, have been reluctant to grant United States concerns permission to utilize Canadian rivers for giant Alaskan power plants. Another Alaskan resource is lumber, but the cost of transportation to the United States is so high that Alaskan wood has little chance of competing with United States or Canadian lumber in the United States market, although the Japanese market offers good prospects.

A final economic value of Alaska to the United States is its potential role as a settlement area, but here again there has been relatively little activity. Only about 11 per cent of the state is considered suitable for settlement, and the principal "pioneer" activity has taken place in the Matanuska Valley, north of Anchorage, where several thousand persons from the United States have undertaken to settle and farm the area since 1935.

The federal government controlled 99.86 per cent of the territory of Alaska, leaving only a small area for private ownership. Federal ownership was set up by Congress to protect Alaska's natural resources against unwise commercial exploitation. Mining and timber rights on government-owned land are leased to private concerns, but throughout the greater part of Alaska little economic development has taken place. One drawback to economic development has been the lack of adequate transportation facilities. There are only two main railroads in Alaska—a 509-mile line connecting Fairbanks with Seward, and the much shorter White Pass and Yukon railroad connecting Skagway with Whitehorse, Canada. The Yakutat and Southern is a small line serving the fishing area at the northern end of the Panhandle. Not until 1942 was a direct overland road completed between Alaska and the United States. The Alcan Highway, forming a major portion of this route, connects Fairbanks with Dawson Creek, British Columbia, a Canadian road and rail head. Ships, operating mostly from Seattle, still constitute the principal link and almost exclusive freight mover between the United States and its largest state. Airlines now represent an important additional means of communication.

Defense Position. Alaska is located close to the Soviet Union; Attu Island, at the western end of the Aleutians, is but 200 miles from the Soviet-controlled Commander (Komandorski) Islands and 600 miles from the Kamchatka Peninsula, while to the north the Alaskan and Siberian mainlands are 56 miles from one another across the Bering Strait.

The development of large-scale military operations in Alaska has been a recent phenomenon. The great-circle route between the United States Northwest and the Japanese islands lies across southern Alaska, and during World War II defense installations were constructed in various parts of the territory. In 1942 Japanese forces occupied several islands in the western Aleutians, and enemy attacks were made on the Alaskan mainland. The conclusion of peace with Japan in 1945 was soon followed by an increase in tension between the United States and the Soviet Union, and again Alaska's military importance became evident. Eventually United States defense officials decided upon an Alaskan "Heartland" defense concept, which called for the maintenance of two large air bases, one in the vicinity of Fairbanks (Eielson Field) and one in the neighborhood of Anchorage (Elmendorf Field). These are supplemented by several smaller fields, among them bases at Nome and on the Aleutians. The presence of radar screens, a strong antiaircraft defense, ground forces to protect the air bases, and, of course, naval support along the coasts constitute the supplementary elements of this "air-defense" project. The locational significance of these bases may be illustrated by the fact that Fairbanks lies 2,900 miles from the Manchurian border, 1,500 miles from Seattle, and 3,200 miles from New York. In United States hands these bases represent a menace to eastern Siberia; in Soviet hands they would be a far greater menace to the United States.

Statehood for Alaska. Following World War II many of the people of Alaska began agitating for admission of the territory into the United States. In 1946 a referendum was held in Alaska on the subject of statehood, and it was approved by a margin of three to two. Statehood, it was argued, would give impetus to the territory's economic development, since most decisions concerning economic activities had to be settled in Washington, rather than Juneau. Permission was necessary from Congress, for example, for any lumbering done on the over 99 per cent of the Alaskan territory which was controlled by the federal government. The rapid growth of Alaska's population since 1940, the area's military development, and the completion of overland connection between Alaska and the United States were cited as justification for statehood.

Opposition to Alaskan statehood came first from traditionalists who disapproved of a noncontiguous state, from some Republicans who felt it would normally be a Democratic stronghold, and from some "States' Rights" Democrats who were concerned about the inclusion of two Alaskan senators and one representative in Congress. Because of its small population the new state would have a disproportionate power in Congress, as there would be one senator for less than 80,000 people, and one representative for

226,000. This same contention of overrepresentation has been used against the admission of virtually every new state into the Union since 1783, but it still has political appeal. It was pointed out that Alaska had more people at the time of admission than did twenty-seven other states at the time they entered the Union. Finally, in January, 1959, Alaska was admitted to the Union as the forty-ninth state.

An important provision of the enabling act admitting Alaska as a state is that Alaska shall have the right to select over 100 million acres of vacant and unappropriated public lands; the state can open these lands to prospectors for minerals, and it is to derive the principal advantage in all gains resulting from the discovery of minerals. Certain federally administered lands, now reserved for the conservation of fisheries and wildlife, are to be transferred to the state, thereby increasing its potential tax base.

The problem of federal-state relationships came up in Alaska in the spring of 1962 in connection with foreign fishing in marginal waters. Two Japanese fishing vessels operating in Shelikof Strait, between Kodiak Island and the mainland, were seized by officials of the Alaska Fish and Game Department without previous notice having been given to federal authorities. Shelikof Strait varies in width from 21 to 30 miles and is claimed by the state of Alaska as inland waters, although no decision on the status of these waters had been made in Washington. Because of the rugged nature of the Alaskan south and west coast, the rich fishing grounds of the offshore waters, and the presence of foreign fishing vessels, the Alaskans desire a liberal ruling on the question of control over marginal waters, while Washington has traditionally been conservative on these matters.

Hawaii

Although begun over half a century ago, the movement for statehood for the Hawaiian Islands gained momentum only after the end of World War II. The noncontiguous location of the territory and the concern of some legislators over the inclusion of new senators and representatives in Congress militated against Hawaii's admission as a state. Moreover, Democrats who felt the area would be a Republican stronghold opposed statehood on the grounds of political expediency.

The Hawaiian Islands, stretching across two thousand miles of the Pacific, are of economic and military significance to the United States. Practically all of the area and population are concentrated on the eight principal eastern islands; Midway, at the western end of the archipelago, is the only other important island group. The islands have a total area of 6,423 square miles and an economy based on highly commercialized agriculture (sugar and pineapples), tourism, and the military bases there, such as Pearl Harbor and Schofield Barracks. In 1959 Hawaii's total dollar earnings with the mainland through exports and services came to 953 million, while the islands' imports from the United States were valued at 923 million. The area is clearly an important component of the United States economy.

One of the great objections to the inclusion of Hawaii as a state was based upon the territory's ethnic character. Approximately 35 per cent of the population is Japanese in origin, 12 per cent is of Filipino descent, and another 6 per cent is Chinese. The great majority of these, however, are United States citizens. Nevertheless, the prospect of an influx of persons of Oriental descent was alarming to certain congressmen, particularly from the western states.

Spokesmen for Hawaii pointed to the area's war record as proof of the people's loyalty to the United States. Throughout World War II not a single case of sabotage by a Hawaiian civilian was reported, and the Asiatic population there contributed significantly to the war effort in terms of labor and military service. The territory has a larger population than four of the mainland states and contributes more to the federal treasury than do nine of the states. The desire of the Hawaiians for statehood was proved in 1950, when a special convention drafted a state constitution which was approved overwhelmingly, first by the territorial legislature and then by the voters of Hawaii. In August, 1959, Hawaii became the fiftieth state of the United States.

Internal and External Boundaries of the United States

The partitioning of the United States (exclusive of Alaska and Hawaii) into forty-eight states was not completed until 1912, when New Mexico and Arizona were admitted. The process of delimiting state boundaries was a complex politico-geographic one in certain areas, reflecting both the nature of the land itself and the interplay of "pressure politics" in the United States Congress, where the decisions as to the limits of new states were ultimately made.[3] The frequent use of rivers, mountain crests, and straight lines, particularly west of the Mississippi, reflects the fact that here, as in Latin American and Africa, political borders are largely of the antecedent type, that is, laid down before the advent of appreciable white settlement in the border areas. As in the case of the external boundaries of the country, the stability of the state boundaries stands out in contrast to the more changeable internal political patterns in such countries as the Soviet Union, India, or China.

Although the United States borders only two other States, the length

---

[3] For accounts of disputes over state boundaries see Isaiah Bowman, "An American Boundary Dispute: Decision of the Supreme Court of the United States with Respect to the Texas-Oklahoma Boundary," *The Geographical Review*, XIII (1923), 161–90; and Benjamin E. Thomas, "Boundaries and Internal Problems of Idaho."

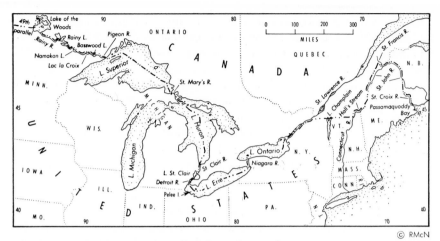

© RMcN

Figure 16. United States–Canadian Boundary—Eastern Sector.

of its boundaries (excluding those of Alaska) totals over 5,900 miles, of which 4,000 are with Canada and 1,900 with Mexico. Over half of the border with Canada follows water bodies, including the St. Lawrence River, the Great Lakes, Lake of the Woods, and the straits of Georgia and Juan de Fuca between Washington and British Columbia (Figures 16 and 17). West of Lake Superior the boundary trends in a general northwesterly direction to the northwestern corner of the Lake of the Woods. This is the northernmost position of the boundary; from here it runs due south for about twenty-five miles until it meets the forty-ninth parallel. In so doing it cuts off from Canada a peninsula which extends into the lake from the western shore. This peninsula, surrounded on three sides by water and on the

Figure 17. United States–Canadian Boundary–Northwestern Sector.

© RMcN

fourth by the province of Manitoba, is, in effect, a United States exclave in Canada. After reaching the forty-ninth parallel south of this peninsula, the boundary turns west and follows the parallel for nearly 1,300 miles until it reaches an arm of the Pacific. Here, twelve miles across Boundary Bay from Blaine, Washington, is a second United States exclave—Point Roberts, the southern end of an otherwise Canadian peninsula which extends for about two miles south of the forty-ninth parallel.

The Mexican border, starting at the Gulf of Mexico, follows the Rio Grande for 1,210 miles to El Paso, Texas. From here it consists of a series of straight lines, except for twenty miles in the west where the Colorado River separates the two countries (Figure 18).

The boundaries between the United States and its two neighbors are unique, first, in that they are completely unfortified and, second, in the ease of border crossing. No passports are required of citizens of the adjoining countries, and millions of persons cross the borders each year as commuters, tourists, and temporary inhabitants. No quotas are maintained on permanent immigration in either direction across the United States–Canadian or United States–Mexican borders, although there are restrictions as to the number who may cross as temporary laborers into the United States from Mexico. Along each border an International Boundary Commission, composed of representatives of the two adjoining States, acts as a permanent body for inspection of the borders, repair or replacement of border markers, and determination of the exact border location in cases of dispute. Along the United States–Mexican border the International Boundary Commission, in addition to its other tasks, also handles water problems involving the two countries. An International Joint Commission maintains jurisdiction over the use, obstruction, diversion, and pollution of joint United States–

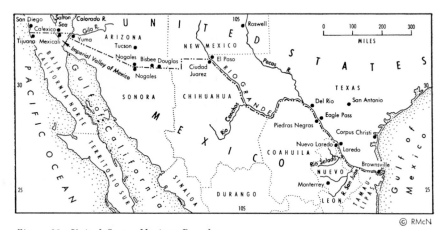

© RMcN

Figure 18. United States–Mexican Boundary.

Canadian waterways and of waters that cross the border.

Several important disputes have arisen between the United States and its neighbors, most of them in connection with common water features. Chicago's diversion of the waters of Lake Michigan, for use in its navigation-sanitation canal running westward to the Illinois River, has brought protests from the Canadian government because of the lowering of the Great Lakes and St. Lawrence River and the resultant navigation hazards. Power development at Niagara Falls and navigation and power developments on the St. Lawrence are also matters which require joint United States–Canadian action.

The division of water for irrigation in both the Rio Grande and the Colorado River has created problems for the United States and Mexico. Although about half the water in the Rio Grande comes from Mexican tributaries, the United States normally takes about 80 per cent of the water used for irrigation. On the other hand, all the water in the Colorado River comes from sources in the United States, yet Mexico's Imperial Valley depends upon the Colorado for irrigation. Treaties were eventually evolved to regulate the quantities of water each country might take out of the Rio Grande and Colorado.

Two other United States–Mexican border problems involve the location of the Rio Grande and illegal immigration from Mexico. The Rio Grande below El Paso flows in part through a broad flood plain, with the river meandering considerably and often changing its course. Not only is the boundary lengthened by the meanders, but with a shift of the main channel areas formerly in one country become included in the other (Figure 19). In 1933 a program was undertaken for flood control and straightening the channel of the Rio Grande, and the middle of the deepest channel now serves to mark the international border.[4]

The problem of the Mexican "wetbacks" (so called because many of them swim the Rio Grande to get to the United States) has been a frequent source of friction between the United States and Mexico. Each year the United States government officially contracts for the temporary services of a certain number of Mexicans as agricultural workers, particularly in the south central and southwestern states. By means of this contract system, smuggling, traffic in narcotics, and the spread of disease can be watched, and the interests of the laborers protected against exploitation by American farmers. By this means, too, the wage levels of contract Mexican laborers, as well as of United States workers, are maintained, for the illegal immigrant will generally work for lower wages than will either of these other two groups. The lure of higher wages in the United States, however, attracts far more Mexicans than are handled by the contract system; as a result hun-

---

[4] In July, 1963, the United States agreed to cede to Mexico the El Chamizal, a 437-acre tract between El Paso and Ciudad Juarez, which was Mexican territory until 1864 when a shift in the Rio Grande resulted in the area's being to the north rather than the south of the river.

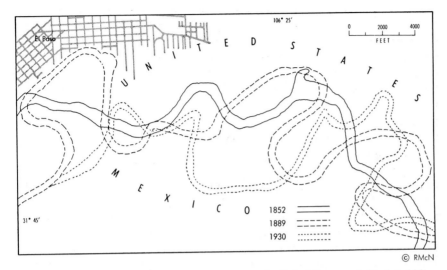

Figure 19. Fluctuations of the Rio Grande Between the United States and Mexico. (After a map by International Boundary and Water Commission, United States and Mexico.)

dreds of thousands cross the border illegally, and, despite the efforts of immigration authorities, probably over half the "wetbacks" escape detection and remain for indefinite periods of time in the United States.

The Alaskan-Canadian Boundary. In 1898 a dispute arose between Great Britain and the United States over the location of the Alaskan-Canadian boundary in the Panhandle section, southeast of Mount St. Elias. The Treaty of 1825 between Russia and Britain fixed the Panhandle boundary ". . . along the summit of the mountains parallel to the coast," leaving ambiguous the allocation of indentations which extended inland past the coastal ranges (Figure 20). When control of Alaska passed to the United States, American statesmen assumed, as the Russians had, that the salt water indentations were part of Alaskan territory; but with the discovery of gold in the Klondike the route north from Skagway, at the head of the Lynn Canal, became one of great significance. British authorities in Canada then claimed that by the terms of the 1825 treaty Skagway and the upper Lynn Canal, as well as the upper portions of the other indentations, were Canadian territory. The dispute was eventually submitted to arbitration, and in 1903 a compromise line was agreed upon which retained the indentations within Alaskan territory.

The Alaskan-Canadian boundary dispute points up the unusual situation of one State having control over much of another State's coast line. Were it not for the fact that Britain—and, more recently, Canada—had no particular need for access to the Pacific through northern British Columbia, it is probable that the Russian and American claims to control of this coast would have been more strenuously opposed than was actually the

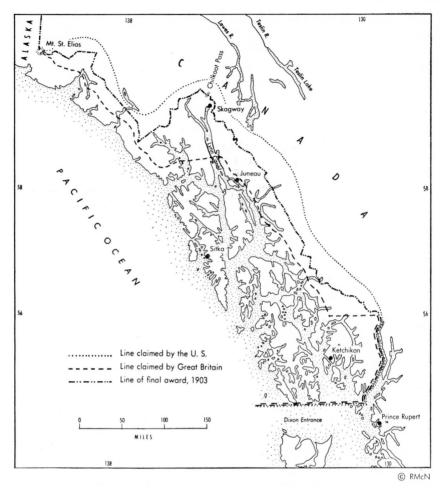

© RMcN

Figure 20. Southeast Alaskan–Canadian Boundary: Controversy and Settlement. Note how the final award denied Canada access to the sea north of Prince Rupert. (After Bemis, *A Diplomatic History of the United States.* Used by permission of Holt, Rhinehart and Winston, Inc., copyright 1936, 1942, 1950, 1955.)

case. There has been some talk of a possible "swap" between Canadian and Alaskan interest here—the award to Canada of a corridor to the sea through the Alaskan Panhandle in exchange for the use of Canadian rivers by Alaskan power plants.

The Submerged Lands Dispute

One of the most complex boundary problems with which the United States has had to contend recently is in connection with the submerged lands (sometimes incorrectly termed "tidelands") off the United States. This problem involves two issues of political control, one between the several states and the federal government, and the other with respect to national offshore boundary claims. Several precedents have been established in the field of international law regarding submerged lands as a result of these disputes.

The impetus for the submerged lands controversy was provided initially by the discovery of petroleum beneath the floors of the Gulf of Mexico and Pacific Ocean and of methods of recovering such petroleum by drilling in water up to several hundred feet in depth. In September, 1945, President Truman issued a proclamation which asserted federal control over mineral resources beneath the continental shelf off the United States mainland, its territories, and possessions. The total area involved in this proclamation amounted to 760,000 square miles. Rough estimates of oil reserves beneath the continental shelf off the United States mainland alone run to as much as one-third of the present *proved* reserves in the United States. It was specifically stated in the proclamation that control of mineral resources did not affect navigation on the high seas above the shelf, nor did it extend the limits of the territorial waters of the United States. In other words, the United States in 1945 claimed jurisdiction over resources alone, not sovereignty over the sea areas involved. Despite this clear distinction between types of jurisdiction, a number of Latin American States subsequently laid claim to sovereignty over large ocean areas off their coasts, in conformity with this "precedent" set by the United States.

At the time of the Truman proclamation, there already were conflicting claims to ownership of offshore areas within the national three-mile limit. Leases on the ocean floor for drilling purposes had been granted to oil companies by the coastal states since the early 1930's. The question of ownership of the ocean floor arose in connection with income received from the leases and the legality of these leases.

By 1937 officials of the federal government had begun to question the rights of the various states (particularly Texas, California, and Louisiana) to issue leases on submerged coastal lands without the consent of Congress. Thus began a three-way political struggle, with Congress passing laws granting title to the states, the President vetoing the measures, and the Supreme Court acknowledging federal ownership of offshore lands until such time as a law was enacted specifically granting title to the coastal states. Finally, in the spring of 1953 the Submerged Lands Act granting the various states title was signed by President Eisenhower and became law.

Officials of certain of the coastal states maintained that their historic state boundaries exceeded the national three-mile offshore limit. Texas claimed control out to ten and one-half miles (three leagues) in the Gulf of Mexico, because prior to 1845 the legislature of the Lone Star Republic had proclaimed this limit as marking the country's seaward boundary. Louisiana and Florida likewise claimed ten and one-half miles as their boundaries in the Gulf of Mexico. The Submerged Lands Act grants the coastal states sovereignty over submerged lands within their "historic" boundaries—to a distance of three miles in the Atlantic and Pacific oceans, and to ten and one-half miles in the Gulf of Mexico.

Since 1793 the United States government has held the three-mile limit as marking the offshore boundary of United States sovereignty. The position was maintained at the International Congress at The Hague in 1930 and is used by the United States delegates in their efforts to dissuade other powers from making unreasonable demands for offshore sovereignty in the case of their own coast lines. Extension of the control of Texas and west Florida to the ten and one-half mile limit carries with it the implication of United States control as well.

The question of the states' offshore limits was ultimately referred by the federal government to the United States Supreme Court. In June, 1960, the Court ruled that the states of Mississippi, Alabama, and Louisiana owned rights to the subsurface resources out to three and one-half miles from their coasts, while Texas and Florida owned the submerged lands to ten and one-half miles out. Estimates of the potential oil reserves in the whole Gulf offshore area are some 15 billion barrels, of which about 10 billion barrels are believed to lie off the coast of Louisiana. Since, at the time of the Court's decision, virtually all of the offshore oil production was from the area adjoining the Louisiana coast, the bulk of it beyond the three-mile limit, this decision was of great importance to the petroleum industry, which had invested an estimated $2 billion in offshore drilling. It also was a blow to Louisiana, since it stood to lose some $300 million in royalties which had been held in escrow pending a final settlement of the case. In addition to oil resources there is also sulphur. In 1960 the first offshore sulphur mine began operation seven miles off the Louisiana coast. Thus the economic value of the submerged lands area in the Gulf of Mexico becomes increasingly great.

Problems of Representation

Although membership in the House of Representatives is readjusted in accordance with population shifts at each decennial census,[5] there are several conditions under which the principle of proportional representation is not followed. The first involves the urban-rural ratio. According to the 1960 census 69.9 per cent of the United States population were classed as urban and 30.1 per cent as rural; yet of the House seats, only 42 per cent

---

[5] There was, in 1960, an average of approximately one representative for each 415,000 persons.

represented urban districts, while 58 per cent were from rural areas. Associated with this is the distribution of electoral votes in presidential elections. Alaska, with a 1960 population of 226,000, has three electoral votes (one for each 75,000 persons), while New York's 16,780,000 people have 45 votes (one for each 323,000 persons). In 1960 President Kennedy won 300 electoral votes to Nixon's 223, although his plurality of votes cast was but 113,000 out of a total of 16,800,000.

A more serious representation problem is that of the Negro. In six southeastern states (Alabama, Georgia, Florida, Louisiana, Mississippi, South Carolina) there were in 1960 an estimated 3,450,000 Negroes of voting age; of these less than 19 per cent were registered to vote. In Mississippi only 5 per cent of those of voting age were registered; in Alabama, 12 per cent; in South Carolina, 13 per cent.

Inequalities in congressional representation are reflected at the state levels as well, where the state legislatures determine the apportionment of senators and representatives. In many states the representation from rural areas has far outweighed that from urban ones, and legislatures have for decades resisted redistricting to conform with population shifts.[6] Finally in March, 1961, the United States Supreme Court ruled that appeals for redistricting of states may be returned to the federal courts if legislatures refuse to act in conformity with population shifts within individual states. Here again is a case of federal pressure on individual states to conform with what might be termed "national norms."

Economic Position of the United States

The tremendous economic strength of the United States is a potent factor in world affairs. War, or threat of war, in the past has often been the final arbiter in international disputes, and the United States' economic status, as a reflection of its military potential, has since 1917 been one of the basic components of world power relations. The economic power of the United States is based primarily upon its possession of essential commodities, such as food, petroleum, and steel, its position as a market, and its control of funds and credits which are advanced to less wealthy countries.

Of the nearly 3 million square miles of land area (exclusive of Alaska and Hawaii), nearly one-quarter is classed as arable. Actually the United States is one of the few States of the world which has been systematically reducing its total amount of cultivated land; about three-quarters of the area classified as arable is actually in crops. In normal times the country produces surpluses of such commodities as wheat, corn, and other grains,

---

[6] For the United States as a whole in 1960, 13 per cent of the population resided in counties having total populations of less than 25,000, yet such counties were represented by 36 per cent of the seats in state senates throughout the nation and 28 per cent of the seats in the lower houses.

and of cotton and tobacco, and is virtually self-sufficient in wool, meats, fruits, and vegetables.

In terms of industrial output the United States steel capacity equals over one-third of the world total. The miracle of this production has resulted in part from the tremendous market available to United States producers. The fifty states are in effect in an economic union with one another, since no trade barriers of any kind exist between them, and production on a mass basis can thus be developed for the large national market. The flexibility of industrial production permits the United States to match the flexibility of military demands and not only keep abreast of technical developments in the military field, but also to expand or contract military or consumer output on short notice when the situation warrants the move.

From 1946 through 1962 the United States extended nearly $98 billion worth of goods and credits to foreign countries in order to build up their economic strength and to aid them in arming against possible attack; this figure is part of a continuing program which represents large-scale United States commitments to foreign areas. Despite this foreign aid, however, the wealth of the United States has been in several respects a detriment to relations with other countries. For one thing, the existence of large agricultural surpluses has tended to create resentment on the part of the peoples in such countries as India, where a large segment of the population has insufficient food. Secondly, the great economic development within the United States tends to build psychological barriers between it and some of the less-developed countries of the world, for the peoples in these areas feel that the people of the United States cannot possibly understand or appreciate their problems of poverty. Finally, because of its market potential and its control of large-scale foreign aid, the United States occupies a position of great power and responsibility with respect to the economies of many other States. Consequently, the United States is frequently criticized for various situations which may adversely affect the economic conditions of individual States, even though these matters (for instance, a drop in the price of copper or coffee) may be entirely beyond the power of United States officials to control.

The Viability of the United States

Internal cohesion is well developed in the United States, although distance and diversity of physical elements have in the past represented important centrifugal forces. Population is distributed unevenly over a large area of land, and peoples in different parts of the country have developed divergent opinions with regard to national and international issues. Evidence may be found in the general distribution of "segregationists," "isolationists," and "high-tariff men."

The most important of the centripetal forces have been the great mobility of the United States population and the development of a strong circulatory system, including modern transportation facilities and the "standardization" of much of United States culture as the result of a common language and mass communication media. The fact that there have been no nearby powers tending to attract segments of the United States away from Washington's control has also contributed to the unity of the country

There were times, of course, in the development of the United States when strong divisive forces did appear. The territories of Kentucky and Tennessee, isolated from the east by the Appalachians, threatened for a time to withdraw from the State, and the Republic of Texas existed for ten years as an independent state before becoming incorporated within the United States. The most serious threat to national unity occurred in 1861, when eleven southern states, comprising one-quarter of the area of the United States and about 18 per cent of its population, seceded from the Union and announced the formation of the new Confederacy (Figure 21). The northern armies, however, succeeded in restoring political cohesion.

Since the end of the Civil War the problems of reconciling regional interests with those of the State as a whole have been reflected both in the patterns of voting in Congress and in the struggle for power between the state and federal governments. Interregional voting blocs, composing such diverse groups as, for example, southern Democrats and midwest Republicans, have succeeded in obtaining the passage of congressional bills favoring

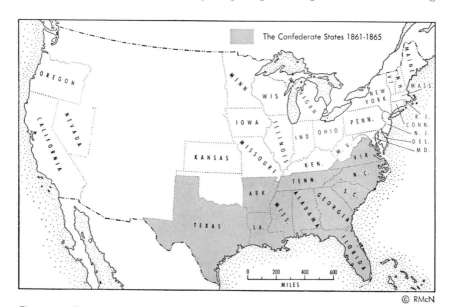

© RMcN

Figure 21. The Confederate States, 1861–65.

the interests of particular geographic areas. The changing distribution of population in the United States has, of course, influenced the activities of regional groups, as evidenced in the relative decline in the political strength of the northeastern urban areas during recent decades. The struggle between the state and federal governments is shown in the conflicts over hydroelectric power developments, taxation policies, and control of the submerged lands off the United States coasts (see page 142). Such a struggle is endemic to any political system in which power is divided between the national and the state or provincial bodies, but it is particularly strong in the United States, due to the relative power of the individual states.

The State's economic stability is also strong. The general prosperity is reflected in statistics of income per capita, in the ability of the United States to finance gigantic foreign aid programs, military defense spending, and in the variety of internal programs financed by the federal, state, and local governments. This prosperity is also reflected in the attraction of the United States for its overseas territories. Only the Philippines has opted for independence; the tendency among the other areas is for closer coordination with the mother country in response, to a great extent, to the economic opportunity offered by the United States.

So far as ability to maintain its territorial integrity is concerned, the United States is the greatest, or certainly one of the two greatest, military powers on earth. But any assessment of relative national power must take into consideration not only the defense capacities so far as territorial United States is concerned, but also the many areas throughout the world allied with the United States. Modern global war is a war of movement, of assault against peripheral as well as central objectives. Acting in terms both of its own direct defense and of the defense of other countries whose loss would greatly weaken its own power position, the United States has committed itself to supporting defense efforts in many parts of the globe, ranging from South Korea to Pakistan and from Greenland to Turkey. These commitments may involve direct military aid pacts (as with Japan), common participation in a multilateral agreement (such as NATO), or the maintenance of United States military bases on foreign soil (as in Iceland or Spain).

The threat of Soviet territorial aggression in western Europe in the years following World War II led to the formation in 1949 of the North Atlantic Treaty Organization (NATO), which united the United States and Canada with thirteen European nations.[7] One major feature of this agreement has been that the United States has undertaken to assist in the military build-up of its European allies, in order to bolster western Europe against possible invasion from the east and to maintain air and naval supremacy over the North Atlantic Ocean itself.

---

[7] Belgium, Denmark, France, Great Britain, Greece, Iceland, Italy, Luxembourg, the Netherlands, Norway, Portugal, Turkey, and West Germany.

Associated with NATO has been the development of United States military bases on foreign soil throughout the general north Atlantic area. These bases serve both the purpose of offense against a potential enemy and of defense for Anglo-America itself. The first group of bases is located in Europe and in Morocco; the second group stretches from Greenland through the central Atlantic; the third group is in Canada, Bermuda, and on some of the Caribbean islands (Figure 22).

All manner of political problems are associated with the development of the network of United States bases; the conduct of military personnel on foreign soil, the continued granting of permission for the maintenance of foreign installations within a country, and the extent of United States sovereignty over the area granted to it. Morocco's achievement of independence

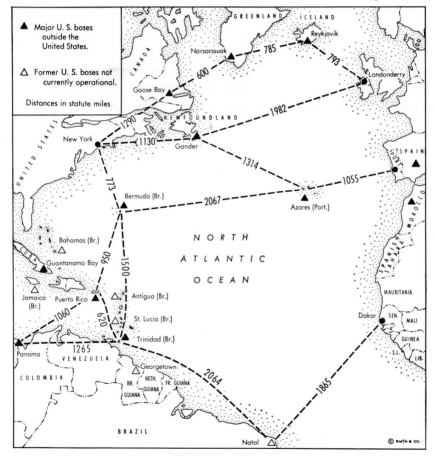

Figure 22. Major United States Bases in the North Atlantic. The two bases in Canada are actually Canadian-controlled, but a portion of each base is set aside for American military use.

in 1956 meant that the treaty between the United States and France providing for the maintenance of American bases in Morocco was no longer effective. In 1963 the last of the United States bases in Morocco will be closed down. In a somewhat different situation, the Icelandic government in 1956 requested that the United States abandon its base on the island. Although the government withdrew its request after the Soviet military action in Hungary in the fall of 1956, the event points up the extent to which "neutralism" may develop even among NATO members, particularly during times in which Cold War pressures are eased. The problem of maintaining United States bases on foreign soil involves not only NATO members but also such countries as Spain, Libya, the Philippines, and Japan, where American military installations are also located.

The Soviet Union has frequently complained of "encirclement" by United States military bases and has on occasion warned countries with such bases of possible countermeasures. It was from Pakistan that Gary Powers, the U-2 pilot, took off in 1961, bound for northern Norway, and the U.S.S.R. reacted to his capture deep within Soviet territory with stern warnings to both countries. In a move for nonalignment in the Cold War, Saudi Arabia insisted that in 1962 the United States cease military activities at the Dhahran base on the Persian Gulf. The government of Panama has repeatedly contested United States sovereignty over the Panama Canal Zone, with its military and naval bases (see page 190), while the possibility of action by Cuba against the Guantánamo Bay base remains a very real one (see page 189).

The problem of maintaining an adequate defense in the face of Communist threats obviously encompasses more than the maintenance of overseas bases. It involves questions of disarmament, of nuclear testing, and of the maintenance of effective striking forces in case of "limited" wars. It also involves the military effectiveness of major allies, such as Britain, France, and West Germany. There is no clear-cut test (except the test of war itself) to determine a State's actual ability to defend itself. New techniques of military offense or defense, shifting alliances, changes in the capacity of a people to resist outside pressures—these and similar factors may vitally influence a State's defensive position; in a situation so diverse as that of the United States vis-à-vis the Soviet Union, Communist China, or other potential adversaries, the degree of territorial security which exists at any one time can only be roughly approximated.

PROBLEMS OF READJUSTMENT

The history of the growth of the United States reads like an almost continuous success story. With its isolated position the State was free to expand, to test, and if necessary reject economic, political, and social ideas, to indulge in what with hindsight might appear as colossal mistakes, to delay in making and implementing unpleasant decisions. Since the end of the 1930's, however, the United States has no longer been able to afford the luxury of isolation. Not only must it assume a major role in the defense of the non-Communist world against the spread of Communism, it must also be acutely aware of the "image" it portrays to the other countries. In the contemporary struggle for men's minds the relative images of the United States and of the Soviet Union are of great importance, since each epitomizes to a certain extent a particular ideology; thus a highly significant aspect of the Cold War are the propaganda moves by each State, and by their allies, continually to improve their image vis-à-vis those of their ideological competitors. Because of this role of the national "image," and because of the relative freedom of press representatives to witness and report on facets of United States life, it follows that various imperfections or inconsistencies in the United States have come to assume global importance. Several of these imperfections will be noted here.

Probably the most serious malady in the United States has been, and still is, the racial question. The action of the Supreme Court in 1954 outlawing segregation in the public schools, and the sentiments of a majority of the members of Congress indicate that the federal government is in favor of ending the inequalities due to race or color as rapidly as possible. Yet, because of the federal nature of the United States government, the central government must move slowly and with caution. The Constitution, rather than the sentiments of congressmen, is the supreme law of the land, and the separate states retain those rights which are not specifically granted to the federal government. Yet eight years after the Supreme Court's decision there had been no integration whatever of Negro and white students in the public schools of four states of the deep South, while in a total of seventeen southern states (including Maryland, Mississippi, and Texas) only 6 per cent of the Negro pupils were in mixed classes. The refusal of restaurants in the South to serve nonwhite dignitaries of foreign states, acts of violence by whites in the United States toward nonwhite citizens, indeed the very continuation of segregation itself on such a massive scale seriously affects the image of the United States, particularly so far as many of the so-called uncommitted states of the world are concerned.

The economic structure of the United States is constantly on display. The problems of agricultural surpluses (and the accompanying tales of large-scale destruction of crops in order to keep up the prices) receive little sympathy in countries where much of the population is hungry. The crash of 1929, and the ensuing decade-long depression with its millions of unemployed, the slow rate of growth of the United States economy in recent years —all these are poor advertisements for the capitalist system, as are also the failure of the United States to match some of the Soviet space achievements and the apparently permanent pool of unemployed in the United States, numbering several millions. To combat such propaganda and to turn attention instead to obvious weaknesses in the Soviet system requires skillful action on the part of American officials.

In its role as a major bulwark against international Communism the United States has faced, and continues to face, serious economic problems of foreign aid and of trade. If foreign aid is to be administered, to what countries should it go, and in what form? The following table gives a breakdown of total United States foreign aid from 1946 through 1962:

Europe	$44.8 billion
Far East	22.2
Near East and South Asia	17.8
Latin America	6.8
Africa	1.8
Others	4.3
Total	$97.7 billion

(About 60 per cent of this total was economic aid and 40 per cent military aid.)

Originally, massive amounts of aid were dispatched to western Europe. Later the emphasis shifted to southern and eastern Asia. More recently there has been growing assistance to Latin America and Africa. The "Alliance for Progress," announced in Washington in 1961, will result in up to $20 billion worth of goods and credits being sent to the countries of Latin America during the ensuing ten-year period.

The foreign trade pattern of the United States may be seen by the following breakdown for 1961:

	Exports	Imports	Total
Europe	$6,506 million	$4,267 million	$10,773 million
Latin America	3,754	3,963	7,717
Canada	3,707	2,902	6,609
Asia	2,720	3,627	6,347
Africa	766	535	1,301
Australia and Oceania	475	266	741

Practically every year the United States faces a payments deficit, that is, more money leaves the country than comes in, with a consequent loss in gold holdings. Although the value of United States exports generally exceeds that of imports, there are such other factors as military spending abroad, economic aid, private investments, and tourist spending in foreign countries to augment the flow of payments. For this reason the United States views with considerable concern the gradual development of the European Common Market, an area of 180 million people to which in 1961 the United States exported over $3.5 billion worth of goods. As the common tariff toward outsiders continues to rise in the Common Market, fewer United States products will be able to compete there. Thus government officials in the United States have strongly urged that attempts be made to work out agreements between the United States and the Common Market to insure as free a movement of trade as possible in coming years, even though this may mean radical changes in traditional United States "protectionist" policies toward foreign goods.

In terms of both foreign aid and of trade the United States faces growing competition from the Soviet Union and other countries of the Soviet bloc (see page 338). The rise of new States, particularly in Africa and Asia, means new instabilities and new demands on the United States for assistance in order to ward off economic collapse or the spread of Communism to the individual countries. The Soviet successes in massive thermonuclear weapons spurs the United States on to even greater efforts, yet forces must be maintained for coping with "brush-fire" wars. In 1961 over half a million United States troops were stationed in fifteen foreign countries throughout the world, while another quarter of a million were "afloat" in the naval forces. Soviet achievements in space have brought pressures for United States crash programs. All of these commitments weigh heavily on the State's economic strength. Thus it is a period of uncertainty which the United States faces— a period in which some of the accepted postulates, such as the efficacy of the "containment" policy against Communism, or the miracle of United States industrial superiority, are being put to the test. One of the strengths of a democratic State should be its ability to readjust to conform with changing conditions. In a sense this is the supreme test for the United States in the next few years.

BIBLIOGRAPHY

BEMIS, SAMUEL FLAGG. *A Diplomatic History of the United States.* New York: Henry Holt & Company, 1950.

An excellent treatise on United States territorial expansion, both domestic and overseas.

BROWN, RALPH H. *Historical Geography of the United States.* New York: Harcourt, Brace & Company, 1948.

Maps and description of the territorial development of the United States.

DEWHURST, J. FREDERIC and Associates. *America's Needs and Resources: A New Survey.* New York: Twentieth Century Fund, 1955.
A detailed discussion of the United States resource base.

HARDWICK, WALTER G. "Changing Corridors to Alaska," *Journal of Geography,* LXI (1962), 49–57.
A discussion, with maps, of transportation links between Alaska and the forty-eight continental states.

HART, JOHN FRASER. "The Changing Distribution of the American Negro," *Annals of the Association of American Geographers,* L (1960), 242–67.
Maps and tables on the changing pattern of America's largest minority group.

HOOPES, TOWNSEND. "Overseas Bases in American Strategy," *Foreign Affairs,* XXXVII (1958), 69–83.
A careful appraisal of the role of American bases.

LAWRENCE, HENRY. "Waterway Problems on the Canadian Boundary," *Foreign Affairs,* IV (1926), 556–74.
An excellent summary of background materials, particularly on the St. Lawrence Seaway and the Chicago Drainage Canal.

PAULLIN, C. O. *Atlas of the Historical Geography of the United States,* JOHN K. WRIGHT (ed.). New York and Washington: American Geographical Society and Carnegie Institution, 1932.
A basic reference on the territorial growth of the United States.

THOMAS, BENJAMIN E. "Boundaries and Internal Problems of Idaho," *Geographical Review,* XXXIX (1949), 99–109.
One of several studies of internal politico-geographic features in the United States.

TIMM, CHARLES A. "The International Boundary Commission—United States and Mexico." Austin: University of Texas Publication No. 4134, 1941.
A detailed study of United States–Mexican border problems.

"U.S.-Russian Convention Line of 1867." International Boundary Study No. 14, May 21, 1962. Washington, Department of State, Office of the Geographer.
Detailed map and description.

8

CANADA AND THE AMERICAN ARCTIC

● Northern Anglo-America is predominantly a pioneer area—one in which resource utilization is in a relatively early developmental stage. It is true that settlements have existed for over three centuries in Canada's Maritime Provinces and along the St. Lawrence waterway, and that fishermen, trappers, and traders have long worked in such areas as southern Greenland, the Pacific Northwest, and the coasts of Hudson Bay. Yet the fact remains that the economic and cultural expansion of the lands north of the United States has been primarily a twentieth-century phenomenon, and that resource utilization has increased markedly since World War II. The American Arctic was long a frozen barrier protecting the northern approaches to the United States and southern Canada. Trapping, fishing, and some mining were the principal activities pursued there. But in recent years this pattern has changed. The shortest air distances between the Soviet Union and Anglo-America lie across the north polar regions, giving rise to elaborate defense installations north of the Arctic Circle. Commercial aircraft cross the Arctic between Europe and the Pacific coast of North America. Geologists have found northern Anglo-America to be rich in mineral wealth and power resources which are gradually being developed, bringing people and transportation media to these recently empty areas. As has happened so often before in North America, the peopling of this region has been accompanied by demands for recognition of the political rights and the economic needs of the indigenous people of the north.

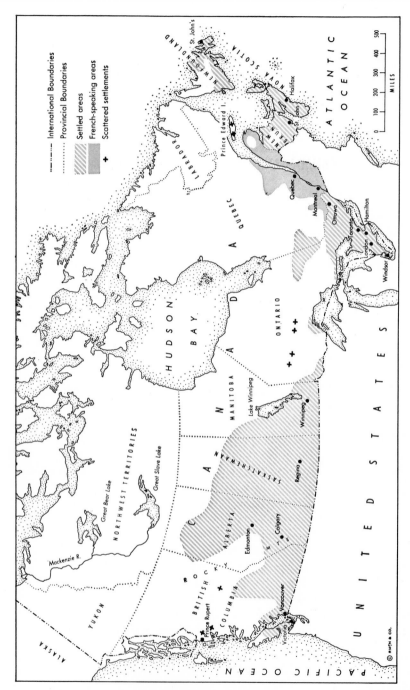

Figure 23. Canada.

CANADA

The Canadian State is not only the third largest in the world, it is also one of the richest in terms of natural resources. With a relatively small and highly efficient population, Canada enjoys one of the highest per capita incomes of any of the world's States. Yet the Canadians do not have the wealth to develop their resources, nor the home markets to absorb them. Canada has long maintained close ties with Britain, yet, because of trade ties, proximity, and the influx of United States capital, it is also strongly oriented toward the United States. Finally, Canada lies on the direct route between the United States and the Soviet Union. Its territory is close to that of the U.S.S.R., and with the Soviets it shares problems of polar development. Canada's greatest problem, perhaps, particularly since World War II, has been how to develop and assert its own individuality in a world of great powers and power blocs.

Physical Features

Canada has an area of over 3,800,000 square miles, throughout most of which there is a population density of less than one person per square mile. Over one-half of the population of 18 million lives within 100 miles of the United States border, and most of the remainder within 200 miles of it (Figure 23). Throughout two-thirds of Canada there are less than four months in summer when the average monthly temperature is above 50° F.; along the northern coast and on the Arctic islands is the tundra, a treeless area covered by grass and bushes, where no month of summer has an average temperature above 50° F. In northwestern Canada summers, although short, tend to be warm, permitting some agriculture, but in the northeast, because of the cold waters of Hudson Bay, summers remain cool, and in Quebec and Labrador there is little settlement more than 100 miles north of the St. Lawrence.

In Canada, as in the United States, distance and variations in the physical landscape are important centrifugal forces. The country measures 2,800 miles from north to south and over 3,300 miles east to west, and consists of several major physiographic regions—the Eastern Mountains, the St. Lawrence Lowland, the Canadian Shield, the Interior Plains, the Western Upland, and the Arctic islands. These regions are important not only because of economic diversity but also because of their effect on population distribution. The latter is particularly true with respect to the Canadian Shield, a 2-million-square-mile area of thin soils and generally poor agricultural potential, although the Shield is rich in minerals. Because of the scarcity of population and transport facilities throughout much of Canada, the difficulties of effective organization of these northern regions represent an important problem confronting the Canadian government and people.

Territorial Development

The development of control by the Canadian government over the vast territory may be studied from two approaches: the growth and unification of Canada itself and the evolution of Canadian independence from Great Britain. By the sixteenth century the Newfoundland fisheries were being utilized by Europeans, and landings had been made on the Newfoundland coast. The first actual claim was made in 1498 by John Cabot—a claim to English sovereignty over the east coast as far south as 34° north latitude. In 1534 Jacques Cartier reached the Gaspé Peninsula, which he claimed for France; he subsequently sailed up the St. Lawrence, visiting the sites of what are now Montreal and Quebec. Thus at an early stage the rivalry for control of Canada developed between Britain and France.

The country was settled during the seventeenth and eighteenth centuries by both French and British colonists. The British were largely in Newfoundland and at settlements in the Hudson Bay area; the French settled in Nova Scotia and the lower St. Lawrence Valley. Warfare between France and Britain in Europe was reflected in the New World by frequent skirmishes between the colonists. In 1713 France yielded to Britain her claims to Hudson Bay, Newfoundland, and Nova Scotia. Fifty years later, as a result of the British victory in the French and Indian War, all of Canada, with the exception of the two small islands of St. Pierre and Miquelon just south of Newfoundland, became the possession of Great Britain.

In its early years as a British colony Canada found it necessary to assimilate three diverse groups—Frenchmen, Scots, and American Tories. The 65,000 Catholic Frenchmen, proud of their language, religion, and customs, were determined to maintain their cultural identity in the new political area. The descendants of the Scottish Highlanders had migrated to Canada in the early eighteenth century as a result of an oppressive policy on the part of the London government toward Scotland. In 1763 these persons considered themselves the logical "heirs" to the new British colony. The third group comprised the approximately 40,000 American Loyalists who left the United States (particularly New England) at the close of the American Revolution and settled in Canada, especially in Nova Scotia, in what is now New Brunswick, and north of the Great Lakes–St. Lawrence waterway, betwen Detroit and Montreal. In 1791 the province of Quebec was divided into two new provinces, Lower and Upper Canada, the latter ultimately developing into the predominantly British province of Ontario, while the former (renamed Quebec) remains basically French in speech and culture.[1]

---

[1] For an excellent account of the political partitioning of Canada, see Norman Nicholson, *The Boundaries of Canada, Its Provinces and Territories* (Ottawa: Department of Mines and Technical Surveys, Geographical Branch, Memoir 2, 1954).

Canada's political unity was slow in coming. Not until 1867 did the area become a federated political region with a parliament of its own; at that time Ontario, Quebec, Nova Scotia, New Brunswick, and Prince Edward Island were joined together.

In Canada east of the Great Lakes, boundary evolution proceeded hand in hand with settlement and development. It was a comparatively slow evolution not only because it occurred in a period when transportation and communication were much less developed than they are today, but also because of the struggles between French and British over control of the area. If political stability in the northern half of North America was retarded by the alternations of French and British supremacy, these alternations did at least allow the political boundaries to evolve until they met the requirements of the populations involved.[2]

Two years later the Hudson's Bay Company relinquished control of the Prairie Provinces to the colonial government, and in 1871, upon the promise by the Ottawa administration to link the two coasts with a transcontinental railroad, British Columbia on the Pacific coast joined the federation. The inclusion of the last province, Newfoundland, illustrates the interesting point that the expense of government operations may be a critical factor in an area's capacity to exist as a self-governing political unit.

During Canada's development Newfoundland, together with Labrador, remained a separate British governorship. In 1926 Newfoundland was awarded dominion status, but eight years later the area found itself economically unable to continue the responsibilities of self-government. The island dominion, with few natural resources, was not involved in the great economic expansion Canada was beginning to undergo. Consequently Newfoundland voluntarily accepted a temporary end to its dominion status and inclusion within the British Empire as a special kind of colony. This return to colonialism was followed in 1948 by a general referendum among the people of Newfoundland to decide among three alternatives: continued colonial status for another five years, confederation with Canada, or return of dominion status as it existed prior to 1934. Proponents of confederation with Canada were successful in the balloting, and in March, 1949, Newfoundland, along with Labrador, became Canada's tenth province. There are few parallel cases in modern history of voluntary renunciation of independence by a country's citizens.

The modern Canadian State is divided politically into two parts, the northern territories and the ten provinces. Most of the region north of the sixtieth parallel consists of two federal areas, Yukon and the Northwest

---

[2] *Ibid.*, p. 117.

Territories. Only a few thousand persons live within this region, which comprises 42 per cent of the dominion. In January, 1962, it was decided that a new territory, to be known as the Mackenzie Territory, would be carved out of the Northwest Territories. Comprising about 45 per cent of the Northwest Territories, it will lie east of Yukon and contain much of the Mackenzie River Valley, the most populated and economically developed area of the Canadian north. In the remaining portion of the Northwest Territories the population is estimated at about 7,000, of whom 5,000 are Eskimos.

South of 60° north are the provinces, where the bulk of Canada's population is grouped in four main areas; the Maritime sector along the Atlantic coast, the upper St. Lawrence Valley and eastern Great Lakes region, the southern and central parts of the Prairie Provinces, and the Pacific coast. These areas are shown quite prominently in Figure 23. The second of the areas (consisting of southern Quebec and Ontario provinces) is the political and economic heart of the country, possessing nearly half the total population. Ottawa, located in this core area, represents a compromise capital between English- and French-speaking Canada, since it lies on the linguistic border between the two.

Population

Canada's population has grown from 2,750,000 in 1851 to over 18 million in 1961, an increase of nearly 600 per cent in a little more than a century. Since 1900 over 8 million persons have immigrated to Canada, most of them from northern and eastern Europe. The structure of the population by national origin in 1955 was approximately as follows: British and American, 48 per cent; French, 31 per cent; German, 4 per cent; Ukrainian, 3 per cent; others, 14 per cent (including about 75,000 Asians and 170,000 Indians and Eskimos). Religiously, Canada is divided into the following faiths: Protestant, 49 per cent; Roman Catholic, 43 per cent; others, 8 per cent. Since the majority of those of French descent retain the French speech and Catholic faith, there would seem to be a basis for national weakness. One Canadian writer has complained that the French-speaking peoples refer to themselves as "Canadien," to the rest as "les Anglais," while the English-speaking majority call themselves "Canadians" and the French-speaking portion "French-Canadian."[3] The French outnumber the English-speaking population only in Quebec Province; there the ratio is better than four to one. The birth rate of the French Canadians is higher than that of the English-speaking groups, and as a result the ethnic composition of Canada is gradually changing, for the French-speaking settlements are expanding into eastern and northern Ontario and northern New Brunswick.

[3] Hugh MacLennan, "The Psychology of Canadian Nationalism," *Foreign Affairs*, XXVII (1949), 417.

The fact that the French- and English-speaking peoples of Canada work together as well as they do is the result of several historical causes. In 1774 Britain's Parliament passed the Quebec Act, guaranteeing to the French Canadians freedom of religion, to preserve their own language, and to continue to practice civil law. This act still forms the basic framework within which the two linguistic groups exist side by side. There are actually few States in the world in which the language and culture of a large minority group have been so carefully protected as in Canada.

A second reason is that France has never tried to work through the French Canadians to undermine British (or Canadian) power, as, for example, the Germans worked through the Sudeten Czechs in 1938. Actually, there are few ties left between France and French Canada; France is in no way a champion of the French Canadians. Thus the French-speaking peoples of Canada represent one of the few minority groups which retain the culture of their former homeland but have severed most of the ties of sentiment and loyalty. Another cause for peaceful relations in Canada has been the remarkable tact and diplomacy displayed by Canadian leaders, among them the long-time Prime Minister, W. L. Mackenzie King, who skillfully managed to avoid head-on collisions between members of the two linguistic groups for over three decades. Finally, both French- and English-speaking Canadians are united in their determination to remain independent of foreign control. The concept of nation is thus quite a strong centripetal force in this country.

Achievement of Independence

Canada became a self-governing dominion only at the end of World War I. At the peace conference of Paris in 1919 the various dominions of the British Empire were accorded representation in the League of Nations as though they were independent States, but not until the imperial conference of 1926 were the dominions officially recognized as equal partners with Britain in the British Commonwealth. Their status of equality with Britain as freely associating members in the British Commonwealth was legally recognized in 1931 by the Statute of Westminister. The Canadians no longer refer to their country as a "dominion"; the Royal Style and Titles Act of 1953 allows each independent Commonwealth member to define its concept of relationship with the Crown. Canada is not a member of the Commonwealth sterling bloc, but retains preferential tariffs in favor of Great Britain and of most of the members of the British Commonwealth.

Canada's Economy

Agriculture, manufacturing, and the extractive industries (mining, lumbering, and fishing) are important aspects of the Canadian economy. In minerals and power fuels the country is unbelievably rich. Canada leads the world in the production of nickel, platinum, asbestos, and radium; stands second in zinc; third in copper, silver, and gold; and fourth in lead and cobalt. It is fourth in potential hydroelectric power, while its reserves of three other important commodities—iron ore, petroleum, and coal—are of vast and undetermined amounts. Canada has advanced to a position of eighth among the industrial nations of the world in terms of steel output. One of the principal facets of Canada's economy is that the State is a major supplier to the United States of industrial raw materials, such as nickel, asbestos, and wood pulp.

Much of the development of Canadian resources has been done in cooperation with the United States. In 1954, for example, a 360-mile railway was completed, linking the port of Sept Isles on the St. Lawrence with Knob Lake on the Quebec-Labrador boundary, where an enormous reserve of high-grade iron ore is being developed. The railroad was built largely with United States capital, and much of the ore will be shipped to steel plants along the United States shores of the Great Lakes to augment the diminishing supplies of iron ore in the Mesabi Range. In 1950 the United States and Canada concluded a treaty providing for considerable increase in the development of hydroelectric power at Niagara Falls, and four years later they agreed to the joint construction of the St. Lawrence Seaway, providing a channel with a minimum depth of twenty-seven feet connecting the Great Lakes with the Atlantic Ocean. As a measure of Canada's economic position, that country was prepared to develop the seaway by itself if the United States were unwilling to cooperate in the program. Finally, in 1961 the two governments concluded a treaty for the joint development of the Columbia River, which rises in the Canadian Rockies but flows through the United States before reaching the Pacific.

Agricultural development is limited by the short growing season, rough terrain, and infertile soils to about one-sixth of Canada's total area, of which less than half is actually in cultivation. Although these limitations are cited as obstacles to Canada's population growth, many experts agree that in the future the State could well support over 40 million persons. Canada is one of the world's leading producers of grains; the wheat crop alone averages over 600 million bushels a year. Like their American counterparts, Canadian farmers are often troubled by the existence of surplus crops, for which no markets can be found. Nearly 50 per cent of the land area is covered by forest, but only two-fifths of this are considered both productive and economically accessible. Over one-quarter of Canada's total exports by value consists of wood, wood pulp, and newsprint. In terms of fishing Canada borders on two prime fishing regions, the northwest Atlantic and the northeast Pacific. Canada's catch normally ranks it fifth or sixth among the countries of the world.

Canada's foreign trade is closely oriented toward the United States. In 1960 the United States accounted for 56 per cent by value of Canada's exports and 67 per cent of its imports, compared with the Commonwealth countries (23 and 16 per cent respectively) and the Common Market (6 and 5 per cent respectively). In addition to wood and wood products, Canada's principal exports include wheat, aluminum, uranium ore, nickel, copper, iron ore, asbestos, and fish. Thus Canada remains primarily an exporter of raw materials and an importer of finished goods (machinery, automobiles, electrical equipment, aircraft). In recent years there has been a fairly even balance between imports and exports.

Many of Canada's manufacturing plants are branches of companies in the United States, and Canadians are at times concerned over the extent of United States investments in their country. Nearly two-thirds of Canada's manufacturing, mining, petroleum, and forest industries are owned by United States companies. The home market is not large, and foreign-owned plants frequently do not plan to produce for export in competition with exports from the plants owned by the same companies in the United States. Thus, despite its potential wealth, Canada's rate of economic growth in recent years has not been high, and Canadians are acutely conscious of restrictions which have been or may be placed on freedom of trade, particularly that with the United States. The United States farm products disposal program (which affects Canada's sizable farm surpluses), restrictions on the imports of Canadian oil into the United States, and the constant threat of higher United States duties on lead and zinc are among the economic differences which exist between the two countries.

Canada as a Middle Power

In the years since World War II Canada and the United States have stood firmly together on the defense of North America against possible attack from the Eastern Hemisphere and on resistance to the spread of world Communism. The two States are joined together in NATO and in NORAD, the North American Air Defense Command, which is a binational air defense system under an American commander-in-chief with a Canadian deputy. The DEW line, an early warning system stretching east to west in the extreme Canadian north, was a joint construction project of the United States and Canada. Although financed by the United States, its operations are largely a Canadian responsibility. Farther south the mid-Canada radar warning line was erected and is maintained by Canada, while the Pine Tree line, just north of the United States border, was erected by the United States but is operated in part by Canadians.

Despite these cooperative efforts many Canadians have been concerned over what they feel is an undue attempt by the United States to force its policies upon Canada. They resent the Pentagon's apparent conviction that it alone is the final judge of what defense installations in Canada are necessary (including the suggestion that missiles with nuclear warheads be based on Canadian soil) and the dispatch of United States forces to any and all parts of Canada. More important, perhaps, is resentment of pressure for them to conform with United States foreign policy in such areas as Cuba or Communist China. When the United States government, for example, decided to impose an embargo on trade with Cuba, the Canadians did not follow suit, since the Canadian government felt an embargo would not achieve the necessary objectives. Canada, like Australia, has sold surplus wheat to Communist China. In seeking a "middle" course, where possible, in world disputes, Canada has been instrumental in the organization of truce agreements and in their supervision. Canada was one of the three states (along with Poland and India) chosen to man the commissions to supervise the agreements of the 1954 Geneva Conference on Indochina; it took a lead in the establishment of a United Nations Emergency Force during the Suez crisis, and Canada supplied one of the largest contingents for this force. Canadian officers were supplied for the United Nations Observer Group in 1958 in Lebanon, and Canadian contingents have also served with United Nations forces in the Congo since 1960. Discussing Canada's role as mediator, John Holmes wrote, "Some middle power had to be involved which could supply communications personnel and air force maintenance. Among those middle powers which habitually contribute to these peace-loving exercises, only a few such as India, Sweden, and Canada are normally able to provide the necessary technical base. The selection of middle powers to act in disputes is, of course, on an ad hoc basis. None of us would be accepted as impartial and disinterested in all circumstances."[4]

It is difficult for the Canadians to play what is, in effect, a dual role—as codefender of North America against the U.S.S.R. and as mediator for the United Nations. It is particularly difficult so far as relations with the United States are concerned, since many United States citizens, accustomed as they are to taking Canada's foreign policies for granted, tend to view deviations by Ottawa as a form of treason. "It is important to bear in mind, however, that countries can be united in a common purpose but differ over tactics. It is, in fact, differences over tactics rather than ultimate ends which have been and will undoubtedly continue to be the cause of dispute between our two countries."[5] With its economic strength and its close ties both to the United States and to the Commonwealth countries, Canada is ably suited to play the role of a middle power amid changing world relationships.

---

[4] John W. Holmes, "Canada and the United States in World Politics," *Foreign Affairs*, XL (1961), 114. Copyright by the Council on Foreign Relations Inc.
[5] *Ibid.*, p. 107.

THE AMERICAN ARCTIC

The sector referred to here as "the American Arctic" extends from roughly 15 to 170° west longitude and includes Greenland, northern Canada, the Arctic islands, and northern Alaska. It is a region of extremely sparse population, but one which has assumed increasing importance in terms both of defense and of resource use. Because of its new importance various questions of sovereignty claims have arisen in recent years.

Greenland

The Danish territory of Greenland has an area of approximately 840,-000 square miles and a population (1958) of 30,600, of whom 2,400 were Europeans and the rest Eskimos. The territory extends from 60° north latitude to nearly 84°, a point about 450 miles from the North Pole. Over three-fourths of the island is covered by a great mass of ice, in some places over 10,000 feet thick. Along the ice-free coast, particularly on the west, dwell the area's inhabitants, engaged for the most part in fishing.

The importance of Greenland to the world political pattern lies in its strategic location, both to trans-Arctic air routes and to the great-circle Atlantic route between Newfoundland and the British Isles (Cape Farewell at the southernmost tip of Greenland lies about 550 miles north of such a great-circle line). The United States air base at Thule in northwestern Greenland is 2,450 miles from New York and 2,800 miles from Moscow. Control of Greenland and its bases is an important element in global air strategy.

The island was settled by Icelanders shortly before A. D. 1000, and during the next two centuries a republic was maintained in southern Greenland. Norway gained control of the area in 1261 and maintained it until 1814, when Denmark was awarded possession. United States interest in Greenland was not particularly strong until April, 1940, when German troops invaded and conquered Denmark. A year later the United States assumed responsibility for the defense of Greenland. The island was subsequently used both as an intermediate stop for air flights across the North Atlantic and as an area for the collection of valuable weather information. In the latitudes above about 30° north most of the weather moves in a general west-east direction, and much of the weather phenomena affecting Britain and northwest Europe have their origin on the Greenland icecaps. The port of Gronnedal was also used as a base by the United States Navy in its North Atlantic operations. In April, 1951, the United States and Denmark signed an agreement providing for the joint defense of Greenland under the North Atlantic Treaty Organization.

Greenland's economy has been strengthened in the past few decades by new developments in the fishing industry. Instead of hunting for seals and walrus, many fishermen are now engaged in commercial fishing for mackerel, cod, and other species which have migrated northward in response to an apparent warming of the ocean waters. There are considerable reserves of low-grade coal in Greenland, lead and zinc have begun to be utilized, and the island is important as the world's major source for the mineral cryolite, used in the manufacture of metallic aluminum and of glass. Political developments have accompanied the growth of its economic and military importance. In 1953 Greenland became an integral part of the Danish realm with the same measure of self-government as the rest of Denmark.

Resource Development in the American Arctic

Economic resources in the American Arctic are severely limited by climate and inaccessibility. Growing agricultural products for export is virtually ruled out by the short growing season, and lumbering in the northern taiga is handicapped by the difficulties of getting the lumber to market. Trapping is important in northern Canada, and, to some extent, in northern Alaska, and there are valuable commercial fishing grounds off the west coast of Greenland. Mining has been carried on since the latter part of the last century in Alaska and northern Canada, starting with the gold operations in the Yukon and extending through oil production at Norman Wells on the Mackenzie River, gold mining at Yellowknife on Great Slave Lake, and the mining of radium and uranium at the town of Radium on Great Bear Lake. Defense needs and the development of economic resources in northern Canada are hastening the construction of transportation facilities in the former wilderness area, and scientists and engineers are becoming acquainted with the climate and other physical handicaps of the region. Airlines are being expanded, often utilizing planes equipped with pontoons or skis in the absence of prepared landing strips. Waterways flowing north to the Arctic Ocean, such as the Mackenzie River, now serve as important transportation routes, and there has been a marked increase in highway and railroad construction in sparsely settled areas of Canada during the past two decades. Research groups are investigating the effects of arctic cold on new types of clothing, shelter, lubricants, and paving material as a prelude to Canada's role as a major economic and military power.

The Arctic area is important both for sea routes and for air transportation. For centuries men have sought for a Northwest Passage across the top of North America, and in 1954 the first icebreaker journeyed from Davis Strait, between Greenland and Canada, to Bering Strait, separating Alaska from Siberia. Nuclear submarines have subsequently operated in this area in the interests of securing both scientific and military information.

Churchill, Manitoba, is a port on the southwest shore of Hudson Bay which is connected by rail with the Canadian wheat districts, and which serves in summer as a port for the shipment of grain through Hudson Bay and Strait and into the Atlantic Ocean.

The first commercial air route across the Arctic between Europe and the west coast of North America was instituted in 1954, connecting Copenhagen with Los Angeles. Subsequent routes have been established, and negotiations have been started for a Washington-Moscow air route which would pass across Greenland. Canadian airfields are now scattered about the northern sectors of the State, and a number of joint Canadian-United States weather stations have been established in the islands north of the Canadian mainland. With its generally good flying conditions, the Arctic should become increasingly important in terms of air travel between the two hemispheres.

Associated with commercial air travel, is, of course, the problem of defense. To the United States and southern Canada the Arctic is important in terms of early warning against enemy attack and of interception systems which might blunt or destroy such an attack. Mention has already been made of the radar networks stretching across Canada and of the joint continental air defense system. In addition to Canadian airfields, the United States maintains large air installations in Newfoundland (Harmon and Gander) and Labrador (Goose Bay) and on Baffin Island (Frobisher Bay). Air protection is further afforded from bases in Alaska, Greenland, and the northern United States. At Clear, Alaska, and Thule, Greenland, the United States maintains ballistic missile early warning system radars, while at Shemya in the Aleutian Islands is a radar installation used to monitor Russian missile tests.

Sovereignty Claims in the Arctic

The Canadian government claims sovereignty over all land areas in a wedge-shaped sector between longitudes 60° west and 141° west (the Canadian-Alaskan border) northward to the pole (Figure 24). The 60° border actually juts westward at one point where a portion of Greenland extends into this wedge-shaped quadrant. Canada apparently does not claim sovereignty over the waters of the Arctic Ocean beyond territorial limits, although in 1937 the Canadian government announced that Hudson Bay and Strait are regarded as territorial waters on the basis of historic sovereignty. The United States has made no claims to the sector north of Alaska, except with respect to President Truman's proclamation of 1945 that the resources of the seabed and subsoil of the continental shelf adjacent to the coasts of the United States and its territories are the property of the federal government. Denmark likewise makes no claims to the sector north of Greenland. Com-

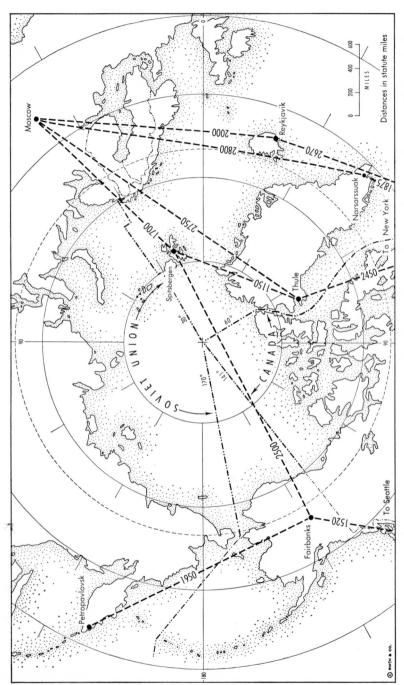

Figure 24. The Arctic Basin: Political Control and Major Air Bases. Spitsbergen, although it has no military installations, is shown because of its strategic location. Distances in statute miles.

menting on the status of sovereignty in Canada's arctic sector, Nicholson wrote, "it has recently come to take on added meaning with the possibility that large areas of sea ice may be used as airfields. If this becomes a reality then the question of sovereignty . . . will no doubt have to be examined, for it will have some of the aspects and uses of dry land."[6] Associated with this is the problem of ice islands on which technicians of the various Arctic countries have drifted over long periods of time, taking scientific observations. These islands often move from one sector to another, but apparently without causing international friction.

BIBLIOGRAPHY

CONANT, MELVIN. "Canada's Role in Western Defense," *Foreign Affairs,* XL (1962), 431–43.

A review of Canada's strategic defense role.

HOLMES, JOHN W. "Canada and the United States in World Politics," *Foreign Affairs,* XL (1961), 105–18.

Penetrating study of United States–Canadian relations.

JOHNSTON, V. K. "Canada's Title to the Arctic Islands," *Canadian Historical Review,* XVI (1933), 24–41.

Background material on sovereignty in the Arctic.

JONES, STEPHEN B. *The Arctic: Problems and Possibilities.* New Haven: Yale Institute of International Studies, 1948.

An interesting geographic evaluation of the area.

McGRATH, SIR PATRICK T. "The Labrador Boundary Dispute," *The Geographical Review,* XVII (1927), 643–61.

A comprehensive treatment of the Labrador-Quebec boundary dispute, including considerable historical data.

MILLER, E. WILLARD. "The Hudson Bay Railway Route: A Geographical Reconnaissance," *Journal of Geography,* LVII (1958), 163–73.

Map and description of this northern rail link.

NICHOLSON, NORMAN L. *The Boundaries of Canada, Its Provinces and Territories.* Ottawa: Department of Mines and Technical Surveys, Geographical Branch, Memoir 2, 1954.

Exhaustive study of Canadian internal and external boundaries.

---

[6] Nicholson, *op. cit.,* p. **48.**

REED, JOHN C. "The United States Turn North," *The Geographical Review*, XLVIII (1958), 321–36.

A discussion of American efforts in northern Canada, Alaska, and the Arctic.

RIGGS, THOMAS. "Drawing the Alaskan Boundary," *The Canadian Historical Review*, XXXVI (1945), 1–24.

Considerable historical detail on the boundary delimitation.

WOLFE, ROY I. "Transportation and Politics: The Example of Canada," *Annals of the Association of American Geographers*, LII (1962), 176–91.

An excellent analysis of the centripetal effects of transportation media on Canadian development.

9

LATIN AMERICA AND THE ANTARCTIC

● Latin America is an area in transition. It includes that portion of the
Western Hemisphere south of the United States,[1] a region roughly equal to
Anglo-America in size and population, although differing from it in the complexity of its political pattern and in levels of economic development. The
States of Latin America for nearly a century following the achievement of
independence underwent relatively little economic, social, and political
progress, and most of the area came under the dominant influence of the
United States. In recent decades, however, although legacies of the past still
remain in many regions of Latin America, powerful forces for change have
come into being in Mexico, Argentina, Cuba, Brazil, and other countries.
Because of the expanded circulatory systems, many people have become
aware of new ideas and new wants and have brought new political pressures
to bear both within and between the various States. Unlike the conditions
in much of Africa and Asia, the drive for political freedom from colonial
rule is not one of the compelling forces there; rather the pressures are for
more complex forms of freedom, such as freedom from starvation, from political oppression, from economic subvervience of one State to another, or
from overt or covert interference in a country's affairs by States located outside of Latin America.

---

[1] The area of Latin America is generally divided into two regions, *Middle America*, consisting of
the mainland countries from the United States–Mexican border south through Panama, as well as
the islands in the Gulf of Mexico and the Caribbean Sea, and *South America*, comprising the area
south of Panama. *Central America* (a part of Middle America), is the mainland area between
Mexico and Colombia.

PHYSICAL FACTORS

Location

The area of Latin America stretches from 32° north latitude to 56° south latitude, but the bulk lies in, or adjacent to, the tropics. Only in Chile, Argentina, and Uruguay does all or most of the national territory lie outside the tropical zone. Because of its location in the low latitudes, much of Latin America experiences a climate which has failed to attract large-scale white immigration, yet one in which tropical and subtropical crops, such as coffee, sugar cane, cacao, bananas, and cotton, can be produced for consumption by the peoples of Anglo-America and Europe. As a result of this, large amounts of foreign capital have been invested in agricultural production in Latin American countries, and the economies of these States have been closely linked with those of the States in the northern mid-latitudes.

The proximity of the United States to Latin America and the existence of ocean masses between the Western and Eastern hemispheres have aided in the maintenance of the United States' position of dominance in the Latin American area. Within recent years expanded facilities for the interchange of goods, people, and ideas have brought the United States into even closer contact with Latin America. These facilities, however, have also affected communications between the Western and Eastern hemispheres; as a result the relative isolation of Latin America, particularly from Europe, is breaking down, with an accompanying decline in the predominant position of the United States in Latin American affairs.

The location of eastern South America with respect to Africa and the south Atlantic is of significance in terms of the over-all defense of the Western Hemisphere against possible attack from the Eastern Hemisphere. The 1,800-mile distance across the Atlantic from Cape São Roque, in eastern Brazil, to Dakar, Senegal, represents the closest the Eastern and Western hemispheres approach one another. Military control of the northeast coast of South America clearly is important to the maintenance of power in the North Atlantic basin, and for this reason the United States and other major world powers have long been interested in the matter of political sovereignty over this vital coastal area. During World War II the United States maintained important military bases at Trinidad, Georgetown in British Guiana, and in the vicinity of Natal in easternmost Brazil. A major function of these bases was to forestall any possibility of an Axis foothold being secured in northeastern South America.

Surface Configuration

The surface configuration of Latin America is characterized by a series of young, rugged mountains, stretching from the United States through

Mexico and Central America, then along the west coast of South America to the southern tip (Figure 25). Few low passes exist through this mountain barrier, particularly in South America, but there are numerous inter- montane basins, some of which contain significant population concentrations. In addition to this mountain chain there are other important features, such as the plateaus and broad river basins in eastern South America, the coastal plains of Mexico and Central America, and the mountain arc which swings east from northern Central America to form most of the islands of the Caribbean. These features have considerable political significance to the individual States, particularly in terms of their effect on communications and population distribution. River valleys and lowlands about inland water

© RMcN

Figure 25. Latin America: Physical Features.

Figure 26. South America: Population.

bodies often serve as nuclei for settlement or as transportation links between populated areas. Highland regions may separate sectors of a country as in Colombia and the Dominican Republic, and thus act as centrifugal forces; on the other hand, because of special climatic advantages, they may serve as core areas for settlement, as in Guatemala and Costa Rica. Surface configuration is also important with respect to economic diversity. Ecuador was cited in Chapter 3 as a State in which the contrasts between mountain and lowland areas have resulted in economic and political differences, a situation which also exists in most other western Latin American States, such as Bolivia and Guatemala.

Climate

The predominance of tropical climates in Latin America has already been noted. Like surface configuration, climate has influenced the distribution of population and has contributed to regional differences within individual States. In Chile, for example, the aridity of the Atacama and the cool, humid conditions in the southern part have contributed to the concentration of over 90 per cent of the population in middle Chile—a potent centripetal force in that 2,600-mile-long country. The wet, tropical Amazon basin of Brazil, Argentina's semiarid Patagonian plateau, and the heat and humidity of the Caribbean coastal lowlands of Central America are other areas in which climate has been a dominant factor limiting settlement.

In Latin America, as in other parts of the world, economic diversity, reflecting climatic differences, can be either a centrifugal or a centripetal force within a country. Argentina may be cited as an example in which diverse economic areas are closely knit into a cohesive national unit.

POPULATION FACTORS

Size

The population of Latin America totals over 200 million persons. Of these, nearly one-half live in the "ABC" countries—Argentina, Brazil, and Chile—and some 50 million more inhabit Middle America. Birth rates are high; death rates are being drastically cut by the application of modern medical practices throughout much of the area. Latin America has one of the most rapidly growing populations in the world. One estimate places the population in the year 2000 at 373 million,[2] an increase of over 125 per cent in less than half a century. With the prospects of such a large population growth in coming decades, the countries of Latin America must prepare to expand greatly both their productivity and the means of distribution

[2] Preston James, *Latin America* (New York: The Odyssey Press, 1950), p. 770.

to satisfy a growing market, or else face mounting discontent, owing to a scarcity of food products and other consumer items.

Type

Three ethnic types have combined to produce the bulk of the Latin American population. These are the whites, the Indians (indigenous at the time of European colonization), and the Negroes (brought to Latin America by the Europeans as slaves). Mixed racial groups include mestizos (white-Indian), mulattoes (white-Negro), and zambos (Indian-Negro). In addition, there are, particularly in Brazil and Peru, people of Mongoloid stock, and East Indians in British Guiana and Trinidad. Of the total population, about one-third is mestizo, and about a quarter is white. Indians and Negroes each comprise slightly less than one-fifth. Whites predominate in Argentina, Uruguay, and Puerto Rico and are in a slight majority in Brazil and Costa Rica. The Indians constitute majorities in many of the western Latin American States and in Paraguay. The Negroes are concentrated primarily in the Caribbean area.

Racial distinctions in Latin America have not resulted in the strong interracial frictions which are characteristic of the United States. Racial interbreeding has long been common, although some Europeans have consistently attempted to maintain as much "racial purity" as possible. Economic class distinctions appear to be more stringent than those based on race or color. Latin Americans, as a rule, have little sympathy with the racial practices in the United States. In their anti-American propaganda beamed at the Latin Americans, the Communists have often played up anti-Negro sentiment in the United States; at the same time they accuse the United States of being "anti-Indian," a theme which finds some reception among the Indian-mestizo peoples of Middle America and western South America.

Distribution

Distribution and density of population vary widely from place to place. Some of the general aspects of the settlement patterns were mentioned under the heading "Physical Factors." In addition to such limiting elements as steep slopes, cold, aridity, and poor soils, inaccessibility and the prevalence of disease (particularly in the tropical rain forest) have also contributed to low population densities in various regions. On the other hand, there are certain environmental conditions which have served to attract settlement, such as the volcanic soils in the Central American highlands, the mineral deposits of Bolivia and northern Chile, and the oases of the Peruvian coastal desert. Only in Uruguay, El Salvador, and some of the island areas can the total national territory be said to be effectively occupied.

In an article entitled "The Distribution of People in South America,"[3] Preston James points out several characteristics of population distribution, all of which are applicable to the mainland nations of Middle America as well. Of these, the most important to a study of political geography is the observation that "each [population] cluster forms the core of effective national or state territory, and the boundaries, with few exceptions, pass through scantily occupied areas which separate the clusters."[4] In discussing this phenomenon, James suggests that the failure of the populations of the various republics to spread out and occupy effectively their national territory may be due in part to the fact that ". . . Throughout the four-hundred-odd years of European settlement . . . essentially the same modes have governed the process of living on the land."[5] In other words, the pattern of economic activities, established in the early agricultural and mining days, has not changed radically throughout most of Latin America, and the land which was not utilized in early colonial times remains today largely undeveloped. Practically all of Latin America was settled by penetrations from the coastal areas, so that the majority of population clusters and lines of transportation extended inland from the coast rather than parallel to it. The factors of distance and ease of communication between settlements are, of course, important to the forces of political cohesion within countries.

The nature of Latin America's population pattern has influenced the history of territorial control there, in that border disputes generally involve larger areas of land than is the case in many of the microterritorial problem areas of Europe and Asia, where the cultural patterns in frontier zones are more complex. Invariably little attention is paid to the wishes of the indigenous peoples in the case of boundary changes; the only major plebiscite ever scheduled for contested territory in Latin America was never carried out (see discussion of the Atacama area on page 194).

ECONOMIC FACTORS

The characteristic economy of the Latin American States is based on the production and export of agricultural goods or of minerals and petroleum. Many of the countries are dependent upon one or two basic commodities for the bulk of their exports, tying their whole economic structure to fluctuating world prices. Venezuela's petroleum, Colombia's coffee, Bolivia's tin, Cuba's sugar, Chile's copper and the bananas of Honduras represent situations where the national economy is particularly sensitive to the export of a single commodity. The predominance of a single market

---

[3] In *Geographic Aspects of International Relations*, pp. 217–43.
[4] *Ibid.*, p. 219.
[5] *Ibid.*, p. 231.

for the exports of many of the countries is evidenced by the fact that the United States normally takes over three-fourths of the exports (by value) of Colombia, Costa Rica, El Salvador, Guatemala, Panama, and Venezuela, and over 50 per cent of the exports of seven other countries.

There are both direct and indirect political consequences of such economic dependence. For example, the United States has heavy investments in such areas as Guatemala and Venezuela and is in a position to exert influence upon these countries' governments.[6] Likewise, the United States may be expected to resist any outbreaks of violence within these and other exporting countries, either of the internal type (riots, revolutions, attempts to destroy the political unity of the state) or of an external type (invasions, territorial wars), for such violence might endanger investments and the normal flow of goods. Attempts by third powers to disrupt these economic bonds by "capturing" some of the exports or by influencing the political and economic policies of the exporting Latin American states are also apt to be resisted strongly by the United States.

Latin America is rich in agricultural and mineral resources. Over one-half the world's coffee and commercially handled bananas are produced here, as well as between one-third and one-half of its cacao and sugar cane. These products form important items of export, along with beef, wool, hides, flaxseed, and citrus fruits. About 15 per cent of the world's petroleum comes from the area. Important minerals include tin, copper, bauxite, lead, vanadium, tungsten, quartz crystals, and industrial diamonds. There are large known reserves of iron ore in Brazil and Venezuela and smaller ones in Chile, Cuba, and the Dominican Republic. Only small amounts of the petroleum and minerals produced in Latin America are used locally; most of them are free to enter the world market. Unfortunately there is little coal in Latin America, and most of the water power potential is undeveloped —one of the major handicaps to the regions' economic development.

The process of industrialization has been slow and spotty. Brazil, Argentina, Mexico, and Puerto Rico are the four areas in which the greatest per capita development has occurred, but even these countries lag by United States or western European standards. Lack of industry has meant three things: first, that no Latin American state is capable of initiating or supporting a major war, since aircraft and heavy armaments cannot be produced in quantity; second, that minerals such as iron ore, manganese, industrial diamonds, and tin, which are important for modern industry, are available for export; and, third, that there has been little development of an industrial "middle class," an element which is generally important to the maintenance of stable, democratic governments. The Latin Americans are

---

[6] Conversely, Argentina, which carries on relatively little trade with the United States, has often pursued violently anti-American policies, one reason perhaps being that the economic system there has less to lose than in most other countries as a result of United States antagonism.

conspicuously either quite rich (the numerically small upper class) or very poor. Average annual incomes per capita throughout most of the countries are less than 20 per cent of those in the United States.

With improved circulatory systems throughout the Latin American states this widespread poverty can have strong political repercussions. Dynamic political groups (particularly the Communists) stand ready to capitalize on popular discontent—against the government, against major business concerns, or against the United States, which plays such an important role in the economic life of many of the republics. "Anti-Yankee" sentiments are quick to be aroused, and countermeasures, designed to reduce these sentiments, are difficult to carry out. Lack of economic diversity and industrialization, poor transportation facilities, unstable political conditions, shortage of capital—these are but a few of the long-term conditions which must be remedied if the annual income of the Latin American is to be substantially improved and his resentment against continued poverty removed. In some areas, such as Puerto Rico and Mexico, strenuous efforts are being made to combat these evils and considerable progress has been made. The United States, through various inter-American agencies, has also contributed to the improvement of economic and social conditions. Much more remains to be done, however. Until the average Latin American is assured that he can look forward to a substantially higher standard of living, he will remain prey to various utopian programs offered him as a means of attaining painlessly a more equitable distribution of wealth.

POLITICAL FACTORS

One of the outstanding characteristics of the political pattern of Latin America during the last century and a quarter has been its relative stability in terms of both national sovereignty and boundary locations. The large number of national political units and the ability of these units to maintain their independence over long periods of time are in sharp contrast with the turbulent conditions of political control which have existed in many other parts of the world since the early nineteenth century. This stability of the political pattern has persisted in spite of the revolutions and changes of administration which take place frequently within the national governments in many of the Latin American states. It also has existed in seeming defiance of internal centrifugal forces caused by the ethnic differences and scattered population patterns in many of the countries.

Various external factors are responsible for the relative permanence in the political pattern of this area. The Monroe Doctrine has had the effect of excluding from Latin America since 1823 much of the same type of colonial activities as have been carried on by European powers in Africa, Asia, and the Pacific basin. As a result, during the past century and a quarter the extension of the intra-European wars to the Western Hemisphere has been largely prevented. Coupled with this has been the development by the United States, particularly since the beginning of the twentieth century, of a "Pax Americana" policy with respect to the States of Latin America. Under this policy the United States has endeavored, wherever possible, to prevent conflicts from breaking out between the Latin American countries, primarily in order to protect foreign investments and to prevent the deterioration of United States influence in this area.

Some of the factors within Latin America which contribute to the stability of the political pattern have already been mentioned. Among these are the lack of population concentrations and of exploitable resources in the boundary areas, and the fact that in most of the Latin American States population totals are small and the national economies are at an early stage of development. Thus few of the countries possess the population and economic strength to wage sustained territorial war against their neighbors. Further, there has been little urge for territorial expansion in order to secure additional "living space." The lack of adequate transportation facilities between many of the neighboring States of Latin America has also served to reduce the possibilities of agressions.

Political History

The Colonial Period. The early explorations and conquests of Latin America were carried out largely by the Spaniards during the sixteenth and seventeenth centuries, except for that portion of South America east of 50° west longitude, where, according to the Treaty of Tordesillas (1494), Portugal was accorded the right to be the dominant power. The conquerors came originally in search of precious metals and stones, and many were accompanied by Roman Catholic missionaries, intent upon converting the Indians to Christianity. The whole pattern of early colonial life was based on a "get-rich-quick" concept, and even today throughout much of Latin America an atmosphere of speculation and quick profits remains. From the sixteenth to the nineteenth centuries the Spanish and Portuguese empires were divided and subdivided into administrative districts, the local boundaries of which were in a state of frequent change. When the States of Latin America achieved their independence early in the nineteenth century, many of the borders of these former administrative districts were taken to mark the international boundaries between the new countries. "The national idea . . . in Latin America got solidified into units whose size was determined by systems of communication and transportation that were available around 1800. By the next century, when methods of communication might have made a unified Spanish America possible the national idea had become so firmly implanted as to make any union seem utterly impractical despite its obvious advantages from every point of view except the maintenance of nationalism."[7] Thus the vestiges of early partitionings are of considerable importance to present political developments in this area.

Colonial efforts on the part of Britain, France, and the Netherlands in Latin America were confined largely to the Caribbean basin and the Guiana coast. Spain and Portugal remained important land powers down to the nineteenth century, but on the coastal lands and islands of eastern Latin America the sea power of the more northerly European nations became increasingly important after 1588 in establishing colonial possessions. One of the principal attractions of this part of the world lay in the products which could be obtained from the area, including sugar, tobacco, indigo, cotton, and dyewoods. Following France's defeat by Britain in 1763, some British statesmen viewed the transfer of the French colony of Martinique to Britain as preferable to British control of French Canada; and at the time of the American Revolution the British island of Jamaica, with its sugar, rum, and molasses, was said to bring more revenue to the mother country than did the thirteen American colonies.

Independence Movements of the Early Nineteenth Century. Achievement of independence among the Latin American States took place almost entirely during a twenty-five year period at the beginning of the nineteenth century, when much of Europe was embroiled in the Napoleonic Wars. In 1804 the government of Haiti declared itself independent of French control. Revolts against European domination were already breaking out in other parts of Latin America, and in the years following Haiti's declaration of independence many of the other colonies also won self-rule. In two cases political units were formed which lasted but a few years. The first was Gran Colombia, 1821–30, comprising Colombia, Venezuela, and Ecuador; the second was the Federation of Central America, 1824–38, consisting of the various Central American States (excluding Mexico). In each case centrifugal forces in the form of relief, differing histories, political leaders, and economic interests were eventually strong enough to break up the political units into separate parts.

One of the problems confronting the newly independent States of Latin America was the delimitation of their boundaries. The individual governments, at least in principle, agreed to accept the *uti possidetis* of 1810 as a basis for future negotiations on territorial disputes. *Uti possidetis* is a term which signified that the newly independent States were the successors of the former provincial units of the Spanish empire, within essentially the same territorial limits as existed at the time independence was established. The principle was also used to apply to the former Portuguese territory of Brazil. Because of the constantly changing pattern of the Spanish sub-

---

[7] Marsten Bates, *Where Winter Never Comes* (New York: Charles Scribner's Sons, 1952), p. 254. Used by permission.

divisions during that country's period of control in Latin America, definite determination of boundaries affected by the principle of *uti possidetis* was often extremely difficult and led to numerous controversies between the new States.

Many of the boundaries of Latin America were based on physical features, such as rivers, mountain crests, and drainage divides. It is far easier to determine boundaries such as these on a map than in the field, for when and if the time comes to demarcate the line all manner of disagreements may arise. Such problems as location of drainage divides, relation of towns to markets or water supply, or of farmers to their fields may prove to be far more complex than was anticipated when delimiting the border on the map. Many Latin American boundaries have never been completely demarcated. Unless population pressure or the utilization of resources demands it, they may remain indefinitely as vague zones of delimitation. "So long as the potential wealth of an area is imperfectly known, the contestant countries hesitate to have boundaries precisely defined lest they later discover that they abandoned valuable resources to a rival neighbor."[8]

Political Patterns Since 1838. In the years since 1838 only seven Latin American States have undergone a complete change in political status. In 1844 the Dominican Republic, at the eastern end of the island of Hispaniola, became independent of Haitian control. Fifty-four years later, at the conclusion of the Spanish-American War, Spanish sovereignty in Puerto Rico and Cuba was replaced by that of the United States. Puerto Rico remained a United States possession, while Cuba was eventually set up as an independent state, although with close ties to the United States (see page 187). In 1903 Panama, with assistance from the United States, broke away from Colombia and became the twentieth independent state in Latin America. In 1917 Denmark relinquished possession of the Virgin Islands to the United States for the sum of $25 million. Finally, in 1962, Jamaica and Trinidad became independent States within the British Commonwealth.

Territorial conflicts in Latin America since the early nineteenth century have been concentrated for the most part in a relatively few areas. Mexico, in the years from 1836 to 1854, lost over 700,000 square miles of territory to the United States. These losses were the result of both American territorial ambitions and centrifugal forces within Mexico itself, occasioned largely by the lack of contract between Mexico City and the country's northern regions.

In South America Paraguay and Bolivia suffered major territorial losses. Paraguay, after a disastrous five-year war (1865–70) against Argentina, Brazil, and Uruguay—during which approximately four-fifths of the country's male population was killed—saw its territory reduced by 55,000 square miles. An inland State, Paraguay has remained since then one of the poorest in Latin America. Bolivia's territorial losses to Chile and to Paraguay are described later in this chapter. Because of these losses Bolivia has been cut off from both the Pacific and from the Paraguay-Paraná river system in eastern South America. In addition, Bolivia in 1903 was forced to cede the rubber-rich Acre territory in the Amazon basin to Brazil, thereby cutting off the country's access to the Amazon. Thus Bolivia, like Paraguay, is a landlocked country, dependent upon the permission of neighboring States for its access to the sea.

There have also been a number of boundary disputes in Central America and northern South America and in the La Plata estuary between Argentina and Uruguay. These disputes generally have involved less territory than did the cases mentioned above, but some of them—for example, the controversy between Guatemala and Honduras over territory containing banana plantations—have never been settled to the mutual satisfaction of the interested States.

Unity and Diversity Within the Latin American States

The location of the national capital and its relation to other centers of population are important aspects of centrifugal and centripetal forces in the individual States. By studying political and population maps, the effects of location and the relative concentrations of populations in capital areas can be ascertained. In each of the countries of Latin America, with the exception of Brazil and Ecuador, the national capital is also the dominant city in terms of population. In Brazil, Rio de Janeiro and São Paulo, located 225 miles to the southwest, are both cities of over 3 million persons. In Ecuador, Quito, the capital, and Guayaquil, the Pacific port, also approximate one another in population (over 200,000 each). In both States this bipolarity operates as a centrifugal force. In Bolivia there are actually two capitals, Sucre, the legal seat, located in the eastern mountains, and La Paz, Bolivia's largest city, the *de facto* capital, on the Altiplano. In Nicaragua the capital, Managua, was selected as a midway point between two rival cities, León and Granada. As all three centers are located within a sixty-five-mile zone in the populous southwestern uplands, there is little divisive force operating between the urban centers.

Most of the Latin American governments have recognized the difficulties of maintaining political control over their national territories because of poor circulatory systems, and have attempted to remedy this by the construction of transportation routes leading out from the capital city. Ecuador had one railroad which travels over a tortuous route to link Quito with the Pacific coast. A second one from Quito to San Lorenzo on Equador's coast near the Colombian border has recently been completed. Bolivia has connected its population centers on the Altiplano at great expense and has constructed two links eastward to serve agricultural communities in the eastern mountains. Peru and Colombia are especially handicapped by the presence of towering mountains and deep valleys. Colombia has been working on a railway system which will greatly improve Bogotá's connections with population centers in the central and western parts of the nation. Buenos Aires has for many years been the hub of an extensive rail net spreading across the Pampas, with connections to many outlying sections of Argentina. The result has been a marked centralization of political and economic affairs in the Argentine capital.

Brazil. In terms of centrifugal forces the most complex of the South American States is probably Brazil—over 3 million square miles in area and stretching about 2,500 miles both in a north-south and an east-west direction. The distribution of population, the diverse relief, climate, and vegetation, the great distances and the lack of adequate transportation facilities, and finally the off-center location of the economic and political metropolises represent major forces of disunity. On the other hand, unifying factors include the use of a common language, a sparsely inhabited interior, and the absence of populated areas across the borders from western and northern Brazil.

The Brazilian State consists of several geographic regions. In the north is the Amazon basin, a lowland tropical rainforest region which contains two-fifths of the country's area but only about 6 per cent of its population. To the south of this basin is an extensive grassland, much of it rolling plateau, which stretches to the southern borders. This central interior area, like the Amazon basin, has attracted little settlement.

Northeast Brazil consists of a humid tropical coast and a dry interior upland. The Natal-Recife-Salvador area along the coast represents one of the core areas of the country; the population is slowly expanding into the dry interior as well. South of this region is the east-central plateau, averaging 1,000 to 3,000 feet in elevation. Within this area are located Brazil's two principal cities, as well as over half the State's population. Here, in the main core area, are well-developed transportation nets, as well as coffee, cotton, iron ore, hydroelectric power, industries, and other facets of Brazil's economic development. The plateau continues into southern Brazil, although in the extreme south it gives way to a low grassland region. In the Curitiba–Pôrto Alegre sector of southern Brazil is the country's third important population concentration.

The problem of tying such a large area together politically is handicapped by the great distances and by the lack of easy surface routes of travel. The Amazon is the only major river navigable for a considerable distance upstream from the sea, and it drains an area whose climate has not attracted white settlement. Many other rivers rise near the coast, but flow inland away from the Atlantic, or, if they enter the ocean, their course is interrupted by rapids close to the mouth. Early settlement was naturally along the coastal area, but much of this sector (particularly in the southeast) is backed by mountains which hinder communications with the interior. James noted the lack of natural transportation hubs in Brazil,[9] a factor which has tended to restrict the development of population clusters in the State. Railroads have been constructed at considerable expense to link various sectors of Brazil together, but the network is far from complete. Only the southeastern portion of the country could be termed well-served; from there, rail lines fan out north and west for about 500 miles, but there is no through line to the northeast coastal area, and most of the interior has no rail service whatever. Airlines are now being developed to make up for some of this deficiency.

Rio de Janeiro, with its magnificent harbor, easily dominates Brazil's foreign trade. Despite the existence of a mountain wall to the west, rail and highway transportation lines link the city with a large hinterland to the south, west, and north. Brazilian leaders have recognized the need for the country to turn its attention inland in order to develop the interior, however. A new federal district, Brasília, located over 500 miles northwest of Rio de Janeiro, the old capital, was inaugurated in April, 1960, and the transfer of all federal government departments and personnel is scheduled for completion by 1963. Moving the capital away from the southeastern core area in order to centralize it more in relation to the interior and the northeast may in time prove beneficial, but if the bulk of Brazil's population and wealth remain in the Rio–São Paulo area there will be a strong force there pulling away from the new capital.

Foreign Control in Latin America

Although most of the Latin American area consists of independent States, foreign control is exercised there by the United States, Great Britain, France, and the Netherlands. The United States has sovereignty over Puerto Rico, the Virgin Islands, and the Panama Canal Zone. The three European powers have territories on the Guiana coast of northeastern South America, and Britain also has sovereignty over British Honduras in Central America and the Falkland Islands in the South Atlantic. In addition, all three European States exercise control over various Caribbean islands.

Within recent decades there has been a trend toward reorganization of dependent territories in Latin America. Movements toward federation have taken place among some of the British possessions in the Caribbean (see page 192) as well as in the Dutch territories, and in the dependent areas of all four controlling powers increasing measures of self-rule have

---

[9] *Latin America*, p. 356.

been granted. In actual practice, however, the trend toward independence for colonial areas seems to be moving more slowly than in many parts of Asia and Africa. In 1954 representatives of the Latin American States adopted a resolution condemning colonialism in the Latin American area.

The position of the United States with respect to Latin America represents an interesting case study in power relations, for, in addition to the establishment of direct sovereignty, the United States has at times maintained various degrees of control of the protectorate type over individual Latin American States. Some aspects of the United States power position in Latin America are considered here.

Puerto Rico. Relations between the United States and Puerto Rico constitute a somewhat unusual variety of colonial control. The island of Puerto Rico has an area of 3,435 square miles and a population of over 2¼ million persons. Because of the high birth and relatively low death rates, this population is increasing at a current rate which would double the total every quarter-century. Much of Puerto Rico's relief is of such rugged character as to handicap agriculture, and there are no known minerals to be profitably exploited on the island. Much of the agriculture is geared to commercial crops, such as sugar cane and tobacco, for which there is generally a higher cash return than is the case with production of food for local use. A land tenure system which permits considerable absentee land ownership also adds to the economic woes of Puerto Rico. On the other hand, the brightest spot in the island's economy has been the concerted effort toward industrialization, together with a government-sponsored land reform system which is breaking up many of the old estates. American industries in particular are attracted to Puerto Rico by the absence of income and other taxes, and by the availability of hydroelectric power and cheap labor supplies. Despite this, however, the problem of a dense population and of competition with neighboring areas for export markets continues to work against Puerto Rico's economic advancement.

After the United States assumed control over Puerto Rico in 1898, the political status of the area was diminished, for the United States Congress failed to recognize the same degree of autonomy for Puerto Rico that it had experienced under Spanish rule. Not until 1917 were the people of Puerto Rico awarded United States citizenship. By the end of World War II political groups in Puerto Rico were divided in their views concerning the island's future political status—complete independence, statehood, or commonwealth status. The advocates of commonwealth status were victorious in the elections of 1948, and four years later Puerto Rico was officially established as a commonwealth of the United States.

Under the terms of the commonwealth arrangement Puerto Rico became free to manage its own local affairs, although defense and foreign relations are still conducted by the United States. Puerto Rico has closer bonds with the United States than do the British Commonwealth members with the United Kingdom, for in the latter instance defense and foreign affairs are handled by the countries themselves.

There is apparently little pressure for independence in Puerto Rico, largely for economic reasons. Under the commonwealth system Puerto Ricans are free to emigrate to the United States. Thousands each year take advantage of this opportunity, the majority of them going to New York City. In Puerto Rico, as in Newfoundland, independence has been rejected by the voters because of the economic advantages to be gained by a political union with a larger country.

Cuba. The island of Cuba, lying to the south of Florida, has an area of 44,218 square miles and a population of close to 6 million. Unlike Puerto Rico, Cuba is not densely populated, and its agricultural potential is high. Much of the land is level or gently rolling, and about one-third of Cuba is in cultivation. Sugar cane is Cuba's principal crop—a product which in the past has found a large market in the United States.

A former Spanish colony, Cuba was under United States control from 1898 to 1901. Accompanying the proclamation of Cuba's independence in 1901 was the Platt Amendment, granting the United States the right to maintain coaling and naval bases on Cuban soil and to intervene in internal affairs "for the preservation of Cuban independence . . . for the protection of life, property, and individual liberty." This right was exercised in 1906, 1912, and from 1917 to 1922.

As a result of the Platt Amendment and of Cuba's economic position

Figure 27. Cuba and the Caribbean.

relative to the United States, the island existed in a protectorate type of status from 1901 until the development of the United States "Good Neighbor" policy in the mid-1930's. Even after the abrogation of the Platt Amendment Cuba continued in a position of economic dependence upon the United States. In 1958 the United States took over half of Cuba's sugar crop and provided three-quarters of Cuba's export earnings. American investments in Cuba totalled over $1 billion and included public utilities, agriculture, mining, petroleum, and manufacturing enterprises.

In July, 1959, after General Batista had been overthrown, and the leader of the revolutionary forces, Fidel Castro, was installed as premier. Dr. Castro immediately set out on a program of land redistribution and of a gradual change-over of Cuba's economy to one of socialism. Within a few months of his coming to power his government embarked on a violent anti-United States campaign. American agricultural enterprises in Cuba were seized without recompense, and as the United States in retaliation began cutting down on its imports of Cuban sugar, Castro turned more and more for economic support to the Soviet Union. Diplomatic relations between Cuba and the United States were ultimately severed, all Cuban exports to the United States were banned, and the Communist countries became Cuba's major trade partners. By 1961 the Soviet Union and the countries within its east European sphere, together with Communist China, accounted for over three-quarters of Cuba's sugar exports.

The abrupt change in relations between the United States and Cuba brought with it the fear on the part of the Americans that Communist influence in Cuba would endanger other countries of Latin America. The Cuban government became increasingly Marxist in nature and in its pronouncements, and in April, 1961, there was an unsuccessful attempt by a Cuban exile army to land on Cuba and start a countermovement against Castro. The United States was deeply committed to this undertaking, having aided in training the soldiers and provided naval cover for the landings. The failure of the attempt was a serious blow to American prestige, both because this was clearly an attempt to interfere with the internal affairs of another State and because, through faulty intelligence, poor management, and lack of adequate supplies and air coverage, the action was a complete failure. Since that time the United States has sought to bring pressure on Cuba through a ban on all trade between that country and the United States and through the Organization of American States to isolate the Cuban government diplomatically and if possible economically.

By the fall of 1962 the Soviets had built missile bases in Cuba with a potential of striking many areas in the United States and in Middle and northern South America. The United States imposed a naval quarantine on the shipment of arms to Cuba, and under threat of invasion of Cuba by United States forces the Soviets agreed to dismantle the bases and remove the missiles from Cuba. Thus the Cuban government has in a sense become

then brought on the United States to abandon its gigantic Chaguaramas naval base on the northwest corner of the island for use as the site for a capital. Ultimately an agreement was worked out whereby the United States abandoned much of the land it had acquired throughout the Caribbean in 1941 for use as bases, but retained most of the Chaguaramas base for use until 1977.

Despite the careful planning for an independent West Indies Federation the project foundered in September, 1961, less than nine months from its scheduled independence, when in a popular referendum 54 per cent of the people of Jamaica voted to withdraw from the federation. With half the land area and half the population of the federation, Jamaica was to have 30 of the 64 senatorial seats. The island has enjoyed full internal self-government since 1959, and in August, 1962, complete independence was granted by Britain.

With its high population density (over 350 persons per square mile) and an annual population increase of close to 3 per cent, Jamaica faces a difficult economic future; thousands of Jamaicans have emigrated to Britain to find work. The island's principal advantages are its enormous bauxite deposits which are being worked, its program for industrialization which includes income-tax concessions and duty-free importation of plants and equipment, and its growing tourist industry. Jamaica's economic potential appears better than that of the other federation members with the exception of Trinidad, and the fear of large-scale emigration to Jamaica from other islands once independence was achieved was a factor in the Jamaicans' decision to withdraw from the federation program.

In August, 1962, Trinidad, having the highest per capita income of the federation, also achieved independence within the Commonwealth, together with the nearby island of Tobago. The two islands have a combined population of over 800,000, but Trinidad's oil and asphalt, together with sugar and rum industries, give the new state a firm base for economic viability. This has left Barbados, together with the various colonies of the Leeward and Windward islands, as the remaining units of the federation. These islands have a combined area of less than 1,500 square miles and a population of 725,000, of whom 30 per cent live on Barbados. Principal exports are sugar, bananas, cotton, and spices; in 1956 the value of exports from these islands came to about $35 million. Nevertheless, a new federation is planned with independence set for 1964. The capital will be in Barbados, the easternmost of the islands. Without Jamaica and Trinidad the new State will face serious economic difficulties and will, for the foreseeable future, be heavily dependent on outside aid.

The break-up of the West Indies Federation points up some of the difficulties of uniting separate political units into a larger State. The principal centripetal force was the British government, which sought to create as economically viable an independent State as was possible in the

Caribbean. Both British Guiana and British Honduras refused from the start to take part in plans for a federation, partly because of their fears of extensive migration of the islanders to the mainland. Although the sea offered the means for communication, there was little incentive for inter-island circulation. Ultimately the "provincialism" of Jamaica and of Trinidad and Tobago disrupted the federation.

TERRITORIAL PROBLEMS

The ability of a capital to control outlying areas can, of course, be demonstrated by the degree of political unity of the country concerned. With the exception of Panama's separation from Colombia in 1903, no State of Latin America since 1844 has had one of its sectors detach itself from the capital's control and become independent. Peripheral areas, however, have been detached from one country and joined to another, often with accompanying wars. In this section Latin America's major territorial conflicts of the past seventy-five years will be considered.

The Atacama

One of the most serious territorial disputes which has taken place in Latin America involved Chile, Peru, and Bolivia in a contest over the northern Atacama Desert area (Figure 29). This dispute was particularly significant, not only because of its violence and of the major territorial changes which followed it, but also because it proved to be one of the few territorial wars of modern times which ultimately was a financial success for the aggressor nation.

Prior to the late 1870's Peru controlled the northern Atacama, including the port of Arica, with its nearby oasis of Tacna. Bolivia had sovereignty over the central sector of the desert, while the southern portion was Chilean territory. The Atacama had been relatively unimportant economically, except for some silver and copper mining and a few coastal ports, but after 1860 the exploitation of the desert's sodium nitrate deposits led to a wild scramble for control of the territory. Both the Chileans and Peruvians were active in developing the nitrates, which had world-wide demand for use as fertilizers, while the Bolivian government was interested in collecting taxes on mines operated by Chilean and Peruvian organizations within Bolivian territory.

Ill-defined boundaries and the opportunity for quick profits inevitably led to conflict. In the bitter War of the Pacific (1879–84) Chile attacked Peru and Bolivia and eventually was victorious. As a result Bolivia lost control of its coastal province, including the port of Antofagasta (Bolivia's only outlet to the ocean), and Chile's northern border was extended 350

Figure 29. The Atacama. (After Borchard, Foreign Affairs, I [Sept., 1922]. Copyright by Council on Foreign Relations, Inc., New York.)

miles along the Pacific coast to the port of Arica. Thereafter the nitrate deposits were entirely within Chilean territory, and for the next thirty years —until the development of a method of recovering nitrogen from the air— Chile realized enormous profits from the export of nitrates from the Atacama. Bolivia, cut off from the sea, was in a serious position, since the country's economy is dependent upon the export of minerals. Eventually the Chilean port of Arica was made a free port for Bolivia's foreign trade. By the terms of the treaty ending the War of the Pacific, a plebiscite was eventually to be held in the Tacna-Arica area to determine its ultimate disposition between Chile and Peru. For over four decades, however, Chile refused to permit the plebiscite, and relations between Chile and Peru became severely strained. Finally, in 1929, as a result of strong diplomatic pressure from the United States, the Tacna-Arica area was divided, with Tacna reverting to Peru.

The Argentine-Chilean Boundary

This second dispute is noteworthy, not only because of the friction it engendered between neighboring States, but also because of the careful treatment given in the final arbitration award to the problem of ambiguous geographic terminology. The Andes Mountains form what seem to be an ideal natural boundary separating Chile from Argentina; only in the extreme south are they sufficiently low to form an ineffective barrier range. Article 1 of the 1881 treaty between Chile and Argentina states, "The frontier line shall run . . . along the highest crests . . . which may divide the waters, and shall pass between the slopes which descend on either side."[12]

Unfortunately, the line joining the highest crests of the Andean cordillera does not always divide the watersheds. Particularly in the southern sector of the boundary, some westward-flowing rivers have eroded their valleys headward to a point where they drain areas well to the east of the line connecting the highest crests. The Chileans claimed that the term "highest crests" should be construed to mean only those highest crests which divided the waters; between such crests the boundary should naturally follow the watershed division. Argentina, on the other hand, maintained that "highest crests" meant just that, regardless of drainage divides. Both Chile and Argentina prepared for war, but eventually they agreed to submit the dispute to the Queen of England, and in 1902 a settlement was reached. In gratitude for the averting of war, the peoples of Chile and Argentina erected a colossal "Christ of the Andes" statue in Uspallata Pass, the main route through the mountains between Buenos Aires and central Chile.

The Upper Amazon

One territorial dispute which has not been completely settled concerns the upper drainage basin of the Amazon, where the borders of Colombia, Ecuador, and Peru meet (Figure 30). Although the international boundaries in the northern sector of the Amazon basin generally follow drainage divides, this is not the case in the western part of the basin. During colonial times Spanish explorers crossed the Andes from the Pacific coast, moving downstream along the Amazon tributaries, and the boundaries of the Peruvian viceroyalty were extended several hundred miles east of the watershed dividing the Atlantic and Pacific drainage areas. The most direct route

---

[12] Quoted by S. Whittemore Boggs, *International Boundaries*, p. 86. For a full discussion of this controversy see this work, pp. 85–93; also Gordon Ireland, *Boundaries, Possessions and Conflicts in South America* (Cambridge, Mass.: Harvard University Press, 1938), pp. 17–27; and Sir Thomas Holdich, *The Countries of the King's Award* (London: Hurst and Blackett, 1904).

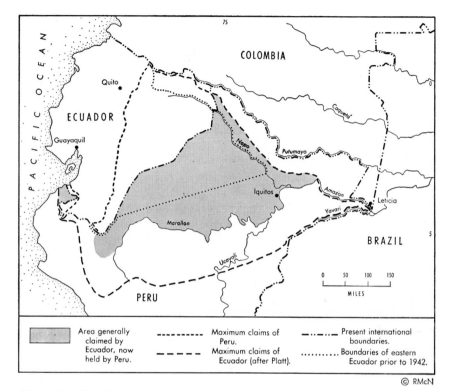

© RMcN

Figure 30. The Upper Amazon. (Adapted from Bowman, *Foreign Affairs*, XX [July, 1942], copyright by Council on Foreign Relations, Inc., New York; and Platt in *Geographic Aspects of International Relations*, ed. Colby, The University of Chicago Press, copyright 1938 by The University of Chicago.)

from Spain's western settlements to the upper Amazon lay across the mountains (at an elevation of over 10,000 feet) through Quito to the main headwaters of the Amazon. The difficulties of this route, however, were increased by the presence of hostile Indians, and gradually a Spanish route was developed from Lima, Peru, eastward across the mountains to the Ucayali River, which is navigable for a considerable distance upstream from its confluence with the Amazon.

As in other sectors of South America, international boundaries in this area were extremely obscure at the time of independence for the countries. Under Spain, title over the disputed upper Amazon basin area was established with the provincial government at Quito, and this jurisdiction was recognized as having passed to the Ecuadorian State after the winning of independence. Although Ecuador continued its claim to the upper Amazon region on the basis of historical jurisdiction, its sovereignty was challenged by Peru and Colombia. During the nineteenth and early twentieth centuries, Peruvian settlers moved down the Ucayali to establish the river port of Iquitos and develop other parts of the upper Amazon basin, while Ecuador, despite its more direct access to the region, did little to colonize what it claimed was the eastern sector of the Ecuadorian nation. After 1900 Peru took active steps to extend jurisdiction over the upper Amazon basin. Eventually these actions led to complications with both Ecuador and Colombia.

Colombia in 1927 agreed to recognize Peru's claims to what had been eastern Ecuador. In return Peru ceded to Colombia a strip of territory in the disputed area, by means of which Colombia's border was moved southward to the Amazon River, giving it control over the port of Leticia. The solution was mutually satisfactory, for Peru's claims to the territory were strengthened and Colombia acquired navigation rights on the Amazon.

The principle of *de facto* control of what used to be eastern Ecuador was demonstrated by the Peruvians who effectively settled the area. In 1942 this control became *de jure,* for Ecuador officially relinquished claims on territory as far upstream on the Amazon tributaries as is navigable to launches—territory containing about 77,000 square miles. By such action Ecuador lost contact with the Amazon River. Peru now claims all of the territory east of the Andes still controlled by Ecuador, again on the basis of settlement, but the Ecuadorian government has remained adamant in its refusal to accede to these demands. In fact, in October, 1960, Ecuador revived the dispute over what had been its eastern territory claiming that the 1942 agreement had been imposed under duress and was therefore null and void. The Peruvians, on the other hand, have been pushing work on a northern trans-Andean highway to link the Pacific with the Maranon River, a tributary of the upper Amazon, thereby opening its northeastern area to greater settlement and economic development.

The Chaco

A territorial dispute which led to a bloody war between Bolivia and Paraguay involved the northern portion of the Gran Chaco, lying north of the Pilcomayo River and west of the Paraguay River (Figure 31). Bolivia's claims to this area were based on the principle of *uti possidetis,* for the original Spanish division of Bolivia had jurisdiction eastward to the Paraguay River. On the other hand, Paraguay claimed the area as hers by virtue of early exploration and settlement. Treaties attempting to divide the northern Chaco between the two countries had been signed in 1879, 1887, and 1894, but none of them had been ratified by both States. In 1932 war between Bolivia and Paraguay broke out, and despite the best efforts of the League of Nations and other international bodies, continued for three years, until both countries were exhausted and a mediation was effected. Paraguay received about three-fourths of the northern Chaco area, although the contested portion of the Andes foothills, containing known oil reserves,

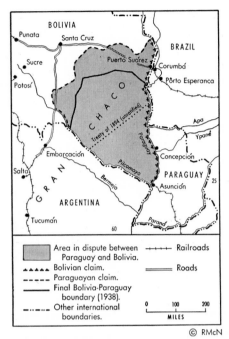

Area in dispute between Paraguay and Bolivia.
▲▲▲▲▲ Bolivian claim.
- - - - - Paraguayan claim.
——— Final Bolivia-Paraguay boundary (1938).
—··—··— Other international boundaries.
+—+—+ Railroads
═══ Roads

0   100   200
MILES

© RMcN

Figure 31. The Chaco. Note the extreme use of rivers to mark boundaries. (After Schurz, *Foreign Affairs,* VII [July, 1929]. Copyright by the Council on Foreign Relations, Inc., New York.)

remained with Bolivia. At Paraguay's insistence Bolivia was effectively blocked from utilizing the Paraguay River route to the Atlantic when it was forced to relinquish control of the west bank of the river to Brazil.

Promises of extensive oil reserves in the Chaco have never materialized, and despite the three-year-long conflict (1932–35) for its control, the region remains of little economic value even today. Throughout the practically level area precipitation is seasonal and erratic; the western portion is both too arid and too remote for the development of an extensive grazing economy, while much of the eastern part is subject to widespread floodings. Unlike the War of the Pacific, the Chaco War was a bitter contest for a practically valueless prize.

British Honduras

The most serious territorial controversy in Middle America concerns Guatemala and British Honduras (Figure 32). Early British claims to what is now British Honduras were based upon exploration and occupation, although the first British inhabitants of the area were mostly pirates and logwood cutters. In the latter part of the eighteenth century Spain granted certain rights to British settlers along this part of the coast, but continued to maintain its rights to sovereignty over the area, and Britain continued to recognize this sovereignty even after Mexico and Guatemala had won their independence from Spain. During the nineteenth century Spain refused to discuss sovereignty claims with Britain. Guatemala as early as

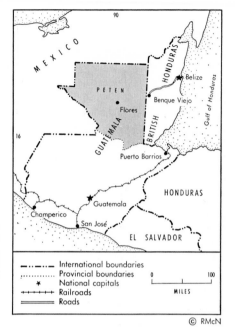

Figure 32. Guatemala and British Honduras. Note the isolation of Petén. (After Harrison-Church, *Modern Colonization,* Hutchinson's University Library and Longmans, Green & Co., 1951. Used by permission.)

the 1820's laid claims to the British-occupied region, however, on the grounds that Guatemala was the rightful heir to all lands which had been under Spanish control between Mexico and the El Salvador and Honduras borders.

Despite the disputed sovereignty over British Honduras a treaty was signed by Great Britain and Guatemala in 1859, defining the international border as that which existed previous to January 1, 1850, and signifying the intentions of the signatory powers to cooperate in the construction of a road from Guatemala City to the Atlantic coast. The road, however, was never constructed, and a British offer to Guatemala of £50,000 in discharge of Britain's obligations for its sector of the road was not accepted within the agreed time limit by the Guatemalan government.

Since 1933 Guatemala has pressed her claims for the "return" of British Honduras to Guatemalan control. These claims are based on more than legalistic maneuvers. British Honduras effectively shuts off the Guatemalan department of Petén, covering one-third of the country, from ready access to the Caribbean. Petén occupies the northern lowland of Guatemala and has few communication links with the highland sector of the country to the southwest. Its normal outlet would seem to lie eastward to the Caribbean, but this route is blocked by the British colony.

In the decade of Guatemala's left-wing government (1944–54) there were indications that the dispute might eventually develop into some forcible expression of Guatemalan nationalism, but since then there has been little active controversy over this question. Britain has constructed the promised road from Belize westward to the Guatemalan border, but no connecting roads have been built in Petén. The political and economic situation might be aided by the improvement of port facilities at Belize, capital of British Honduras, and the designation of its harbor as a free port for Guatemalan products. British plans to give eventual independence to the colony of British Honduras (with a 1960 population of 90,000 compared to Guatemala's 3,760,000) has led to increased Guatemalan bitterness and a request that the United States mediate the dispute between Guatemala and Britain.

Other Disputes

A border dispute between Honduras and Nicaragua along their Caribbean coast was submitted to the International Court of Justice in 1958. The area involved, measuring about 7,000 square miles and inhabited largely by the Mosquito Indians, is a sparsely settled tropical forest region fronting the Caribbean for 150 miles and extending inland about 175 miles as a wedge between the two states. It is bordered in part on the north by the Patuca River and on the south by the Coco River. There have been some indications that oil might be found in the disputed area; otherwise at the present time it is of very little economic value to either state. In 1906 the King of Spain, who had been asked to arbitrate a dispute over sovereignty in this area between Honduras and Nicaragua, awarded the territory to Honduras. Nicaragua refused to accept the decision, and in the intervening years both Nicaraguan and Honduran settlers moved into the area. The decision by the two governments to take the dispute to the International Court was made at the suggestion of the Organization of American States, and the subsequent award was in favor of Honduras. Nicaragua's acceptance of the Court's decision has ended one of the long-standing boundary controversies of Central America. In line with this agreement the government of Honduras has been pressing the United States to cede the two tiny Swan Islands, about 100 miles off shore in the Caribbean to the north of the area disputed with Nicaragua. The islands have been claimed by Honduras since 1921. They are virtually uninhabited except for United States citizens who work there in connection with a weather station and a radio station, the latter used to transmit news programs to Cuba by Cuban exiles.

In the southwestern Atlantic controversy over the Falkland Islands has involved Argentina and Great Britain. Although the islands were claimed by Argentina at the time of its independence, Britain landed troops on the Falklands in 1833 and declared them to be British territory. The local population was forced to emigrate to Argentina, and in time Britain developed the area into a major naval, coaling, and wireless station. In the years since World War II Argentina has revived the issue of sovereignty over the Falklands, the Argentinians insisting that Britain occupied the islands illegally over a century ago and should therefore evacuate them in

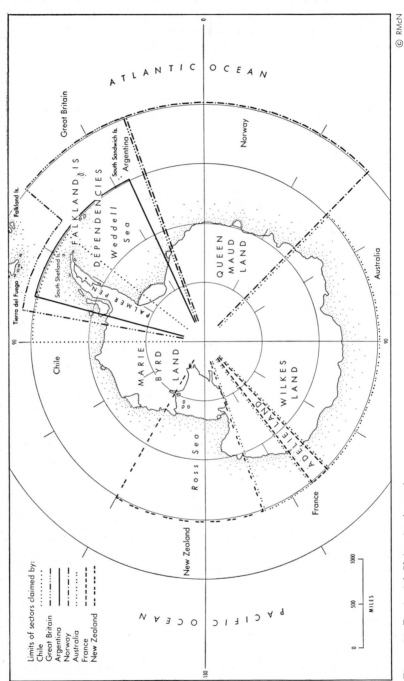

Figure 33. Territorial Claims in Antarctica.

favor of their rightful owners. This dispute has perhaps less potential for trouble than have the Guatemala–British Honduras and the upper Amazon controversies, though it would certainly add to Argentina's prestige if the country were successful in dislodging Britain from the area.

Rival Claims in Antarctica

The Antarctic continent, with an area of over 5 million square miles, has, until recently, been completely uninhabited. There are no known areas in which plant life of any kind can exist. Mineral and fuel deposits are still largely unknown, and the entire continent is of little economic consequence. Bases for fishing fleets are not located on the Antarctic mainland itself but on nearby island groups, such as the South Sandwich and South Orkney islands and Deception Island. The only present value the area would seem to possess is in connection with weather stations, since Antarctica is of importance to meteorologists in making long-range weather forecasts.

The prospects of the future economic and military value of Antarctica, however, have led to announcements of territorial claims by various States since the beginning of the twentieth century. Each of the claimants has resorted to the use of polar sectors, the various boundaries of which radiate out from the South Pole (Figure 33).

Within recent years disputed territorial claims on this barren area have led to incidents which might easily have precipitated armed conflict. In 1925 Argentina laid claim to a sector south of the western Atlantic and of South America, despite the fact that this sector was part of an area which had previously been designated as the Falkland Island Dependencies by the British. In 1940 Chile also claimed a sector of Antarctica, although much of it coincides with the region claimed by Argentina.

The British, French, Norwegian, and Australian claims to sovereignty are based for the most part on the principle of discovery, although in the case of the Falkland dependencies there is some controversy as to the nationality of the captain who first sighted the mainland there. On the other hand, Argentina and Chile base their demands for sovereignty on the grounds of effective occupation. The Argentinians have operated a weather station on an island close to the mainland since 1904, and the Chileans have had a whaling station on Deception Island since 1906, although neither establishment was actually on the Antarctic mainland. In more recent years, however, both Chile and Argentina have begun to operate year-round weather stations on the Antarctic mainland itself, thereby fortifying their respective claims to effective occupation. The British also have a year-round weather station on Palmer Peninsula within the sector claimed by all three contesting nations.

During the 1957–58 International Geophysical Year various countries of the world took part in cooperative scientific studies of Antarctica, and in December, 1959, an Antarctic Treaty was signed by twelve States,[13] providing for a thirty-year moratorium on territorial claims in all the area south of 60° south latitude, except the high seas. "No activities taking place while the present Treaty is in force shall constitute a basis for asserting, supporting or denying a claim to territorial sovereignty in Antarctica; no new claims, or enlargement of an existing claim . . . shall be asserted while the present Treaty is in force."[14] The treaty establishes Antarctica as an area to be used exclusively for peaceful purposes, for international cooperation in scientific investigation, and for the preservation of living resources of the area. Nuclear explosions and the dumping of radioactive wastes are prohibited, and a mutual inspection system is set up to prevent military activities. Any signatory State has the right to appoint observers with complete freedom of access to all areas and installations in Antarctica to carry out inspections for military activity, and complete exchange of scientific information is guaranteed between the signatory States.

The Antarctic Treaty is a unique arrangement in the current bipolar world and has been made possible only because of the fact that the Antarctic is as yet of no economic or strategic value. If and when the day should come that recoverable resources are discovered there, or plans are drawn up by one or more governments calling for military use of the area, the 1959 treaty will then be put to a severe test.

BIBLIOGRAPHY

AUGELLI, JOHN P., and TAYLOR, HARRY W. "Race and Population Patterns in Trinidad," *Annals of the Association of American Geographers,* L (1960), 123–39.

A detailed study of Trinidad's racial problems.

HAYTON, ROBERT D. "The Antarctic Settlement of 1959," *American Journal of International Law,* LIV (1960), 349–72.

Well-documented discussion of the Antarctic Treaty.

International Boundary Studies, Washington, Department of State, Office of the Geographer:

"Dominican Republic–Haiti Boundary," No. 5, May 23, 1961.

"British Honduras–Guatemala Boundary," No. 8, July 21, 1961.

Maps and detailed descriptions of the boundaries.

---

[13] Argentina, Australia, Belgium, Chile, France, Great Britain, Japan, New Zealand, Norway, Union of South Africa, U.S.S.R., and the United States.

[14] Quotation from the treaty taken from Robert D. Hayton, "The Antarctic Settlement of 1959," *American Journal of International Law,* LIV (1960), 359.

IRELAND, GORDON. *Boundaries, Possessions and Conflicts in Latin America.* Cambridge, Mass.: Harvard University Press, 1938.

———. *Boundaries, Possessions and Conflicts in Central and North America and the Caribbean.* Cambridge, Mass.: Harvard University Press, 1941.
Two basic reference books for detailed descriptions of Latin American boundaries and territorial disputes.

JAMES, PRESTON E. *Latin America.* New York: The Odyssey Press, 1950.
The outstanding regional geography of Latin America.

———, and Faissol, Speridiao. "The Problem of Brazil's Capital City," *The Geographical Review,* XLVI (1956), 301–18.
The geographic factors of the site of Brazil's new capital city.

LOWENTHAL, DAVID. "Population Contrasts in the Guianas," *The Geographical Review,* L (1960), 41–59.
Detailed treatment of population distribution in the Guianas.

PLATT, ROBERT S. "Conflicting Territorial Claims in the Upper Amazon," *Geographic Aspects of International Relations,* C. C. COLBY (ed.). Chicago: University of Chicago Press, 1938.
A detailed account of this border dispute prior to World War II.

TRAVIS, MARTIN B., and WATKINS, JAMES T. "Control of the Panama Canal: An Obsolete Shibboleth?" *Foreign Affairs,* XXXVII (1959), 407–18.
An interesting analysis of the strategic role of the Canal.

WASHINGTON, S. WALTER. "Crisis in the British West Indies," *Foreign Affairs,* XXXVIII (1960), 646–56.
A discussion of the factors in the break-up of the proposed West Indies Federation.

10

WESTERN EUROPE

● Western Europe consists of a series of peninsulas and islands extending from the western portion of the great Asian land mass. It is a region of physical, ethnic, economic and political diversity—a region which by the sixteenth century had become the world's major power centers, and from which explorers, settlers, and governments went out to organize the other continents and islands of the globe. In time the wealth which flowed into and through western Europe made it the richest area on earth; only in the past few decades has the power position shifted. The rise of non-European "super-States," the break-up of European empires, and two disastrous world wars have combined to alter radically western Europe's position with respect to the rest of the world. The adjustments the countries have made to these changing conditions are the principal theme of this chapter.

The term "western Europe" is taken here to include the area west of the so-called Iron Curtain, that is, west of the Communist countries. The eastern limits follow the eastern boundaries of Italy, Austria, and West Germany. Finland, Greece, Turkey, and Cyprus, although non-Communist in ideology, are left for consideration as part of eastern Europe. As defined here, the total area of western Europe measures about 1,200,000 square miles with a 1960 population of some 300 million. Included are twenty-one independent States.[1]

---

[1] Austria, Belgium, Denmark, France, Great Britain, Ireland, Iceland, Italy, Luxembourg, the Netherlands, Norway, Portugal, Spain, Sweden, Switzerland, West Germany, plus Andorra, Liechtenstein, Monaco, San Marino, and the Vatican City. In discussing background elements of Germany, the area now organized as East Germany is also included here.

PHYSICAL BASE

Location, climate, and access to the sea are three important characteristics of western Europe. Despite its broad latitudinal spread (from 36° north latitude in southernmost Spain to 72° north latitude in northern Norway), the bulk of the population lives between 40° and 55° north latitude, a belt approximately 10 degrees north of the most populous zone of the United States. Proximity to Africa has been a factor in western Europe's settlement of that continent, while the north Atlantic serves as a bridge between Europe and Anglo-America—a bridge whose importance may be seen in the historic ties binding the two areas together. The Mediterranean also has served as a link between Europe and the Middle East and, beyond Suez, to southern Asia as well. Finally, it is a shorter distance from western Europe to the east coast of South America, south of Cape São Roque, than it is from the United States. Thus, from a vicinal point of view, western Europe is well located with respect to sea and air connections with much of the rest of the world.

Despite its northerly location, much of western Europe experiences a relatively "temperate" climate with average monthly temperatures in winter above freezing and with cool summers. Precipitation is well distributed throughout the year; only in parts of Spain do extensive areas with desert, or even semidesert, conditions appear. The Italian Peninsula and parts of southern France have hot, dry summers when agriculture may be limited by availability of water for irrigation, while in northern Scandinavia and parts of Iceland temperatures and poor soils combine to rule out farming almost entirely. But in general western Europe enjoys a very "liveable" climate in which neither extreme cold nor extreme dryness severely limits settlement.

Access to the sea is provided by the many coastal indentations and by the existence of offshore islands and peninsulas. Only Switzerland, Austria, and Luxembourg, among the sixteen major States, are landlocked. Navigable rivers, such as the Rhine, the Seine, and the Elbe, connect inland areas with the sea, and along much of the coast line good harbors are associated with the hills and mountains bordering the water. Outside of the Baltic–Gulf of Bothnia area relatively little of the seas bordering on western Europe is normally frozen, except for short times during the winter. The availability of the sea and the presence of rich fishing grounds off many of the coasts has been an important factor in western Europe's cultural development, in terms of circulation among countries of this region and between western Europe and other parts of the world.

Much of the area consists of plains or of low hills, permitting dense settlement patterns. The major coastal plain starts in southwestern France and swings northeastward about the Massif Central into Belgium, the

Figure 34. Western Europe.

Netherlands, and Germany. Southern England, southern Sweden, and Denmark are also a part of this plain. Among other prominent lowlands are the Po, Rhine, and Rhone valleys, the Andalusian Valley of southern Spain, the central basin of Ireland, Portugal's coastal plain, and the Scottish lowland, which includes Glasgow and Edinburgh. Many of the hill areas are habitable, as evidenced by conditions in eastern France, central and southern Germany, southwestern England, and southern Italy. With the advantages both of landforms and climate much of western Europe is both settled and in agriculture. Moreover, despite the presence of mountain barriers, such as the Alps, the Pyrenees, and the Sierra Nevada of southern Spain, numerous overland transportation routes exist within and between the various states of western Europe, thereby reducing the incidence of "isolation" of particular areas.[2]

The major mineral and power resources of western Europe are coal, timber, water power, and iron ore. These commodities are divided unevenly among the various States, with few countries having an abundance of more than one or two items. In addition to the commodities noted above Spain has lead, zinc, and copper, Italy has sulphur, and France has important bauxite deposits. These and lesser reserves contribute to the area's wealth. When measured against demand, however, western Europe is not particularly rich in such resources; it is a net importer of coal, timber, and iron ore and must depend almost exclusively on outside supplies of petroleum, copper, tin, uranium, and other industrial raw materials.

POPULATION

The 300 million people of western Europe are unevenly distributed throughout the area. The major concentration includes southern Britain, northern France, Belgium, the Netherlands, and northwestern Germany. Here is the industrial heart of Europe, with the densest transportation net, and with one-third of the total population, yet from Liverpool to the German Ruhr is a distance of but 400 miles. The Po basin and the western coast of the Italian Peninsula are important population centers, as are also the agricultural and industrial belt across East Germany and coastal areas of Spain and Portugal. These great population clusters are highly vulnerable to attack, particularly to attack by air, a factor of great significance in view of the development of thermonuclear weapons with wide ranges of destructiveness.

Much of the population is highly developed in terms of education and skills, as well as of consumer demands. Average per capita incomes are

---

[2] Switzerland, although often cited as an example of isolation, is, in reality, an extremely cosmopolitan country with good connections with its neighbors. Andorra, high in the Pyrenees, is a more valid example of national isolation.

highest about the southern North Sea area, gradually diminishing to fairly low levels in Ireland and parts of the Iberian and Italian peninsulas. Much has been written about "overpopulation" in such areas as England, the Netherlands, and Italy, but great care should be taken in the use of this concept. It is true that many of the west European States are unable to grow sufficient food to feed their populations, but they produce other goods and services for export in order to purchase food. In sophisticated economies such as these overpopulation is not evidenced by large-scale starvation; rather its existence would be more apparent in the inability of a country to deal with widespread unemployment or to raise the general per capita income of its people materially over a long period of time. Even here, however, the cure may lie, not in reducing the size of the population, but rather in finding ways of improving the country's production and exchange of goods and services.

Most of the major language groups have their own independent countries, although there are notable exceptions. English is generally spoken in the Republic of Ireland (although an effort is being made to revive Gaelic), the Swiss speak four languages (of these only Rhaetian, a minority tongue, is exclusively Swiss), and the Belgians two, French and Flemish. German is the language of both Austria and Luxembourg. More important, perhaps, than this question of "mother tongues" is that of the relationships between ethnic and political borders. German-speaking peoples inhabit the Tyrol of northern Italy, as well as Alsace and parts of Lorraine, while the Basques, residing in both Spain and France, seek to maintain as much cultural and national identity as possible. Germans and Danes are mixed in the area of their common border, as are also Frenchmen and Italians between Switzerland and the Mediterranean. Several of these ethnic mixtures have led to important border disputes in the past and could conceivably cause international friction in future years.

From the end of the Middle Ages down to the mid-twentieth century the ethnic complexities of western Europe have fostered the growth of nationalism. Such States as France, Spain, Britain, Denmark, and Sweden became unified and self-governing at early stages in the nationalist movements; others, such as Belgium, Germany, and Italy, were considerably later in their development. Norway, Ireland, and Iceland are twentieth-century additions to the independent States of this area. To each of the States of western Europe the test of national viability might with profit be applied.

In the sections which follow it may be seen that most of the States of western Europe have relatively few problems so far as the maintenance of internal cohesion is concerned. Economic viability, on the other hand, is a difficult goal for many of these countries, as is also territorial security, both in terms of border disputes with neighbors and of the threat of Soviet expansion from the east. The economies of most of the west European States are heavily dependent on foreign trade, and a number of countries have suffered severely in the past few years from losses both of overseas territories and of trading partners and potential areas for investment in Communist eastern Europe, the Soviet Union, and Communist China. These losses are in addition to wartime destruction and loss of overseas investments. Thus the question of economic development has, for most of these countries, been an extremely serious one in the years since World War II.

Coupled with these problems have been those of defense against possible Soviet aggression. Communist encroachments in eastern Europe, culminating in the Czech *coup d'état* in 1948, served to weld much of western Europe together in a mutual defense pact which includes also the United States and Canada. The growth of the North Atlantic Treaty Organization (NATO)[3] has served both to reduce border friction between member States and to impose greater economic burdens on these states in the maintenance of defenses. There still are actual or latent problems of territorial control in western Europe, but a number of disputes have been settled, or else laid aside in the interests of unity. Defense costs have, to some extent, been offset by foreign aid from the United States; on the other hand, defense expenditures for some countries have risen considerably due to colonial problems such as those in Algeria, Indochina, or the former Dutch East Indies.

The States of western Europe, urged on by economic and military necessity, have gradually been moving in the direction of united action in the military and economic realms. In 1957 Italy, France, West Germany, and the three Benelux countries entered the first stage of an economic program designed to lift the barriers on the free movement of goods, capital, and labor between them. This union, embracing an area with a population roughly equal to that of the United States, will when completed, constitute one of the three great economic units of the world, along with the United States and the Soviet Union. Its development has been one of the major postwar events in western Europe.

The process of recent economic integration in western Europe goes back first to the Organization for European Economic Cooperation, set up in 1947 at the suggestion of the United States. This organization was designed to coordinate the needs of the European states in terms of the aid they were to receive from the United States under the Marshall Plan. The following year the Netherlands, Belgium, and Luxembourg entered into the first stage of the Benelux customs union in which tariffs and other restrictions on the movement of goods between member states were to be removed, and a common tariff policy be adopted in relation to goods entering the union from the outside. In 1953 the three Benelux countries, together with France,

---

[3] The European members of NATO are Belgium, Denmark, France, Great Britain, Greece, Iceland, Italy, Luxembourg, the Netherlands, Norway, Portugal, Turkey, and West Germany.

West Germany, and Italy established the European Coal and Steel Community (Schuman Plan), a customs union with respect to coal, iron, and steel. This community helped to heal the wartime breach between France and West Germany and to pave the way for the eventual solution of the Saar problem (see page 224). Four years later the Coal and Steel Community was expanded to a union involving all commodities exchanged among the various States.

Reductions in empires, the loss of most of eastern Europe to Soviet control, and the controversies between the Soviet Union and the United States have tended both to isolate western Europe as a whole and to reduce the relative power positions of its individual States. Yet with its long history of nationalism, and with the many divergencies of opinion existing there, western Europe would seem to be facing a long and difficult road to unification, except in specific cases. Five of the sixteen countries are not in NATO, and for all its accomplishments the Common Market embraces but six of the States of this area. Ultimately, all or most of the so-called Outer Seven[4] may join the Common Market as full or associated members, thus bringing economic unity to all States but Iceland, Ireland, and Spain, but such a move would probably take years to complete. Beyond this is political union, a "United States of Western Europe," a goal toward which as yet no concrete steps whatever have been taken. In the following pages individual States, or groups of States, are considered in terms both of their internal structure and of their relations with other countries of western Europe. These are combined as follows: France, Benelux, and Switzerland; the "Middle Kingdom"; Germany and Austria; the Mediterranean area; the northern States. In this way elements of unity and diversity within and among the regions of western Europe can be discussed.

FRANCE, BENELUX, AND SWITZERLAND

France

The French State faces on three bodies of water—the Atlantic, the Mediterranean, and the English Channel—while on its land borders it touches eight countries. For over a thousand years portions of France's land borders, particularly in the east, have been the scenes of frequent warfare and territorial change. Three disastrous wars with Germany in less than seventy-five years have affected both the material and the psychological position of the French, and many of France's internal and external problems since 1945 can be traced to the devastating aftereffects of German aggression.

As a result of the historical rivalry between France and Germany, the economic position of the French State has been of particular importance to

---

[4] Austria, Denmark, Great Britain, Norway, Portugal, Sweden, Switzerland.

its political development. Economic production, particularly in the industrial fields, represents one of the major elements of a State's war potential, and France's ability to defend itself against German aggression (either by maintaining high levels of French output or by reducing those of the Germans) has been a significant aspect of the nation's security.

The French State possesses considerable natural resources, including iron ore, potash, coal, bauxite, and forests, as well as large areas where both soil and climate render conditions suitable for agriculture. The country's energy output has been augmented in recent years by increased development of its water power potential. French industrial production, however, is normally less than that of Germany. After World Wars I and II France sought to gain control of industrial facilities in the Saar, primarily to effect a greater equalization of output with Germany. In 1945 France also sought to impose limits on the degree to which German industry could expand in its postwar recovery, but these efforts were largely unsuccessful, and by 1950 steel production in West Germany had surpassed that of the French.

Population potential is another aspect of France's power position. The population has grown relatively slowly during the past century. In 1861 it numbered 37,400,000; by 1960 it was 45,700,000, representing an increase of 22 per cent in about a century. This slow population growth has had an adverse effect on France's power status, in that it has been a check on the availability of manpower to maintain the State's economy and to serve in its armed forces. France has an area of 213,000 square miles with an average population density of just over 200 persons per square mile—a figure which is low for the countries of northwest Europe. The lack of population pressure has been partly responsible for the relatively small-scale emigration of colonists to France's overseas possessions, with the exception of those in North Africa.

France has been a unified State for over six centuries, and there are strong centripetal forces based on national sentiment, centralization of power, and ethnic unity. The Paris basin, which is the principal core of the country, also serves as the economic and political center of France. The centralization of control there is augmented by the political subdivision of the country into 90 departments, no one of which is in a position to challenge seriously the authority of the national government. Despite physical and economic differences throughout the country there is a well-developed circulatory system, based primarily on the transportation facilities and on the extensive use made of radio, newspaper, and other communication media.

Religion also constitutes a unifying element, since practically all of the French are Roman Catholic. Language, on the other hand, does not produce the same degree of cultural cohesion. Although over 90 per cent of the inhabitants speak French, there are important minorities along the borders which speak foreign tongues. In Alsace and eastern Lorraine much

© RMcN

Figure 35. France: Language Minorities. (After Van Valkenburg, *Elements of Political Geography*, copyright 1939 by Prentice-Hall, Inc., Englewood Cliffs, N.J. Used by permission.)

of the population speaks either German or Alsatian, a dialect akin to German, and in the eastern part of the French Riviera are many Italian-speaking groups. There are thousands of Spanish-speaking people in southern France at the eastern end of the Pyrenees, while in the western end are the Basques, a distinct ethnic group also inhabiting northern Spain. Finally, in the northwest are people who speak Celtic, or Breton (Figure 35). In France, as in other countries, these ethnic differences represent centrifugal forces, which, particularly in times of crisis, tend to weaken the unity of the State.

Benelux

The three Benelux States (Belgium, the Netherlands, Luxembourg) illustrate well the principles of unity and division within a border area. Location has proved both a blessing and a curse, for in peacetime proximity to Germany, France, and Britain has enabled the Benelux countries to achieve high levels of economic development. In wartime, on the other hand, parts of the region have repeatedly suffered from invading forces. In the face of recurrent danger from bordering powers, the Benelux States have long been under pressure to unite their efforts economically, militarily, and politically. Differences in their cultural, economic, and historical backgrounds, however, have served in the past to keep them apart.

Protestant Holland won its independence from Spain in 1648, and subsequently developed one of the great colonial empires of the world. The Catholic States of Belgium and Luxembourg remained under foreign domination until the Congress of Vienna (1815), following the defeat of Napoleon, when the victorious powers, desiring a strong buffer state along France's northeastern border, united the two areas with Holland into what was then termed the United Netherlands. This attempt at political unity soon failed, and in 1830 the peoples of Belgium and Luxembourg revolted. Nine years later the independence of Belgium was officially recognized. Luxembourg maintained a personal union with the Netherlands until 1868, when a constitution was drawn up declaring the former an independent State. Memories of the ill-fated United Netherlands served to dampen enthusiasm among the peoples of all three countries for subsequent attempts at unification during the remainder of the nineteenth century and in the early part of the twentieth.

The Netherlands itself is a relatively small European State, with a high population density of nearly 800 persons per square mile. The Dutch economy—based on intensive utilization of domestic resources—consists primarily of commercial activities (both intra-European and overseas), agricultural exports, such as dairy products, fruits and vegetables, and flowers, and high-grade manufactured goods, particularly ships, machinery, and electrical equipment. The Netherlands has few resources for heavy industry; coal production is insufficient for domestic needs, and there is practically no iron ore, ferroalloys, or petroleum. Belgium has an area of nearly 12,000 square miles and a population of some 9,200,000 persons. Despite the high average population density, Belgium's industrial structure—based on the presence of extensive coal deposits—normally provides sufficient employment opportunities for the bulk of Belgian workers. Thus the country has had little need for an empire as a settlement area for surplus population. Luxembourg, with less than 1,000 square miles, has about 300,000 people. The Grand Duchy is an important producer of iron ore, since within its borders are included the northernmost portions of France's Minette reserves.

Switzerland

The Swiss State represents a unique politico-geographic situation, for despite its intricate political pattern and the presence of diverse linguistic and religious groups within its borders, the country has overcome the internal centrifugal forces so common to this sector of Europe and has maintained its boundaries intact through several major European conflicts (Figure 36). Independent since the late thirteenth century, Switzerland has had no serious territorial problems since 1815, and has been involved in none of the wars which have been waged since that time among the States of Europe.

Although often thought of as a predominantly Alpine country, Switzerland has three principal geographic regions—the Alps in the south, the Jura Mountains in the west, considerably lower in relief, and the Swiss Plateau, comprising about one-third of the country, which extends northeast-south-

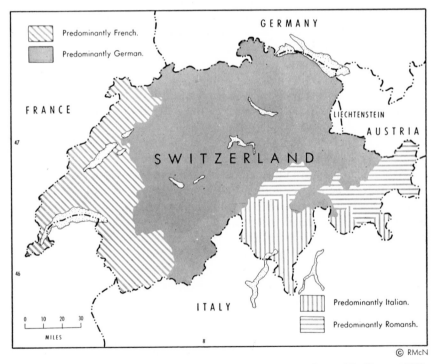

Figure 36. Switzerland: Language Patterns. (After a map in *Focus*, VI [Sept., 1955]. Courtesy of *Focus*–American Geographical Society.)

west between the Jura and the Alps. Within this plateau area, most of which is less than 2,000 feet in elevation, live over three-quarters of the State's population. There are practically no valuable mineral resources in Switzerland, and hydroelectric power is the only important source of energy. With a population of over 5 million Switzerland must depend on high-grade manufactures, such as machinery and watches, on specialized agriculture, on international transit freight, and on tourism as major sources of revenue.

Location in and adjacent to the Alps once helped to isolate the Swiss from their more powerful neighbors, but with modern transportation the nation has become an important link in Europe's east-west and north-south road, rail, and air routes. By its long-term policy of neutrality Switzerland has developed a role as the site for international organizations and conferences. During its lifetime the League of Nations was located at Geneva, as are now the headquarters of the International Red Cross and certain agencies of the United Nations. Major international conferences have been held at Geneva, Lausanne, Montreux, and other Swiss cities.

Switzerland's borders are typically complex and irregular, like many others in this part of Europe. In the north a Swiss bridgehead at Schaffhausen extends across the Rhine toward Germany, and within this are two tiny enclaves of German territory. To the northwest a glacis stretches across the main crest of the Jura Mountains toward France, while to the south a much larger glacis projects into the north Italian plain. Thus, like the Benelux countries, Switzerland retains vestiges of medieval political units, some of which appear anachronistic in the current world political pattern, with its emphasis on efficiency of economic and political operations. A further example of the complexity of this area is the existence of Liechtenstein, a sixty-one-square-mile country lying between Switzerland and Austria. Independent since the early eighteenth century, Liechtenstein is joined with Switzerland in a customs union.

The attitude of the Swiss people is one of the most remarkable features of this State. Despite the diversities of language and religion, the sense of unity contrasts sharply with the shifting political loyalties of many other peoples of Europe. One reason for this may be the national pride of the Swiss people in the fact that their forefathers achieved independence without help from outsiders and that this experience has been maintained for over six and a half centuries. Another reason for the lack of stronger centrifugal forces in Switzerland is the factor of neutrality—the benefits of freedom from entanglement in Europe's conflicts provide a strong motive for continued national unity. Associated with this are the advantages of Switzerland's economic position, particularly in international banking, investments, and trade. Thus in Switzerland, as in Belgium, Canada, and other areas, the economic and political benefits of national cohesion outweigh the divisive forces of cultural differences.

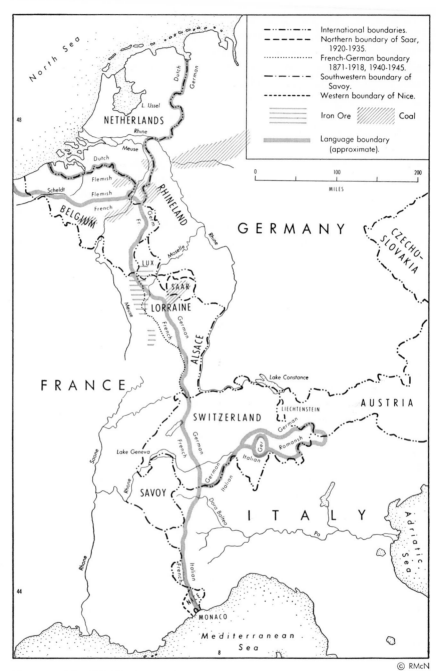

Figure 37. The "Middle Kingdom."

WESTERN EUROPE'S "MIDDLE KINGDOM"

Between the Mediterranean and the North Sea lies one of the most complex politico-geographic areas of the world. Here in western Europe's "Middle Kingdom"[5] boundaries of language, religion, and nationality overlap one another in complicated patterns. Political units have been characterized by complex shapes and by frequent border changes, and problems of territorial control are often magnified to the point where bitter international disputes have arisen over the possession of small pieces of territory. The scars of past conflicts are still much in evidence in the desires and fears of the local inhabitants, in the patterns of political control, and in the attitudes of the western European governments toward matters of present and future sovereignty in this area.

The area of Lothar's Middle Kingdom included what is now eastern France, western Germany, the Benelux countries, Switzerland, northwestern Italy, and Monaco. Only once during its long history was the entire area unified under its own ruler. That was from 843 to 855, when Charlemagne's empire was divided among his three grandsons after the Treaty of Verdun. Charles received the western portion, Louis the eastern, while the Middle Kingdom, lying between the two, was given to Lothar (Figure 37). After Lothar's death in 855 the Middle Kingdom was divided between the eastern and western empires. France eventually evolved out of what had been the western portion of Charlemagne's empire, while the eastern zone is now included in Germany, Austria, and northwestern Italy. The central belt between these two sectors has never been effectively absorbed by its more powerful neighbors, however, nor has it been reunified. Possibly all the area, except for Switzerland, may in time be incorporated within a unified west European political organization. For the sake of clarity the Middle Kingdom is considered here in terms of the following problem areas: the Benelux-German border; the Saar; Alsace-Lorraine; and French-Italian border area.

The Benelux-German Border

The border area between Germany and the three Benelux countries points up the nature of microterritorial disputes in this part of the world. At the end of World War I the Belgian-German boundary, which had been delimited in 1815, was rectified in favor of Belgium, the recent victim of German aggression. In addition to annexing the former neutral territory of Moresnet, Belgium received control of the small areas of Eupen, Malmédy, and St. Vith (Figure 38). These areas totaled about 400 square miles, but

---

[5] So called because it corresponds generally to the Middle Kingdom awarded to Lothar at the break-up of Charlemagne's empire.

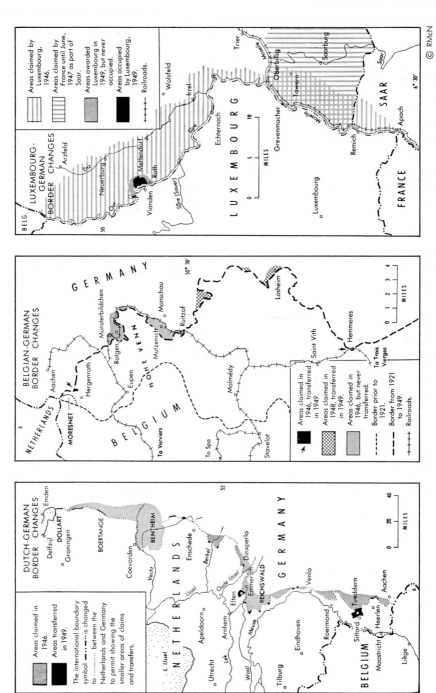

Figure 38. The Benelux–German Border. In 1956 most of the Belgian-held territories were returned to Germany. (After Alexander, *The Geographical Review,* XLIII [Jan., 1953]. Courtesy of American Geographical Society.)

they brought timber and water power resources within the Belgian borders. Between the towns of Eupen and Malmédy was a railroad which, although Belgian-controlled, passed several times across the German border, thus creating enclaves of German territory between the right-of-way and the Belgian border.

Several thousand German-speaking people living in the Eupen area were included within Belgium following the territorial transfer. After the rise of Hitler in the early 1930's German political propaganda was directed toward the return of these areas to the Fatherland. In 1940, following Germany's second invasion of Belgium in twenty-six years, the Eupen-Malmédy sector (including St. Vith) was reannexed by the Germans. Five years later it was returned to Belgium. Territorial shifts such as these are typical of this Middle Kingdom area.

During World War II the Netherlands, Belgium, and Luxembourg were invaded and occupied by the Germans. At the end of the war the Netherlands demanded 648 square miles of territory from Germany as compensation for the more than $14 billion worth of damage done to that country by the Germans between 1940 and 1945. Luxembourg asked for 140 square miles of land, while the Belgians desired 11 square miles. The total German-speaking population involved in these claims amounted to about 150,000 persons.

Many officials in the Benelux countries, as well as elsewhere, were frankly doubtful of the feasibility of these demands. They were worried about the inclusion of so large (and presumably unfriendly) a German minority within the lowland countries. They were also apprehensive lest Germany move to reconquer these lost areas as soon as it was in a position to do so. In March, 1949, a commission of the Western powers sanctioned a series of 31 minor changes in the Benelux-German border, involving a total of 52 square miles and some 13,500 German-speaking inhabitants (Figure 38). The largest share of this territory (26 square miles) went to the Netherlands. Although the final border readjustments were to be confirmed or modified by a peace treaty with Germany, it would appear with the passage of time that no additional land will be ceded by Germany; in fact in 1956 Belgium returned most of the areas it had annexed and in 1960 the Dutch did likewise. As part of the contemporary spirit of cooperation in western Europe this border problem, once a burning issue to the people involved, is now largely forgotten.

The Saar

The Saar, located to the southeast of Luxembourg, has been one of the historic disputed areas between France and Germany. Since late in the ninth century the region has been associated with the Germans, although for brief periods during the reigns of Louis XIV and Napoleon it was included within France. The great majority of the people are German in speech and culture.

The Saar is of military importance to its neighbors, since it controls the eastern approaches to the Lorraine Gate, a lowland passageway between Germany and France which has figured prominently in wars between the two areas. It is of economic importance because of its great coal reserves and its steel mills (Figure 39). It is also something of an economic link between France and Germany: international rail and waterways pass through the Saar, much of the area's coal (mixed with coking coal from the German Ruhr) is used to smelt the iron ore of the French province of Lorraine, and the Saar's deficiencies in food are normally met by imports from Lorraine.

The French government at the time of the Versailles Conference in 1919 put forth claims to the Saar, partly on the grounds of war reparations and partly in order to reduce Germany's national power potential. French

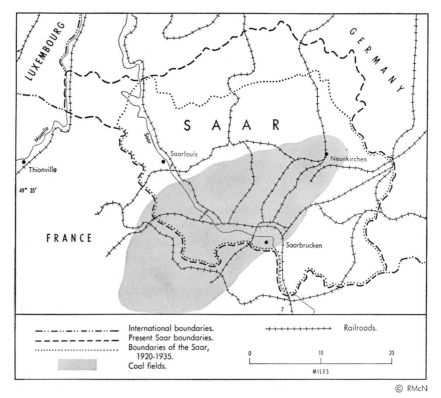

© RMcN

Figure 39. The Saar. (After Held, The Geographical Review, XLI [Oct., 1951]. Courtesy of American Geographical Society.)

coal fields in the northeastern part of the country had been badly damaged by the Germans, and the French government feared that without ready access to coal reserves France would be seriously handicapped in any future efforts to maintain industrial equality with Germany. In the final peace settlement in 1920 a 730-square-mile area within the Saar basin was taken from Germany and placed under the administration of the League of Nations for a period of fifteen years. The French were awarded ownership of the coal mines during the fifteen-year period in order to satisfy their economic demands.

Several important questions may be raised with respect to the treatment of the Saar problem after Warld War I. First, should a defeated State be divested of an integral part of its national territory in order to weaken its power potential? Second, can a State achieve security by acquiring territory or resources from a rival power? Third, in a buffer zone such as the Middle Kingdom is international control of disputed areas a workable solution to territorial conflicts?

The answers are difficult to find, for national power is a complex and changing phenomenon, and each territorial dispute has its own individual elements of motives, desires, and justice. The delegates at Versailles apparently had some concern for the feelings of the Saarlanders, first, when they placed the area under League supervision rather than awarding it directly to France and, second, when they provided for a plebiscite to be held in 1935 to determine the Saar's future status. Some of the weaknesses of international control of territory were illustrated in the case of the Saar. Although international organizations generally provide well-run administrations, the national aspirations of the peoples of the internationlized area often remain unsatisfied. Furthermore, the conflicting powers themselves are frequently dissatisfied with a solution involving international control of a disputed area, for it fails to satisfy either one's territorial demands. One power, however, may in time accept international administration, if the alternative is that the other power will obtain complete control over the area.

In the 1935 plebiscite over 90 per cent of the voters favored return of the Saar to Germany. The exchange was effected in the same year, and control of the coal mines was returned to the Germans. The resources and industrial output of the Saar contributed to Germany's economic and military build-up prior to and during World War II.

The territorial problems of the Saar following World War II differed in certain respects from those of the post-World War I era. French troops took over control of the area from the Americans in July, 1945. After some border rectifications, the Saar territory measured 991 square miles in area, somewhat larger than the region detached from Germany in 1920. The population numbered 943,000, most of them German-speaking. In the fall of 1947 a local parliament was elected, with a large majority of the votes going to parties committed to economic union with France. Candidates of pro-German political parties, however, were denied the right to seek office in the Saar. In December of that year French occupation troops were withdrawn, and in January, 1951, an autonomous Saar was officially established.

In the years following World War II the French made several moves to strengthen the bonds between France and the Saar. They invested heavily in the area, they denied themselves the privilege of dismantling Saar factories, and they made efforts to improve the living conditions of the Saarlanders and to hasten the revival of industries in the area. On the other hand, they continued to deny the right of pro-German political parties to take part in the Saar government. Within a few years the Saarlanders— many of whom had been glad to accept French help in 1945–46—grew increasingly restless under France's control.

During the early 1950's, as France and West Germany became member States in international economic and military organizations, the Saar situation grew increasingly tense. The area's industrial importance to France may be illustrated by the fact that in 1955 the Saar produced 32 per cent as much coal and 25 per cent as much steel as the French nation itself. Including the Saar output, France's steel production that year equaled 73 per cent of West Germany's; if the Saar were included with West Germany the French percentage would have dropped to 51.

After many consultations between French and West German officials over the area's future, the Saarlanders in the fall of 1955 were offered a plebiscite, in which they were to accept or reject an international status for the area under the administration of the Western European Union, until such time as a final German peace treaty was worked out.

In October, 1955, the Saarlanders rejected the proposed statute by a vote of just over two to one. There were many reasons for this, among them a lack of faith in the newly organized Western European Union, the cultural affinities of the Saarlanders with the Germans, and the continually expanding economic strength of West Germany. Pro-German political parties soon won control of the Saar parliament, and in June, 1956, a Franco-German agreement was finally drawn up providing for the return of the Saar to Germany on January 1, 1957, and its establishment as the tenth state in the West German Republic. The economic union with France was to be abolished gradually over a three-year period. The French, however, were assured of access to coal from mines in the Saar for at least twenty years, and trade between France and the Saar remains duty-free. The only stipulation was that, if the value of exports or imports between the two areas exceeds the respective values of 1955, duties will be levied against the excess amount. Also included in the agreement was a provision for German assistance in canalizing the Moselle River, thereby affording the Lorraine industrial district ready access to the Ruhr coal supplies and markets of West Germany.

Alsace-Lorraine

The name Alsace-Lorraine refers to a 5,600-square-mile area to the south and southeast of Luxembourg and the Saar, which, like the Saar, has several times been a source of bitter dispute between France and Germany. The province of Alsace stretches to the west of the Rhine River and includes not only the Rhine lowlands paralleling the river but also the eastern slopes of the Vosges Mountains. The region is important for agriculture (grain, tobacco, fruit), for potash, most of which is manufactured into fertilizer, and for its small petroleum reserves. It is also of military importance because of its control of the Saverne Gap through the Vosges Mountains into east central France. Lorraine is a gently rolling plateau area, whose major economic significance lies in its great iron ore deposits. Like the Saar, it is strategically located with regard to the Lorraine Gate between France and Germany. In the territorial disputes only the Moselle department in eastern Lorraine has been involved; the rest of the province has remained French during all boundary shifts (Figure 40).

Alsace-Lorraine has been a historic transition area between French and German cultural and political developments. After the break-up of Lothar's kingdom Alsace was included in the Germanic realm for the greater part of eight centuries, although for some years during the thirteenth century the ten major cities of Alsace were practically independent units within the Holy Roman Empire. In 1648 Alsace was officially joined to France; two centuries later, however, a majority of the inhabitants still continued to speak a German dialect. Sectors of Lorraine also won varying degrees of independence during the Middle Ages, although throughout much of the province's history it was included with the German-speaking areas which lie to the east. In 1766 Lorraine passed under French control. The interaction of cultural forces there is illustrated by the fact that in modern times the French language has predominated throughout most of the province, except in the Moselle department where German is the principal tongue.

Alsace-Lorraine has changed hands between France and Germany four times since 1870. By the Treaty of Frankfurt (1871), ending the Franco-Prussian War, victorious Germany annexed the Alsace-Lorraine area, thereby weakening France's defensive position and at the same time gaining control of Lorraine's valuable iron ore reserves. The inhabitants of Alsace-Lorraine were, for the most part, strongly opposed to the German move, but their opinions were never solicited. At the time of the delimitation of the French-German border in 1871, considerations of military strategy and, to

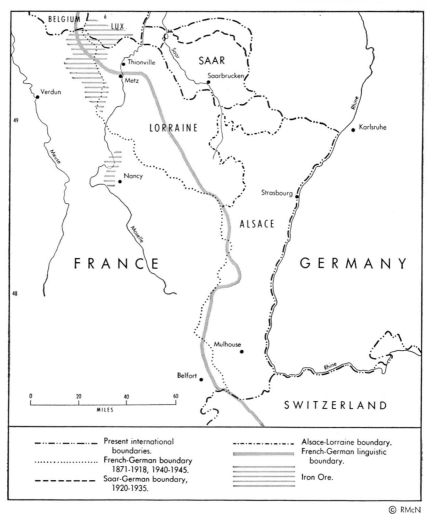

Figure 40. Alsace-Lorraine. (After Hartshorne, *World Politics*, II [Jan., 1950]. Used by permission.)

a lesser extent, the location of the French-German language boundary were of greater importance to the German officials than were the iron ore resources.[6] Control of a part of the Lorraine resources, however, was of great significance to Germany's industrial build-up in the years prior to World

---

[6] See Richard Hartshorne, "The Franco-German Boundary of 1871," *World Politics,* II (1950), 209–51. The inclusion of much of the iron ore within Germany appears to have been almost accidental, a coincidence resulting from locating the border according to strategic considerations. In 1871 the Lorraine ores were being used by the French for iron production, but until the discovery of the Thomas-Gilchrist process in 1878, it was not possible to utilize the resources with their high phosphorous content for the production of steel.

War I, for Germany possessed good coking coal, particularly in the Ruhr area, but few supplies of iron ore.

The French, of course, were extremely bitter over Germany's annexation of the territory, for they saw a Germanized generation grow up in what they considered to be their own national territory. Not until the close of World War I was France in a position to demand reannexation of the lost areas from Germany. The return of Alsace-Lorraine did not end the territorial problems. The French government has always been highly centralized, with a great degree of power vested in Paris, while prior to World War I Alsace and Lorraine had been permitted by the Germans to set up their own local parliaments. In Alsace particularly a movement developed in the 1920's in favor of autonomy for the area. Many Alsatians felt that their land would continually oscillate between France and Germany unless the local inhabitants were free to manage their own affairs.

The third war between France and Germany in less than seventy years broke out in 1939, and after the Nazi conquest of France in June, 1940, Alsace-Lorraine was reannexed by the Germans. Five years later, Germany was again a defeated nation and the territory was returned to France.

In unhappy areas such as this the principal sufferers are the inhabitants themselves. Not only is the political structure of the region damaged, but also the economic and social foundations. New tariffs and government policies suddenly present themselves to the businessman. Old markets are gone and new ones must be found; health and education facilities suffer. Persons in responsible positions may be removed from their jobs, imprisoned, and sometimes executed. If this happens once in a generation the results may be serious. If it happens four or five times the entire social framework of the area is severely tested.

The French-Italian Border

Along the French-Italian border disputes over territorial control have involved two sectors, the 6,500-square-mile Savoy area in the north and the small province of Nice along the Mediterranean coast. Between Switzerland and the Mediterranean the Maritime Alps trend north-south in an unbroken chain with few practical passes across them. Mountainous areas at lower elevations extend for a considerable distance east and west of the main chain, and within these upland regions relatively isolated political units have developed. Savoy, located south of the Swiss border and to the west of the main chain of the Alps, is perhaps the most famous of these political units. Communications between Savoy and France are considerably easier to maintain than between Savoy and Italy. The principal markets for Savoy's exports are in France, and the majority of the population is French-speaking. Nevertheless, throughout much of its history the area has been

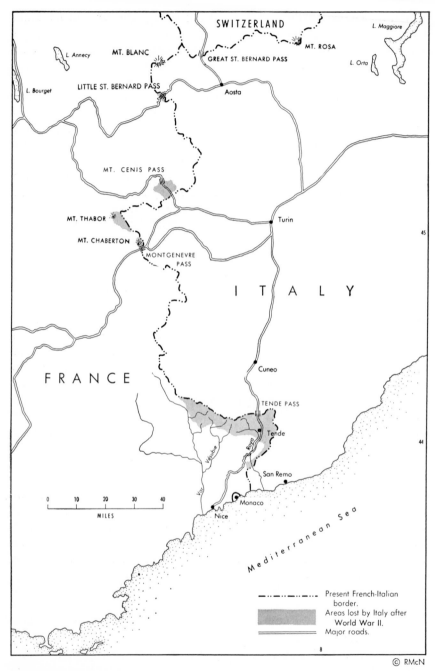

Figure 41. The Franco-Italian Border Following World War II. (Courtesy of Secrétariat Général du Gouvernement, Direction de la Documentation, Service Cartographique, France.)

politically associated with the Italian states to the east. Nice to the south is also separated from Italy by mountains. As in the case of Savoy, lines of communication with France are more easily maintained than are connections via the coastal road with Italy.

In 1859 the French emperor agreed to support the Italian states in their struggle for independence from Austria in exchange for the territories of Nice and Savoy. The French forces were withdrawn from the struggle before victory for the Italians had been achieved, however. Despite Italian protests the French held plebiscites in the two areas to determine popular sentiment concerning union with France. The results of both plebiscites were in favor of France, and Savoy and Nice subsequently incorporated within the French State. The areas were later the source of considerable friction between Italy and France. Mussolini used them to build up anti-French propaganda in the 1930's, reminding the Italians that both areas were historically a part of Italy and that France annexed them after a broken promise.

The French-Italian border problems have never been as serious as those between Germany and her western neighbors, partly because of the mountain chain between France and Italy and the relative lack of recources in the border areas. The linguistic boundary corresponds fairly closely to the political one, and the Alps form a rather effective barrier between France and Italy. At the end of World War II France annexed from Italy five small areas along the crest of the Alps as compensation for war damages. These areas contained a total of 370 square miles and a population of 3,620 persons (Figure 41), most of them Italian-speaking. From north to south these areas were: (1) Little St. Bernard Pass, (2) Mount Cenis Plateau, (3) Mount Thabor, (4) Mount Chaberton, including the Montgenèvre Pass, and (5) the upper valleys of the Tinée, Vésubie, and Roya rivers, including the Tende Pass.

Through these border changes France gained control of several important passes as well as water power sites. Special clauses were included in the treaty to insure that Italy would continue to receive electricity from her former hydroelectric installations. The moderate nature of the French demands and the fact that provisions were made to prevent undue hardship to the Italian economy because of the territorial transfers have resulted in an apparent absence of bitterness on Italy's part with regard to its losses.

Monaco

Along the Mediterranean coast is Monaco, another relic of the medieval political pattern. This country, with an area of 370 acres and a population of 23,000, is joined in an economic union with France. It is famous for its gambling casino. Perhaps Monaco's reputation as a distinct political entity has helped to prevent French attempts to incorporate it within the territorial jurisdiction of the French nation, which surrounds it on all but its seaward side.

GERMANY AND AUSTRIA

Germany

The territorial area of Germany has changed many times during the twentieth century. Most Germans think of the German State as comprising the area which was contained within the 1935–38 boundaries. Following World War II this territory was divided into the following parts: West Germany (the German Federal Republic), a sovereign democratic State; East Germany (the German Democratic Republic), a Moscow-oriented Communist State; the area east of the Oder-Neisse line, now a part of Poland, except for a small sector annexed by the U.S.S.R.; Berlin, with a special four-power status; and the Saar, which became an autonomous area joined politically and economically with France. On January 1, 1957, the Saar was united politically with West Germany and became one of its constituent states.

Germany occupies a central position in Europe, touching nine States and bordering on both the North and Baltic seas. Its location with regard to neighboring States has been both an asset and a liability (Figure 42). With its central location and with lowland routes and waterways connecting it with other areas, Germany has been able to profit from cultural associations with its neighbors, notably in political ideas, scientific developments, and philosophic and artistic trends. It has also, of course, benefited from economic ties with adjoining States. On the other hand, this location, together with the diversity of relief (particularly in central and southern Germany), contributed to the late political unification of Germany, for the region has long been a transit area for foreign armies and peoples, and it lacks well-defined boundaries within which cohesive forces could operate for political unity. A central location also involves the possibility of a two- or three-front war, as occurred in 1944–45 when Germany had to defend its western and eastern borders as well as its southern flanks.

Since 1871 no country bordering Germany has been as strong economically as the Reich itself. As a result Germany has been in an advantageous economic position with regard to trade with its neighbors, particularly Luxembourg, the Netherlands, Switzerland, and Austria. German industrial exports have found ready markets in these and other adjacent States, and from them Germany has been able to obtain needed commodities, such as dairy products, fruits and vegetables, iron ore, and grains.

In many respects Germany's economic strength was developed only after physical limitations had been overcome. Most of the soils are of moderate to poor fertility, but with wise agricultural practices these have

Figure 42. Germany and Austria: Physical Features.

been made productive to the point where the country during the two world wars was able to achieve a high degree of self-sufficiency. One important element in Germany's economic power has been the development of science and technology, particularly in the electrochemical fields, enabling the State to utilize its great coal resources for the production of needed commodities and to derive substitutes for such products as sodium nitrate and petroleum, which in time of war have been unobtainable. Wartime needs have greatly stimulated German economic development, particularly since the end of the nineteenth century, focusing attention on the build-up of heavy industries, on the role of government aid and supervision in strengthening the economic base, and on the search for new processes and commodities to aid Germany in time of conflict.

German economic power has been felt in other countries as well, often with political or military overtones. During the 1930's, for example, Germany achieved a position of economic dominance over many of the countries of southeastern Europe, and German overseas trade with Latin America, the Middle East, and the Orient was also greatly developed at that time. Economic contacts were frequently utilized as bases for espionage or dissemination of Nazi propaganda. In some countries, for example, Hungary, the powerful role Germany played in the national economy aided the local Nazi party in eventually assuming control of the country's government.

A large population has always been one of the elements of German power in terms of labor and military forces. The German people have an intense national consciousness, bolstered by a common language. This sense

Table 2

GERMAN-SPEAKING PEOPLES LIVING BEYOND
GERMANY'S BORDER IN THE EARLY 1930's

Country	Population	
Czechoslovakia	3,200,000	(1930)
Poland	1,300,000[a]	(1935)
Russia	1–1,200,000	(1935)
Romania	745,000	(1930)
Yugoslavia	499,000	(1930)
Hungary	479,000	(1930)
Latvia	62,000	(1935)
Lithuania (excluding Memel)	33,000	(1931)
Memelland	25,000	(1930)
Estonia	16.000	(1934)
(Practically all German-speaking peoples in the areas listed above have fled, been removed, or killed since the beginning of World War II.)		
Austria	6,330,000	(1931)
Switzerland	2,900,000	(1930)
France	1,250,000[b]	(1930)
Saarland	770,000	(1927)
Luxembourg	297,000	(1935)
Italy	250,000[c]	(1939)
Belgium	69,000	(1930)
Denmark	20,000[b]	(1930)
Netherlands	12,000[b]	(1930)

Census figures vary widely according to the particular definition of "German-speaking" peoples.

[a] Approximate figure. Includes Danzig.

[b] Approximate figure.

[c] Including Ladins.

Sources: Joseph B. Schechtman, European Population Transfers, 1939–1945 (New York: Oxford University Press, 1946); The Statesman's Yearbook, 1941; information services of the Netherlands, Belgium, and Denmark.

of unity has developed despite religious differences[7] and postwar territorial divisions. The 1945 division of the nation, dictated by outside powers, runs counter to the strong feelings of unity, and to a majority of the German people reunification remains an essential goal.

Two aspects of the German population factor have been utilized by propagandists in justifying the State's territorial demands. One is the need for living space or *Lebensraum* for the large energetic population. The concept of life as a fight for space was developed in the writings of Ratzel and his followers, and has been utilized by more recent German scholars and officials in explaining the nation's needs for additional territory. Associated with this *Lebensraum* has been the desire by German leaders to unite German-speaking groups living beyond the country's borders within the framework of Germany itself, even at the cost of destroying other national units and incorporating large non-German groups as well.

The Development of the German State. The various German states of central Europe were late in merging into one political entity. In 1815, at the Congress of Vienna, a Germanic Confederation, including both the German states and Austria, was organized under Austrian domination. By this time, however, the German state of Prussia, occupying much of north central and northeast Germany, had so increased in power that already it represented a challenge to Austria's position in central Europe. In the decades following the Vienna Congress Prussia moved gradually to eliminate Austria from the Confederation and to unite the German states in a Prussian-dominated nation.

As a first step toward German unification the Prussians promoted a customs union (*Zollverein*) in 1833, which eventually united the German states into an economic unit, from which Austria was excluded. Next, in 1864 Prussia attacked Denmark, and the cooperation of the other German states in the war effort furthered the bonds of German unity. Two years later Prussia again brought on war, this time against Austria, and once more the other German states came to Prussia's aid. Austria was soon defeated, the old Germanic Confederation was dissolved, and a new Prussian-dominated confederation was formed, in which Austria did not participate.

In 1870 Prussia instigated a war with France. For the third time in six years the other German states cooperated in the conflict, and within a few months the French were defeated. In the aftermath of the Franco-Prussian War the German states decided to unite politically into the new German nation under the sovereignty of the Prussian king. As war booty, Germany received from France the border province of Alsace, together with a part of neighboring Lorraine.

---

[7] The population of pre-Hitler Germany was divided roughly three to two in favor of Protestants over Catholics. In addition there were 500,000 Jews, of whom less than 25,000 now remain in the two German republics.

During the decades following its unification Germany worked to build up its economic strength in Europe and to expand its political and economic power abroad. Industrialization proceeded at a rapid rate, and the population increased from 41 million in 1871 to 65 million in 1914. Growth in German agriculture, foreign trade, and armaments kept pace with these other increases.

Overseas, Germany moved rapidly to develop a colonial empire in Africa and the Pacific. During the 1880's German settlements were established in Africa, and gradually Germany's claims were recognized over Southwest Africa, the Cameroons, Togoland, and German East Africa (most of which now comprises Tanganyika). In the Pacific Germany annexed the northeastern shore of New Guinea, as well as the Bismarck Archipelago and the northern Solomons. In less that a decade and a half after its formation as a unified State Germany had developed the third largest colonial empire in the world at that time. Later acquisitions in the Pacific included western Samoa, the Marshall Islands, the Carolines, and the Marianas.

In 1914 Germany, Austria-Hungary, and the other Central Powers entered World War I against France, Britain, and their allies. Four years later the Central Powers surrendered. Germany's defeat put a temporary stop to the country's expansion and led to a major reapportionment of the areas under German control (Table 3). The country was stripped of all its overseas possessions. Territorial losses in Western Germany have already been noted; consideration is given here to losses in the east.

THE GERMAN-POLISH BORDER. The area ceded to Poland by Germany in 1919 returned the German-Polish border to approximately its

Table 3

EUROPEAN TERRITORY LOST BY GERMANY AFTER WORLD WAR I

	Area (in sq. mi.)	Population (Census of 1910)
Alsace-Lorraine	5,607	1,874,014
Saar Basin (under League of Nations for 15 years)	744	713,105*
Belgium (Eupen and Malmédy)	400	60,003
Poland	17,816	3,854,971
Memel	1,026	141,238
Danzig	739	330,630
Denmark (Schleswig—northern zone) . .	1,542	166,348
Czechoslovakia (part of Upper Silesia) .	122	48,446
Total	27,996	7,188,755

*Census of 1922.
From Isaiah Bowman, *The New World*, p. 273. Copyright 1928 by World Book Company. Used by permission of R. G. Bowman.

Table 4

DISTRIBUTION OF GERMAN COLONIES AFTER WORLD WAR I

Colony	Mandate Power	Class of Mandate
German East Africa (Tanganyika)	Great Britain	B
Ruanda-Urundi	Belgium	B
Cameroons	France, Great Britain	B
Togoland	France, Great Britain	B
Southwest Africa	Union of South Africa	C
North Pacific islands	Japan	C
German New Guinea and nearby South Pacific islands	Australia	C
Western Samoa	New Zealand	C
Nauru	Joint Administration: Great Britain Australia New Zealand	C

location in 1772, at the time of the first partition of Poland. In the area along the Baltic coast border delimitations were particularly difficult, for most of the inhabitants here were German, while the new Polish State insisted that it have access to the Baltic Sea. This conflict of self-determination versus economic needs was eventually settled by Germany's retention of East Prussia as an eastern outlier along the Baltic, by the creation of a Polish Corridor to the sea between East Prussia and the rest of Germany, and by the establishment of the German-inhabited port of Danzig (lying within the Polish Corridor) as a Free City under League of Nations administration. In the Allenstein-Marienwerder area of southern East Prussia (Figure 44) a plebiscite was held in 1920 to determine the wishes of the local people. The predominantly Protestant population voted to remain with the Germans rather than join Catholic Poland. To the northeast of East Prussia, Memelland, a German-speaking area on the Baltic, was eventually annexed by Lithuania (see page 291).

Danzig, a city of 400,000 inhabitants at the mouth of the Vistula River, was cut off from its former hinterland, and even after the final delimitation of the German-Polish border the people of Danzig continued their agitation for reunion with Germany (Figure 44). Largely because of the hostility of these peoples, Poland began construction in 1921 of a rival port, Gdynia, located a few miles northwest of Danzig on the Polish-held portion of the Baltic coast. After the port's completion Danzig's commercial activities practically ceased. Because of the economic distress there the Free City during the 1930's was an important center for the Nazi party, with its demands for renunciation of the Versailles Treaty and the return to Germany of its prewar territories.

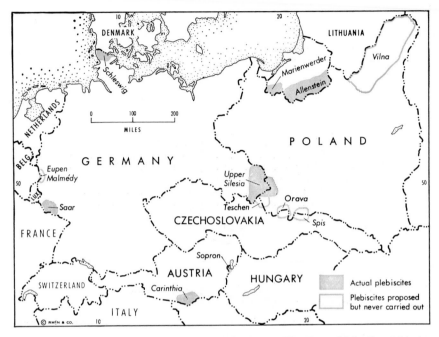

Figure 43. Plebiscites in Europe After World War I. The Eupen-Malmédy plebiscite was only partially carried out. (After Wambaugh, *Plebiscites Since World War I,* Carnegie Endowment for International Peace, 1933. Used by permission.)

Hitler exploited the discontent of the Germans in Danzig and the Polish Corridor in his demands on Poland for return of these areas. At the beginning of World War II German forces occupied western Poland, which was subsequently annexed to the Reich. Toward the end of the war, however, Soviet forces, moving westward across Poland, forced the Germans from this area. In 1945 the German-Polish border was shifted westward to the Oder-Neisse line, and the Germans living to the east of this line were repatriated. Thus the boundaries of Poland were extended considerably farther west than they had been prior to Hitler's invasion of 1939.

In Upper Silesia, at the southern end of the German-Polish border, problems arose over boundary delimitations through what was basically a unified economic region. Although there was talk of awarding the entire area to Poland, German spokesmen argued that without at least a part of Upper Silesia their nation's economic future would be in jeopardy. Yet if division were agreed upon, there remained the task of drawing the boundary so as to include as many persons as possible within the country of their choice, while at the same time avoiding undue strains on the area's economy and on the maintenance of border functions.

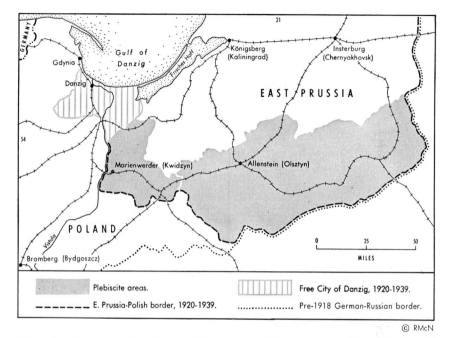

Figure 44. Danzig and the Allenstein-Marienwerder Plebiscite Areas. (After Wambaugh, *Plebiscites Since World War I*, Carnegie Endowment for International Peace, 1933. Used by permission.)

A plebiscite was held in a part of Upper Silesia in 1921. Despite the fact that a majority of the inhabitants there were Poles, the results showed 700,000 votes for union of the plebiscite area with Germany and about 470,000 for annexation to Poland. The pro-German victory in this predominantly Polish area demonstrated the fact that there, as in other parts of western and central Europe, economic considerations often outweighed cultural factors in influencing political choices. The final German-Polish border decided upon by the League of Nations split the plebiscite area, leaving 572,000 Poles in Germany and 350,000 Germans in Poland (Figure 45). Since the end of World War II the entire Upper Silesian area has been included within Poland.

THE GERMAN-DANISH BORDER. The territorial problems between Germany and Denmark at the end of World War I involved the Schleswig-Holstein area. Taken from Denmark in 1864, Schleswig-Holstein received a large influx of German settlers, so that by 1919 the ethnic character of its population had changed considerably from what it was in the mid-nineteenth century. Danish claims to Holstein itself were considered too weak by League of Nations officials to justify a plebiscite, but it was decided that to the north, in Schleswig, a vote would be taken. The province was

Figure 45. The Upper Silesia Plebiscite
Area. (After Bowman, The New World,
World Book Co., 1928. Used by permission of R. G. Bowman.)

Upper Silesia plebiscite area.

International Boundaries
1921-1939.

Boundaries of Teschen area.

Final Polish-German border
in plebiscite area.

Coal Basin.

© RMcN

divided into two parts for the plebiscite: the people of the northern portion decided three to one in favor of joining Denmark, but those in the south elected to stay with Germany. Despite Danish protests the province of Schleswig was divided (Figure 46).

When Nazi Germany annexed Denmark in 1940, northern Schleswig was returned to German control, but five years later the Danes reannexed it. In this fairly homogeneous agricultural area boundary delimitation along ethnic lines is difficult. Barring large-scale population transfers, the complex ethnic pattern there seems likely to continue. Thus at some future date it may again erupt into a territorial dispute between the two States.

Expansion of Germany Under Hitler, 1935–39. During the first decade and a half following World War I an attempt was made to develop a successful democratic government in Germany. The failure of this attempt was the result of many factors, including Germany's continued economic difficulties. The economic structure had suffered heavily from the war and from the readjustments which followed it, and, unlike conditions which existed after World War II, there was no large-scale foreign aid for defeated enemies during the 1920's. In 1933, at the depth of the world-wide depression, Adolph Hitler became the German chancellor and capitalized on the

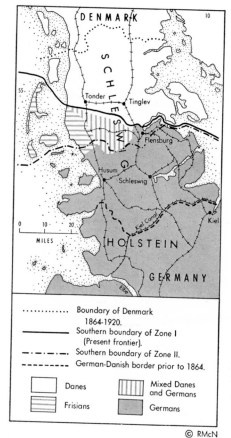

Figure 46. The Schleswig Plebiscite Area. (After Bowman, *The New World,* World Book Co., 1928. Used by permission of R. G. Bowman.)

popular discontent in the nation. He embarked on a program to revive Germany's national power and was determined to strengthen the nation internally and to expand its territorial holdings. His efforts, like those of Frederick the Great, Bismarck, and Kaiser Wilhelm II, were aided by the blind following of many of the German people. Through skillful use of mass propaganda Hitler and his National Socialist (Nazi) party were able to win continued support of the German people for their internal and external policies.

Germany's first territorial acquisition under Hitler occurred in 1935, when the people of the Saar voted nine to one for the return of German control (Figure 47). The following year Germany began to rearm the Rhineland, the area between the Rhine River and the western border, which had been permanently demilitarized by the Versailles Treaty. No active opposition to this move on the part of the Allied powers was encountered, and Hitler felt encouraged to continue his renunciations of the

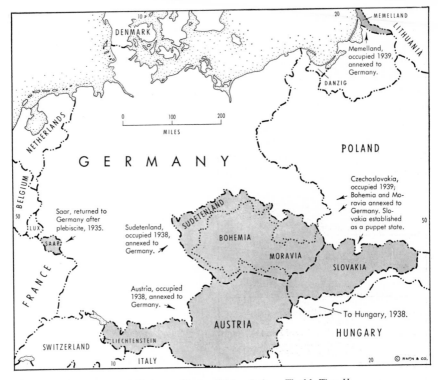

Figure 47. Expansion of Germany Under Hitler Before World War II.

Versailles terms. In February, 1938, German military forces occupied Austria. This bold venture to establish a German-Austrian *Anschluss* was carried out despite opposition on the part of many Austrians, who considered the German act one of conquest rather than unification.

By constant utilization of the Pan-German theme, the Nazis were able to stir up discontent among German groups residing in other European countries. In the fall of 1938, after a bitter propaganda campaign, Germany annexed the Sudeten area of western Czechoslovakia with its more than 3 million German inhabitants. By this time demands were also being made on Poland to restore to Germany the Polish Corridor and Danzig with their large numbers of German-speaking peoples.

Despite Nazi claims at the time of the acquisition of Sudetenland that all of Germany's territorial ambitions were now realized, the Germans within a few months moved to annex new areas. In March, 1939, Hitler occupied the remainder of Czechoslovakia, except for the easternmost province, Ruthenia, which Hungary seized. Memelland on the Baltic coast was then taken back from Lithuania, and by June the enlarged German State contained a population of 86 million people. Within a few weeks of the Czech occupation the German government had stepped up its propaganda campaign for the return of western Poland to Germany. The British and French, determined at last to halt Germany's territorial aggrandizement, supported Poland in its refusal to comply with Nazi demands. On September 1, 1939, German forces invaded Poland, and two days later, in fulfillment of their obligations to the Poles, Britain and France declared war on Germany.

Territorial Problems Since World War II. At the end of World War II Germany, a defeated nation, was divided into occupation zones, and a cease-fire line was delimited between Soviet forces in the east and those of the United States, Britain, and France in the west. This line, drawn as a temporary border, followed no particular pattern of physical or historical boundaries. Local political areas were split by the border, villages and towns were separated from their hinterlands. Inability on the part of the great powers to agree on the nature and function of an all-German government led to the hardening of this cease-fire line into a political boundary, and eventually into a sector of the Iron Curtain, across which virtually no traffic moves. Such a dividing line has worked considerable hardship on the people of the border areas and illustrates clearly the difficulties attendant on ill-conceived boundaries drawn across a unified physical, cultural, and economic region. In 1949 the German Federal Republic (West Germany), comprising the three western occupation zones, came into existence, with its capital located at Bonn. In the same year the German Democratic Republic was established in the Soviet occupation zone, with its capital in East Berlin.

In addition to internal political division, Germany suffered several territorial losses at the end of the war, as shown in Table 5. These losses totaled over 51,000 square miles of territory, containing a predominantly German-speaking population of about 10½ million. Most of the people living in the areas lost to Poland and the U.S.S.R. have been forced to emigrate to Germany; thus the Germans in the future will no longer have claims to those areas on the basis of ethnic ties.

West Germany (The Federal Republic of Germany). In May, 1955, West Germany became a sovereign independent State. With over 56 million inhabitants it has the largest population of any country in Europe outside the Soviet Union; it has also the strongest industrial economy in Europe. Its area of just under 95,000 square miles approximates that of the United Kingdom (which has about 4 million less people), but unlike Britain West Germany has no overseas territories or Commonwealth members with which it can tie its economy. It does, however, have coal, lignite, iron ore, potash, and small amounts of petroleum, as well as a dense network of transport facilities and a strong industrial base. Coupled with this are the energies and skills of the German people, and the policies and plans of the

Table 5

GERMAN TERRITORIAL CHANGES FOLLOWING WORLD WAR II

*A. Territory Lost by Germany**

	Area (sq. mi.)	Population
To Poland	44,215	9,000,000
To Soviet Union	6,100	500,000
To the Netherlands	26	13,000
Saar	991	943,000

B. Territorial Division of Germany

	Area	Population (1959)
West Germany (German Federal Rep.) .	94,634	53,049,100
East Germany (German Democratic Rep.)	42,392	16,203,553
Berlin		
West		2,208,000
East		1,082,349

C. Economic Comparison of post-World War II German Areas in Terms of 1938 Production (figures represent percentages of national total)

	Coal	Coal & Steel	Food
West Germany	74	67	43
East Germany	3	3	30
Polish- and Soviet-controlled eastern territories	17	11	25
Saar	6	19	2

*The Germany of 1935–38, after the return of the Saar. The Saar was again returned to Germany in 1957.

postwar government which have made possible the rapid economic rise of the country after the destruction and defeat of World War II.

The re-emergence of West Germany as a power would not have been possible without the cooperation and support of other Western states, notably France, Britain, and the United States. The animosity of the early postwar years was gradually replaced by a sense of urgency that West Germany regain its strength in order to supplement western Europe's power position against the Soviet-dominated east. The treaties under which West Germany became independent stipulated a contribution of West Germany to Western defense within the framework of NATO—a contribution which, it is planned, will ultimately be greater in numbers of troops than that of any other NATO member. The lack of defense expenditures prior to 1955 aided the Germans in their economic build-up, and by 1960 West Germany was the third among the states of the world in steel production, turning out nearly half again as much steel per year as Britain, which was in fourth place.

The position of West Germany in a divided Europe poses a number of serious questions. Under Chancellor Adenauer the State has adhered closely to the Western anti-Soviet policies, and Germany is also an important member of the Common Market. Its postwar territorial problems with its western neighbors have been amicably solved (see pages 221 and 224), and Germany is again accepted by most of the non-Communist States of the world. But three problems remain to plague the West German government; West Berlin, the reunification of Germany, and return of the lost territories east of the Oder-Neisse line. In the case of West Berlin, American, British, and French military power stands as a symbol of resistance to future Soviet encroachments. Reunification is in many respects more of an emotional than a practical problem under current conditions, although the Soviets at times suggest possible "compromises" under which reunification of East and West Germany might be considered (see page 299). Return of the eastern territories would appear to be even less of a possibility, although they will probably remain for a long time as German "irredenta." (See page 298 for a discussion of East Germany.)

WEST BERLIN. West Berlin, comprising the British, French, and American zones, has an area of 188 square miles and a population of about 2 million (Figure 48). It is governed as a single unit, and although represented in the legislature of the West German republic, it is not actually a state of the republic, but a separate political entity. In 1945 it was divided into four occupation zones, under the authority of a committee comprising the four Allied commanders. Actually the basic document on Berlin was the protocol drawn up by the European Advisory Commission in 1944 and ratified by the United States, Britain, the Soviet Union, and later by France, providing an Inter-Allied Governing Authority to administer jointly the Greater Berlin area. When the Western powers recognized West Germany's sovereignty in 1954, they reserved their rights and responsibilities relating to Berlin; the following year, however, the Soviet Union recognized East Germany's sovereignty over East Berlin, and that city is now the capital of East Germany. The United States, Britain, and France have never acknowledged East Germany's rights in administering the area on the grounds that the 1944 agreement is still in effect.

The problems connected with the maintenance of a Western outpost deep within Soviet territory were amply demonstrated by the airlift of 1949–50, when all surface communications between West Germany and West Berlin were cut off by the Soviets and supplies had to be brought in by air. In normal times a fixed number of freight and passenger trains is permitted over the rail line from Helmstedt in West Germany to West Berlin; also an *autobahn* connecting the same cities is kept open, and some barge traffic is permitted. In addition, three air corridors twenty miles wide are kept open between Berlin and West Germany. Only over these airways has traffic remained unimpeded throughout the occupation.

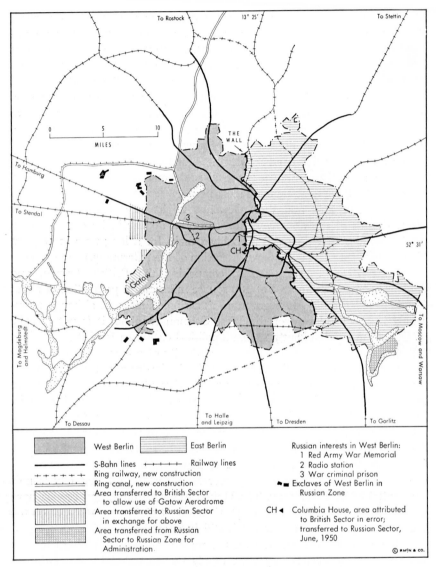

Figure 48. The Division of Berlin. (After Robinson, *The Geographical Review,* XLIII [Oct., 1953]. Courtesy of American Geographical Society.)

At the end of World War II no explicit, written documents were ever drawn up guaranteeing Western rights of access to Berlin; the only actual agreement was that flights between Berlin and West Germany could take place in three air corridors without advance notice. The location of these corridors and of the overland routes to West Berlin was assigned to the Western powers by the Soviets. At the time of the ending of the Berlin blockade in 1949 it was agreed that all restrictions imposed on communications between Berlin and West Germany, as well as those between West and East Berlin, would be removed. In subsequent years hundreds of thousands of refugees streamed across the border from East to West Berlin, most of them to be flown from West Berlin to West Germany. Faced with a shortage of professionals and skilled workers, the East Germans eventually moved to shut off this exodus and in August, 1961, the flow of East Germans was halted when a wall was constructed dividing East and West Berlin. West Berlin then became an island surrounded by East Germany, an island to which the East Germans (in most cases) could no longer escape nor even visit. Thus its function as a "showcase" of democracy within East Germany no longer exists.

The future of West Berlin revolves about two considerations. First, what pressures will the Soviets exert in order to change its status? They have suggested that West Berlin become a demilitarized "free city" under some form of international administration, and that in exchange for guarantees of freedom of access to the area the United States agree to recognize the East German regime. The Western powers, on the other hand, have little room for maneuverability, since they are committed to the defense of West Berlin; abandonment of the West Berliners would have serious repercussions on the people of West Germany itself. It would also be a serious defeat for the West in the over-all Cold War struggle, since it would represent a gradual retreat by the Western powers in the face of relentless Communist pressure, until at last they were forced out of Berlin. Such a process might then be repeated in other parts of the world as well.

Figure 49. Berlin: Routes of Access to West Germany.

There is also the problem of West Berlin's economy. Approximately one-half of the city's expenses are covered by the export of goods and services; the rest must be met by grants from the West German government and the United States. West Berlin may continue to develop its manufactures, particularly those of high-cost, low-bulk goods, although such development must take place in competition with similar expansions in many other parts of the world. Along with economic viability goes the factor of morale. If the people of West Berlin become apprehensive of the future, there may be a mass exodus from the city to West Germany, particularly an exodus of young people, leaving West Berlin as the shell of a once-great capital, surrounded by a hostile country and maintained only by expensive and dangerous means.

Austria

Austria's location in central Europe has been of great importance to the State's development. Major north-south and east-west transportation lines pass across the area, and Austria has served as a historic marchland protecting central and western Europe against attacks from the east and southeast. The Romans established Vienna as a fortress guarding the Danube route, and later Charlemagne developed the Austrian area as a defense zone against hostile forces to the southeast. In the sixteenth and seventeenth centuries Vienna was besieged by the Turks moving up the Danube Valley; the city's successful resistance to these invaders prevented Mohammedan control from spreading west of the Vienna basin. The Brenner, Tauern, and Semmering passes in Austria are major links in the north-south routes between the Mediterranean basin and the lands to the north of the Alps. These routes are traversed by important rail lines, as are the east-west routes through Austria connecting Switzerland and southern Germany with the Danube basin.

Despite its nodal position Austria suffers from certain disadvantages. The State has no seacoast and must depend on foreign ports, such as Trieste and Hamburg, for its overseas trade. Culturally and economically Austria maintains close bonds with three of its neighbors—Germany, Hungary, and Italy—yet geography and history have combined to keep it politically and economically separated from each of the three. Language and economic ties bind it with Germany; Hungary, with its foodstuffs and potential markets, is a former political and economic partner; Italy, in which many former Austrian citizens live and through whose territory passes one of Austria's principal links with the sea, has historically been an enemy of the Austrian State. Instead of representing a focus of power in central Europe, Austria has often been forced to accept the role of buffer area between the major power blocs which surround it.

The area of Austria is about 32,000 square miles. Its 7 million people are overwhelmingly German-speaking and Roman Catholic. The Jews, most of whom had fled or been exterminated by 1945, were the most important minority group in the nation prior to World War II. The annual population increase is less than three per thousand, reflecting the low birth rate. Resources include iron ore, timber, salt, graphite, lignite, petroleum, and water power potential. The country is Europe's third largest producer of petroleum, and although the output is only about 40 per cent of Romania's, it fulfills domestic needs and permits some exports as well. Austria also exports timber and electric power, but it must import considerable quantities of coal for local use. Approximately 22 per cent of the total area is devoted to agriculture; since World War I Austria has been a food-deficit country, producing at best only about three-fourths of its total food requirements.

Before World War I Lower Austria (with Bohemia, in what is now Czechoslovakia) served as the industrial and commercial heart of the Austro-Hungarian Empire. With the break-up of the empire the Austrians were separated from prewar markets, food sources, and industrial raw materials. Vienna, with a population of nearly 2 million people, had been the leading city of an area of 51 million persons; in 1919 it became the center of a country whose total population was only about three times as great as that of the city itself.

The defeat of Austria-Hungary in World War I completely shattered the Empire. Austria and Hungary were separated from one another, and Austria was stripped of 70 per cent of its territory. Prewar Austrian areas contributed to the formation of three new States—Poland, Czechoslovakia, and Yugoslavia—as well as to the expansion of Italy and Romania.

The Carinthia and Sopron Plebiscites. In the Carinthian basin of southeastern Austria and in the Sopron area along the Austro-Hungarian border two plebiscites were held after World War I. In Carinthia the dispute involved Austria and Yugoslavia. In the Drava River lowland of southeastern Austria both Austrians and Slovenes were settled. Some League of Nations experts argued against any territorial changes which would split the economic unity of the basin, but a vote was nevertheless taken in the area south of the river, with the results six to four in favor of the continued inclusion of Carinthia in Austria (Figure 50). Following World War II Yugoslavia sought to annex a portion of the Carinthia area measuring nearly 1,000 square miles and containing a population of about 190,000. No mention was made of a plebiscite, although neutral estimates placed the number of Slovenes at less than 20 per cent of the total population. Despite strong Yugoslav claims the Carinthia basin continued to remain with Austria.

The Sopron plebiscite involved the transfer of Burgenland from Hun-

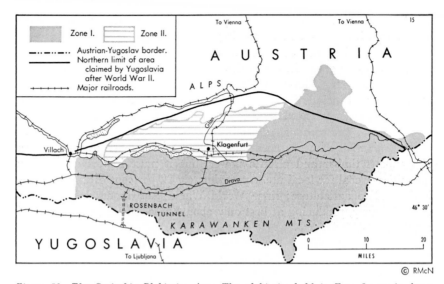

© RMcN

Figure 50. The Carinthia Plebiscite Area. The plebiscite held in Zone 1 was in favor of continued union with Austria. If the vote had been pro-Yugoslav, a plebiscite would then have been held in Zone 2. (After Wambaugh, *Plebiscites Since World War I*, Carnegie Endowment for International Peace, 1933. Used by permission.)

gary to Austria in 1919. This 1,558-square-mile district, with a largely German-speaking population of 218,000, was a rich agricultural area and an important asset to a food-deficit State like postwar Austria. A plebiscite was held in 1920 among the people in the Sopron area in the eastern sector of Burgenland, and the pro-Hungarian vote resulted in the separation of this small area from Burgenland and its retention in Hungary.

South Tyrol. These two plebiscites did not end Austria's problems, for in the South Tyrol section of northern Italy were 200,000 German-speaking Austrians, residents of what had been a part of Austria up to 1919. The Tyrol was a historic "pass" region, lying across one of Europe's most important north-south routes from southern Germany and the Inn Valley of Austria south through the Brenner Pass into Italy (Figure 51). From South Tyrol strategic passes connect to the north with Austrian Tyrol and east with the Drava Valley, as well as south with the North Italian Plain. From 1363 to 1919 the South Tyrol was an Austrian glacis extending south of the main crest of the Alps.

Following World War I no plebiscite was held among the inhabitants of South Tyrol to determine their wishes. Italy's northern boundary was moved to the main crest of the Alps (in this section to the Brenner Pass), thereby including former Austrian territory in the Italian regions of Alto Adige and Trentino. Under Italy's Fascist government (1923–43) attempts were made to Italianize South Tyrol, first, by transferring large numbers

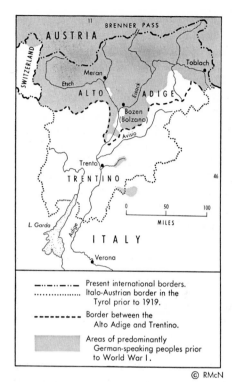

Figure 51. The South Tyrol. (Based on Marinelli, *The Geographical Review*, VII [March, 1919]. Courtesy of American Geographical Society.)

of Italians to the area and, second, by interfering with the customs and economy of the German-speaking inhabitants. In governmental positions and in public services Germans were replaced by Italians. The use of German in the schools was forbidden, street names and public signs were changed to Italian, and Germans were forbidden to engage in various cultural activities, such as the wearing of traditional costumes or membership in German social clubs. With the gradual industrialization of South Tyrol, Germans were generally excluded from employment in the new industries and power projects which developed after 1923.

In 1939, a year after the Austrian union with Germany, the governments of Germany and Italy agreed to a plebiscite to be held among the German-speaking persons of the South Tyrol to determine whether they wished to be repatriated to Germany or remain in Italy. Approximately 185,000 persons, or 70 per cent of the voters, elected to return to Nazi Germany, while some 80,000 others voted to stay in Italy. About 40 per cent of those who voted to return to Germany were actually repatriated before World War II halted the operations. Many of the returned Germans were subsequently settled in those sections of eastern Europe which were overrun by German armies in the opening years of World War II, but by 1945 most of them were back in Germany itself. Some of the former Tyrolese attempted to return to the South Tyrol after the war, but the Italian government refused permission on the grounds that these people when given the opportunity had chosen German rather than Italian sovereignty.

In 1946 Austria put forth claims to the northern province (Alto Adige) of South Tyrol. Although even the Italian government admitted that a plebiscite in this area would show a majority of the inhabitants favoring reunion with Austria, neither the Western powers nor the Soviet Union actively supported Austria's claims, and the area remained with Italy. The Italians eventually agreed to grant local autonomy to the Tyrol, to respect the German culture there, and to readmit most of the former German-speaking inhabitants who had left in the years 1939–43.

Since 1946 the German language has been permitted in the South Tyrol schools, and discrimination against German-speaking peoples there has largely disappeared. In granting local autonomy to South Tyrol, however, Italy has included the area administratively with the province of Trentino to the south; thus the German-speaking people are greatly outnumbered by the Italians. Finally, the Austrian government contends that Italy, although encouraging emigration of Italians to South Tyrol, has still refused to admit all but a few of the German-speaking people who voluntarily left the Tyrol in the early 1940's.

Austria Since World War I. Following the dismemberment of the Austro-Hungarian Empire, Austria struggled to develop its resources and to increase its industrial output, but the nation's economy never regained its prewar economic stability. In 1921 the Austrians officially requested an *Anschluss* of their country with Germany, hoping thereby to prevent a collapse of the national economy, but the move was blocked by France, which feared it might produce too great an increase in Germany's power potential. Seventeen years later, when the *Anschluss* did take place, Austria's economic structure became geared with that of Nazi Germany.

After World War II the Austrians were faced with serious economic problems. The ties with Germany were dissolved, and German assets in Austria were seized by the Allied powers.[8] Although in 1946 the United States, Britain, and France returned to the Austrians the industrial facilities which they had previously dismantled, the Soviets permanently removed an estimated 12 per cent of the nation's total industrial equipment. For ten years the Soviets siphoned off most of the wealth of their occupation zone, and by the terms of the 1955 peace treaty the Austrians were forced to

---

[8] Austria's position with respect to war reparations was complicated by the fact that German capital, particularly after the 1938 *Anschluss*, had built up much of the nation's economy. In some cases the Germans had confiscated through technical purchases many former Austrian enterprises. After World War II all German assets in Austria were classed as enemy property, subject to confiscation as war reparations.

Figure 52. Germany and Austria.

supply the U.S.S.R. with $152 million worth of free goods in the ensuing six years and 1 million tons of oil a year (approximately one-third of the country's oil output) for a period of ten years, as well as an additional 200,000 tons a year for six years in payment for the return of German assets in Austria which the Russians had previously confiscated. Austria was forced to become a permanently neutral State and was forbidden to join Germany in any future political or economic union.

Austria's future development is restricted by a number of factors. Ideological differences block the creation of any type of Danubian federa-

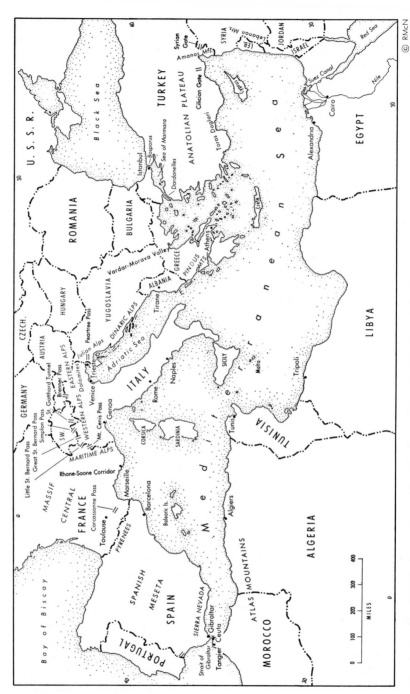

Figure 53. The Mediterranean Basin, Showing Surrounding Highlands and Lowlands.

tion, in which Austria might once again become associated with Hungary and other States of the Danube basin. Unification with Germany has been specifically prohibited. The legacy of past differences with the Italians and the lack of strong economic bonds between Austria and Italy preclude the development of particularly close ties there. Although it is now a neutralized State, Austria does not enjoy Switzerland's long history of neutrality and its climate of stability, which has served to attract foreign economic activities. The Austrians are particularly concerned over developments in the Common Market. Over 40 per cent of Austria's imports are from West Germany and a quarter of her exports go to Germany: thus the erection of a tariff wall against Austria would seriously affect her foreign trade. On the other hand, the Russians hold that Austrian participation in the Common Market would violate the 1955 treaty, prohibiting Austria from pursuing policies which might lead to another union with Germany. In 1960 Austria joined the "Outer Seven," a move which may in time mean further trade barriers between Austria and Germany. As a result the Austrians face serious problems in their efforts to evolve a stable economic and political system in what once again has become a position exposed to dynamic and potentially hostile forces to the east.

THE MEDITERRANEAN AREA

Italy

The peninsular State of Italy has often experienced territorial instability and change. Its relations with the areas which surround it on its land and sea borders have been greatly influenced by two historical trends, first, the fear that these areas might be used as bases for launching attacks against Italy itself and, second, Italian desires to expand the country's political control to nearby areas, some of which have in part been occupied by Italians, and which were once part of the Roman Empire. On its land borders the State is separated by the Alps from four neighbors—France, Switzerland, Austria, and Yugoslavia. Across the narrow Adriatic Sea lie Yugoslavia and Albania. The French island of Corsica is situated 50 miles west of the Italian mainland, and the formerly French-controlled North African coast is less than 100 miles across the Mediterranean from Sicily. Finally, 60 miles to the south of Sicily is the British island of Malta.

Italy's location makes it something of a transition area between central Europe and the Mediterranean. The climate of northern Italy is continental rather than Mediterranean, and much of the economy of this area is closely tied with that of France, Switzerland, and Austria. Although the Alps virtually surround Italy on its land boundaries, communications through and around the mountains are not difficult to maintain; the numerous valleys of the Italian border regions are populated by French-, German-, and Slavic-speaking peoples as well as Italians. Italy's continental neighbors, particularly France and Austria, for many centuries controlled important sections of what is now the Italian State, and the political and military activities of these countries in Italy constituted one of the principal causes for the late unification of the peninsula into an independent national unit.

The country possesses few of the important requirements for national power. There is virtually no petroleum in Italy, only small amounts of low-grade coal, and insufficient iron ore to meet domestic needs. Water power is the only readily available power source, although utilization of natural gas is becoming increasingly important. Much of Italy's soil is exhausted or subject to severe erosion, the system of land tenure is only gradually being modernized, and, although 45 per cent of the country's land is in crops, food production is insufficient to satisfy domestic needs.

Italy's population of some 49,500,000 places considerable strain on its resources. Large numbers of Italians have emigrated to foreign countries; Italian workers also migrate as "temporary residents" to other European States in order to secure employment. It was an Italian hope that the acquisition of overseas territories would provide an outlet for surplus population. Prior to the outbreak of World War II, however, less than 200,000 Italians (0.4 per cent of the population) resided in Italy's colonial areas. One of the important political aspects of Italy's population pressure is, of course, the effect of this pressure on the State's economic structure. There is in Italy a large Moscow-oriented Communist party, which skillfully capitalizes on the fears and discontents of the Italian people.

Italy's political features reflect the complicated pressures which exist there. Major centripetal forces include a strong concept of nation, a single language and religion, and a relatively well-developed circulatory system. The capital is centrally located geographically, although it is too far south in relation to the political or economic balance. The principal core area of Italy is the Po basin, containing approximately 40 per cent of the State's population. Other core areas are Tuscany (including Florence and Pisa), the Tiber lowlands around Rome, and Campania in the southwest, centered on Naples. The northern Italians, with their greater economic development, often feel themselves to be culturally superior to the people of central and southern Italy; one political effect of this has been the resentment among north Italians toward government-sponsored programs for the economic and social betterment of the south.

Since the end of World War II the Italian government has sought to protect the interests of certain "peripheral" areas through the creation of autonomous regions in which local governments are given jurisdiction over such affairs as education, public works, planning, and industrial development. There are four such regions—Trentino-Adige (South Tyrol), Val d'Aosta in the northwest, Sicily, and Sardinia. The Trieste area, including the provinces of Gorizia and Udine, may in time become a fifth region.

Territorial Development. After the unification of Italy in 1870 the Italians, like the Germans, desired an overseas empire as a mark of national prestige, as an area for investments, and as a market for exports. In Africa Italy acquired Eritrea along the Red Sea coast by conquest and Italian Somaliland by occupation and treaties, while Libya was won from the Turks just prior to World War I. In 1935 Ethiopia, one of Africa's few independent states, was invaded and conquered by Italian forces based in Eritrea and Italian Somaliland. The success of Italian moves there was occasioned in part by the fact that these African areas had not been effectively claimed by other European powers, since they had little demonstrable economic or strategic value. They also proved to be of little economic importance to the Italians in terms of resources, settlement areas, or markets. Following World War II the territories were taken from Italy, although the Italians were later awarded a ten-year trusteeship over Somalia—the former Italian Somaliland (see Chapter 14).

In the eastern Mediterranean Italy won from Turkey the Dodecanese Islands (including the island of Rhodes) at the same time it acquired Libya. The islands, inhabited by Greeks, are of little economic value, but the Italians hoped to use them as a springboard for the expansion of their power into Turkey—an operation which was never successful. For over three decades the Dodecanese remained an Italian outpost in the eastern Mediterranean, but in 1944 Italy, by this time a defeated Axis State, ceded them to the Greeks. Finally, in the Adriatic area Italian territorial ambitions involved both Trieste and the Istrian Peninsula in the north and various islands and coastal points in the central and eastern parts of that area.

The Trieste controversy is one of the outstanding examples of Italian irredentism. The area about the head of the Adriatic, sometimes referred to as the Julian region, has been a maritime outlet for regions to the north and to the east, and from Trieste rail lines extend eastward to the Danube lowland, north to the Drava Valley and Vienna basin, and westward to the Po lowlands. The close ties between this area and central Europe are illustrated by the fact that even in 1956 over two-thirds of the trade handled by Trieste was Austrian.

The ethnic pattern in the Julian region reflects its historical development as a marchland area. Roman colonists came to the Adriatic littoral in the first centuries of the Christian era, while Slovenes moved there from the east during the seventh and eighth centuries. From such ancient roots the modern ethnic division developed, with surprisingly little variation or intermixture. In general, the Italians inhabited the coastal lowlands from the Isonzo River to Pola at the tip of the Istrian Peninsula, while the Slovenes, a Slavic people, lived in the uplands behind the coastal plains.

For nearly three centuries prior to 1919 Trieste and most of the Istrian area were under Austrian control. At the end of World War I both Italy and the newly created State of Yugoslavia put forth claims in this area.

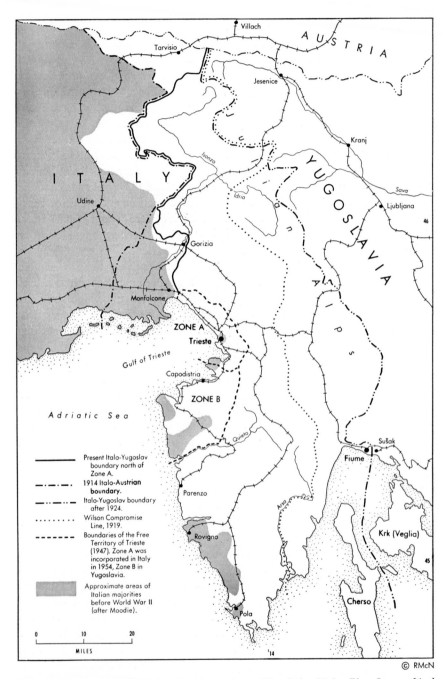

Figure 54. The Italo-Yugoslav Boundary Area. (Based on Kish, *The Geographical Review*, XXXVII [Jan., 1947], courtesy of American Geographical Society; and Moodie, *The Italo-Yugoslav Boundary*, George Philip & Son, 1945. Used by permission.)

The Yugoslavs maintained that their State was heir to this part of the former Austro-Hungarian Empire, and further that Trieste and Fiume were the only seaports available to them, while Italy had other harbors to develop. Italy, however, insisted on its ethnic and strategic rights, and the Italo-Yugoslav boundary was eventually delimited so as to give Italy control of almost the entire Julian region. Over half a million Slovenes thus came under Italian jurisdiction. The nearby port of Fiume was set up as a "free state," but within a few years the Italians annexed this as well (Figure 54).

With the ending of World War II the question of sovereignty over Trieste and the surrounding areas was raised once again. Much the same arguments were used as in the years following World War I. Eventually, by the terms of the Italian peace treaty Yugoslavia received most of the area which prior to 1919 had belonged to Austria-Hungary, although Trieste and the coastal regions near it—containing a predominantly Italian population—were constituted as the Free Territory of Trieste and placed under United Nations control.[9] Until such time as a governor could be appointed for the Free Territory, the area was divided into two zones—Zone A, included Trieste itself, which was occupied by American and British forces, and Zone B, to the southeast, occupied by the Yugoslavs. Most of the Italians living in the coastal areas east of Trieste subsequently moved to Italy itself, thus breaking the historical ethnic pattern.

As in Korea and Germany, the provisions for a unified territory of Trieste were never carried out, due to the inability of the Western and Communist powers to agree on the details of implementation. In October, 1954, after numerous proposals for the area's future had been considered, the territory was permanently divided, with Zone A being incorporated within Italy and Zone B into Yugoslavia. A minor correction in the border between the two zones, involving six square miles and about 4,000 Slovenes, was made in favor of Yugoslavia.

As has often happened in the past, the principal victims of the settlement may be the Triestans themselves. Trieste has been maintained as a free port, but Yugoslavia is improving the facilities of its own port at Fiume (Rijeka) and uses this as the country's outlet to the Adriatic. The occupation forces were subsequently withdrawn from Trieste, and the economy of the city (population about 250,000) has since declined. With the advent of economic depression may come widespread discontent on the part of the Triestans against the terms of the territorial settlement.

At the close of World War I, in addition to claims in the Trieste area, Italy demanded control of certain Adriatic islands as well as territorial concessions along the Dalmatian coast of Yugoslavia. Eventually the Italians

---

[9] The compromise on Trieste was closely tied to the question of the Italian Tyrol at the end of World War II. Austria had demanded return of the Tyrol from Italy, and the successful resistance by the Western powers to these demands partially compensated the Italians for their losses in the east to Yugoslavia.

were granted (1) an enclave about the Yugoslav city of Zara (now Zadar); (2) three northern Dalmatian islands (Cherso, Lussino, and Unie) controlling the entrance to Fiume; (3) Lagosta and another southern Dalmatian island; and (4) the Pelagosa Islands in the mid-Adriatic, forty miles southwest of Lagosta. These unconnected points assured Italy of naval dominance in the Adriatic.

During World War II Italy extended its power farther east by annexing the western areas of defeated Yugoslavia and establishing a protectorate over the central portion of the State (Figure 53). The end of the war, however, saw the evacuation of Yugoslavia and the return of Zara and the Italian-controlled Adriatic islands to the Yugoslavs, coupled with a rising interest by Yugoslavia in the development of its maritime activities. Thus once again Italy is confronted by a strong power across the narrow Adriatic.

Despite the historic conflicts which have for so long divided Italy from other countries of western Europe, the Italian government, in the years since World War II, has led the country into various economic and military agreements with its neighbors, the most significant being the European Common Market.

Malta

Britain's island base of Malta, lying to the south of Italy, faces an uncertain political future. With an area of 122 square miles (including the nearby islands of Gozo and Comino) and a population of some 330,000, Malta must import two-thirds of its food requirements. The major source of income is from the British dockyard, which employs nearly half of the total working force. In recent years the British have been reducing their naval activities in the Mediterranean, and a private British company has taken over and begun reconstructing a part of the dockyard to handle ordinary maritime repairs. Meanwhile the government of Malta has been proceeding with long-range industrial development plans which, it is hoped, may ultimately result in the establishment of twenty new factories and industrial plants in the area.

The Maltese, descended from the ancient Phoenicians, are divided in their political aspirations. One group favors dominion status for the island, while another is striving for incorporation within the United Kingdom—a status resembling that of Northern Ireland. In the latter case Malta would stand to gain from British social welfare benefits, although, on the other hand, the people would also have to pay high income taxes. The Maltese are Roman Catholics, and some opposition to the integration plan has come from the Catholic Church, which fears that its dominant position in matters of religion, education, and family life in Malta might be endangered if the island were a part of Protestant Britain. In February, 1956, a referendum was held in Malta, which resulted in a three to one vote in favor of union with Great Britain. This union never materialized, and with hopes of economic improvement in Malta, feelings there have lately turned more toward independence either within or outside the Commonwealth. An independent Malta might in time face serious economic problems, particularly if plans for industrialization do not work out. Although the average standard of living there is higher than in most of the other countries bordering the Mediterranean, separation from Britain—and the possible loss of British income to the island—might turn more and more of the Maltese in the direction of Communism.

The Iberian Peninsula

The Iberian Peninsula, sparated from France by the Pyrenees barrier, forms a relatively isolated geographic unit, yet one in which centrifugal forces have been effective in preventing political and cultural cohesion. Among these forces are diversity of landforms and differences in climate, economic activities, and historical development. Five principal languages are spoken: (1) Catalan, in northeast Spain, (2) Castilian, in central and southern Spain, (3) Galician (a dialect of Portuguese), in northwest Spain, (4) Portuguese, in Portugal, and (5) Basque, the language of approximately 2 million people who inhabit the western Pyrenees in both Spain and France. Although they have no history of political independence, the Basques have for many centuries resisted efforts to assimilate them within the cultures of the French and Spanish States.

Madrid, the Spanish capital, was purposely located during the late Middle Ages in the geographic center of the Iberian Peninsula, in order to strengthen centripetal pressures in that area. As early as the thirteenth century, however, Portugal, facing the Atlantic, had become an independent State, and except for a sixty-year period of union with Spain, it has remained a separate country since that time. A third political unit on the peninsula, the British possession of Gibraltar,[10] was established early in the eighteenth century. In addition to the physical and cultural forces of diversity is the fact that there is no one primary core area in Iberia and that even in modern times the circulatory system is poorly developed there. Thus regional differences continue to influence strongly the attitudes and desires of a majority of the people.

---

[10] The mountain State of Andorra in the east-central Pyrenees might also be considered part of the peninsula. Protected by surrounding mountains, this Catalan-speaking country, with an area of less than 200 square miles and a population of about 5,000, has a history of independence which dates back to 1278.

Portugal has an area of 35,000 square miles and a population of about 9 million. The people are united by language and religion, and Lisbon, the capital, is also located in the major core area. Thus Portugal, unlike Spain, has few centrifugal forces within its borders to threaten national cohesion. Much of the country is mountainous, and little of its estimated mineral wealth has yet been exploited. Except for textiles, industrialization is not well developed, and the per capita income is low compared with that of the States of northwestern Europe. Although the country has a long, indented seacoast on the Atlantic and is important for its fisheries, Portugal has not been a major maritime power for nearly four centuries. Its governments have lacked the resources needed to administer a large and far-flung empire, and much of the impetus for colonial development has been furnished by the Catholic Church or by chartered commercial companies, such as the Mozambique Company, which up to 1942 exercised political control over a large portion of Mozambique.

Portugal's historic alliance with Great Britain provided the protection of the British fleet and saved at least a part of the Portuguese African possessions from annexation by other European powers. In recent years Portugal has also maintained close military relations with the United States. Portugal is a member of the North Atlantic Treaty Organization, its principal contribution being the granting of permission to the United States to build and maintain an air base in the Azores Islands. Portugal's willingness to permit continued American use of the Lajes air base in the Azores has been tempered by what the Portuguese feel is a lack of American sympathy toward Portugal's colonial problems, however, both through the refusal of the United States to support the Portuguese when their colonial policies are attacked in the United Nations, and American failure to react at the time of the Indian take-over of Goa on the west coast of India (see page 471).

Although they were once important world powers, Spain and Portugal have made relatively little economic or political progress within recent times. The harbors of the two countries no longer serve the great trade routes of the world. Both States have for many years been controlled by dictators, and the long acceptance by the Spanish and Portuguese of existing conditions contrasts sharply with many other areas of the world, where, since the mid-1930's, continued poverty and political oppression have led to widespread popular unrest and violence. The factors of location and of protection behind the Pyrenees have meant that Spain and Portugal are less exposed to the dangers of possible invasion from the Soviet Union and its satellites than are other States of western Europe. In 1953 the Spanish government agreed to permit the United States to construct and maintain air and naval bases in Spain in return for American economic aid to that country, and Spain has now become an important military bastion for the United States, guarding the western Mediterranean.

The Strait of Gibraltar

One of the most strategically important areas in the western Mediterranean basin is the Strait of Gibraltar, a waterway eight miles wide at its narrowest point, which connects the Atlantic with the Mediterranean. Spain occupies the northern coast, except at the extreme east, where the British-controlled peninusula of Gibraltar is located. The southern coast is occupied by the former Spanish Morocco, which since 1956 has been a part of the independent State of Morocco. The Spanish continue to maintain sovereignty over a coastal enclave about the town of Ceuta. At the western end of the African coast is located the city of Tangier (see page 361).

For centuries the strait has been a historic passageway for political and military movements both in a north-south direction between Europe and North Africa, and east-west between the Atlantic and the Mediterranean. The Vandals moved southward across the strait early in the fifth century in an encircling movement toward Rome. Three centuries later the Moors advanced northward from Africa to Europe. The waterway represents a transition point between European and North African cultures, and something from each continent has managed to filter across to the other.

The British Rock. Great Britain occupied the 2¾-mile-long Gibraltar Peninsula (including the famous Rock) in 1704, and has retained it ever since, despite periodic pressures from Spain for its return (Figure 55). Composed of limestone, the Rock rises to over 1,400 feet and is honeycombed with corridors, rooms, ammunition and storage dumps. The normal peacetime population is about 25,000. Although a majority of the population

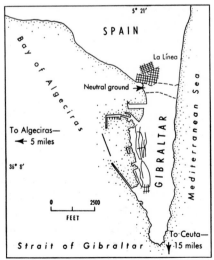

Figure 55. Gibraltar.

© RMcN

speaks Spanish, the people are not Spaniards by origin or in sympathy. When Britain first established Gibraltar as a fortress, the Spanish population living there voluntarily withdrew, and the area was repopulated by immigrants, mostly from the Italian city of Genoa. Gibraltar is connected by a land bridge with the Spanish mainland, and many Spanish workers who earn their living on Gibraltar live in the Spanish city of La Línea at the northern end of this bridge.

Spanish nationalism in recent years has manifested itself in sporadic demonstrations and in demands for the return of Gibraltar to Spain. The indigenous people of Gibraltar apparently have no wish for such a move. Nor would the 12,000 Spanish workers who commute daily to the Rock welcome the transfer, for wages on Gibraltar are far higher than could be earned in Spain. For the British the Rock is still important as a supply and maintenance base and as a symbol of British power, but its military significance has declined in relation to other less vulnerable bases of the British Commonwealth. In any future world conflict Gibraltar might be completely neutralized by hostile control of the Spanish mainland or by atomic attack on the base itself.

THE NORTHERN STATES

The Northern States are taken here to include the Scandinavian Peninsula (Norway and Sweden), Denmark, Iceland, and the British Isles. These areas are removed from the primary axis through Europe, extending from the Soviet Union through France, and all except Denmark are separated from Germany or France by physical barriers. To some extent, then, they are "peripheral," and it is interesting to note that none of these States was a charter member of the Common Market. Yet despite their locations each of these States faces problems of economic development and of defense against possible Soviet expansion. Several also have latent problems of boundary delimitation with their neighbors.

Norway and Sweden

The Scandinavian Peninsula consists primarily of a block of mountains which rise steeply on the western (Atlantic) side and slope much more gradually to the Baltic Sea and the Gulf of Bothnia. The crest of the mountains, which marks the border between Norway and Sweden, is close to the western coast. This Norwegian coast is deeply indented by fjords, with thousands of islands and rocks in the immediate offshore waters. The steep slopes and abundant precipitation give Norway a large water power potential, but there is little level land available for agriculture or for towns. The principal lowlands of Norway are in the vicinity of Oslo, bordering on the Skagerrak at the entrance to the North Sea.

Despite the centrifugal forces resulting from shape, from the location of the capital, Oslo, in the southeastern part of the State, and from poor land communications to the northwestern and northern areas, Norway is a relatively cohesive state. Most of the people are united by ties of language, religion, and national sentiment. The majority live in the central and southern parts of the country, and there are no large population centers across Norway's land borders in Sweden or the Soviet Union to attract the Norwegians away from Oslo. With an area of 125,000 square miles and a population of about 3,400,000, Norway's resources (in addition to water power) include moderate amounts of iron ore, pyrites, copper, lead, and zinc. Arable land is limited to less than 5 per cent of the total area, but fishing and shipping activities are important. One of the Norwegian government's problems has been to protect the country's offshore sovereignty (claimed out to the four-mile limit) from encroachment by foreign fishermen (see page 80).

Sweden, on the eastern side of the peninsula, has an area of 173,000 square miles and a population of 7,500,000. Northern Sweden is largely in forest, but lowlands appear in the central and southern portions with good agricultural possibilities. Swedish farmers produce over 100 per cent of the calorie needs of the population. With its rich iron ore deposits, particularly those at Kiruna north of the Arctic Circle, its timber, and its water power resources, Sweden is in a potentially strong economic position. Neutrality in two world wars has spared it the destruction much of the rest of western Europe has suffered; Swedish skill and economic organization have resulted in a highly efficient productive system and the highest standard of living in Europe. Exports include metals and machinery, wood, wood pulp and paper, and iron ore—commodities needed by much of the rest of Europe —as well as metals, machinery, and automobiles. Despite its well-organized economy Sweden is very dependent on foreign sources for oil and on a high volume of foreign trade in order to maintain its prosperity. The latter factor is important in Sweden's relationship with the Common Market (see page 272).

As a Baltic power Sweden has long been concerned with efforts to regulate the use of this water body. In the years following World War II the Soviet Union has been interested in establishing a "mare clausum" (closed sea) regime for the Baltic, at least to the extent that its use is controlled by a commission consisting of representatives from the various States bordering the sea. To such proposals the Swedes have remained firm in their opposition, claiming that national rights extend only out to territorial limits.[11] Sweden has never joined NATO, following instead its traditional policy of neutrality. But Sweden's neutrality is, in a sense, linked with that of

[11] See Gene Glenn, "The Swedish-Soviet Territorial Sea Controversy in the Baltic," *American Journal of International Law*, L (1956), 942–49.

Finland. Should Finland be occupied by Soviet forces (on the grounds that the U.S.S.R., threatened by attack from the northwest, must maintain defenses in Finland to protect its own territory), Sweden might well decide to join an anti-Soviet alliance. On the other hand, should Sweden decide to join such an alliance first, the Soviets might feel compelled to set up bases in Finland for protection. Thus there is something of a neutrality balance in the Baltic which has remained in force for over a decade.

Denmark

Located on the sandy Jutland Peninsula and its offshore islands between the North and Baltic seas, Denmark has a physical environment characterized by relatively infertile soil (which Danish farmers at great expense have made extremely productive), a long coast line, and a virtual absence of minerals and power fuels. With a population of about 4,600,000, Denmark has a national economy based on intensive agriculture and the export of dairy products, bacon, eggs, and vegetables, on high-grade manufactured goods (ships, diesel engines, china), on fishing, and on the maintenance of a moderate-sized merchant marine which is important in international shipping activities.

Denmark's border problems with Germany are described on page 237. The Danish people are united in language and religion. Perhaps equally important as a centripetal force, however, has been the need for national cohesion in the face of German expansionist pressure to the south. Unlike most peninsular areas, Jutland is politically partitioned, and the Danes have no natural defenses against the Germans. Denmark's national sovereignty has in the past depended largely upon the cultural and political strength of the Danish people and upon the support Denmark has received from other countries at times when its existence has been threatened. The nation's capital, Copenhagen, is located on an island in the eastern part of the State. It is, however, the historical political and cultural center, about which is concentrated over one-quarter of Denmark's population.

Despite its recent history of invasion and occupation by the Germans, Denmark is united with West Germany in NATO. Both Denmark and Norway have refrained from permitting American military bases to be established on their soil, although the positions of both countries in terms both of the entrance to the Baltic and of the eastern North Sea make them strategically valuable to West European defenses.

Iceland

Lying close to the Great Circle route between northeastern United States and the British Isles, Iceland is an important link in North Atlantic air defenses for Anglo-America and western Europe. It also is an unusual country because of the adjustments its people have made to a difficult environment. With an area of 39,700 square miles, Iceland consists largely of plateaus and mountains, including some 5,000 square miles covered by glaciers. About 18 per cent of the land is potentially arable, but of this only 200 square miles are in cultivation. Because of the proximity of the warm North Atlantic Drift the west, south, and east coasts enjoy January temperatures slightly above freezing, leaving most of the waters about the island ice-free for fishermen throughout the year. Mineral resources are practically nonexistent, except for the hot springs which are used for heat in and around Reykjavik, the capital.

Iceland's population totals less than 200,000. Despite the poor resource base Iceland has one of the highest average per capita incomes in Europe, a factor attributable in part to the richness of the fishing grounds and in part to the extension of goods and credits from the United States and the income derived from the American air base at Keflavik in the southwestern part of the island. Over 90 per cent of Iceland's exports normally consist of fish and fish products, making the Icelanders acutely aware of competition from foreign fishermen off their coasts. The controversy with Great Britain over the extension of Iceland's fisheries limits to twelve miles was treated in Chapter 4. The resulting shift of trade from Britain to the Soviet Union brought with it pressures for Iceland to abandon its NATO ties and adopt a more neutralist policy. The Icelanders have retained their defense alignment, however, including giving permission to the United States to continue military operations at Keflavik—thereby maintaining strong sea and air defenses in the northern Atlantic.

The United Kingdom

The United Kingdom, located off the coast of northwestern Europe, is composed of Great Britain (England, Wales, and Scotland), Northern Ireland, and the Isle of Man and Channel Islands. The last two are special political units, with their own legislatures and with governors appointed by the Crown. Location, resources, and the early pre-eminence of this part of Europe in the fields of science, navigation, and commerce have contributed to Britain's[12] development as a great colonial power. Although location close to the mainland of western Europe enabled the British to enjoy the advantages of association with the States of that area, the presence of the English Channel permitted them the opportunity to withdraw from continental affairs whenever conditions warranted such action. Thus the British have remained neutral in some continental wars, and have succeeded in

---

[12] The term "Britain" is used here synonomously with the United Kingdom.

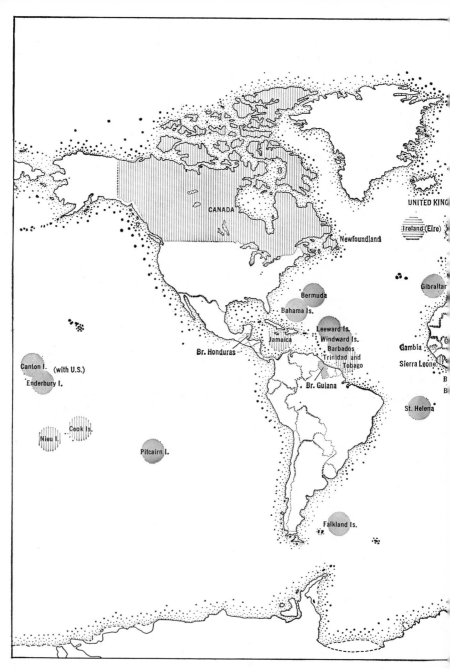

Figure 56. The British Commonwealth: Changes Since 1921.

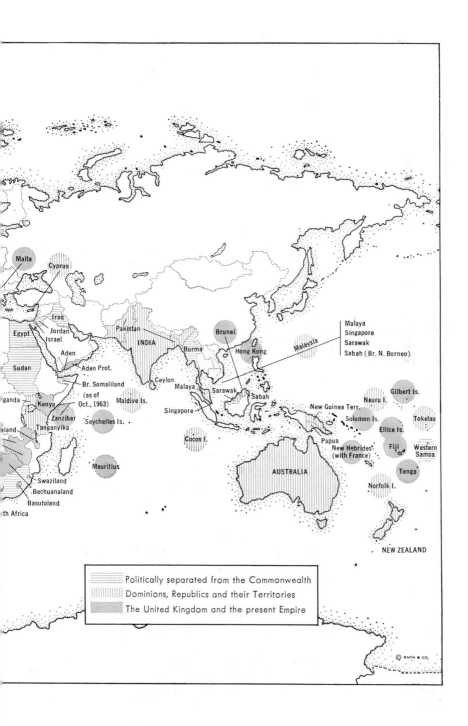

Malta
Cyprus

Iraq
Egypt · Jordan
Israel
Aden
Sudan
Aden Prot.
Br. Somaliland
(as of
Oct., 1963)
ganda · Kenya
Zanzibar
land · Tanganyika
Seychelles Is.
Swaziland
Bechuanaland
Basutoland
th Africa
Mauritius

Pakistan
INDIA
Burma
Ceylon
Malaya
Maldive Is.
Singapore
Cocos I.

Brunei
Hong Kong
Sarawak
Sabah

Malaya
Singapore
Sarawak
Sabah (Br. N. Borneo)
Malaysia

New Guinea Terr.
Solomon Is.
Papua
New Hebrides
(with France)

Nauru I.
Gilbert Is.
Tokelau
Ellice Is.
Fiji
Western
Samoa
Tonga

AUSTRALIA

Norfolk I.

NEW ZEALAND

Politically separated from the Commonwealth
Dominions, Republics and their Territories
The United Kingdom and the present Empire

© RM$N & CO.

withdrawing their land forces from the mainland during others, when faced with the prospects of defeat. Since 1066 no foreign army has successfully invaded Britain.[13] In addition to defense the waters surrounding Britain have provided opportunities for overseas trade and commerce. Some of the major trade routes of the world pass close to the British Isles, and since the middle of the seventeenth century Britain has been a leading maritime power.

The advantages of Britain's insular location are partially offset by the country's small area and limited resources. Including Northern Ireland, the total area amounts to 94,000 square miles, and with a present population in excess of 52 million, Britain has an average density of over 540 persons per square mile. Climate, soils, slope, and the relative costs of agriculture have limited crop land to about 30 per cent of the total area, thereby affecting the country's capacity to feed itself. During World War II, when strenuous efforts were made by the British people to produce as much food as possible, well over 50 per cent of the State's food requirements still had to be imported from overseas.

The United Kingdom represents a situation in which centripetal forces are well developed. The limited area, the strong circulatory system, and the sense of national unity on the part of the British outweigh the centrifugal forces created by regional differences or differences in historical development, as in Scotland and Wales. Northern Ireland, inhabited largely by the descendants of settlers from Scotland, is bound to the British Isles not only by economic and cultural ties but also by the desire of the majority of the people there to remain free of political domination by the Republic of Ireland.

Britain's limitations in agriculture have been compensated in part by industrial and commercial activities and by the earning of "invisible income" through such services as tourism, insurance and banking activities, and foreign investments. The Industrial Revolution came early to Britain, and its development was aided by the presence of extensive coal deposits as well as by a moderate amount of iron ore. In the nineteenth century Britain became a coal-exporting country. By the mid-twentieth century, however, many of the more accessible deposits have been exhausted, labor costs are high, and the process of mechanization has been slow; as a result the British must normally import a portion of their coal. Other mineral and fuel resources are almost completely absent in Britain, adding to the list of commodities the British must import in order to maintain their in-

---

[13] The waters which protect Britain from invasion by enemy armies have, of course, had little effect on air operations. During World War II the German Luftwaffe proved that the barrier function of the English Channel was fast disappearing, and the development of rocket artillery toward the close of the war further established this fact. Postwar experiments with atomic and hydrogen bombs have virtually ended the possibility of British isolation in the event of future warfare on the Continent.

dustrial economy. Before World War II Britain was able to maintain a favorable balance of payments, but in the years since 1939 this has generally not been true. Loss of foreign investments and overseas markets, together with wartime destruction and the expense of maintaining armaments for the Cold War, has hindered postwar economic recovery, with the result that considerable financial assistance from the United States since the end of World War II has been necessary to permit Britain to fulfill its domestic and overseas commitments.

In the development of its empire the British State has been fortunate in both the number and the quality of its population. From the early seventeenth to the early nineteenth century, while Britain still possessed a primarily agricultural economy, there was a considerable excess of population in terms of available employment. Thus there was a strong incentive for emigration overseas. The advent of the Industrial Revolution in the nineteenth century meant increased opportunities for employment in Britain itself, but at the same time the population also increased rapidly. During the half-century from 1851 to 1901 the combined population of England and Wales increased by over 80 per cent.

The concern of British settlers in overseas territories for the advancement of orderly government and for the development of the land they inhabited led them to establish stable political and economic systems in these areas. Despite certain weaknesses in some regions, such as economic exploitation and retention of the color bar, the British have ranked among the best colonizers in the world in terms of effective utilization of the land, treatment of colonial peoples, and political administration.

In July, 1960, the United Kingdom joined with six other countries, Sweden, Norway, Denmark, Switzerland, Austria, and Portugal, to form the "Outer Seven," or European Free Trade Association (EFTA), a project in which the member states would progressively reduce trade barriers on the exchange of industrial goods among themselves. Designed as a counter to the Common Market, this agreement is to take ten years to fulfill; unlike conditions in the Common Market, agricultural products are largely excluded, and there is no attempt to prepare a common external tariff or commercial policy, nor are there any plans for eventual political union. The total population of the seven countries is just over half that of the Common Market States, but on the average they have a higher standard of living, and their gross national product is approximately two-thirds that of the six states of the Common Market. Britain is clearly the giant in this association, and within a year of the inception of the EFTA the British government was beginning talks with the Common Market leaders on the possibilities of British entrance into that body.

One of the principal stumbling blocks to British entry into the Common Market is the problem of trade preference ties with the Commonwealth members. Several of these members, such as New Zealand and Australia, are highly dependent on Britain as a market for their agricultural exports; in 1960 over one-half of New Zealand's exports went to Britain, most of them in the form of wool, butter, or mutton. Over a quarter of Australia's exports—again largely agricultural goods—go to Britain.[14] Should the British enter the Common Market and begin adopting the common tariff against exports of such goods, several of the Commonwealth members would be in serious economic straits. Also, should Britain eventually enter the Common Market, many of the other members of the "Outer Seven" would presumably become associated with the "Inner Six."

Ireland

The turbulent history of the island of Ireland is reflected in its political division into a northern and a southern sector, and in the continued agitation in the south for unification of the entire area into one State. The island has an area of 31,840 square miles and a population of 4,300,000. About one-quarter of the land is in cultivation. In the past Ireland has had difficulty in feeding its people: in 1830 there were more than 8 million inhabitants on the island, but repeated potato famines during the next two decades resulted in the emigration of over half the population—a majority of them to the United States. Other than agricultural land Ireland has few resources, except peat and some water power potential. The Irish have thus experienced considerable difficulty in developing industries, and, particularly in the central and southern parts of the island, they have preserved a predominantly agricultural economy. Northern Ireland has undergone some industrilization and is important for its shipbuilding and linen industries. The economic advances made there are significant in terms of possible unification of the island.

The Republic of Ireland, occupying the central and southern portions of the island, contains 84 per cent of the total area and 68 per cent (1960 figures) of the population, and is overwhelmingly Catholic, while Northern Ireland, an integral part of the United Kingdom, has a population which is about 70 per cent Protestant (Figure 64). The island was divided in 1920 in response to demands by the people of the central and southern sectors that they receive self-government. Plebiscites were held in each of the island's thirty-two counties, and in six northern counties a majority elected to remain with Britain. The boundary was finally delimited on the basis of old county boundaries, so that many people who had wished to be in southern Ireland found themselves included in the north. Although from the

[14] In 1961, 43 per cent of Britain's exports went to the Commonwealth, compared to 19 per cent to the Common Market. From 1959 through 1961, however, British exports to the Common Market had increased by 30 per cent, while those to the Commonwealth members had declined slightly.

Figure 57. The Partition of Ireland. (After Stoneman, "The Partition of Ireland," Doctoral dissertation, Clark University, 1950. Used by permission.)

standpoint of origin the Ireland–Northern Ireland border was historical in nature, it represented a superimposed boundary with respect to the cultural aspects of the area, for it failed to separate effectively the Catholics from the Protestants. As a result the border has contributed to the tension existing between the northern and southern counties.

The central and southern portion of the island has been known by several names—the Irish Free State (1922–37), Eire (1937–49), and the Republic of Ireland (since 1949). It was set up as a dominion in 1922, but later it chose to sever all connections with the Commonwealth, except those of an economic nature. Since 1922 the people of the Republic of Ireland have agitated continuously for elimination of the island's division and inclusion of Northern Ireland within the Republic. This proposal has been resisted both by the British, who wish to maintain military and economic ties with Northern Ireland, and by a majority of the people of Northern Ireland itself. The latter are not attracted by the possibility of being a definite religious minority in a united Ireland; more important, perhaps, is the fact that the standard of living in the north is considerably higher than in the south. Political unification with the other units of Great Britain has been important to Northern Ireland's economy; if union with the Irish Republic ever were carried out, the average income per capita might undergo a considerable decline. The Republic, however, may in time succeed in deriving some wealth of its own through its program of industrialization. In the western area, particularly around Limerick (in connection with the Shannon free port) there has been considerable industrial development in recent years, particularly of branch plants of foreign concerns.

WESTERN EUROPE—UNITED OR DIVIDED?

The threat of Soviet aggression in the years since World War II, coupled with pressing economic needs, has resulted in moves toward greater cooperation among the countries of western Europe than at any other time in modern history. The various peninsulas and islands extending westward from the Communist Eurasian bloc have in recent years become thoroughly accustomed to the needs for united action, aided and supported from across the Atlantic by the United States and Canada. Such unity has, however, been incomplete because of the actions of certain "isolationist" countries, such as Spain, Switzerland, and Ireland, which have failed to participate in many of the united efforts; more important, this unity has been threatened by the creation in western Europe of competing economic blocs.

The Common Market is well on its way to becoming a highly successful organization. In 1961 the area had a combined population of 180 million a gross national product (the value of all goods and services produced), of $190 billion, and an export trade of $31 billion, or approximately one-sixth of the world's total. Its combined steel output was 75 million tons, slightly higher than that of the Soviet Union, placing it second only to the United States. In recent years its gross national product has averaged a greater annual increase than that of either the United States or the U.S.S.R.

The gradual reduction of tariffs among the member States of the Common Market has been moving ahead of schedule. By the summer of 1962 tariffs on industrial goods had been reduced by 50 per cent, and on agricultural products by 35 per cent. Thus the Common Market is rapidly developing into one of the three great economic units of the world along with the United States and the Soviet Union.

Along with this development has come the question, What of the other 40 per cent of the people of western Europe? How will their countries' interests be protected in the face of this new economic giant? One key to the answer lies in the development of Britain's policies. The European Free Trade Association is far less dynamic in nature than is the Common Market; in time such EFTA members as Norway, Sweden, and Denmark may find it more to their advantage to become associated with the Common Market than to remain in the Free Trade Association. What of those countries that are neither in the Common Market nor EFTA, that is, Greece, Spain, Ireland, and Iceland? Greece is already becoming an associate member of the Common Market, and the Spanish government is attempting to establish some sort of association with that body. If the members of EFTA become associated with the Common Market as well, presumably Ireland and Iceland would follow suit (although the Soviet Union might block Austria's entry into an economic organization that includes West Germany). In the event of complete (or even partial) economic unification of western Europe, there remain such questions as (1) Would Finland be permitted by the Russians to enter such a union? (2) Would Yugoslavia be forced into closer economic ties with the Soviet Union and eastern Europe? (3) What steps would the United States, Canada, and Japan take with regard to such a west European union?

Whatever the final form the Common Market takes, it is clear that new patterns of circulation will be formed in western Europe as a result of its creation. The movement of people, ideas, and goods throughout the area will be reoriented with resulting changes in the landscape and in the attitudes and ideas of the people themselves. This is true not only for western Europe itself but for other areas of the world as well. The United States, for example, which for years supported the principle of cooperation in western Europe, may in time face a united economic area which not only is the greatest trading bloc on earth, but which also has closer economic ties with most of the new states of Africa than does the United States itself. Will the Common Market develop sufficient economic strength to act as a true "third force" along with Anglo-America and the Communist bloc, so that new countries in Africa and Asia need not look merely to the West or the East for economic, military, and political support, but have the alternative of turning to the Common Market as well? Will western Europe become one of the two balances of an anti-Communist north Atlantic fulcrum? Will western Europe continue indefinitely as part of the North Atlantic anti-

Communist bloc, or might it in time turn more toward "neutralism," seeking to balance between the United States and the U.S.S.R., and come to enjoy the benefits of aid and assistance from both groups? Questions such as these arise as the various States seek to adjust to the growth of this new organization.

BIBLIOGRAPHY

ALEXANDER, LEWIS M. "Recent Changes in the Benelux-German Boundary," *The Geographical Review*, XLIII (1950), 29–36.
A discussion, with detailed maps, of the territorial claims by the Benelux countries against Germany after World War II.

"The Barrier Across Berlin and its Consequences," *The World Today*, XVII (1961), 459–71.
An interesting analysis of the effects of the wall in Berlin.

DIEBOLD, WILLIAM, JR. "Britain, the Six, and the World Economy," *Foreign Affairs*, XL (1962), 407–19.
A penetrating discussion of Britain's position with respect to the Common Market.

DIEM, AUBREY. "The Economic Basis of Autonomy in the Val D'Aosta, Italy," *Journal of Geography*, LVII (1958), 5–13.
A geographic summary of one of the "peripheral" areas of northern Italy.

FREYMOND, JACQUES. *The Saar Conflict, 1945–1955*. New York: Frederick A. Praeger, 1960.
A basic reference on the Saar, with an excellent bibliography.

GOTTMANN, JEAN. *A Geography of Europe*. 3rd ed. New York: Holt, Rinehart and Winston, 1962.
A sound regional geography of Europe.

HARTSHORNE, RICHARD. "The Franco-German Boundary of 1871," *World Politics*, II (1950), 209–51.
A thorough, well-documented examination of the delimitation of this boundary.

———. "Geographic and Political Boundaries in Upper Silesia," *Annals of the Association of American Geographers*, XXIII (1933), 195–228.

A detailed boundary study. One of the outstanding pieces of research of its kind in political geography.

HELD, COLBERT C. "The New Saarland," *The Geographical Review,* XLI (1951), 590–606.
A regional study of the area with a map of changes in the Saar boundaries, 1945–49.

HOFFMAN, GEORGE W. (ed.). *A Geography of Europe.* 2nd ed. New York: The Ronald Press Company, 1961.
A very good regional geography text.

———. "The Survival of an Independent Austria," *The Geographical Review,* XLI (1951), 606–22.
A concise regional study of Austria after World War II.

International Boundary Studies, Washington, Department of State, Office of the Geographer:
"France-Italy Boundary," No. 4, May 19, 1961.
"Belgium-Germany Boundary," No. 7, June 30, 1961.
"France-Switzerland Boundary," No. 11, October 18, 1961.
"Italy-Switzerland Boundary," No. 12, October 23, 1961.
Maps and detailed descriptions of the boundaries.

JOHNSON, JAMES H. "The Political Distinctiveness of Northern Ireland," *The Geographical Review,* LII (1962), 78–92.
A rewarding study of regional uniqueness.

JONES, EMRYS. "Problems of Participation and Segregation in Northern Ireland," *Journal of Conflict Resolution,* IV (1960), 96–106.
The effects of partition in Northern Ireland.

KISSINGER, HENRY A. "The Unsolved Problems of European Defense," *Foreign Affairs,* XL (1962), 515–42.
An interesting analysis of Europe's military problems.

MOODIE, A. E. *The Italo-Yugoslav Boundary.* London: George Philip and Son, 1945.
A detailed account of this border by one of the experts on the problem.

POUNDS, NORMAN J. G. *Divided Germany and Berlin.* Princeton: D. Van Nostrand Company, 1962.
A well-written summary of the Berlin problem.

————. "The Origin of the Idea of Natural Frontiers in France," *Annals of the Association of American Geographers,* XLI (1951), 146–58.
The historical evolution of the concept of France's eastern frontier.

ROBINSON, G. W. S. "West Berlin: The Geography of an Enclave," *The Geographical Review,* XLIII (1953), 540–58.
A detailed study of the geography of West Berlin and its relationships with East Berlin. Some of the material has become dated since the erection of the wall.

SHAUDYS, VINCENT K. "The External Aspects of the Political Geography of Five Diminutive European States," *Journal of Geography,* LXI (1962), 20–31.
A study of an aspect of these microterritorial areas.

WEIGEND, GUIDO C. "Effects of Boundary Changes in the South Tyrol," *The Geographical Review,* XL (1950), 364–76.
A well-knit survey of South Tyrol, particularly since World War I.

11

EASTERN EUROPE

● Eastern Europe[1] is one of the great transit areas of the world. Across this important region a great number of armies and migrating peoples have moved, each leaving its imprint upon the cultural landscape. Thus, in addition to physical diversity, particularly in its central and southern portions, eastern Europe also contains a wide variety of ethnic groups as well. The political pattern in turn has been characterized by complexity and by frequent change, as ethnic groups have struggled for self-rule, as States have vied with one another for territory, and as major powers bordering on eastern Europe have expanded or contracted their control in this area. Three trends dominate in the political partitioning here; the drive for ethnic self-determination, the struggle for economic viability of the individual States, and the attempts by countries bordering on eastern Europe to establish control over all or a part of the region.

PHYSICAL ELEMENTS

Surface Configuration

Eastern Europe, as defined here, stretches through nearly thirty degrees of latitude from the northernmost part of Finland to the Mediterranean

---

[1] Eastern Europe here comprises the tier of states located between the Soviet Union and what was described in the preceeding chapter as the "western Europe" area, with the Arctic Ocean to the north and the Mediterranean Sea to the south. Within this region are approximately 680,000 square miles of territory and a population of some 130 million persons. Estonia, Lativa, and Lithuania, although treated here as part of eastern Europe, are now actually included within the borders of the Soviet Union. The physical and historical background elements of East Germany were considered in Chapter 10. Turkey, with only a small sector in Europe, is treated at the end of this chapter.

coast (Figure 58). North of the Carpathians along the Czech-Polish border eastern Europe consists of plains and low hills. Except for the Scandinavian Shield of Finland and the uplands of southern Poland, few parts of this northern sector rise above 1,000 feet in elevation. Between the Carpathians and the Baltic coast of Poland lies the historic "invasion gateway" to Russia —the route followed by Napoleon, Hitler, and other would-be conquerors

© RMcN

Figure 58. Eastern Europe: Physical Features.

of the Russian State. Because of the relative uniformity of surface configuration north of the Carpathians, there are no effective physical barriers
to mark national boundaries; settlement patterns are often intermixed with
one another, and few national units have managed to survive for more
than a short time there.

In southeastern Europe surface configuration is more diverse, and there
is a variety of mountain and basin areas. The largest of the basins is the
Hungarian Plain. This region is drained by the Danube and its tributaries,
and includes not only Hungary itself but also portions of Yugoslavia, Romania, southern Czechoslovakia, and eastern Austria. Since 1945 the Soviet
Union, by means of its control of the former Czech province of Ruthenia,
has also had a foothold in the Hungarian Plain.

Downstream from the Hungarian Plain the Danube drains the lowlands of Wallachia and Moldavia in Romania. These fertile regions, which
slope away from the mountain arc of central Romania, form the nucleus
of the Romanian State. They also lie on the historic transit route between
southeastern Europe and southern Russia and, like the North European
Plain, have been the scene of many invasions and settlements.

The Bohemian basin of Czechoslovakia and the Transylvanian basin
of west central Romania are also important areas of settlement and economic development. Other principal lowland areas of southeastern Europe
are the Maritsa Valley of Bulgaria, the Vardar Valley of southern Yugoslavia, the Drava Valley in northern Yugoslavia, the Morava Valley of
central Czechoslovakia, and the coastal lowlands of Greece. In addition
to their function as settlement and economic areas, each of the basins of
southeastern Europe has formed the nucleus for the development of political areas. Thus Hungary has developed on the Hungarian Plain; Bohemia—and later the Czech State—focused on the Bohemian basin; while
Serbia developed largely about the Morava Valley extending southward
from the Danube. The political partitioning of eastern Europe after World
War I resulted in the inclusion of several lowland nuclei within individual
States, such as the Bohemian basin and the Morava Valley in Czechoslovakia, and the Wallachia-Moldavia lowland and the Transylvanian basin
in Romania. The strong sense of regionalism which had been developed in
these separate areas continued even after political unification, however, and
often represented a powerful divisive force within the east European States.

One of the significant aspects of the political geography of southeastern
Europe has been the conflicts for control of the various passes and lowland
routes leading to and from the basin areas. There are several important
physiographic "gates," for example, to the Hungarian Plain; among them
are the Vienna Gate from the northwest, the Sava Corridor in northern
Yugoslavia, the Vardar-Morava route leading north from the Aegean, the
Iron Gate where the Danube cuts through the Transylvanian Alps along the

Romanian-Yugoslav border, and a number of passes through the northern mountain rim, including the Yablonitsa Pass in the northeast, the Moravian Gate leading to Polish Silesia, and the Elbe Gate between Bohemia and Germany.

Natural Resources

Eastern Europe has several areas in which soil fertility is extremely high and in which climate, slope, and drainage combine to produce nearly optimum conditions for agriculture. Countering these, however, are large areas in which the physical environment prevents, or greatly limits, agricultural production.

In mineral and power resources the area is relatively rich. Romania has oil and natural gas. Hungary has bauxite and some oil. Yugoslavia has a wide variety of minerals, including chromite, bauxite, copper, mercury, and iron ore, as well as coal and some oil. Czechoslovakia and Poland both have coal and iron ore. East Germany contains uranium and potash, while Poland has important deposits of lead and zinc. In addition there is considerable hydroelectric power potential, particularly in the countries of southeastern Europe.

Only recently has extensive utilization of most of the mineral and power resources in eastern Europe been started. Romania's oil and the coal and iron ore of Czechoslovakia and Poland were the major commodities developed prior to World War II. Since 1945 both Yugoslavia and the Soviet-oriented Communist States have placed increasing emphasis on industrial development; as a result, the agricultural, mineral, and power resource base of eastern Europe is coming to assume great importance to the over-all power status of this part of the world.

CULTURAL GROUPS

The major cultural groups in eastern Europe are shown in Table 6. The actual numbers in each group are for the most part only approximations, for there has been considerable movement of populations in eastern Europe since 1939. The great variety of peoples emphasizes the corridor location of the area, through which many groups have moved during the past two thousand years. Migrations of peoples westward from the grassy steppes of Asia have been countered by movements eastward on the part of Scandinavian groups, Germans, and Mediterranean peoples. In recent centuries eastern Europe has been a zone of conflict between Germanic and Slavic peoples, with the boundaries between them continually shifting from east to west.

Since 1918 there have been a number of major population changes.

Table 6

MAJOR CULTURAL GROUPS IN EASTERN EUROPE

Country and People by Language	Approximate Number	Percentage of Total Population	Racial and Religious Characteristics
Finland (1958)			
Finns	3,918,525	89.5	Baltic; Protestant
Swedes	383,575	8.5	Nordic; Protestant
Kareliens	87,900	2.0	Baltic
Lapps	5,000	–	Origin not known
TOTAL	4,395,000		
Estonia (1940)			
Esthonians	1,134,000[a]	100	Baltic; Protestant
Latvia (1940)			
Latvians	1,944,506[a]	100	Baltic; Protestant and many Roman Catholics
Lithuania (1940)			
Lithuanians	2,879,070[a]	100	Slavic; Roman Catholic
Poland (1957)[b]	27,000,000	98	Slavic; Predominantly Roman Catholic
Poles[c]			
Byelorussians and Ukrainians	245,000	1	Slavic; Eastern Orthodox
Germans	240,000	1	Germanic; Protestant
TOTAL	27,445,000		
Czechoslovakia[b] (1957)			
Czechs[d]	8,500,000	65	Slavic; Predominantly Roman Catholic
Slovaks	2,900,000	23	Slavic; Roman Catholic
Hungarians	590,000	4.5	Magyar; Roman Catholic
Ruthenians	170,000	1.4	Slavic; Eastern Orthodox
Others	840,000	6.1	Poles, Germans, and Jews
TOTAL	13,000,000		
Hungary[b]			
Hungarians	9,500,000	97	Magyars; approx. 68.7% Roman Catholic and 30% Protestant
Germans	200,000	2	Germanic; Protestant
Others	100,000	1	Slovaks, Serbs, Croats
TOTAL	9,800,000		

Table 6—(Continued)

Country and People by Language	Approximate Number	Percentage of Total Population	Racial and Religious Characteristics
Romania[b]			
Romanians	15,000,000	86	Romanic; 80% Romanian Orthodox; 19% Greek Catholic
Hungarians	1,600,000	9.4	Magyars; Protestant
Germans	382,000	2.2	Germanic; Mostly Protestant
Others	510,000	2.4	Czech, Slovak, Serbs, Croats, Ukrainians, Turko-Tartar
TOTAL	17,492,000		
Bulgaria[e]			
Bulgars	6,800,000	92	Slavic; Eastern Orthodox
Turks	500,000	7	Altaic; Moslem
Others	200,000	1	Gypsies, Jews
TOTAL	7,500,000		
Albania[b]			
Albanians	1,400,000	100	Albanians; 71% Moslem; 20% Eastern Orthodox; 9% Roman Catholic
Yugoslavia[f]			
Serbs	7,064,000	40.3	Slavic; Predominantly Serbian Orthodox
Croats	3,970,000	22.5	Slavic; Predominantly Roman Catholic
Slovenes	1,492,000	7.8	Slavic; Predominantly Roman Catholic
Macedonians	897,000	5.2	Slavic; Predominantly Macedonian Orthodox
Montenegrins	467,000	2.6	Slavic; Predominantly Serbian Orthodox
Albanians	852,000	4.7	Albanians; mostly Moslem
Magyars	507,000	2.9	Magyar; mostly Protestant
Undeclared	992,000	5.9	Mainly Moslem in Bosnia and Herzegovina
Others	1,445,000	8.1	Turks, Slovaks, Gypsies, Germans, etc.
TOTAL	17,686,000		

Table 6—(Continued)

Country and People by Language	Approximate Number	Percentage of Total Population	Racial and Religious Characteristics
Greece[g] (1958)			
Greeks	4,829,680	96	Mediterranean; Eastern Orthodox
Others	203,320	4	
TOTAL	5,033,000		

[a] Figures cited are pre-World War II. The numbers of Baltic peoples still living in these countries is not known.

[b] Statistics for Poland, Czechoslovakia, Hungary, Romania, Bulgaria, Albania, and Yugoslavia from George Hoffman, "Eastern Europe: A Study in Political Geography," *The Texas Quarterly*, II (Autumn, 1959), 63–64. Used by permission.

[c] Since 1939 the approximately 2,500,000 Polish Jews have been killed or have left the country, and over 9,000,000 Germans have been repatriated. Border shifts and population exchanges have also removed Ruthenian, White Russian, and Lithuanian minorities.

[d] 450,000 Ruthenians, included in the Czech nation prior to 1945, were transferred with the province of Ruthenia to the Soviet Union at the end of World War II. Approximately 3,000,000 Germans and 200,000 Hungarians have been repatriated since World War II.

[e] Nearly 250,000 Turks living in Bulgaria at the end of World War II were forced to emigrate to Turkey in 1950.

[f] The 500,000 Germans who once lived in the northeastern lowlands of Yugoslavia have been repatriated, as has a majority of the 4,800 Italians who lived in the Adriatic coastal areas.

[g] Approximately 350,000 Turks and 185,000 Bulgars living in Greece after World War I were repatriated.

Turks, Bulgars, Greeks, and Macedonians were involved in mass movements during the early 1920's, and Turkish groups have continued to be repatriated from Bulgaria since that time. The slaughter or exile of Jews in Poland, Czechoslovakia, Romania, and other east European countries before and during World War II removed at least 3 million persons from the area. In 1939 German groups were repatriated from the Baltic States, and in 1945 they were sent to Germany from Poland, Hungary, Czechoslovakia, Romania, and Yugoslavia. Many Latvians, Lithuanians, and Estonians have been killed or exiled since the Soviet absorption of the three countries in 1940. There have been other population shifts since World War II, such as the repatriation of Hungarians from southern Czechoslovakia and Italians from Yugoslavia. Boundary changes have also affected the ethnic composition of east European States. The transfers of minorities and of territories, particularly since World War II, have resulted in a greater cultural unity in most of the east European countries than existed at the end of World War I. In Poland, for example, the Poles in 1920 numbered 68 per cent of the population; now they number close to 100 per cent.

Within the complex cultural patterns of eastern Europe the factor of weakness in diversity is clearly recognizable in the struggles of small national units to remain independent and to keep their borders intact. Of the several major groups only the Poles number over 20 million, and only the Romanians and Hungarians (scattered throughout four countries) over 10 million.

As a result all these States lack the population requirement for a strong power status. If they choose to seek a position of strength the countries of eastern Europe have had two alternatives: alliance with one another in a regional bloc, or the acceptance of military and economic support from Germany or the U.S.S.R.

ECONOMIC FEATURES

Throughout most of eastern Europe agriculture still forms the dominant economic base, despite recent Communist efforts to speed industrial development. Although the soil of the lowlands is inherently fertile and agriculture is dominant in the general economy, the average yields per acre are generally lower than in western Europe. This is the result of more backward agricultural techniques and less investment per acre in fertilizers. The average per capita income in eastern Europe is considerably lower than that in the West. The educated middle class in most countries represents a minority of the total population. One political effect is that democracy has never gained much headway in eastern Europe. During the interwar years only Czechoslovakia, Finland, and Estonia were successful in maintaining democratic governments for more than a short time.

Since Russia's absorption of most of eastern Europe within its power sphere, the U.S.S.R. has attempted in three ways to alter the economic basis of the area: (1) by forced collectivization of farms; (2) by industrialization; and (3) by orienting the economy to the Soviet Union. The presence of a large landholding class throughout much of eastern Europe, representing something of a holdover from feudalism, was a cause of peasant unrest, particularly during the late nineteenth and early twentieth centuries when new political and social ideas began to permeate the area. The Communist program, with its emphasis on land redistribution, won considerable popular support among the landless farmers. In their first steps after the communization of eastern Europe the Communists broke up the large estates and distributed land to the peasants (a process which in some areas had begun even before the war), after which they worked to collectivize the peasant holdings in order to gain greater political and economic control over the farmers and to increase the total agricultural production. The peasants in varying degrees have resisted collectivization, and the total agricultural production of some parts of Soviet-oriented eastern Europe is lower than it was before 1940. Most of the agricultural land in the Soviet-dominated States is now either in collectives or in state farms, with percentages still in the private sector ranging from about 30 for East Germany to less than 5 in Bulgaria. In Poland the process of collectivization has been reversed; only 12 per cent of the agricultural land in 1960 was in collectives or state farms.

The Hungarians, although they have collectivized nearly 90 per cent of the arable land, have left in private hands the areas from which a substantial portion of their total crops are derived. In 1960 the private farms supplied nearly all of Hungary's meat, vegetables, fruit, and potatoes, indicating that there as in other of the Communist states by far the most efficient production is still in the private areas.

Although industrialization throughout eastern Europe has proceeded at a much faster rate since 1945 than it did prior to World War II, the area still has a long way to go before it will approach western Europe in the production of heavy industrial goods or consumer products. Czechoslovakia and the Silesian district of what has become southwestern Poland had important industrial economies even before World War II. The Communists have large-scale plans for industrialization of other Communist areas as well, in order to aid the Soviet Union in its own economic and military build-up and to provide for a higher standard of living of the peoples in Soviet-dominated eastern Europe, thereby lessening the chances for popular discontent against the Communist regimes.[2] Industrialization has also advanced rapidly in Yugoslavia since the end of World War II, but here again, because of the limits of capital and of certain raw materials and the lack of an important prewar industrial base, the total output has only in recent years begun to be significant.

Finally the orientation of the Communist bloc of eastern European countries to the Soviet Union has meant that the U.S.S.R. is in a position to benefit from exportable surpluses from the area. In the early postwar years a great deal of the foreign trade of the seven Soviet-oriented Communist states was with the U.S.S.R.; in recent years the pattern has shifted to more trade between the states themselves, as well as to trade outside the bloc. The Soviets are in a position to benefit from natural resources (such as Hungary's bauxite or Czechoslovakia's uranium) as well as from such manufactured goods as the U.S.S.R. might require. Further, the Soviets may engage in "triangular" trade with outside countries, such as sending Czech machinery to an African or Asian State, importing food or raw materials from that State into the Soviet Union, and then sending goods or credits to Czechoslovakia to complete the transaction. In 1949 the Council for Mutual Economic Aid (Comecon) was set up, consisting of the Soviet Union and the seven Soviet-dominated east European States. By periodic meetings and exchange of information and by joint planning the council has endeavored to coordinate as much as possible the economic development of its member States. The council does not concern itself with the detailed trade arrangements relating to the exchange of commodities between members, but it does act as a unified clearing house for the registration of exportable surpluses.

---

[2] The standard of living in Czechoslovakia, and probably Poland, is higher than in the U.S.S.R.—an example of the less-developed helping the more-developed areas.

POLITICAL FEATURES

The political diversity of eastern Europe is clearly shown by the existence of a large number of States, by the centrifugal forces which are present in many of the countries, and by the territorial problems which have been so characteristic of this part of Europe. The legacies of past conflicts and of former political units are much in evidence there, as they also are in other parts of the Continent. Many of the boundaries correspond to historical lines, and contested areas, such as Transylvania and Southern Dobruja, have had histories of political vacillation which are equally complex as those of some of the west European regions.

Forces of unity and diversity in eastern Europe have not followed the same patterns of development as in western Europe. Following World War I the area (excluding Greece and Turkey) was divided into eleven independent States, many of them containing two or more important ethnic groups within their borders. For two decades these States struggled with the problems of economic development and of internal cohesion; some of them also engaged in increasing their territories at the expense of their neighbors. Under such conditions united military and political action on the part of the eastern European countries was virtually impossible, and they eventually fell prey to the expanding power of Germany, Italy, and Russia. Since World War II there have been but nine national units in the area as defined above—seven of them dominated by the U.S.S.R.

The establishment of most of eastern Europe as a Soviet-oriented area has, of course, greatly diminished the divisive forces existing there. There is little room in the Soviet system for the operation of centrifugal forces within Communist States, nor for boundary disputes between these countries. The complete elimination of nationalist pressures is a difficult, if not impossible, task, yet one which the Soviets, at least in their early years of control in this area, appeared determined to accomplish. One of the most significant political aspects in eastern Europe is the degree of unity on both national and international levels which can be maintained there by the U.S.S.R. The long-range effectiveness of Soviet control in eastern Europe will be measured in part by the development of centrifugal forces within and between the States of this area.

DEVELOPMENT OF THE PRESENT POLITICAL PATTERN

The origins of the present political pattern in eastern Europe go back to the nineteenth century. The slow disintegration of the Ottoman (Turkish) Empire led to the creation of new and relatively weak States in southeastern Europe—Montenegro, Greece, Serbia, Romania, Bulgaria, and Albania—thereby forming something of a power vacuum into which major powers

Table 7

TERRITORIAL CHANGES IN EASTERN EUROPE AFTER WORLD WAR I

1. Territorial Division of the Austro-Hungarian Empire

Political Entity	Area (sq. mi.)	Per Cent	New Sovereignty
Austria	115,832	100.0	
	30,844	26.6	Austria*
	84,988	73.4	*Countries listed below:*
	30,670	26.5	Poland
	30,366	26.2	Czechoslovakia
	10,815†	9.3	Yugoslavia
	9,106	7.9	Italy
	4,031	3.5	Romania
Hungary (Kingdom of Hungary comprising Hungary proper, Fiume, and Croatia-Slavonia)	125,641	100.0	
	35,893	28.6	Hungary
	89,748	71.4	*Countries listed below:*
	39,586	31.5	Romania
	24,578	19.6	Yugoslavia
	23,801	18.9	Czechoslovakia
	1,558	1.2	Austria (Burgenland)
	220	0.2	Poland
	5	—	Italy

2. Russian Territorial Losses‡

Political Entity	Area (sq. mi.)
Finland	130,094
Estonia	17,463
Latvia	25,262
Lithuania	20,395
Poland	101,471
Bessarabia (to Romania)	17,143

3. Bulgarian Territorial Losses

Political Entity	Area (sq. mi.)
Greece	2,332
Yugoslavia	888

* Austria also received Burgenland (1,558 sq. mi.) from Hungary in 1919.
† Also Bosnia-Hercegovina (19,758 sq. mi.).
‡ Russia also lost 10,128 sq. mi. to Turkey in 1918.
Source: Sophia Saucerman, *International Transfers of Territory in Europe* (Washington: U.S. Government Printing Office, 1937), pp. 6, 53, 100. Used by permission.

sought to extend their control. With the defeat of Germany, Austria-Hungary, Bulgaria, and Turkey and the collapse of Russia in World War I, most of the immediately adjacent antagonists were eliminated, at least temporarily, from the power struggle in eastern Europe, leaving only Italy, Britain, and France, together with the countries within the area, as major contestants for control.

Between the Two World Wars

By the terms of the treaties ending World War 1 the political map of eastern Europe was almost completely redrawn (see Table 7). Serbia and Montenegro disappeared as separate political entities, and the new States of Finland, Estonia, Latvia, Lithuania, Poland, Czechoslovakia, and Yugo-

Figure 59. Territorial Division of the Austro-Hungarian Empire After World War I. In addition, Fiume and its immediate environs passed from Hungarian to Italian control in 1924. (Based on Saucerman, *International Transfers of Territory in Europe*, U.S. Government Printing Office, 1937. Used by permission.)

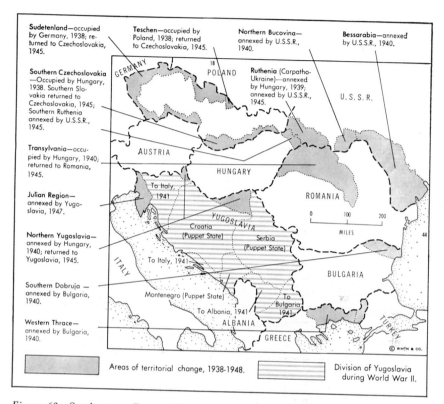

Sudetenland—occupied by Germany, 1938; returned to Czechoslovakia, 1945.

Teschen—occupied by Poland, 1938; returned to Czechoslovakia, 1945.

Northern Bucovina— annexed by U.S.S.R., 1940.

Bessarabia—annexed by U.S.S.R., 1940.

Southern Czechoslovakia —Occupied by Hungary, 1938. Southern Slovakia returned to Czechoslovakia, 1945; Southern Ruthenia annexed by U.S.S.R., 1945.

Ruthenia (Carpatho-Ukraine)—annexed by Hungary, 1939; annexed by U.S.S.R., 1945.

Transylvania—occupied by Hungary, 1940; returned to Romania, 1945.

Julian Region— annexed by Yugoslavia, 1947.

Northern Yugoslavia— annexed by Hungary, 1940; returned to Yugoslavia, 1945.

Southern Dobruja — annexed by Bulgaria, 1940.

Western Thrace— annexed by Bulgaria, 1940.

Areas of territorial change, 1938-1948.

Division of Yugoslavia during World War II.

Figure 60. Southeastern Europe: Territorial Changes, 1938–48.

slavia were created. Romania gained territory at the expense of Hungary, Austria, and Russia; and Bulgaria lost eastern Thrace to Greece as well as some small territories to Yugoslavia (Figure 59).

During the 1920's and early 1930's, while Germany, Italy, and the Soviet Union were absorbed in their own internal problems, the political pattern of eastern Europe remained relatively unchanged except for border areas in Poland and Lithuania, the Italian annexation of Fiume, and the Sopron plebiscite. During this time no one State was in a position to embark on a program of territorial expansion against its neighbor, but after the mid-1930's both Germany and the Soviet Union loomed as threats to the existing political pattern in this area. By the fall of 1938 the Germans had begun to expand their borders eastward, and eventually they were joined in this process of aggrandizement by both the Soviets and the Italians (Figure 60). Ultimately the countries of eastern Europe became embroiled in World War II.

Since 1945

The defeat of Germany and Italy in World War II removed them as immediate contenders for power in eastern Europe. Soviet forces occupied most of the area, and Soviet power became firmly established there. Estonia, Latvia, and Lithuania had been absorbed into the U.S.S.R. in 1940. After the war the Soviets annexed territory in eastern Finland, Poland, Czechoslovakia, and Romania (see Table 11). Pro-Soviet Communist governments were subsequently established with the assistance of the Red Army in Poland, Czechoslovakia, Hungary, Romania, Bulgaria, and Albania.[3] Eastern Europe was thus set up by the Soviet Union as a broad buffer area against the West. In a future world conflict this area may serve as a defense zone for the U.S.S.R., in which much of the fighting and destruction would take place rather than within Russia itself. In the absence of war this zone forms an area in which Western and Soviet territories and influence come into closest contact with one another, and as such it is a region of potential political and cultural tension.

In the sections which follow the individual States of eastern Europe will be considered in the light of territorial developments since World War I, with particular emphasis on post-World War II problems. In this way greater insight may be gained into the complex political pattern of the region and its role as a buffer area between great powers.

Political Areas of Eastern Europe

For the sake of clarity, the States of eastern Europe will be considered here under the following headings: the Soviet-dominated area; Finland; Yugoslavia; the northeastern Mediterranean—Greece, Turkey, and Cyprus.

THE SOVIET-DOMINATED AREA

The Baltic States

The three Baltic States—Estonia, Latvia, and Lithuania—had short and troubled histories of independence before they were reabsorbed into the Soviet Union. Created from Russian territory at the end of World War I, the Baltic States illustrate well the principle that population differences alone are not sufficient grounds for the establishment of independent units, unless (1) the territorial integrity of the new States is guaranteed by major powers, and (2) sufficient attention is given to the countries' potentialities for developing a sound economic base. Estonia, Latvia, and Lithuania

---

[3] In Yugoslavia Communist partisan forces established a Communist type of government there. In 1948 the Yugoslav government broke with the Soviets.

not only suffered from economic depression and a lack of trained personnel to carry out the tasks of government during their two decades of independence, but their strategic location between Russia and the Baltic coast was almost certain to result in reabsorption into the U.S.S.R., without an effective safeguard of independence on the part of the Western powers.

The boundaries of the Baltic States as set up in 1919 corresponded fairly closely to the cultural pattern, except in southern and western Lithuania, where Poles, White Russians, and Germans were included in the new country. Some Lithuanian groups were also left within Poland. The three Baltic States were essentially agricultural, although before 1914 the Latvian port of Riga had been an important outlet for Russian foreign trade and there was some industrial development there and in the Estonian city of Tallinn. German landowners played major roles in the economies of the Baltic States, particularly in Latvia and Estonia, and even after Germany's surrender to the Allies in 1918 these persons continued as important groups in the newly created countries.

Vilna and Memelland. At the end of World War I the new country of Lithuania found itself involved in territorial controversies over the territory centering on the city of Vilna (Vilnyus) along the frontier with Poland and over Memelland on the Baltic coast (Figure 61). These disputes are of politico-geographic interest, since they illustrate both the difficulties involved in delimiting a mutually satisfactory boundary in a complex ethnic area, and the fact that an unarmed international organization is powerless to enforce its authority, even with respect to small States, in the face of determined national resistance.

In the Vilna area Lithuanians, Poles, and White Russians were intermingled, and it was impossible in 1919 to draw a true cultural boundary separating them. During the process of delimiting the Polish-Lithuanian boundary both States claimed the Vilna territory (11,500 square miles in area), the Poles on the basis of population composition,[4] and the Lithuanians on the grounds that Vilna was their historic capital and their largest and most beautiful city. After four years of bitter debate and of military campaigns in the area, the Poles, whose military power was stronger than that of the Lithuanians, officially incorporated the Vilna territory into the Polish State. In the face of Polish resistance the League of Nations was unable to carry out a plebiscite or even to effect a mediation between Poland and Lithuania, and all relations between the two neighboring States were completely suspended for many years.

The dispute over Memelland, a 1,026-square-mile area on the Baltic coast north of the Nemunas (Neman) River, involved primarily Lithuania

---

[4] Of a total population of 1,600,000 in the Vilna area, the Polish census of 1919 (which in detail is open to question) listed 54 per cent of the inhabitants as Poles, 21 per cent as White Russians, 8 per cent of Jews, and 7 per cent as Lithuanians.

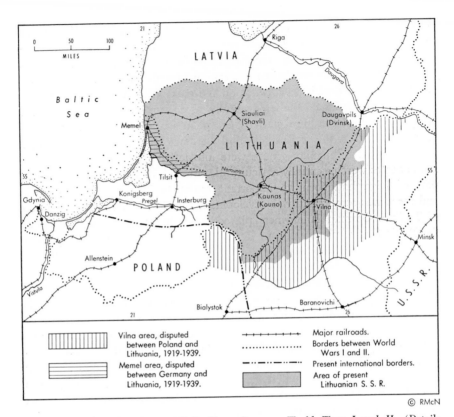

Figure 61. Lithuania: Territorial Problems Between World Wars I and II. (Details of Vilna area after Lord, *Foreign Affairs*, I [Jan., 1923]. Copyright by Council on Foreign Relations, Inc., New York.)

and Germany. Of the 150,000 inhabitants of Memelland about 25,000 were Germans, the rest Lithuanians. By the Treaty of Versailles Germany ceded Memelland to "the Principal Allied and Associated Powers," and while the Vilna controversy was raging the transfer of Memelland to Lithuania was delayed by the League of Nations. Finally, in January, 1923, when Poland annexed Vilna, Lithuania, in defiance of the League, occupied Memelland and declared the area to be part of the Lithuanian State.

By their refusal to cooperate in settling territorial disputes States often place themselves in positions in which united military and political action become impossible. The resultant weakening of their resistance to potential aggressors often means that in time these border disputes become academic; in 1939 Memelland and Vilna were incorporated into what had become the Lithuanian S.S.R. of the Soviet Union.

The Collapse of the Baltic States. The strategic position of the three Baltic countries in relation to Soviet defense became increasingly important with the growth of German power under Hitler. In the fall of 1939 the Soviet Union demanded that the Baltic States change the composition of their governments and make them friendly to the U.S.S.R. The Soviets also insisted that Russian air and naval bases be established within the borders of the Baltic States as defense against possible German attack. Later, as a result of Russian pressure, the nearly 140,000 German-speaking inhabitants of the Baltic States were repatriated to Germany, thus ending over five centuries of German influence in that area. The three countries were unable to resist Soviet demands, and pro-Soviet governments were installed. In July, 1940, Estonia, Latvia, and Lithuania were officially incorporated as republics within the Soviet Union. In an effort to destroy any semblance of nationalism, the Russian government reportedly uprooted a large proportion of the Baltic peoples from their homes and resettled them deep within the Soviet Union.

Poland

The problems of maintaining the political independence of an ethnic group located between powerful neighbors are well illustrated by the tragic history of Poland. To the north of the area originally inhabited by Poles is the Baltic Sea, along which large German concentrations existed until 1944. To the south are the Carpathians, which form both a physical and cultural boundary. The plains of Poland merge into Germany in the west and into Russia in the east (although the Pripet Marshes offer something of a "natural" border in White Russia). This lack of physiographic obstacles not only hinders defense and boundary delimitation, but also influences settlement patterns. In the west Germans and in the east Ruthenians, White Russians, and Lithuanians were intermixed with Poles in complex settlement patterns along the borders of the major bloc of Polish-speaking peoples (Figure 62).

Territorial Problems of the Polish State. When Poland was formed at the end of World War I from Russian, German, and Austrian territory, two principal factors were taken into consideration: (1) the State should include areas inhabited by Polish populations, and (2) it should have access to the Baltic Sea. In its northern and central sections the Polish-German border followed the linguistic boundary fairly closely. In the southwest territorial control in Upper Silesia was eventually settled by plebiscite (see page 236), with Poland receiving most of the coal, lead, and zinc resources. The final delimitation of Poland's western border left over 900,000 Germans in Polish territory and nearly 600,000 Poles within Germany (see Table 8).

The problem of Poland's access to the sea was complicated by the presence of a large German population along the Baltic. East Prussia remained with Germany; the German-inhabited port of Danzig and its im-

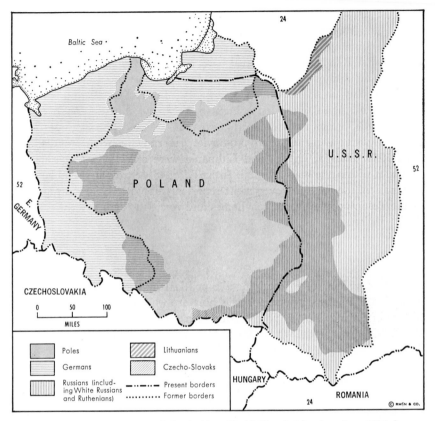

Figure 62. Ethnic Patterns in Poland After World War I. Map based on 1918 figures. (Adapted from Bowman, *The New World*, World Book Co., 1928. Used by permission of R. G. Bowman.)

mediate hinterland was made a Free City under administration of the League of Nations; and a Polish Corridor, averaging twenty to fifty miles in width, was created between Germany and the Danzig–East Prussian border. (See page 235 for a further discussion of this area.)

The delimitation of Poland's eastern boundaries was as great a complication as the delimitation of those in the west. In the face of population patterns, natural resources, and strategic demands, historical boundaries which had existed a century and a half before had little significance in determining new political borders. At the Paris peace conference a British expert, Lord Curzon, was called upon to aid in fixing the new Polish-Russian border. The resulting "Curzon Line" was drawn to conform as closely as possible with the distribution of Poles and Russians. In the spring of 1920 the Poles, dissatisfied with the territorial arrangements, invaded western Russia. After considerable vacillation of military lines, the Polish-Russian

Table 8

TERRITORIAL AND POPULATION STRUCTURE OF POLAND, CZECHOSLOVAKIA,
AND YUGOSLAVIA FOLLOWING WORLD WAR I

Area (sq. mi.)	Per Cent	Former Sovereignty	Ethnic Group	Percentage Breakdown into Ethnic Groups

Poland (1921 population, 27,000,000)

149,958	100.0		Poles	68.0
101,223	67.5	Russia	Ruthenians	14.0
30,723	20.5	Austria	Jews	10.0
17,809	11.9	Germany	Germans	3.5
203	.1	Hungary	White Russians	3.5
			Others (incl. Lithuanians)	1.0

Czechoslovakia (1921 population, 14,000,000)

54,206	100.0		Czechs	50.0
30,304	55.9	Austria	Slovaks	16.0
23,781	43.9	Hungary	Ruthenians	4.0
121	.2	Germany	Germans	23.0
			Magyars	5.0
			Others	2.0

Yugoslavia (1921 population, 12,000,000)

95,576	100.0		Serbs	50.0
30,573	32.0	Austria	Croats	22.0
24,578	25.7	Hungary	Slovenes	9.0
888	.9	Bulgaria	Macedonians	4.0
34,194	35.8	Serbia	Magyars	4.0
5,343	5.6	Montenegro	Germans	4.0
			Albanians	3.5
			Others (incl. Montenegrins)	3.5

Statistics on territorial structure from Sophia Saucerman, *International Transfers of Territories in Europe* (Washington: U.S. Government Printing Office, 1937). Used by permission. Statistics on population from *The Statesman's Yearbook,* 1922.

See Table 6 for post-World War II population figures.

boundary was fixed by the Treaty of Riga (1921) well to the east of the Curzon Line, and over 4,750,000 White Russians and Ukrainians were included in the new Polish state.

The difficulty over Vilna has already been discussed. A final territorial problem involved the new Polish-Czech border in the former duchy of Teschen, where a small disputed area proved to be a source of considerable friction between the neighboring States. The Teschen district, with an area of 853 square miles, contained coal deposits and industrial facilities and was an important rail center as well (Figure 63). Both Poland and Czechoslovakia claimed it, but eventually it was divided, Czechoslovakia obtaining

Figure 63. The Teschen Area. (After Bowman, *The New World*, World Book Co., 1928. Used by permission of R. G. Bowman.)

the coal and the railroads and Poland most of the city of Teschen and a majority of the industrial facilities. Spis and Orava, two small areas to the east of Teschen, were also divided. Approximately 80,000 Poles were included within Czech territory, and during the Munich crisis of 1938 Poland capitalized on Czech weakness and occupied all of the Teschen area.

With conditions of disputed control along practically all its borders, the new State of Poland represented a complex politico-geographic area, whose independence had been achieved mainly as a result of the collapse of both its powerful neighbors, Germany and Russia. Lacking effective support from other major powers, Poland's independence was jeopardized as soon as these two countries regained power. With its population of 30 million, its coal, lead, zinc, petroleum, timber, and agricultural land, and its growing industrial strength, Poland struggled to become a strong national unit between 1920 and 1939. Centripetal forces within the country were strong. Warsaw, the capital and leading city, was located near the geographic center of the State, and communication was easy between it and other core areas, such as the Vilna region to the northeast, Poznan to the west, and the Krakow and Silesian districts in the southwest. Despite differing histories of past political allegiance, the Polish majority was bound together by ties of national sentiment, as well as by language and religion. The State, however, was plagued by large minorities and by the growing pressures from Germany and the Soviet Union to recover their lost territories.

The Destruction of Polish Independence. In September, 1939, western Poland was invaded and conquered by the Germans, eastern Poland was occupied by the Russians, and the country was divided between the two States. In June, 1941, German armies swept eastward across Russian-held Poland in the opening of the invasion of the U.S.S.R.; three years later the Russians were driving them back across the Polish plains. The collapse of Germany in May, 1945, and the occupation of both eastern Germany and Poland by Soviet troops ended any hopes the Poles might have had for a revival of independence after the war.

Efforts by the United States and Britain after World War II to re-establish the prewar Polish republic were frustrated by the Soviets, who installed a Communist administration in Warsaw, so that by 1946 Poland had become a full-fledged Soviet-oriented State. At the Yalta Conference (February, 1945) the Russians claimed the Curzon Line as a basis for the Polish-Russian border. Since the Western powers had accepted this line in 1919 as one dividing Russians and Poles, they were in no position to oppose Soviet demands a quarter-century later. To the Soviet Union Poland ceded nearly 69,000 square miles and a population of about 11 million, in-cluding over 5 million Ruthenians and White Russians and about 4 million Poles. The Poles, however, were eventually repatriated to Poland. With the ceding of this eastern territory Poland lost some of its best agricultural and forest land, as well as most of its oil reserves, to the Russians.[5]

Other Polish border lands were also affected by postwar changes. Ger-man East Prussia was divided between Poland and the Soviet Union, the Russians gaining the port of Konigsberg (renamed Kaliningrad). The Pol-ish-German boundary was moved westward from the 1939 location to the Oder and Neisse rivers. By this move Poland gained 44,215 square miles of territory, including the German portion of the Upper Silesian industrial area, the port of Stettin, and the Free City of Danzig, as well as con-siderable agricultural land. Over 9 million Germans living in the areas which became Polish were forced to leave their homes and to become refugees in Germany itself. Finally, Poland was forced to return southern Teschen to Czechoslovakia. As a result of these territorial changes, Poland's area of 120,359 square miles was but 80 per cent of the country's size prior to World War II.

The establishment of the Soviet power system in eastern Europe has at least temporarily ended Poland's boundary problems, for the State's ter-

---

[5] In 1951 Poland and Russia exchanged territories, amounting to about 260 square miles, in the southern portion of their common border. This gave Russia control of territory containing a link in the Lvov (Lemberg)-Kovel railroad in the area east of Lublin, while Poland received an oil and natural gas area southeast of Przemysl.

ritorial integrity is backed by the power of the U.S.S.R. Likewise, the mass exchange of upwards of 13 million persons has resulted in the creation of ethnic unity in Poland and the removal of minorities from within its borders, a step which would seem to eliminate further friction. German reluctance to accept the Oder-Neisse line as the eastern border with Poland is the greatest potential threat to the present Polish political area. If Germany regains its normal power position in central Europe, this boundary will undoubtedly be challenged. Despite this threat, however, the Poles violently expressed their resentment against Soviet rule in 1956, and succeeded in winning some measure of freedom from Moscow's direct control.

East Germany (The German Democratic Republic)

East Germany has an area of 41,357 square miles and a 1960 population of just over 17 million, some 2 million less than the peak population it had in 1948. On the one hand East Germany was forced to receive over 4 million "expellees"—former residents of eastern Europe who had been forced to flee; on the other hand East Germany, since 1950, has lost over 1½ million refugees to Berlin and West Germany. The stream of refugees, which in July, 1961, reached a monthly peak of over 30,000, served to drain the country of many of its skilled workers and professionals. The erection of the wall dividing Berlin has ended this exodus.

As noted on page 242, East Germany, when it was constituted, received areas producing about 3 per cent of prewar Germany's coal, iron, and steel, and 30 per cent of its food. The country has enormous supplies of lignite (brown coal) as well as potash, uranium, and salt, and before World War II its industries specialized in chemicals and machinery. The rich soils of the south are noted for sugar beets and wheat, and with domestic supplies of fertilizer and agricultural machinery East Germany might be expected to achieve a strong agricultural economy. Yet actually under the Communist agricultural policies East Germany has failed to do this and remains a net importer of foods, particularly grains, meats, and vegetables. The chronic labor shortage, the lack of incentive on the part of much of the population, the poor economic planning, and the loss of Silesia's raw materials and industries to Poland have combined to keep the State's growth rate far below that of either West Germany or Poland. With the closing of the escape route to West Berlin the people of East Germany face an extremely drab future in a rump State which is controlled by Moscow and lacks the economic potential of either its eastern or western neighbors.

The artificial nature of East Germany points up its political difficulties. As a true "satellite" of the Soviet Union, it is occupied by Soviet forces, and its economic and political policies are formulated in Moscow. To the Poles East Germany stands as a "promise" that the former German lands east of the Oder-Neisse line will not be reannexed by Germany, since East Germans are in no position to demand such a move, and their country effectively blocks West Germany from these eastern lands. The West Germans are committed to the reunification of Germany on the basis of free elections, which would probably mean the end of Communist domination in the east. The Soviets could never agree to this, although at times they have talked of possibly uniting East Germany's 17 million people with West Germany's 56 million on a basis of equality. Even such a move by the U.S.S.R. seems highly unlikely. There are those in West Germany who actually question the economic wisdom of reunification, since the West Germans would then be responsible for the economic well-being of the 17 million East Germans with their relatively low per capita incomes.

Czechoslovakia

The Czech State presents an outstanding example of centrifugal forces operating within a national unit. At the time of its establishment in 1919 on territory of the former Austro-Hungarian Empire, Czechoslovakia was a long, narrow country in which the obstacles of distance and surface configuration prevented easy communication between the three major Slavic groups—Czechs, Slovaks, and Ruthenians. The Czechs were concentrated in the Bohemian basin and the Morava Valley, the Slovaks were settled largely in the uplands of Slovakia, while the Ruthenians were in the Carpathian uplands and in the valleys which opened southward to Hungary (Figure 64). Each of these groups had its own language, and feelings of national unity were not sufficiently developed to act as a strong unifying force among them. The national capital was at Prague, the former Bo-

Figure 64. Ethnic Patterns in Czechoslovakia After World War I. Map based on 1918 figures. (Adapted from Bowman, *The New World*, World Book Co., 1928. Used by permission of R. G. Bowman.)

hemian capital and center of Czechoslovakia's principal core area. Prague's disadvantage as a capital city, however, lay in its location in the western part of the State. Only through strong leadership and the determination of the Czechs was the country able to remain united.

The formation of the Czech State, like that of other east European countries in 1919, was based theoretically on the principle of self-determination for ethnic groups. Economic and military factors, however, also figured prominently in the determination of the Czech borders: as a result Slovaks and Ruthenians were included with the Czech majority, while several foreign minorities were also incorporated within the territory of Czechoslovakia. At the time of the country's establishment about 35 per cent of the population consisted of foreign minorities—principally Germans, Magyars, and Poles (Table 8).

Despite the limitations of the population structure, of shape, and of poor communications, Czechoslovakia remained a democracy with a comparatively high standard of living during its interwar independence. Developing its resources of coal, iron ore, timber, and agricultural land, as well as its skilled labor force, it became the leading industrial State of eastern Europe, specializing in iron and steel, textiles, shoes, glass, and beer. The Czech government was careful to avoid discrimination against its foreign minorities. However, the country lay in the path of German expansion, and in the late 1930's, despite its record of internal achievements, Czechoslovakia was eventually overwhelmed because of its minority problems, German territorial aggression, and the lack of military support from the Western powers in the face of German pressure.

The Gradual Destruction of Czech Independence. As early as 1934 Nazi Germany in its drive for territorial conquests began to foment discontent among the more than 3 million Sudeten Germans living in Czechoslovakia, descendants of settlers who migrated to the area during and after the thirteenth century. Although these people had been well treated by the Czech government, propaganda was built up around the "repressions" they were supposedly undergoing, and the German government sought to "liberate" the oppressed minority by annexation of the territory they inhabited. The Czechs prepared to resist the Germans by force if necessary, and looked for support to France and Britain. But at Munich in September, 1938, the French and British agreed to Germany's territorial demands on Czechoslovakia in exchange for a promise by Hitler of "peace in our time." The shattered Czechs not only saw Germany annex the Bohemian rimland, but they were also forced to cede the southern rim of Slovakia to Hungary and southern Teschen to Poland on the grounds of the ethnic composition of these areas. Six months later the remainder of Bohemia and Slovakia was occupied by the Nazis without the formality of explanation, while Ruthenia was seized by Hungary.

The dismemberment of Czechoslovakia in 1938–39 illustrates what may be termed the "jackal" principle of territorial aggrandizement, that is, if a State proves itself unable to resist territorial encroachment, it may become the victim of territorial losses to several of its neighbors. This process sometimes occurs after a country has suffered defeat (for example, China after the Opium War in 1842, Russia after World War I, and Yugoslavia in World War II), or, as with Czechoslovakia and Romania, it may take place in time of peace.

At the end of World War II Czechoslovakia was occupied by Soviet troops. Germany, Hungary, and Poland returned the areas they had seized, but the Russians demanded and received the eastern province of Ruthenia (4,921 square miles) on the grounds that the Ruthenians were in reality Ukrainians and should be under Soviet control (Figure 50).[6] In another territorial change, Czechoslovakia received from Hungary 30 square miles of territory on the south bank of the Danube opposite Bratislava for an industrial expansion of this city. At that time the Czechs had not forgotten the prewar annexations by Germany, Hungary, and Poland, or the sellout at Munich by France and Britain, and despite the loss of Ruthenia to the Soviets relations with Russia were friendly in the early postwar years. The Communist party in Czechoslovakia was the country's largest, having polled 38 per cent of the votes in the 1946 national elections. In February, 1948, the Communists effected a complete *coup d'état,* ousted the democratic government, and brought Czechoslovakia within the power sphere of the U.S.S.R.

Hungary

The people of Hungary never became reconciled after World War I to the territorial losses which their country had suffered. They therefore seized the opportunity offered by Hitler during the 1930's to extend their borders at the expense of their neighbors, thereby compounding the international tensions existing among the eastern European States prior to World War II. The aggressive attitude of the Hungarians proved to be a decided asset to Nazi Germany in its drive for power in southeastern Europe in the years preceding World War II.

The Hungarians are a non-Slavic ethnic group, which since the ninth century has occupied the center of the fertile Danube plain. Before World War I Hungary was joined politically with Austria, but following the war the Austro-Hungarian Empire was broken up and the size of the Hungarian portion reduced by over 70 per cent. To its neighbors Hungary lost its agricultural land, its mines, and most of its timber, as well as control over

---

[6] In 1944, with the Red Army occupying the territory, a plebiscite was held in Ruthenia, with 99 per cent of the votes in favor of union of the area with the Soviet Union.

the upper courses of the rivers which cross the Hungarian lowlands. The new frontiers cut rail and highway lines; and in the absence of international action joint projects for irrigation, power, and flood control in the Danube basin became impossible. The economic unity of the area was completely destroyed. Besides its agricultural land the postwar Hungarian State had few resources left to it except bauxite, a small amount of oil, salt, and timber in the Bakony Forest. Cut off from Austria, its economic partner, Hungary also found itself stripped of Ruthenia, Slovakia, Transylvania, and those areas which became part of northeastern Yugoslavia. The final delimitation of the national borders in 1920 resulted in the separation of over 2,500,000 Hungarians (or Magyars, as they are sometimes called) from Hungary itself (Figure 65).

The much-reduced Hungarian State was a closely knit political unit, in which most of the people were united by language, religion, and national sentiment. Several hundred thousand Germans and Slovaks formed the only important minority groups. Upland areas did not interfere with the transportation systems throughout the country. Budapest, the capital and leading city, was unrivaled in political and economic power by any other

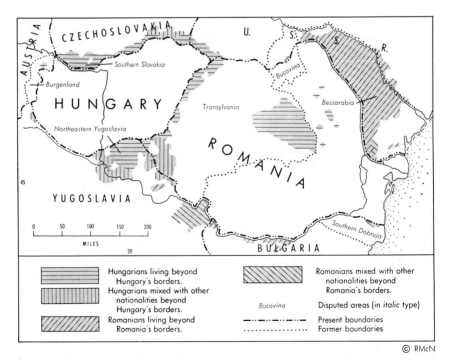

© RMcN

Figure 65. Ethnic Patterns in Hungary and Romania After World War 1. Map based on 1918 figures. (Adapted from Bowman, *The New World*, World Book Co., 1928. Used by permission of R. G. Bowman.)

region within the country. With its strong internal unity Hungary waited for the day of retribution when it could reannex its lost borderlands.

In 1938 the Hungarians shared in the dismemberment of Czechoslovakia, reannexing about 750,000 Magyars in this move. In the following year Ruthenia was occupied, and in 1940 the Germans forced Romania to return northern Transylvania with its Magyar and German minorities to Hungary. For their help in the conquest of Yugoslavia, the Hungarians in 1941 received two provinces, Backa and Banat, in the northeastern plains region of that country.

In the closing months of World War II Hungary was overrun by Soviet forces, and a Moscow-oriented Communist party gradually assumed control of the country. The areas which Hungary had seized from its neighbors were returned to their former owners, and by 1946 Hungary had become firmly welded to the Soviet power bloc. Many Hungarians, however, continued to remain outside the national borders, thus presenting the possibility of future Hungarian expansionist drives. The uprisings of 1956 clearly demonstrated the powerful forces of opposition to Soviet control in this non-Slavic country, the steps to which the Soviets are willing to go to maintain their power position in eastern Europe, and the policies of the United States and other Western powers against actively supporting uprisings within the Communist bloc.

Albania

Least developed of the east European Communist States is Albania, bordering the Adriatic, with an area of 11,000 square miles and a 1960 population of about 1,600,000. It is a mountainous country having a fairly broad but poorly drained coastal plain. With slightly over 10 per cent of the area classed as arable land, no important mineral resources, and a poor circulatory system, Albania has one of the lowest average per capita incomes in Europe. Regional loyalties are often stronger than national ones, and large parts of the area have never been effectively organized either politically or economically. The principal *raison d'être* for Albania's independence was the international rivalry existing over the control of this strategic portion of the Balkans.

During World War I Italy's ambitions to establish permanent control over Albania were eventually blocked by pressure from Britain, France, and the United States, and in 1919 the Italians were forced to content themselves with possession of the Albanian port of Valona (Vlonë), across the Strait of Otranto from Italy, and of the island of Saseno (Sazan), at the mouth of the Bay of Valona. In this way Italy secured control of both sides of the Strait of Otranto.

Between the two world wars Italy expanded its influence in Albania, first by economic means, and later by assisting in the training of the Albanian army. To both Yugoslavia and Greece this Italian encroachment on the Balkan Peninsula was viewed with alarm. On Good Friday, 1939, Italian forces invaded Albania and soon subdued the country. From there they later launched an unsuccessful attack against the Greeks, and in 1941 Albania provided a base for Italian forces for their part in the Axis invasion of Yugoslavia.

Italian influence in Albania has not returned since World War II. Communist partisans in Albania helped to liberate the country from the Axis forces. A pro-Moscow government was installed, and by 1946 Albania's government had become Moscow-oriented. Saseno and Valona were returned to Albania by Italy, thus ending Italian dreams of supremacy in the Strait of Otranto. Since 1956 Communist China has become increasingly important in Albania, leading to speculation as to a possible rift in the Soviet east European power sphere.

Bulgaria

Bulgaria, like Hungary, is a country which has suffered territorial losses and which has anxiously awaited the time when it could recover its former lands. Many of the boundary problems in southeastern Europe during the twentieth century have been associated directly or indirectly with Bulgarian territorial aspirations.

The original Bulgars migrated to the area from Asia in the seventh century A.D., but with repeated incursions by other groups they came to lose much of their original identity. The modern Bulgar language is a Slavic tongue, and modern Bulgarians are often considered to be Slavs.

The inhabitants of Bulgaria form a fairly compact ethnic group, united by language and religion. The principal minorities are in the northeast, where there are Turks and some Romanians. Although there are some agricultural plains, particularly in the central portion of the country, much of Bulgaria is composed of low, forested hills and mountains trending in an east-west direction. The country lacks industrial resources, and the level of its agricultural production is low when compared with that of areas in western and central Europe. In per capita income Bulgaria ranks among the lowest of any of the States of the Continent. The mountains have not only influenced settlement patterns in Bulgaria, but have also made communications between the various parts of the country more difficult than is the case in Hungary or Poland. The capital and leading city, Sofia, lies in a basin in the western portion of the mountains. The political effects of this physical diversity and off-center location of the capital have, however, been more than offset by the strong feelings of national unity among the Bulgars.

The Bulgarian people were under the control of the Turks from the fifteenth century until 1878, when the northern part of the country became independent. In the following thirty-five years the present central and southern sections were also acquired by the Bulgar State. During World War I Bulgaria fought on the losing side, for which it was forced subsequently to yield territory to its neighbors. By the Treaty of Neuilly (1919) Bulgaria lost some small areas along its western border to Yugoslavia, but, more important, it was forced to cede eastern Thrace to Greece, thereby cutting off Bulgaria's access to the Aegean Sea. Although the Bulgars were later offered the port of Dedeagach (Alexandroupolis) on the Aegean as a free port, they declined to accept the gesture.

When the memory of military defeat dies and national pride is rekindled, countries often strive to regain political prestige by agitating for the return of lost territory. Bulgaria was no exception. Bulgarian terrorists operated in Yugoslav and Greek Macedonia during the interwar years (see page 307), and in 1940 Bulgaria became a willing ally of Nazi Germany, hoping thereby to regain its national prestige. The territories it acquired in 1941 at the expense of Yugoslavia and Greece were returned to those States at the end of the war, however. On the other hand, Southern Dobruja, an area bordering the Black Sea which was taken from Romania during World War II, remained with Bulgaria after 1945. The region is peopled largely by Bulgars and Turks and has been a scene of disputed sovereignty since before World War I.

Although Bulgaria did not declare war on Russia, it was occupied by Soviet forces in 1944 as the German armies were forced westward. Within two years a Soviet-oriented government was established, and Bulgaria passed within the Soviet sphere. Control of Bulgaria puts Russian forces within less than twenty miles of the Aegean coast and about eighty-five miles of the Turkish Straits.

The Evacuation of Turks from Bulgaria. A potent Communist weapon against non-Communist countries is the expulsion of thousands of minority peoples from Communist States, thereby placing a tremendous strain on the economy of the non-Communist areas which must receive them. These refugees are generally compelled to leave behind practically all of their possessions, to which the Communist State then falls heir. In 1950, 250,000 Turks, or about one-third of the total Turkish population in Bulgaria, were ordered from the country by the Bulgarian government. These people were transported to the Turkish border, and Turkey was forced to accept the refugees, many of whom had no ties with modern Turkey except those of language and religion, and to provide food, shelter, and eventually employment for them. In time the other half-million Turks in Bulgaria may also be expelled.

The forced evacuation of minorities can under certain conditions stabilize international borders and remove troublesome elements, as in the Czech Sudetenland. Such mass evacuations, if they are to be carried out in an orderly and humane fashion, require careful planning between the sending and receiving countries, and provisions for compensation to the evacuated groups. The use of a quarter-million destitute refugees as a political weapon indicates the extremes to which the Soviet Union and the east European Communist States will go in order to burden countries outside the Soviet bloc.

The Macedonian Question

A special territorial problem, which involves four southeast European States, is that of Macedonia, the area centered on the Vardar Valley from Skopje, Yugoslavia, to Salonika, Greece, and extending east and west to include easternmost Albania and southwestern Bulgaria (Figure 66). Macedonia thus occupies a strategic location in control of the southern portion of the historic Vardar-Morava lowland route from the Aegean Sea to the Danube basin.

The area of Macedonia is about 26,000 square miles, of which 50 per cent is in Greece, 40 per cent in Yugoslavia, just under 10 per cent in Bulgaria, and a small fraction in Albania. Greek influence had spread into the area by the fourth century B.C., and later Macedonia was part of the Roman Empire. In the seventh century Slavs settled there, and shortly afterward the Bulgars also colonized the area. At various times from the ninth to the fourteenth centuries it was part of both the Bulgarian and Serbian empires; then in 1371 it was conquered by the Turks and remained under Turkish control until 1913.

The Macedonian question has been one of the most persistent and

Figure 66. Macedonia. (After Kostanick, "Macedonia: A Study in Political Geography," Doctoral dissertation, Clark University, 1948. Used by permission.)

© RMcN

perplexing territorial problems in eastern Europe. During the past half-century historical, ethnic, economic, and strategic claims have been put forth at various times by the four contesting countries (Yugoslavia, Greece, Bulgaria, and Albania), and disputes over political control have been an important source of friction between the neighboring States. Serbia, and more recently Yugoslavia, claimed the area on the grounds that the Macedonian Slavs are essentially Serbian in speech, while the Bulgars insisted that the Macedonian tongue closely parallels Bulgarian. Actually, the Macedonian language represents something of a transition between Serbian and Bulgarian. Both States have also pressed historical claims (dating back to before 1371) and "strategic needs," based on vague requirements for national security. The Greeks have at times claimed Macedonia on the grounds that Greek culture was there first and that southern Macedonia is predominantly Greek in culture. Albania has based its claims on the presence of 100,000 Albanians in the general area of Macedonia.

Besides the claims of the four States are, of course, those of the Macedonians themselves, many of whom have long desired independence (as have other ethnic groups politically divided between two or more States, such as the Armenians, Basques, and Kurds), while others favor a political role within one of the existing States. Thus the claims and desires of the various countries and peoples in this area add up to an extremely complex territorial situation, the solution of which would appear to be almost impossible within the framework of the traditional concept of national control.

Following World War I large transfers of population were made in the Macedonian area, with the result that political patterns came to correspond fairly well with ethnic boundaries. Of 1,500,000 persons in Greek Macedonia, all are Greek except for 80,000 Macedonian Slavs; in Bulgarian Macedonia the 250,000 persons are almost entirely Bulgarian; while in Yugoslav Macedonia there are about 750,000 Macedonian Slavs and 100,000 Albanians.[7] Although Bulgaria was thus excluded from control over the Macedonian peoples, the State did not abandon hope for future sovereignty in the area. A Bulgarian-supported "International Macedonian Revolutionary Organization" was responsible for waves of terrorism in non-Bulgarian Macedonia, particularly between the two world wars, in an effort to undermine political authority and ultimately to win territory for Bulgaria itself.

In December, 1944, warfare broke out between Communist guerrillas and the Greek army in northern Greece. After two years of fighting Greece brought the case before the United Nations. A UN commission found that

---

[7] In mountainous areas such as this, settlement patterns are often complex. Within Greek and Yugoslav Macedonia are also Romanian shepherds (Vlachs) who move seasonally with their flocks, and in Yugoslavia some Turkish groups still remain. The small area of Albanian Macedonia is practically uninhabited.

the three Soviet-dominated neighbors (Albania, Yugoslavia, and Bulgaria) were giving assistance to the guerrillas. In 1947 American military aid was granted to the Greeks; eventually the guerrilla threat subsided. This aspect of the "Macedonian problem" differed from earlier ones in that the three Soviet-oriented States had no quarrel with one another over possession of Macedonia, but were using this territorial problem as a means of extending Communist control into Greece.

Tito's break with Moscow in 1948 removed some of the Macedonian threat to Greece, since Yugoslavia could not be used as a base for Soviet-inspired hostilities. Agitation in Greek Macedonia can still be directed from Bulgaria and, to a lesser extent, from Albania, but a strong, centralized Greek government and an effective military force have succeeded in preventing serious trouble along the northern borders. In Yugoslav Macedonia Tito's government has expended large amounts of time and money in developing the area and in uniting the Macedonian Slavs within the country. From all reports these activities have met with considerable success.

Romania

Romania, like Poland, is located between militant neighbors—in this case the Soviet Union and Hungary and Bulgaria—and its various borders have vacillated back and forth with the political fortunes of these States. Like Poland, it has also looked to the powers of western Europe for support in its efforts to maintain its territorial integrity; at times, however, this support has been ineffective, and Romania has suffered important losses.

Among the original settlers of Romania were Roman colonists, and the Romanian language is a Romance tongue. As in Bulgaria, the constant flow of diverse groups through the area has profoundly altered the characteristics of the inhabitants, so that the present Romanian is a mixture of many ethnic strains. Romania passed under Turkish rule in the sixteenth century; not until 1866 did the country gain complete independence.

Romania is cut by the Carpathian mountain chain which trends northwest-southeast through two-thirds of the country, then swings west as the Transylvanian Alps. East of the mountains is the plateau of Moldavia, and to the south is the Wallachian lowland. These two areas, inhabited largely by Romanians, form the core of the State. Bucharest, the capital and largest city, is located in the Wallachian lowland.

To the east of Moldavia is Bessarabia, with its Romanian, Russian, Bulgarian, and Turkish population. To the northeast is Bucovina, an area of mixed Romanian-Ruthenian-German population, which adjoins Bessarabia and controls the eastern approaches to a portion of the Carpathians. To the west is the basin of Transylvania, long the scene of disputed sovereignty between Romania and Hungary. In this basin are approximately

2,800,000 Romanians, 1,500,000 Hungarians, 500,000 Germans, and 300,000 others. Finally, in the southeast, control of Southern Dobruja has frequently been contested by Romania and Bulgaria. Thus both terrain and ethnic differences represent powerful centrifugal forces in Romania (Figure 65).

Territorial Changes Since World War I. At the end of World War I Romania, which had sided with the Allies in the conflict, found itself in possession of all four of its border areas—Bessarabia, Bucovina, Transylvania, and Southern Dobruja. With an area of 122,000 square miles and a population of over 12 million, Romania was the largest State in southeastern Europe. Within its borders were valuable resources, including oil, gas, timber, and fertile soils. The development of these resources, however, was not far advanced except for petroleum, and the standard of living was low.

With the rise of Russian and German power in the 1930's Romania's boundaries were threatened. In June, 1940, the Soviet Union demanded and received Bessarabia and northern Bucovina from Romania. The primary cause of these demands was the Soviet desire to establish a defense zone against Germany. Even though Bucovina had never been a part of Russia, the population of the northern part was largely Ruthenian rather than Romanian, and the area represented a connecting link between Bessarabia and Russian-controlled eastern Poland. Two months later northern Transylvania was returned to Hungary at Germany's insistence. Hungary was by now a German ally, and this territorial move foreshadowed the expansion of German power into southeastern Europe. Similarly, the Bulgarian annexation of Southern Dobruja in September, 1940, was a further German-inspired move, for Bulgaria was also a German military ally. Thus Romania, in its buffer position, became the victim of great-power rivalries. The country was forced to cooperate with the Axis powers in the war on Russia, and in 1944 Romania was occupied by the Red Army.

The post-World War II history of Romania is similar to that of most of the east European States. Two years after its occupation by the Soviets it became incorporated within the Communist bloc. Transylvania had been returned by the Hungarians to Romania at the end of World War II, but Southern Dobruja, Bessarabia, and northern Bucovina—all annexed in 1940—were not reunited with Romania. The power of Britain, France, and other Western countries after World War II was unable to restore Romania's territorial losses or to prevent its absorption within the Soviet power system.

*Contributions of the Moscow-Oriented East European States
   to the U.S.S.R.*

The contributions to the Soviet Union of the seven Moscow-oriented east European States—Albania, Bulgaria, Czechoslovakia, East Germany, Hungary, Poland, and Romania—can be considered under the following headings: strategic location, population, natural resources, agricultural and industrial production, and armaments and armed forces. Since these States exist in a dependent status to the U.S.S.R., they are in a position to assist the Soviet Union in any extension of its present economic, military, and political power.

Strategic Location. The combined area of the Soviet-bloc countries in eastern Europe is 393,000 square miles. This area provides defense in depth along Russia's western borders (the "gateway" to the Heartland). With the exception of northern Norway and northeastern Turkey, NATO territory is now removed from the Soviet Union by a wide "buffer zone" through which Soviet forces could fall back in the face of enemy pressure. Soviet military power is in a strong position with regard to the southern shore of the Baltic, to Denmark and West Germany, Austria, Yugoslavia, and Greece. Albania, a Communist State, controls the eastern shore of the Strait of Otranto, and thus poses a threat to Allied activities in the Adriatic and central Mediterranean. Russian forces are also close to the Aegean (through Thrace) and to the Turkish Straits.

Population. The population of the Soviet-oriented area is over 100 million, providing reserves for both labor and armed forces—assuming, of course, that centripetal pressures within the area remain strong. Some of these people are miners or industrial workers with specialized training and technical skills, engineers, or scientists, but the great majority are farmers. When added to that of the Soviet Union this population increases the total for the Soviet bloc to over 300 million.

Natural Resources. In addition to good agricultural lands, the east European States have other valuable resources, including oil (Romania, Hungary), coal (Poland, Czechoslovakia), bauxite (Hungary), uranium (East Germany), and iron ore (Czechoslovakia, Poland). The large areas of fertile agricultural land probably represent the area's greatest natural resource.

Agricultural and Industrial Production. The Soviet-bloc area has long been noted as an important agricultural region. Prior to World War II important exports included wheat, corn, and meat. Theoretically, these surpluses could go now to the Soviet Union, where food production is falling behind the needs of the growing population, but actually agricultural production in some of the east European States since 1945 has been insufficient to do much more than meet domestic demands.

The countries contain two important industrial areas, Polish Silesia and western Czechoslovakia, although the Communists are working to increase the industrial output in other areas as well. Steel production from the east European States amounted to over 22 million tons in 1960. Other important manufactures include chemicals, machinery, textiles, armaments, and electrotechnical supplies. These manufactures are used to strengthen the economies of the eastern European countries as well as that of the Soviet Union.

Armaments and Armed Forces. Among the industrial resources now available to the U.S.S.R. are the armament plants of the Communist States, including the famous Skoda works of Czechoslovakia, once the foremost armament producer of the Austro-Hungarian Empire. These armament plants are now operating at capacity in order to equip the armies of the various countries. It is estimated that there are over a million men in the combined armies of the East European bloc. Some military experts question the effectiveness of these troops in an offensive war, although they might fight in defense of their homelands and with the Soviet Union, if they were convinced that by so doing they could profit economically or politically.

The extent and value of these contributions are, of course, dependent upon future Soviet–east European relations. The discontent in Poland in 1956 led to an apparent weakening of Soviet control in that country and the creation of a more independent Communist regime in Warsaw—somewhat analogous to the situation in Yugoslavia. The Hungarian uprisings of 1956, on the other hand, were met by fierce Soviet resistance, thereby emphasizing the mythical nature of independence in this country. The long and bitter struggle by the Hungarians against the Soviet forces served to point out the underlying hatred for the U.S.S.R. existing throughout the dominated area, and the necessity for perpetual Soviet vigilance and force if the unity of eastern Europe and the Soviet Union is to be maintained. Because of the scarcity of official information it is difficult to assess changes taking place in the relations between the Soviet Union and the seven States. The apparent easing of Soviet dominance in Poland has been accompanied by the granting of goods and credits to that country from the United States. There has been a considerable increase of trade between these countries and the non-Communist world, as well as of exchanges of students and other visitors. Nevertheless, in two respects the seven States remain tied to Moscow, first, through their support of Soviet foreign policy and, second, through their unswerving acceptance of Communism as the ruling political ideology.

FINLAND

Finland, together with Yugoslavia, is something of an anomaly in eastern Europe, in that only a small portion of its territory was temporarily occupied by Soviet forces during World War II and it has remained outside of the Soviet bloc since that time. Finland's continued independence is due in part to the stubborn character of the Finnish people, who agreed to surrender to the Russians in 1944 only on the grounds of continued national survival, and who subsequently refused to support the local Communist party in its bid to acquire control of the national government.

The Finns, whose ancestors had migrated to northeastern Europe from Asia by the eighth century, are unlike the Slavic peoples to the east and the Scandinavians to the west. With their own language and culture they are a distinct ethnic group, occupying something of a buffer position between Sweden and Russia. Prior to 1809 Finland was for many years a possession of Sweden, and from 1809 to 1919 it was joined to Russia. Following World War I Finland was one of the tier of independent States which was created along the Soviet Union's western border.

The Finnish State has few resources except forests, water power, and fish. Climate and soil limit the land in agriculture to but 7 per cent of the total area. Population is concentrated largely in the southern and western areas. Helsinki, the capital, is also the largest city. Most of the nearly 4½ million Finns are united by language, religion, and national sentiment; this strong sense of nationalism has been one of the most important factors contributing to Finland's continued independence since 1919. In addition to the Finns there is an important Swedish-speaking minority (totaling about 9 per cent of the population), which lives along the west coast of Finland. Since World War I relations between Sweden and Finland have generally been friendly, and this minority has not posed a threat to Finland's national unity. The principal threat has come from the east, where the Soviets have twice pressed for reannexation of a part of the territory of their former possession.

Despite its record of political and economic development and of neutrality in foreign affairs during the interwar years, Finland was invaded by the Soviet Union in 1939 and was defeated after a short war. As a result the Russians gained valuable territory along the Finnish border, including the Karelian Isthmus northwest of Leningrad, within which was located Viipuri (later named Vyborg), Finland's second city (Figure 67). In an effort to regain these lands Finland joined Germany in 1941 in the attack on the U.S.S.R. Again Finland was defeated, and in 1944, after its second surrender, the country was forced to cede additional land to the Soviets, including territories in the Petsamo area in the north which contained Finland's valuable nickel deposits. Petsamo was an ice-free port and Finland's only sea outlet to the north (for a listing of Finnish losses in World War II see Table 11). After the two defeats 450,000 refugees from areas ceded to the U.S.S.R. fled to Finland, placing a tremendous strain on the country's already disturbed economy. Although the Communists within Finland sought to capitalize on the State's economic and political problems and to overpower the democratic government (as they did in Czechoslovakia), the Finns resisted the pressure and thereby prevented their country from becoming a Soviet-dominated State.

Since World War II Finland has maintained as neutral a position as possible with respect to the Cold War. The State has paid off in full the

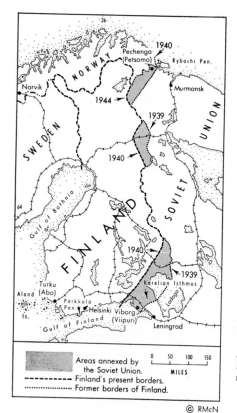

Figure 67. Finland's Territorial Losses to the Soviet Union, 1940–44. The Porkkala Peninsula was returned to Finland in 1956. (After Van Valkenburg, "European Jigsaw," *Headline Series* No. 53, Foreign Policy Association, 1945. Used by permission.)

heavy war reparations demanded by the Russians. In 1948 the Finns were compelled to sign a treaty of mutual assistance with the U.S.S.R., providing for joint defense in the event of enemy attack on either nation. Under adverse conditions the Finns have been successful in maintaining an independent democratic State in the northern portion of this historic east European buffer area. One condition of such independence, however, is that Finland does not adopt a government unfriendly to the Soviet Union. One third of Finland's foreign trade is with the countries of the "Outer Seven," another third with the Common Market States, and less than one-fifth with the Soviet Union and Communist east Europe. Thus the Finns face many trade difficulties in the gradual division of Europe into economic blocs.

YUGOSLAVIA

In its politico-geographic structure Yugoslavia has certain aspects in common with two other east European States. Like Finland it has remained outside of the Soviet-dominated orbit, and like Czechoslovakia it has been troubled in the past by complex centrifugal forces brought on by ethnic and physical diversities. These centrifugal forces have been compounded primarily of four interrelated factors: (1) diversity in language, alphabet, religion, and national sentiments; (2) difficult communications due to the mountainous character of much of the country; (3) important foreign minorities; and (4) frequent border disputes with neighboring States.

The Yugoslav State

Yugoslavia—the former Kingdom of the Serbs, Croats, and Slovenes—was created at the end of World War I, partly from territory of the Austro-Hungarian Empire and partly from the two independent States of Serbia and Montenegro. In 1919 the three major Slavic groups—Serbs, Croats, and Slovenes—together accounted for about 81 per cent of the total population. There were differences not only of language, religion, and alphabet among these three groups, but also of historical development. Before the formation of the Yugoslav State Croatia and Slovenia had for many years been part of the Austro-Hungarian Empire, while Serbia had been under the rule of the Turks from the fourteenth to the early nineteenth centuries and then had become independent. Education and technical training among the Croats and Slovenes had been more highly developed than in Serbia, thus contributing to the mutual antagonism between the numerically superior Serbs on the one hand and the Croats and Slovenes on the other.

The delimitation of the Yugoslav borders in 1919 resulted in controversies with Italy, particularly in the Trieste and Fiume areas (see page 255), and with Austria (see page 248). In both instances Yugoslavia failed to get the territory it desired. In the northeast the final borders with Hungary and Romania were drawn so as to include 450,000 Hungarians, 500,000 Germans, and 200,000 Romanians in the new country. In the south over 500,000 Macedonians and more than 400,000 Albanians, together with Turks and Bulgars, came under Yugoslav sovereignty (Table 8).

Yugoslavia consists of five major regions—the northeastern plain (a part of the Danube lowlands), the Vardar-Morava Valley, leading southward to the Aegean, the central (Dinaric) upland, the Adriatic littoral, and the mountain and hill areas of the northwest. The northeastern plain is inhabited largely by Serbs, together with Hungarian and Romanian minority groups. There is located Belgrade, the national capital and center of the country's principal core area. Serbs also occupy the northern portion of the Vardar-Morava Valley, while in the southern part of this lowland are the Macedonians, a Slavicized group with their own language and culture (see page 307). In the central uplands and on the Adriatic littoral are Croats, a third Slavic group, whose language is the same as that of the Serbs, but whose alphabet and religion differ. The Serbs are Serbian Orthodox, while the Croats are Roman Catholic. Finally, in the northern part of Yugoslavia are the Slovenes, also Slavic and Roman Catholic, with the same alphabet as the Croats, but with their own distinctive language. Albanians live in the southern part of the central uplands, and there is a small Turkish minority in the southeast. Italians, Germans, and Jews, who once formed additional minorities in Yugoslavia, have largely disappeared since World War II.

Economic and strategic considerations were important in the formation of the Yugoslav State, as they were in the creation of Czechoslovakia. Yugoslavia is well supplied with mineral resources—chromite, bauxite, copper, mercury, and iron ore—although most of these have as yet been only partly utilized. About one-third of Yugoslavia's petroleum requirements is met by local production. The country also has low-grade coal and abundant water power potential. At the time of Yugoslavia's formation its economy was still at a low stage of development and transportation facilities were poor. Only since World War II has there been a marked development of the State's mineral resources, improvement of land utilization techniques, and appreciable expansion of industrial activities. With its 98,766 square miles of territory, its population of over 18 million persons, and its varied resource base, Yugoslavia may in time become one of the economically strong countries of eastern Europe.

Yugoslavia's Development as a State

From 1919 to 1941 Yugoslavia struggled to develop internal unity and to strengthen its economy. The ruggedness of the terrain, the poor contacts with the Adriatic because of mountains and poor transportation facilities, the general backwardness of the economy, and finally the political upheavals within the government itself all combined to prevent Yugoslavia from developing into a strong unit during the interwar years. The Croats desired a federal political structure in order to prevent political domination by the Serbs, who comprised over 40 per cent of the national population, but the Serbian concept of a centralized administration formed the basis for the government. There were movements for an independent Croatian republic, but no permanent political unit developed, and in spite of continued rivalries between the various groups, Yugoslavia remained a State intact until June, 1941, when it was invaded and conquered by Germany and its allies. Following its defeat Yugoslavia disappeared as a separate entity, its several parts apportioned out among Germany, Italy, Hungary, Bulgaria, and Albania as direct territorial annexations or as puppet states (Figure 60).

In 1945 Yugoslavia regained its prewar political shape. Eventually about 3,050 square miles of former Italian territory were incorporated into the country. Postwar Yugoslavia was set up as a federation of six autonomous republics—Serbia, Croatia, Slovenia, Bosnia-Hercegovina, Macedonia, and Montenegro, with two additional autonomous areas within the Serbian republic—but political control still remained firmly centered within the national Communist government. The emphasis on national unity rather than on regional differences is a potent force working to overcome the various divisive pressures which existed in Yugoslavia from 1919 to World War II. Although the State was originally within the Soviet orbit, Tito broke with Moscow in June, 1948, and the Yugoslav government, while still Communist in form, has since maintained its own independence.

Yugoslav resistance to the U.S.S.R. is compounded of various factors. Diversity of relief has fostered relatively isolated, closely knit cultural groups, whose spirit of resistance to foreign control is strongly developed. The rugged terrain served as a base for guerrilla activities. Yugoslavia had its own army in the closing months of World War II, and the country was not occupied by Soviet forces. Moreover, its continued independence from Soviet control has been partly due to the determined leadership of Marshal Tito. Yugoslavia stands out as a symbol of resistance to Soviet imperialism in that it is the only country of eastern Europe which, after having become a part of the Soviets' power sphere, has managed to regain its independence of action.

THE NORTHEASTERN MEDITERRANEAN— GREECE, TURKEY, AND CYPRUS

Greece

Greece, like Italy to the west, contains elements of both continental and maritime environments. On its northern borders the State adjoins Albania, Yugoslavia, and Bulgaria. The mountainous character of the border areas and the complex ethnic patterns there have resulted in historic conflicts of boundary location between the Greeks and their three northern Balkan neighbors. On the northeast Greece also adjoins Turkey: here again many territorial and ethnic problems have arisen. The mainland possesses a long coast line and is surrounded by many Greek-inhabited islands.

With an area of 51,182 square miles, Greece has relatively few resources to support its population of about 8 million. Much of the land is mountainous and less than 32 per cent is classed as arable land. Level areas are often swampy and require extensive drainage operations before they can be made productive. There, as in Italy, agricultural production suffers not only from the lack of available land, but also from poor agricultural techniques and lack of capital for such things as good seed and fertilizers. Greece has no coal or petroleum, and the water power potential is not yet well developed. The State has a wide variety of minerals, such as iron ore, lead, zinc, and chromium, but none of these occurs in large quantities. The population increase is about 90,000 per year, and many Greeks have emigrated overseas in search of better economic opportunities. Others have turned to the sea for their livelihood, but the Mediterranean is not one of the rich fishing areas, and Greece is not one of the great mercantile countries of the world.

Most of the people living within Greece are united by language, religion, and national loyalty. The frequent need for resistance to foreign aggression has also contributed a significant unifying element to the country. The principal areas of ethnic differences occur in the northern border regions. Centrifugal forces are strong there, due to the complex terrain, the differences in economic interests, particularly between northern and southern Greece, and the lack of transportation and other communication facilities throughout the State. Athens, both the ancient and modern capital, is located in the principal core area, but because of the diverse topography population concentrations are scattered throughout the country. Greek Macedonia, centering on Salonika in the northeast, represents a secondary core area, while among the less important ones are the various lowlands of Peloponnesus in the south and the plain of Thessaly northwest of Athens.

After nearly four centuries of Turkish control the Greeks finally won their independence in 1829. During the following ninety years they were able to extend gradually the territory of their country, winning control of various Aegean islands, Crete, Corfu, and the Ionian Islands, as well as both western and eastern Thrace, all of which were inhabited largely by Greeks. At the end of World War I the Greek-inhabited eastern Aegean islands, including Lemnos, Samos, and Samothrace, were ceded to Greece. Return of the Dodecanese Islands at the end of World War II brought another segment of Greek population under the State's control.

Before World War I many Greeks also lived in the vicinity of Smyrna on the western coast of Turkey. Following the war Greek troops occupied the Smyrna area in anticipation of the creation of a Greek "influence zone" there, but they were soon forced to withdraw after defeat in battle. In 1923 there was an exchange of over 1¾ million Greeks living in Turkey with some 350,000 Turks living in Greece. Thus the Greek ethnic "bridgehead" in Anatolia was largely removed.

Land Boundaries of Greece. Greece's land boundaries have often caused difficulties to the country. Because of the complex ethnic patterns existing in the border area, conflicts have arisen with Bulgaria over Thrace, with Yugoslavia over Macedonia, and with Albania over northern Epirus.

THRACE. In 1913 Greece gained control over the former Turkish territory in western Thrace, and after World War I defeated Bulgaria was forced to cede eastern Thrace to the Greeks. This narrow strip of Greek territory, reaching eastward to Turkey, separates the territory of Bulgaria, a Soviet-dominated State, from the Aegean. The territory is inhabited for the most part by Greeks, although in the mountain areas along the Greek-Bulgarian frontier there are nomadic peoples of Bulgarian and Romanian origins.

Northwestern Thrace includes a portion of the region known as Macedonia, a complex ethnic and political area. Greek Macedonia was the scene of a major population change in 1923, when over half a million Greek refugees from Turkey were settled in the northern part of this area. Immediately following World War II the mountainous area of Macedonia, bordering on northern Greece, Albania, Yugoslavia, and Bulgaria, was the site of guerrilla warfare, as Communist forces from countries to the north of Greece sought to overrun the State. The presence of Macedonians, Albanians, and other non-Greek groups along the borders complicates the political situation, especially when Greece's neighbors use them to stir up trouble for the Athens administration (see page 306 for a discussion of the Macedonian problem).

NORTHERN EPIRUS. Relations between Greece and Albania have been strained for many years as a result of disputed sovereignty over northern Epirus, a mountainous area of about 3,000 square miles in southern Albania containing some 320,000 people. When the Albanian State was set up just prior to World War I, its southern boundary was delimited in such a way that a number of people having cultural affinities with Greece were included within the new country. Since 1913 Greece has frequently pressed for border rectifications so as to include these people within the Greek State.

The ethnic characteristics of the people of northern Epirus have never been carefully determined. Surveys based on religion at the time of World War I showed that about 40 per cent of the population were Greek Orthodox. Whether all of these, if given the choice, would prefer Greek to Albanian rule is, of course, impossible to predict. Another survey, made after World War I, estimated that about one-sixth of the population of southern Albania spoke Greek in their homes. In this case Greece might have fairly strong claims to the loyalty of most of the people. On the other hand, there is also a large number of Albanian-speaking people (sometimes estimated as high as 100,000) in northern Greece, thereby further contributing to the problems of delimiting an ethnic boundary between the two States.

The problem of the Albanian-Greek border must be viewed today in the light of its role as a sector of the Iron Curtain and therefore an area of tension in the Cold War. Greece has for the time abandoned its claims to parts of northern Epirus, but the ethnic problem may eventually be revived, as each country still has sizeable minorities in the other's territory.

Turkey

Turkey's location in the northeastern sector of the Mediterranean basin is strategically important because of the Straits, the country's proximity to the Soviet Union, and its relationship to the States of the Middle East. As a result of its military alignment with the United States and other NATO powers, Turkey has become an extremely significant area of Western influence in this part of the world—a check to Soviet expansion to the Aegean Sea and the Middle East, and a base for United States military strength in the troubled eastern Mediterranean.

With its population of over 23 million and its reserves of chrome, molybdenum, and manganese, as well as its coal and water power potential, Turkey possesses the basis for a relatively strong economic system. Because of its history and the mountainous terrain throughout most of the country, however, modernization of Turkey's economic, social, and political structure has been slow, with the result that the average annual income remains very low. Much progress must still be made in such fields as education, health, and agricultural techniques before Turkey will have reached the level of development and per capita income of the nations of western and central Europe.

Centrifugal forces of distance, mountain barriers, and poor communication systems have hampered the development of strong political cohesion in Turkey. During the 1920's the national capital was moved from Constantinople to the ancient capital city of Ankara in the center of the State, in order to promote a sense of independence from foreign control and to help in the unification of the various sectors of Turkey. With the expulsion of the Greeks in 1923 greater cultural unity was obtained among the Turkish population. The principal ethnic minorities remaining in Turkey are the Armenians and Kurds in the rugged eastern part of the country.

Changing Power Status of Turkey. The Ottoman Empire, of which Constantinople (now Istanbul) was the capital, began its growth during the mid-fifteenth century, and about 200 years later had reached its maximum extent. At one time the Turks controlled an area from the Atlantic to the Persian Gulf and from the Hungarian Plain and the southern Ukraine to the southwestern corner of Arabia. By the end of the seventeenth century the empire had begun to decrease in size, but not until after World War I did it completely disappear. Thus for nearly 500 years Turkey was a major power in the Mediterranean basin.

From 1914 to 1918 Turkey fought on the side of Germany and its allies, after which Turkey was a thoroughly beaten country, in no position to bargain at the peace conference. Control of the Straits was taken from the Turks in 1920 and placed in the hands of an international commission, and foreign zones of occupation (French, Italian, and Greek) were established along the State's western and southern coasts.

The rebirth of Turkish power began in 1920, when a spirit of nationalism (occasioned in part by the severity of the terms of the Turkish peace treaty) began to sweep the country. Foreign occupation forces were eventually defeated by Turkish troops, and by 1923 Turkey was in a position to reassert its sovereignty. Under the strong leadership of Kemal Ataturk,

Turkey adopted many customs of the Western countries, developed a strong military force, and by 1939 had again become an important power in the Middle East.

During World War II the State remained neutral until the closing months of the conflict, when it declared war on Germany. Immediately following the war Turkey was subjected to heavy pressure by the U.S.S.R., particularly in connection with the Straits, for the Soviets wanted a share in the control and defense of the waterway. With the backing of the United States, Turkey resisted Soviet pressure. American military and economic aid was granted to the Turks, and eventually Turkey became a member of NATO. One of the most powerful States of the Middle East area, Turkey has regained much of its former significance as a key State in international power alignments.

The Straits.   One of Turkey's most critical problems of territorial control has concerned the waterway connecting the Black and Aegean seas. This waterway lies entirely within Turkish territory, although the right of passage through it vitally affects all the countries which border the Black Sea. The Straits consist of three sections: the Dardanelles in the west, a 47-mile-long passage, at one point less than a mile wide; the Sea of Marmara, 125 miles long; and the 18-mile-long Bosporus in the east, less than 2,500 feet wide at its narrowest point (Figure 68). Istanbul stands on both the European and Asiatic sides of the Bosporus at its entrance into the Sea of Marmara. Since

© RMcN

Figure 68. The Straits.

the middle of the fifteenth century Turkey has retained control of the Straits and holds the threat of being able to bottle up Black Sea navigation when and if Turkish leaders deem such action necessary.

The history of Turkish policy toward the passage of foreign ships through the Straits is a long and intricate one. The defeat of Turkish forces late in the eighteenth century led to a relaxation of restrictions on foreign shipping in 1774 and the granting of permission for Russian merchant vessels to utilize the waterways. In 1859 permission was extended to all neutral shipping to pass through the Straits, thereby opening the Black Sea for the first time to world commerce. During World War I Turkey, a belligerent, closed the Straits to all Allied shipping, and Russia was cut off from Allied supplies. British naval and land units tried to force the Straits in 1915, but despite high losses their efforts were unsuccessful. By the Treaty of Sèvres (1920) the Straits were demilitarized and Turkey lost complete control of their administration.

Two subsequent international conferences served to return control of the Straits to Turkey. The resurgence of Turkish nationalism led to the Treaty of Lausanne (1923), returning the waterway to Turkish administration. Thirteen years later Turkey found itself in a strong bargaining position, and the Lausanne Treaty was superseded by that of Montreux, permitting Turkey to fortify the Straits and to close them to warships of all countries when Turkey was at war or threatened by aggression. Soviet warships were to use the Straits in peacetime without restriction, but non-Black Sea powers could send only a limited naval tonnage at one time into the Black Sea.

During World War II Turkey exercised its right of closure, although Allied officials maintained that German vessels at times dismantled their armament, sailed through the Straits, and then reassembled it. The passage of Soviet warships through the Straits was denied, and in 1945 the Russians put forth demands for increased control of the Straits. They asked for a confederation, composed of powers bordering the Black Sea, to administer the waterway, although these powers consisted only of the U.S.S.R., the Soviet-dominated States of Bulgaria and Romania, and Turkey. The Russians demanded that a joint Soviet-Turkish defense be set up for the Straits and that they be open in peacetime only to warships of the Black Sea powers. The Turks, however, have resisted Soviet demands, and the Straits are still administered according to the Montreux Convention of 1936.

The Turkish-Russian Border Area. The mountainous region of northeastern Turkey is one of the most isolated parts of the country, and an area in which strong centrifugal forces have at times developed with respect to Turkish control. The Armenians, an ethnic group which numbers about 2,500,-000, inhabit the valleys and basins of northeastern Turkey and of the southwestern sector of Soviet Transcaucasia. Their isolation has helped them to retain their distinctive language and culture in the face of the numerous military activities and political changes which have taken place there through past centuries.

The Turkish-Soviet border stretches for 322 miles through this upland region (Figure 69). Controversy between Turkey and Russia over the location of this border dates back to 1878, when the Russians completed a century-long advance southward by annexing a Turkish-controlled sector, including the port of Batumi on the Black Sea coast. During World War I Russia and Turkey faced one another across the border. Russian forces advanced into eastern Turkey and were aided by Turkish Armenians, still recovering from the terrible massacre inflicted on them by the Turks in 1894. The collapse of Russia in 1917 brought the return of Turkish troops and renewed pillage. In the Treaty of Brest-Litovsk, which defeated Russia signed with Germany and its allies, the Kars-Ardahan region, part of the sector won by Russia from Turkey in 1878, was returned to the Turks. The new boundary practically split the Armenians in two. After the surrender of Germany and the other Central Powers in November, 1918, the Brest-Litovsk Treaty was abrogated, but because of Russian internal difficulties the Turks continued to hold the Kars-Ardahan area.

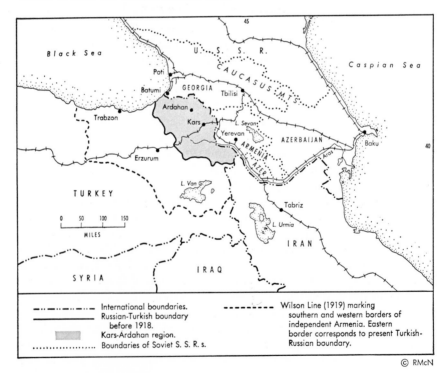

© RMcN

Figure 69. The Turkish-Russian Border Area. (Boundaries after Bowman, *The New World*, World Book Co., 1928. Used by permission of R. G. Bowman.)

Following World War II the Soviets asked for the return of Kars and Ardahan from the Turks. Despite its rugged terrain the area could be utilized by powers hostile to Russia for the construction of air bases only a few minutes flying time from the industrial oil fields and transportation lines of Soviet Transcaucasia. The Turks have held firm in their resistance to Soviet territorial demands. Although in 1953 the Soviet government officially abandoned its claims to changes in its border with Turkey, the region still remains a source of potential dispute, particularly if relations between Russia and Turkey should deteriorate at some future time.

Cyprus

The Republic of Cyprus was constituted as an independent State in August, 1960, after years of controversy and civil disorders. The island had been conquered by the Turks in 1571 and remained under Turkey until 1878, when it was ceded to Britain for administrative purposes. At the outbreak of World War I the British formally annexed it. The area measures about 3,500 square miles and as of 1960 had a population of 561,000, some 80 per cent of Greek origin and 20 per cent Turkish. The political problems in Cyprus following World War II revolved about this ethnic split. The outbreak in civil violence in Cyprus began in 1955 and was associated with Greek demands for "enosis," that is, union of the island with Greece. Greeks have inhabited Cyprus since ancient times, and the Greek Orthodox Church is very strong there; Archbishop Makarios of the Orthodox Church was a leading spokesman for enosis. The Turkish population, on the other hand, resisted any move for incorporation within the Greek State, and as a counter to enosis the Turks pressed for partition of Cyprus into Turkish and Greek sectors. The British were concerned with their two bases on the island and its role as a last remaining British defense area in the eastern Mediterranean area.

The disorders in Cyprus lasted for four years and cost over 600 lives before agreement was reached on the island's future. In 1959 it was decided that Cyprus would be prepared for independence, an independence guaranteed by Britain, Greece, and Turkey, with prohibition against union of Cyprus with another State, or partition of the island into two or more parts. The president of Cyprus was to be Greek with a Turkish vice-president. British sovereignty would be retained over the two areas used as bases. Thus a seemingly hopeless impasse was overcome through the use of common sense on all sides. In March, 1961, the independent republic was admitted to the British Commonwealth of Nations.

Independence for Cyprus has not ended its problems. Although disorders have not reappeared on the island, there is as yet little concept of nationhood; the citizens still think of themselves as Greek or Turkish

Cypriotes. More important, perhaps, the economy has not been strong, and there is a chronic unemployment problem. Agriculture is the mainstay of the island, although there is some mining and export of copper. The largest trade union is Communist-oriented, and by late 1961 it was estimated that in a state-wide election the Communist party might poll as high as 35 to 40 per cent of the votes. Here is a country which has had statehood thrust upon it largely as a compromise among foreign States which quarreled over its political future. Cyprus has no army, but is garrisoned by British, Greek, and Turkish forces. Its supreme constitutional court consists of a neutral president and two judges, one Greek and one Turk. As an area of balance between the interests of three countries Cyprus faces a difficult task in working out the intricate problems of representative self-government and of the development of a national consciousness.

BIBLIOGRAPHY

"Backs to the Wall: East Germany's Economy in 1962," *The World Today,* XVIII (1962), 242–49.

A summary of East Germany's economic dilemma.

BRZEZINSKI, ZBIGNIEW, and GRIFFITH, WILLIAM E. "Peaceful Engagement in Eastern Europe," *Foreign Affairs,* XXXIX (1960), 642–55.

Interesting analysis of the problem of military planning in Europe.

CAMPBELL, JOHN C. "The European Territorial Settlement," *Foreign Affairs,* XXVI (1947), 196–219.

Maps and descriptions of the territorial settlements at the end of World War II involving Italy, Romania, Bulgaria, Hungary, and Finland.

HARTSHORNE, RICHARD. "A Survey of the Boundary Problems of Europe," *Geographic Aspects of International Relations,* C. C. COLBY (ed.). Chicago: The University of Chicago Press, 1938. Pp. 163–217.

Considers border disputes throughout all of Europe following World War I.

HOFFMAN, GEORGE W. "Eastern Europe, a Study in Political Geography," *The Texas Quarterly,* II (1959), 57–89.

This article concentrates primarily on populations and territorial control since World War II.

MELAMID, ALEXANDER. "Partitioning Cyprus: A Class Exercise in Applied Geography," *Journal of Geography,* LIX (1960), 118–23.

A summary of the problems which might have been raised if Cyprus had been partitioned into Greek and Turkish sectors.

"Progress East of the Oder-Neisse," *The World Today,* XVI (1960), 491–501.

A description of changes taking place in western Poland.

ROUCEK, JOSEPH S. "Central-Eastern Europe," in *Approaches to an Understanding of World Affairs, Twenty-Fifth Yearbook of The National Council for the Social Studies,* Howard R. Anderson (ed.). Washington, 1954. Pp. 138–56.

A good descriptive article on this area.

SKENDI, STEVRO. "Albania and the Sino-Soviet Conflict," *Foreign Affairs,* XL (1962), 471–79.

Albania's problems with the U.S.S.R.

TORNGREN, RALF. "The Neutrality of Finland," *Foreign Affairs,* XXXIX (1961), 601–10.

An analysis of the extent of Finnish neutrality.

12

THE SOVIET UNION

● The Soviet Union, or the Union of Soviet Socialist Republics (U.S.S.R.), ranks with the United States as one of the two great power centers of the world. Its area is the largest of all countries, and its population is surpassed only by those of China and India. The country's central location in the Eurasian land mass, its rich resource base and growing economic might, and its role as the center of the world Communist movement are factors which also contribute to the great strength of the Soviet State. Internally the U.S.S.R. is faced with the problem of welding its diverse ethnic groups into a strong national unit. Externally it is confronted with a variety of opposing forces, many of which have arisen as a result of Soviet moves for territorial aggrandizement since the summer of 1939. Because of the dynamic nature of its foreign relations, and because of the great power potential which it possesses, the Soviet Union represents a force of primary importance in the pattern of territorial control throughout the world.

LOCATION

The location of the U.S.S.R. in the Heartland of Eurasia is, of course, of great significance to its power potential. To the west lie the countries of Europe, with their large populations and their great industrial development. To the south are the oil resources of the Middle East and the Suez land bridge to Africa, as well as peninsular India and southeast Asia, with their great concentrations of people and natural resources. To the east lie China, with its 700 million inhabitants, and Japan, with its dense population and economic strength. Thus Russia is centrally located with respect to much of the people, resources, and economic development of the Eastern Hemisphere. Because of this location, it is often in a position to exert powerful influences on economic and political developments within the great belt of countries which borders it on three sides. On its fourth side the U.S.S.R. faces Anglo-America across the Arctic.

The physical elements of a State are important both as assets and as liabilities to national development. For the Soviet Union the effects of these elements may be measured in terms of economic strength, defense, and internal unity and diversity.

Economic Strength

As a result of Russia's northern continental location its climate is an important limiting factor to agricultural and commercial development. Long, severe winters exist throughout much of the country, and there are large areas of arid or semiarid conditions, particularly in the south central parts. Approximately two-thirds of the U.S.S.R. is normally too cold for agriculture and another sixth is too dry. Commercially Russia's climate has meant that the State has few ice-free ports and that many of the rivers are frozen during several months of the year. Much of Russia's history of territorial expansion since the late seventeenth century has been interpreted in part as a quest for warm-water ports on open water bodies, although explanations may also be found in other economic and political drives, such as desire for security, for national prestige, for control of resources, and (since 1918) for the spread of Communism.

Areas of steep slope and of infertile soils and poor drainage also place limitations on agriculture. East of the Yenisey River in Siberia and along the southern borders of the State much of the land is mountainous. Large sectors of European Russia and of western Siberia, however, are flat or gently rolling, and within this region there are extensive areas in which the soils are of moderate to high fertility. The belt of fertile chernozem soils in the U.S.S.R. is probably the largest of any country in the world.

Geologic findings have indicated that the Soviet Union has within its borders a considerable supply of practically every major mineral except tin. In addition, it has large reserves of coal and petroleum. Certain ferroalloys, particularly molybdenum, tungsten, and vanadium, are in short supply, but the last two are thought to be available from Communist China.

Forests and water resources are two other physical aspects of Soviet economic strength. Russia has one of the greatest forest reserves in the world, although the small annual rate of growth in the northern areas, combined with their inaccessibility, restricts the potential value of much of these vast forested areas.

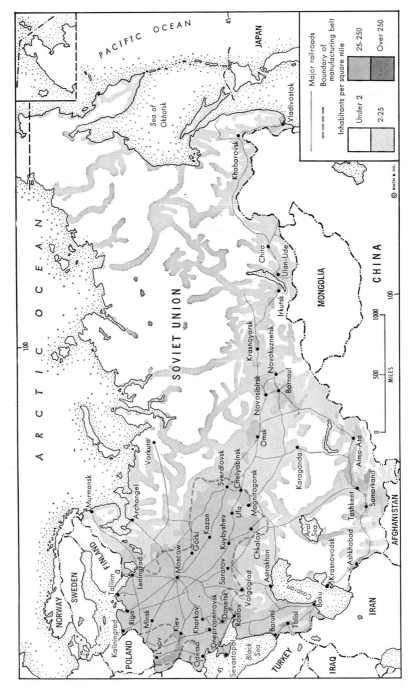

Figure 70. The Soviet Union.

Many of the great rivers of Russia are navigable for considerable distances, but three of the largest (Ob, Yenisey, and Lena) flow north to the Arctic Ocean, while the Volga discharges into the Caspian Sea, from which there is no outlet. In addition to transportation, Soviet rivers are important for water power and irrigation. The rivers of the central and eastern Siberian uplands are particularly valuable for their hydroelectric potential, while the Volga in European Russia and the Amu and Syr rivers in southern Siberia are used extensively for irrigation. The U.S.S.R. and China have arranged for the joint devolopment of the Amur River in the Far East for transportation and hydroelectric power. One of the major Soviet engineering projects being developed is the diversion of the waters of some of the northward-flowing rivers to the southern steppes and deserts, where they can be used for irrigation projects.

Size, climate, and surface configuration also affect surface transportation facilities in Russia. From Brest on the western border to Vladivostok on the Pacific it is over 6,000 miles by railroad, and for a country which has only recently entered the Industrial Age, distances such as this can pose tremendous problems in the development of transportation systems. The difficult climate and terrain and the problems of construction in areas of permafrost have slowed the progress of railroad-building, particularly in the northern and northeastern parts of the U.S.S.R.

Defense

Russia's size, climate, and physical borders are important assets in terms of national defense. Because of the great area of the State (about 8,600,000 square miles) Russian armies have been able to fall back in the face of invading forces without being conquered or destroyed, as they did before Napoleon in the nineteenth century and Nazi Germany in the twentieth. The severe Russian winters have also been a defense factor, for the military operations of the invaders have been severely limited by the cold. In the Air Age large size permits greater dispersion of bombing targets; at the same time, however, it also may mean longer borders to defend against air attacks.

The defense value of the mountain regions and water bodies surrounding Russia was an important factor in Mackinder's concept of the Heartland area. From the eastern end of the Black Sea to Vladivostok on the Pacific the Soviet Union's borders are marked almost continuously by mountains, and they are also generally removed by considerable distances from large population centers in neighboring States. From the Black Sea north to the Arctic terrain barriers are much less effective, and it is there in the east European lowland that Russia has suffered the most from invasion. Water bodies, such as the Black and Baltic seas, have provided protection for Russia only if the country has had military control of these areas. The assault on Crimea during the nineteenth century, for instance, illustrated the danger of foreign control of the surrounding water bodies, and the Soviet Union, particularly since World War II, has made strenuous efforts to assure itself of naval and air supremacy in the waters which surround it.

Russia's central location is important in terms of both defensive and offensive operations. Eleven countries have territory adjoining the Soviet Union.[1] Japan is separated by less than ten miles from the Soviets in the Kuril Islands, and the American state of Alaska is but two miles from the easternmost island of Siberia. Although physical barriers exist between the Soviet Union and its neighbors to the south and east, the existence of so many countries along the borders of the Soviet Union could represent a serious threat to Russian security in the event that all or most of them were united in military action against the U.S.S.R. It was this possibility that underlay Spykman's thesis of the predominance of power in the Rimland area of Eurasia. Added to this list of potential enemies is Anglo-America, separated from Russia by the Arctic wastes, but close to it in terms of air operations.

For Russia, as formerly for Germany, this ring of surrounding States may also offer possibilities for territorial aggression—assuming that these States are not united militarily in defense against such a move. The weakness of disunity has been amply demonstrated by repeated Soviet successes in expanding into adjoining territories, such as Finland, the Baltic States, Poland, Manchuria, and Japan.

Internal Unity and Diversity

Russia's size and shape have contributed greatly to the centrifugal forces in the State, first, because of the difficulties of politically uniting such a vast area and, second, because between the Black and Caspian seas the country extends across a strong natural boundary—the Caucasus—to include an area whose climate and population differ in many respects from those of the rest of the U.S.S.R. It is in this Transcaucasian area, containing the republics of Georgia, Armenia, and Azerbaijan, that some of the strongest opposition to Moscow's control has developed, particularly since 1917.

In European Russia, north of the Caucasus, and in western Siberia the lack of landform diversity has been a contributing factor to political unity. Climatic conditions change slowly, and diversity of agricultural and commercial interests is not so strong here as in areas such as eastern United States. In central and eastern Siberia and in the southern Siberian border regions, however, distance, surface configuration, and even climate do con-

---

[1] Russia has on occasion claimed the eastern panhandle of Afghanistan, which would bring the Russians to the borders of Kashmir, adding one more political unit to the list of those touching the U.S.S.R.

stitute important centrifugal forces. Following World War I, for example, there was a move (sponsored largely by the Japanese) to set up a separate State in the Maritime Province along the Pacific. Resistance to Moscow's authority has also been encountered many times among the mountain peoples along the borders of China and Afghanistan. The government's answer to these moves has been to improve the circulatory systems there, not only railways and highways, but also educational facilities, motion pictures, political rallies, and other communication media to indoctrinate the inhabitants with a sense of national loyalty to the Russian State.

POPULATION

The population of the Soviet Union is an important power factor in terms of size, age structure, and the increasing degree to which the people are becoming educated and trained. The use of women in the labor force and army is much more widespread than in the United States and western Europe and thus adds further to the available supply. This large population, of course, represents a centrifugal force within the State, particularly since ethnic characteristics differ, and the distribution pattern is such that large sparsely settled areas separate the major populated regions. One of the major tasks of the Communists has been to foster local cultures in order to reduce dissension within the vast territory, while at the same time preventing the formation of strong divisive political forces.

The first complete Soviet census since World War II took place in 1959. According to this census the Soviet population in January, 1959, totaled 208,800,000, an increase of only 9.5 per cent over the 1939 population. These figures indicate enormous Soviet war losses in population, losses which may have run as high as 45 million, including 25 million dead from war causes and another 20 million not added to the population as a result of the decline in the normal birth rate. In January, 1961, the Soviet population was estimated at 216 million, a figure approximately one-sixth larger than that for the United States. The birth and death rates in the U.S.S.R. have dropped considerably since the 1920's, reflecting the higher standard of living, the increased urbanization, and the greater effectiveness of health measures. In 1926 the birth and death rates were 47.0 and 20.3 per thousand, respectively; in 1957 they were 25.3 and 7.8, respectively, indicating a drop in the annual rate of population increase in Russia over a thirty-one-year period from 26.7 to 17.5 per thousand. Thus in 1961 the annual population increase amounted to about 3,700,000.

In terms of age structure the Soviets benefit from the fact that there is a large number of persons in the 18–45 age group—the age group with the greatest production and military potential. Twenty-five per cent of the total population in 1959 was in the 18–31 age group (compared with 18 per cent for the United States). The young, virile population in the Soviet Union is reflected in the continuing high birth rate, the challenge to traditionalism, and the emergence of a "pioneer" spirit among many of the Russian people.

The population of the U.S.S.R. comprises a large number of ethnic groups. Approximately 50 per cent are Great Russians, over 18 per cent are Ukrainians or Little Russians, and just under 5 per cent are White Russians (Belorussians), making a total Slavic majority of about 73 per cent. Within this Slavic majority, however, the political unity tends to obscure certain divisive elements. Ukrainians have in the past sought independence from Moscow and the Great Russians, and in the present Communist State centrifugal forces in the Ukraine still appear in the resentment of many Ukrainians of Moscow's control. The non-Slavic groups, listed in Table 9, are generally too small in number to offer serious competition to the political dominance of the Slavs.

The many differences of language, religion, and customs among the peoples of the Soviet Union represent significant elements of potential dis-

Table 9

SOVIET POPULATION STRUCTURE ACCORDING TO ETHNIC GROUPS

Major Groups	Per Cent of Total
Slavs	76
Great Russians	55
Ukrainians	18
Belorussians	3
Turkic and Iranic Peoples	8
Uzbeks	3
Tatars	2.5
Kazakhs	1.5
Tadzhiks	*
Kirghiz	*
Turkmens	*
Caucasians	3.5
Azerbaijanis	1.5
Armenians	1
Georgians	1
Baltics	2
Lithuanians	1
Latvians	*
Estonians	*
Others	11.5

(Within this category are Jews—1 per cent—as well as smaller groups such as Moldavians, Germans, Chuvashes, Mordvinians, Bashkirs, Yakuts, Mongols, Tuvinians, and Tungus.)

* Less than 1 per cent.
Approximate Soviet population (1961): 216,000,000.
Source: *The Statesman's Yearbook, 1961–62*, ed. S. H. Steinberg, by permission of St. Martin's Press, Inc., and Macmillan & Co., Ltd.

unity. The U.S.S.R. is divided politically into 15 Soviet Socialist Republics (S.S.R.'s), each one based—in theory—upon cultural differences. Within each republic the local language, religions, and customs are retained (providing they do not lead to political separatist movements). The Soviets use the theme of cultural liberalism as a propaganda weapon, but in reality the government's attitude toward such groups as the Jews or the Baltic peoples has been anything but liberal. Many cultural groups in the Soviet Union, the Jews, Bashkirs, Tatars, and Tuvinians, for example, have failed to receive political recognition in the form of separate republics, although some have been included in autonomous units within the major republics. The ethnic make-up of the various republics is shown in Table 10. From this table the expansion of Great Russians beyond the borders of the R.S.F.S.R. becomes evident.

The attitude of the Soviet government toward religion has often varied. The Russian Orthodox Church is by far the largest in the State, and because of its national affiliations is permitted to operate relatively freely.

Table 10

ETHNIC COMPOSITION OF THE SOVIET REPUBLICS, 1960

R.S.F.S.R.	Russians (80%); Others (20%)
Ukraine	Ukrainians (77%); Russians (17%); Others (6%)
Belorussia	Belorussians (81%); Russians (8%); Poles (7%); Others (4%)
Azerbaijan	Azerbaijanis (67%); Russians (14%); Armenians (12%); Others (7%)
Georgia	Georgians (64%); Armenians (11%); Russians (10%); Others (15%)
Armenia	Armenians (88%); Azerbaijanis (6%); Russions (3%); Others (3%)
Moldavia	Moldavians (65%); Ukrainians (15%); Russians (10%); Others (10%)
Estonia	Estonians (75%); Russians (20%); Others (5%)
Latvia	Letts (62%); Russians (27%); Others (11%)
Lithuania	Lithuanians (79%); Russians (9%); Poles (9%); Others (3%)
Kazakhstan	Kazakhs (30%); Russians (43%); Ukrainians (8%); Others (19%)
Turkmenistan . . .	Turkmenians (60%); Russians (17%); Others (23%)
Uzbekistan	Uzbeks (62%); Russians (14%); Others (24%)
Tadzhikistan	Tadzhiks (53%); Uzbeks (23%); Russians and Ukrainians (15%); Others (9%)
Kirghizia	Kirghizians (41%); Russians (30%); Uzbeks (11%); Others (18%)

Source: *The Statesman's Yearbook, 1961–62,* ed. S. H. Steinberg, by permission of St. Martin's Press, Inc., and Macmillan & Co., Ltd.

The 20 million Moslems are generally left alone so far as religion is concerned, but toward the Jews, the Armenians, and the non-Orthodox Christians, government policy has ranged from considerable liberalism (particularly during World War II) to strong interference. Since 1945 the Russian Jews have been the victims of several vicious anti-Semitic movements.

The population distribution in the Soviet Union has changed significantly since the mid-1920's. At that time the population was concentrated largely in European Russia, in a triangle whose base ran along the western border from Leningrad to the Black Sea and whose apex was roughly in the central Ural Mountains. With the development of the Soviet Five-Year plans and the gradual industrialization of the State, great numbers of people have moved away from this triangle into the grasslands of western Siberia, the Maritime Province, the Kuznetsk basin of central Siberia, the Kazakh steppes, and the areas close to the borders of southern Siberia. The Lake Baykal region, centering on Irkutsk, and districts north of the Arctic Circle have also increased greatly in population since the start of the first Five-Year Plan. In 1959, 31 per cent of the population lived in or east of the Urals. The Soviet government has encouraged these population movements in order to organize more effectively the national territory and to permit greater utilization of resources. Increased intermingling of ethnic groups throughout Russia will also have the effect of lessening the regional differences between various peoples. Associated with this dispersal has been a great growth of the urban population, largely in response to industrialization efforts and to the attraction of higher living standards in the large cities. The urban population amounted to 48 per cent of the total in 1959, compared with 32 per cent of the total twenty years earlier.

ECONOMIC STRUCTURE

The rapid economic growth of the Soviet Union, measured by any one of several indices, has been an outstanding development of the past few decades. In 1928 the U.S.S.R. produced 4 million tons of steel; by 1960 the figure had risen to 65 million tons, placing the Soviet Union second among world producers. In coal output the figure for 1928 was 35 million tons, and for 1960 over 500 million tons. Statistics for oil output, railroad mileage, and textile production indicate a similar expansion.

The economic advances made by the Russians during the past quarter-century are attributable in part to the Five-Year plans, in which the whole economic program of the Soviet Union for the ensuing half-decade was determined in advance. Production goals were set, and the requirements of industry, agriculture, commerce, and the military were worked out in such a way as to insure maximum efficiency. The first plan lasted from 1928 to 1933, and has been followed by a series of additional ones.

Industry

The U.S.S.R. possesses in considerable quantities the prime requirements for industrial growth—raw materials, power, labor, capital, technical know-how, and markets. The availability of raw materials and of power facilities has already been noted, as has also the fact of Russia's huge population, particularly in the 18–45 age group, which provides a large labor pool for the nation.

The flow of capital is controlled by the government, whose economic power for over a quarter-century has been geared primarily to industrial expansion. Much of the capital for industrialization was until recently obtained from the farmers, whose products were purchased by the government at low prices and then resold to consumers at high prices—the difference providing an important source of government revenue. Technical training in Russia has been extended to many people, and concerted efforts have been made to enhance the status of the technical class. The U.S.S.R. is turning out approximately 50,000 trained engineers each year, thereby building up a large supply of skilled workers for its industrial expansion. Finally, the market potential in Russia is tremendous for armaments and heavy manufactures, as well as for consumer goods. As a result industrial growth can presumably continue for a long time before any saturation point in the market is reached.

The effects of Russia's industrial growth on its power potential are of course extremely significant. During World Wars I and II the industrial strength and flexibility of the United States proved to be a decisive factor in Allied victory. In any future world conflict Soviet industrial strength will also be an extremely formidable weapon.

A significant aspect of Soviet industrial development has been the gradual dispersal of industries (Figure 70). Much of the impetus for this dispersal occurred during World War II, when the Donets basin—then Russia's foremost industrial area—was threatened by the German armies advancing eastward across the southern Ukraine. Part of the Soviet industrial plant was moved to the central and southern Urals, and cities such as Sverdlovsk, Chelyabinsk, and Magnitogorsk became important industrial producers. Following World War II this area continued to increase its output, and in addition other sectors of Russia also were developed as industrial centers. Among these were the Kuznetsk basin, 1,200 miles east of the Urals; the Amur Valley in the Far East; Karaganda in the Kazakh steppe; Transcaucasia; the Murmansk district across the border from northern Finland; Tashkent in southern Siberia; and the Irkutsk region near Lake Baykal. This dispersal of industries has affected population distribution, transportation needs, and the vulnerability of the Soviet Union's productive means to enemy air attack.

Agriculture

In the process of Russia's planned economic development, industrial expansion has received a higher priority than agriculture. Moreover, Communism has proved itself better equipped to organize industrial than agricultural workers, and as a result agricultural production in Russia has failed to register significant growth since 1928. During the first Five-Year Plan the Soviet government began the process of collectivization, gradually abolishing private holdings and setting up large collective farms, on which the workers receive a share of the profits, or state farms, where the workers are paid a fixed wage. The resistance of the farmers to these measures was accompanied by widespread suffering. During the winter of 1932–33 several million persons, principally in the Ukraine, died of starvation because of government-induced famine conditions and government measures to stamp out peasant resistance to official agricultural policies.

In an effort to provide for the great increase in population, the Russian government has been working on a number of large-scale agricultural projects. One is to increase the mechanization of agriculture, a process for which parts of Russia are well suited, particularly sectors of the Ukraine and western Siberia. A second is to improve agricultural methods by providing training and advice to the farmers. A third is to bolster farmer's incentive by increasing the prices he receives for his produce, to permit more ·private gardens and stock-raising, and to impart enthusiasm through closer party discipline. Soviet economic development has involved great sacrifices from the working groups. Of course the farmer has probably suffered the most in the past quarter-century.

Still another method for increasing food production has been to bring additional land under cultivation through irrigation, drainage, and the utilization of areas with low precipitation and short growing seasons. Government leaders hope to bring over 70 million new acres under cultivation. Low agricultural production represents a major weakness in the Soviet economy, and a difficult problem to solve, yet one which, if unresolved, may cause widespread resentment and unrest on the part of the mass of the Russian people.

Transportation and Commerce

In transportation Russian progress since 1925 has been steady but not spectacular. By 1960 rail mileage had increased over four times what it had been thirty-five years before, but the total was still small for an industrial State of the size of the U.S.S.R. The Trans-Siberian Railroad has been double-tracked, and several international rail lines now link Russia with its eastern European satellites. On these lines the gauges are being broadened to conform with the Russian width, thereby permitting more effective transportation between the U.S.S.R. and these areas. There are also rail connections between Russia and other adjacent areas, including Finland, Turkey, Iran, Outer Mongolia, and Manchuria.

Railroads form the strategic arterial system of the country, but they are supplemented by highways, rivers, and canals. Among the most important of the latter are the Volga-Don Canal at Volgograd (formerly Stalingrad), linking the Volga system with the Black Sea; the Baltic–White Sea Canal, running northeast from Leningrad; and the Moscow-Volga Canal. The improvement of canals and canal equipment permits increased use of Soviet waterways (except during winter months), thereby helping to take the pressure off the railroads. The Russian air network has also been greatly expanded in order to handle both passengers and freight. Despite these advances, however, the Soviet transportation system is still underdeveloped, particularly east of the Urals. In any future conflict inadequate transportation lines would be a serious handicap to Soviet military operations.

In order to reduce the strain on its transportation system the U.S.S.R. has undertaken a nationwide program for economic regionalization, in which several economic regions have been established, each of which is to become as self-sufficient as possible. Although this compartmentalizing applies particularly to critical industries, there are also efforts to achieve limited self-sufficiency in agriculture, particularly in dairy products, meat, and feeds. Such a regional program may have political as well as economic repercussions, for by reducing the economic interdependency of the various parts of the State a potential situation is created in which forces for political independence might also come into play.

Since the end of World War II the Soviet Union has not been one of the leaders in international trade. This has been the result partly of the government's efforts to achieve national self-sufficiency, and partly of the embargo on trade in various "strategic" commodities imposed on the Soviet bloc by the Western countries. In 1958 the total Soviet foreign trade was valued at $8.5 billion, compared with $30.7 billion for the United States and $19.8 billion for the United Kingdom. Of the Soviet total, $4.5 billion was with eastern Europe, $1.75 billion with Asian Communist countries, and $2.25 billion with non-Communist States. The Soviet Union looks upon foreign trade primarily as a source for raw materials (for example, rice and rubber), machinery, transportation equipment, and consumer goods ranging from butter to refrigerators. The Russians have relatively few commodities available for export except pulpwood, fish, and furs to pay for imported commodities, although in recent years they have been building up their exports of petroleum. Pipelines are planned from the U.S.S.R. to non-Communist Europe, and in time the Soviets may become an important supplier to Europe of this needed commodity.

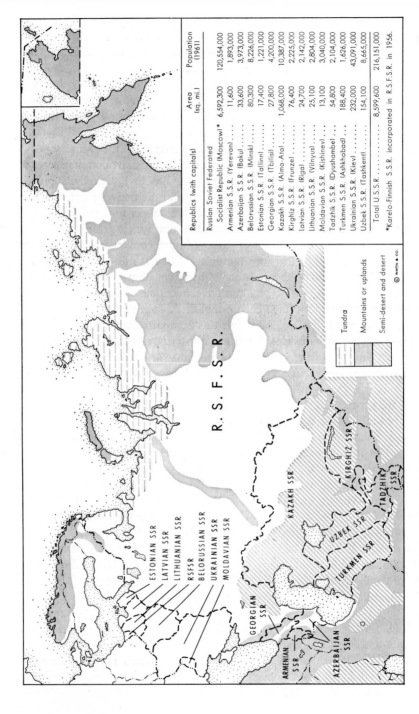

Republics (with capitals)	Area (sq. mi.)	Population (1961)
Russian Soviet Federated Socialist Republic (Moscow)*	6,592,300	120,554,000
Armenian S.S.R. (Yerevan)	11,600	1,893,000
Azerbaijan S.S.R. (Baku)	33,600	3,973,000
Belorussian S.S.R. (Minsk)	80,300	8,226,000
Estonian S.S.R. (Tallinn)	17,400	1,221,000
Georgian S.S.R. (Tbilisi)	27,800	4,200,000
Kazakh S.S.R. (Alma-Ata)	1,068,000	10,387,000
Kirghiz S.S.R. (Frunze)	76,400	2,225,000
Latvian S.S.R. (Riga)	24,700	2,142,000
Lithuanian S.S.R. (Vilnyus)	25,100	2,804,000
Moldavian S.S.R. (Kishinev)	13,100	3,040,000
Tadzhik S.S.R. (Dyushambe)	54,800	2,104,000
Turkmen S.S.R. (Ashkhabad)	188,400	1,626,000
Ukrainian S.S.R. (Kiev)	232,000	43,091,000
Uzbek S.S.R. (Tashkent)	154,100	8,665,000
Total U.S.S.R.	8,599,600	216,151,000

*Karelo-Finnish S.S.R. incorporated in R.S.F.S.R. in 1956.

Figure 71. The Soviet Union: Political Divisions.

The Russians have at times utilized international trade for political purposes: (1) by exporting food and other needed commodities to countries, such as India and Iran, in time of crisis, thereby winning friends for the U.S.S.R.; (2) by "dumping" oil on the world market at prices below that established by Western exporters; and (3) by capturing markets from Western exporting nations by the conclusion of various types of bilateral agreements. Some of the bilateral agreements are associated with Soviet "foreign aid," through which certain goods and services are extended to less-developed countries in exchange for long-term agreements covering exports to the U.S.S.R. By the end of 1960 the Soviet Union had extended economic aid to non-Communist countries outside the Sino-Soviet bloc amounting to over $4.6 billion. Among the major recipients were Yugoslavia, India, Egypt, Indonesia, Iraq, Cuba, and Afghanistan.

Russia's economic viability has been amply demonstrated during recent years by statistics of national output, by the continually rising standard of living of its citizens, by its ability to carry out an impressive foreign aid program, and by its achievements both in space science and in military growth. The Soviet gross national product appears to have been growing at a rate of some 6–8 per cent annually during the past decade, compared with a figure averaging 3–4 per cent for the United States, a comparison which has occasioned considerable concern among American leaders. Clearly its great economic strength is a major source of Soviet power. In future years the rate of Soviet economic growth may be affected by agricultural difficulties, by labor shortages, or possibly by depletion of certain resources, such as high-grade iron ore. But in general there is little to indicate any marked slowdown in coming years in the rate of growth or in the resultant power potential of the U.S.S.R.

POLITICAL FEATURES

The U.S.S.R. consists of fifteen republics which, altogether theoretically independent, are actually under the strict political control of the Moscow government (Figure 71). The facade of independence in the republics is formalized by the representation of two of them—Ukraine and Belorussia—in the United Nations. Of the fifteen republics, the Russian Soviet Federated Socialist Republic (R.S.F.S.R.) is by far the largest in area and population. Among the units at lower administratve levels are the *autonomous republics, krays* (territories included only in the R.S.F.S.R.), *autonomous oblasts, okrugs,* and other subdivisions, each representing a particular ethnic group or groups.

A study of the internal political structure of the Soviet Union offers a broad field of investigation for students of political geography. The boundaries of the republics and of the oblasts and other subdivisions are subject

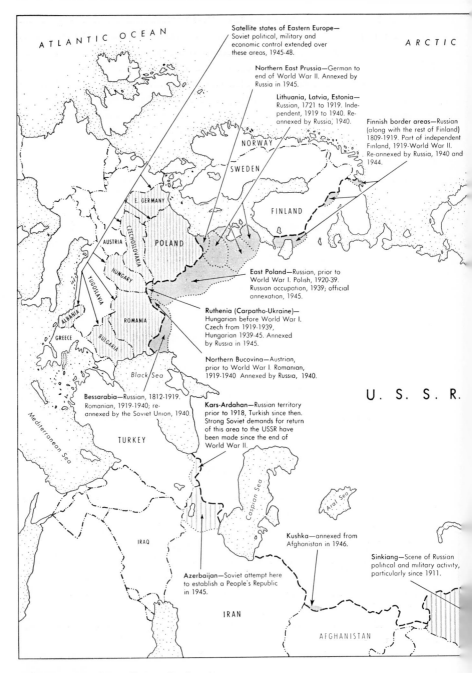

Satellite states of Eastern Europe—
Soviet political, military and
economic control extended over
these areas, 1945-48.

Northern East Prussia—German to
end of World War II. Annexed by
Russia in 1945.

Lithuania, Latvia, Estonia—
Russian, 1721 to 1919. Independent, 1919 to 1940. Re-
annexed by Russia, 1940.

Finnish border areas—Russian
(along with the rest of Finland)
1809-1919. Part of independent
Finland, 1919-World War II.
Re-annexed by Russia, 1940 and
1944.

East Poland—Russian, prior to
World War I. Polish, 1920-39.
Russian occupation, 1939; official
annexation, 1945.

Ruthenia (Carpatho-Ukraine)—
Hungarian before World War I.
Czech from 1919-1939,
Hungarian 1939-45. Annexed
by Russia in 1945.

Northern Bucovina—Austrian,
prior to World War I. Romanian,
1919-1940 Annexed by Russia, 1940.

Bessarabia—Russian, 1812-1919.
Romanian, 1919-1940; re-
annexed by the Soviet Union, 1940

Kars-Ardahan—Russian territory
prior to 1918, Turkish since then.
Strong Soviet demands for return
of this area to the USSR have
been made since the end of
World War II.

Kushka—annexed from
Afghanistan in 1946.

Sinkiang—Scene of Russian
political and military activity,
particularly since 1911.

Azerbaijan—Soviet attempt here
to establish a People's Republic
in 1945.

Figure 72. The Soviet Union: Border Areas.

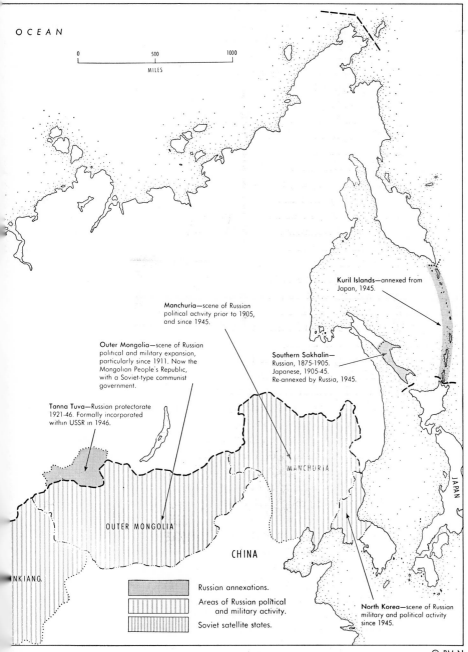

OCEAN

0   500   1000
MILES

Kuril Islands—annexed from Japan, 1945.

Manchuria—scene of Russian political activity prior to 1905, and since 1945.

Outer Mongolia—scene of Russian political and military expansion, particularly since 1911. Now the Mongolian People's Republic, with a Soviet-type communist government.

Southern Sakhalin— Russian, 1875-1905. Japanese, 1905-45. Re-annexed by Russia, 1945.

Tanna Tuva—Russian protectorate 1921-46. Formally incorporated within USSR in 1946.

MANCHURIA

JAPAN

OUTER MONGOLIA

CHINA

NKIANG.

Russian annexations.

Areas of Russian political and military activity.

Soviet satellite states.

North Korea—scene of Russian military and political activity since 1945.

© RMcN

to change, not only because of shifts in Russia's external borders, but also because of realignments of the country's internal administration, such as the transfer in 1954 of Crimea (Krym) from the R.S.F.S.R. to the Ukraine, or the absorption of the Karelo-Finnish S.S.R. within the R.S.F.S.R. in 1956. From a careful study of boundary shifts within the republics one can gain considerable insight into the relationships between economic and political regions, the contests for power between Moscow and the provincial capitals, and the centrifugal forces existing within the State.

Moscow, the capital and leading city of the Soviet Union, is centrally located with respect to European Russia, but is geographically removed from the area east of the Urals. As the historic seat of Russian power, Moscow exerts a great sentimental pull, although for nearly two centuries St. Petersburg (now Leningrad) was the capital city. Peter the Great moved the capital to St. Petersburg in order to benefit from contacts with Western countries, but in 1918 Moscow again became the seat of government, thus symbolizing a reorientation of Russian policy after the fall of the czar.

Since August, 1939, the Soviet Union has annexed a total of almost 263,000 square miles (Figure 72), containing a population of over 23 million persons, of which about 40 per cent belong to non-Slavic groups (Table 9). In addition, the country has developed a power sphere in Europe totalling nearly 393,000 square miles in area with a population of over 100 million. These Moscow-oriented States, although directly subjected to Moscow's control, are technically independent (all but East Germany are represented in the United Nations), which absolves the Russians from accusations of imperialism in the historical sense of the term.

Unlike the Germans of past decades, the Russians have never engaged in many theoretical justifications for aggrandizement, such as the State's "organic borders" or its "place in the sun." The only Russian justifications have been constant reiterations of the requirements for national security, and an occasional rigged plebiscite, as in the Baltic States and Ruthenia. Even the theme of Pan-Slavism is of little value, for except in Yugoslavia there are no large Slavic groups left in Europe beyond the borders of the Soviet-oriented bloc.

Officially the Soviet Union has no colonies. The Kuril Islands and Sakhalin are administered as parts of the R.S.F.S.R., whose territory also includes eastern Siberia. With no colonies the Russians are in a position to pose as the champions of peoples in dependent areas. This process of incorporating new areas into the political structure of the State, rather than considering them as dependent units, is an interesting variation of the traditional imperialism, and one which has blinded many people, particularly in dependent or recently independent areas, to the realities of Soviet imperialism policies.

THE TERRITORIAL DEVELOPMENT OF RUSSIA

The evolution and expansion of the Russian State to its present size and extent is a complicated history of the interaction of internal and external forces. Since the fifteenth century Russia has undergone a gradual process of territorial growth, which has been particularly successful under its Communist administrations. In order to present some of the basic factors of this territorial development in condensed form, the history of Russia can be arbitrarily divided into three phrases: (1) the establishment of the Russian State and its expansion prior to 1900; (2) territorial losses to 1919; (3) the Soviet Union since World War I.

The Establishment of the Russian State and Its Expansion Prior to 1900

The history of the Russian people can be traced back to the first centuries of the Christian era. At that time Slavic groups occupied an area northeast of the Carpathians between the Vistula and Dnieper rivers. Under the pressure of invading groups the Slavs began to spread out after the second century. A western group moved across Germany as far as the Elbe[2] and southwestward into Slovakia and Bohemia; the eastern Slavs moved eastward to the Dnieper and Don valleys, and northward to the vicinity of the present city of Moscow; and the southern Slavs migrated into the Balkan Peninsula. The Slavic peoples were prolific, and from their several branches came the Poles, Czechs, Bohemians, Moravians, Slovaks, Ruthenians, Serbs, Croats, Slovenes, and Macedonians, as well as the three Slavic groups of present-day Soviet Russia—the Great Russians, Ukrainians, and White Russians.

The Russian people were under Tatar control from the early thirteenth to the latter part of the fifteenth century, when the grand duke of Moscow succeeded in establishing an independent political unit. During the next four and a half centuries Moscow's borders were gradually extended in all directions, particularly during the reigns of Peter the Great (1682–1721), Catherine the Great (1762–96), and Alexander I and II during the nineteenth century. The history of Russian expansion is shown graphically in Figure 73. The absence of strong political units within Russia to compete with Moscow, the continued military and cultural development of the Russian State, the steady growth of its population, and the skill of Russian leaders in capitalizing on the weaknesses of neighboring States were important factors in the expansion of the country from 15,000 square miles in the

---

[2] The Wends, a group of western Slavs living near Berlin, have kept some of their ancient customs and continue to speak a distinct Slavic dialect to this present day.

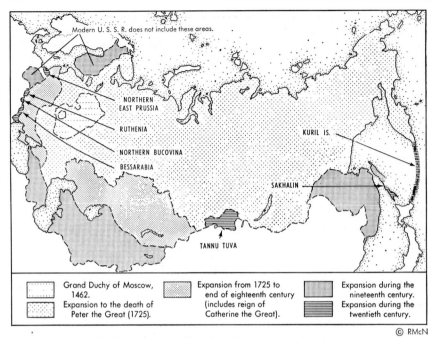

Grand Duchy of Moscow, 1462.

Expansion to the death of Peter the Great (1725).

Expansion from 1725 to end of eighteenth century (includes reign of Catherine the Great).

Expansion during the nineteenth century.

Expansion during the twentieth century.

© RMcN

Figure 73. Territorial Expansion of the Soviet Union.

fifteenth century to 8½ million square miles by the mid-twentieth. The centralization of political and military power in the capital, despite the country's great distances and inadequate transportation, has meant that at no time in Russia's history since 1462 has there been a serious challenge from some other part of the State to the political control of the central government.

The vast areas of sparse population in central Asia were important to Russia's territorial growth, particularly during the nineteenth century when the State moved its borders southward and eastward until stopped by opposing pressures from Britain, China, and Japan. Alaska, Russia's one holding in the Western Hemisphere, was sold to the United States in 1867. Along the western and southwestern boundaries the process of territorial expansion was considerably slower, however, because of strong opposing forces from such countries as Sweden, Germany, Austria-Hungary, and Turkey.

Territorial Losses to 1919

The process of territorial growth was temporarily halted during the early twentieth century, first, by the military defeat by Japan, and, second, by Germany. In 1904 Japan launched an attack against Russia in the Far East in order to eliminate Russian power in this area. As a result of its defeat Russia was forced to cede the southern part of Sakhalin Island to the Japanese and to abandon its attempts to establish a power sphere in Manchuria (see page 535).

Less than a decade later Russia entered World War I on the side of Britain and France, but was again defeated, this time by Germany in 1917. By the Treaty of Brest-Litovsk, signed with Germany and its allies in March, 1918, Russia lost heavily in the west and southwest. Seven territories were detached from Russia and created into an east European buffer zone. These territories—Finland, Estonia, Latvia, Lithuania, White Russia, Poland, and Ukraine—were to be German-oriented in their foreign affairs, and Germany was to have strong influence in their over-all national development. In addition, the Kars-Ardahan region along the Russo-Turkish border was joined to Turkey (see page 322).

It is interesting to note the similarities between the terms of this agreement and those of the Versailles Treaty with regard to Russia's western borders. Germany's surrender in November, 1918, nullified the Brest-Litovsk Treaty, but the victorious Allies, fearful of Russia's new Communist regime, favored the isolation of Russia as much as possible. By the Versailles Treaty Finland, Estonia, Latvia, Lithuania, and Poland were confirmed as independent States, although without German supervision and control.

In the southwest the province of Bessarabia was annexed by Romania, and the Russo-Turkish border, as delimited in the Brest-Litovsk Treaty, remained unchanged. Most of the territorial gains made by Russia in eastern Europe during the two preceding centuries were thus removed.

The Soviet Union Since World War I

The development of the Soviet State since World War I can be summed up in three phases: internal political consolidation, reacquisition of lands lost after World War I, and expansion into new areas. The first period lasted until 1939, the second from 1939 to 1941, and the third has taken place since 1941.

During the first period (1918–39) Russia's borders remained fairly stable.[3] For fifteen years after the end of World War I there was little contact between Russia and other countries of the world. Within the Soviet Union, meanwhile, political activities were confined largely to overcoming all significant opposition to the new Communist regime. By 1933 the Soviet Union was again playing an important role in world affairs, and as the

---

[3] In 1921 the western border with Poland was established. During the same year Tannu Tuva became a Russian protectorate, and Outer Mongolia moved within the Soviet sphere of influence (see page 542).

menace of fascism increased in Europe during the late 1930's, political leaders, particularly in France and Great Britain, began to look to the Soviet Union as a possible ally in resisting Germany's territorial expansion. Misunderstandings and distrust between the democratic Western governments and the Soviet Communist regime precluded any East-West military alliance, however. In August, 1939, after German dismemberment of Czechoslovakia, the Soviet Union concluded a nonaggression pact with Germany, principally to gain time for further development of Soviet defenses against the possibility of an eventual German invasion.

The second phase of postwar Russian history opened in September, 1939, when German forces invaded Poland. The Poles fell back in the face of the attack, but after seventeen days of resistance the defenders found themselves overwhelmed, as Soviet forces invaded from the east. Once again the Polish State was partitioned, this time between Germany and Russia, and Russia's border was moved west to the Bug River. Two months later the Soviets invaded Finland, and after a short war Finland was defeated and forced to cede territory along its eastern border to the Russians (see page 312). The U.S.S.R. was thus able to improve its northwestern defenses, particularly around the city of Leningrad. In June, 1940, Russia presented Romania with a twenty-four-hour ultimatum which resulted in the return of Bessarabia and the cession of northern Bucovina, and in the following month the three Baltic States of Lithuania, Latvia, and Estonia were annexed by the Soviets (see page 392).

Thus in ten months the Russians had succeeded in reoccupying much of the territory in eastern Europe which was lost to them after World War I, and in erecting a defense zone against the Germans. Like the dismemberment of Czechoslovakia in 1938–39, here was an example of the "jackal" theory of territorial aggression, for the Soviet advance into eastern Europe did not begin until after Germany had inaugurated its penetration of this area in 1939. The historical process of great-power rivalry in eastern Europe was also clearly demonstrated. Despite the detailed work of Allied and League of Nations officials after World War I, local territorial problems in the east European area were completely submerged in the race for territory between the Soviet Union and Germany in 1939–40.

The third phase—that of Soviet expansion into new territories— began in 1944, as Soviet forces, after falling back in some areas nearly 1,000 miles in the face of the German attack, now drove the Germans westward across the Russian border and occupied what later became the "satellite" States. Eventually, the retreat of the enemy forces across eastern Europe provided the Soviets with the opportunity to occupy all the countries of that vital area except Greece, where United States and British forces were brought in by sea, and Yugoslavia and Albania, where local partisan forces liberated the areas. Finland remained free of Soviet occupation through the terms of its surrender agreement in 1944. With the gradual collapse of Germany and its allies there were no armies in eastern Europe to challenge the Soviet advance, and the westward expansion of Russian-occupied territory was halted only upon contact with other Allied forces advancing eastward from France and north from Italy. Within a short time Soviet-occupied eastern Europe, together with Yugoslavia and Albania, where local Communist groups gained political dominance, came under the *de facto* political control of the Soviet Union.

Contact of Soviet and Western forces occurred roughly along a line running from Stettin on the Baltic south to Trieste. Russian armies were given the honor of "liberating" Berlin, Prague, and Vienna, and the American forces which had entered Czechoslovakia were withdrawn across its western border. In Germany and Austria cease-fire lines had been laid down between Soviet and Western armies, and the countries were divided into military occupation zones. In Germany the cease-fire line eventually came to mark the border between West Germany and Communist-dominated East Germany.

At the end of World War II the Russians advanced their borders in Finland, in the territory of former East Prussia, and in Czechoslovakia (see Chapter 11). The Finns were also forced to lease the Porkkala Peninsula in the Gulf of Finland to the Soviets as a naval base. This area was returned to Finnish control in 1956. In addition the Soviet Union succeeded in establishing an east European power sphere to the west of its borders, composed of States controlled by Moscow-oriented Communist governments. In central Asia Tannu Tuva, a Russian protectorate, was completely absorbed within the Soviet Union in 1946, and Soviet power was also extended into Outer Mongolia and, for a time, western Sinkiang (see Chapter 20). In the Far East the U.S.S.R., which had declared war on Japan a few weeks before that country's surrender in 1945, gained control of all of Sakhalin Island and of the Kuril Islands northeast of Japan. Thus the Soviet Union emerged from World War II as the dominant State of Eurasia. Most of its potential enemies had been seriously weakened by the war, and the Soviets moved into a powerful position with respect to Europe, central Asia, and the northwestern Pacific. Much of the history of international relations since World War II has revolved about the readjustments of the States of the world to the new power status of the U.S.S.R. (see Table 11).

Obviously the establishment of Soviet control over many non-Soviet areas carries with it the danger of centrifugal tendencies in these areas, and it is this danger, particularly in the Communist States of eastern Europe, which has forged one of the weakest links in the Soviet bloc. One important factor has been the morale of many of the peoples in eastern Europe as a result of their reduced standard of living under Soviet control. Several

Table 11

SOVIET TERRITORIAL GAINS SINCE 1939

Area and year of annexation	Area (sq. mi.)	Population
*Finland (1940)**		
Karelian Isthmus	10,570	486,365
Four islands in the Gulf of Finland . .	19	2,935
Salla sector (central Finland)	3,010	5,550
Rybachi Peninsula (1944)	45	9,401
Petsamo (Pechenga) district	4,288	c. 10,000
Total	17,932	514,251
Estonia (1940)	17,463	1,134,000
Latvia (1940)	25,262	1,994,506
Lithuania (1940) (excluding Vilna area)	20,395	2,879,070
Germany (1945) Northern East Prussia .	6,100	830,000
Poland (1945) (including Vilna area) . .	68,667	10,900,000
Czechoslovakia (1945)		
Ruthenia (Carpatho-Ukraine) . . .	4,921	725,000
Romania (1940)		
Northern Bucovina	2,195	650,000
Bessarabia	17,143	3,000,000
Afghanistan (1946)		
Kushka area	c. 1,000	—
Tannu Tuva (1946)	64,000	65,000
Japan (1945)		
Southern Sakhalin	13,935	332,000
Kuril Islands	3,944	17,550
Total gains	262,957	23,041,377

°The Porkkala Peninsula, near Helsinki, leased to the Soviets as a naval base after World War II, was returned to Finland in 1956.

devices have been employed to weld the recently acquired areas to the Soviet Union, including an emphasis on Soviet language and culture, establishment of firm economic bonds, removal of potentially hostile elements, particularly among the middle class, and propaganda campaigns which play on the fears of the east European peoples against their historic enemies in non-Soviet Europe. These devices serve as centripetal pressures, designed to counteract such centrifugal forces as national sentiment, hatred of the Russians, and resentment of Communism and the confiscation of private property. These smoldering contrifugal forces, however, occasionally erupt into violence, as in the East Berlin riots of 1953 and the Polish and Hungarian uprisings of 1956.

SOVIET PRESSURES ALONG THE IRON CURTAIN

Since the establishment of the Soviet bloc in its present form, various Soviet expansionist pressures have continued to be exerted along the borders between this bloc and non-Soviet areas. These pressures have been associated with the trend toward the extension of Soviet territory outward into adjacent areas, and appear in several forms or combinations of forms.

1. Direct Support for Communist Minority Groups Seeking Control. The support given to communist guerrilla forces in Greece, to the North Koreans before and during their invasion of South Korea, and to the Chinese Communists prior to their victory over Chiang Kai-shek's forces are all illustrative of this form of pressure. Military support has in the past also been given to antigovernment forces in the Chinese province of Sinkiang.

2. Demands for Boundary Changes. These demands reflect the movement outward of Soviet borders, and since 1945 they have involved Turkey, Iran, and Afghanistan. From Turkey Russia has sought the return of the Kars-Ardahan area. In Iran Russia claims six small boundary areas. In Afghanistan Soviet demands culminated in an agreement in June, 1946, which provided for the rectification of the Afghan-Soviet border, with Russia gaining uncontested control of the Kushka area. More recently, unofficial Soviet claims have been made for the eastern Afghan panhandle between Russia and Pakistan.

3. Propaganda for Political Unification of Divided Areas. This has been demonstrated in both Germany and Korea, where the Communists occupy a part of the area and where pressure exists for the re-establishment of political unity, particularly from within the divided sectors. Capitalizing on this pressure, the Soviets have offered to permit unification, but only under conditions which would lead to the eventual establishment of Communist governments in the reunified States.

4. Establishment of Cultural Bonds with Border Peoples in Order to Weaken Political Unity. A major objective of Soviet cultural activities in Azerbaijan has been to lessen Tehran's control over the area. Similarly in Armenia (where Soviet activities have been less direct than in Azerbaijan) Russia has sought to disrupt the unity of the Turkish State and, if possible, establish Soviet control in Turkish Armenia.

5. Attempts to Disrupt Normal Economic and Political Operations. This type of pressure accompanies military activities (South Korea, Greece), but it also may take the form of restrictive devices, such as the blockade of West Berlin, or of local Communist-inspired strikes and riots, as in Iran.

6. Extension of Economic Aid. The Soviet economic offensive against neighboring States has taken the form of advancing large amounts of foreign aid and then applying economic pressure to orient the country's policies toward those of the Soviet Union. The outstanding example has been

Afghanistan, where Soviet foreign aid has amounted to about twice that from the United States. The principal Soviet objective here has been to wean Afghanistan away from a pro-Western position (an objective aided by the territorial dispute between Afghanistan and Pakistan, a military ally of the United States).

7. Intimidation with Soviet Military Power. To a certain extent this type of pressure has been exerted all along the Soviet borders, but with varying degrees of success. In Finland the pressure has been relatively effective; in Norway, West Germany, Austria, Greece, Yugoslavia, Turkey, and Japan it has been less so. The specter of Soviet power can be a potent force against small countries—particularly those which have not joined in military alliances with powerful non-Communist States.

BIBLIOGRAPHY

CRESSEY, GEORGE B. *Soviet Potentials: A Geographic Appraisal.* Syracuse: Syracuse University Press, 1962.
A discussion of the various factors of the Soviet Union's power potential.

EAST, W. GORDON. "The New Frontiers of the Soviet Union," *Foreign Affairs,* XXIX (1951), 591–608.
A summary of conditions along the Soviet borders after World War II.

HODGKINS, JORDON A. *Soviet Power: Energy Resources, Production and Potentials.* New York: Prentice-Hall, 1961.
Well-documented discussion of Soviet coal, petroleum, and other power sources.

JACKSON, W. A. DOUGLAS. "The Virgin and Idle Lands Program Reappraised," *Annals of the Association of American Geographers,* LII (1962), 69–80.
An excellent account of the virgin lands program.

KISH, GEORGE. *Economic Atlas of the Soviet Union.* Ann Arbor: University of Michigan Press, 1960.
Excellent maps of Soviet economic activities.

LONSDALE, RICHARD E., and THOMPSON, JOHN H. "A Map of the USSR's Manufacturing," *Economic Geography,* XXXVI (1960), 36–53.
Description and statistics of the pattern of Soviet industry.

Nove, Alec. "Soviet Agriculture Marks Time," *Foreign Affairs*, XL (1962), 576–95.
A clear discussion of the agricultural problem.

Roof, Michael K., and Leedy, Frederick A. "Population Redistribution in the Soviet Union," *Geographical Review*, XLIX (1959), 208–22.
Maps and statistics on Soviet population.

Schwartz, Harry. *Russia's Soviet Economy*, 2nd ed. New York: Prentice-Hall, 1954.
A summary of the Soviet economy as of 1954. Many observations are still pertinent.

Shabad, Theodore. "Political-Administrative Divisions of the U.S.S.R., 1945," *Geographical Review*, XXXVI (1946), 303–12.
Discussion and detailed map of administrative divisions and subdivisions of the Soviet Union.

Taafe, Robert A. "Transportation and Regional Specialization: The Example of Soviet Central Asia," *Annals of the Association of American Geographers*, LII (1962), 80–99.
A regional study of one aspect of Soviet transportation.

Wheeler, G. E. "Russia and the Middle East," *International Affairs*, XXXV (1959), 295–305.
An analysis of the Russian position with regard to the Middle East.

Wiles, Peter. "The Soviet Economy Outpaces the West," *Foreign Affairs*, XXXI (1953), 566–81.
An interesting hypothesis of future Soviet power. Although some of the conclusions are open to debate, this article should be read by all persons interested in Cold War problems.

13

THE ARAB WORLD

● The regions of southwest Asia and northern Africa constitute one of the world's principal zones of tension. Here at the junction of three continents are located the spiritual centers for nearly half the peoples of the globe, over 65 per cent of the world's estimated petroleum reserves, and the sea link between the Mediterranean and Indian Ocean basins. Here also are over a dozen and a half separate States in various stages of political evolution. Because of its location, resources, and religious importance the area now occupied by the Arab World is one of the historic prize areas of the globe, for the control of which men have struggled since the beginning of recorded history.

Recent political developments within the Arab World are of great importance to global power relations. Under pressures from local nationalism, European political control has been gradually disappearing, although even in areas now independent the legacies of European colonialism still remain in the fragmented political structure, the foreign military bases and alliances, and the prominent European position in local economies. Since 1945, however, United States and Soviet influences have substantially increased, and the region now represents a major focus of conflict between Soviet and anti-Soviet power spheres.

Several geographical names have been applied to this part of the world. W. B. Fisher[1] has suggested that the term "Near East" lost its significance with the end of the Ottoman Empire, and that "Middle East" has several

---

[1] "Unity and Diversity in the Middle East," *The Geographical Review*, XXXVI (1947), 414–36.

ambiguous definitions. In addition to a core area of Syria, Lebanon, Israel, Jordan, and Iraq, the term "Middle East" generally includes Iran, Egypt, Cyprus, and the Arabian Peninsula. It may also include Turkey, Afghanistan, Libya, and countries to the south of Egypt.

In this chapter another term, the "Arab World," is used. The Arab World here includes the region from the Iran-Iraq border west to the Atlantic shores of Morocco, and from the southern boundary of Turkey south through the Arabian Peninsula, Egypt, and Sudan. The non-Arab State of Israel is thus within this area. In north central and northwest Africa the southern borders of Libya, Algeria, and Morocco are generally considered the southern limit of the Arab World (Figure 74). A special section on Iran is included at the end of this chapter; otherwise Iran is considered only in connection with the oil developments in the Persian Gulf area.

PHYSICAL ELEMENTS

The location of the Arab World is of great significance to an understanding of the political forces operating in this region. Extending over 3,000 miles from west to east, it straddles the major transportation routes southward out of Europe, and the question of political and military control in the area is of importance to the British air and sea links to the Indian Ocean–southern Asia area and the French links to northern and eastern Africa. The Suez Canal reduces the sea distance from Europe to southern Asia and eastern Africa by thousands of miles, and Cairo has become one of the great air terminals of the Eastern Hemisphere, serving both north-south and east-west connections between the three continents.

In terms of Cold War activities the location of the Arab World is also significant. Because of its position with respect to Europe and the U.S.S.R., this area has figured prominently in Western plans for the "containment" of Soviet power. On the other hand, it is also important in Soviet plans for outflanking the containment moves and for interfering with communication links between western European powers and the countries of Africa and southern Asia.

The North African–Asian desert belt stretches 4,000 miles from India westward to the Atlantic shores of Morocco. Some areas within this belt receive adequate moisture for agriculture either from mountain slopes intercepting rain-bearing winds or from rivers across the desert lowlands. Lowland areas close to the Mediterranean coast in Israel, Lebanon, and Syria, and to the west from Tunisia to the Atlantic also contain belts of moderate precipitation. In the hills of Syria and northern Iraq, western Jordan, southern Morocco, western Yemen, and southwestern Arabia are other areas of ample moisture for crop cultivation. In Egypt's valley of the Nile and along the Tigris-Euphrates system in Iraq the fertile soil, level

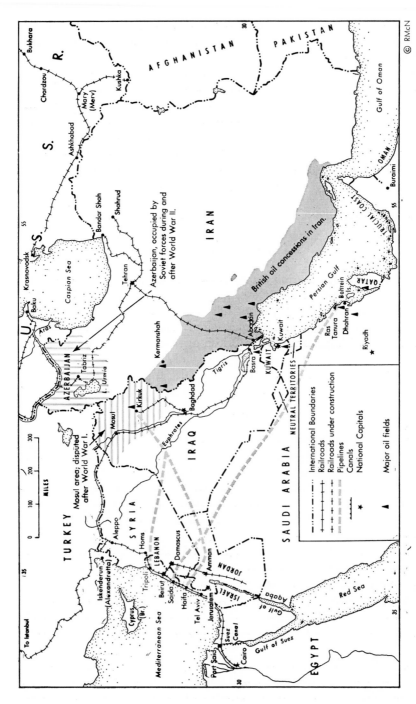

© RMcN

Figure 74. The Middle East. (Adapted from Cressey, *Crossroads: Land and Life in Southwest Asia*, 1960, by permission of the publisher, J. B. Lippincott Co.)

land, and year-round water supply combine to produce nearly optimum agricultural conditions. To the south of Egypt the Sudan extends into the tropical rain forests of central Africa.

Water supplies are unevenly distributed, giving rise to widely scattered regions of population settlement; these are often separated from one another by long distances of sparsely inhabited area. In many parts of the Arab World the people are nomadic, moving frequently in search of pasturage and water for their flocks. To such persons the existence of international boundaries in the areas through which they move usually means very little. Tribal loyalties are often stronger than State or national loyalties, and armed conflict between tribal groups is still a common feature of parts of the Arab World.

Most of the minerals and power resources are concentrated within a relatively few areas. Oil is present in the Persian Gulf region, Algeria, and Libya; iron ore, phosphate, and manganese exist in the western portions of North Africa; Egypt has some iron ore reserves; and Israel has potash. The Nile and the Tigris-Euphrates rivers possess water power potential, as do such well-watered mountain areas as those in northern Algeria and Morocco. Much of the area has not been adequately mapped, so that the extent and variety of resources are imperfectly known. The general scarcity of minerals and power fuels throughout large areas of the Arab World, however, has been a factor contributing to the shortage of investment capital in all but a relatively few areas.

POPULATION FACTORS

The inhabitants of the Arab World are for the most part Arabic-speaking Moslems, although there are a number of important minority groups. The Moslems themselves are divided into two main branches—the Shiites, who reside in many sections of Iraq and along the southeast coast of Arabia and who predominate in Iran, and the Sunnites (by far the larger branch) in the other parts of the area. Within the Arab World, where religion plays such an important role in the lives of the people, this division, roughly analogous to the Catholic-Protestant division in Christianity, represents a force for cultural and political diversity, particularly in Iraq, where the numbers of Sunnites and Shiites are believed to be about equal. There are also smaller sects, such as the Druses and Alawi of Syria, which contribute further to religious disunity. In addition, there are Christian groups in all countries, as well as Jews, predominantly in Israel but also in most of the Arab States.

Egypt contains over 26 million persons, or about one-third of the total population of the Arab World. Algeria, Morocco, Sudan, and Saudi Arabia have between 5 and 10 million persons each, while the remaining States have less than 5 million each. It must be remembered, however, that most of the States have relatively small areas suitable for agriculture. Thus, despite what may seem to be small population totals (except for Egypt), there are high average population densities in terms of arable land throughout most of the Arab World. The population is increasing rapidly as a result of continuing high birth rates and gradually lowering death rates. In Egypt the birth rate in 1956 was 41 per thousand, compared with 43 in 1920, while the death rate during the same period dropped from 26 to 16. The State's population nearly doubled in four decades (1920–60).

Population distribution throughout the Arab World is extremely irregular, with large concentrations along river courses and on well-watered coastal plains, and with great expanses of practically uninhabited land. The bulk of the population inhabits those regions enumerated on page 353, in which water can be obtained from precipitation, from rivers, or from wells. There are also a number of oases, such as in the Fezzan area in central Libya and at Riyadh in Saudi Arabia, where settlement has developed in response to water supply. Population distribution, of course, has had political repercussions both within and between States. Most of the major population concentrations have formed the foci for the development of individual political units. In some States there is more than one important concentration, a factor which contributes to the existence of strong centrifugal forces.

ECONOMIC CONDITIONS

The economy of the Arab World is essentially an agricultural one, in which the poverty of the great mass of the people is reflected in the low average incomes which prevail there. The following quotation sums up the economic conditions existing throughout most of the Arab World:

> The basic cause for the poverty of the countries of the Arab World lies in the semi-feudal structure of their economy. This economy is predominantly agricultural, as shown by the fact that over two-thirds of the population derive their livelihood directly or indirectly from the land. . . . The backwardness of the agrarian structure limits agricultural productivity and so keeps down the living standard of the majority of the people. . . . The semi-feudal structure . . . manifests itself in the existence of large landholdings owned by a small number of landlords who are mostly absentee owners and who constitute a rentier class drawing comfortable incomes from the land but taking little or no interest in its utilization. . . . Besides the class of absentee landlords there is the class of poor share-tenants and landless agricultural workers who cultivate the land and constitute the great majority of the rural

population. The share-tenants, who are usually burdened with debts contracted at excessively high interest rates, have no incentive to improve the land.[2]

Many of the countries of the Arab World must rely on food imports to satisfy domestic demands, and there are relatively few agricultural exports except cotton from Egypt, citrus fruits from Israel, wheat and wine from Algeria, and dates from Iraq. The impact of commercialized agriculture upon a subsistence economy has presented difficulties in several areas, notably in Egypt, where many farmers now raise cotton as a cash crop. Most of the cotton is exported, and in return for the low prices the farmers receive for their sales, they must purchase high-priced manufactured articles as well as seed and fertilizer. Frequently dependence on a cash crop has only further increased their proverty and also has led to serious depletion of the soil.

Except for Israel and Egypt, where much of the earlier traditional social and economic system has been overthrown, there has been little industrialization within the Arab World. Lack of investment capital has been an important factor limiting the development of industries. Throughout most of the Arab World any surplus capital which is accumulated is likely to be siphoned off by powerful individuals or groups for their private use, so that little finds its way into public improvements, social welfare, or industrial growth.

Because of rigid social systems and a shortage of educational and technical training facilities, much of the human resources of the Arab countries are not being adequately utilized. The training of civil servants, the establishment of an effective electoral system, even the maintenance of law and order in time of crisis, are difficult problems for most of these States. One of the tragic circumstances of history is that some of the countries of the Arab World, whose greatest need is for peace and internal development, are still involved in social and political tensions, burdened by thousands of refugees, and with many of their normal trade patterns disrupted through international dissension.

POLITICAL FEATURES

The modern political pattern in the Arab World is of recent origin, for even at the beginning of the twentieth century the Ottoman Empire still controlled much of the area, while France and Britain held sovereignty over most of the remainder. Since that time two world wars and the rise of Arab nationalism have greatly altered this pattern. The limits of many of the political units were established at the end of World War I. Political

---

[2] Charles Malik, "The Near East and the Search for Truth," *Foreign Affairs*, XXX (1952), 248, 249. Copyright by the Council on Foreign Relations, Inc.

fragmentation in the Arab World was partly the result of conflicting great-power interests, particularly British and French, which led to the partitioning of the former Turkish territories. Transjordan, for example, was a largely artificial creation by the British which lacked a strong *raison d'être,* a significant core area, or the resources necessary for the development of a viable economic structure. From 1918 through 1962 thirteen States became independent, twelve of them Arab and one Jewish.[3] As in other parts of the world, the question arises of whether or not these States have the internal cohesion and the economic stability necessary to function effectively as separate political units. Can they also defend their territorial integrity against outsiders?

Many of the boundaries in the Arab World are antecedent in nature, for they were delimited through regions in which settled areas did not exist. Considerable use has been made of straight-line boundaries. In some areas, particularly on the Arabian Peninsula, the exact—or even approximate—location of boundaries has never been fixed. Few of the boundary lines have been demarcated, and throughout much of the desert areas little attempt is made to guard them against illegal crossings.

Despite the empty areas through which many of the boundaries pass, and the general lack of valuable resources in boundary zones, there have been quite a few border disputes in the Arab World since the end of World War I. Two controversies involved the delimitation of Turkey's southern border after World War I. Turkey and Britain disputed the location of the Turkish-Iraqi border in the oil-rich Mosul area, while France and Turkey were involved in the delimitation of the Turkish-Syrian border, particularly around the port of Alexandretta. Both of these disputes are discussed later in this chapter. Israel's border conflicts have posed a major threat to peace in this part of the world since 1948. Still another dispute centers on the Buraimi Oasis in the southeastern Arabian Peninsula, where Saudi Arabia and Britain have conflicting claims of sovereignty over an area with rich oil deposits. In addition to these disputes, local controversies often exist—particularly over water rights—along the many poorly defined boundaries.

ELEMENTS OF UNITY AND DIVERSITY

Within the Arab World there exists a wide and often conflicting variety of unifying and divisive elements. Among the Arab peoples there is what Charles Malik has referred to as a feeling of "mystical unity."[4] The political effects of this sense of unity are difficult to determine, although in time of

---

[3] Syria, Lebanon, Jordan, Iraq, Egypt, Libya, Saudi Arabia, Sudan, Yemen, Tunisia, Morocco, Algeria, and Israel.
[4] *Op.cit.,* p. 240.

crisis it can apparently be a potent force for united action on the part of the member States of the Arab League.[5]

The tangible results of unity in the Arab World may be measured in two respects—the adoption of common policies toward world problems and the reduction of boundary functions. These results apply only to the Arab States themselves and not, of course, to Israel. Although common policies have developed among some of the Arab areas with regard to relations with the Communist bloc, Britain, and the United States, only in their hostility to Israel has there been any unanimity of approach to foreign affairs on the part of all the Arab governments. As far as boundaries are concerned, the Arab countries have held closely to the political patterns of preindependence days. Steps have been taken toward reducing economic barriers between states, but in general the forces of local nationalism have been too strong to permit the unification of the Arab States. Proposals for a Greater Syria, embracing Syria, Lebanon, Jordan, and Iraq, although possessing considerable economic validity, have never been seriously considered by the respective governments, while in northeastern Africa, Sudan has rejected any suggestions that it be politically united with Egypt. In 1958 Egypt and Syria did unite to form the United Arab Republic, but three years later this union was dissolved. Only in Morocco, where the former Spanish and French zones have been merged, had there, by the end of 1962, been a unification of territories in the Arab World.

Forces of disunity within and between the Arab States are often as strong or stronger than those of unity. In several states strong centrifugal pressures exist which may threaten national cohesion. In Libya the widely separated centers of population might eventually bring about a political partitioning of the country. In Sudan and Morocco the presence of diverse ethnic groups represents potentially divisive forces. On the international level the historic competition between the Nile Valley and Mesopotamia has been reflected in recent times by the rivalry between Egypt and Iraq. Both have vied for influence in Syria, Jordan, and Lebanon, as well as Yemen and other peripheral areas of the Arabian Peninsula. Yet in the changing power complex of the Middle East neither has been successful in becoming a "core area" for the coalescence of Arab power. Nasser's socialism in Egypt finds few friends among the Moslem traditionalists to the east, any more than did Kassim's socialist approach in Iraq. Monarchist and pro-Western Libya blocks expansion of Egyptian influence to the west in North Africa, while the Kurdish rebellion in Iraq, the intransigence of Western-oriented Iran, and British power in the sheikdoms to the south of Iraq curtail that country's activities beyond its own borders.

---

[5] Formed in 1945 and eventually including Syria, Lebanon, Jordan, Iraq, Egypt, Saudi Arabia, Yemen, Libya, and Sudan.

DEVELOPMENT OF THE ARAB STATES

The Decline of Turkish Power and Expansion of European Control

The history of the area dates back thousands of years, but for the purposes of analyzing the present political pattern the changing aspects of territorial control will be considered only since the beginning of the nine-teenth century. For three hundred years prior to that time Turkish con-trol of the Arab lands had remained virtually unchallenged. The maritime powers of western Europe saw little profit to be gained from the Middle East, and rather than battle the Turks for control of the barren land they had turned to other continents in search of empires.

The establishment of European control in the Arab World during the nineteenth and early twentieth centuries produced a complex history of conflicting power forces. Expanding westward from India in the early part of the nineteenth century, Britain became the first of the European powers to secure areas of permanent political control in this part of the world. Commercial and political treaties were signed with the local sheiks and sultans of southern Arabia, and the port of Aden, lying close to the mouth of the Red Sea, was annexed as a British colony; thus with the opening of the Suez Canal in 1869 between the Mediterranean and the Red Sea, Britain was provided with a new and well-guarded lifeline to her eastern possessions. A few years later the island of Cyprus in the eastern Mediterranean was leased to Britain by Turkey, and in 1882 British troops occupied Egypt, in order to put down serious riots which were sweeping the country and to protect European lives and property. The country eventually became a British protectorate, and Port Said, at the northern end of the Suez Canal, was established as an important British naval base, thereby further safeguarding Britain's lifeline to the East.

To the south of Egypt nearly a million square miles of territory were also added to the British Empire in the closing years of the nineteenth cen-tury, when British and Egyptian troops gained control of the Sudan. The Sudan controls the middle portions of the Nile, its Red Sea coast could be used for naval bases between Suez and Aden, and at the time of its annexa-tion it served as a check on French territorial ambitions in east central Africa. In 1899 a British-Egyptian condominium was set up over the Sudan, whereby the two governments shared in its administration, although Britain actually was the predominant power.

While Britain was expanding its power in the eastern Mediterranean–Red Sea area, French influence was being established in western North Africa. In 1830 French forces landed on the Algerian coast across the Mediterranean from France and began a drive inland to subjugate all of North Africa. The coastal lowlands afforded considerable opportunities for agriculture, and much of the better land in Algeria was taken over by French settlers. To the east of Algeria the State of Tunisia was administered by a native ruler. Although nominally a part of the Ottoman Empire, Tunisia by the mid-nineteenth century enjoyed virtual independence. In 1881 France forced the ruler to accept the establishment of a French protectorate over his country, so that, although he retained nominal powers, actual control in Tunisia passed to the French resident-general and his staff.

In northwestern Africa French interests during the nineteenth and early twentieth centuries conflicted with those of Britain, Spain, and Germany. Only through various compromises was France able eventually to establish undisputed control of the area of French Morocco. At the end of the nineteenth century Britain withdrew its claims there in exchange for French withdrawal from the Anglo-Egyptian Sudan, Spain was granted a strip of Moroccan territory in the northwest facing the Spanish coast, and Germany abandoned its demands in northwest Africa after territory had been transferred from French Equatorial Africa to the German Cameroons. Territorial compromises such as these were characteristic of the political partitioning of all of Africa during the late nineteenth and early twentieth centuries.

Morocco was ultimately divided into three zones in 1912. Most of the area became a French protectorate under the nominal control of the native sultan. About 5 per cent was constituted as Spanish Morocco. Ceuta and Melilla remained as Spanish coastal enclaves under Spain's direct sovereignty, and Ceuta was developed as a Spanish naval base close to the Strait of Gibraltar. Control of the city of Tangier, located at the northwestern tip of Africa, became a source of international controversy, since the harbor is on the southern shore of the Atlantic approach to the Strait of Gibraltar. Finally, in 1925 Tangier and the territory adjacent to it were established as an international zone. With an area of 225 square miles and a population of 150,000, the zone was placed under the control of a committee composed of the consuls of eight European powers. Tangier, the only international area of its kind in the world, represented a unique arrangement for control of an area disputed among several States.

Another European country to acquire territory in the Arab world was Italy. This State was late in its drive for colonies, and by the time it began to expand most of the territory in Africa had already been claimed by other European powers. In 1911 Italian troops landed at Tripoli on the North African coast; simultaneously the annexation of Turkey's province of Libya was announced in Rome. War with Turkey followed, but within a year the Italians were victorious, and Libya was subsequently recognized as an Italian colony.

By 1914 the Turks had lost all territorial holdings in North Africa, as well as in much of the southern and eastern parts of the Arabian Peninsula. The British, pursuing a policy of "marginal control," had concentrated their power in key areas within their territorial possessions, maintaining relatively small but mobile military units and administering wherever possible through local rulers. To Britain the Arab World was important because of its military value in protecting the sea routes to India and the Far East and as a buffer between rival European empires—notably German and Russian—and their own in India. France, Italy, and to a lesser extent, Spain were interested in their possessions as settlement areas. Many Frenchmen had moved to North Africa, but the Italian government, both before and after World War I, was less successful in its colonization efforts in Libya. The Italian people had little interest in permanent settlement in Africa, and Libya had much less to offer as a settlement area than did the French North African territories. The Germans, although controlling no territory in the Arab World, sought to extend their influence in the area through cultural and economic contacts with the Arabs, including the proposed and partly constructed Berlin-Baghdad Railway. As centrifugal forces grew stronger in what remained of the Ottoman Empire both before and during World War I, various European States began making preparations for expanding their control in the Arab World.

World War I and the Palestine Dispute

During World War I Turkey joined Germany and the other Central Powers against France, Britain, Italy, Russia, and their allies. Early in the fighting the British began a campaign to enlist the aid of Arab groups in the struggle against the Turks. As an incentive for their cooperation the British held out the promise of eventual Arab independence once Turkey was defeated. In 1915 Sir Henry McMahon, High Commissioner for Egypt, wrote to the sherif of Mecca promising British support for Arab independence in the Middle East. Sir Henry was forced to recognize the existence of historical French interests in Syria and Lebanon, and he therefore stated that the future independence of those areas lying west of the districts of Damascus, Homs, and Aleppo could not be guaranteed by the British government at that time.

British commitments were accepted by the sherif and his associates, and Arab forces were soon battling against the Turks. The British government made another commitment in the Middle East, however, this one to the Jews. In the years preceding World War I several thousand Jewish immigrants came to settle permanently in Palestine in the hope of establishing a Jewish homeland there. As reward for Jewish contributions to the war effort the British government in 1917 issued the Balfour Declaration:

His Majesty's Government view with favour the establishment of
a National Home for the Jewish People . . . in Palestine.

To the Arabs the Balfour Declaration was in direct contradiction with the
promises made to them in the McMahon letter. Palestine lies west of the
Damascus-Aleppo line, but also to the south of Syria. The MacMahon and
Balfour declarations became a source of British embarassment during the
next thirty years, and the dispute eventually erupted into the Arab-Jewish
War of 1948–49.

The High Point of European Power, 1919–39

Turkey's defeat in 1918 heralded a complete political realignment in
the eastern part of the Arab World. Britain and France, the leading
European States in the Allied coalition of World War I, became the dominant powers in this part of the world and shared between them the territorial spoils of the old Ottoman Empire. The area south of Turkey itself,
between Egypt and Iran, was divided into five small political units—Syria,
Lebanon, Palestine, Transjordan, and Iraq. This political partitioning seriously weakened any potential unity which the Arab peoples might have
experienced after liberation from Turkish rule.

It was felt by the Allied officials that independence for these Arab
areas should eventually come about, but only after an indefinite "training
period." These countries were deemed ill-prepared immediately after World
War I for the responsibilities of self-government. Therefore, they were set
up as Class A mandates of the League of Nations, with Britain and France
as administering powers. Under the terms of the mandates, the Arab countries were to be governed during the interim period before independence by
the European States under the supervision of a League of Nations commission. Palestine, Transjordan, and Iraq were set up as British mandates,
and Syria and Lebanon became French mandates.

No provisions were made for the establishment of mandates on the
Arabian Peninsula, for much of the area had not been under Turkish
control before the war and, except for Aden, the peninsula was then considered to be of little economic value. The regions of Nejd, al-Hasa, Hejaz,
and Asir were later combined into the independent kingdom of Saudi
Arabia. Unlike events in other parts of the Arab World, this unification
took place through internal means (the military campaigns of Ibn Saud)
rather than as a result of action by foreign powers. Except for some of its
coastal areas the Arabian Peninsula has always been relatively isolated from
foreign control. Centrifugal forces there are illustrated by the existence of
two Saudi Arabian capitals—Riyadh, the political capital, in the desert

250 miles inland from the Persian Gulf, and Mecca, the religious capital, in the west.

In addition to Saudi Arabia the peninsula contains a number of small political units. Yemen, a mountainous area on the southwestern coast, has been independent since 1925. The port of Aden and the territory around it is a British colony, and much of the southern Arabian Peninsula consists of the British-supervised Aden Protectorate (see page 387). Kuwait in the northeast was an independent State under British protection—a protection which terminated in 1961. The Bahrein Islands in the Persian Gulf are also independent but under British protection, as, in the southeast, are the sheikdoms of Qatar, the seven sheikdoms of Trucial Oman, and the sultanate of Oman (or Muscat and Oman). Political patterns in this area are in a state of frequent change; even the number of these small political units varies according to the fortunes of local wars, although in recent years attempts have been made to stabilize political and military conditions in order to facilitate oil exploration and development.

Along Saudi Arabia's northeastern border two Neutral Zones were established after World War I. The word "neutral" is a misnomer, for the Zones are actually condominiums, controlled in the one case by Iraq and Saudi Arabia and in the other by Kuwait and Saudi Arabia. The Neutral Zones, like the former Anglo-Egyptian Sudan, are compromises of territorial claims. In the Kuwait–Saudi Arabian area oil is now being developed.[6]

To the north of the Arabian Peninsula the territorial dispute between Turkey and Britain over the determination of Iraq's northwestern border has already been noted. The Mosul area there is part of the Tigris-Euphrates Valley (Mesopotamia) and contains some of the country's most promising oil resources. With a mixed Arab-Turkish-Kurd population, the Mosul region was tied economically more closely with Iraq than with Turkey at the end of World War I, although the Turks claimed—possibly with some justification—that a plebiscite in this area would have shown a predominance of the population favoring continued Turkish control. Britain was interested in obtaining the Mosul area for Iraq, first, in order to strengthen its friendship with the Iraqi government and, second, because of British claims to the oil resources there. In 1926 the final boundary was delimited, awarding practically the entire area to Iraq.

The Beginnings of Arab Independence

The gradual establishment of independence in the Arab World was the result of three principal factors: (1) the terms of the mandate agree-

---

[6] See Alexander Melamid, "The Economic Geography of Neutral Territories." The original condominiums set up in 1922 were with Nejd, which later became the core region of the new state of Saudi Arabia.

ments, which called for eventual self-rule, (2) local pressures for an end to foreign control, and (3) changing policies and conditions within the European countries themselves. In many cases, of course, independence resulted from a combination of two or even of all three of these elements.

During the period between the two world wars Britain was the only European power to grant independence to Arab states—to Egypt in 1922 and to Iraq in 1932—and even there the withdrawal of British political control was accompanied by military treaties, whereby Britain was permitted to maintain bases and use the resources of the two countries in time of war. Britain also retained a strong economic position in Egypt and Iraq.

The French did little in the way of advancing self-government for their two mandates, Syria and Lebanon. Through their insistence on special political and economic privileges for French citizens in these two areas, the French created considerable antagonism among the Syrians and Lebanese, and thereby accentuated the local demands for independence. Shortly before World War II the French government further alienated the people of Syria by permitting Turkey to annex the coastal district of Alexandretta (now called Iskenderun). French authorities maintained that the district's population was predominantly Turkish in character, and despite France's obligations under the League of Nations to protect Syria against loss of territory, the transfer was agreed to in 1939. Iskenderun is now the third largest Turkish port.

In other parts of the Arab World there was little progress toward self-rule between the two world wars. All the dependent areas were governed according to the economic and political policies of the various mother countries, with the result that during this period regional differences between the states were accentuated and the possibilities for Arab unity diminished.

World War II and the Postwar Changes

When World War II broke out in September, 1939, the Arab World became of great strategic importance to the contesting powers. The defeat of France in June, 1940, and Italy's entrance into the war on the side of the Germans were serious threats to Britain's position in the Middle East. To the British the Arab World was of great value because of its oil supplies, its position with respect to reinforcement lines from India, Australia, and New Zealand, and its role as a base for resisting German pressures south and southeast from occupied Europe. After 1943 the Arab World also served as a staging area for the reinvasion of Europe. To the Germans the Arab World also was a source of much-needed oil supplies, as well as a base for operations against southern Russia and British supply lines from the East. The Germans were never able to win military control of this area, however. Finally, to the peoples of the Arab World, many of whom were more concerned with independence demands than with Axis aggression, World War II appeared both as a continuation of foreign exploitation of their resources and location and as an opportunity to further their own political goals.

Since World War II several major changes of sovereignty have taken place in the Arab World. Syria, Lebanon, Libya, Transjordan, Israel, Morocco, Tunisia, the Sudan, and Algeria have achieved independence, and the British have evacuated the Suez Canal Zone. The gradual decline of European power there has been further accentuated by such actions as the Egyptian nationalization of the Suez Canal, by anti-British moves in the former mandate of Transjordan, by the adoption of neutralist policies with regard to the Cold War by some of the Arab States, and by the abortive invasion of the Suez by British, French, and Israeli forces. In the sections which follow the changes of sovereignty in the Arab World since World War II will be considered in detail.

The Partition of Palestine and Creation of Israel. The steady influx of Jewish immigrants into Palestine after the establishment of the British mandate in 1920 increased the Jewish proportion of the population from 16 per cent in 1922 to 24 per cent in 1947. In general the Jewish arrivals were better educated than the local Arab inhabitants. Outside funds were solicited by the World Zionist Movement to be used in the settlement of Palestine. The hardworking immigrants developed land reclamation projects, new farming techniques were instituted, and Palestine's agricultural production rose substantially during the quarter-century following World War I.

Resentment between Jews and Arabs in Palestine continued to rise. During the interwar years the Jews gained ownership of nearly all of the country's commercial enterprises. In 1939 in response to Arab demands the British placed restrictions on future Jewish immigration, limiting the number of immigrants to 15,000 per year. By 1945 thousands of European Jews who had survived the horrors of fascism and war were desperately eager to reach Palestine, where future security and hope awaited them. While the British navy attempted to intercept ships laden with illegal immigrants, Zionist and Arab underground organizations in Palestine were conducting campaigns against one another and against the British.

A United Nations Palestine Commission eventually was established with the task of seeking a just and equitable solution to the problem. The commission's recommendation was for partition of Palestine into three Jewish and three Arab sectors. The future of Jerusalem, holy city to Jews, Arabs, and Christians alike, was left for subsequent discussions. In November, 1947, this partition plan was approved by the United Nations General Assembly. Jewish leaders accepted the UN partition plan, but the Arabs denounced it bitterly. In May, 1948, Britain surrendered its mandate, and British forces withdrew completely from the area. Fighting immediately broke out between the Jews and Arabs, the latter supported by the armies of Jordan, Egypt, Syria, Lebanon, and Iraq. More than 600,000 Arab civilians living in the Jewish sectors of Palestine evacuated their homes and retreated behind the Arab lines.

In the months which followed the Arab attack, the Jewish armies were able not only to stand up against the Arab forces but also to drive them back in many sectors. In the spring of 1949 separate armistice agreements were signed between the Jews on the one hand and the several Arab States on the other. Hostilities ended and military truce lines were set up. At that time the Israelis controllel an area about 2,200 square miles greater than that which had been awarded them in the 1947 partition scheme.

The new Arab-Jewish border followed the old Palestine frontier throughout much of its length. One exception was in eastern Palestine, where a 2,300-square-mile area west of the Jordan–Dead Sea line remained in Arab hands, and another in the extreme west, where the Egyptians re-tained a coastal strip about eight miles in width (Figure 75). The six-zone concept of the UN Palestine Commission disappeared, and all the Jewish territory was now contiguous. The temporary cease-fire boundaries have

Figure 75. Israel. (After Alexander, *World Politics*, VI [April, 1954]. Used by permission.)

remained as permanent political features of the landscape. In Jerusalem the Jews controlled the New City, while the Arabs retained the old part with its religious relics, including Gethsemane, the Church of the Holy Sepulcher, and the Jewish Wailing Wall.[7] Bethlehem was also in Arab hands.

The erratic political pattern in the former Palestine area has caused a number of potentially dangerous situations. Like the "iron curtain" across Korea, the military cease-fire line has formed a closed boundary across what used to be a unified region, with resultant hardships to the peoples and economies of the border areas. Violence has broken out repeatedly between Jews and Arabs across the border, and a United Nations commission has supervised the border functioning and, where possible, negotiated between Jews and Arabs in an effort to control the border warfare.

Assuming the 1949 borders of Israel become permanent, several outstanding problems remain to be solved. First, there is the matter of the Arab refugees who once lived in what is now Israel.[8] The Arabs have insisted that before peace negotiations can take place these people must be returned to their former homes. The Jews have contended that such repatriation is impossible, since the refugees left their homes voluntarily in 1948 hoping to return with the victorious Arab armies, and that because of the influx of Jewish immigrants to Israel since 1948 there is no room left for the readmission of these former Arab inhabitants. By the end of 1960 the independent State of Israel had received 989,000 immigrants, approximately half from Europe and the United States and half from Asia and Africa. Since many of these immigrants have come from Arab lands, presumably some of the Arab refugees could be settled in the areas vacated.

A second problem is that of water scarcity. Any long-term proposal for the increase of agricultural areas in Israel and the neighboring Arab States (thus providing among other things for the resettlement of Arab refugees) is related to this problem. The most promising source of water for Israel and western Jordan is the Jordan River and its tributaries. Most of the headwaters of the Jordan actually rise in Syria and Lebanon; they unite in the Huleh Marsh area of northern Israel to form the major stream, which flows south partly in Israeli territory, partly along the Israeli-Jordan border, and in its southern sector entirely within the territory of Jordan (Figure 75). The utilization of the waters of the Jordan system could best be

---

[7] The United Nations in 1949 passed a resolution calling for the internationalization of Jerusalem under a UN commission. Neither the Jews nor the Arabs would acquiesce in this proposal. The Jews announced that Jerusalem was the legal capital of Israel, while Jordan proceeded to annex eastern Jerusalem, as well as the other Arab-held portions of Palestine (except Egypt's Gaza strip in the extreme west), and to make them integral parts of the Kingdom of Jordan. After a year of fruitless negotiations the United Nations admitted it was unable to implement the 1949 decision.

[8] Natural increase (and the addition of "refugees" who actually never lived in the territory which is now part of Israel) has swelled the number of Arab refugees by 1961 to over 1,200,000. The UN Relief and Works Agency has been caring for these displaced persons in refugee camps located in the Arab States bordering Israel. About 70 per cent of the cost of caring for these people is borne by the United States.

accomplished through some form of international agreement between the Jews and the Arabs, but since the Arabs refuse to negotiate with Israel, such agreement is impossible, and both groups are preparing plans for separate irrigation and power developments within their own areas. The Israelis have been proceeding with plans to divert much of the water of the Jordan by pumping from the Sea of Galilee, while the Arabs might divert the waters of the Yarmuk above its confluence with the Jordan and use this both in Jordan and in Syria.

A third problem involves the economic position of Israel, as additional Jewish immigrants continue to arrive. The Israeli nation is committed to the support of all Jews, yet there are limits to the number of persons who can be adequately cared for by a State with less than 8,000 square miles of territory and few natural resources. Hundreds of millions of dollars have already been advanced to Israel by Jews living in other parts of the world, particularly by those in the United States, western Europe, and South Africa. One of the major sources of Israel's strength is the financial and political support it receives from the approximately 10 million Jews living outside its borders. The State must eventually become self-supporting, however, if it is to be a strong national unit in this part of the world. Since Israel's creation all efforts to improve the country's economic position have, of course, been handicapped by the economic blockade imposed on Israel by the Arab States.

Another problem concerns the Gulf of Aqaba, extending south from Israel to the Red Sea. Jordan, Egypt, and Saudi Arabia also border on the gulf, and thus it is an international waterway. The only navigable channel between the gulf and the Red Sea, however, is through the Strait of Tiran, a three-mile-wide waterway, both sides of which are controlled by Arab countries. In 1949 Egypt established fortifications along the strait and prevented Israeli shipping from using the waterway in passing to and from the port of Elath in southernmost Israel. Blocking an international waterway is contrary to the generally accepted rules of international law, but there, as in the case of Israeli shipping passing through the Suez Canal, Egypt resisted all efforts by the United Nations to bring about a relaxation of restrictions on passage by Israeli vessels. Since 1956 United Nations forces have been deployed in Egyptian territory along the west shore of the Strait of Tiran, thereby enabling Israeli shipping to enter and leave the Gulf of Aqaba.

Syria and Lebanon.   French claims to predominance in Syria and Lebanon were based largely on France's historical role as protector of Christianity in this part of the world. Lebanon, occupying a well-watered mountain area along the Mediterranean coast, has a population of 1,850,-000, which is over 50 per cent Christian. Because of its importance as a commercial and financial center, Lebanon is a relatively prosperous country and has long maintained close ties with the European nations. Beirut, its capital and leading city, is an important harbor, and two other Lebanese ports serve as Mediterranean outlets for pipelines from oil fields in Iraq and Saudi Arabia.

Syria, on the other hand, is a much poorer country. Like Lebanon, it has no mineral or petroleum wealth. In addition, it has no good harbors along the Mediterranean, having lost Beirut to Lebanon and Alexandretta to Turkey. The bulk of its 4,825,000 inhabitants are settled inland from the coast along a north-south axis running from Aleppo, close to the Turkish border, to Damascus, the capital, in southern Syria. Both cities are approximately equal in size—a significant centrifugal factor, since each is an important regional center. The population is largely Moslem and includes three important minorities—Turks, who live in northern Syria, Kurds, inhabiting the mountains of the northeast (see page 390), and the Druses, who inhabit a mountain area in south Syria and often engage in armed conflict against the Damascus government.

French control in both Syria and Lebanon was marked by strife and rebellion. The Syrians, among other things, resented the political partitioning of their country by the separation of Transjordan, Palestine, and Lebanon from what had been the prewar Turkish province of Syria, by the subdivision of postwar Syria into theoretically autonomous regions, and finally by the loss of Alexandretta.

No definite steps were taken by France prior to World War II to terminate the mandates in Syria and Lebanon. In 1941 France, then under a pro-Axis administration, officially withdrew from the League of Nations. The governments of Syria and Lebanon announced that as a result of this withdrawal the areas were no longer to be considered French mandates. At the end of World War II the independence of these countries was officially acknowledged by France, and French political and military power was thereby eliminated from the eastern Mediterranean.

By the mid-1950's strong Soviet influence was apparent in Syria. Arms from the Communist bloc were being delivered to the Syrians, economic ties had been strengthened between the two areas, and a left-wing government had come into office in Damascus. A power vacuum had existed in Syria since the withdrawal of the French, and Soviet activities there posed a potential threat to the position of the Western nations in the Middle East. Were Syria to align its foreign policy with that of the Soviets, Turkey would be outflanked, and aircraft based in Syria would be in a position to threaten Iraq, Jordan, Lebanon, Cyprus, and the United States naval base at Iskenderun. The oil pipeline from Iraq could be permanently cut, and raiders from Syria could easily cross the border into Israel. In 1958, partly in response to Communist pressures, the government of Syria agreed to a political union with Egypt, under the name "United Arab Republic"—a union which lasted approximately three years (see page 388). The break-up of the UAR, engineered largely by elements of the Syrian army, has done little to bring economic or political stability to this small but strategically located State.

Lebanon, despite its relative prosperity, has also experienced internal political turmoil and the threat of a Communist take-over. In 1958, one week after the pro-Western government of Iraq had been overthrown by a coup, United States forces were landed in Lebanon for the purpose of preventing what appeared to be a potential anti-Western revolution there as well. Although foreign forces were soon withdrawn, there still exist in Lebanon, as in the other states of the Arab World, strong anti-Western feelings, based in part on extreme Arab nationalism, in part on association of the West with the Israelis, and in part on admiration for the Soviet Union, or more simply for the tenets of Marxism itself.

Jordan. Formerly the British mandate Transjordan, Jordan is one of the poorest of the Arab countries. The eastern and southern portions are desert, and only in the western uplands is there sufficient precipitation for agriculture and extensive grazing. Phosphate is the only important mineral resource. Prior to 1948 the population of about 400,000 was concentrated largely in the western sector, centering on the capital city of Amman. The British mandate was ended in 1946, at which time the area became independent. British bases were retained there, and Britain was granted the right to utilize Jordan's territory in time of war. In return, the State's annual deficit was to be met by payments from the British treasury.

In 1949, as a result of the Israeli war, Jordan acquired an additional 2,300 square miles of the former Palestine mandate, containing approximately 400,000 persons. At the same time, Jordan also received over 450,-000 Arab refugees, so that the nation's population actually trebled within a short space of time. The acquisition of the eastern section of Jerusalem and other regions of eastern Palestine has been an economic asset to Jordan; on the other hand, the refugees (whose number in 1960 was given at 535,-000) are in one sense a drain on the economy, although they are also an important source of needed skills. Foreign help will be needed to provide for the permanent settlement of these refugee peoples in Jordan and the other Arab States. The presence of these diverse groups in Jordan has constituted a powerful centrifugal force within the country, since the cultural, economic, and political interests of these people differ widely from those of the majority of the inhabitants of pre-1948 Jordan.

Early in 1957 the Jordanian government announced it would terminate its economic treaty with Britain. The annual subsidy made to Jordan by the British was to be provided by Egypt, Saudi Arabia, and Syria. This economic assistance, however, was not forthcoming, and although the British evacuated their bases in Jordan in 1958, the yearly budgetary deficits have continued to be made up by grants from Great Britain and the United States. For a period of five months in 1958 Jordan and Iraq were at least officially joined in a political union, the Arab Federation; this union terminated after an armed *coup d'état* in Iraq in July, 1958, ended the reign of King Faisal II and established a republic under General Kassim. Jordan, even more than Syria, remains a poor and loosely organized State, without much *raison d'être* or economic viability.

Iraq. Based on the fertile delta of the Tigris and Euphrates rivers, Iraq is potentially a relatively rich area, both because of the possibilities of irrigated agriculture and of the oil production which in 1960 amounted to over 4 per cent of the world's total. With an area of 171,000 square miles and a 1960 population of close to 7 million, Iraq may be divided physically into four regions: (1) the folded mountains of the north which continue into Turkey and Iran; (2) the western desert which merges into Syria, Jordan, Saudi Arabia, and Kuwait; (3) a rolling upland (the "Jezira") northwest of Baghdad, where agriculture is possible only if the rivers are dammed for irrigation waters; and (4) the delta, below Baghdad, where soil and water supply combine to form excellent agricultural possibilities.

The major oil field in Iraq is at Kirkuk in the north, about 100 miles southwest of Mosul. From there oil is sent by pipeline to the Mediterranean. There are also smaller fields near Mosul and in the south near Basra. The Iraq Petroleum Company is foreign-owned, with Iraq itself receiving 50 per cent of its profits before the deduction of foreign taxes.

Iraq's foreign policy was in general closely tied to that of the British until a military coup in July, 1958, resulted in the execution of the reigning King, Faisal II, and the establishment of a republic under General Kassim. Since 1958 the government has sought (1) to establish a socialist type of economy in Iraq (including the possible nationalization of the Iraq Petroleum Company); (2) to expand Iraq's power in the Arab World, a move which carries with it the threat of territorial expansion southward through neighboring Kuwait; (3) to maintain internal cohesion in the face of a Kurdish rebellion (see below); and (4) to follow a "neutralist" line with regard to the Cold War. Military aircraft have been received from the Soviet Union, and in 1959 the British evacuated their air base at Habbaniyah, west of Baghdad. Yet Iraq is in no sense a Soviet-dominated State.

In July, 1961, a delegation from the Kurdish area of northern Iraq demanded that General Kassim establish an autonomous "Kurdistan" in the mountains east and north of Mosul. The delegation was led by Mullah Mustata, a Communist who fled to the Soviet Union in 1946 and returned to Iraq with 1,500 Kurdish refugees in 1958 at General Kassim's invitation. When demands for an autonomous Kurdish area were refused by Baghdad, fighting broke out in northern Iraq, and by the summer of 1962 was becoming increasingly serious. Iraqui planes, seeking to end the rebellion, have clashed with Turkish jets along the sensitive border between the two States. Kassim's failure to put down the Kurdish rebellion has jeopardized Iraq's image as a power center in the Arab World and represents a threat both to the oil fields at Kirkuk and to boundary stability in northern Iraq (see also page 390).

The Territorial Problems of Egypt.   Since the end of World War I the Egyptian people have gradually established control over the area and resources of their country. In 1922 the British protectorate was ended, although Britain continued to maintain certain rights in Egypt, including that of stationing troops there. Eighteen years later British forces were withdrawn from the country after the conclusion of a treaty which permitted them to remain in the Suez Canal Zone and gave Britain the right to reoccupy Egypt in time of war. This right was exercised during World War II. Although the Egyptians did not declare war on the Axis powers until the spring of 1945, their country was used as a base of operations by Britain and its allies from 1939 to the end of the war by virtue of this Anglo-Egyptian military treaty.

During the decade following the war Egyptian nationalism manifested itself in the abrogation of the Anglo-Egyptian military treaty, and in pressuring the British to evacuate their military forces from the Suez Canal Zone and to terminate their political control in the Anglo-Egyptian Sudan. In 1952 King Farouk of Egypt was replaced by Naguib, an army general, who two years later was in turn replaced by Gamal Nasser, one of the outstanding contemporary figures of the Arab World. By following both a nationalistic and (in terms of Cold War politics) a neutralistic policy, he has endeavored to strengthen Egypt's position both internally and externally and to make it a leading power in the Middle East and North Africa.

The pressure of population on Egypt's meager resources has already been noted. With a shortage of minerals (iron ore is the only important resource) and petroleum and a rapidly increasing population total, Egypt faces a difficult economic future. One of the proposed projects for alleviating Egypt's land problem has been the construction of a high Aswan Dam on the Nile, 400 miles upstream from Cairo, at a cost of $1,300 million. The dam would provide for the irrigation of 2 million acres, an increase of nearly one-third of Egypt's cultivated area, and would also be an important source of hydroelectric power. Two problems, however, are associated with this project. First, there is the need for funds to finance the dam; second, permission for its construction was necessary from Sudan, since the dam would back up water 100 miles across the Sudanese border, inundating the town of Wadi Halfa and the agricultural lands to the south of it. In order to obtain funds for the construction of the dam President Nasser turned first to the United States and the International Bank. When these sources, in the summer of 1956, withdrew their offers of financial support, the Egyptian government nationalized the Suez Canal, hoping thereby to obtain the needed funds. Two years later the Soviet Union advanced $100 million to start construction on the dam, and in 1961 a second loan of $130 million was negotiated. The principal repayment of these loans will be the export of Egyptian cotton to the U.S.S.R.

The Sudan. The controversy which arose between Egypt and Britain after World War II over control of the Anglo-Egyptian Sudan is of politico-geographic interest, since it illustrates the conflict of power forces in northeastern Africa. During the discussion which took place between British and Egyptian officials, two solutions appeared to be the most feasible for the Sudan: first, complete independence for the area or, second, political unification with Egypt. The reduced power position of Britain in this part of the world was evident, for in either case the British stood to lose their share in the control of the Sudan, with its area of nearly one million square miles.

Egypt's claims to the Sudan were based primarily on conquest, ethnic ties, water rights, and the need for additional land for settlement. In addition, Egypt was interested in obtaining a position of power in northeastern Africa. Egyptian forces conquered the Sudan in 1821, and Egypt controlled the area for sixty-four years. A majority of the population is of Arabic origin. The two main sources of the Nile, although rising outside the borders of the Sudan, flow for a long way through Sudanese territory before crossing the border into Egypt. Since 96 per cent of Egypt's population lives in the Nile Valley, the Egyptian government is naturally concerned over the control of the upper reaches of the river. Finally, if the Sudan were joined politically to Egypt, it might offer potential areas for the settlement of Egyptians, thereby relieving the population pressure in Egypt.

There were other factors, however, which served to weaken Egyptian claims. First, although the Egyptians once controlled the Sudan, they were forced out by local uprisings in 1885, and it was the British who did the bulk of the fighting which subdued the area from 1898 to 1917. Second, about 30 per cent of the Sudanese are pagan Negroes rather than Arabs and have almost no cultural ties whatever with the Egyptians. Finally, even the Sudanese Arabs would oppose large-scale immigration of Egyptians into their country. The British thus felt that it would be unfair for the Sudanese to be forced against their will to join politically with Egypt. Eventually British and Egyptian representatives agreed to grant the Sudan local self-government, and in January, 1956, after native Sudanese leaders had registered their opposition to union with Egypt, the independent State of Sudan came into existence (see Figure 74).

Sudan faces enormous internal problems as an independent State. In the absence of adequate transportation, education, and health facilities, of trained personnel, and of a sound economic base, the process of political development may take many years to accomplish. The poorly trained Arabs and the primitive peoples of the south must be united into a single, cohesive political unit, otherwise the southern sector may break away from the rest of the State and perhaps join the Negro country of Uganda. A future division of the Sudanese nation into two physical-ethnic units might prove to be a sound move, for the old Anglo-Egyptian Sudan was an artificial creation with little justification as a single political unit. Such a move would have to wait until considerable development has taken place in the southern sector, however, since there has to date been little economic, political, or social progress among the Negroid peoples there.

Relations between Sudan and Egypt have been complicated by the problems of the Nile and by a border dispute east of the Nile. With respect to the latter the Sudanese claim that the easternmost section of their boundary with Egypt extends northward from the twenty-second to approximately the twenty-third parallel in conformity with existing tribal boundaries in the area. This "administrative boundary," although never formally adopted by treaty, was for years the *de facto* border and has been commonly represented on maps. The Egyptians, however, hold that the boundary follows the twenty-second parallel to the Red Sea as defined by the treaty of 1899. The area in dispute, measuring approximately 600 square miles, has been occupied since 1958 by Egyptian troops.

So far as the Nile is concerned, an Egyptian-Sudanese agreement of 1959 provides for a payment by Egypt to Sudan of approximately $43 million as compensation for the flooding of the Nile Valley some 100 miles south of the Egyptian-Sudanese border as a result of the completion of the Aswan Dam, and the necessary resettlement of over 40,000 Nubians— citizens of Sudan who inhabit the area in and near Wadi Halfa which will be inundated. The dam will result in a saving of some 22 billion cubic meters of water per year which normally would be lost to the Mediterranean. Of this amount Sudan will receive 14.5 billion cubic meters, or approximately two-thirds. In terms of total allocation of Nile water, after the dam is completed Sudan will receive 18.5 billion cubic meters, or 25 per cent, and Egypt will get 55.5 billion cubic meters, or 75 per cent.

The Suez. While they were withdrawing from the Sudan, the British also made plans to evacuate the Suez Canal Zone in order to appease local nationalist aspirations. Constructed in 1869, the 105-mile-long waterway greatly reduces the sea voyage from western Europe to the Indian Ocean and the Far East. From London to Kuwait on the Persian Gulf, for example, is 7,488 miles via the Suez and 13,437 miles around South Africa; and the distances to Singapore are 9,392 and 13,314 miles, respectively. The Suez Canal handles over 100 million tons of cargo a year, more than twice the amount handled by the Panama Canal. Of this tonnage about 65 per cent consists of oil and oil products, most of it bound from the Persian Gulf area to Europe. Ownership of the canal rested with the Suez Canal Company, an international organization in which French interests controlled a majority of the stock, while the British government owned about 40 per cent. In the Constantinople Convention of 1888 nine States (not including Egypt) laid down the principle of freedom of navigation for all vessels through the waterway in peacetime and in war.

Not only is the canal a vital link in seaway communications between Europe and the Indian Ocean basin, but it also crosses the land connection between Africa and Asia. Thus British military strength in the Suez Canal area was centrally located with respect to the Arab areas to the east, northeast, west, and south. The evacuation of British forces from the Suez Isthmus removed a major focus of European power in the Arab World.

In October, 1954, an agreement was concluded between British and Egyptian authorities, providing for the gradual withdrawal of all British forces from the Suez Canal Zone. The agreement, which was to last for seven years, further stipulated that, in the event of a hostile attack on Turkey or any of the Arab States, Britain could reoccupy its Suez bases and remain there until hostilities ended, and that Egypt would keep installations in the Canal Zone "in efficient working order and capable of immediate war action." Thus the British, who previously had abandoned Palestine as a major base, were forced to leave the Suez area as well and concentrate their Middle East forces on Cyprus. Although the Suez Canal was to become by treaty the property of the Egyptians in 1968—99 years after its completion—the Egyptian government announced the nationalization of the canal twelve years before this date, thus following a trend established by Iran in 1951, in which European holdings in this part of the world are gradually being taken over by the Arab countries themselves.

In October-November, 1956, the Suez area was invaded by the forces of Britain, France, and Israel, in an effort to bring to a head such problems as the future status of the canal, the continued violation of Israel's borders by Egyptian raiders, and the steady drift of the Arab States away from Western influence. In the face of United States pressure and Soviet threats, the invading armies halted after a brief campaign, and the existing Egyptian government—whose anti-Western actions had provoked the invasion—remained in power. The foreign troops were eventually withdrawn, and United Nations forces were sent to occupy both the Gaza strip (to prevent raids into Israel) and the western shore of the Strait of Tiran. These forces have continued to be on duty in Egypt since 1956.

At the time of the invasion the Egyptians blocked the Suez waterway by sinking ships in the channel. Approximately one-half of Europe's normal oil requirements are brought by tanker through the Suez; another 20 per cent are transported by pipelines from Iraq to the Mediterranean coast and then by tanker to Europe. The Iraqi pipelines were cut by Arab nationalists during the Suez fighting, and with the canal blocked, most of Europe's oil imports from the Persian Gulf region were brought by ship around Africa. In view of the shortage of tankers for this long haul, Europe's oil imports were seriously curtailed as a result of the military action in Egypt, and the price of oil for the European States was increased. This was a severe blow to the economies of these countries, necessitating increased oil shipments to Europe from the Western Hemisphere. At the same time some of the Middle Eastern governments were deprived of very important revenues from their oil operations.

Despite some predictions that the Egyptians would be unable to operate the Suez Canal successfully, the waterway has handled an increasingly greater tonnage in recent years than it did prior to 1956. The shareholders of the Suez Canal Company in 1958 accepted an agreement providing for a compensation payment by Egypt of approximately $58 million. The following year the World Bank granted Egypt a loan of $57 million for the deepening, widening, and general improvement of the canal and Port Said harbor.

Libya. The independent State of Libya is of little value economically, but it is of great strategic importance in the Arab World. Libya borders the Mediterranean for over one thousand miles and also adjoins Egypt, Tunisia, and Algeria. As a result political and military developments in Libya have had strong repercussions in other parts of North Africa.

This former Italian colony is a desert country of 1,150,000 inhabitants with three widely scattered centers of population, each forming the nucleus of a large administrative division: Tripolitania in the west along the Mediterranean coast, with Tripoli as its center; Cyrenaica nearly four hundred miles to the east, also on the Mediterranean coast, with Benghazi its main population center; and the distant oases of Fezzan, four hundred miles south of Tripoli. Over 70 per cent of the population (including most of the Italians) lives in Tripolitania, 25 per cent lives in Cyrenaica, and less than 5 per cent inhabits the southern area. The existence of two important core areas is, of course, a factor of considerable significance to political cohesion within the State.

During World War II British forces occupied portions of northern Libya, while French forces were in the Fezzan. Following the war the British proposed a ten-year interim period during which Libyans could be trained for independence, but this proposal was blocked in the United Nations by other countries (particularly France, Egypt, and the Soviet Union), which were jealous of Britain's power in the area. No workable solution could be found for a trusteeship status for the area (among other things it was feared that under a trusteeship arrangement Soviet power might be able

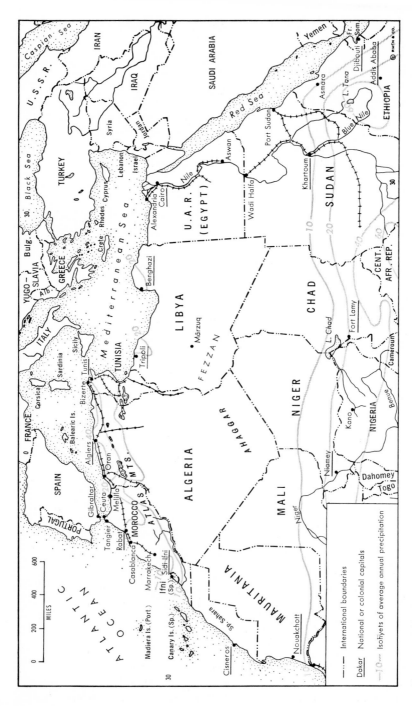

Figure 76. North Africa.

to establish itself in North Africa), and thus Libya was eventually granted independence by the United Nations.

In the brief time between the United Nations decision for Libyan independence (November, 1949) and the actual start of self-rule, Libyan authorities were faced with the problem of obtaining trained personnel for the necessary government posts. The emir of Cyrenaica was eventually chosen as king by the national assembly, and the cities of Tripoli and Benghazi were designated as twin capitals, with the parliament meeting alternately in each city. In December, 1951, Libya became an independent State.

Libya's poverty was even greater than that of Tunisia or Egypt. Over 90 per cent of the country's inhabitants were illiterate at the time of independence. There is no defense force; Libya's independence must be guaranteed by American, British, and French forces. The United States operates the Wheelus Air Base in northwestern Libya, near Tripoli, the only American-controlled air base in this part of the Arab World. The British have an important naval and air base in northeastern Libya in the Tobruk area. The French also maintain forces in the country. The revenue from these bases represents an important source of income for the Libyan government. Libya's budget is also aided by subsidies from the British treasury, and Britain thus continues to maintain influence here in North Africa. Oil exploration has been in progress for several years, largely by American companies, and late in 1961 Libya began exporting oil from a field 105 miles inland from the coast. Although the exact nature of the Libyan reserves is not known, it is expected that they may be of considerable size, thus in a few years elevating Libya from a position of poverty to one of considerable prosperity.

Independence for a disputed area (in contrast with condominiums, neutral zones, and United Nations administration) is an unusual method for solving problems of political control. A decision to establish independence may, of course, fail to take into account the inability of the inhabitants to maintain effective independence due to a lack of internal organization, economic stability, or military power. In the light of the intense nationalist efforts in such areas as Indochina, Indonesia, and Algeria, it seems ironic that Libya should have received independence almost as if by default.

Tunisia. Tunisia is a relatively poor country, with a population of about 4 million and an agricultural area which is greatly limited by climate and surface configuration. Tunisia's population includes over 300,000 Europeans, divided almost equally between Frenchmen and Italians. The Europeans here, as in Algeria and Morocco, have tended to settle on the best agricultural lands, leaving the poorer sections for the Arab population. Agricultural practices among the Arabs are often backward, and much of the land is in need of redevelopment. Iron ore, phosphate, lead, and zinc are the principal mineral resources. With its rising population, Tunisia, like many other Arab States, faces difficult problems ahead in its economic structure.

Education and training in Tunisia are relatively advanced, and among the African population there do not exist the strong centrifugal forces which are present between the Arabs and Berbers of Morocco. In 1957 Tunisia abolished the office of the bey, or native ruler, and adopted a republican form of government. The trend away from monarchical rule in the Arab World may eventually spread to other countries as well, such as Morocco, Libya, and Saudi Arabia.

At the time of Tunisian independence (1956) French forces were withdrawn, except for those at the important naval base at Bizerte. In the ensuing years Tunisia's government followed a policy of friendship both with France and other countries of the West. Nationalist pressures continued to grow, however, and in 1961, after failing to win from France a date for evacuation of the base, Tunisia began armed attacks on the installation. In retaliation French forces temporarily occupied the city of Bizerte, and in the fighting close to 1,000 Tunisians were reported to have lost their lives. Tunisia later broke off diplomatic relations with France, although the French, having evacuated the city, continue to remain in force at the naval base. In July, 1962, diplomatic relations were re-established. The French have agreed to the ultimate evacuation of the Bizerte base—another indication of the gradual withdrawal of French power in North Africa.

Algeria. The Algerian conflict, which led to an agreement for independence for the country, cost an estimated 250,000 deaths and an expenditure by France of some $20 billion. As a result of independence nearly a million Europeans (most of them Frenchmen) found themselves a political minority among 9 million Arabs—a total which is expected to double in approximately twenty years.

Although Algeria has an area of nearly 850,000 square miles, the bulk of the country is desert, with less than 4 per cent actually in cultivation. Of the area in crops over one-third was in the hands of European farmers, although only about 25,000 European families were engaged in agriculture. Algerian exports, the bulk of which go to France, include iron ore, phosphates, wine, fruits and vegetables, and, in the past several years, petroleum. The Algerian oil fields are connected by pipeline with Mediterranean ports and may in time become a very valuable source of income. There is low-grade coal and considerable water power potential in the northern mountains. But although Algeria has important agricultural and mineral resources, it also has a large and rapidly growing Moslem population, an agricultural structure to a considerable extent in the hands of the French, and very few industries to absorb the nonagricultural peoples.

The Algerian conflict began in 1954 when the Moslem National Liberation Front (FLN) revolted against French rule. Despite the presence of what finally grew to an estimated 400,000 French troops in Algeria, France was unable to end the guerrilla activity. Support for the insurrectionists eventually came from other Arab States as well, and ultimately France's President de Gaulle began working toward an agreement leading to independence for Algeria, if possible in some form of association with France. Although the people of France, weary of the long struggle, generally came to support (or at least did not actively oppose) independence for Algeria, de Gaulle was faced with bitter resistance from right-wing elements of the French in Algeria who stood to lose many of their privileges if French control terminated. De Gaulle also faced opposition from the underground Algerian leaders who had for years been conducting the struggle against France, since they mistrusted the French and feared that independence might come with many conditions attached to it. One of the key points was sovereignty over the vast southern Sahara area which France began administering separately from populous northern Algeria in 1957, and which contains the bulk of the oil and natural gas deposits. The 1962 agreement between the French and Algerian nationalist governments called for a cease-fire, a referendum to be held in Algeria to determine its future status and—should the Algerians choose independence—for Algerian sovereignty over its southern area, although the Sahara's gas and oil production would be shared equally between Algeria and France. In July, 1962, Algeria became completely independent. France is to lease the use of its military base of Mers-El-Kebir (close to Oran) for a fifteen-year period, renewable by agreement between the two countries, and Algeria will also grant France the use of a number of airfields and other military sites. How long this military agreement will remain in effect is difficult to predict in the light of French problems over military rights in Tunisia and Morocco.

The French living in Algeria are to enjoy Algerian civic rights for a period of three years after achievement of self-determination, after which they will either elect to become Algerian nationals or will in effect be foreigners in Algeria. For one million people (the largest European minority in Africa except for the Republic of South Africa) the time is fast approaching when they must choose (1) to go back to France, where few of them were born and which most know only as visitors; (2) to become Algerian citizens; or (3) to stay on as a foreign minority in a country where they once were in a powerful position. Such choices have, of course, faced Europeans and Americans in other countries as well, but seldom have such a large number of people been involved. Rather than accept such a future, a French underground army, the OAS, began carrying out terrorist attacks as soon as the cease-fire agreement had taken effect, hoping to wreck the treaty, discourage the moderates who had concluded it, and, through the military, continue French control in Algeria. These attacks failed to halt the move toward independence, and by August, 1962, half the French population in Algeria had returned to France. With the loss of Algeria France's African empire is reduced to the coastal territory of French Somaliland, approximately 8,500 square miles in area.

Morocco. The former protectorate of Morocco—including both the French and Spanish areas—became an independent State in 1956. With a population of over 11 million (including some 400,000 Europeans, most of whom are French), Morocco has a large area of cultivable land, as well as phosphate, iron ore, manganese, coal, and hydroelectric resources. The population pressure on the land is not excessive, and the area offers good possibilities for further economic development.

There are several important centrifugal forces in this country. The African population is divided between the Arabs, located largely in the plains areas, and the Berbers, who inhabit the mountains. Because of the concessions granted to them by the French, some of the Berber chieftains remained loyal to France during times of Arab resistance to French control. Rabat, the Moroccan capital, is a coastal town, and is surpassed in size by Casablanca, Marrakech, and Fès. To the rivalry between these regional centers may eventually be added a major contest for power between the Berber and Arab peoples.

The country's location both on the western Mediteranean and on the Atlantic places it in a strategic military position. Following World War II the United States constructed four large air bases in Morocco. Permission for these bases was, of course, secured from France, and in 1963 the United States ends its use of these bases and returns them to Moroccan control.

Less than 20 per cent of the population can read or write, and France for many years contended that these people were unready to assume the responsibilities of self-rule. Nevertheless, in late 1955 local uprisings in Morocco became so intense that the French were forced to recall from exile Morocco's former sultan (deposed by the French for being too nationalistic) and to consent to an ending of Morocco's protectorate status.

The repercussions of independence for French Morocco affected the other dependent areas of North Africa as well. The French protectorate over Tunisia was also ended, as was Spain's protectorate in northwestern Morocco. Ceuta, Spain's naval station on the African side of the Strait of Gibraltar, was not included in the transfer of sovereignty to the Rabat government, nor were the port of Melilla east of Ceuta, Villa Sanjurjo, and the Chafarinas Isles, a group of three small islands in the Mediterranean near Melilla. Spain also continues to control the enclave of Ifni on Morocco's southwest coast, as well as Spanish Sahara to the south of Morocco (see page 406).[9]

---

[9] In July, 1963, Morocco announced it had annexed all of the enclave of Ifni, except for the city of Ifni itself, which was remaining under Spanish control.

Since independence the Moroccan government has made numerous claims to control of the various Spanish territories along its borders. On the basis of historic rights it also has claimed the westernmost portion of the Algerian Sahara, the newly independent (formerly French) State of Mauritania lying south of Spanish Sahara, and the northwestern portion of the Republic of Mali, also a former French territory. These claims represent an explosively divisive force in northwestern Africa.

The Persian Gulf Oil Area

To the west and north of the Persian Gulf is located one of the major oil-producing areas of the world, consisting of southwestern Iran, Iraq, and the eastern part of the Arabian Peninsula.

The first discovery of oil in this area was made by a British company in 1908 in western Iran. By 1914 this region had become an important oil producer, and a pipeline had been constructed between the oil wells and Abadan, where a refinery had been built and from which overseas shipments could be made. By this time the search for oil had also begun to the west of Iran in what is now northern Iraq. Between 1918 and 1939 oil production in the Persian Gulf area expanded rapidly. In both Iran

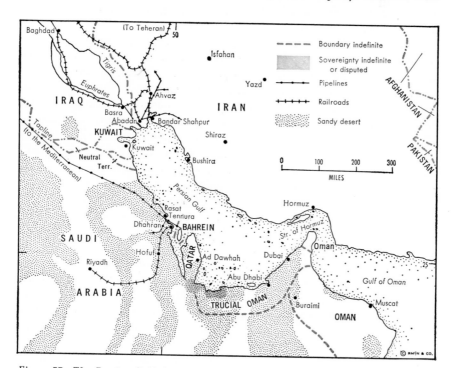

Figure 77. The Persian Gulf Area.

and Iraq revenue from the oil companies came to play a major role in national finances. During the 1930's oil exploration was undertaken along the Persian Gulf coast of the Arabian Peninsula, while to the north the Iraqi fields were connected by pipeline with the Mediterranean coast in order to facilitate their exploitation. During World War II oil production in the Persian Gulf area was an important asset to Allied military operations, particularly in the Middle East.

Hundreds of millions of dollars have been poured into the oil-rich Arab States, and from the expanded impact of Western culture upon these countries a whole new set of sociological and political problems has emerged. The contrasts between the rich and the poor have been accentuated as a result of the oil revenues, many Arabs have received educations in Western nations, and in countries such as Kuwait much of the new wealth has been directed toward improvements in health, education, and other social services. Several of the Arab States are now in a position to purchase sizable quantities of military equipment from foreign powers.

With the increased oil activities Arab leaders have demanded a greater share in the wealth from oil operations. In 1951 the Anglo-Iranian Oil Company was nationalized, and in other oil-producing States Arab officials have frequently pressed foreign oil companies for higher production quotas and increased profits, which, if not forthcoming, might result in further nationalization movements.

By the end of 1960 the Middle East accounted for approximately 25 per cent of the world oil production (see Table 12 for production by countries). Much of the oil is sent in crude form to refineries in other parts of the world, although the bulk of Iran's production is refined at Abadan, and there are smaller refineries near Dammam in Saudi Arabia and on Bahrein Island. To facilitate transportation the Trans-Arabian Pipeline (Tapline), over 1,000 miles in length, was constructed across northern Saudi Arabia, linking the American-controlled fields on the Persian Gulf with the Lebanese port of Saida (Sidon) on the Mediterranean.

The oil companies controlling production in the Persian Gulf area are European and American. Although the British have abandoned their protectorate over Kuwait, their influence remains strong in Bahrein and the southeastern Arabian Peninsula. The United States has close relations with Saudi Arabia, primarily as a result of American investments in the oil company in that State. For a number of years following World War II the United States maintained an air base at Dhahran on the Persian Gulf, but in 1962 it was closed to the use of all military traffic.

Because of its great oil wealth Saudi Arabia has come to occupy a significant position in international politics in this part of the world. In contrast with the poverty existing in most of the Arab countries, the Saudi Arabian government receives several hundred million dollars annually in

Table 12

WORLD CRUDE OIL PRODUCTION, 1962

Continent and Country	Annual Production (in 1,000 metric tons)	Year's Production as per cent of World Total
North America	409,200	*33.83*
Canada	34,000	2.8
Cuba	18	*
Mexico	16,180	1.3
United States	359,000	29.7
South America	203,530	*16.83*
Argentina	13,500	1.1
Bolivia	390	*
Brazil	4,320	0.4
Chile	1,480	0.1
Colombia	7,200	0.6
Ecuador	330	*
Peru	2,900	0.2
Trinidad	6,900	0.6
Venezuela	166,500	13.8
Europe	31,844	*2.65*
Albania	724	*
Austria	2,470	0.2
Bulgaria	200	*
Czechoslovakia	170	*
France	2,400	0.2
Germany, West	6,790	0.6
Great Britain	110	*
Hungary	1,600	0.1
Italy	1,780	0.1
Netherlands	2,150	0.2
Poland	200	*
Romania	11,600	0.9
Yugoslavia	1,650	0.1
Soviet Union	186,000	*15.38*
Africa	39,155	*3.25*
Algeria	20,400	1.7
Angola	500	*
Egypt	4,625	0.4
Gabon	950	*
Morocco	130	*
Nigeria	3,300	0.3
Asia, Total	339,361	*28.06*
Asia, Middle East	305,541	*25.26*
Bahrein	2,250	0.2
Iran	65,000	5.4
Iraq	48,021	4.0
Israel	130	*
Kuwait	93,000	7.7
Neutral Zone	12,000	1.0
Qatar	5,800	0.7
Saudi Arabia	75,000	6.2
Turkey	540	*

Table 12—(Continued)
WORLD CRUDE OIL PRODUCTION, 1962

Continent and Country	Annual Production (in 1,000 metric tons)	Year's Production as per cent of World Total
Asia, Far East	33,820	*2.80*
Burma	580	*
India	980	*
Pakistan	470	*
China	4,500	0.4
Indonesia	22,400	1.8
Japan	750	*
New Guinea	140	*
Sarawak-Brunei	3,800	0.3
TOTAL WORLD	1,210,550	100.0

°Less than 1 per cent.
Source: *The Statesman's Yearbook, 1962–63*, ed. S. H. Steinberg, by permission of St. Martin's Press, Inc., and Macmillan & Co., Ltd.

oil royalties, only a small percentage of which is spent on public improvements and on domestic health and education projects. The government has generally followed the Egyptians in neutralist policies toward the Cold War, in attempts to reduce British influence in this part of the world, in rivalry toward Iraq, and, of course, in hostility to Israel. Thus, on the one hand, Saudi Arabia derives great wealth from United States–managed oil operations, while on the other it pursues a course of action which is often inimical to the interests of the United States and of Britain.

The development of oil resources on the Arabian Peninsula has resulted in a boundary controversy between Saudi Arabia and two small states along the Persian Gulf. These states are Abu Dhabi, one of the Trucial States, and Muscat (Oman), an independent sultanate. The dispute involves the location of Saudi Arabia's boundaries with respect to the Buraimi Oasis, an area containing valuable oil reserves. If the oasis is located within the territory of Saudi Arabia, the Arabian-American Oil Company will develop the oil; if it is not, the Iraq Petroleum Company, in which the British are strongly represented, will carry out the exploitation. Boundaries in this area have never been clearly delimited. One of the interesting aspects of the dispute was the British complaint that the Saudi Arabians have been spending enormous sums of money bribing local chieftains in this area to switch their allegiance from the ruler of Abu Dhabi and the sultan of Muscat to the king of Saudi Arabia. British-led troops from the Trucial Oman states have been in occupation in the oasis for several years to prevent its absorption by Saudi Arabia, although as yet no oil reserves have been developed in the area.

The changing nature of oil politics in the Persian Gulf area was illustrated in 1961 by the discovery of what may turn out to be an extremely valuable oil field at Murban in the sheikdom of Abu Dhabi. Exploratory work was carried out by the Iraq Petroleum Company; if estimates of the oil reserves prove correct, the new field may reduce Britain's dependence both on Iraq (where the government has repeatedly threatened to nationalize foreign oil holdings) and on Kuwait, which may in time become the victim of Iraqui irridentism. About half the field is in territory which is claimed by Saudi Arabia. The potential there and in the offshore field being developed in the Persian Gulf near Das Island will greatly enhance Abu Dhabi's importance to the British.

The unusual political pattern along the western shore of the Persian Gulf is subject to disturbances not only from Saudi Arabia to the west but also from countries to the north and east. Iran has laid claim to the oil-rich Bahrein Island, since it was ruled by the Iranians until late in the eighteenth century. Iraq in 1961 claimed Kuwait on the basis of historic control of that area, a move opposed strongly by the British. Later the Iraqui government made vague assertions of sovereignty over areas along the western shore of the Persian Gulf to the south of Kuwait. In these areas the British advise the ruling sheiks and assist them in the maintenance of their defense forces. In the Trucial Oman States, where some 90,000 Arabs are controlled by seven sheiks, there is a British-officered army, known as the "Trucial Oman Scouts"—a highly mobile force which keeps the peace among warring sheiks, and, as in the case of the Buraimi dispute, protects the area against outsiders. But here, in this strategic and (in some parts) oil-rich area, where the British maintain a light control over the local sheiks, and they in turn wield absolute control over their subjects, the winds of change are also bound to come, whether through popular unrest or expansion into the region by neighboring States.

In August, 1962, an agreement was reached in London on the merger of the British colony of Aden (area, 75 square miles) with the Federation of South Arabia, the western portion of the Aden Protectorate, which stretches along the coast from Aden to the borders of Muscat and Oman. Within the total protectorate are 23 sheikdoms, sultanates, and emirates, all of which are under some degree of British control or influence. Ten of these are included in the Federation of South Arabia, which is being more closely organized politically both as a move against Yemeni irridentism and as a step toward what may in time become independent statehood. The eastern Aden Protectorate, which includes the Hadhramaut—a 300-mile-long canyon in which are a string of ancient oases—is very loosely organized, and the boundaries between this area and Saudi Arabia have never been determined. In time various units of the eastern protectorate may elect to join the Federation of South Arabia.

CHANGING POWER PATTERNS IN THE ARAB WORLD

Since the end of World War II the decline of British and French power in the Arab World has been accompanied by the rise of Arab nationalism, the creation of Israel, the growth of United States influence in the area, and the incipient pressures of the Soviet Union. With Algeria's independence French influence has virtually ended except for military bases in Tunisia, French economic cultural ties in its former North African territories, and France's share in the oil and natural gas of the Algerian Sahara. Britain retains a hold along the eastern and southern borders of the Arabian Peninsula as well as some indirect influence in Libya.

Arab nationalism has been expressed not only in the achievement of independence but also in the adoption of "neutralist" policies on the part of most of the Arab States. In both Egypt and Iraq pro-Western rulers were overthrown by revolution. Jordan, Syria, and Morocco have terminated agreements with Western states for the maintenance of military bases on their soil, and Tunisia has in effect done likewise, although the French continue by force to utilize the Bizerte base. The Arab States still maintain an economic blockade on Israel and have at times harassed the Israelis from across the border.

Yet the growth of Arab nationalism has also led to diversities within the Arab World. Egypt, with the largest population of any of the Arab States, has attempted to become a dominant force, through the United Arab Republic[10] and through maneuverings for leadership of the "neutralist" policies of the Arab World. In this latter task Egypt has been challenged, first, by Iraq, which since 1958 has also sought a position of power, and, second, by Morocco. While Iraq looks south to the oil areas of the Persian Gulf, Egypt has sought to expand its influence southward through Sudan and northern Eritrea, and Morocco has been pressing its territorial claims southward at the expense of Spanish and former French territories.

Soviet influence in the Arab World has been more indirect than direct, that is, it has sought more to weaken Western ties there than actively to expand Soviet power. In most of the Arab States there are local Communist parties; at times these have achieved temporary positions of importance, as in Iraq, Egypt, and Syria. The Soviets have built a new port, Hodeida, for Yemen, and have given military aid to the Yemeni as well. The British in Aden have cause for concern over the prospects of an armed Yemen, since that country has a long-standing border dispute with the British over the northern limits of the Aden Protectorate.

---

[10] The United Arab Republic, consisting of Egypt and Syria, included for a time the Kingdom of Yemen on the southeastern shore of the Red Sea as well. During this time the republic was officially designated as "The United Arab States." Yemen, a mountainous country ruled by one of the world's last absolute monarchs, continued to maintain its internal status but cooperated with the UAR in defense and foreign policy. This artificial union was dissolved some months before the final break-up of the United Arab Republic. By the spring of 1963 there were efforts to re-establish the United Arab Republic, linking Egypt with Syria and Iraq.

United States policy toward the Arab World has been complicated by several factors, among them American support for Israel, the difficulties of choosing which groups to support in the various controversies between Arab countries and America's west European allies, and the problems of erecting an anti-Soviet military alliance (CENTO) of the countries between Europe and India which are close to the Soviet borders. Such an alliance has at times included Turkey (also a NATO power), Iraq, Iran, and Pakistan. The 1958 revolution in Iraq, with its anti-Western consequences, destroyed an important link in this defense system, and there is reason to doubt the efficacy of Iran in any military "containment" scheme. Finally the loss to Britain of its bases in Jordan and to the United States of its military rights in Saudi Arabia serve further to weaken the West's military position there.

IRAN

Iran lies beyond the limits of the Arab World as defined here, but it is considered in this chapter because of its role in the oil developments and because of its geographic location.

Forces of Unity and Diversity

Iran consists of a vast plateau, divided by numerous highland areas into a series of cultivable tracts, and a few coastal lowlands. The terrain offers no central unifying area for the State; rather there are several core areas. Most of Iran is desert or semidesert, and communications between the capital, Tehran, and other population centers are poor. The movement of people and of ideas thoughout much of the country is not well developed, and Tehran's control is weak in many provincial areas.

From a cultural point of view there is remarkable unity throughout Iran on the basis of tradition and religion. It is this cultural unity, more than any other factor, which has preserved Iran as a cohesive political unit. Unlike the inhabitants of most other Moslem States, the Iranians belong largely to the Shiite sect. Major minority groups among the total population of over 20 million include some 2 million Azerbaijanis and 800,000 Kurds in the northwestern part of the State, as well as over 500,-000 other persons belonging to various tribes throughout Iran whose languages differ from that of the majority of Iranians. Tribal leaders still exercise considerable control over their people, and only recently has Tehran's authority become strongly felt in these non-Iranian-speaking areas.

Foreign Control in Iran

At the beginning of the twentieth century Iran, then known as Persia, was a weak but independent State. The principal external pressures exerted on it at this time were from Great Britain and Russia, the former moving northward from the Arabian Sea–Persian Gulf area, and the latter pressing south from the Caspian Sea region and its long border with Iran. British military power was also stationed in India, along Iran's eastern border. In 1907 the British and Russian governments agreed to establish zones of influence in Iran, thus developing the country as a buffer between the power spheres of the two States. Although the foreign spheres of influence in Iran were abandoned after World War I, a Soviet-Iranian agreement was concluded in 1921 whereby Russia was permitted to send armed reinforcements to Iran in case that country should be invaded by a third power and used as a base for aggression against the Soviet Union.

During World War II Soviet forces occupied northern Iran to protect military supply lines running north to the U.S.S.R. from the Persian Gulf. By agreement with the Iranian government foreign occupation troops were to leave the country within six months of the end of World War II, but in the spring of 1946 Russian forces were still in Azerbaijan Province in northwestern Iran. Inhabited largely by Turkic-speaking peoples, Azerbaijan (area 41,000 square miles; population 2¾ million) is one of the best-watered parts of Iran and thus an important agricultural area. Past relations between Azerbaijan and Tehran have not always been friendly, and the Soviets, during their period of occupation, sought to establish an autonomous people's republic in the area with close ties to the U.S.S.R., where there is also an Azerbaijani population. In the face of strong pressure from the United Nations, the Soviets finally withdrew their forces from Iranian Azerbaijan in May, 1946, and the movement for a people's republic there quietly collapsed.

The Kurds

The Russians also fostered an independence movement among the Kurds, a cultural group of about 2½ million people spread out over five States—Iran, Iraq, Syria, Turkey, and the U.S.S.R. The Kurds, united by the common use of the Kurdish language, are primarily nomadic tribesmen, living in the mountain masses southeast of the Black Sea and adjoining areas to the south. Because of their relative isolation and their military traditions, they have managed to retain considerable independence of action in their rugged homeland, regardless of the power or powers nominally controlling the territory in which they live. A delegation allegedly representing the Kurds appeared before the Versailles Conference in 1919 and the San Francisco Conference in 1945, seeking an independent Kurdish State to be created from parts of Turkish, Syrian, Iraqi, and Iranian territory. The political demands of the Kurds appealed to the Soviets after the occupation of Azerbaijan in 1941, and the Russians assisted the Kurdish nationalists, hoping thereby to weaken Iran, Iraq, and Turkey in the areas close to the Soviet frontier.

The Oil Crisis in Iran

Iranian nationalism, which reached a climax in the 1951 nationalization of the Anglo-Iranian Oil Company, eventually resulted in widespread economic and political difficulties for the country. In response to what they termed the illegal seizure of the company, the British established a worldwide boycott of Iranian oil. Since profits from the sale of oil normally represented about 40 per cent of Iran's national revenue, the boycott created enormous financial hardships for the State. Because of internal political and economic problems the Iranian Communist (Tudeh) party became the strongest political group in the country.

By 1953 strikes and riots were a frequent occurrence, and the State appeared to be in danger of a Communist-inspired revolution. Yet if a major Communist uprising took place, British and American forces could not intervene (even at the invitation of the Iranian government) without risking Soviet armed intervention by right of the 1921 Soviet-Iranian agreement. In August, 1953, an army-led revolt resulted in the establishment of a pro-Western government in Tehran, and gradually the danger of a Communist revolt subsided. An arrangement was worked out to compensate the British for their loss of investments in the Anglo-Iranian Oil Company, the boycott was lifted, and eventually Iran concluded military agreements with Britain and the United States. A consortium was formed to handle Iranian oil production and international sale. Iran, however, still faces internal problems, which have been brought on by the extreme poverty of most of its people, the presence of a strong landholding class which opposes major land-reform programs, and the existence of a strong, though illegal, Communist party, ready to capitalize on popular discontent at the earliest opportunity. Because of the country's location and resources, its political future is a matter of great concern to all the major world powers.

BIBLIOGRAPHY

ALEXANDER, LEWIS M. "The Arab-Israeli Boundary Problem," *World Politics*, VI (1954), 322–38.

Historical and geographical background of the conflict along Israel's borders.

"The Break-up of the United Arab Republic," *The World Today,* XVII (1961), 471–79.

An interesting summary of the centrifugal forces which eventually led to the republic's dissolution.

CLARKE, JOHN I. "Economic and Political Changes in the Sahara," *Geography,* XLVI (1961), 102–20.

New trends and events in the Sahara.

CRESSEY, GEORGE B. *Crossroads: Land and Life in Southwest Asia.* Philadelphia: J. B. Lippincott Company, 1960.

A good regional geography of the area.

International Boundary Studies, Washington, Department of State, Office of the Geographer:

"Algeria-Libya Boundary," No. 1, April 28, 1961.
"Libya-Niger Boundary," No. 2, May 4, 1961.
"Chad-Libya Boundary," No. 3, May 5, 1961.
"Afghanistan-Iran Boundary," No. 6, June 20, 1961.
"Morocco-Spanish Sahara Boundary, No. 9, September 14, 1961.
"Libya-Sudan Boundary," No. 10, October 16, 1961.
"Chad-Sudan Boundary," No. 15, June 15, 1962.

Detailed maps and descriptions of the boundaries.

KELLY, J. B. "Sovereignty and Jurisdiction in Eastern Arabia," *International Affairs,* XXXIV (1958), 16–25.

A summary of this complicated political area.

MELAMID, ALEXANDER. "The Political Geography of the Gulf of Aqaba," *Annals of the Association of American Geographers,* XLVII (1957), 231–40.

A well-documented discussion of the gulf.

———. "Political Geography of Trucial Oman and Quatar," *The Geographical Review,* XLIII (1953), 194–207.

A comprehensive description; includes a detailed map.

MOUNTJOY, ALAN B. "The Suez Canal at Mid-Century," *Economic Geography,* XXXIV (1958), 155–68.

General summary of the role of the canal.

SOUSTELLE, JACQUES. "The Wealth of the Sahara," *Foreign Affairs,* XXXVII (1959), 626–37.

Like Clarke's article, a valuable appraisal of the Sahara.

WHITTLESEY, DERWENT. "Lands Athwart the Nile," *World Politics,* V (1953), 214–42.

A concise politico-geographic study of the Nile basin.

14

AFRICA—THE WEST AND NORTHEAST

● Between Arab North Africa and the belt of equatorial States lies a broad transition zone measuring nearly 4,500 miles from east to west, and 1,200–1,500 miles north to south. Within this zone are nearly 100 million people, as well as almost half the States which have achieved self-rule since World War II. Colonialism remains now only in a few coastal enclaves and in the extreme northwest in the desert strip of Spanish Sahara. Here is an area which has experienced more rapid political changes in recent years than almost anywhere else on the globe, an area in which the final patterns of political and economic adjustment are obviously not yet completely evolved. Many of the newly independent States would score poorly on the test for political viability; yet because of contemporary power relationships they were permitted to achieve, and (at this writing) to retain, independence in the face of enormous obstacles. In this chapter some of these obstacles to national viability will be examined.

The area to be considered here extends from the southern boundaries of the countries bordering the Mediterranean (Morocco, Algeria, Libya, and Egypt) to the northern borders of the Congo (the former Belgian Congo),[1] Uganda, and Kenya. Such a classification puts Gabon and Congo as parts of west Africa, although by location, climate, and vegetation they are "equatorial" countries. Politically and historically, however, they are more closely associated with the areas to the north and west than they are with the former Belgian Congo. An arbitrary division has been made between

---

[1] To avoid confusion the former Belgian Congo will be referred to as "the Congo," while the neighboring former territory of French Equatorial Africa will be "Congo."

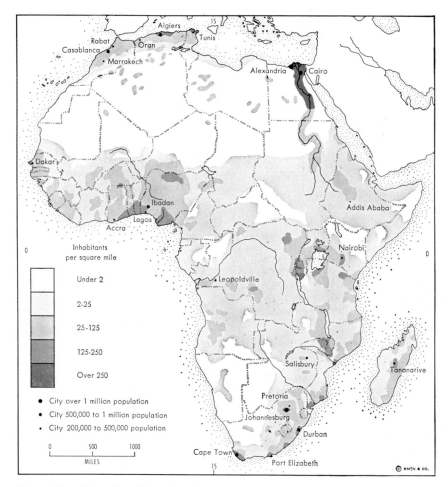

Figure 78. Africa: Population Distribution.

west and northeast Africa, the boundary being Sudan (former Anglo-Egyptian Sudan), which extends southward from Egypt to Uganda and Kenya, separating Chad and the Central African Republic on the west from Ethiopia on the east. Because of its close ties with Egypt Sudan was treated in the chapter on the Arab World, and will thus be omitted from detailed treatment here.

WEST AFRICA

West Africa embraces over 3½ million square miles and has a population of about 75 million, of whom 45 per cent live in the one State of Nigeria. No other west African State, except Ghana, in 1960 had as many

Table 13

POLITICAL UNITS AND PEOPLES IN CENTRAL AFRICA

Unit	Area (sq. mi.)	Population—1960		
		Natives	Whites	Others
Independent States				
Burundi	10,500	2,500,000	2,000	
Central African Republic	238,000	1,192,000	1,000	
The Congo	904,991	13,540,000	3,000 (est.)	
Ethiopia	457,800	18.000,000 (1958 est.)	3,000	
Federation of Nigeria	350,291	35,290,000	7,000	
Gabonese Republic	103,000	420,000	1,000	
Ghana	91,840	6,687,000	4,000	
Islamic Republic of Mauritania	416,100	261,000	500	466,000 Arabs
Liberia	43,000	2,500,000 (1958 est.)	2,000	
Malagasy Republic	227,950	5,110,000	74,000	
Republic of Cameroun	184,000	3,207,000	16,000	
Republic of Chad	496,000	2,571,000	5,000	
Republic of the Congo	132,000	794,000	1,500	
Republic of Dahomey	43,800	2,000,000	3,000	
Republic of Guinea	94.945	2,725,000	2,000	
Republic of Ivory Coast	123,000	3,100,000	15,000	
Republic of Mali	460,500	4,300,000	7,000	
Republic of Niger	494,600	2,800,000	3,000	
Republic of Senegal	80.600	2,590,000	7,000	
Republic of Togo	22,002	1,090,000	1,000	
Republic of Upper Volta	106,000	4,000,000	4,000	
Rwanda	10,400	2,385,000	1,000	
Sierra Leone	27,924	2,500,000 (1960 est.)	2,000	
Somali Republic	266,275	1,870,000	1,000	
Tanganyika	362,274	9,123,000	23,000	87,000 Indians
Uganda	93,981	6,437,000	11,000	72,000 Indians 4,000 Arabs
British Possessions				
Bechuanaland	275,000	293,000	4,000	
Gambia	4,003	326,000	500	
Kenya	224,960	6,269,000	68,000	174,000 Indians 39,000 Arabs
Northern Rhodesia	290,300	2,345,000	75,000	10,000 Indians
Nyasaland	48,442	2,808,000	9,000	11,000 Indians 2,000 Colored
Southern Rhodesia	150,327	2,840,000	215,000	15,000 Indians
Zanzibar (incl. Pemba)	1,020	280,000	500	18,000 Indians
French Possessions				
French Somaliland	8,500	60,000	4,000	3,000 Arabs
Portuguese Possessions				
Angola (and Cabinda)	481,350	4,255,000	120,000	
Mozambique	297,731	6,200,000	70,000	
Portuguese Guinea	13,948	567,000	3,000	
São Tome and Principe	372	59,000	1,000	

Table 13—(Continued)

POLITICAL UNITS AND PEOPLES IN CENTRAL AFRICA

Unit	Area (sq. mi.)	Population—1960		
		Natives	Whites	Others
Spanish Possessions				
Spanish Guinea	10,831	209,000	4,000	
Spanish Sahara	102,703	23,000	1,000	

Source: *The Statesman's Yearbook, 1961–62*, S. H. Steinberg (ed.) (New York and London: St. Martin's and Macmillan), and *Goode's World Atlas*, Edward B. Espenshade, Jr. (ed.) (11th Edition; Chicago: Rand McNally, 1960).

as 5 million inhabitants. Except for a few specific areas there was relatively little economic development of west Africa by the Europeans prior to 1957. In southern Ghana and in parts of Nigeria are the only extensive road or rail facilities; only two railroads in west Africa extended inland to serve landlocked regions, one from Bamako in French Sudan (now Mali) to Dakar, Senegal, and the other from Ouagadougou, Upper Volta, to the port of Abidjan in Ivory Coast. Prior to 1957 the one independent State was Liberia. In March of that year the former British colony of Gold Coast became the self-ruling State of Ghana; since then eighteen other French and British territories in the area have achieved self-rule. Only British Gambia, Portuguese Guinea, and Spanish Guinea remain along with the desert strip of Spanish Sahara as relics of the complex colonial pattern which existed there for nearly three-quarters of a century.

Physical Features

The dominant physical aspect of west Africa is the climate. North of 15° north latitude (in the vicinity of Dakar) the average annual rainfall is less than 20 inches per year. Yet a few hundred miles to the south, in Sierra Leone and Liberia and again in southeastern Nigeria and Cameroun, the annual rainfall is over 80 inches per year. The distribution of rainfall, between the desert and the humid tropics, is shown in Figure 79. This distribution is important both to the pattern of natural vegetation and of economic activities. The equator passes 300 miles south of Liberia, thus temperatures throughout the year are generally high. Along the Guinea coast the annual range of temperature is less than 10°F., but in the drier interior it ranges up to 25°F. The cool Canary Current off the northwest coast of Mauritania and Spanish Sahara tempers the coastal climate and brings frequent fog but no rain. Although there is precipitation every month of the year along the Guinea coast (accompanied by high humidity), in the interior the rainy season is in summer, with winter drought. This seasonality of precipitation not only affects agriculture but also the level of rivers,

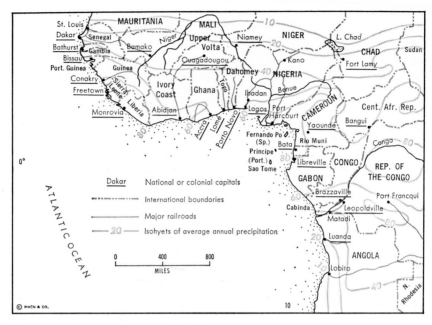

Figure 79. West Africa.

causing severe floodings in parts of the Niger, Senegal, Gambia, and other rivers rising in the interior.

In the southwest from Portuguese Guinea to Ivory Coast is a belt of tropical rain forest which yields valuable timber, including mahogany. The oil palm is also important there; in Liberia, portions of the rain forest have been cleared for rubber plantations. The rain forest reappears in Nigeria, Cameroun, Spanish Guinea, and Gabon. Agriculture in the rain forest is frequently of the "milpa" type; the natives clear the land and farm it for a few years, after which the soil becomes exhausted and they must move on. In this way much of the original rain forest has disappeared to be replaced by second-growth jungle. Inland from the rain forest is the more open forest with many deciduous trees which lose their leaves during the dry season. This in turn gradually gives way to the grassland (savanna), first the tall grasses and then, generally beyond the 20-inch annual rainfall line, the low grasses. Finally this, too, gives way to the true desert shrub or barren areas of the Sahara Desert, occurring in the northern portions of Mauritania, Mali, Niger, and Chad, as well as in Spanish Sahara.

The relief of west Africa is characterized by coastal plains rising to uplands in the interior—stretching from the Guinea Highlands in the west to the Jos Plateau of Nigeria in the east, with elevations generally below 2,000 feet. The Cameroon Mountains, on the coast of the Gulf of Guinea, rise to over 13,000 feet, and to the northeast, along the Cameroun-Nigeria border, are other hills to over 5,000 feet. Most of the area east of Nigeria is part of the Central African Plateau, ranging from 2,000 to 4,000 feet in elevation. Along the entire coast of west Africa there are very few natural harbors. Mangrove swamps, mud flats, sandbanks, and offshore bars make this an inhospitable coast with very few good anchorages. Among the major rivers are the Niger, which rises in the Guinea Highlands and flows through four countries to the sea, the Senegal, the Gambia, the Benue, a tributary to the Niger, and the Volta, the major river of Ghana.

Historical Background

West Africa was for many years an area of penetration by Arabs from Egypt and the North African coast. The Arabs came not only as conquerors and merchants but also as settlers and even now the peoples of the northern areas are largely Arab. The west African Negroes, divided into many tribal groups, were frequently at the mercy of the Arabs. Among the major empires of the pre-European era were the Ghana Empire of the tenth and eleventh centuries and the Mali Empire of the fourteenth century, both based in the semiarid interior near the Niger River. By the middle of the fifteenth century Portuguese seamen had passed south of the Sahara barrier and explored the Guinea coast, and in 1481 the first permanent settlement had been made on the Gold Coast. By the Treaty of Tordesillas (1494) Portugal had been granted title to all newly discovered lands east of 50° west longitude—an area which included all of west Africa. At this early date the States of northwestern Europe had not yet developed their maritime facilities to the point where they were ready to undertake expeditions to the west African coastal region, so that Portugal had a relatively free hand in the early exploration and development of the area. A string of forts was established on the Guinea coast to guard the Portuguese trade in gold, ivory, and slaves, while other settlements were located further south on the west coast (in what is now Angola) and on the east coast (Mozambique and Kenya). Portuguese colonial interests, however, were directed more toward Brazil and the Far East than toward Africa, and little effort was made to halt the gradual expansion in this area of other European States during and after the seventeenth century. In 1618 the British established a fort at Gambia in west Africa, and soon settlements were also developed along the Guinea coast by Holland, France, Denmark, and the German state of Brandenburg-Prussia.

The chief objectives of the European powers in this part of Africa from the mid-seventeenth to mid-nineteenth centuries were (1) to develop the lucrative trade in slaves, gold, and ivory and (2) to safeguard their sea lanes to the Indies. The European development of the African coastal areas continued slowly during the eighteenth and nineteenth centuries, and little effort was made to investigate the interior of the continent, either for commercial exploitation or for the establishment of political control. The lack of major indentations in the coast, of good harbors, and of navigable waterways extending inland into the continent, the obstacles of tropical forests and hostile tribes, the absence of readily available riches, and finally the greater opportunities for wealth in the New World and the Orient combined to discourage European penetration into west Africa until four centuries after the first settlement of the coasts.

Nineteenth-century explorers finally acquainted European governments and businessmen with the wealth of Africa. "When European industrialization had developed a need for raw materials that yearly grew more active, when vacant spaces in the Pacific, the Far East, and southern and western Asia had been allocated, with South America a politically closed world on account of the Monroe Doctrine, Africa was the only large free realm in which political power and colonial trade could yet be won together."[2] Not until 1870 did the political division of west Africa finally get under way, and within thirty years practically the entire area had been partitioned.

There were various motives for the rapid movement to acquire territories in the late nineteenth century. Among these were commercial exploitation, desire for national prestige, attempts to suppress the illegal slave trade, missionary activities, and jealousy over the expansion of territorial control by rival powers. The race for territorial expansion was at first a rather haphazard affair, with numerous and conflicting claims, but at the Berlin Conference of 1884–85 the European powers agreed to regularize their imperialism in order to avoid serious clashes. The treaty which was drafted at the conference made no mention (other than to denounce slavery) of the rights of the Africans themselves, but it drew up a code of ethics for territorial expansion by providing that no State was to establish a new claim in Africa without first notifying the other powers, that recognition of territorial claims must depend on effective occupation, and that all disputes were to be settled by arbitration.

The territorial scramble in west Africa during the late nineteenth century involved France, Germany, Italy, Belgium, Portugal, and Britain. Spain, the seventh colonial power in Africa, merely retained the small possessions it had acquired in the early years of overseas explorations in the Gulf of Guinea area and to the north along the Atlantic coast. France, having suffered defeat at the hands of the Germans during the Franco-Prussian War (1870–71), wished to regain its national prestige, and from

---

[2] Isaiah Bowman, *The New World* (New York: World Book Company, 1928), p. 637. Used by permission of R. G. Bowman.

their bases along the Atlantic and Guinea coasts the French pressed inland to acquire control over what became French West Africa and French Equatorial Africa. France also established a base on the lower Red Sea coast as a nucleus for what later became French Somaliland.

The German states were unified in 1871, but until the mid-1880's the German government had little interest in acquiring colonies in Africa because of the difficulties and expense involved and the general lack of knowledge about the area's potentialities. After the Berlin Conference, however, the Germans began moving rapidly to secure their country's "place in the sun." Treaties were signed with native rulers along the Guinea coast, in southwest Africa, and in the eastern sector of the continent, which placed these areas under German protection and set up commercial establishments to develop Africa's resources.

Portugal also partook of the new imperialist spirit in the closing years of the nineteenth century. In Portuguese Guinea on the northwest African coast and on the islands of São Tome and Principe in the Gulf of Guinea Portugal strengthened its colonial holdings. The British, after 1870, expanded their power in the Gold Coast and Nigeria in the face of opposing claims by Germany and France, as well as retaining their coastal holdings of Gambia and Sierra Leone, dating back to the seventeenth century. Only Liberia remained free of European control. Established as a home for freed American slaves early in the nineteenth century, it became a republic in 1847 and was subsequently recognized by several European States. American interests in the area undoubtedly contributed to the reluctance of the European powers to annex the country.

By the beginning of the twentieth century the political map of west Africa had been completed. France controlled two enormous areas—French West Africa and French Congo (later French Equatorial Africa)—which were subdivided into territories, later to become independent countries. The boundaries of these territories were frequently superimposed on existing tribal patterns. Germany controlled Togoland on the Guinea coast and the Cameroons east of Nigeria. Portugal, Spain, and Britain also had unconnected coastal holdings, in addition to which the British controlled Nigeria, by far the most populous area of west Africa. Following World War I Germany's two territories were divided between Britain and France.

The drive for independence began in 1957 with the establishment of Ghana under the leadership of its president, Dr. Kwame Nkrumah. In the following year the peoples of France's Overseas Territories were given the choice of either (1) separating completely from the French Community, (2) remaining as Overseas Territories, (3) becoming Overseas Departments (and thus more closely integrated with France), or (4) becoming autonomous states in the French Community. Of the twelve territories in French West and French Equatorial Africa, eleven chose to become autonomous

States; French Guinea alone opted to separate from the Community, and in September of that year Guinea became an independent State.

In the months following Guinea's withdrawal from the French Community, pressure mounted on the Paris government to permit other Overseas Territories to achieve self-rule but also to remain within the Community. Eventually the French constitution was amended, permitting an autonomous State of the Community to become independent within the Community, providing a resolution to that effect has been adopted by the State's legislative assembly and confirmed by a popular referendum. During 1960 the remaining eleven territories of French West and French Equatorial Africa became independent. The former French Sudan had joined with Senegal in January, 1959, to form the Federation of Mali—a union which lasted until August, 1960, when they became separate independent States.

The political futures of Togoland and the Cameroons were a problem for the United Nations Trusteeship Council. In 1956 the people of British Togoland had voted to join the soon-to-be-constituted State of Ghana—a union which was carried out in March, 1957, at the time of Ghana's achievement of independence. French Togoland became the independent Republic of Togo in 1960. The French Cameroons became the independent Republic of Cameroun on January 1, 1960, in accordance with the wishes of its people. In February of the following year a plebiscite was sponsored by the United Nations in both the northern and southern portions of the British Cameroons to decide their political future. A majority of the voters of the southern Cameroons opted in favor of union with the former French Cameroon (in part because of their fear of domination by the Ibo peoples of neighboring Nigeria), while the vote in the northern portion was for integration into Nigeria.

Britain in 1961 granted independence to Nigeria and in the same year to Sierra Leone, leaving only Gambia among the former British colonies in West Africa. France's colonies there are now gone. The territories of Spain and Portugal, however, remain politically unchanged, except for the cession by Spain of the protectorate of Southern Morocco to the State of Morocco in April, 1958.[3] Here then, as in Latin America, are a series of predominantly small, weak, independent States, but (unlike the case in Latin America) States which do not enjoy the physical and political isolation which Latin America did during most of the nineteenth and early twentieth centuries.

---

[3] The protectorate of Southern Morocco separated Morocco itself from Spanish Sahara. In January, 1958, the Spanish government changed the status of Spanish West Africa (which included Spanish Sahara, the enclave of Ifni to the north, and the protectorate of Southern Morocco) so that both Ifni and Spanish Sahara became African provinces, administered directly by Madrid—as are the two provinces comprising the Canary Islands off the coast of Spanish Sahara. Southern Morocco was then ceded to its northern neighbor.

Economic Structure

The economy of most of west Africa is based on agriculture—both subsistence agriculture and grazing, as well as commercial agriculture for export. Largely because of its climate west Africa has never attracted large-scale European settlement for farming; thus the problem of "white reserves" and of large European communities is not present there. Efforts have been made to train native farmers in order to check soil erosion and soil exhaustion, as well as to halt the burning of large areas and the overstocking of grazing grounds. So far as commercial crops are concerned, west Africa is important for peanuts, rubber, cacao, coffee, bananas, cotton, and palm oil, as well as timber, particularly in Gabon and Sierra Leone. Hance, Kotschar, and Peterec, in their description of export production in Africa,[4] noted the existence of productive "islands" in vast seas of emptiness. Among these are:

1. The peanut area of Senegal and Gambia.
2. The banana and mineral area of the Iles de Los and the rail belt in the Republic of Guinea.
3. The Firestone rubber plantations in Liberia.
4. The coffee, cacao, banana, and forest-product areas of the Ivory Coast.
5. The cacao and timber area of Ghana, one of the richest mineral zones of Africa and the leading cacao-producing area of the world.
6. The cacao and timber areas of the Western Region of Nigeria and the palm-products area of the "Oil Rivers" district of the Eastern Region.
7. The timber area of Gabon.
8. The islands of the Gulf of Guinea (cacao and coffee).[5]

They also noted other islands, such as the peanut and cotton regions of northern Nigeria and the cotton belt of the Central African Republic and Chad, then cited the following mineral islands:

1. The bauxite and iron-ore area of Guinea.
2. The Bomi Hills of Liberia—iron ore.
3. Southwestern Ghana, where west Africa's major mineral production is centered within a remarkably small radius. Manganese, gold, diamonds, and bauxite are produced.
4. The iron-ore and diamond areas of Sierra Leone.
5. The Nigerian Jos Plateau tin-columbium area.[6]

---

[4] W. A. Hance, V. Kotschar, and R. J. Peterec, "Source Areas of Export Production in Tropical Africa," *The Geographical Review*, LI (1961), 487–500. Note particularly the map of sources of export production.
[5] *Ibid.*, pp. 495–96.
[6] *Ibid.*, pp. 498–99.

In addition to these are the rich manganese reserves now being developed in Gabon, the iron ore deposits of Mauritania, as well as such other resources as copper (Mauritania), manganese (Mali), and oil (Gabon). Much of west Africa has received only superficial attention from geologists, and the area may in time become one of the world's important sources for minerals and power fuels.

The lack of economic development throughout a majority of west Africa is evidenced by the shortage of roads, railroads, port facilities, power plants, and manufacturing establishments. Only southern Ghana, western Senegal, and parts of Nigeria can be said to have anything approaching an adequate transportation network to serve their economic needs. Each of the coastal States has a major port (frequently the capital and largest city); Nigeria has two ports, Lagos and Port Harcourt, while Ghana has Accra and Tokoradi. Since economic penetration of these coastal States took place largely from the sea, it is not surprising that much of their economic development and population concentration are located close to the water. In Cameroun, however, the capital, Yaoundé, is situated about 200 miles inland from the hot, humid coast, in an upland region of cacao production, while Nigeria's Northern Region is a center for cotton and peanuts. Many of the coastal states extend inland to what Harrison Church described as "The Poor Intermediate or Middle Belt of West Africa." Concerning this, he wrote:

> . . . it is estimated that several million, perhaps twelve million, Africans were taken out of Africa in the course of a thousand years of Arab slave-dealing and of five hundred years by Europeans and Americans. Vast areas were depopulated, by actual removal of people, by peoples fleeing from slave raiders, and as a result of slave raiding which left the populations too small to reduce the vegetation harbouring tsetse flies and mosquitoes.
>
> For this and other reasons, vast areas of low population density are among the outstanding features of modern Africa. The interior of West Africa suffered from the Arab and European slave trades. One of its major modern problems is the Intermediate or Middle Belt between the rain forests and the savannah. On a population map it is startlingly clear. Not only are people few, but the soils and the vegetation degraded. The belt has all the liabilities of the rain forests and savannah (*e.g.,* their diseases), but none of their assets. From the Ivory Coast to Nigeria, this is a vast negative zone which, for example, the railways cross without finding any significant traffic.[7]

[7] R. J. Harrison Church, "The Impact of the Outer World on Africa," in East and Moodie (eds.), *The Changing World*, pp. 733–34.

Five States have no seacoast. These are Mali, Niger, Chad, Upper Volta, and the Central African Republic. Both Mali and Upper Volta are connected by rail with seaports, while the Central African Republic borders on the navigable Ubangi River, a tributary to the Congo. Niger and Chad must send their products to the rail system of Nigeria and via this to Lagos or Port Harcourt.

The Countries of the Arid North

This first subdivision of west Africa is taken to include six states— Mauritania, Mali, Niger, Chad, Senegal, and Upper Volta—as well as two colonial territories, Spanish Sahara and Gambia.

Mauritania. The Islamic Republic of Mauritania has an area of 419,-000 square miles and a population of about 700,000, divided between nomadic Moors in the northern and central areas and Negro farmers in the south along the Senegal River. The country is almost completely undeveloped with no paved roads, no newspapers, two secondary schools, and one small fishing port. Before 1957 the capital was at St. Louis, across the border in Senegal; in that year it was moved to Nouakchott, a desert town a few miles inland from the Atlantic coast. Mauritania is completely arid or semiarid. Off its coasts are rich fishing grounds, and in the north central area, near Fort Gouraud, rich iron ore reserves have been discovered. A railroad is being constructed between this area and Port Etienne on the border of Spanish Sahara in order to develop the iron ore, which the government hopes will provide much-needed capital for the country.

Mauritania is claimed by Morocco on the grounds that it was a historic part of Morocco and was administered by the French as a part of the protectorate of Morocco until as late as 1920. In the southeast the Hodh region, Mauritania's richest livestock area, was transferred from what is now Mali in 1946 and may form the basis for another territorial claim against the country.

Mali. East of Mauritania is the landlocked state of Mali, whose capital, Bamako, on the upper Niger River, is linked by rail with Dakar. The north is desert, the south largely savanna. The upper Niger is being utilized for irrigation, although Mali's chief export crop, peanuts, is concentrated in the northwest along the upper Senegal. With over 4 million people and few agricultural or mineral resources, Mali has actively sought political union with other States. Its federation with Senegal failed because of strong centrifugal forces, among them the fact that Senegal is richer and more pro-French in outlook than its eastern neighbor. After the break-up of the federation rail traffic ceased across the Mali-Senegal border. Since 1960 the Bamako government has sought closer ties with Guinea (which it borders) and Ghana (separated from it by Upper Volta). In 1962 Soviet engineers began surveying for a railroad to link Bamako with Guinea's rail system at the town of Kouroussa.

Niger and Chad. Lying east of Mali are two large States, predominantly arid or semiarid, each with populations of over 2 million concentrated largely in the south. Niger's capital, Niamey, is in the extreme southwest, on the Niger River. The principal export crop is peanuts, grown in the vicinity of the southern border with Nigeria. The country has reserves of iron ore, manganese, copper, and possibly uranium—all of them undeveloped due in part to lack of transport facilities. Here, as in Mauritania, Mali, and Chad, most of the international boundaries pass through empty desert or semidesert territory. Fort Lamy, Chad's capital, lies close to the northern extension of Cameroun to Lake Chad. Actually, Chad's territory extends south of the 20-inch rainfall line to an area where cotton is an important crop for export. Like Niger, Mali, and Mauritania, it has large areas which are practically uninhabited.

Senegal and Gambia. Senegal, bordering the Atlantic, is the most developed of the countries of the arid north. Its capital, Dakar, is a "Westernized" city with an excellent harbor and with an airport which is important to trans-Atlantic travel to South America. Senegal's chief export is peanuts. The State surrounds on three sides the British territory of Gambia, consisting of the colony (Bathurst and its suburbs) and the protectorate, where local tribes are left largely untouched. The British, having established the port of Bathurst, promised the chiefs inland along the Gambia River protection within 10 miles of the river. The result was a territory varying from 7 to 25 miles in width and extending inland for about 300 miles. There, as in other States of the arid north, peanuts are the principal export product. The colony has little economic viability, and there has been little progress toward independence. But although Gambia's most logical future would seem to be some form of union with Senegal, Britain in 1963 announced that Gambia's 300,000 people would achieve self-rule early in 1964.

Upper Volta. This country consists of a semiarid plateau, the rain coming only for a short time during the summer. With a population of some $3\frac{1}{2}$ million, Upper Volta has few resources except cattle, peanuts, and cotton. Its capital, Ouagadougou, is linked by rail with the Ivory Coast port of Abidjan, 500 miles away, but the largely grassland country has little economic or political *raison d'être*. Flanked by six states—Mali, Ivory Coast, Ghana, Togo, Dahomey, and Niger—it appears likely to be linked in time with one or more of its neighbors in some form of political union.

Spanish Sahara. This is a largely barren territory which includes the colonies of Saguia el Hamra and Rio de Oro. It is administered from the Canary Islands and has a small (mostly Arab) population. Villa Cisneros, the only port, is noted as a fishing harbor. Spanish Sahara is claimed by

Morocco; if, in time, valuable mineral wealth is discovered there (as was done just across the border in Mauritania), the area may become a source of considerable friction between Morocco and Spain.

The Humid Western Coast

Starting with Portuguese Guinea, this area includes the States of Guinea, Sierra Leone, Liberia, Ivory Coast, Ghana, Togo, and Dahomey.

Portuguese Guinea. With 14,000 square miles and 580,000 people, this is an area of coastal swamps, rain forest, and deciduous woodland, which has been developed for rice, peanuts, and palm oil. Unlike Angola and Mozambique, Portuguese Guinea has attracted few Europeans for settlement, but there has been no move there yet for eventual independence. Indeed, as a separate political entity Portuguese Guinea would have a difficult time achieving economic viability. Should Portuguese control end there, this coastal enclave might conceivably join Guinea which adjoins it on two sides.

The Republic of Guinea. Guinea is the only French territory in west Africa to leave the French Community. In the humid coastal region palm oil, rice, bananas, and coffee are produced, while further inland in the savanna uplands are peanuts and cattle. Iron ore, mined along the coast near Conakry, Guinea's capital, is an important export as is also bauxite from the offshore Los Islands. Significant iron ore deposits exist in the extreme southeast and may in time be exported through Liberia, while bauxite occurs (but is undeveloped) in the Fouta Djalon in north Guinea.

With its various resources and its population of over 2½ million Guinea has considerable potential for development. At the time of its independence the country sought aid first from France and other Western powers and then from the Soviet Union. Communist equipment and technicians began arriving in large numbers in Guinea, and its president, Sekou Touré, adopted what was considered to be a generally anti-Western foreign policy. By 1960 there were rumors of a possible agreement to give the Soviets a submarine base and radio installations in the country which would threaten the Western military position in the Atlantic. Guinea has never become Communist-oriented, however. The Soviet foreign aid program has not been functioning well, and in December, 1961, the Soviet ambassador to Guinea was expelled from the country because of his alleged espionage activities. In November, 1958, Guinea and Ghana proclaimed a union of the two countries, and in April, 1961, Mali joined them in the "Union of African States," a political entity whose details have as yet to be worked out.

Sierra Leone. South of Guinea is Sierra Leone, a former British territory, which was founded in 1787 as a home for freed slaves from Britain. The population of 2½ million consists of native tribes and of "Colony Africans," the descendants of the liberated slaves, who have remained largely about Freetown, the capital and leading port located on the best natural harbor in west Africa. Both iron ore and diamonds are exported from Sierra Leone, as well as palm oil and some coffee, but agriculture for export needs greater development. Freetown, with its excellent harbor, is an important port of call and is in a sense more "Westernized" than some of the other port cities of west Africa. Sierra Leone, surrounded as it is by countries which were not under British control, is, like adjoining Liberia, in a sense "isolated" and has not been strongly involved in most of the recent unification moves in west Africa.

Liberia. The independent Republic of Liberia, located along the Guinea coast, was established during the 1820's by the American Colonization Society as a haven for freed slaves. The present economic, social, and political conditions of the country illustrate some of the arguments *for* colonial rule of undeveloped areas. Liberia is extremely poor. Roads and railroads are practically nonexistent, and the only major airfield in the country was constructed by the United States for military use during World War II. Political control of Liberia rests in the hands of a small Americo-Liberian minority, probably representing less than 2 per cent of the total population, plus about twice as many coastal Negroes, who also have come in contact with Western culture.

Health and education facilities are severely limited by Liberia's shortage of capital. Prior to World War II the only major economic development in the State was in connection with the Firestone rubber plantations. More recently a concession has been granted to the Republic Steel Corporation to mine iron ore in Liberia. In spite of these activities, however, Liberia remains a poor and undeveloped area, although it has one of the longest records of independence of any State in Africa.

Ivory Coast. The typical forested coastal lowlands and the grassland uplands of the countries along the Guinea coast are found there also. Abidjan, the capital, has a very good harbor and is the terminus of the railroad running north through the coffee and cacao area south of Bouaké, ultimately connecting with Upper Volta. The country is important for the export of timber and bananas. There, more than in most of the new States of West Africa, commercial life remains mostly in the hands of the French. President Felix Houphouet-Boigny has invited the French to remain for a time in the country; France has a near-monopoly on trade, and French military units continue to be stationed in the Ivory Coast. But despite its pro-French position Ivory Coast borders on Guinea, Mali, and Ghana, all members of the neutralist "Casablanca Group" (see page 414). Although outwardly calm, Ivory Coast has experienced considerable internal friction as political groups contest the absolutism of its president, and as tribal peoples seek to break away from control by the central government. The kingdom of Sanwi, for example, occupying some 3,000 square miles of territory in the eastern part of the State, has announced its desire for annexation by neighboring Ghana.

Ghana. The State has a population of over 6½ million people and a considerable resource potential. Cocoa is its major agricultural export; timber and palm products are also exported. In addition Ghana has developed its gold, diamonds, manganese, and bauxite. Manufactures have been built up, including textiles, food processing, and machinery, giving Ghana a considerable economic lead over the other countries of west Africa, with the exception of Nigeria. Its per capita foreign trade is the highest of any of the west African States. The Volta River, flowing through Ghana, has considerable water power potential, and with its bauxite reserves Ghana is in a position to develop an important aluminum industry, providing capital can be obtained for the Volta River project.

The population is divided into numerous tribal groups, and as yet there is relatively little concept of nation in Ghana. In and around Accra, the capital and leading city, are many detribalized natives and the bulk of the educated, intellectual Africans. Farther north Ashanti, economically important for its cacao, gold, and bauxite, is still dominated largely by its tribal chiefs. The people of Ashanti have been much concerned about a centralized political system in Ghana, since a large portion of the country's wealth comes from the cacao production of this area, yet much of the federal revenue is spent in the Eastern Region around Accra. In northern Ghana tribal conditions also prevail, and there is a large Moslem population; tribal chiefs have feared loss of power and a change of cultural patterns under the domination of Accra. Politically, Ghana has been divided into the Eastern Region, a Western Region, Ashanti, and the Northern Territories. It is, however, a unitary State rather than a federation.

Togo. Lying to the east of Ghana, Togo is a country about 50 miles wide and 400 miles long with a population of over one million. Coffee, cacao, and palm products are its principal exports, although there are known to be extensive phosphate deposits within 20 miles of the coast. One of Togo's most serious problems concerns the Ewes, an important tribe numbering over 2 million, some 200,000 of whom live in Togo. Before World War I the Ewes were practically united under German rule (although a small proportion of their number were included in the Gold Coast), but the division of Togoland in 1922 into British and French mandates split the Ewes, resulting in considerable hardships for this group. The Ewes have repeatedly protested this artificial division of their people but to no avail (see Figure 80). In 1957 British Togoland was incorporated within the new State of Ghana, in accordance with the results of a plebiscite held under United Nations auspices. French Togoland had, the year before, been established as an autonomous republic within the French Union, and this move was subsequently approved by 71.5 per cent of the Togolese voters in a referendum held in that

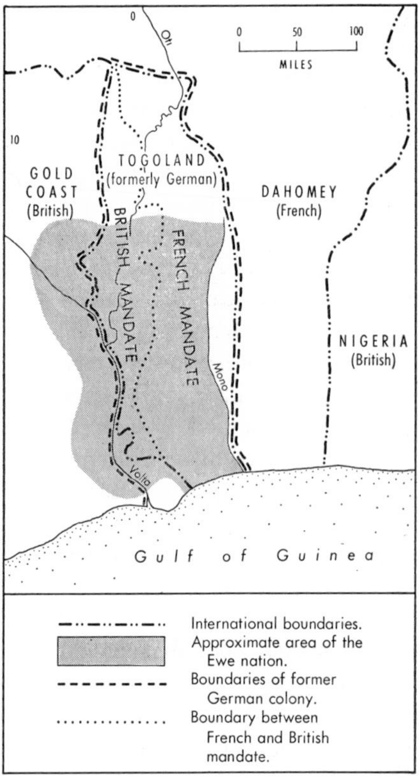

Figure 80. Togoland. (After Fischer, *World Politics*, I [Jan., 1949]. Used by permission.)

area. The United Nations refused to accept the results of the plebiscite on the grounds that the opposition groups had boycotted it and the alternatives offered the voters were so worded as to influence their choice. Nevertheless the French continued to treat the trust territory as a part of the French Community, and in April, 1960, it became an independent State. Ghana may in time use the Ewe question as a basis for pressuring Togo to join it as one of its provinces.

Dahomey. A former territory of French West Africa, Dahomey is, like Togo, a long, narrow State, having a population of 1¾ million. Most of its population is concentrated in the southern half of the country, where palm products form the principal export crop. Dahomey was one of the last areas in west Africa to be politically organized and represented a seaward extension of French control between the British and German Togoland. It adjoins the relatively advanced Western Region of Nigeria, with whom it logically should have economic, if not political, ties. But here again one is faced with the problems of history, for with its largely tribal structure and its lack of economic viability, Dahomey nevertheless has been permitted to become a separate independent State.

Nigeria

Nigeria, richest and most populous of the States of west Africa, was considered in some detail in Chapter 5 (see page 88). Its territory extends from the forested coastal lowlands to the grassland uplands of the north, and includes "Westernized" Negroes in the south (particularly the southwest), more primitive tribal groups in the central areas, and Moslems in the north, still largely under the influence of local rulers. There is a fairly extensive rail system covering most of the country except the northwest. Cacao, timber, palm products, and rubber are export crops of southern Nigeria, peanuts and cotton of the north. Nigeria is an important source for tin, and there are small deposits of coal and petroleum, as well as uranium and the rare mineral columbite. But the country lacks sources of cheap power for industrialization.

With its large population the Federation of Nigeria seems destined to play a major role in west African affairs, although it must also solve its own problems of internal cohesion and economic consistency. The centrifugal forces caused by its many diverse ethnic groups form a serious handicap to its development as an independent federal State. Agriculture is not well developed, despite the large and relatively dense population; Nigeria could grow far more both for its own needs and for export. The Niger and its tributaries offer possibilities for both irrigation and water power, although considerable capital is needed to develop these. In western Nigeria is an urbanized and sophisticated population which has relatively little in common with the Ibos of the southeast or the Hausa, Fulani, and other tribes of the north. Although pro-Western in its outlook, the Nigerian federal government has indicated it will welcome investment capital from all foreign sources. Because of the State's relatively well-developed circulatory system, Nigerians are perhaps better acquainted with their economic inadequacies than are many of the other peoples of West Africa; thus pressures on the popularly elected government for economic improvement are also stronger.

The Eastern Area

Included here are the former French trust territory of Cameroons and three states of former French Equatorial Africa—Gabon, the Republic of the Congo, and the Central African Republic (formerly the territory of Ubangi Shari). The Spanish enclave of Rio Muni is also located here, while in the Gulf of Guinea are several Spanish and Portuguese islands. The Central African Republic and much of the State of Cameroun are located in the tall grass savanna, with annual rainall of 40–60 inches; the rest of the area is covered by equatorial forest. There is a broad coastal plain extending southward through Gabon, behind which is the Central African

Plateau. Much of the area is drained by northern tributaries of the Congo, although in the north are the Shari and Logone rivers emptying into Lake Chad.

Cameroun. This country embraces several hundred tribal groups, with Moslems in the north and Negroes in the central and southern areas. Tribal loyalties are particularly strong there, and the French did little to develop a concept of nation among the people before granting Cameroun independence. One result has been almost constant dissension within the new State, one of the strongest centers being among the Bamileke tribe in the south, which is in revolt against the centralized government at Youandé. With nearly 4 million inhabitants Cameroun has had a fairly intensive economic development, under first the Germans and then the French. Cacao is produced for export in the uplands around Youandé, coffee, bananas, and palm products in the southwest. Cotton is grown in the northern extension between Nigeria and Chad, although transport facilities are poor between this area and the more populous south. Douala, the chief port, is linked by rail with the capital. No minerals of value have as yet been discovered in Cameroun. With its large and diverse population the country faces difficult problems in the achievement of political viability as an independent State.

Gabon. A small, forested State along the Gulf of Guinea, Gabon contains some forty ethnic groups, and had until recently undergone relatively little economic development. Exports include timber, cacao, and small amounts of petroleum, the oil production coming from fields near Port Gentil in the central part of the country. Gabon is rich in minerals, however, the greatest reserve being the manganese at Moanda in the southeastern part of the State. To export the ore a combined 180-mile railway-cableway is to be constructed southward through the forested uplands, crossing the Republic of the Congo to connect with the Brazzaville–Pointe Noire railroad which follows the Congo River. At Pointe Noire docking facilities will be expanded to handle the export of the manganese. Iron ore is also known to exist at Belinga in the extreme northwest, and a 435-mile railroad has been proposed across Gabon to the coast just south of Libreville, the capital. With mineral wealth and the prospects of considerable rail construction Gabon faces a brighter economic future than do some of its neighboring States.

Spanish Guinea. Sandwiched between Gabon and Cameroun is the Spanish coastal enclave of Rio Muni, a survival of Africa's slaving era. Coffee, timber, and some cacao are produced for export. Fernando Po, an offshore volcanic island, which, with Rio Muni, forms the territory of Spanish Guinea, is noted for its cacao production. Farther south are Portugal's islands of Principe and São Tome, also important for cacao production and export.

Congo. The Republic of the Congo is covered for the most part by tropical rain forest, in which there has been little economic development. For over a thousand miles it is separated from the former Belgian Congo by the Congo and Ubangi rivers. Population and economic activities are concentrated in the southeast between Brazzaville, the capital, and Pointe Noire. Gold is obtained inland from Pointe Noire, and there is a small export of palm products. Otherwise, this country, with over 800,000 people, has as yet little economic *raison d'être*.

Central African Republic. An inland State, this also faces a difficult future. The capital, Bangui, is on the Ubangi River, which furnishes the principal outlet to the sea. Cotton is grown, particularly in the northwest near the Chad border, and there is some coffee in the south. There is also a small export of diamonds. In the grasslands of the north there are Moslems, although most of the population is Negro. On the east the republic borders southern Sudan, but most of its contacts are to the west and south with Congo and Cameroun.

Moves for Unity and Disunity in West Africa

From the above discussion it would appear that (1) many of the west African States are artificial political units, composed of many diverse ethnic groups without any real economic or political *raison d'être;* and (2) the greatest needs of these States are time and outside development capital, permitting them to raise their economic levels substantially. Development capital is being made available by the United States, the Soviet Union, France, Britain, and West Germany in varying amounts, and several of the west African States are in relatively good bargaining positions for these funds. Time, of course, is another matter—first because of the possibility of internal dissension, second, because of potential border problems with neighboring states, and, third, because of the desires of countries from other areas to extend or solidify their influence in west Africa.

Internal stability has been extremely difficult to achieve in many of the new States. Writing in the magazine *Foreign Affairs*, Chief H. O. Davies of Nigeria has stated:

> Perhaps the most fundamental problem that has confronted the newly independent states is the difficult task of fitting their people to the alien constitutions which have been adopted. The colonial powers have greatly influenced the former colonies in the making of their constitutions. The educated elite in the colonial territory and the representatives of the metropolitan country who negotiated and drafted the constitutions had both been bred in the climate of the metropolitan constitution, and were *ad idem* in the belief that a carbon copy of that constitution was all that was required. Little did they realize that their outlook on life generally

was completely foreign to that of the ordinary citizen of the colony. In the end, the constitutions that were made were not only alien to the nature and needs of the ordinary citizens of the new states, they were so advanced and complicated as to be completely misunderstood. The net result is that, in the absence of constitutions suitable for the people, the people have to be suited to their new constitutions. This arduous process is still going on.[8]

After discussing the results of this problem, Chief Davies concluded:

The pattern of constitution which is evolving on the African continent is therefore "democracy with strong leadership." . . . Africans obviously believe that the commencement of independent life calls for a united and disciplined people under a strong and dedicated leadership. . . . The stress is not on "the people" but on "the leader" and the leader unmistakably speaks with the tongue of the millions of his people.[9]

With so many small independent States it is only natural that efforts have already been made toward unification of one form or another. Mention has been made of the Mali Federation, uniting the former French Sudan (Mali) with Senegal, and, after that had ended, of the union of Mali, Guinea, and Ghana. These three States are members of the so-called Casablanca Group (including also Morocco, Egypt, and the provisional Algerian government), a militant, neutralist organization which has been pressing for economic, military, and political unification as rapidly as possible. Opposed to these is the "Monrovia Group" with Nigeria in the lead and including all the independent countries of Africa, except Sudan, the former Belgian Congo, the Republic of South Africa, and the members of the Casablanca Group. The Monrovia countries are in favor of solving practical problems of integration first, such as those related to economies, transportation facilities, and health and education. They do not see political integration as a necessary end product of this cooperation, and are more moderate in their views toward the former colonial powers.

Among the Monrovia Countries is the "Brazzaville Group," comprising those States which still have strong links with France. In all of the former French territories except Guinea and Mali there are close cultural links with France (the African elite speak French and were generally educated in France), as well as the ties of trade and aid. The French traditionally maintained a near-monopoly on the trade of their overseas ter-

[8] "The New African Profile," *Foreign Affairs*, XL (1961), 293–94. Copyright by the Council on Foreign Relations, Inc.
[9] *Ibid.*, p. 302.

ritories, and in most cases this relationship continued after independence. France has also given substantial aid to its former colonies, all of which, except Guinea, are associated with the Common Market. This economic division between the French-oriented and nonoriented States of west Africa creates a powerful divisive force there. The British never maintained the trade monopoly with their colonies that the French did, nor has Britain advanced foreign aid to Sierra Leone and Nigeria on the per capita basis that France has done. Added to this are (1) Liberia, (2) the Spanish and Portuguese territories, and (3) Guinea and Mali, which have severed many of their ties with France; the result is an extremely complex system of interrelationships among the various west African States.

There are obvious differences in the viability of the various political units, and, presumably, in their future courses of action. Guinea and Ghana, for example, have strong economic potentials, as does Nigeria, assuming it is not split by internal forces. Gambia, on the other hand, has few of the basic requirements for independence, and for several States such as Upper Volta, Togo, Dahomey, and the Central African Republic, there are cogent reasons for eventual integration with a neighboring country. Because of the absence of strong unifying points in west Africa, it is difficult to suggest trends in the arrangement of political units. Despite what might appear to be the logic of union of many of the States with one another, it should be pointed out that since World War II there have been very few cases of such union, except of a small country with a larger one, or of colonies uniting as they achieve independence. Once self-rule is attained, the practice is to avoid political integration with other States.

NORTHEAST AFRICA

Northeastern Africa, or the "African Horn" as it is sometimes known, is divided physically into two parts: the well-watered highlands of northern and central Ethiopia and central Eritrea, and the semiarid hills and coastal plains in the remainder of the sector (Figure 76). Ethnically there is a division between the Christians and other peoples loyal to the Ethiopian crown and the Moslem Somalis occupying the coastal regions from Eritrea around to northern Kenya. Politically the Horn of Africa includes Ethiopia (with which the former Italian colony of Eritrea has been federated), the French overseas territory of French Somaliland, and the newly independent Somali Republic, incorporating the former Italian and British Somalilands into a right-angled country of 246,000 square miles and some 2 million impoverished Somalis.

Northeastern Africa occupies a strategic location with respect to surrounding areas. To the northwest is Sudan and beyond it the growing power of Egypt, seeking to exert influence over the Islamic peoples of Eritrea and the Somalias. To the east is the Strait of Bab el Mandeb, entrance to the Red Sea, and beyond it Yemen, Aden, and other areas of the Arabian Peninsula. To the south is Kenya, newly emerging from British control. The Blue Nile rises in the highlands of Ethiopia, and from Ethiopia it is but a few hundred miles to the Negro areas of southern Sudan, to Uganda, and to the borders of the former Belgian Congo.

Within northeastern Africa recent political developments have revolved primarily about (1) the gradual withdrawal of foreign control and (2) the controversies between Ethiopia and the Somalis. Ethiopia is an empire, divided administratively into twelve provinces. The capital is located at Addis Ababa, at an elevation of over 8,000 feet. About half the population of Ethiopia are Coptic Christians (the Coptic Church is an autonomous Eastern faith which recognizes the bishop of Alexandria as its patriarch), and there is a large Moslem majority in the northern and eastern part of the country. With its agricultural possibilities, its hydroelectric potential, and indications of coal and considerable mineral wealth (including gold, silver, and iron ore), Ethiopia possesses a resource base which, if adequately developed, could place it in a strong economic position.

The country has had a long history. Political unification, however, took place toward the close of the nineteenth century, at the time when the British, French, and Italians were establishing footholds along the coasts of the Red Sea and Indian Ocean. The result was that Ethiopia emerged as a unified independent State, cut off from the sea by European colonies. With its great physical and ethnic diversity and its lack of a strong circulatory system, Ethiopia was a loosely knit political area, whose emperor, acknowledged as the "King of Kings," exercised only nominal control over much of the territory.

During the 1930's the Italian fascist government became interested in expanding Italy's empire as a symbol of Italy's growing power and prestige. On the pretext of moving in to "civilize" Ethiopia, Italy invaded and conquered the country in 1936, but five years later, during World War II, British forces drove out the Italians and restored Ethiopia's independence.

After World War II the disposition of Italy's two colonies Eritrea and Somaliland produced a series of compromises between the claims of the interested powers and local groups. In Eritrea the population is divided between Coptic Christians (with historical and cultural ties with Ethiopia) in the central highlands and the Moslem peoples in the northwest and along the Red Sea coast. At the end of World War II the Christians desired union of Eritrea with Ethiopia, while the Moslems, fearing they would be submerged in a non-Moslem State, favored independence or some type of federation, at least of the Moslem-inhabited areas, with the Sudan. Unwilling to split Eritrea along ethnic lines, the United Nations in 1948 ruled that the area should be federated with Ethiopia as an autonomous state, with Ethiopia responsible for defense, foreign affairs, and finance, and in 1952 this federation became effective. The acquisition of the Eritrean Red Sea littoral strengthened Ethiopia's economic and strategic position. Since then the country has developed a strong military force, including American and Swedish jets. Haile Selassie, the Ethiopian emperor, has sought for himself a position of leadership in the emergence of African nationalism, in part, perhaps, as a block to the power of Egypt's Nasser. Still the absolute ruler of his country, he has been forced to institute political reforms in the wake of a bloody uprising in 1961 which nearly cost him his throne.

About 500,000 people in the Ogaden sector of southeastern Ethiopia are Somalis, and thus ethnically akin to the inhabitants of the Somali Republic. Somalia, as the former Italian Somaliland was known, is an arid coastal strip along the Indian Ocean, across which several rivers flow from the Ethiopian highlands to the sea. Along the course of these rivers and around numerous wells which have been drilled agriculture is carried on, with bananas (particularly in the vicinity of the capital, Mogadishu) the principal export product. Over two-thirds of the people are nomads, moving their cattle frequently in search of water and pasturage. No recoverable minerals have been discovered there, and the principal economic hope for the area appears to lie in greater development of irrigated crops.

The former protectorate of British Somaliland is also largely arid, although about 15 inches of summer rain are received in the uplands around Hargeisa close to the Ethiopian border. No year-round rivers cross this area to the sea, and the economy is even more dependent upon grazing than is the case in Somalia. Actually the best winter grazing lands for the Somalis are in the so-called Haud, a region obtained by Ethiopia in agreement with Britain in 1897 along with the neighboring "Reserved Areas"— one of the few areas close to British Somaliland where rainfall is sufficient for agriculture. Somali herdsmen frequently take their flocks across the border into Ethiopia, and fighting has broken out on occasion between Ethiopians and Somalis in the area of Wal Wal where important wells are located. Farther south, in the Ogaden sector, nomads from the former Italian territory annually migrate across the Ethiopian borders; the government of Ethiopia does not obstruct these movements, but it refuses to permit the foreigners to own grazing lands, and, in the case of strong separatist movements on the part of the Somalis of Ogaden, some restrictions might in time be put upon entrance from the Somali Republic.

In addition to the people of the Somali Republic and of the Ogaden area are the Somali people of French Somaliland and of northeastern Kenya. French Somaliland consists primarily of the port of Djibouti and its environs. Djibouti is the terminus of the only railroad linking the Ethiopian capital with the coast; thus the Ethiopians are concerned with any changes in the political status of the area. French Somaliland is unique in that, alone

among the French possessions in Africa, it chose to remain an Overseas
Territory rather than become an autonomous republic (or, as in the case
of Guinea, to leave the Community). Half the population lives in Djibouti,
whose economy is largely dependent upon the transit trade from Ethiopia.
About 40 per cent of the people are Somalis; thus one of the goals of Somali
nationalism is the annexation of France's coastal enclave.

About 60,000 Somalis inhabit Kenya, but to date there has been little
sign of Somali irridentism in that direction. The border there passes through
a semiarid grazing region, but herdsmen from the Somali Republic are not
permitted into Kenya. Considering the resource potential of the republic
it might seem logical for a considerable number of Somalis to emigrate to
Kenya, where there are stretches of sparsely settled land, but such a move
would be opposed by both the whites and the Negroes of Kenya.

Prior to independence both Somalia and British Somaliland were
heavily subsidized by their respective mother countries—subsidies which
amounted to close to half the annual budgets. Combining two poor areas
into one political unit does nothing toward settling the economic problems.
"Hence the Somalis are left primarily with the sale of their strategic vantage
points to foreigners—a commodity that can be a dangerous domestic irritant
in a nationalist era."[10] Many countries would be glad to establish an influence sphere there—Egypt, Britain, the United States, Italy, and the Soviet
Union, to mention the major contenders. But any move in the Horn of
Africa must take into account the interests of Ethiopia, a country of growing military strength and importance, a country with serious border problems involving the Somalis, and a country intent on maintaining its outlets
through Somali territory to the sea.

BIBLIOGRAPHY

BUCHANAN, KEITH. "The Northern Region of Nigeria: The Geographical
Background of its Political Duality," *The Geographical Review,* XLIII
(1953), 451–74.

A regional description of this political area.

"Central African Republic–Sudan." International Boundary Study. No. 16,
June 22, 1962. Washington, Department of State, Office of the Geographer.

Detailed map and description of the boundary.

---

[10]Leo Silberman, "Change and Conflict in the Horn of Africa." *Foreign Affairs,* XXXVII (1959),
654. Copyright by the Council on Foreign Relations, Inc.

DAVIES, CHIEF H. O. "The New African Profile," *Foreign Affairs*, XL (1962), 293–303.

An African view of the problems of statehood in Africa.

JACKSON, BARBARA WARD. "Free Africa and the Common Market," *Foreign Affairs*, XL (1962), 419–31.

A summary of the relations between Africa and the Common Market.

PERHAM, MARGERY. "White Minorities in Africa," *Foreign Affairs*, XXXVII (1959), 637–49.

Careful treatment of the subject.

PRESCOTT, J. R. V. "Nigeria's Regional Boundary Problems," *The Geographical Review*, XLIX (1959), 485–506.

Excellent maps and description of the boundaries.

SENGHOR, LEOPOLD. "West Africa in Evolution," *Foreign Affairs*, XXXIX (1961), 240–47.

Trends and problems among the West African States.

SILBERMAN, LEO. "Change and Conflict in the Horn of Africa," *Foreign Affairs*, XXXVII (1959), 649–60.

A very good summary of conditions in this area.

STAMP, L. DUDLEY. *Africa, A Study in Tropical Development*. New York: John Wiley & Sons, 1953.

A basic regional text for all of Africa.

WILLIAMS, DAVID. "How Deep is the Split in West Africa?" *Foreign Affairs*, XL (1961), 118–28.

A concise treatment of regional divisions.

15

EQUATORIAL AFRICA

● The central and eastern portions of Africa, roughly between 5° north latitude and 10° south latitude, are considered here as equatorial Africa. The combined area approximates 1,600,000 square miles and the population about 40 million. Political units include the Congo (formerly Belgian Congo), Rwanda and Burundi, Kenya, Uganda, Tanganyika, and Zanzibar.[1] In the west the Congo is separated from the coast by the former French territories north of the Congo and Ubangi rivers, by the Portuguese enclave of Cabinda (administratively a part of Angola) at the mouth of the Congo, and by the northwestern extension of Angola itself between the Kwango River and the Atlantic. In the east an extension of Somali Republic limits Kenya's coastland, and even a part of this coastal strip is technically under the sovereignty of Zanzibar (see page 432). Such territorial complexities as these indicate the relative values placed on coastal and inland areas in central Africa at the time of its political partitioning.

Three European powers were primarily involved in the establishment of control there—Belgium, Germany, and Britain. The Congo River basin was largely ignored by European governments until late in the nineteenth century. In 1878 Leopold II, King of the Belgians, recognizing the economic potential of this area, established the International Association of the Congo, an organization over which he exercised dominant control. The following year he sent Stanley, the American explorer, on an expedition to the Congo

---

[1] The Malagasy Republic (formerly Madagascar), although physically and politically separated from the area described here as equatorial Africa, is included at the end of the chapter, since its development differs considerably from that of the areas of southern Africa.

basin, and in 1884 the Independent State of the Congo was established under the control of the International Association. Non-Belgian interests in the Congo were bought out by Leopold in 1887, and for 21 years this area of over 900,000 square miles was held as virtually the private property of the Belgian monarch. The brutal treatment of the Congolese, together with other excesses in the administration of the area, finally led a reluctant Belgian government to annex it as a colony in 1908.

In east Africa the coastal areas had long been dominated by the sultan of Zanzibar. Largely in an effort to suppress Arab slave traffic, the British in the 1840's began exercising influence over Zanzibar, and eventually supported the sultan's efforts toward expanding his power on the mainland. In 1890 Britain established a formal protectorate over Zanzibar and the neighboring island of Pemba. The expansion of Arab control in east Africa was ultimately checked by the rise of German power, which, through the German East African Association, succeeded in securing a protectorate in 1889 over German East Africa—later divided into Tanganyika and Ruanda-Urundi. Germany's colonial drive northward was eventually blocked by the conclusion of British protectorates over Uganda (1893) and Kenya (1895) through the actions of the British East Africa Company. The sultan of Zanzibar was permitted, however, to retain sovereignty for himself and his heirs and successors over a coastal strip along the Indian Ocean 10 miles wide, including 170 miles of the Kenya coast south of the Tana River, as well as a part of Tanganyika. In 1895 the Germans purchased the strip south of the Kenya border from Zanzibar, but the British established the area in Kenya (which includes the port of Mombasa) as a protectorate, and have paid the sultan an annual rental amounting to about $47,000.

Germany's defeat in World War I led to the establishment of a British mandate over Tanganyika and a Belgian mandate over the northwestern area, known as Ruanda-Urundi. After World War II the mandates became trust territorities of the United Nations.

Unity and division in equatorial Africa are clearly reflected in its political units. Since independence the Congo has struggled to remain united in the face of powerful centrifugal forces; Ruanda-Urundi has split into two small, independent States, while the three emerging entities of mainland east Africa, rather than facing division, are making plans for closer union with one another. The results of this are of no small importance to the political power balance in central Africa.

THE CONGO

The former Belgian Congo covers an area of 900,000 square miles and has a population of close to 14 million. It occupies most of the basin of the Congo River, a waterway 3,000 miles long which possesses the greatest water

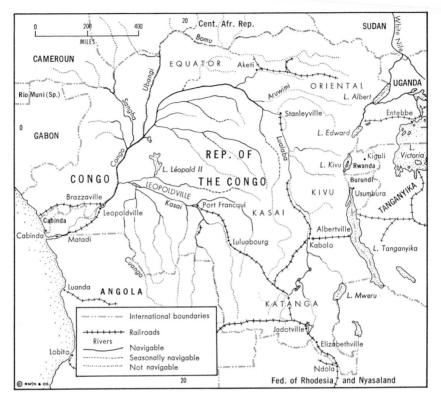

Figure 81. The Congo.

power potential of any river in the world. Much of the basin is a plateau less than 2,000 feet in elevation, although in the southeast and the east the plateau rises, culminating in highlands near the boundary of Northern Rhodesia, and in the east bordering Lakes Tanganyika, Kivu, and Edward. The equator passes through the northern Congo, and the climate for the most part is hot and wet; thus only the interior highlands have been major areas of European agriculture. Nearly 40 per cent of the Congo is covered by equatorial rain forest, although in the extreme north and in the south central and southern areas are more open forest and grassland.

Much of the Congo River and its tributaries are navigable, but below Léopoldville, capital of the country, are rapids preventing navigation down to the sea. A railroad has been built to connect Léopoldville with Matadi, the head of navigation on the river, and there are railroads in the interior as well, particularly in the mineral-rich Katanga area of the southeast, and linking the eastern uplands with Lake Tanganyika.

The Congo includes over 200 different tribes, speaking nearly 40 main languages, and ranging in level of development from skilled urbanized workers to illiterate forest pygmies. Tribal loyalties are strong, and, as in many other parts of Africa, there is little concept of nation among a majority of the inhabitants. Some tribes, such as the Bakongos of the west, numbering over one million, the Luluas of Kasai in the south central Congo, or the Batetela of North Kasai, represent strong centrifugal forces in the country. The four major cities, representing regional centers, are Léopoldville, on the lower Congo across from Brazzaville, Congo; Elisabethville in Katanga Province; Luluabourg in Kasai, the diamond-rich province west of Katanga; and Stanleyville in Oriental Province in the northeast. Only Elisabethville and Luluabourg among the four cities are connected with one another by railroad. The poorly developed circulatory systems, the ethnic complexities, the off-center location of the capital, and finally, since independence, the rivalries of political leaders, have served to pull the country apart.

The Belgians were originally interested in the Congo for ivory and wild rubber. Later the demand for vegetable oils led to the establishment of plantations for palm products, and this in turn was followed by the growing of coffee, tea, cocoa, cotton, bananas, and chinchona—the bulk of these by Europeans, concentrated for the most part in the southeastern and eastern highlands. But the Congo was also found to be rich in minerals, particularly copper, uranium, diamonds, cobalt, tin, silver, and gold. Copper, cobalt, and zinc are concentrated in the Katanga and diamonds in Kasai. To develop Katanga's minerals there is the gigantic Union Minière du Haut Katanga, a Belgian corporation with shareholders in Britain and other European countries.

To the Belgians the Congo, particularly after World War I, came to represent a source of considerable revenue. Belgian development capital began to be poured into the area, and agricultural and mineral resources were exported throughout the world. The Congo became the world's leader in cobalt production and is a major source of radioactive minerals and industrial diamonds, as well as copper. Unfortunately there is little iron ore and almost no power sources except water power, which the Belgians did little to develop.

Much of the wealth of the Belgian Congo remained in the hands of the Europeans, and it was not until after World War II that the Belgian government began seriously to consider the future status of the natives. Agricultural experts began working to improve the agriculture of the Africans, and more and more natives were drawn to the industries and urban areas. The Belgians held that the Africans should be trained and educated before they could have a voice in governing themselves, and by 1950 strenuous efforts were being made through the establishment of schools and the elimination of color bars in economic activities to achieve the goal of native advancement as rapidly as possible. In the meantime the white minority in the Congo was not allowed to control the area's destinies; rather political power was firmly retained in Brussels.

Belgium's reform, however, came too late to be of much aid to the Congo. Few Africans received any training in managing governmental affairs, and at the time of independence only a dozen Congolese had risen to administrative positions in the colonial government. There were no Congolese doctors, lawyers, engineers, or army officers; Belgian officers ran the Congolese army, as well as its health services, communications, transportation, and commerce. Although the Belgians had sought to isolate the Congo from other areas in order to proceed carefully with preparations for self-rule, the independence of the French territories adjoining the Congo set off a series of bloody riots. These culminated in a conference in January, 1960, at which the Belgians agreed to independence at the end of six months. It has been claimed that this precipitous haste on the part of the Belgians was in part an effort to avoid further bloodshed and to permit business in the Congo to suffer as few interruptions as possible.

Independence for the Congo was followed immediately by (1) a mutiny by units of the Congolese army against their Belgian officers, (2) widespread rioting throughout the country, and (3) the secession of Katanga Province from the new State. Units of the Belgian army moved to restore order and protect Belgian citizens; in response, Premier Lumumba of the new Congolese government asked the United Nations to intervene and force the Belgian troops out of the country. In July, 1960, the first United Nations forces began arriving in the Congo. The Belgians soon withdrew their troops, leaving the multinational United Nations contingent as the strongest military unit in the new country.

Since the summer of 1960 the Congo has remained in a state of chaos. The Province of South Kasai, with its diamond wealth, followed Katanga's lead in seceding from the Congo, while in Stanleyville in the northeast a left-wing government was set up under Antoine Gizenga. The struggle for power between such men as Gizenga, Kasavubu, Lumumba, Tshombe, and others has done much to set back Congo unity. The secession of Katanga and South Kasai represented a serious economic blow to the central government, since these two areas are the most important sources of foreign currency in the country. European mining firms continued to pay to local banks in these areas, instead of to Léopoldville, since provincial military forces rather than the Congolese army exercised effective control in Katanga and South Kasai. In 1961 Katanga's revenue came to $60 million, compared to the central regime's receipts in the same year of only $78 million.

The solution of the Congo's political problems may lie in some form of federation rather than in attempting a unitary State. The Belgians had divided their colony into six provinces, with many boundaries cutting across tribal areas. It would not be illogical to rearrange the internal political pattern to conform more closely with ethnic divisions, although agreement among political leaders on the details of such a change might be very difficult to achieve. There are few neighboring areas with which border districts of the Congo might join, and, outside of Katanga, it is doubtful that any one province could for long maintain its independence in the face of strong action by the central government. The United Nations is apparently committed to upholding the unity of the Congo under the Léopoldville regime—an interesting objective for this organization in the light of the political divisions taking place in so many parts of the world.

RWANDA AND BURUNDI

The former Belgian trust territory of Ruanda-Urundi lies to the east of the Congo, across the rift valley which contains Lakes Kivu and Tanganyika. The area is primarily upland, with a central plateau averaging 4,000–5,000 feet in elevation and mountains to over 8,000 feet in the west. In the extreme west is a tropical lowland, lying between Lakes Tanganyika and Kiva. On the shores of Lake Tanganyika is Usumbura, the former capital of the territory and now the capital of Burundi (formerly Urundi). From there goods may be sent via the lake to Kigoma, Tanganyika—the terminus of the trans-Tanganyika railroad to Dar es Salaam—or to Albertville, Congo, and by rail to the west coast port of Lobito, Angola. The capital of Rwanda (formerly Ruanda) is the town of Kigali, located in the central plateau on the main road from Usumbura north to Uganda.

The area of the two countries totals 21,000 square miles, with a population of over 4 million, indicating the high carrying capacity of this agricultural land. Cattle and coffee are the principal export crops; in the past most of the trust territory's trade had been with the neighboring Congo. Since World War I the Belgian government has paid annual subsidies to Ruanda-Urundi, although little has been done to develop export agriculture of the natives. There are no valuable mineral or power fuels (other than water power), and with its inland location the area, although good for subsistence agriculture, does not have a strong economic potential.

The population is divided into two major groups. The Watusi, comprising about 15 per cent of the total, emigrated to the area some 400 years ago and became the ruling economic and political people; the Bahutu, making up some 80 per cent of the population, were the indigenous inhabitants. Smaller tribes, including "pygmoids" (resulting from interbreeding between pygmies and Bahutus), comprise the rest of the population. Only about 8,000 Europeans lived there, and with the approach of independence practically all of them departed. The Watusi, measuring up to seven feet in height, have long dominated Ruanda-Urundi, owning most of the cattle and controlling the government. Friction was greater in Ruanda between the ruling Watusi and the Bahutu peoples than was the case in Urundi. In 1959 riots broke out in Ruanda between the two groups,

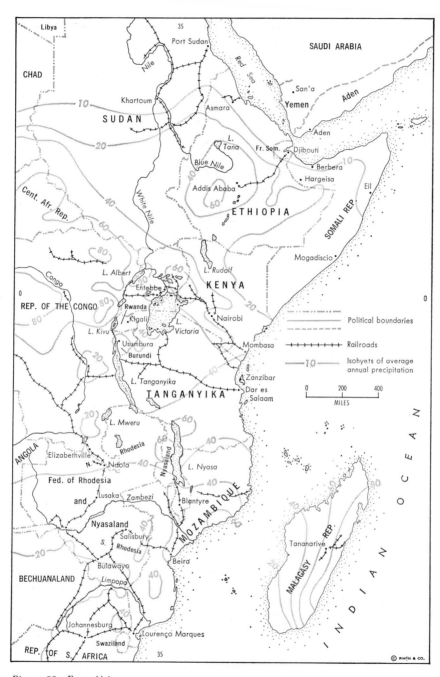

Figure 82. East Africa.

and many Watusi were forced to flee to the Belgian Congo. The Belgians, as a step toward preparing Ruanda for eventual self-rule, gave their support to the predominant Bahutus, and in 1961 the Watusi king was deposed.

With approaching independence for Ruanda-Urundi the United Nations sought to keep the territory together, but was opposed largely by the rising nationalism of the Bahutus in Ruanda. This area was intended by the Bahutus as a republic, while Urundi was to become a monarchy in which the Watusi aristocracy would retain their power. Thus in July, 1962, two landlocked States were created, each measuring in the neighborhood of 10,000 square miles. Each is faced with difficult economic problems, including the mere task of feeding their large populations. In the face of Bahutu nationalism in Rwanda it is difficult to envision long-term Watusi political dominance in Burundi, since this nationalism will undoubtedly spread southward across the new border. Equally important is the fact that here, in the uplands of central Africa, political and tribal borders do not coincide, and from the neighboring territories of the Congo, Uganda, and Tanganyika centrifugal forces may soon move to challenge the authorities in Kigali and Usumbura. Political viability may be a long time in coming to the two new States.

EAST AFRICA

The three mainland countries of east Africa—Kenya, Uganda, and Tanganyika—consist of an extensive plateau area over 3,500 feet in elevation, with lower areas in southern Tanganyika and northeastern Kenya, and with a coastal plain running along the Indian Ocean. Rising above the plateau are scattered highland areas of over 6,000 feet, particularly in southern Kenya, northern Tanganyika, and along the Uganda-Congo border. The Kenya highlands, near the capital, Nairobi, are the home of thousands of European settlers, who were attracted by the climate and agricultural opportunities. In Tanganyika is an isolated volcanic bloc, including Mount Kilimanjaro, highest point in Africa, while in western Uganda are the Ruwenzori Mountains ("Mountains of the Moon").

Rainfall is a critical factor in much of east Africa. Few areas receive more than 60 inches of rain per year, and much of the region has less than 30 inches. The predominant vegetation is savanna grassland or open woodland. Only along the coastal strip and north of Lake Victoria is there tropical rain forest. Northeastern Tanganyika and eastern Kenya are semidesert scrub, suitable only for grazing. Unlike conditions in western Africa there are no large rivers. Along the borders of the Congo are long, narrow lakes— Tanganyika, Kivu, and Albert, while in the center of the plateau is the large, shallow Lake Victoria, forming a natural reservoir from which the White Nile flows northward to the Mediterranean. In northern Kenya is Lake Rudolf, an inland water body from which there is no outlet. In the absence of major river systems lakes such as these played important roles in the exploration and settlement of east Africa.

The Nile River, 4,000 miles in length, has its major source in the east African highlands, and thus is of importance to that area. Its most remote headstream is the Kagera River, rising in Burundi near Lake Tanganyika, and flowing north and then east to Lake Victoria. Other headstreams rise in the highlands to the north, including the rainy Ruwenzoris. From Lake Victoria the Nile flows over Ripon and Owen falls, through Lake Kioga, and then over Murchison Falls to Lake Albert. These falls represent excellent water power sites and some use has already been made of the potential. From Lake Albert (elevation 2,030 feet) the Nile continues northward through the Nimule Gorges, and across Sudan and Egypt to the sea. At Khartoum, Sudan, it receives the Blue Nile, coming from Lake Tana in Ethiopia. The Nile's 1-million-square-mile drainage area also includes southwestern Sudan and the highlands of western Ethiopia. The Sudan-Congo border actually follows the watershed between the Nile and Congo rivers.

During the low water season 80 per cent of the water of the lower Nile comes from the White Nile, rising in east Africa, although in flood season the major source of water is the Blue Nile.[2] Since almost all of the Nile water originates in east Africa or Ethiopia, the Egyptians, whose economic life depends on the Nile, have long been anxious over control of the upper parts of the river. The British in 1929 concluded a Nile Waters Agreement, under which it agreed to do nothing that would interfere with the flow of the White Nile without first obtaining the consent of Egypt. At that time practically all of the areas from which the waters of the White Nile originated were under British control. Conditions have now changed. Lake Victoria, the "reservoir" for the White Nile, is bordered by Tanganyika, Kenya, and Uganda—areas where British control has, or shortly will, disappear. Uganda is interested in developing hydroelectric power from an estimated potential of 2 million kilowatts in the White Nile's 1,700-foot drop between Lakes Victoria and Albert, while all three countries are concerned with the use of waters in the area around Lake Victoria for irrigation. The Egyptians, in order to increase Lake Victoria's value as a reservoir in low water season, would like to see the lake level raised 3½ feet, thereby flooding lowlying coastal areas. Ethiopia has refused to enter into agreements with Egypt so far as the Blue Nile is concerned, and the gradual disappearance of British control in east Africa may eventually cause difficulties between Egypt and the east African countries over future use of the waters of the White Nile.

Economic development in east Africa has depended to a considerable extent on transportation facilities. The two major railroads are the one across southern Kenya and southern Uganda, focusing on the port of Mom-

---

[2] See the discussion and diagrams of the Nile in L. Dudley Stamp, *Africa: A Study in Tropical Development* (New York: John Wiley & Sons, 1953).

basa, and the trans-Tanganyika line with its outlet at Dar es Salaam. The
Kenya line serves the white settlers in the highlands northwest of Nairobi,
as well as the coffee and cotton areas about the northern shores of Lake
Victoria and the copper region of southwestern Uganda. Tanganyika's railroad reaches both Lake Victoria (and the diamond area to the south of the
lake) and Lake Tanganyika, across which is the eastern terminus of the
railroad to Lobito on the Atlantic. Railroads also serve the Kilimanjaro uplands, focusing on the port of Tanga in northeastern Tanganyika, and there
is a line extending inland a short distance from the port of Lindi in the
south. In addition to Tanganyika's diamonds and Uganda's copper there
are few other important minerals in east Africa, although Kenya has some
iron ore and gold is mined in Tanganyika. All three countries have considerable water power potential in their highland areas. Agriculture continues to be the major economic source, with coffee, cotton, and tea the
principal exports.

Kenya

This northernmost of the three east African countries has an area of
224,000 square miles and a population of 6½ million, of whom 68,000 (in
1960) were Europeans, 175,000 were Indians, and 39,000 were Arabs. Although fewer than 5 per cent of the total population are non-Africans, their
special economic and political positions have constituted a major racial
problem in the area. Not until 1895 was the territory placed under British
administration by the sultan of Zanzibar.

At the start of the twentieth century the British began the construction
of a railroad from Mombasa to Lake Victoria. "It was prompted," wrote
M. F. Hill of the *Kenya Weekly News,* "partly in order to discharge
Britain's responsibilities under the Act of Brussels to put an end to the slave
trading by establishing law and order in the interior; partly to make possible the retention of Uganda—where missionaries of the Church Missionary
Society had been precariously settled since 1876—as a British 'sphere of influence' and later as a protectorate; and partly to secure Britain's position
at the source of the Nile waters. . . . In reaching the decision to build the
railway no heed was paid to the possible development of the Highlands of
Kenya."[3] Within a few years, however, it was evident that the only way to
pay at least in part for the railroad's construction and maintenance costs,
and to provide revenue for the Protectorate of Kenya, was to encourage the
settlement by white farmers in the lands along the railroad; by World War I
some 3,000 Europeans had settled in the highlands of southern Kenya. Construction of the railroad was carried out largely by laborers imported from
India. These and their descendants have remained in Kenya, largely in the

[3] "The White Settler's Role in Kenya," *Foreign Affairs,* XXXVIII (1960), 638. Copyright by the
Council on Foreign Relations, Inc.

urban areas. The Arabs, inhabiting the coastal strip, are remnants of the days when Zanzibar's power extended over much of east Africa.

The Africans themselves are divided into various tribes, of which the Kikuyu, numbering about 1,500,000, are the largest. They inhabit the agricultural central province in the vicinity of Nairobi. The Luo, totaling more than 800,000, are settled on the shores of Lake Victoria, while the Masai, a nomadic, cattle-raising group, numbering just under 500,000, live along the Kenya-Tanganyika border. In 1911 the British concluded a treaty with the Masai, reserving 15,000 square miles of territory along the border for members of their tribe. Another 23,000 square miles in adjacent Tanganyika was also reserved for them. With approaching independence in Kenya the Masai are concerned that they might lose their reservation and have talked of creating a single Masai Province straddling the border within the framework of a yet-unformed East African Federation. In arid eastern Kenya 50,000 Somalis fear domination of the African government in Nairobi; one possible solution, they feel, would be the cession of northeastern Kenya to the Somali Republic. In both of these situations may be found illustrations of the fears of minority groups that their interests are far better protected under a colonial regime than when their own countrymen are in control.

The Land Problem in Kenya. In the highlands of southern Kenya

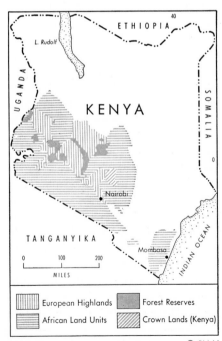

Figure 83. Kenya: Land Distribution. (After map in *Focus*, III [June, 1953]. Courtesy of *Focus*–American Geographical Society.)

© RMcN

racial tension, leading to widespread acts of terrorism, has resulted from the conflict between white and native interests. At altitudes generally above 5,000 feet lands reserved for white settlement are located in the midst of native agricultural holdings (Figure 83). Although comprising but a small fraction of the total highland area of southern Kenya, the white reserves generally consist of good agricultural land, and, perhaps more important, much of the land is unused—reserved for future farmers.

The first European farmers arrived in Kenya in the early 1900's. Land was acquired from various tribes in the Kenya highlands, among them the Kikuyu, who occupied areas close to the capital city, Nairobi, and whose reserves there became intermeshed with those of the Europeans. Although only about 100 square miles of the European reserves ever belonged to the Kikuyus, the people of this tribe have been the principal fomenters of trouble for the whites. The white farmers have engaged in scientific farming, producing coffee, grains, tea, and cattle, while most of the natives, with their primitive land-use practices, have contributed to soil erosion and exhaustion. Average densities per square mile are far higher on native than on white reserves.[4] The native population in Kenya has increased rapidly (more than doubling since World War I), and on his crowded, overworked land the African could not help noticing the discrepancy between the land resources available to him and those reserved for the European.

A few of the Kikuyus were educated at European universities. Many of them work for the Europeans in Kenya, and their close association with the whites and their knowledge of the tools and techniques of the white culture made them formidable opponents. A secret society, the Mau Mau, was formed among the Kikuyus, dedicated to throwing the white man out of Kenya. Beginning in 1952, an undeclared war engulfed the Kenya highlands, as the murder and destruction wrought by the Mau Mau against the whites and against fellow Kikuyus who refused to join in the struggle were met by stern countermeasures on the part of the British.

By 1956 the combination of strong military action and increased opportunities for native education and economic and political betterment had succeeded in almost eliminating Kikuyu terrorism. The British have inaugurated an extensive program for bringing the Africans into greater contact with Kenya's expanding economy, thereby enabling them to obtain better wages and a higher standard of living. Among the steps taken are instruction of the African in modern farming methods, increased native participation in local government, and large-scale rehabilitation programs for Kikuyus imprisoned during the armed conflict. By 1962 the Kikuyus, under the leadership of Jomo Kenyatta (who had been imprisoned in connection with the Mau Mau uprising), were in control of the African National Union, Kenya's dominant political party, which was working for a strong,

---

[4] Derwent Whittlesey gave the figure of 285 per square mile as the average density for the Kikuyu Reserve. See "Kenya, the Land and Mau Mau," *Foreign Affairs,* XXXII (1953), 88.

centralized government in what was soon to be constituted as an independent country. Opposing this group is the African Democratic Union, an amalgamation of several smaller tribes, which is fearful of Kikuyu supremacy and was pressing for a federation in Kenya with considerable self-government for the individual tribes. There, as in the Congo, the issue of centralism versus regionalism is a very real one in such a multiethnic country. But in a federation can the central government work effectively to develop the economy, raise the general standard of living, prevent separatist movements, and defend the borders against foreign infringements? For the Africans Nigeria may in time provide the test.

Another problem for an independent Kenya is the future of the Arab-owned strip along the southeastern coast. The strip includes Kenya's leading port, many sisal and sugar plantations which are of considerable economic value, and some 35,000 Arabs who fear domination by an African Nairobi government. Some Arabs have suggested that this coastal strip be made an independent state federated with Kenya, although such a move is virtually unthinkable to the Africans, who would then lose control of their major outlet to the Indian Ocean. The British are concerned over the future of their Royal Navy depot at Mombasa, as well as the air force station and large army installations in the vicinity of Nairobi. With recent withdrawals of both air and naval units from the Middle East and from the Indian sub-continent, the British have come to rely heavily on Kenya as a base for mobile military units to cover the Persian Gulf–Indian Ocean areas. It was from Kenya, for example, that British units moved northward in 1961 in response to Kuwait's request for military assistance in the face of Iraqi irridentism. Britain still retains military bases in Cyprus and Aden, as well as an air base in the Maldive Islands southwest of Ceylon, but these lack the space necessary for the establishment of a large military complex.

The future of the British agricultural settlers in Kenya remains uncertain, but the problem is obviously related to the future of European agriculture in Southern Rhodesia, in Algeria, and in the Republic of South Africa, the other three areas to which they have come in large numbers. The Africans may first seek to expropriate those areas of the "White Highlands" (reserved for European ownership and occupation) which are not being used for agriculture; later, the European agricultural lands may also be sought. What compensation will be paid to the European farmers for this land is an important part of the problem.[5] It has been estimated that over two-thirds of Kenya's total exports by value consist of agricultural products raised by the European farmers. Should this production decline markedly, the economy of an independent Kenya would obviously suffer. Yet in the face of these economic statistics is the fact of African nationalism, the long-

---

[5] A British proposal made in the summer of 1962 called for Britain's purchase of at least a million acres of farmland owned by whites in Kenya and the transfer of this land to the Kenya government for resettling landless Africans.

smoldering resentment against the European way of life and superior productive methods, and, with it, the possibility that the Europeans in Kenya may in time be blamed for the various economic difficulties with which the new States will have to cope.

Uganda

The landlocked country of Uganda won its independence from Britain in October, 1962. Within its 94,000 square miles are over 6½ million people, indicating that there, as in neighboring Rwanda and Burundi to the south, the carrying capacity of the land is high. Except in the Ruwenzori range in the extreme west and some isolated lands along the northern and eastern borders, Uganda does not have elevations comparable to those in Kenya. There are few European agriculturists, only a small number of Arabs, and about 40,000 Indians. Ninety-eight per cent of the population is African, divided into fourteen principal tribes, speaking five major languages. Of these tribes, the Buganda, comprising nearly one-third of the total population, is both the largest and the most economically developed. One of the problems in planning for an independent Uganda has been the status of the Buganda within such a State.

Most of Uganda is warm and relatively moist with a vegetation of open forest, or grassland with trees. Subsistence agriculture and grazing are the principal economic activities, although about the shores of Lake Victoria the Africans grow cotton, coffee, and some tea as cash crops for export via the only major link with the sea—the railroad across Kenya to Mombasa. The soils and climate of Uganda, both conducive to agriculture, are offset to some extent by serous epidemics of sleeping sickness and other insect-borne diseases, as well as by the depredations of the tsetse fly on the natives' cattle. The British have attempted to leave the tribal structures alone as much as possible, although quite a number of Africans are being attracted to the towns and cities where beginnings are being made to industrialization, particularly in the food-processing lines. Because of the falls of the White Nile Uganda has considerable water power potential; it also has some copper and a little tin ore, but lacks the great mineral wealth of some of the west African States.

Within the new country Buganda is governed as a separate federated state with its own parliament. It is in turn represented in the federal parliament by just over one-quarter of the total of elected members. The parliament is responsible primarily for conditions in the other, less-developed areas; foreign affairs, defense, and control of the armed forces will, for a time, remain the responsibility of Great Britain. Uganda thus represents an unusual form of independence in Africa, with one area (the richest and most populous) being virtually self-governing, and with defense and foreign affairs still controlled by the former mother country. Kampala, located on

Lake Victoria, is the capital. The country lacks road and rail development in its northern areas and in parts of the southeast, but it is far more intensively settled than are either Kenya or Tanganyika. Uganda's major agricultural exports are subject to price fluctuations and to oversupply, and its future trading position depends on close association with Kenya. Although native agriculture there (particularly in Buganda) is better developed than in most other parts of Africa, Uganda faces a difficult economic future in acquiring foreign currency and in caring for its large and rapidly expanding population.

Tanganyika

Largest of the three countries of the east African mainland is Tanganyika, with 363,000 square miles and over 9 million people. The country was a British mandate and later trust territory, receiving its independence in 1961. Like Uganda, the State consists largely of a plateau 2,000–4,000 feet in elevation, with isolated mountain areas in the northeast near the Kenya border and in the south near Lake Nyasa. In the extreme east are the coastal lowlands with 40–50 inches of rain per year and equatorial rain forest. Inland is the plateau country with open savanna or dry forest, much of it the scene of grazing or shifting native agriculture. In the few highland areas rainfall is sufficient for forests, and the climate is attractive to European settlement, although not to the extent of that in Kenya. There were 22,000 Europeans in 1960, 87,000 Indians, and some 30,000 Arabs, in addition to the 9 million Africans, divided ethnically into more than 100 tribes, each with its own dialects and customs. Swahili, the language of Zanzibar, is spoken throughout the country, as it is also in the eastern and some central areas of Kenya. No one of the tribes, however, is in a position of dominance, as are the Buganda of Uganda or the Kikuyus of Kenya. The Europeans have dominated much of the economic life of Tanganyika, while the Indians occupy many of the civil service positions, giving rise to some racialism in Tanganyika since independence and the decision by many Indians to leave the country.

Tanganyika's economy is based primarily on agriculture, with important export crops being sisal, coffee, cotton, tea, and hides and skins. The country contains one of the world's richest diamond mines as well as some gold, tin, cement, soda ash, copper, and gold. Although wealthier in minerals than Kenya or Uganda, Tanganyika cannot rely heavily on these exports to take care of the needs of its large population. Over most of the plateau area climate and soils, while not inimical to agriculture, are not particularly tempting. Except for a few highland sectors Tanganyika is not a country attractive to white settlers, nor does it offer particularly favorable conditions to the Africans. Because of the long years of uncertainty over the area's political future, foreign capital was not attracted in large quantities. There are inadequate road and rail networks. Population concentrations are scattered—in the highlands along the Kenya border, on the shores of Lake Victoria and the extreme northeast, and in coastal areas, particularly about the ports. Much of central Tanganyika has very few inhabitants. The capital, Dar es Salaam, is located in the extreme east. Railroads connect the port with Lakes Tanganyika and Victoria, but do not adequately serve the densely populated sugar, rice, and cotton areas about Lake Victoria or the coffee-producing highlands of the east and the extreme northeast. In time distance may become a powerful centrifugal force in this country.

The East African Federation Plan

Uganda, Kenya, and Tanganyika have been gradually strengthening their economic bonds. The three territories are united in a customs union, so that no tariffs exist on the movement of goods across their common borders. In 1948 an East Africa High Commission was established with authority over certain activities in the three countries, such as transportation, postal and telegraph services, and customs and excise. There is a common income tax system as well as common excise rates. Thus, in effect, a limited federation already exists there. Such economic cooperation might in time, of course, lead to political integration as well. It is also possible that economic cooperation might be extended to neighboring countries. The most logical region would be Rwanda and Burundi, although the government of Tanganyika has done little so far to encourage such a move. In fact, in 1961, it was announced that Belgian port facilities at Dar es Salaam, leased at one time "in perpetuity," must, by 1963, be handed over to Tanganyika in exchange for adequate compensations. Nyasaland and the Somali Republic are two other neighbors which might in time establish economic links with the federation. In the meantime it stands as the one really serious economic federation in Africa, a program on which considerable study and compromise have already been spent and which may serve as a guide to similar movements among other countries of the continent.

ZANZIBAR

The British protectorate of Zanzibar lies 22 miles off the coast of northern Tanganyika and includes both Zanzibar and Pemba islands. In a humid, tropical area of just over 1,000 square miles live 300,000 people, including about 50,000 Arabs, who own most of the land and control the government, 19,000 Indians, who carry on much of the trade, and some 230,000 Negroes, whose standard of living is generally lower than that of the other two groups. Once a major power in eastern Africa, Zanzibar later became an important point for the transshipment of goods to and from the east African ports. The economy of the two islands is now largely dependent upon the export of cloves and coconut products, as well as the handling of a certain amount of Indian Ocean trade. The people of Zanzibar Protectorate have been restless under the rule of the sultan, and in December, 1963, the area is scheduled for independence within the Commonwealth. When this occurs there are three points to be considered. First, will the Arabs succeed in retaining their position of economic and political power? Second, if they do, Zanzibar, like the Somali Republic, will constitute a "legacy" of Arab coastal control in east Africa and a possible target for "pan-Arab" movements emanating from Cairo. Third, with its high population density, can Zanzibar afford the costs of independence without subsidies from some foreign State, be it Britain, Egypt, the East African Federation, or some other political unit? There, as in the Somali Republic, there may be an economically unstable State whose very existence invites foreign intervention into eastern Africa.

MALAGASY REPUBLIC

The island of Madagascar, known since independence from France as the Malagasy Republic, is located 250 miles off the southeast coast of Africa. With an area of 228,000 square miles, it has a population of just over 5 million, including some 60,000 French, 15,000 Indians, and 7,000 Chinese. The Africans are divided into many tribal groups, the most important of these being the Merina (or Hova), who ruled much of the island before the establishment of French control. The capital city, Tananarive, located in the central highlands, was the former Merina capital.

Madagascar was first sighted by the Portuguese in 1500, but it was late in the nineteenth century before France moved to secure control over the area. Several military campaigns were waged by the French between 1882 and 1895 before the island was completely conquered. In 1896 Madagascar became a French colony, and its subsequent economic development was closely tied to France. In 1960 it achieved its independence.

Madagascar consists of a hot, humid eastern coastal lowland, a central highland area, consisting largely of savanna grasslands, and a drier western lowland, culminating in semiarid conditions in the extreme southwest. There are no well-defined "core areas" on the island. Population is concentrated along the east coast and in the central highlands around and to the south of Tananarive. Since Madagascar is nearly 1,000 miles long, distance represents a major centrifugal force. The island lacks good harbors (except for Diégo-Suarez in the extreme north) as well as navigable rivers, and its upland character makes overland transportation difficult. Hance, in describing the road facilities, wrote, "Fully three-quarters of the roads are of irregular practicality; even the main roads are tortuous and rough except for stretches of 20 to 30 miles near the larger cities. In the rainy season washouts are common . . . ferry service is abandoned or disrupted; roads become pitted or ravined, and many are entirely impassable, or at best only 'jeepable'."[6] The major railroad links the Tananarive area with the east coast port of Tamatave, 150 miles away. Another line, farther south, connects the central highlands with the coast at Manakara, a secondary port. In the absence of adequate transport facilities Madagascar's economic development has been seriously handicapped.

The island exports coffee, rice, cloves, sugar, sisal, and other agricultural goods; mineral products, including graphite, mica, and quartz, make up but a small proportion of the total value of its exports. Much of the area could be utilized more than it is for the production both of subsistence and of export crops, but Madagascar lies off most of the world's shipping lanes, far from the markets of Europe or Anglo-America. Except for its ties with France the country is to a considerable extent isolated, located off a continent which is gradually forming various systems of regional integration. Its nearest neighbor is Portuguese Mozambique, with which it has no political, ethnic, or economic ties. As a young State it has many of the characteristics of west African countries; as an underdeveloped island off southeastern Africa it would appear for some time to have need of considerable foreign economic assistance before indications of national viability may appear.

BIBLIOGRAPHY

CARRINGTON, C. E. "Frontiers in Africa," *International Affairs*, XXXVI (1960), 424–40.

A survey of ethnic and political boundaries.

CARTER, GWENDOLEN M. *Independence for Africa*. New York: Frederick A. Praeger, 1960.

A readable account of the achievement of independence of the African States.

"Economic Problems During the Transfer of Power in Kenya," *The World Today*, XVIII (1962), 164–76.

A summary of Kenya's contemporary economic problems.

HANCE, WILLIAM A. "Transportation in Madagascar," *The Geographical Review*, XLVIII (1958), 45–69.

A regional account of the island's geography.

---

[6] William A. Hance, "Transportation in Madagascar," *The Geographical Review*. XLVIII (1958), 48.

————, KOTSCHAR, VINCENT, and PETEREC, RICHARD J. "Source Areas of Export Production in Tropical Africa," *The Geographical Review,* LI (1961), 487–500.

An excellent map and description of African exports.

HILL, M. F. "The White Settler's Role in Kenya," *Foreign Affairs,* XXXVIII (1960), 636–48.

Excellent review of the white settler's problems.

KIMBLE, GEORGE H. T. *Tropical Africa,* 2 vols. New York: Twentieth Century Fund, 1960.

A detailed reference on African geography.

VAN BILSEN, A. A. J. "Some Aspects of the Congo Problem," *International Affairs,* XXXVIII ((1962), 41–52.

Interesting account of the issues in the former Belgian Congo.

16

SOUTHERN AFRICA

● The area of southern Africa—including South Africa, the federation of the Rhodesias and Nyasaland, and Portuguese colonies of Angola and Mozambique—represents the last major stronghold on the continent of non-African control. Portugal has made no move to grant independence to its colonies, nor have the whites of South Africa or Southern Rhodesia permitted nonwhites to share in the control of these areas. Only in Nyasaland and to some extent in Northern Rhodesia (both still under British sovereignty) have starts been made toward granting Africans an important share in the area's administration. Sweeping political changes are often difficult to arrest at national boundaries; from the Congo and Tanganyika, and from the newly independent territories north of these, the tide of African nationalism presses southward toward the northern "buffer zone" of this region, and beyond it to the Republic of South Africa as well.[1] In this chapter this northern buffer zone (or "northern tier," as it will be referred to collectively here) will be considered first, followed by a discussion of the Republic of South Africa.

THE NORTHERN TIER

The belt of territory extending across Africa from approximately 10° south latitude to the northern borders of Southwest Africa and the Republic of South Africa is, for the most part, a continuation of the central African

---

[1] The name of the former Union of South Africa was changed to the Republic of South Africa in May, 1961, two months before the country withdrew from the British Commonwealth of Nations.

upland, with elevations of 3,000–5,000 feet, entrenched rivers, and occasional highland areas above the plateau, particularly in Nyasaland, sections of the Rhodesias, and central Angola. Most of the area is drained eastward by the Zambezi system, which empties into the Indian Ocean in Mozambique. Because of the prevailing winds and the existence of a cold current along the west coast, the western portion of this area (Angola, Bechuanaland, western Northern Rhodesia) is arid or semiarid. The eastern part, on the other hand, receives considerable precipitation. There has been far greater mineral development there than in the eastern sector of central Africa: copper, lead, asbestos, chrome, coal, and iron ore are valuable commodities, particularly in the Rhodesias.

As late as 1885 the interior of this southern sector between the Congo Free State and the Limpopo River (now the northern border of the Republic of South Africa) remained unsettled and unclaimed by the Europeans. In the following decade, however, practically all the territory was divided politically among the European powers. Concessions for mineral development in what later became the Rhodesias were granted to Cecil Rhodes in 1888 by Lobengula, king of the Matabele, and with this wedge British authority was gradually established in the upper basin of the Zambezi. Bechuanaland became a British protectorate in 1890, in order to protect the route from the Cape Colony north to the Zambezi, and Nyasaland was also annexed as a British protectorate in the following year. Many years were to pass before precise boundaries were worked out between the British and Portuguese territories, but by 1895 the general political pattern of this area had been established, and a British-controlled corridor extended north from Capetown to Tanganyika.

Racial Problems

The relationships between racial groups in the "Northern Tier" differ in certain respects from those in east Africa. The Indian population is not nearly as large and does not constitute a significant political force, while the Arab element is practically nonexistent. Within the territories of Portugal and Britain there is considerable variation in governmental racial policy.

The Portuguese, in their efforts to develop their colonial territories, have been working slowly to bring an end to racial discrimination, although their efforts may in time turn out to have been too little and too late. Angola, on the west coast of Africa, has a Portuguese population of some 120,000 and an African total of over 4,250,000. Both white and nonwhite residents are regarded as Portuguese citizens, but Africans must attain certain standards of education and training before they may enjoy full rights of citizenship. By the end of 1961 about 30,000 of the Africans had graduated to this class. In Mozambique, with 70,000 Europeans and 6 million Africans, less than 1 per cent of the nonwhite population are classed as *assimilados* to be brought into the Western society and live on terms of relative equality with the Europeans. Thus the prospects of equality for the individual African are exceedingly dim. On the other hand, there has been considerably less discrimination of agricultural lands there than in some of the former British territories. In Mozambique, for example, only 4 per cent of the area has been set aside as white reserves. There and in Angola the Portuguese government is undertaking irrigation and land reclamation projects and is opening the region to settlement by both Europeans and natives, the only major conditions being that the natives must agree to follow European-approved agricultural practices on the improved land.

Portugal's colonial policies must be considered in the light of its traditional conservatism toward native advancement as well as shortages of capital and trained personnel to carry out an ambitious *assimilado* policy. Only recently have the Portuguese begun extensive development programs for their two large African territories. In 1953 the government announced a Six-Year Joint Development Plan for Portugal and its overseas territories which resulted in an expenditure of over $100 million for Angola alone. Portugal subsidizes about 11,000 immigrants a year to Angola and assists the area in its production of coffee, diamonds, manganese, and maize—all of which are exported. In the highlands of central Angola and the irrigated areas to the south there is considerable land for future settlement by Portuguese from the homeland.

Mozambique has been less developed than Angola, although there is good agricultural land for tropical plantations as well as highlands in the northwest where European farmers are concentrated. Cotton, sugar, and sisal are important plantation crops which are exported. Mozambique possesses one of Africa's good coal reserves, and the recent construction of a dam on the Limpopo River has opened up rich alluvial lands in the south for European settlement. Finally, both Lourenço Marques and Beira are important ports for handling trade with the African interior. Thus both Mozambique and Angola offer good possibilities for settlement from Portugal (where the annual population increase is close to 50,000 per year), providing additional development funds are forthcoming and political stability can be maintained.

Since 1951 Portugal's overseas possessions have had the status of overseas territories and are considered to be integral parts of the homeland. The generally low economic and cultural levels of the Africans under Portuguese control, combined with the effective police work of the Portuguese themselves, has acted to prevent native uprisings. In March, 1961, however, revolt broke out in northern Angola, in an area inhabited by the Bakongo tribe which also occupies territory across the border in the former Belgian Congo. Approximately 1,000 Portuguese citizens were killed, several hundred coffee plantations were burned, and the bulk of Angola's coffee crop was destroyed. Portuguese army and air units went into action against the rebels, but movement was hampered by the difficult terrain and the forest. Since that time guerrilla warfare has been intermittently in progress in northern Angola, and by August, 1962, a military training camp for Angolan rebels had been established near Thysville, the Congo, about 100 miles north of the Angolan border. The camp was set up with the knowledge and consent of the Léopoldville government. Here, then, is the first direct assault against the non-African tier of states bordering the Republic of South Africa.

Two British protectorates in which there are few Europeans and little racial conflict are Nyasaland, to the north of Mozambique, and Bechuanaland, south of Angola (see page 452). In Nyasaland some 4,000 Europeans are concentrated in the Shire Highlands south of Lake Nyasa and are engaged primarily in plantation agriculture. The remainder of the country is rather densely populated with natives, many of whom remain little affected by the European culture. Northern Rhodesia is a British protectorate which has never attracted large-scale white immigration, partly because of the warm climate (few places are much over 3,000 feet in elevation), the prevalence of disease, particularly malaria, and the relative isolation of the area. In the northwest, however, a sizable white settlement has grown up about the important copper mines, while to the south, at Broken Hill, the mining of lead and zinc has attracted additional Europeans. Altogether there are about 40,000 whites in Northern Rhodesia, and since their major interests are not agricultural, the problem of white and native reserves has never become an acute one. On the other hand, friction exists between white and native miners, since the average wages for the former are considerably higher than for the latter, and relatively few opportunities exist for native advancement in the mining industries. There is an African trade union, and the Africans have gone out on strike to secure better working conditions. A labor agreement in 1955 broke the monopoly position of the white miners' union and opened the way for important advancements by nonwhite workers. Trends such as these are in direct contrast with the position of African labor in the mines of the Republic of South Africa.

In Southern Rhodesia, a self-governing British colony, 140,000 Europeans constitute about 6 per cent of the total population. Since only the whites have the vote, they alone exercise political power, and there is a greater degree of color discrimination there than in other parts of the "Northern Tier." With its iron ore and coal resources Southern Rhodesia has experienced a modest industrial development. Agricultural activity in this country is far more important to the whites than it is in Northern Rhodesia and Nyasaland, however, and Southern Rhodesia, like Kenya, has been faced with the difficult problem of protecting the interests of both white and native farmers. Portions of Southern Rhodesia have been set aside as native reserves, and the whites are divided among themselves on the question of future native policy—whether to follow a "liberal" trend toward the Africans or to adopt more of the restrictive measures which are practiced in the neighboring Republic of South Africa.

The Federation of Rhodesia and Nyasaland

In 1953 Nyasaland and the two Rhodesias were formed into a loose political unit, in which such functions as customs duties, currency, and railways were unified. Within this federation Nyasaland and Northern Rhodesia retained their political status of protectorates, and Southern Rhodesia that of a self-governing colony. A federal parliament was established in Salisbury, Southern Rhodesia, but its duties were limited largely to the economic sphere. Many local problems, including white-native relations, remained within the domain of the individual units.

The primary aims of the federation were to attract greater investment in the new political area and to prepare the region for eventual independence. The impetus for political unification of the three territories came in part from the government in London, which was interested in strengthening the economic basis of its possessions, and in part from local groups in southern Africa. The whites in Nyasaland, faced with serious economic conditions in their protectorate, favored federation in order to bolster the area's position, while the whites of Northern Rhodesia, fearing a decline in the price of copper, were anxious to broaden their territory's economic base by an alignment with the agricultural and industrial economy of Southern Rhodesia. On the other hand, native groups in both Nyasaland and Northern Rhodesia opposed strengthening of the federation because they feared their present protected status would be replaced by more restrictive policies and they might lose their lands and be crowded on native reserves.

By the fall of 1963 the federation had all but broken up. In Nyasaland an interim constitution had permitted internal affairs to be handled largely by Africans under the leadership of the Malawi Congress Party. African political leaders in that country were planning for secession from the federation and for independence by early 1964. In Southern Rhodesia the white-dominated government has indicated it will not accept any solution to the federation problem which will permit African domination of the area. Northern Rhodesia, with its mineral wealth, was in a sense the key to the situation, since with an African-dominated government it would probably not associate politically with Southern Rhodesia, while if the whites continued to control the government it might well have remained in the federation, even if Nyasaland should secede. An interim constitution for Northern Rhodesia, drawn up in March, 1962, provided for increased African par-

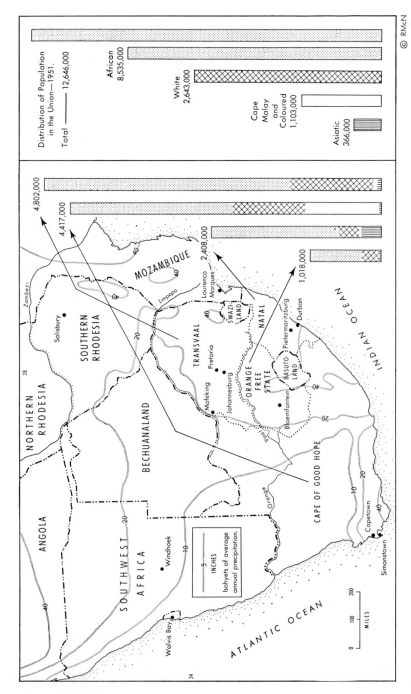

Figure 84. *The Republic of South Africa and Southwest Africa.* (After maps in *Focus,* IV [Oct., 1953]. Courtesy of *Focus*—American Geographical Society.)

ticipation in the territory's affairs (there are more Africans than Europeans in the new Legislative Council) although it remains practically impossible for one African party to form a government unless it relies on the help of the Europeans. Independence for Northern Rhodesia has now been scheduled for early 1964.

The economic future of the area of the Rhodesias and Nyasaland depends in part upon accessibility to the sea. Within recent years the Portuguese have undertaken considerable development of rail and port facilities in Mozambique in order to prepare it as an outlet for the mineral and agricultural exports of the federation. Mozambique is better located to service this area than are the ports of the Republic of South Africa. Moreover, the transportation systems of the Rhodesias have also been improved and have been linked more closely with those of the Portuguese territory. Lourenço Marques in southern Mozambique has a good harbor and has been connected by rail with Southern Rhodesia and through it with Northern Rhodesia, while the port of Beira, four hundred miles to the north of Lourenço Marques, will concentrate on the overseas trade of Nyasaland. Such regional economic cooperation in Africa may lead to the increased development of resources and greater opportunities for political and social advancement for both the European and native peoples.

THE REPUBLIC OF SOUTH AFRICA

At the southern tip of Africa lies that continent's most important and most powerful State. Over one-half of the white residents of Africa live there in the midst of a majority of nonwhites—Negroes, Colored, or half-castes, and Indians—who, taken together, comprise nearly 80 per cent of the Republic of South Africa's population. Rich, strategic, isolated: these terms characterize the republic. Rich in terms of its reserves of minerals and power fuels; strategic because of its location with respect to the south Atlantic and south Indian oceans, as well as to south central Africa; isolated because of its physical removal from other Westernized nations, because of the trend of its racial policies, and because a majority group of its whites has developed a culture of its own, which is neither British nor Dutch but Afrikaans.

Physical Elements

The Republic of South Africa has an area of 472,733 square miles and consists of four provinces—the Cape of Good Hope (or Cape Province), Natal, Orange Free State, and Transvaal (Figure 84). In terms of white population Cape Province and Natal, bordering the coast, have a majority of English-speaking people, while the Orange Free State and Transvaal, in the northeastern uplands, include a predominance of Boers—a name given to the descendants of the original Dutch settlers of South Africa. This population distribution reflects the history of English settlement in the coastal regions during the nineteenth and early twentieth centuries and the migration (trek) of Boers to the interior during the 1830's. There is also a large English concentration in the Johannesburg area of Transvaal, the so-called Rand district, which is the world's greatest gold-producing area.

Within the borders of South Africa there are also two large British-controlled areas, Swaziland and Basutoland, which have been established as native reserves. These areas have a combined population of about 800,-000, and their economies are tied for the most part with that of the Republic.

South Africa's location at the southernmost part of the continent is of great importance both to the republic itself and to its external relations. Its isolation has enabled the republic to enjoy a certain independence in its national development, as evidenced, for example, by the distinctive Boer culture and by the refusal of the present South African government to liberalize its policies toward the nonwhites, despite the trend in this direction throughout other parts of the African continent. Although South Africa was awarded a League of Nations mandate over Southwest Africa at the end of World War I, it has consistently refused since 1945 to accede to United Nations requests to change the area's status to that of a trusteeship territory—another indication of South Africa's independent course of action. In the present era of global interdependence the luxury of national isolation, whether it be of external or internal policies, is one which is becoming increasingly difficult to defend from either a practical or moral point of view. South Africa's position might perhaps be defined as "partial isolation," in that in some respects, such as economic affairs, the country is willing to work closely with other powers, while in other matters it chooses to pursue its own course.

The Republic of South Africa consists largely of a plateau, averaging 3,000 to 6,000 feet in elevation, with a narrow coastal plain in the west, south, and east. Capetown is located at about the same distance from the equator as Cape Hatteras, North Carolina. Because of its latitudinal location and the upland character of most of the country, the climate approaches that of mid-latitude areas. Thus South Africa is one of the relatively few parts of the continent which has attracted permanent white colonization on a large scale. Rainfall is a major factor determining settlement. The western half of the state is arid, but in the east grassland plateaus, utilized for sheep and cattle grazing, merge into forested mountains rising to over 10,000 feet. Wheat, corn, and cotton are important products in eastern South Africa, but the country is not a major food exporter. In minerals the republic is an important producer of gold, diamonds, copper, asbestos, and, to a lesser extent, manganese and platinum. Uranium ores are also being mined. With its reserves of iron ore and coking coal (as well as some hydro-electric power potential) South Africa is in the process of developing its heavy industry. Already it is the major industrial power on the African continent and, although agricultural production is restricted by the physical environment and by poor farming practices, the republic's economic potential is a very good one.

Population Structure

Three basic problems exist in the republic which reflect, in part, the country's ethnic complexity: conflict between the Boers and the British, internal relations between the white and nonwhite peoples, and external relations with Great Britain and the Commonwealth. The population in 1960 was divided as follows: 3 million whites, including about 1,900,000 Boers and 1,100,000 British; approximately 10,800,000 Negroes; 1,490,000 Colored; and 477,000 Indians.

The Boers, who comprise about 63 per cent of the white population, have historic ties with the Dutch culture, although the Afrikaans language which they speak differs from Dutch. A majority of them are members of the Dutch Reformed Church. There are today few sentimental ties between the Boers and the Netherlands; if anything, the Boers have closer sympathies with the Germans. They are strongly nationalistic, but the concept of their country as many of them envision it is not the South Africa of the past. Rather they see it as a future Boer republic, in which little room is left for Englishmen of any sect, for Roman Catholics and Jews, and for non-whites, except in the capacity of unskilled laborers. A majority of the Boers are determined to keep the nonwhites indefinitely in a state of political, social, and economic inferiority, although utilizing their labor for white-controlled enterprises. In the mid-twentieth century concepts such as these can have powerful political repercussions.

The British are somewhat divided concerning South Africa itself and the nonwhite population. Some of the more conservative elements still envision the country as a British-oriented area, complete with British traditions and culture; others are ready to concede the trend toward nationalism, but, with a minority of the Boers, they are anxious to retain South Africa's multicultural character, rather than see it develop into an isolationist, anti-English state. With regard to the nonwhites, only the most liberal of the British are ready to move rapidly along the path of racial equality, but the majority of them are opposed to the reactionary policies of the Boers. Any solution, they feel, lies in a slow but steady education and training of the Negroes and a gradual lifting of restrictions for them as well as for the Colored and Indians, with a distant but eventual goal of complete racial assimilation.

A third group in South Africa are the Negroes, whose population is increasing rapidly and by 1963 will have reached 12 million. The Negroes are the great underprivileged mass in the republic. They have no vote and are represented in the parliament by white officials. Although nearly 70 per cent of the State's population is made up of Negroes, their representatives in the Senate number 4 out of a total of 89 members and in the House of Assembly 3 out of 159. The Negroes are forbidden to own land outside of the native reserves, yet these reserves, comprising but 13 per cent of the country's territory, have large areas which are unsuitable for cultivation. The Negroes are subject to conscription for labor in the South African mines, and their wages throughout the republic are far below those paid to the whites.

Unlike the situation existing in former French Equatorial Africa, where the African society was left largely untouched, the South African whites have exploited the Negro's labor, but have largely destroyed his old tribal society (except in parts of the reserves) and have failed to substitute a new social order in its place. At present about 40 per cent of the Negroes still live on the reserves under conditions of extreme poverty, about 30 per cent live in the cities where most of them work for the whites, and another 30 per cent are tenant farmers on white-owned farms. Despite these drawbacks, however, South Africa attracts large-scale illegal immigration of Africans, particularly from countries adjacent to the republic, since wages here are higher than in the Rhodesias or the Portuguese territories. In addition, there are hundreds of thousands of legal Negro immigrants in South Africa, who also have been attracted by the wages—especially in industry—and by the health, education, and welfare benefits, which are greater there than in most other parts of the continent south of the Sahara.

The Colored (persons of mixed Negro-white ancestry) occupy a slightly higher social position than the Negroes. Nearly 90 per cent are concentrated in the Cape of Good Hope Province, where they work primarily as servants, craftsmen, and manual laborers. Unlike the Negroes, the Colored were for many years permitted to vote in the Cape Province. Since the approximately 40,000 Colored voters generally voted against the Nationalist party candidates, the Boer-controlled government in 1956 established separate voting rolls for the Colored and for the whites. The Colored voters, as well as the Negroes, are now represented in parliament by a fixed number of white officials. The government has also undertaken a reclassification of the republic's Colored population, with the result that some have had their official status changed to Negro.

The Asians in South Africa are the descendants of immigrants who were brought to the area prior to 1913 as indentured laborers to work in the sugar plantations, particularly in Natal Province. Over four-fifths of the Asiatic people in South Africa are still concentrated in Natal, where they find employment as field laborers, small-scale market gardeners, or laborers (mostly unskilled) in industry. In Natal and in the other provinces the Asians are also important as peddlers and as proprietors of small businesses. They are denied the right to vote and are not represented in the South African parliament. Outside of Natal the law forbids Asians from owning land, and the Nationalist government has been setting up restricted areas for those Asians who live and work in the cities. Immigration quotas now prevent all but a small number of Asians from entering the republic.

South African History

The first Europeans to settle in South Africa were the Dutch, who established a watering station at the Cape of Good Hope in 1652 to service their shipping route to the East Indies. In the decades which followed many settlers came from Holland under the auspices of the Dutch East Indies Company and took possession of the lands about Capetown. The inhabitants they found were aboriginal Bushmen. Not until 1770 did the Europeans clash with the Bantus, a more advanced Negro group, whose members were migrating southward from central Africa. In the ensuing clash of cultures, the Europeans, with their greater technical knowledge and training, eventually triumphed, although the Bantus were neither decimated nor driven away, in contrast to conquered native groups in other parts of the world. The Dutch settlers were stern Calvinists, convinced by their reading of the Scriptures that the whites were destined to rule and the non-whites to be ruled. Many of their descendants still hold to this conviction today.

In 1814 Great Britain obtained possession of southernmost Africa. In reaction to British control many Boer settlers soon began to move north and east away from the Cape of Good Hope. The climax came in 1836 when 7,000 Boers began a trek to the Transvaal area. During the nineteenth century, while thousands of British colonists were coming to the southern and eastern coastal areas, the Boers subdued the Bantu armies and developed agricultural areas in what are now Transvaal and the Orange Free State. In 1853 the independent South African Republic was established in the Transvaal. The following year the independence of the Orange Free State was also recognized by the British.

Proud of their culture, the Boers had no wish for interference from the British, but their hopes were in vain, for in 1867 diamonds were discovered in the Orange Free State and twenty years later gold was found in the Transvaal. The subsequent efforts of British miners and financiers—among them Cecil Rhodes—to develop these resources led to growing friction with the Boer settlers. In 1880, after Britain had annexed the independent Transvaal republic, war broke out between the Boers and the

British. After a few months of fighting the British agreed to restore Transvaal's independence, but after the discovery of the enormous gold deposits in the Witwatersrand (at Johannesburg) the conflict of British and Boer interests grew increasingly severe. The rapid influx of British whites and of British capital into the Transvaal was countered by increasing Boer resistance, and finally in 1899 the second Boer War broke out. With the British victory in 1902 the two independent Boer republics were abolished. Eight years later these were joined with Natal and the Cape of Good Hope in the Union of South Africa.

The Rise of South African Nationalism. At the time of the establishment of the union the British inhabitants of the new country were greatly outnumbered by the Boers. Thus a situation existed in which a people who had been defeated militarily might through representative means gain political domination of a country. Equal voting rights were allocated to each of the two white groups, and South Africa became a bilingual area, with legal recognition given to both the English and the Afrikaans languages. The dual nature of South African society was reflected in the establishment of two capitals—one the administrative capital at Pretoria in Transvaal and the other the legislative capital at Capetown. For nearly four decades English was the language generally used in government, education, and economic life, and South Africa was primarily British-oriented in economy and foreign policy. Many Boers, of course, resented the predominant British character of the union, and a pro-Boer political party— the Nationalists—gradually gained strength in the country. After South Africa's achievement of dominion status in 1926 the British government was no longer able to affect policy directly in South Africa, but statesmen such as Louis Botha and Jan Christian Smuts succeeded for a time in unifying the two European elements in South Africa and piloted a course for the country consistent with the spirit and ideas of the rest of the British Commonwealth.

Before World War II the pressure of Boer nationalism grew increasingly strong. Associated with the greater use of Afrikaans were the formation of secret Boer societies and the appearance of violently pro-Boer papers and periodicals. In 1939 the South African parliament approved the country's participation in World War II by a one-vote margin, and during the war many Boers openly supported the German cause. Finally, in 1948 the moderate United South African party of Field Marshall Smuts was voted out of office, its place taken by the Nationalist party, headed by the Boer leader Dr. Daniel F. Malan. Since that time the government has worked to implement its policy of suppression of the nonwhites and of a resurgence of Boer culture. Under the leadership of the Nationalist party South Africa has undertaken a program of increased racial suppression, with no apparent end in sight except the establishment of a permanent white-controlled police state. South Africa thus represents a variation in modern nationalism, in that British power in the area is being replaced, not by a native nonwhite majority as in other parts of Africa and Asia, but by a non-British white minority, whose policies toward the nonwhites are more reactionary than those of the British.

An interesting question, of course, is why, after nearly four decades of cooperation, did the situation develop which the founding fathers of South Africa feared most—namely, that the Boer majority would turn on the British and jeopardize their cultural and political position in the country? A latent spirit of Boer nationalism has existed ever since 1902, but why should it erupt so violently under Malan and his successors? Possibly some Boers have been able to identify the British with liberalism in racial matters. The respect many of the Boers had for the Nazis stemmed in part from the latter's racial concepts. Economics also enter into the picture; much of the wealth in the State is British-controlled, but by the end of World War II many Boers had acquired greater political and economic power. Finally, since the retirement of Field Marshal Smuts from the political scene, there have been no strong leaders for the cause of unity among the South African whites.

The strengthening of the Nationalists' grip on South Africa has actually been carried out by constitutional moves. The Nationalist-dominated South African parliament voted to increase the membership of the Senate from 48 to 89 (thus giving their party an overwhelming majority in that body) and to expand the Supreme Court from 5 to 11 members, the new members being appointed by the Nationalists. Thus as the political opposition was gradually rendered ineffective, the Boers, representing less than one-sixth of the total population, have moved into a position of dominance over the Republic.

In the years since 1948 the Nationalist-controlled government has sought to institute a policy of *apartheid* (literally "apartness") as a solution to South Africa's racial problem. Since there is obvious friction between races attempting to exist side by side, the logical step, government officials contend, would be to separate them into areas where they can live with people of their own kind. Such a drastic move would, however, deprive the whites of nonwhite labor (as well as deprive many nonwhites of the means of employment), so that the government has modified the true *apartheid* concept and turned to what might be termed a policy of partial *apartheid*. Under this policy, embodied in the Group Areas Act passed in 1950 by the South African parliament, the Negroes would be encouraged to live in their reserves, where they would have local autonomy, although government inspectors would be permitted to enter and government troops to maintain order if necessary.

In addition to the reserves, restricted areas would be set up in the

South African cities in which Negroes live. Wherever possible the restricted areas would be moved well beyond the city limits, so that, except during their working hours, the Negroes would be excluded entirely from white-occupied portions of the city. The establishment of these restricted areas would alleviate population pressure on the reserves. It would also, of course, make available a supply of cheap labor for white-owned industries. Negro laborers would also continue to work in the mines and on white-owned farms; again in both instances their living quarters would be carefully restricted from those of the whites. Although aimed primarily at South Africa's Negroes, *apartheid* also works to the detriment of the Colored and Asians. No special reserves are provided for these groups, but they too are to be restricted to certain areas within the cities.

There are 264 separate areas in South Africa reserved for residence by Africans; taken together these constitute but 13 per cent of the country's total area, on which live some 40 per cent of the African population. The South African government contemplates consolidating these reserves into seven "Bantustans" in which the Negroes could live apart from the whites, although under white jurisdiction. Eventually the reserves would achieve provincial self-government. The incorporation of the British High Commission Territories of Basutoland and Swaziland, as well as the Protectorate of Bechuanaland, within the republic would increase the potential area for the reserves by nearly 300,000 square miles, although the bulk of this, comprising Bechuanaland, is arid or semiarid. Obviously the reserves could not provide livelihoods for all of the Africans; many would be forced to seek work for the whites in the republic, but they would be permitted out of the reserves only as "temporary laborers" to live in restricted areas near the mines, on the farms, or on the outskirts of the cities.

In 1963 the South African government plans to establish the first of its reserve areas, the Transkei, some 16,000 square miles in extent, to the south of the city of Durban. Lying between the Drakensberg Mountains and the Indian Ocean, this area is the home of the Xhosa tribe; under the proposed constitution, there would be a representative assembly with jurisdiction over such matters as agriculture, education, and health and welfare services, although foreign affairs, defense, and the administration of justice would remain the responsibility of the South African government. More than 40 per cent of the area's 1,500,000 inhabitants normally work outside the proposed reserve. Presumably these conditions would continue, although in time other Africans would be moved to the Transkei as well.

Unfortunately few substitute proposals have originated in South Africa for solving the racial questions. Boers and English alike are united in their fear of black domination. The cultural level of the Negroes and of many of the Colored is abysmally low when compared with white standards, and the task of raising these levels to a point approaching that of the whites appears to many South African leaders as too expensive and time-consuming to be practical. On the other hand, an indefinite continuation of racial suppression contains many elements of potential danger. As fear and unrest among the nonwhites increases, so also does government resistance. Law-enforcement measures are becoming increasingly severe against persons of all races who oppose government policies, civil liberties are gradually suppressed, and the country moves toward a fascist type of regime.[2]

South Africa's External Relations. South Africa's relations with other countries of the world have been complicated not only by its racial policies, but also by its territory of Southwest Africa, by the continued British control of Bechuanaland, Swaziland, and Basutoland, and by South Africa's economic and political significance in world affairs. The gradual estrangement of South Africa from Britain was marked, first, in 1955 by the turnover of British control of the Simonstown naval base located near Capetown to the South African government, with the provision that it could be reoccupied by the British in the event of war, even if South Africa remained neutral. Six years later the South African government voted to become a republic (the Queen was no longer recognized as the sovereign head of the country), and shortly thereafter it left the Commonwealth entirely. There is still an important pro-British element in the population, and economic ties with Britain remain strong, but over the years South Africa has gradually moved into a position of complete political and military separation from Britain.

Of the three British-held protectorates, Basutoland and Swaziland are virtually surrounded by South Africa and are closely linked with it economically. Nearly half the able-bodied males of Basutoland normally work in South Africa, and considerable numbers from Bechuanaland and Swaziland do likewise. The British have been trying to develop the territories politically along nonracial lines and thus permit African political parties to operate there, although such parties are banned in the republic. In keeping with the treaty of 1910 the British have consistently refused to turn over sovereignty of these areas to the Republic of South Africa until the wishes of the local inhabitants can be clearly determined. Here, then, is a potentially explosive situation. Even without direct military action the republic could cripple economic conditions, particularly in Swaziland and Basutoland, by imposing an economic blockade and refusing to permit laborers from these areas to work in South Africa. Yet the British are committed to resist any South African take-over, and with relations between

---

[2] By 1962 the South African government had begun an active drive to recruit white settlers from Europe, hoping by the year 2000 to have 10 million whites in the republic as a balance against the nonwhites.

Britain and the republic apparently growing cooler with time, there is less inclination even than several years ago for Britain to reverse its position.[3]

SOUTHWEST AFRICA. Southwest Africa is the only post-World War II mandate that has not become a United Nations trusteeship territory. The country, which lies to the north and west of the Republic of South Africa, has an area of 325,000 square miles, consisting almost entirely of desert, and a population of 525,000, of which nearly 90 per cent are nonwhites. Walvis Bay, a South African enclave on the coast, is administered by Southwest Africa and is the leading port. There are some grazing lands in the central sector, and Southwest Africa exports wool, karakul skins, and other pastoral products and is also noted for its diamond and vanadium resources.

Of the 75,000 whites in the area over two-thirds are Boers and the rest mostly German-speaking. Like most of the Boers the Germans are generally in favor of a policy of white supremacy. Because of its poor economic prospects, Southwest Africa was one of the last of the African areas to be settled by Europeans: colonization was finally begun by Germany in the 1880's. A bitter four-year war raged from 1903 to 1907 between the German army and the local tribes, so that by 1911 the African population had been reduced to less than 30 per cent of what it had been in 1904. The Negro's resentment against the white man was further increased by the extremely harsh treatment meted out by the German colonial administration, particularly after 1911. When the League of Nations selected the Union of South Africa to take on the mandate of the area in 1919, it was generally anticipated that conditions among the Negroes would improve substantially.

Since that time, however, South Africa has failed to carry out the provisions of its mandate. South Africa was directed to "promote to the utmost the material and moral well-being and the social progress of the inhabitants." Nevertheless, the system of reserves and conscription of Negro labor as practiced in the republic is also in force in Southwest Africa. The reserves themselves are overpopulated. The country needs industries, irrigation projects, and increased agricultural training for the Africans. Through its exports Southwest Africa has developed a favorable balance of trade, but, rather than utilize this surplus for the betterment of the mandate, the republic employs most of the credits to supplement the economy of South Africa itself—a major factor in the republic's reluctance to report to the United Nations on its administration of the territory.

Since 1945 the republic has governed Southwest Africa as part of its own territory. For a short time South Africa did submit reports on the territory to the UN Trusteeship Council, but after the inauguration of Dr.

---

[3] Should South Africa take over Swaziland and establish it as a native reserve, there would be a problem concerning the 6,000 whites living there who own 45 per cent of the land and who would resist losing this to the Africans.

Malan in 1948 even this practice ended. In the following year Southwest Africa was assigned six seats in the South African parliament, and in 1954 the Nationalist party announced that the mandate over the territory was terminated. The United Nations has specifically refused permission to the republic to annex Southwest Africa, and the International Court at The Hague has handed down an opinion advising South Africa that it is obligated to submit annual reports to the United Nations and that it should not undertake any change in the status of the mandate without United Nations consent. Despite these moves, however, the Nationalist party has come out in favor of creating Southwest Africa as the fifth province within the republic. The former mandate is already a *de facto* territory within the republic, but here, as in the case of the British protectorates, the government has resisted any moves for formal annexation.

BIBLIOGRAPHY

BALLINGER, MARGARET. "The Outlook for the South African Republic," *International Affairs*, XXXVIII (1962), 295–304.
A concise account of the country's problems.

BUCHANAN, KEITH and HURWITZ, N. "The Asiatic Immigrant Community in the Union of South Africa," *The Geographical Review*, XXXIX (1949), 440–50.

———. "The 'Colored' Community in the Union of South Africa," *The Geographical Review*, XL (1950), 397–415.
Valuable maps, charts, and discussions of the racial problems of South Africa.

DE BLIJ, HARM J. *Africa South*. Evanston, Ill.: Northwestern University Press, 1962.
A good regional treatment of southern Africa.

———. "Notes on the Geography of South West Africa," *Journal of Geography*, LVII (1958), 333–41.
Summary of Southwest Africa.

DUFFY, JAMES. "Portugal in Africa," *Foreign Affairs*, XXXIX (1961), 481–94.
A discussion of political and economic trends.

GRAAFE, SIR DE VILLIERS. "South African Prospect," *Foreign Affairs,* XXXIX (1961), 670–83.

A general survey of the republic's future.

HOUK, RICHARD J. "Recent Developments in the Portuguese Congo," *The Geographical Review,* XLVIII (1958), 201–22.

A good regional politico-geographic study.

SCOTT, MICHAEL. "The International Status of South-West Africa," *International Affairs,* XXXIV (1958), 318–30.

Historical and legal approach.

"The Statutory Background of Apartheid," *The World Today,* XVI (1960), 181–94.

Like Scott's article, a careful appraisal of the historical and legal aspects of the problem.

17

THE INDIAN SUBCONTINENT

● In 1947 the subcontinent of India was partitioned into two independent States—India and Pakistan—along the lines of the religious division which exists there. The subcontinent, surrounded by mountains and by the sea, forms a distinct geographic unit, which under British control had been developed as a unified economic and political area. Since the partition, however, millions of persons in India and Pakistan have become refugees, conflicting claims to territorial control have arisen in various parts of the subcontinent, and relations between the two States have been severely strained. As a result the Indian subcontinent has become one of the outstanding politico-geographic problem areas of the world.

THE GEOGRAPHIC BASIS OF THE SUBCONTINENT

The Indian subcontinent occupies a transitional location in southern Asia between the humid States of southeastern Asia and the desert areas which lie to the west. Many people from India have settled in Burma, Malaya, and other southeast Asian countries, and since 1947 India has occupied a position of leadership in international affairs among a number of the states in this area. Pakistan, on the other hand, with its arid western portion and its large Moslem population, has more elements of affinity with Iran and the Arab World to the west than with the countries which lie to the east of it.

The physical structure of the Indian subcontinent reveals both the unity and the diversity of the area. There are three major surface features:

(1) the mountain wall in the northwest, north, and northeast; (2) the block of old resistant rock of the Deccan Plateau in the central and southern portions; and (3) the Indus-Ganges lowland, forming an arc about the northern end of the plateau from the mouth of the Indus River on the Arabian Sea to that of the Ganges on the Bay of Bengal. The mountain wall and the Indus-Ganges lowland are shared by both India and Pakistan. The Deccan Plateau lies entirely within India (Figure 85).

The mountain wall consists of numerous highland structures (including the Himalaya and Karakorum ranges, the loftiest mountain system in the world) and fertile valleys, which have served as core areas for the development of individual cultural and political units. Relatively few passes exist through the mountain borders: the Khyber and Bolan passes to Afghanistan, the Makran coastal route to Iran, and the road through Sikkim to Tibet

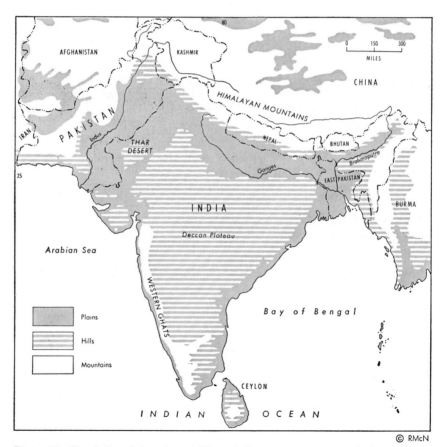

© RMcN

Figure 85. The Indian Subcontinent: Physical Features.

and southern China. Beyond the highland rim are generally inhospitable areas, notably the deserts of Iran and Afghanistan, the plateau of northeastern Afghanistan and Tibet, and the forested mountain ranges of Burma, all of which have added to India's relative inaccessibility by land.

The Deccan Plateau is a region of considerable physical diversity—coastal highlands, canyons, and forested hills—which have contributed to the ethnic differences among its population and to the historical development of its political units. Since 1947 one of the principal tasks of the Indian government has been to weld together the various groups inhabiting the Deccan within the framework of a cohesive national unit.

The lowlands of the Indus-Ganges area exhibit greater topographic homogeneity than the other principal physical regions, but climatic differences, despite the smoothness of transitions, are great. West Pakistan occupies the major share of the Indus lowland; India controls the Ganges plain, except in the eastern sector of the delta area which forms part of East Pakistan. Thus, despite their elements of physical unity, these lowlands are divided by political borders.

Virtually all of the republic of India is influenced by the summer monsoon, with moderate to heavy rainfall during the summer months. East Pakistan is also affected by the monsoon. In parts of the central Deccan Peninsula (in the lee of the Western Ghats) and in most of West Pakistan semiarid to arid conditions occur. The mountains which border the subcontinent have their own peculiar climates. Natural vegetation reflects the climatic pattern and ranges from the tropical forests of the west Deccan coast and eastern India to the drought-resistant plants of the western deserts. Soils also vary widely, according to conditions of climate, vegetation, and underlying rock. Among the many varieties of soils is the fertile alluvium of the Ganges flood plain and delta, which supports some of the most densely populated agricultural areas in the world.

The distribution of minerals and power fuels is uneven, with most of the reserves located on the Deccan Plateau or to the northeast in the general Calcutta area. The Indian State has thus come to possess a majority of these resources. Hydroelectric power potential exists in the mountain rim, but inaccessibility and lack of good sites for power stations have ruled out much development in these areas. It is also present in some of the well-watered upland areas, such as the Western Ghats and the hills of Assam, and, of course, in connection with the great river systems of the subcontinent.

Although differences in physical features throughout the subcontinent are reflected in regional economic differences, before partition there had gradually evolved in India a pattern of economic unity, based on rail and road nets, irrigation systems, and the movement of goods (cotton, jute, oil seeds, and wool) from agricultural to industrial areas. The distribution of investments became nationwide, and a potential market of 400 million customers stimulated economic growth. Across this geographic and economic unit a political border was superimposed in 1947.

THE POLITICAL DEVELOPMENT OF THE SUBCONTINENT
The Colonial Period

In spite of the mountain rim which surrounds it on its land sides, the Indian subcontinent was invaded many times by peoples from the northwest before the arrival by sea of the Portuguese at the end of the fifteenth century. Among the invading groups were the Macedonians under Alexander the Great, the Arabs, bringing with them the Moslem faith, and the Moguls under Tamerlane. Sailing east after rounding the tip of Africa, the Portuguese navigator Vasco da Gama reached the coast of India in 1498, and for the next two hundred years India was the scene of commercial—and, to a lesser degree, political—competition among Portugal, the Netherlands, France, and Britain. Eventually British sea and land power triumphed: Dutch rivalry was eliminated, and the possessions of Portugal and France were reduced to a few coastal enclaves.

At the beginning of the nineteenth century British control in India was still administered through the East India Company, a government-chartered commercial organization. In 1858 the British government assumed the responsibilities of administration, and the subcontinent was divided politically into (1) British India, containing about 55 per cent of the total area and approximately 75 per cent of the population, which was administered as a colonial region; and (2) the Native States and Agencies (numbering well into the hundreds), which continued to exist as protectorates of the British.

During the 1870's a nationalist movement got under way in India, and by 1900 Indian leaders were agitating for the country's independence. As in other units of the empire, the British gradually instituted measures granting increasingly greater self-rule for the Indian peoples. The British government, however, insisted that workable arrangements had to be devised to protect the interests of the various cultural groups within the subcontinent before independence could be achieved. The majority of the population was Hindu, but there existed a large Moslem group in the country, as well as Christians, Sikhs, and smaller minority groups. The Moslem leaders were opposed to the creation of a united, Hindu-dominated state in which Moslems would be in a definite minority.

Following World War I the political power of the Moslems grew increasingly strong, and in 1940 the Moslem league officially demanded the creation of an independent Moslem State. Two years later, the British Parliament offered independence to India, but neither the Hindu nor the Moslem political leaders could agree on conditions for self-government. After many conferences between British, Hindu, and Moslem representatives, a plan was eventually worked out for the partition of India into two States—India, a Hindu nation, and Pakistan, a Moslem one. Finally, in August, 1947, the partition plan went into effect, and two new dominions were created (Table 14).

Table 14

AREA AND POPULATION OF INDIA AND PAKISTAN

(Pop. (1941) in thousands; area in sq. mi.)

	Area	Pop.	Density	Moslems	%	Non-Moslems	%
Western Pakistan	306,977	28,258	92	22,328	79.5	5,930	20.5
Eastern Pakistan	54,030	41,845	775	29,381	67.8	12,464	32.2
Total, Pakistan	361,007	70,103	194	51,709	72.7	18,394	27.3
Indian Union	1,138,551	315,480	277	38,965	12.4	276,192*	87.6
Kashmir	82,258	4,022	48	3,074	77.1	948	22.9

*No data available for religious beliefs of 323,000 persons, formerly in French India, now in the Indian Union.

Source: O. H. K. Spate, "The Partition of India and the Prospects of Pakistan," *The Geographical Review*, XXXVIII, No. 1 (January, 1948), 17. Courtesy of the American Geographical Society.

The Division of the Subcontinent

The political partitioning of the Indian subcontinent was an extremely complicated process, for, on the one hand, religion was the essential basis for division, yet, on the other hand, economic and strategic factors also had to be taken into account in the delimitation of the new boundaries. In several areas Hindu and Moslem groups were so intermingled with one another that no workable boundary could be laid down separating them from one another.

The Position of the Provinces. In the course of partitioning, the provinces of what had formerly been British India were assigned to the two States on the basis of the religion of the majority of the population. In three cases—Punjab, Bengal, and Assam—the individual provinces were divided, however.

In Punjab, in the north central part of the subcontinent, the new boundary cut across a unified agricultural region (Figure 86). The Punjab (99,000 square miles, with a population of over 28 million) produced the largest grain surplus of the Indian provinces, and much of its agriculture was dependent on its extensive irrigation system which was fed by the waters of the eastern tributaries of the Indus River. Punjab was also the home of over 5 million Sikhs, and in the partition Sikh territory, including a large number of holy places, was divided. The political division of the Punjab left 75 per cent of its Moslem population in Pakistan (as well

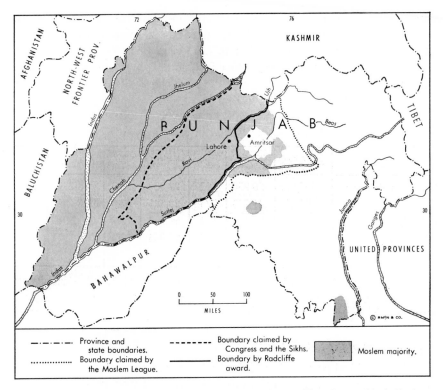

Figure 86. The Partition of the Punjab. (After Spate, *The Geographical Review,* XXXVIII [Jan., 1948]. Courtesy of American Geographical Society.)

as 4 million non-Moslems). Most of the canal irrigation works, as well as about 70 per cent of the irrigated land, also were awarded to Pakistan. Control of the waters for the irrigation systems, however, remained in Indian hands, since the headwaters of the eastern Indus tributaries flow through India. The Radcliffe Award[1] thus split a unified irrigation system, but it granted to Pakistan the basis for its present food surplus.

In Bengal Province (77,000 square miles and 60 million people), located to the east in the Ganges Delta, the partition left approximately 71 per cent of the Moslems in Pakistani territory, together with 11,500,000 non-Moslems (Figure 87). The boundary severed direct communications between Calcutta and the Indian province of Assam east of the Pakistani territory and left practically all the industrial developments in India, while Pakistan won the better agricultural land and most of the jute- and rice-producing areas. Thus not only was the unified communication network

---

[1] A name applied to the lines partitioning Punjab and Bengal; so called because of Sir Cyril Radcliffe, chairman of the boundary commissions for both areas.

centered on Calcutta divided by the new boundary, but so also was the agricultural-industrial unity destroyed, with India controlling the processing plants (particularly for jute) and Pakistan the raw materials. The division of Assam Province (62,800 square miles, population 8 million) resulted in the inclusion of most of Sylhet District in East Pakistan. With an area of 4,600 square miles, this district, to the northeast of Dacca, contained about 1,700,000 Moslems and 1 million non-Moslems.

The Native States and Agencies. The various Indian states and agencies were given the choice of acceding to either India or Pakistan. Eventually all but four were joined to India. Bahawalpur, Khairpur, the North-

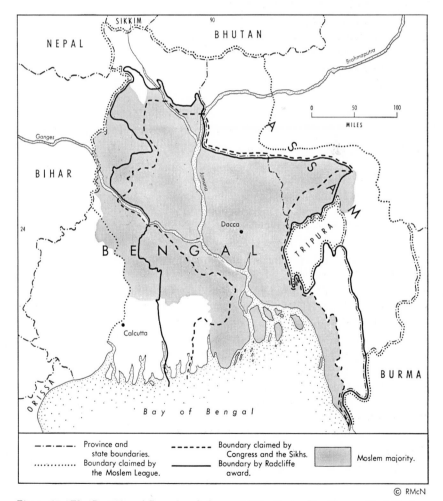

Figure 87. The Partition of Bengal and Assam. (After Spate, *The Geographical Review,* XXXVIII [Jan., 1948]. Courtesy of American Geographical Society.)

West Frontier Agencies, and the Baluchistan states, located in the western part of the subcontinent, acceded to Pakistan. Hyderabad, in the central portion of the Deccan Peninsula, and Kashmir, in the northwestern sector of the subcontinent, delayed joining either country, but in 1948 Hyderabad was occupied by Indian troops and was subsequently joined to India. (For a discussion of Kashmir see page 472.) With the inclusion of Hyderabad, India acquired three-quarters of the prepartition area of the subcontinent and 78 per cent of its population, as well as a majority of its mineral and power resources, while Pakistan, whose two parts were separated from one another by nearly 1,000 miles of Indian territory, received approximately one-quarter of the subcontinent's area and population, as well as those districts which normally produce a surplus of grains, cotton, and jute, but the new State contained practically no minerals and few power resources.

The Nature of the Indo-Pakistan Boundary. The boundary between India and Pakistan was one of the greatest politico-geographical problems the world has ever known. Although this boundary was based primarily on religious considerations, approximately 50 million persons were left on the wrong side of the boundary as a result of its delimitation. Since 1947 an estimated 16–17 million people have crossed between India and Pakistan as political refugees, and some 300,000 persons have been killed in border conflicts.

Much of the boundary follows the political borders of prepartition provinces and Native States. Two tributaries of the Indus—the Sutlej and Ravi rivers—mark portions of the border in Punjab, and in Bengal the Ganges and tributaries of the Meghna are similarly used. In East Pakistan the river boundaries have given rise to local problems of delimitation, as a result of shifting courses and of inadequate descriptions in the Radcliffe Award. In the northern East Pakistan area are 130 small Indian enclaves (with a total area of 33 square miles) and 93 Pakistani enclaves (19 square miles); approximately 23,500 persons inhabit these various enclaves.[2]

Much of the Indo-Pakistan boundary has yet to be demarcated. Because of continued friction between India and Pakistan since 1947, various restrictions have been imposed on the movements of peoples and products across the borders. Such restrictions magnify the problems of normal economic and cultural contacts in the subcontinent. Settlement patterns and economic activities have gradually adjusted to the existence of the boundary lines, but in many parts of the subcontinent the scars of these superimposed lines are in evidence in road and rail blocks, unused irrigation systems, and deserted farms and villages.

The Causes and Effects of Partition. In view of the magnitude of this

---

[2] Figures from P. P. Karan, "Indo-Pakistan Boundaries," *The Indian Geographical Journal*, XXVIII (1953), 19–23.

political problem, the question might well be asked, Was partition necessary, or could India have developed as a united, independent State? Out of a total Indian population of about 390 million in 1941, about 94 million, or some 25 per cent, were Moslems. The Hindus, comprising the bulk of the non-Moslem population, were in favor of a unified State but shortly before World War II the Moslems came out in favor of partition. Ninety-four million Moslems in a predominantly non-Moslem nation would represent the largest minority group in the world.

Although religion was often cited as the principal reason behind the Moslem demands, political and economic factors were probably of greater importance. Hindus had taken the lead in the struggle for independence, they were more advanced than the Moslems in education and the professions, and in the national government Hindus would have been in a permanent majority. Moslem business and financial groups feared that they would be in a poor competitive situation with regard to the more entrenched Hindu interests. Factors such as these formed the basis for a tremendous popular movement, which, fanned by religious fervor, succeeded in bringing about the partition of the Indian subcontinent.

INDIA

The Republic of India, faced with a population increase of about 80 million per decade, is hard put to provide even the basic necessities of life for its people. With an area about 40 per cent of that of the United States, India has a population two and one-quarter times as great. Its over 440 million persons make it second only to China in size of population. Because of its population, its location, and its economic potential, independent India has become one of the important powers of the world, a leading country in the rapidly changing political and economic area of Asia.

The process of modernizing the Indian State has meant that many of the traditional customs and political systems must be changed. For example, the gradual abolition of the worst abuses of the caste system will eventually mean that approximately 50 million "untouchables" (persons of the lowest Hindu caste) must be assimilated into the country's social structure. The population–food supply ratio remains a pressing problem. Some Indian experts favor birth control as a means of easing the strain on India's resources, although such a practice would conflict with the tenets of the Hindu faith. Major changes in India's system of land ownership could lead to a more efficient distribution of crop land among the farmers. Much work has also been necessary in educating the great masses of the Indian people to the responsibilities of self-government and in acquainting them with important issues.

Agricultural Problems and Trends

In order to provide additional food for a growing population, a State must either expand the area of cultivated land, increase the average yield in areas already in production, or depend on large-scale imports of food to supplement domestic production. In India, where intensive cultivation has been going on for many centuries, much of the potentially arable land is already in crops. Maximum utilization in many agricultural areas is hindered by the shortage of fertilizers, small dispersed farm holdings (a result of inheritance laws), and ignorance of modern farming methods.

In their efforts to obtain fuel for heating and cooking the Indian farmers burn cow dung, which might better serve as fertilizer on the fields, or use even small trees and bushes, thereby hastening soil erosion. Food production is further hindered by the failure to rotate crops (and thus prevent soil exhaustion) and by local concentrations on cash crops, such as cotton and jute, rather than on grains or vegetables. A final factor is the uncertainty of rainfall in India, where a delay of the summer monsoon can spell crop disaster and famine for millions of people in large areas of the country.

It has been estimated[3] that in 1951, 250 million persons in India were dependent upon agriculture. Of these, over 75 million were classed as landless laborers. Among this tremendous group of farmers such political philosophies as communism often have considerable appeal.

The Indian government has been making impressive headway in its battle to overcome the obstacles to increased food production, but it still has far to go before the mass of the Indian population can be assured an adequate diet. Large-scale irrigation projects, increased fertilizer production, technical training for farmers, better distribution of food—these and similar projects requiring capital, skilled personnel, and a change in traditional Indian ways of life must be undertaken if India is to bring the general standard of living of its increasing population even remotely in line with that of Western countries. Under the first five-year plan, which ended in March, 1956, 8 million additional acres of land were put under irrigation. During this same time the Community Development Program sent thousands of trained workers into Indian towns and villages to educate and train the people in modern agricultural techniques.

It has been estimated that India must increase its food production by at least 2 per cent per year in order to keep pace with the rising population. Although during the first five-year plan expansion in agricultural output was sufficient to at least match the population rise, the rate of growth tended to fall off during the late 1950's. The Indian government hopes during the third five-year plan (which ends in 1966) to increase food output

---

[3] George Kuriyan, "India's Population Problem," *Focus,* V (1954).

50 per cent over the record harvest of 1958–59, although such a goal will require substantial expenditures of capital and technological training.

India has supplemented its domestic production by annual imports of food from grain-surplus areas, such as the United States and the Soviet Union. Because of India's shortage of foreign exchange, a part of these imports has been made possible by the granting of long-term credits to India. As a result of the country's strategic position in world affairs, both the United States and the U.S.S.R. have made important contributions toward alleviating India's food shortages, despite the fact that its government has consistently refused to align itself with either of the power blocs in the Cold War.

Industrial Growth

In addition to its agricultural resources, India has many of the essentials for industrialization, including minerals, power resources, labor, markets, and transportation. Its minerals include a large reserve of good iron ore, as well as manganese (essential to the production of some types of steel), bauxite (aluminum ore), salt, and mica. The country has a great water power potential, of which less than 10 per cent is developed, and a relatively small amount of coal. Petroleum is almost nonexistent, along with copper, lead, zinc, and several ferroalloys. Before partition native and British capital was responsible for the establishment of a large number of industries in India, including iron and steel, textiles, jute, and food processing, and for the construction of an extensive rail system throughout both India and what is now Pakistan.

India's third five-year plan calls for an investment (both public and private) of over $22 billion, an increase in the national income of 29 per cent, and the achievement of self-sufficiency in grains. Increasing India's industrial facilities can provide additional employment for the growing population as well as make available more products for the home market.

India is in a sense engaged in an economic race with its neighbor Communist China to determine which socio-economic system can best provide for the needs of the respective countries' populations. Success in such a race may be measured by several variables; the gross national products of the two States, their industrial outputs, average per capita incomes, or simply the abilities of the two governments one way or another to provide for the basic needs of their inhabitants. China, through Communist coercion, has adopted one course of action for meeting its present economic requirements, while India has chosen another path, one which respects individual liberties, at the same time seeking to raise living standards as rapidly as possible. China has a far greater population than India; it also has more coal and petroleum than India as well as more potentially arable land. India has had the advantages of large-scale foreign aid which China has in general been denied. Through its program of investment in heavy industry China is pulling ahead of India in terms of industrial output; on the other hand, China faces staggering problems of food procurement, either through domestic sources or from abroad. Soviet aid to China has declined considerably in recent years (see page 530). India also faces such problems, but its population is not as great and it is in a position to receive grain and other food imports from the United States.

Internal Political Problems

Centrifugal forces in India include the diverse physical features, the many languages which exist there, and the presence of two great cities, Bombay and Calcutta, which tend to rival one another in power. The national capital, located at New Delhi in the northwest of India, is the center of many transportation routes. The shifting of the seat of government from Calcutta (where the British had originally located it) to New Delhi in 1912 was a symbol of India's gradual independence from overseas influence and power.

One of the great tasks facing the Indian government since 1947 has been to simplify the pattern of the former Native States, in order to form a more efficient national economic and political structure. Local rulers were urged to surrender control over their historic political units and were "pensioned off" by the Indian government, with the result that the number of states in India was eventually reduced to 28. The resultant savings in local government expenditures and the increase in efficiency of economic operations have reaped considerable benefits to the Indian government.

A new internal political problem has appeared in India in the form of demands for new states to be set up along linguistic lines. Fourteen major languages are spoken in India, but Hindi has been designated as the official tongue (Figure 88). The issue of political divisions on the basis of local languages was considered at the time India attained independence, but little was done until 1953, when the government, after considerable pressure, agreed to the creation of a new Telegu-speaking state of Andhra in southeast India, comprised of territory formerly belonging to Madras state.

Recognition of the political rights of 20 million Telegu-speaking persons brought demands for similar concessions from other linguistic groups throughout the country. To the government this linguistic regionalism represents a potential force for national disunity. Less than half of the population as yet speaks Hindi, and Indian officials have been trying to de-emphasize the cultural differences among the country's inhabitants, rather than strengthen them by yielding to demands for linguistic sectionalism. On the other hand, many of the Indian people have a strong sense of loyalty to

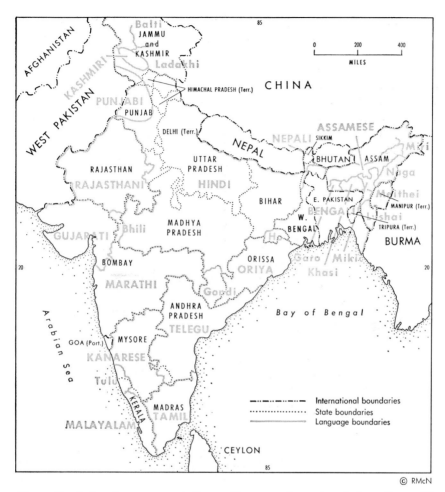

Figure 88. India: Languages and States. (Language data adapted from *Focus,* VI [Feb., 1956]. Courtesy of *Focus*–American Geograpical Society.)

their particular language, and the government was under great pressure to redraw the political map of India, even though by following linguistic patterns in the determination of states it might destroy some of the economic cohesion which existed within the political units as they had been delimited.

After considerable discussion—and occasional outbreaks of violence—the Indian government effected a major revision of the internal political pattern. As of November 1, 1956, the number of states was reduced to 14 (including Kashmir). Hyderabad and eight other states were abolished, and Bihar, in northeast India, relinquished two pieces of its territory to West Bengal. These efforts failed, however, to settle all the problems of internal control. In Punjab some 5½ million Sikhs use Punjabi written in the Gurmukhi script, while 10 million Hindus, also speaking Punjabi, use the Devangari script; some Sikhs have advocated that Punjab be split into two states, one Sikh and one Hindu. Difficulties have also developed in Assam between 4½ million Assamese-speaking people and 3 million who speak Bengali and who are educationally and economically better off than the Assamese. Along the northeastern border the Indian government has for years been engaged in fighting against Naga tribesmen who desire a separate state for some 400,000 people in this remote area of hills and forests. In 1960 the government finally agreed to the formation of an advisory council to draw up a constitution for the eventual establishment of a new state of Nagaland.

The only major change in the pattern of internal political units in India since 1956 took place when Bombay was split in 1960 into two states —Gujerat and Maharashtra. Prepartition Bombay was the largest of the Indian states and included some 18½ million persons speaking Gujerati, inhabiting the north and west of the province, and 29½ million who speak Marathi in the southern and eastern areas. The problem of dividing the province involved the future of the city of Bombay, whose industry and trade is controlled largely by the Gujeratis, but a majority of whose population are Maharashtrians. At first the Indian government suggested dividing Bombay province linguistically, with the city of Bombay set up as a federally administered district, and thus not in either of the two new states. Bloody riots followed the suggestion, and ultimately it was decided that Bombay should go with the Maharashtrians, with the Gujeratis receiving financial compensation for the loss of the great port. Obviously, as in the case of other areas, Indian leaders would hope that in time a spirit of nationalism might come to replace that of regional and linguistic loyalties so that, in addition to the many other problems it faces, the government would not continually be concerned with disputes of internal partitioning. One method of reducing the incidence of such disputes would be the gradual spread of one national language to all parts of India.

External Problems

Since achievement of independence India has faced a variety of external problems—with Pakistan, with other units of the British Commonwealth, with Portugal, with Communist China, and finally with the various members of the Cold War power alignments. As an expression of its national freedom the Indian government in 1948 changed the country's status within the British Commonwealth from that of a dominion to a republic. Military bases on Indian soil are no longer available for use by British forces, and, in opposition to Britain's anti-Soviet policies, India has assumed a position of leadership among the so-called neutral countries which are committed neither to the Soviet Union and its allies nor to the United States and other Western powers. Such neutrality has become difficult to maintain when, for example, China is pressing southward along its borders both with India and the southeast Asian states or when Soviet troops are used to crush the Hungarians. Likewise, threats of force from Pakistan or Communist China have been met by India's determination to defend those areas which it feels that it rightfully owns (see page 478).

The political, social, and economic rights of the over 4 million "overseas" Indians have contributed to friction between India and South Africa, the countries of East Africa, Malaya, Trinidad, and British Guiana, in which Indians form sizeable minorities, and in which they are generally subjected to various forms of racial discrimination. With France and Portugal the Indian government found itself in controversy soon after independence over the political future of the foreign enclaves which still existed as relics of the sixteenth and seventeenth centuries. France controlled five separate regions—Pondichéry, Karikal, Mahé, Yanaon, and Chandernagor —with a total area of 196 square miles and a population of about 320,000; while Portugal had three possessions—Goa, on India's west coast south of Bombay, Damão, and Diu—with a total area of 1,537 square miles and a combined population of 638,000. Of these European enclaves, Goa, in which Portuguese sovereignty dated back to 1510, was the most important in size, population, and economic activity. All of the enclaves bordered territory awarded to India in 1947.

In 1947 the Indian government demanded that these European enclaves be ceded to India. An agreement was subsequently worked out with the French calling for referendums to be held in the French possessions, but only in Chandernagor did a vote actually take place, with the result in favor of union with India. Chandernagor was subsequently turned over to India. In 1954 the other areas were ceded to India without referendums being held. The French government was apparently under no strong pressure to retain these relics of its former empire, particularly since they were costly to administer and were of little economic or military value to France.

With respect to the Portuguese possessions the Indians were less successful. Portugal refused even to consider the transfer of its territories to India, since under the Portuguese constitution all overseas territories are classed as integral parts of Portugal itself, and it is legally impossible to cede them to other powers. Such reasoning held little appeal to Indian nationalists, who saw in the enclaves, particularly Goa, continued vestiges of the hated foreign control to which India was for so long forced to submit. The threats of economic blockades or of "liberation marches" by Indian groups on Goa had no effect on Portugal's stand.

Portugal's defiance of the march of nationalism in southern Asia attracted world attention. Neither Portugal nor India wished a plebiscite to be held, Portugal on the grounds that the alternative of accession to India was not possible, and India because a referendum among the over 600,000 Goans could very possibly end in victory for Portugal. Most of the people are Indian, or mixed Indian-Portuguese, and Hindus outnumber Roman Catholics by only a small majority. The standard of living in Goa was higher than in India, and the enclave, with its harbor of Mormugão and its resources of iron ore and manganese, was a relatively prosperous economic area. Goa is also an important center of Roman Catholicism in the Far East. In its cathedral the remains of the Portuguese missionary St. Francis Xavier are enshrined. The Portuguese, in stating their case for Goa, sometimes referred to the inappropriateness of a Hindu country gaining control of an important Christian shrine.

In December, 1961, the Indian army invaded and occupied Goa and the other two Portuguese enclaves. The army encountered little opposition from the Portuguese and was thus able swiftly to eliminate the last of the foreign holdings on the Indian subcontinent. The occupations raised two questions; first, the relevance of such action to India's traditional role as a champion of peace, and, second, the future of such other enclaves as Macao, Hong Kong, Gibraltar, and the Spanish holdings in northwest Africa. Naval powers were once able to dominate important coastal points and offshore islands in the interests both of trade and naval operations and to control the adjacent land area inland from the coast. Since World War II the trend has been away from such forms of control. Italy, for example, relinquished its coastal holdings in the Adriatic to Yugoslavia and Albania, Spain ceded Spanish Morocco to the new state of Morocco, and Zanzibar may soon relinquish sovereignty over its coastal strip on the African mainland to Kenya (see page 432). As a form of enclave are the bases which still exist on foreign soil, such as Guantánamo Bay, Bizerte, and Mers-el-Kebir, although here again such control is becoming more and more of an anachronism in the modern era of nationalism.

The Kashmir Dispute. The Vale of Kashmir was once famous as a retreat for members of the British Civil Service in India seeking to escape the heat and rainfall of the summer monsoon. Since 1947 it has been the most serious source of conflict between India and Pakistan. Kashmir—or, more properly, the State of Jammu and Kashmir—comprises the provinces of Jammu (including the dependency of Poonch) and Kashmir, as well as the administrative districts of Gilgit and Ladakh (including Baltistan) (Figure 89). It lies in the northwest corner of the Indian subcontinent bordering India, Pakistan, Afghanistan, and China. Kashmir has an area of 82,258 square miles and a population of about 4½ million, of whom over three-quarters are Moslems.

GEOGRAPHIC AND HISTORICAL BACKGROUND. Most of Kashmir consists

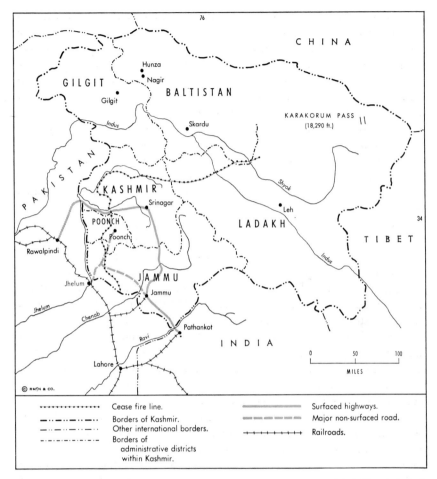

Figure 89. Kashmir. (After Mayfield, *The Geographical Review*, XLV [April, 1955]. Courtesy of American Geographical Society.)

of uplands, varying in altitude from 3,000 to 6,000 feet in the southwest to the Karakorum Range in the north, where much of the land is above 15,000 feet. Only in Jammu Province in the extreme southwest is there a strip of territory with elevations below 3,000 feet. The Vale of Kashmir lies to the north of Jammu at an average elevation of 4,000 to 5,000 feet. This famous resort area, containing the state's capital, Srinagar, and about 40 per cent of its population, is something of a physical and cultural unit, surrounded on three sides by mountains, and with practically all its people united by language and by the Moslem religion. To the south, Jammu, with nearly one-half the state's population, has a Hindu concentration in the south and

Moslems elsewhere. The over-all majority in Jammu is Hindu. The remainder of Kashmir, containing less than 10 per cent of the total population, is inhabited by mountain peoples, living for the most part in isolated valleys. The Pathans of Gilgit and western Baltistan speak Pushtu and are culturally akin to the peoples of the North-West Frontier Province and eastern Afghanistan, while those of Ladakh are mongoloid Buddhists whose linguistic and cultural affinities are with Tibet.

The historical background of the present dispute began in August, 1947, when the governments of the various Native States of prepartition India were instructed to decide whether they would join India or Pakistan. In most states the decision was made by the ruling head. In Kashmir, despite its predominantly Moslem population, the ruling house was Hindu. At the time of partition the maharaja of Kashmir did not declare in favor of either State, but sought to maintain a political *status quo*. Shortly after the subcontinent's partition riots broke out among Moslem groups in Kashmir against the maharaja's administration, and as fighting spread throughout much of the area, Pathan tribesmen from Pakistan entered the state to assist the Moslems. The Kashmir government appealed to India for assistance, and after the marahaja had agreed to accede to India, Indian troops were flown into the Vale of Kashmir to quell the rioters. Shortly afterward regular Pakistani troops were also sent to Kashmir, and fighting between Indian and Pakistani forces went on for over a year. Finally, in January, 1949, a cease-fire line was established as a result of United Nations intervention, leaving two-thirds of Kashmir's area (including the Vale) and four-fifths of its population under Indian control.

Since 1949 Kashmir has remained divided, and all attempts to effect an amicable settlement of this dispute have been unsuccessful. Both India and Pakistan claim the entire area on the basis of ethnic, economic, political, and historical factors. The Kashmir problem has been a major obstacle to the resumption of friendly relations between the two countries, and at times war has appeared imminent. The United Nations has frequently pressed for an all-Kashmir plebiscite to determine the wishes of the Kashmiri people, but such a move has consistently been blocked by India.

CONFLICTING CLAIMS. The Pakistan government based its claims to Kashmir on the following major points: (1) the majority of the population is Moslem. (2) Prepartition Kashmir was linked by road and rail with what is now Pakistan, and its normal trade outlets would be with the Moslem nation. (3) Indian control of Kashmir would jeopardize West Pakistan's vital irrigation system and the opportunities for hydroelectric power development, for the upper Indus River and the headwaters of two of its five major tributaries flow through Kashmir. (4) India's control of Kashmir would threaten Pakistan's national security, because of the lack of natural defenses between southern Kashmir and Pakistan; moreover, Pakistan's control is essential to the security of the North-West Frontier Province against the claims of the Pathan tribesmen (see page 483). (5) With its military links to the West, Pakistan should control Kashmir in order to defend it against Soviet and Chinese expansion. Countering these were the Indian arguments: (1) the Kashmir government legally acceded to India in 1947. (2) Since 1947 India has undertaken an extensive program for developing Kashmir's economy and communications network and has inaugurated a large-scale land distribution program; both Jammu and the Vale of Kashmir have been linked by road with India, and Kashmir's future economic interests can be better served by India, with its greater markets and industrial facilities, than by Pakistan. (3) Pakistan's claims to the use of river waters for irrigation and hydroelectric power development can be met by international agreement. (4) The interests of approximately 1 million Hindus, mainly living in Jammu, must be protected.

The problem of allocation of the waters of the Indus system was settled by an agreement between India and Pakistan in September, 1960, whereby India eventually receives 20 per cent of the total Indus system's waters and Pakistan 80 per cent. The Upper Indus River rises in Tibet, traverses Kashmir amid the towering Himalayas, and does not cross Indian territory in its course southward. One Indus tributary, the Jhelum, drains the Indian-held Vale of Kashmir, while a second tributary, the Chenab, crosses Indian-held Jammu. Two other Indus tributaries—the Ravi and Bease—rise in India rather than Kashmir, while the Sutlej rises in Tibet and flows across Indian territory to its confluence with the Indus.

Before partition an elaborate irrigation system had been developed whereby some 30 million acres were under irrigation. The political division of the subcontinent left about two-thirds of this irrigated land in Pakistan, but interrupted much of the operations of the over-all system. Some 40 million people in Pakistan and 10 million in India are dependent, directly or indirectly, on irrigation from the Indus system, and after eight years of discussion under the auspices of the World Bank, the governments of India and Pakistan finally came to an agreement whereby the waters of the Indus, the Jhelum, and the Chenab will go to Pakistan, while those of the three eastern rivers will be used by India. Such a division requires the construction of water works, link canals, power stations, and other facilities, costing a total of $1 billion, of which the United States will contribute about one-half. While this agreement does not solve the Kashmir dispute, it permits a wise utilization of the Indus waters regardless of what course the Kashmir problem may eventually take.

Several alternatives exist for the over-all settlement of the Kashmir problem:

1. An all-Kashmir plebiscite, which would require the prior withdrawal of most of the Indian and Pakistani troops. India has refused to evacuate the area in which it has *de facto* control.

2. Award Hindu Jammu and Buddhist Ladakh to India, Moslem Baltistan and Gilgit to Pakistan, and hold a plebiscite in Poonch and the Vale.

3. Independence for Kashmir, which would probably produce a power vacuum in this vital area.

4. A special United Nations status for Kashmir—or for the Vale—leaving the remainder of the nation as presently divided.

5. Continued division of Kashmir along the 1949 cease-fire line, and incorporation of the two parts within India and Pakistan respectively. In 1956 Prime Minister Nehru came out in favor of this solution.

Economic activity between India and the India-controlled portion of Kashmir has greatly increased since 1949. Large sums of money have been spent to strengthen India's position by orienting Kashmir's economy toward India and by winning the loyalty of the Kashmiri people—both Hindu and Moslem—who may come to realize that it is to their economic interest to remain within the Indian republic. Pakistan, on the other hand, has made little effort at economic improvement in its portion of Kashmir, since the government has continued to view the 1949 partitioning of Kashmir as only a temporary situation. In January, 1957, India announced the formal incorporation of Kashmir as a constituent Indian state, thereby adding a new element to the already complex nature of this dispute.

The India-China Border. The southern border of China stretches along the Himalaya Mountains and, in its westernmost sector, the Karakorum Range, for a distance of nearly 2,500 miles. To the north of the border is Tibet, except in the west where the Chinese province of Sinkiang lies across the Karakorums from Kashmir. Few passes cross the border between China and India, and there are relatively few people inhabiting the border area, except in the central portion in the three mountain countries of Nepal, Bhutan, and Sikkim. The boundary claimed by India is the so-called McMahon line, which was negotiated in 1914 by Sir Henry McMahon, although never formally accepted by China. Much of this border has never been demarcated. For nearly four decades after the establishment of the McMahon line India faced a semi-independent Tibet and a largely unorganized Sinkiang as its northern neighbors, but since the communization of China in 1949 and the military occupation of Tibet two years later, the Indian government has been confronted with a far more intensive political and military organization than had hitherto been the case. The Peking government has been working rapidly not only to strengthen its position in Tibet and Sinkiang, but also to press for advantages south of its border with the Indian subcontinent.

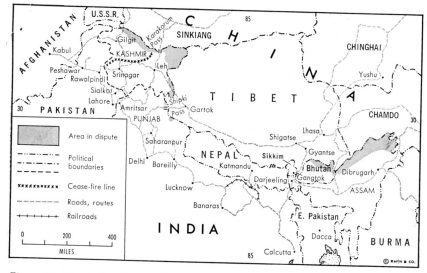

Figure 90. The Indian-Chinese Border Area.

Starting in 1954 there were reports of incursions by the Chinese south of the McMahon line, but in keeping with his avowed neutralist policies India's Prime Minister Nehru did his best to play down these incidents as honest misunderstandings. New Delhi had been among the first capitals to recognize the Communist regime in China, and since 1950 India had been pressing for China's admission to the United Nations. By 1959, however, the Chinese had occupied a number of areas south of the McMahon line, and official Chinese maps were showing a new southern border of Tibet and Sinkiang which had the effect of adding some 51,000 square miles of territory to China. Most of this territory is Indian, although small areas of Pakistan and Bhutan were also involved. Since 1959 there have been periodic incidents involving Indian and Chinese troops, and India has been working rapidly to improve its northern defenses. Meanwhile much of the disputed territory has been under Chinese occupation.

In the northwest the Chinese claim about 15,000 square miles of the Indian province of Ladakh, a remote area of Kashmir through which pass the eastern Karakorums, including Mount Godwin Austen, second highest peak in the world. Chinese troops have occupied some 12,000 square miles of the disputed area, and the Indians have been working rapidly on improvement of roads into it from the Vale of Kashmir. High priority has been given to the completion of a 170-mile road from Srinagar to Leh, the capital of Ladakh, as well as an 80-mile road from Leh eastward to Chusul, close to the border with Tibet. In addition to military uses such roads will lead to greater economic development of Ladakh itself. Through easternmost Ladakh the Chinese have constructed a part of a road linking Gartok in western Tibet with Yarkand in western Sinkiang.[4]

In southeastern Ladakh, and between Ladakh and Nepal, there are also small areas of Chinese claims. Nepal in 1960 reached a border accord with China, but farther east, in Bhutan, the Chinese claim two areas along the northern boundary and another in the southeastern portion of the country. Finally, in Assam, east of Bhutan, the Chinese claim some 36,000 square miles of mountainous territory, parts of which, as in the case of Ladakh, are occupied by Chinese troops.

For three years Indian and Chinese troops were involved in sporadic clashes, but in October, 1962, the Chinese launched full-scale military offensives against the Indians both in Ladakh and in the northeast area. Within a few weeks the Indians had been forced to yield important territory particularly in Ladakh, and the Indian government, abandoning its traditional policy of neutrality, turned to the United States and Britain for military aid. The Chinese did not press their military advantage. Having cleared the Indians from northeastern Ladakh they announced a "cease-fire" which left them in possession of 12,000 square miles of former Indian territory in Ladakh.

Since the areas involved are generally of little economic value, the question arises, Why has China turned on India, one of the few powers with which it has had friendly relations, and laid claim to parts of its territory? Are the Chinese building up along their southern border as a prelude to military invasion of India, are they merely intent on impressing India and Southeast Asia with their new stature as a military power, or, by annexing territory, particularly to Tibet, are they in a sense trying to win approval from the Tibetans of Peking's policies? One theory, expressed specifically with respect to Ladakh, is that the Chinese hope that propaganda may infiltrate across the border to the peoples of the remote areas to the south. "Actually it is not so much the ideology that is likely to arouse a response in the local people; they are perhaps too backward for it. It is the report of the 'fantastic' development evidently taking place in Sinkiang and Tibet that has the simple Ladakhi agog with wonder and envy."[5] The following statement sums up the general situation existing all along China's southern border:

> No Communists are yet in Ladakh but the basic problem
> there is that of all new democracies: established order is very old,
> very weak and very tottering. Its powerful elements are also the

---

[4] The Chinese also claim a small portion of northernmost Gilgit which, since the division of Kashmir, Pakistan has occupied. India does not recognize Pakistan's sovereignty there, but in June, 1962, Pakistan agreed to negotiate with China over their disputed border—a move which infuriated the Indians. A final border settlement was concluded between Pakistan and China in May, 1963.

[5] Kusum Nair, "Where India, China, and Russia Meet," *Foreign Affairs*, XXXVI (1958), 336. Copyright by the Council on Foreign Relations, Inc.

reactionary elements, and although they can be depended upon to oppose Communism tooth and nail, because it will have no place for them, they must also become the first victims of any truly democratic reform. The choice for the Indian Government is therefore not easy. It is either to leave these interests intact, indeed bolster them further, and permit them to continue oppressing the population and holding it in ignorance and backwardness; or to destroy them and rapidly "democratize" the society and in so doing destroy the only existing social bulwark against Communism.[6]

Whatever their intent, there have been no indications that the Chinese will withdraw from their demands, or that the Indians will acquiesce peacefully in the loss of their territory. The greatest "natural" land border in the world is now being organized politically and militarily as the two States, having between them nearly two-fifths of the people of the globe, face one another in a seemingly insoluble dispute.

Bhutan, Sikkim, and Nepal. The three mountain countries along India's northern border are also potential areas of expansion of Chinese influence, regardless of the position of their political boundaries with Tibet. Bhutan is an independent State which in 1949 agreed to accept Indian "guidance" in defense and foreign affairs, while Sikkim was for many years a British protectorate, with the British accepting responsibility for defense, foreign affairs, and communications, and with a British political officer residing in Gangtok, Sikkim's capital. In 1949 India assumed Britain's responsibilities with regard to Sikkim. Thus India is committed to defend the territorial integrity of both countries against China. Nepal is an independent kingdom without military or political alliances with either India or China. All three countries have only recently been emerging from centuries of isolation.

Bhutan has a population of close to 800,000, nearly four-fifths of whom are of Tibetan stock. Speaking a language allied to the Tibetan, they are predominantly Lamaist Buddhist, recognizing the Dalai Lama as their spiritual leader. The country is led by a young, energetic maharajah, who, with Indian financial aid, is seeking to develop Bhutan's economy. Several roads link Bhutan with Tibet, but only in 1961 did work start on a highway system connecting Punakha, Bhutan's capital, with Indian cities to the south.

Of Sikkim's 150,000 people, over three-quarters are first- or second-generation Nepalese, while another 12 per cent are immigrants from Tibet. There, as in Bhutan, there has been considerable economic and political progress since 1949, but with this has also come increased agitation against the government and discontent over India's role in Sikkim's affairs. Through

---

[6] *Ibid.*

Sikkim runs the best route between Tibet and China, and since 1951 thousands of Tibetan refugees have come into the country. Although there is no dispute over the location of Sikkim's border with Tibet, India has been concerned over the possibility of Chinese incursions into Sikkim, and it has improved connections with the country and has stationed troops close to the border of Sikkim in case of trouble here.

The Kingdom of Nepal has an area of 54,000 square miles and a population of some 9 million, the majority of whom are Hindu. Only in 1953 was a motor road completed linking Katmandu, the capital, with India, and in the years since then Nepal has been undergoing considerable political and economic development. Much of the trade is with India, and overseas exports and imports must be handled through Indian ports. Yet despite the receipt of goods and credits from India the government of Nepal has not pursued a particularly pro-Indian foreign policy in recent years. Nepal has resented Indian criticisms of its internal policies as well as India's refusal to return to Nepal political exiles who, it is held, are carrying on guerrilla warfare against the kingdom.

In 1961 an agreement was signed between Nepal and Communist China providing for Chinese help in the construction of a road linking Katmandu with Tibet. To many Indian officials such an agreement might eventually pave the way for a spread of Chinese influence in Nepal. At the same time some 4,000 Khampa tribesmen in northern Nepal have been described as forming a sort of guerrilla army of the Dalai Lama, the Tibetan spiritual and temporal leader who fled to India in 1959 after an unsuccessful revolt against the Chinese. Should these tribesmen eventually assume military importance, the Chinese might have a pretext for demanding the right of entry of their troops into Nepal to destroy the hostile force. Thus, like other neutrals sandwiched between major powers, Nepal, with its emerging development, faces difficult security problems in the face of growing Communist power to the north.

PAKISTAN

Pakistan is a State in which the various forces of diversity require extremely skillful handling on the part of the national leaders. The country is divided into two parts, differing physically, ethnically, and economically from one another, and separated by a thousand miles of Indian territory. Pakistan is not richly endowed with natural resources. Like India, it has a rapidly increasing population. Pakistan also is confronted by territorial problems with India and with Afghanistan.

The division of Pakistan into eastern and western sectors was occasioned by the existence of large Moslem concentrations in and about the delta of the Ganges and in the western portion of the subcontinent. In the establishment of the new country, West Pakistan received 85 per cent of the total territory and 40 per cent of its 77 million people.

Because of the concentration of Moslem power in West Pakistan, this area was chosen as the one in which the national capital would be located. Lahore, in the Punjab, had a central location with respect to the population distribution of West Pakistan, but the city lies close to the Indian border and was therefore considered to be in too vulnerable a position. Karachi, at the mouth of the Indus, was eventually selected as the capital city. Although it is the largest city of Pakistan, it was in an isolated position with respect to both West Pakistan and East Pakistan. In August, 1960, the federal capital was shifted 700 miles to the northeast of Karachi to an area on the Potwar plateau near the city of Rawalpindi. The new capital is to be called "Islamabad," and lies close to the borders both of disputed Kashmir and of the area of Pakistan claimed by Afghanistan (see page 483).

Since partition Pakistan has faced three major problems: (1) how to develop the over-all economy of the country; (2) how to weld East Pakistan and West Pakistan closely together; and (3) how to realize its territorial ambitions in Kashmir.

Pakistan's Economic Structure

West Pakistan is a predominantly arid region, in which there are small reserves of coal, petroleum, and chromium, as well as some salt deposits. Most of the region is drained by the Indus River and its tributaries. Large-scale irrigation works, utilizing the waters of the Indus system, were developed in prepartition years, primarily by British capital. West Pakistan's major economic asset is that it produces high-grade cotton and, in normal times, a grain surplus. In order to capitalize on its agricultural advantage, West Pakistan must continue to increase its irrigated lands, a process requiring both capital and the assurance of available water supply.

East Pakistan is a region of heavy monsoonal rainfall, in which rice and jute are the principal cash crops. With its large population it is a food-deficit area and must import needed supplies from either West Pakistan, India, or southeast Asia. There are no known significant mineral deposits in East Pakistan, although there are reserves of peat, limestone, and natural gas. Before 1947 the region was tied economically even more closely to India than was West Pakistan, and its economy has suffered more from the political partitioning.

Pakistan's over-all economy is handicapped, first, by the scarcity of minerals and power facilities within the country and, second, by the disruption in the former economic ties of the Pakistani and Indian areas. As already noted, the present Pakistan area was an important producer of jute and cotton, which were processed by mills now located in India. Since

1947 trade has been severely disrupted between the two countries. As a result India has been developing its domestic sources for jute and cotton, while Pakistan is constructing its own processing mills. The State does not, however, possess the major requirements for extensive industralization, as India does. On the other hand the Pakistani government, through sound fiscal policies and the receipt of extensive foreign aid, has in recent years succeeded in developing a fairly stable monetary system in the State, despite the fact that the average per capita income remains very low.

Internal Political Forces

Political unity between East Pakistan and West Pakistan has been under severe strain since 1947. Because the national capital is located in West Pakistan, the people of East Pakistan often feel their interests suffer as a result of the distance between them and the seat of political power. Although Pakistan was unified on the basis of religion, the centrifugal forces of language and economic differences serve to divide it. In West Pakistan Urdu is the official language, while in East Pakistan Bengali, a language not closely related to Urdu and written in a different alphabet, is used. Not until 1954 did the Pakistani government elevate Bengali to the status of an official language and thus counter the charge that East Pakistan's cultural interests were being neglected. The standard of living in East Pakistan is considerably lower than that in West Pakistan, and the people in the east regard with suspicion any decision made by the government with regard to prices and controls on such items as rice and cloth, important commodities in the East Pakistan economy. Centripetal forces include the strong central regime led by General Ayub Kahn[7] and the government's decision that in Pakistan's second five-year plan recognition be given to the necessity of maintaining minimum rates of economic growth both in East and West Pakistan—a policy which will involve far greater allocation of funds to the east than had previously existed.

Only two-thirds of the people in East Pakistan are Moslems, and the ties of religion are thus weaker than in West Pakistan, where over 95 per cent of the people are Moslems. Communism has gained a foothold in the east, particularly among the 10 million Hindus who inhabit the area. In the 1954 elections the United Front party, in which the Communists have considerable strength, won control of the East Pakistan legislature from the Moslem League, the political group which originally formed the Pakistan nation. Leaders of the United Front organization soon began to talk of East Pakistan's "colonial" status and of possible independence for the area. In view of the wide acceptance such views received in East Pakistan,

---

[7] General Ayub became the military dictator of Pakistan in 1956; four years later he permitted general elections for the presidency and was himself voted into office as Pakistan's first president.

the Pakistani government undertook to strengthen the ties between the two areas, both by recognizing Bengali as an official tongue and by developing a broad economic expansion program in East Pakistan.

External Relations

Pakistan's official relation with the British Commonwealth was changed in 1956, when it ceased to be a dominion and became the Islamic Republic of Pakistan. The country has become a military ally of the United States and of other western powers against possible Soviet aggression, and is a member both of the Southeast Asia Treaty Organization (SEATO) and of the Central Treaty Organization (CENTO). Because of Pakistan's Western military organization, the United States and Britain have been confronted with a difficult decision with regard to the Kashmir dispute between Pakistan and India. This dispute is very important to both States, and should the Americans or the British openly back Pakistan, India would be greatly antagonized; conversely, support for India might destroy Pakistan's military ties with the West.

Although Pakistan has the greatest population of all the Moslem countries (94 million in 1961), its location and its foreign policy have combined to keep it from assuming a role of leadership among the Moslem States. Egypt or Iraq are more centrally located with respect to the Moslem peoples than Pakistan. More important, perhaps, is the fact that many of the States of the Arab World have espoused a neutral approach to the Cold War problems, while Pakistan has openly aligned itself with the non-Communist countries.

The Pakistan-Afghan Border Area. The northwestern portion of Pakistan is a mountainous area inhabited by Moslem tribes, of whom the Pathans form the largest group. These peoples speak Pushtu and are culturally akin to the Pathans to the west, who comprise about 45 per cent of Afghanistan's population. In 1893, when the Afghan-Indian border was delimited, special political concessions were made to the tribal people in the North-West Frontier Province. When Pakistan was created in 1947, the province was incorporated into the new country. Since that time there has been frequent fighting in the Khyber Pass area in connection with a movement for an independent Pushtunistan (or Pathanistan or Pakhtunistan), to be composed of 5 to 7 million people, of whom probably less than 2½ million would actually be Pushtu-speaking.

The area envisioned for Pushtunistan would include all of the North-West Frontier Province, as well as northern Baluchistan (including Quetta) and Punjab west of the Indus (Figure 91). With an area of 45,000–50,000 square miles, the new State would control the eastern approaches to the Khyber Pass and would serve as a buffer between Afghanistan and Pakis-

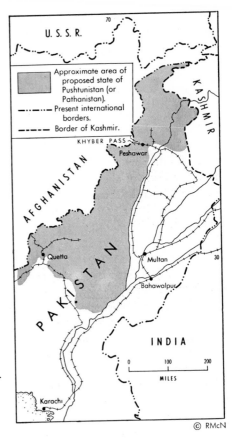

Figure 91. The Afghan-Pakistan Border Area.

tan. Although Pakistan refuses even to consider the possibility of Pushtun-istan, the government of Afghanistan (with the encouragement of the Soviet Union) has actively supported the idea, thereby creating considerable fric-tion between Rawalpindi and Kabul. The Afghans claim that the North-West Frontier Province was illegally joined to Pakistan in 1947, and that the rights of self-government should be granted to the Pathans living in Pakistan.

Although there appears to be little possibility that an independent Pushtunistan State will be created, the situation illustrates the problems of political cohesion in the mountain areas of central Asia. The power of the Karachi government is felt scarcely, if at all, in some of the remote Pathan areas of the North-West Frontier Province. The lack of unity be-tween these people and the rest of Pakistan is matched by a similar lack of cohesion between them and the Afghan Pathans to the west of the Khyber Pass. The government of Afghanistan in its propaganda for Pathan unity is in a dangerous political position, for in northern Afghanistan are Uzbeks and Turkmens whose union with their cultural brothers in Soviet Uzbekistan and Turkmenistan the Soviet Union could urge with equal logic. The Communists, of course, are interested in this dispute between two countries close to the Soviet Union's southern borders, since, like the Kashmir issue, it tends to prevent united action in this area. Pakistan's closing of its border with Afghanistan drove that country into close economic ties with the U.S.S.R. Moreover, the Soviets would be interested in doing what they could to weaken the position of Pakistan, a United States military ally in southern Asia.

CEYLON

The island of Ceylon lies but a few miles off the southeast coast of India, and its interests have been closely tied with those of its neighbor. One of the important problems facing Ceylon, however, is the presence of a large Indian majority within the country and the prospect of a future influx of Indians from the mainland. With an area of 25,000 square miles and an over-all population of over 9 million, Celyon does not approach the population density of parts of southern India. The difference in population densities between Ceylon and India may in time come to be an important factor in the island's relations with India.

Ceylon was not administratively a part of prepartition India, but its independence followed that of India and Pakistan by eight months. Because of its location, Ceylon has long been of importance to British naval operations in the Indian Ocean. Britain maintained a naval base at Trincomalee on the northeastern coast of Ceylon. In 1956, however, the Ceylonese government, following India's neutralist lead, requested that the British evacuate the Trincomalee base, as well as the Katunayaka air base, which was an important staging post for long-distance air travel. As a result, Britain is reviving its air base on Gan in the Maldive Islands, 400 miles southwest of Ceylon in the Indian Ocean, for use by long-range aircraft.[8]

Economic Position

Ceylon is important for tropical plantation agriculture. Its major export crops include tea, rubber, and coconut products (all of them subject to considerable price fluctuations), in exchange for which Ceylon imports over one-half of its food supply. The population is rising at an estimated 3 per cent per year, which in time may place considerable strain on the island's resources. Ceylon's agricultural potential could be considerably

---

[8] The Maldives came under British protection in 1887; since 1960 only external political relations have remained a British responsibility. Britain's decision to reactivate its wartime airfield on Gan Island led to internal difficulties, since the sultan at first refused to acquiesce in Britain's plans. In 1960 the Maldivian government ceded the island to Britain for a period to last until 1986, and the British have developed there a major air base linking Africa with the Far East.

increased by opening up new areas to crops (particularly rice) and improving the present yields.

Although there are no domestic coal supplies, Ceylon's water power and iron ore could help to support future industrial development. In 1962 the government nationalized the foreign-held oil refineries and began importing petroleum from the Soviet Union. The commercial significance of the island is augmented by the fact that Colombo, its capital and leading city, is also an important port of call between Suez and the Far East, and its harbor ranks high in terms of tonnage of shipping handled.

Ceylon's Indian Minority

Some 2 million Hindus reside in the predominantly Buddhist State of Ceylon. About half of these are from families which have been in Ceylon for centuries, while the other half are descendants of immigrants brought in by the British in the nineteenth century to work on the tea and rubber plantations. In general the Hindus are not popular on the island; citizenship rights have been withdrawn from the more recent arrivals from India, and an embargo has been placed on the remittance of money by these people to India. Quite a number of persons from south India have entered Ceylon illegally, and many of those with Indian ancestry are suspected of pro-Communist sympathies.

The conflict between Indian and Ceylonese is reflected in the division of the island's population into some 2½ million Tamil-speaking Hindus and 6½ million Sinhalese-speaking Buddhists. Sinhalese has become the official language of Ceylon, and severe riots have occurred as the Tamils seek to retain their ethnic and economic rights. There is considerable unemployment in Ceylon, and the economic discrimination against the Tamils (who form nearly 30 per cent of the population) has acted as a powerful centrifugal force in the new State. Ceylon's future development would seem to lie along the lines (1) of greater ethnic and economic tolerance of its Tamil minority, (2) of more extensive development of its agricultural and hydroelectric potential and greater efforts to provide for its own food needs, and (3) of agreements with India to control illegal immigration to Ceylon and for repatriation of a given number of Indians from Ceylon.

AFGHANISTAN

Afghanistan, like Iran, is one of the historic buffer areas of Asia. The landlocked country borders the Indian subcontinent on the south and east, the U.S.S.R. on the north, and Iran on the west. On the east it barely touches the Chinese province of Sinkiang. It has an area of 250,000 square miles and a population of some 12 million. Despite its isolation as a result of mountains and deserts, Afghanistan is of considerable importance to all of its neighbors in terms of the conflicting power elements in this part of the world.

Afghanistan has a complex physical structure, resulting in the existence of several core areas. The main range of the Hindu Kush passes through the central part of the country. There is a relatively narrow plain to the north, sloping northward to the Amu Darya (Oxus River), and a broad desert area in the south. Although the majority of the population is united in religion (Sunnite Moslems), it is divided on the basis of language and culture. Among the various groups are the Afghans and Pathans in the east and south, whose language, Pushtu, is the official language of the State;[9] the Tadzhiks, of Persian origin, in the Kabul area and to the north; and the Hazaras, descendants of Mongol Tatars, in the central section of the country.

Afghanistan is still relatively backward, with no railroads, few industries, and very little resource development, although it is known to possess a variety of minerals, including gold, iron ore, copper, and asbestos. There are considerable coal reserves, as well as hydroelectric potential. One of Afghanistan's great needs is capital for development of its water power and irrigation facilities. Transportation links are poor between Kabul, the capital city, and other population centers, such as Kandahar in the south central area and Herat in the northwest. Poorly developed road systems also connect Kabul with Pakistan and Iran. New highways are being constructed, however, from the Soviet border southward to Kabul and other Afghan cities. In contrast to the mountain barriers separating Afghanistan from Pakistan, the Soviet-Afghan border, to the northeast of Kabul, lies in the flood plain of the Amu Darya, permitting much easier communications between the two countries.

History of Foreign Influence

The modern Afghan State dates back to the eighteenth century, when the Persians were expelled from the area and the Afghan Empire was established. Frequent warfare between groups within the country, and later between Afghan armies and Russian and British forces, hindered the economic and political development of the State. During the nineteenth century British efforts to establish a sphere of influence in Afghanistan (and thus protect the northwestern approaches to India) led to the two Afghan wars (1839–42 and 1879–81), as well as to almost constant border warfare in northwest India between British and Afghan forces. In the 1880's Afghanistan consented to British protection, and the Russians in 1907, in exchange

---

[9] Farsi (Persian) is the language of the court.

for a sphere of influence in Iran, agreed to regard Afghanistan as outside Russia's influence sphere. Afghanistan's role as a buffer state was further emphasized by the extension of the country's border eastward in a curious projection to the boundary of Sinkiang, thereby separating India and Russia by about twenty-five to fifty miles of Afghan territory (Figure 91).

Following World War I Afghanistan became completely independent of British control, and in order to strengthen its position relative to both Britain and Russia, the government looked for assistance and advice to a third power—Germany. German engineers and advisers were active in Afghanistan prior to World War II—a role which American technicians filled for a time following the war. The withdrawal of the British from India in 1947 and the creation of independent India and Pakistan affected Afghanistan's position, for no longer was the country a buffer state between British and Russian power. The decline of British influence was partially compensated by an increase of United States interest, largely through loans and technical aid to develop Afghanistan's economy.

Extension of Soviet Power. Since early 1956 Afghanistan has strengthened its economic ties with the Soviet Union. The boundary dispute with Pakistan eventually led to Pakistan's closing the border. No longer was the country in a buffer position between opposing forces. By mid-1961 the Soviet Union had granted or lent a total of $217 million to Afghanistan, compared to $180 million from the United States. In planning their second five-year plan to run through 1966, the Afghans decided to seek some $700 million in foreign exchange, roughly half to come from the Soviet bloc and half from the United States and other Western powers. In September, 1961, however, Afghanistan severed diplomatic relations with Pakistan, resulting in the *de facto,* if not *de jure,* closing of the Afghan route of transit to the outside world through the Pakistan port of Karachi, the major port for Afghanistan's foreign trade. As a result of this closing practically all trade to Afghanistan must come through the Soviet Union, leading Western officials to doubt the possibility of the Afghans receiving large-scale shipment of heavy machinery, wheat, and other supplies from the United States. Unless the trade routes through Karachi can be reopened, Afghanistan seems in a position to be drawn closer and closer into the Soviet sphere of influence.

BIBLIOGRAPHY

Ahmad, Nafis. "The Indo-Pakistan Boundary Disputes Tribunal, 1949–1950," *The Geographical Review,* XLIII (1953), 329–38.

A short but detailed study of disputes along the boundary between India and East Pakistan after the partition.

ARMSTRONG, HAMILTON FISH. "Thoughts Along the China Border: Will Neutrality Be Enough?" *Foreign Affairs,* XXXVIII (1960), 238–61.
A survey of Indian neutrality in the face of Chinese pressures.

————. "Where India Faces China," *Foreign Affairs,* XXXVII (1959), 617–26.
A good general account of the border area.

BRUSH, JOHN E. "The Distribution of Religious Communities in India," *Annals of the Association of American Geographers,* XXXIX (1949), 81–99.
Excellent maps and discussion of religious patterns in India prior to partition.

GINSBERG, NORTON (ed.). *The Pattern of Asia.* New York: Prentice-Hall, 1958.
A good regional text of Asia.

JACKSON, BARBARA WARD. "India on the Eve of its Third Plan," *Foreign Affairs,* XXXIX (1961), 259–71.
Summary of India's economic problems.

KARAN, P. P. "The India-China Boundary Dispute," *Journal of Geography,* LIX (1960), 16–21.
Contains a good map of the border area.

MAYFIELD, ROBERT C. "A Geographic Study of The Kashmir Issue," *The Geographical Review,* XLV (1955), 181–97.
A comprehensive survey of the issues involved in this dispute.

SPATE, O. H. K. "The Partition of India and the Prospects of Pakistan," *The Geographical Review,* XXXVIIl (1948), 5–30.
One of the most comprehensive articles to appear on the partition.

WILBER, DONALD M. "Afghanistan, Independent and Encircled," *Foreign Affairs,* XXXI (1953), 486–95.
A political history of Afghanistan, particularly since World War I.

18

SOUTHEAST ASIA

● In that part of Asia which lies south of China and east of the Indian subcontinent three basic trends have developed since the end of World War II: the gradual disappearance of European political control, the achievement of independence by several States, and the growing significance of Chinese expansion under the guise of international communism. The area is one in which the physical and cultural environments contain many aspects of diversity, but in which there are also important unifying forces which tend to draw together the peoples and countries which are located there. The political pattern of Southeast Asia[1] is in many respects a product of the conflicting forces of unity and diversity in this part of the world.

FORCES OF UNITY AND DIVERSITY

The regional unity of southeast Asia is based primarily on climate, economic development, and a history of colonialism. Most of the countries in this area have recently become independent, and they share with one another many problems of national development, including the threat of Chinese expansion. Southeast Asia also contains many elements of disunity, such as landforms, ethnic types, and conflicting colonial interests, which in

---

[1] Southeast Asia here comprises Burma, Thailand, Indochina, Malaya, Singapore, Indonesia, and British Borneo. The name Thailand was officially adopted in 1949, replacing Siam. Indochina, although no longer a single political unit, is used here to designate the former French-controlled area embracing Vietnam, Laos, and Cambodia. Because of their close ties with the Pacific area and with the United States, the Philippines are considered in the chapter on the Pacific Basin (Chapter 22).

turn have been reflected in political differences between and within the countries of this area. To these countries the diversities of their physical and cultural environments present major obstacles to regional collaboration.[2] As a result, progress toward coping with common social, economic, and political difficulties has been delayed, and the ever present dangers of internal revolt and the spread of Communist control are thereby increased.

Physical Features

The climate of southeast Asia is an important unifying element. Most of the region is influenced by the tropical monsoon, with its alternating wet and dry seasons. Bamboo and palm trees are characteristic vegetation forms, and the cultivation of paddy rice and the development of tropical plantation agriculture are economic responses to this climate. Variations in the climatic pattern exist primarily in upland areas, or along northward- and eastward-facing coasts where the season of heavy rainfall is the reverse of that which exists throughout most of southeast Asia.

The sea also offers a kind of physical unity, since it tends to bind islands and coastal regions together economically, culturally, and politically. Examples of this unifying trend are to be found in the spread of Islam throughout the coastal areas of Malaya and most of Indonesia during the fifteenth century, and the political unification of the Indonesian archipelago by the Dutch three hundred years later.

In contrast to these unifying elements are the landforms and soils. The terrain of southeast Asia is compartmentalized into relatively small lowlands, separated by blocks of rough hill country or mountain cordilleras (Figure 92). The principal plains on the mainland are located on the deltas of great rivers which have their sources within the heart of the Asian continent: the Irrawaddy and Salween of Burma, the Menam (Chao Praya) of Thailand, and the Mekong and Yuan (Red) rivers of Indochina. Although the narrow river valleys afford poor routes into the interior, the broad deltas which have been formed by each of these rivers, except the Salween, contain major population concentrations and represent focal points for political and economic activities. The rugged terrain of the mainland area also extends south through the Malay Peninsula and out onto the islands of Indonesia. The diversity of soil fertility is associated in part with the uneven distribution of volcanic activity, so that even in lowland areas there may be wide differences in soil types. These physical elements naturally affect population distribution. Areas of concentrated settlements are often separated from one another by sparsely inhabited territory in which national governments may exercise little or no effective control.

---

[2] See Jan O. M. Broek, "Diversity and Unity in Southeast Asia," *The Geographical Review*, XXXIV (1944), 175–96, for an excellent discussion of this problem.

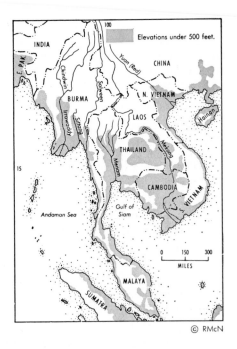

Figure 92. Southeast Asia: Physical Features.

© RMcN

Population Features

The ethnic complexity of southeast Asia is a result of the many waves of peoples—coming both from the Asian mainland to the north and northwest and by sea from the west—which have passed through and across this area. In addition to the major population types, such as Malays, Thais, Burmese, Annamese, Laotians, and Cambodians, there are a great number of smaller ethnic groups, which, because of their isolated locations, have managed to maintain their cultural individuality. There are also three important "foreign" peoples in southeast Asia: the Chinese, the Indians, and the Europeans.

The patterns of language and religion are shown in Figures 93 and 94. The white population of southeast Asia, and those nonwhites dealing directly with them, generally speak the languages of the present or former colonial powers. The Chinese often use their native dialects, and many of the Indians speak Tamil. The Malay language group predominates throughout much of southeast Asia, yet within this framework many variations occur. In Indonesia, for example, there are some twenty-five different languages. Religious diversity is evidenced by the presence of Islam, Buddhism, Christianity, and many other sects. Differences in language and religion, of course, reflect the great diversities of cultural interests—diversities which have often been magnified by certain States (for example, China, India, Thailand) in an effort to further the interests of their respec-

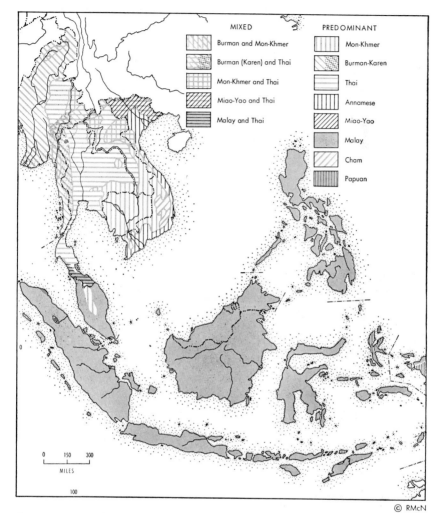

Figure 93. Languages in Southeast Asia. (After Broek, *The Geographical Review,* XXXIV [April, 1944]. Courtesy of American Geographical Society.)

tive "national" groups in southeast Asia, often at the expense of other peoples in this area.

Population distribution is also an important factor fostering political diversity in southeast Asia, for in most of the countries there exist two or more core areas. In addition, many people are settled in small towns and villages which, because of the poor transportation facilities, are practically inaccessible to effective political control from the national capital. This isolation, of course, is heightened by the ethnic differences between inhabitants of provincial areas and those of the urban centers, and by the continu-

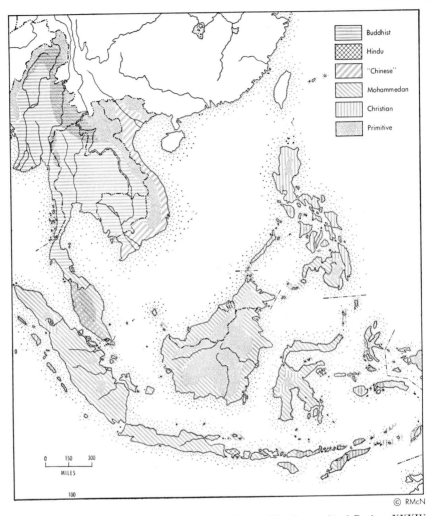

Buddhist

Hindu

"Chinese"

Mohammedan

Christian

Primitive

0   150   300

MILES

100

© RMcN

Figure 94. Religions in Southeast Asia. (After Broek, *The Geographical Review,* XXXIV [April, 1944]. Courtesy of American Geographical Society.)

ing armed warfare which has been carried on in some of the more inaccessible areas, particularly in Burma, Indonesia, Malaya, and parts of Indochina, since the end of World War II.

Economic Features

Climate and land utilization in southeast Asia have produced great similarities of economic activities and interests throughout much of the region. Agriculture forms the predominant basis of the economy, supplemented in some areas by mining and in a few large cities by commerce and light industries. The national economies have been geared primarily to the export of agricultural and mineral raw materials to the industralized countries of the world. The realization of common goals, however, has been at least partially blocked by competing, rather than complementary, economies. During their years of colonial control the British, Dutch, and French oriented the economic structures of their possessions toward the respective mother countries, and little trade was carried on regionally.[3] With the advent of independence, this economic orientation to foreign markets has continued. Communication lines, particularly railroads, tend to focus on the commercial centers of each individual State rather than to cross international boundaries. The only important transportation links between countries are coastal and interisland shipping, and, particularly since World War II, the growing international air routes.

Political Features

The political pattern of southeast Asia reflects its history of foreign control (Figures 95 and 98). The Europeans were responsible not only for the political partitioning of the area but also, to a degree, for the unification of various groups into national units, as in Burma, Indochina, Malaya, and Indonesia. The pressures of colonialism beyond its borders also represented a cohesive force in the independent former buffer State of Thailand. Political unification had varying effects among the countries of southeast Asia: in general it meant greater economic development, although at the same time differing ethnic groups were brought together within one political unit, which resulted in the creation of strong centrifugal forces. In the case of Burma not only were various peoples included within one country, but prior to 1937 Burma itself was joined administratively to India, a fact which was bitterly resented by many of the Burmese.

The political structures of the colonial areas reflected the desire for administrative efficiency on the part of the European States. The French organized Indochina into four protectorates—Cambodia, Laos, Tonkin, and Annam—and one colony, Cochin China. In creating Tonkin, Annam, and Cochin China the French gave political recognition to geographic divisions in eastern and southern Indochina, but they also split the Annamese people into three separate states. The Dutch combined a large number of ethnic groups into the Netherlands East Indies, and since that area's independence there have arisen strong centrifugal forces (see page 517). In Malaya the British governed part of the area indirectly, by means of protectorates, and the rest directly through a crown colony. The protectorates comprised a

---

[3] The major exception to this generalization is rice, which moves from surplus areas in Indochina, Thailand, and Burma to Indonesia and Malaya.

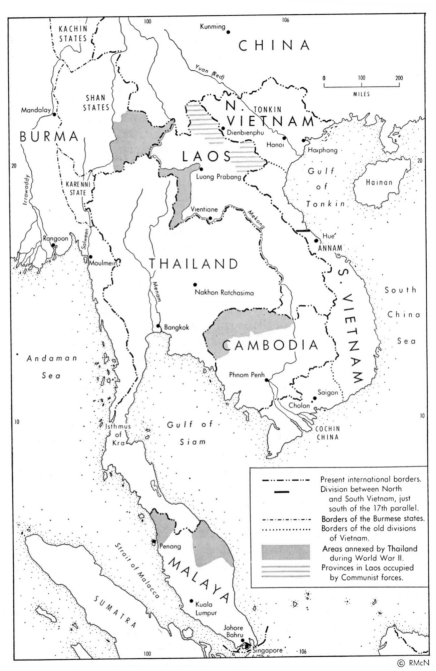

Figure 95. The Mainland States of Southeast Asia.

total of nine states. The crown colony, known as the Straits Settlements, consisted of Singapore (together with Cocos Islands and Christmas Island in the Indian Ocean), Penang Island (including Province Wellesley on the mainland), Malacca, a port to the northwest of Singapore, and Labuan Island, off the coast of British Borneo. This political grouping was actually a legacy of the East India Company, which had organized the area largely for the sake of expediency; not until 1946 were the Straits Settlements broken up.

In the political partitioning of southeast Asia international boundaries were in some instances so delimited as to divide ethnic groups (Thais, Shans, Cambodians, Malays) among two or more countries. These super-imposed boundaries later caused considerable conflict between some of the countries of the area. In many of the more isolated parts the exact location of boundaries has never been clearly determined, and to local peoples the existence of these dividing lines probably means very little. An increase of economic and political development and the possibility of future friction between Communist and non-Communist States will lead eventually to more exact boundary demarcations than now exist.

Centrifugal and centripetal forces within the individual countries of southeast Asia are included in the regional discussions later in this chapter. Distance, mountain barriers, poorly developed circulatory systems, and diverse ethnic groups represent powerful divisive forces in some of these areas, within which the people have only begun to develop a strong sense of nationhood. Associated with the internal aspects of unity and disunity are those of an external nature. With the rise of the independence movements many of the peoples of southeast Asia were drawn together by the common bond of anticolonialism. This bond is still strong and serves also to link this area with India, Ceylon, and other States in southwestern Asia and Africa. Most of these States have been reluctant to align themselves militarily with the Western countries in any alliance against the Soviet bloc, for fear of bringing on a return of foreign control in one form or another.

The State of Thailand is somewhat of a divisive factor among the countries of southeast Asia, for the Thais have not come under direct Western political control and thus they do not share the anticolonial feelings of their neighbors. Thailand, for example, is a member of the Southeast Asian Treaty Organization (SEATO) and is thus allied militarily with the United States, Britain, and France. The country was involved in considerable territorial expansion at the expense of its neighbors during World War II and, although at the end of the war these areas were returned to their former owners, some of them continue to represent regions of potential Thai irredentism.

Another force for international diversity has been the creation of a Communist type of government in North Vietnam and the possibility of the extension of communism into other parts of southeast Asia. Because of past antagonisms, the non-Communist states of Indochina (South Vietnam, Cambodia, Laos) have made no efforts for united action in the face of this Communist threat. The basic philosophy of much of the population is one of nonviolence. There, as in other parts of southeast Asia, the opportunity exists for the Communists to emphasize the tensions existing between the various countries and thus to forestall future international action in this area against the expansion of Communist power.

BACKGROUND TO THE INDEPENDENCE MOVEMENTS

The Era of Colonial Expansion

Southeast Asia is separated from both India and China by such physical obstacles as mountain ranges, forested hills, and difficult limestone terrain. Despite these handicaps a great number and variety of peoples have migrated south and east into what are now Burma, Thailand, and Indochina, settling in the lowland areas or moving down through Malaya and the island archipelago stretching to the southeast.

During and after the thirteenth century Moslem traders came to southeast Asia by sea and propagated the Mohammedan faith in the area. By 1500 the Portuguese, the first of the European colonial groups, had reached the Indies, and a century later the Dutch appeared. The Dutch gradually established their control over islands and coastal points, and in time, since Holland was the stronger maritime power, the Portuguese empire was eliminated, except for a part of Timor Island. By the mid-seventeenth century Holland had become the dominant power in the area. At this time Britain and France were concerned primarily with India, and not until after 1800 did these countries begin to expand in southeast Asia.

The acquisition of territory in southeast Asia, first by Portugal and Holland and later by Britain and France, was motivated primarily by the desire for trade and the development of the area's resources. The British were also interested in protecting sea routes to China and the eastern approaches to India, while the French came to Indochina in the late nineteenth century partly in hopes of establishing overland routes to China and thus bypassing British-controlled Hong Kong. Prior to the nineteenth century there was little desire on the part of any of the European States to gain large territorial holdings, and for a time only a few strategically located ports were actually occupied.

In 1819 Singapore was founded, and two years later parts of southern Burma passed into the hands of the British East India Company. Subsequent British expansion in Malaya and Burma was countered by French conquests in the Mekong delta of southern Indochina. Throughout the remainder of the nineteenth century Britain and France expanded their territorial holdings in southeast Asia, partly by military campaigns and partly by concluding treaties with local rulers which established protectorates over the small, individual States. Thailand was permitted to remain an independent kingdom as a buffer between British and French possessions. Independence, however, could not protect Thailand from territorial encroachments on both the east and the west. The British, expanding their holdings in Burma, eventually annexed the Shan States in northwestern Thailand, while in the south four small Thai border states—Kelantan, Trengganu, Kedah, and Perlis—with a predominantly Moslem Malay population, were later added to British Malaya. Likewise, the French, moving inland from the coast of Indochina, acquired from Thailand the Laotian states east of the Mekong as well as the Battambang area west of Cambodia. In 1896 the Mekong River north of Thailand was taken to mark the border between Burma and Indochina.

The political organizations of the several colonial areas varied considerably. The principal concern the colonial powers had in these areas was in their trade potential, particularly with the mother country. The tendency of the European powers to lump together differing ethnic groups within one national unit in order to serve their particular economic interest often led to considerable antagonism on the part of the people of southeast Asia. In addition to unification, the Europeans also brought about in some countries a reorientation from the interior lowlands to the coast. In Burma, for example, Mandalay, 450 miles north of the Irrawaddy mouth, was the historical capital, but after the arrival of the British Rangoon, located within the Irrawaddy delta, became the political and commercial center of the country.

The Effects of Commercial Development

Agricultural and mineral exploitation by the Europeans gradually expanded in line with the discovery of new resources, methods of development, and additional markets in other parts of the world. Eventually southeast Asia became a major producer of a variety of valuable commodities, most of which were exported to Europe or North America. Among the most important of these were tin, rubber, spices, tea, sugar, palm oil, cinchona (for quinine), copra, petroleum, and tungsten. In terms of investments and foreign trade the southeast Asian colonies came to play significant roles in the economies of Holland, Britain, France, and, to a lesser extent, Portugal. As the most important rice surplus area of the world, southeast Asia has been, and still is, an extremely significant source of food for its own urban centers as well as such major countries as Japan, China, and India.

Although small numbers of both Indians and Chinese had been in contact with southeast Asia for hundreds of years prior to the nineteenth century, a great influx of people from India and China came after 1850 in response to the demand for cheap, tractable labor by European agricultural and mining enterprises, as well as to population pressures existing within India and China. The Indians came mostly to Burma and Malaya: in Burma many of them are in business and landlords, while in Malaya they have been important as laborers on the rubber plantations. Their political influence in these two countries has not been as great as their numbers might indicate, for a majority of them are temporary residents, who return home as soon as they can afford to do so.

In contrast with the Indians, the Chinese are for the most part permanent inhabitants (Table 15). Like the Indians, they came largely as labor-

Table 15

ETHNIC CHINESE IN SOUTHEAST ASIA, 1947

Nation	Chinese Population	Total Population	Per Cent of Chinese
Burma	300,000	17,000,000	2
Thailand	2,500,000	17,359,000	14
Indochina	850,000	27,000,000	3
Malaya	2,615,000*	5,849,000	45
British Borneo	220,000	878,000	25
Indonesia	1,900,000	69,000,000	3
Total	8,385,000	137,086,000	

*Federation of Malaya: 1,885,000 out of a total of 4,908,000 (39 per cent). Singapore: 730,000 out of total of 940,824 (78 per cent).
   Source: Victor Purcell, *The Chinese in Southeast Asia,* Oxford University Press, 1951, p. 2. Used by permission.

ers for the European enterprises, but they also congregated in many of the new commercial cities—Singapore, Rangoon, Bangkok, Saigon, and Hanoi— where they performed many of the menial tasks necessary in these urban areas (Figure 96). The Chinese began to dominate the merchant class in much of southeast Asia and soon held there monopolies in a number of retail and wholesale establishments and in rice milling. They also developed importance as craftsmen and skilled laborers. Like the Indians of east Africa, many of them came to occupy a middle position between the indigenous peoples and the Europeans.

The First Demands for Self-Rule

The development of the independence movements in southeast Asia did not begin until after World War I. By that time the European powers had begun to train and educate certain Asians to play greater roles in the economic and political activities of their countries. Along with this went a gradual liberalization of administrative policies (particularly in the British and Dutch territories), so that local political organizations began to assume

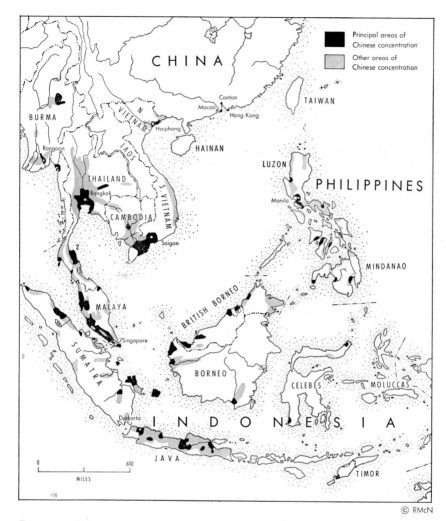

Figure 96. Chinese in Southeast Asia. (After Unger, *The Geographical Review*, XXXIV [April, 1944]. Courtesy of American Geographical Society.)

responsibilities of self-government. Eventually some of the Asians—particularly those who had received education in Europe—grew restive under the restrictions of foreign control and became leaders in the movements for independence.

The Repercussions of World War II

World War II had been in progress for two years in Europe before it spread to southeast Asia. In September, 1941, the Japanese, with the consent of the pro-Nazi government of Vichy France, occupied Indochina. After the attack on Pearl Harbor in December of that year, Japanese forces began to move south and west into Malaya, Indonesia and Burma. By late 1942 Japanese-controlled territory extended westward to the mountains separating Burma from India and southward through Indonesia to southern New Guinea and the Solomon Islands.

During the three years of Japanese occupation, several significant developments took place in southeast Asia. For the first time in history the entire region was united under a single political authority, and through their "Greater East Asia Co-Prosperity Plan" the Japanese aimed at a regional economic development of the area. They played on the theme of Thai nationalism by permitting Thailand to expand its borders and reoccupy some of the lands lost to its neighbors during the late nineteenth and early twentieth centuries. They also combined the three easternmost Indochinese states into the new state of Vietnam, and they administered Cambodia, Laos, and Vietnam as separate political units, thereby destroying the myth of Indochinese unity. Finally, before their withdrawal the Japanese supported local independence movements, particularly in Indonesia and Indochina, so that by the time the European powers reoccupied their former colonies the seeds of revolt were already well sown.

POLITICAL UNITS AFTER WORLD WAR II

Burma

The independent State of Burma is an example of a political area in which centrifugal forces have constituted serious threats to national unity. With an area of about 262,000 square miles, Burma consists of a central lowland enclosed on all sides but the south by uplands. The central lowland is drained by the southward-flowing Irrawaddy, Chindwin, and Sittang rivers, and is subdivided into a northern dry zone, containing the city of Mandalay, and a southern wet zone, centered on Rangoon, the capital and largest city. The upland areas of Burma are for the most part wet and forested, and transportation facilities there are generally poor. These uplands have helped to isolate Burma from land contacts with neighboring countries, and as a consequence Burma's communications with other areas have been carried on largely by sea. Burma's territory extends northward along the borders of China's Yunnan province into the inaccessible mountains of the Kachin area; a narrow projection also extends south for nearly 400 miles along the Tenasserim coast. Thus distance, in addition to climate, surface configuration, and ethnic and economic diversity, is a centrifugal force in the country.

Within Burma's central lowland the diversity which results from climatic differences and from the competition between two urban areas is matched by differing economic and political conditions as well. In the dry northern zone millets, tobacco, peanuts, and cotton predominate, whereas in southern Burma rice is the chief crop. Many farmers in the north own their own land and are considerably more prosperous than the debt-ridden tenant farmers in the Rangoon area. Such differences are reflected in the political parties and platforms existing within the country.

Less than two-thirds of the population of over 20 million persons are Burmese, and these are concentrated for the most part in the Irrawaddy lowlands and along the coast. Minority groups include over a million Karens east and northeast of Rangoon, another million Shans living north of the Thai border, plus several hundred thousand Kachins in the extreme north and Nagas and Chins along the Indian border. These groups are differentiated from the Burmese and from one another by language, customs, and religion, and their incorporation within the Burmese State was a result largely of administrative expediency on the part of the British. The Chinese in Burma form about 2 per cent of the total population, and as such are not a significant political force. Many of them are in retail and wholesale businesses, but as an important economic and political minority group they are outweighed by the more than one million Indians, who handle much of the nation's business and make up a large proportion of the craftsmen and skilled laborers.

The people of Burma emerged from World War II determined to obtain independence. The British government drew up plans for the development of Burma as a dominion at the end of a three-year preparatory period, but the proposal was met by strong protests and violence. Rather than face armed rebellion, the British acceded to Burmese demands. In January, 1948, the independent Union of Burma came into being, completely separate from the British Commonwealth.

Provisions were made for the principal minority groups by the creation of three semiautonomous states—Shan, Kachin, and Karenni. Within a few months of Burma's independence the Karens were in open revolt, seeking to expand the borders of their area and obtain a greater degree of political autonomy. Local Communist groups also staged armed revolts, and for a time the country was threatened with internal collapse. Some political analysts suggested that Burma received its independence before it was actually ready to cope with the problems of self-rule. Although by 1954 the warring elements in Burma had been driven into the more inaccessible areas and had been split up into small groups, guerrilla warfare has continued in various parts of the country, thereby limiting the areas in which the government exercises effective control and hindering the development of Burma's resources. Thus one of the country's principal needs is for a well-developed circulatory system, although this can come about only as a result of large expenditures of capital and the successful conclusion of a nationwide military campaign against the rebel forces.

Burma is important for its rice exports, as well as for teak, petroleum, lead, zinc, and tungsten. The average population density is far lower than that of many areas in eastern China. With the removal of British power from Burma in 1948, a situation has been created which might lead to Chinese expansion into all or parts of Burma in the guise of international communism. In 1956 Chinese Communist troops moved across the northeastern borders of Burma in two places and occupied parts of the Kachin and Wa areas. Both are extremely isolated and inhabited largely by mountain tribes. A British-Chinese convention at the end of the nineteenth century recognized Burma's sovereignty over the Wa area, but the legal status of the Kachin area was never clearly defined.

One of the problems relating to northern Burma was the fact that units of the Chinese Nationalist army had crossed into Burma at the time of the Chinese Communist victory and in the years following 1949 had been making hit-and-run raids into China. In 1953 the United States cooperated in flying some 7,000 of these troops to Taiwan, but others remained in Burma and maintained an airstrip in the remote Shan States. Finally, in March, 1961, the United States airlifted some 4,200 additional Nationalist troops to Taiwan, but still others are believed to have infiltrated into Laos.

In 1960 Burma and Communist China reached a border agreement under which Burma ceded 132 square miles of territory to China in exchange for full title to 85 square miles of former Chinese territory held by the Burmese on a perpetual lease originally negotiated with China by the British. The tract which Burma acquired includes an important road link between the Shan and Kachin states. In addition to the border agreement Burma received $80 million in economic aid from China. Thus, at a time when anti-Chinese forces exist in South Vietnam and Thailand, Burma appears to have been effectively "neutralized" so far as the Cold War in southeast Asia is concerned.

Thailand

In Thailand, as in Burma, physical and ethnic differences create strong divisive forces. Unlike Burma, however, Thailand has not been a European colonial possession, and both its power status and its degree of internal unity have been greater than that of the new Burmese State.

Thailand consists of a central lowland surrounded on three sides by hills and mountains. The lowland is drained by the Menam River (Chao Praya), within the delta of which lies Bangkok, the nation's political and commercial center. In the northern and eastern parts of the country are plateau areas which are inhabited not only by Thais but also by Cambodians, Laotians, and Shans. In these areas there are no clear-cut physical or ethnic dividing lines, and boundaries have shifted several times since the latter part of the nineteenth century. Thai territory extends over 600 miles southward onto the Malay Peninsula. In southern Thailand, adjoining Malaya, are over half a million people whose economic and cultural interests lie more with the Federation of Malaya to the south than with the Thai State, the major core areas of which lie several hundred miles to the north.

Over three-quarters of the approximately 26 million people in the country are Thais, and, except for the Chinese and Malays in the southern part of the State, most of the non-Thai minority groups have close cultural links with the Thais. In the northwest the border with Burma cuts through territory inhabited by Shan peoples; in the northeast that with Indochina leaves many Laotians in Thailand; and in the east Cambodians live within the Thai State. About 14 per cent of Thailand's population is Chinese, many of whom live in and about Bangkok. These people control most of Thailand's retail trade and practically all of its rice distribution and milling. An economically powerful minority group, they have often been the victims of discrimination by the Thai government.

The history of the Chinese in Thailand contains many features which are common to Chinese minorities in other parts of southeast Asia (Figure 96). The influx of Chinese into Thailand began about the middle of the nineteenth century, when they migrated to the area to work in the cities, on European-owned plantations, and in the mines. Practically all of the immigrants were men; many of them married Thai women, and they and their offspring gradually became assimilated into the Thai State. By 1909 approximately 10 per cent of the country's population was estimated to be Chinese, many of whom were already in powerful economic positions.

The end of Chinese assimilation began about the time of World War I, when the Chinese influx increased substantially, Chinese women began to arrive in Thailand in large numbers, and the status of China itself was enhanced by changes in political regime and increased resistance to foreign encroachments. From then on the Chinese began to adhere more closely to their own cultural characteristics, sending their children to Chinese schools and regarding themselves as a non-Thai national group. In recent years there has been more and more resentment of the Chinese in Thailand because of their habit of sending money back to China ("draining off" Thailand's wealth), their apparent willingness to undergo all manner of privations for the sake of money, their economic strength, and their associations (both real and imagined) with communism.

Thailand, like Burma, is normally a major rice-exporting area, and since World War II the country has gradually revived this export trade. Its average population density is about the same as Burma's, with the result that Thailand is not a "crowded" State. With its surplus food production and available land for settlement, this country, again like Burma, is a rich prize in the path of Chinese expansion. Since World War II Thailand, under a firm dictatorship, has become one of the key anti-Communist areas of southeast Asia. Although the per-capita income there, as in other parts of Asia, is still very low, Thailand is an area of relative economic and political stability, in contrast with the turbulent conditions existing in the countries which border it. With instability existing in neighboring Laos, however, Thailand itself cannot help being affected. Nearly one-third of the country's population lives in the primitive, underdeveloped northeastern area adjoining the borders of Laos. Many of these people are closer in language and customs to the Laotians across the Mekong River than they are to the Thais, and there is considerable resentment there toward the more prosperous inhabitants of Thailand to the south and west. Communications with Bangkok are poor, and Communist agents from Laos have been reported in this area stirring up villagers against the central government. When, in May, 1962, Communist-led forces in Laos had spread westward to the Thai border, United States marines were rushed into Thailand and stationed in the northeastern area in an effort to prevent the spread of Communist control to the west of the Mekong.

Indochina

The former French possession of Indochina was an area in which strong centrifugal forces existed and in which both nationalism and communism contributed to the postwar political turmoil. Three major ethnic groups lived within the Indochinese borders—the Laotians, the Cambodians, and the Annamese. Prior to World War II the Laotians and Cambodians each had their own separate political region, while the Annamese were divided into three areas—Cochin China, Tonkin, and Annam. During the war the ethnic unity of the Annamese was recognized in the formation of the country of Vietnam; in 1954 conflicting ideologies led to a partition of Vietnam into North and South.

Geographically as well as administratively, Indochina consisted of five regions. The lowlands of the Red and Mekong rivers are important agricultural areas, particularly the Mekong lowland, where the bulk of Indochina's rice exports was produced. Cochin China, located at the delta of the Mekong, contained Saigon, Indochina's capital, and included most of Indochina's 850,000 Chinese. Concentrated in and about Saigon, the Chinese never played as important a part in the French territory's economic development as they did in Indonesia, Thailand, and Malaya. In the Red River delta of northern Indochina was Tonkin, with its major city of Hanoi and its dense population concentration. This region was one of the poorest areas in southeast Asia. Between these two areas was Annam, consisting of sparsely settled mountains and a narrow coastal plain interrupted by mountain spurs which come down to the sea. Cambodia, to the west of the Mekong delta, is principally an inland basin centering on a lake—Tonle Sap. Much of the region contains good agricultural land. Cambodia also extends west to the Korat Plateau, which it shares with Thailand. The fifth geographic and administrative unit, Laos, is a dissected hilly area bordering the upper Mekong River. One of its principal drawbacks is its inaccessibility, which has been intensified by its quarrels with Thailand and by the communization of North Vietnam, which borders it on the east.

The Japanese occupied Indochina in 1941 and remained there for nearly four years. Toward the end of the war Japan combined Cochin China, Tonkin, and Annam into a new political unit—Vietnam—containing 80 per cent of Indochina's population and most of its potential wealth. Prior to the arrival of Allied occupation troops the Japanese also encouraged independence movements there and in Laos and Cambodia as part of their general policy of hindering the return of European power to southeast Asia. Economic motives were important in the Japanese efforts in Indochina and in Indonesia, for if the Europeans were forced to give up their colonies (and thus end various commercial restrictions in these areas), Japan might enjoy greater trade and investment advantages after peace had been established. For six months after Japan's surrender Chinese troops occupied Vietnam north of the sixteenth parallel. Like the Japanese, they did little to put down nationalist activities, and by the time the French forces returned a widespread independence movement was under way in northern Vietnam.

The Battle for Independence.   In the struggle for self-government in Vietnam two trends were of particular importance: the increasing Communist nature of the conflict and the eventual involvement of Chinese and American interests. The French attempted to re-establish the political unity of Indochina and incorporate Laos, Cambodia, and Vietnam as Associated States within the French Union, but these efforts were blocked, both by the refusal of the Laotians and Cambodians to join in a new Indochinese state and by the growing independence movement in Vietnam. A *de facto* Viet Minh government was set up in Vietnam by the independence fighters under Ho Chi Minh, a Moscow-trained Communist, and in December, 1946, widespread fighting broke out between French troops and the guerrilla forces of the new independence group.

The military struggle for independence lasted for seven and a half years and imposed a severe strain on France's economy. The French could never bring themselves to grant complete independence to Vietnam, and many non-Communist patriots supported Ho Chi Minh out of their desire for self-government for the area. As time went on, however, the Viet Minh government became more openly Communist in character. Eventually it was recognized by the Soviet Union and Communist China, and military supplies began to move across the border from China for the Viet Minh

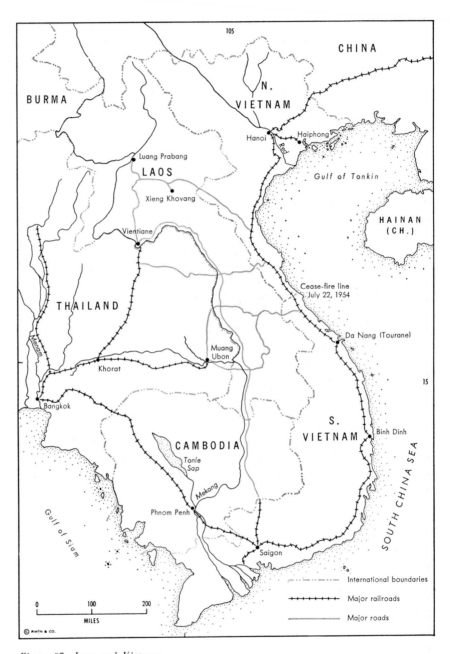

Figure 97. Laos and Vietnam.

forces. Despite considerable military aid from the United States, the French were unable to stem the expanding power of the Viet Minh, and by the spring of 1954 France was forced to ask for a truce.

The Partition of Vietnam.   In the ensuing peace treaty at Geneva in July, 1954, Vietnam was divided roughly along the seventeenth parallel: North Vietnam, with an area of 77,000 square miles and a population of 12 million, passed under the control of the Communist Viet Minh government, while South Vietnam (with 50,000 square miles and 10 million population) remained under the administration of the non-Communist Vietnam government. The Communists agreed to recognize the French-sponsored governments of Laos and Cambodia, but with the provision that these States be neutralized, that is, that they enter into no military alliances with other countries and maintain no more than the minimum number of troops necessary for national security. Communist forces, which had penetrated across the Vietnam border into Laos, were not required to evacuate Laotian territory but established themselves in two provinces adjoining the North Vietnam border. It was also decided that elections would be held both in North and South Vietnam during or before July, 1956, in order to select a national government for a united Vietnam State which would then come into existence. Such elections were never held.

Since 1954 North Vietnam has become a virtual satellite of Communist China, a base from which men and supplies can move west and south through the rugged forested terrain both to Laos and through Laos to South Vietnam. One of the most difficult problems facing South Vietnam after the partition was the establishment of a strong central government capable of gaining the confidence of the people. Over a million refugees from North Vietnam added to the economic and political problems of the South. Internal security was threatened by armed sects, including the Binh Xuyen, a bandit group which controlled the ministry of the interior and the police force. Gradually these outlaw groups were disbanded by strong government action and in 1956 the status of Vietnam was changed to that of a republic with Ngo Dinh Diem as its first president.

In the years following 1956 Diem was able to strengthen the role of the Saigon government in Vietnam, and, with the receipt of considerable American aid, gradually to improve its economic conditions. Refugees were settled in new villages, and although the concept of popular government was far more theoretical than actual in South Vietnam, conditions by 1961 had improved to a considerably greater degree than had been generally anticipated at the time of the division of Vietnam. But by 1961 South Vietnam was coming to face a new and more serious threat—the infiltration of thousands of Communist guerrillas into the country from Laos.

The Communist forces in South Vietnam (known as the "Viet Cong") are to some extent a re-establishment of those the French faced in their long and bitter struggle from 1946 to 1954. These forces are trained guerrillas who terrorize the remote villages of South Vietnam, set up bases in the forests, and engage in hit-and-run raids against units of the regular army. Many of them reach South Vietnam from the north by passing through a strip of Communist-held territory in eastern Laos which adjoins the borders of both North and South Vietnam. Bases have been set up by the Viet Cong in eastern Laos, and at times Viet Cong forces are believed to have retreated in the face of superior forces across the border into Cambodia. The forests, the hills, and in the south the swamps and islands of the Mekong delta hamper large-scale military operations by the South Vietnamese army against the guerrillas.

By early 1962 military aid from the United States was beginning to pour into South Vietnam to bolster Diem's efforts to halt the Communist invasion. Several thousand United States personnel were in South Vietnam acting as instructors, advisers, engineers, and in other capacities with the South Vietnamese troops. A major resettlement program was also being undertaken to move villagers away from the remote areas of the country, where they were easy prey for the Viet Cong, into more concentrated areas where they could be better protected.

Laos. A second State in which Communist control has gradually been expanding is the former French territory of Laos. Communications in Laos are even less developed than in South Vietnam: there are no railroads and only some 3,500 miles of roads, about half of them impassable in the rainy season. A narrow-gauge railroad from Bangkok connects with a ferry across the Mekong River to Vientiane, the administrative capital. The only other connections with the outside are a road to North Vietnam, another along the Mekong through Cambodia to Saigon, and four airfields.

Laos has one long border with North Vietnam and another with Thailand. It also borders on China, Burma, Cambodia, and South Vietnam and thus lies at a focal point in southeast Asia. Its 2 million people belong to a variety of tribes and have developed little sense of nationalism. The struggle for political control of Laos has largely swirled around and over them. This struggle, since 1954, has involved a bewildering number of personalities and political factions, only a few of which will be noted here.

When Laos became independent the royal government was set up under Prince Souvanna Phouma, while Communist-dominated Pathet Lao rebels were led by his half-brother, Prince Souphanouvong. The king, Savang Vathana, was largely a figurehead ruler who lived in the royal capital, Luang Prabang, located some 125 miles to the north of Vientiane. Much of the troubled political history of Laos since independence has revolved around the two rival princes, as well as General Phoumi Novasan, leader of troops backed by the United States.

Negotiations at the time of independence between the Laotian government and the Pathet Lao for the formation of a unified national regime led eventually to elections and the establishment in 1958 of a coalition government; the uneasy truce between the various political elements soon led to the ousting of the Pathet Lao representatives and the beginning of a two-year period of domination, largely by right-wing elements. In the summer of 1960 a neutralist-oriented regime came to power with Prince Souvanna Phouma as prime minister. This government established diplomatic relations with the Soviet Union and was soon suspected of leading Laos toward a dangerous *rapprochement* with the Communists. A rival government was then set up under General Nosavan, with strong United States backing, and after a brief period of fighting was established in Vientiane. By the following year troops loyal to Novosan's right-wing regime were under heavy attack from the Pathet Lao which had been organized and supplied both from North Vietnam and from Communist China. Gradually the Pathet Lao spread out over Laos, and, from the point of view of supply, there was little the United States or other Western powers could do to counter the aid moving across the borders from Communist countries.

In July, 1962, after a fifteen-month conference, representatives of fourteen countries signed at Geneva agreements guaranteeing Laotian neutrality and independence under a coalition government representing both left- and right-wing factions, to be led by the neutralist premier, Souvanna Phouma. Foreign troops are to be withdrawn from Laos, and the signatory states agree to respect the kingdom's neutrality status. American acquiesence in the agreement followed the defeat of General Novasan's forces by the Communists; with the Communists in the ascendancy future neutrality for Laos may be difficult to maintain. Although American troops are withdrawn from the country, what guarantees are there that the Pathet Lao forces will also be disbanded? Through eastern Laos runs the "Ho Chi Minh" supply trail from North Vietnam to the Viet Cong in South Vietnam. Will Vietnamese be kept from using this trail? Clearly the Laotian government will be hard pressed to maintain its neutralist and territorial integrity in the form of Communist activities in the areas adjoining its country's borders.

A take-over in Laos by Communist-dominated forces would seriously affect the positions both of Thailand and of Cambodia. The latter is largely a delta country, relatively undeveloped and with poor communication systems except through its waterways. The government of Cambodia has consistently sought to follow a neutrality policy with regard to the ideological struggles raging about it, but it finds itself faced along the borders with the twin threats of the Viet Cong in South Vietnam and of the Pathet Lao in Laos. The Cambodians have long mistrusted the Thais to their west (who have frequently warred on the Cambodians),[4] and their years of association with the Vietnamese under French control failed to strengthen their re-

---

[4] In June, 1962, the International Court of Justice, acting on a boundary dispute between Thailand and Cambodia, awarded the twelfth-century temple of Preah Vihear to Cambodia. The decision served to alienate further the two countries, since the Thais have for years considered the territory on which the temple is located as within their own boundaries.

lations with what is now South Vietnam. Here again physical and historical isolation makes difficult any united action in the face of Communist infiltration into Southeast Asia.

The Federation of Malaya

The changing pattern of sovereignty in southeast Asia has not only affected Burma, Indochina, and the border areas of Thailand, but also the British territory of Malaya. With its exports of tin and rubber, as well as iron ore, coconuts, pineapples, and palm oil, Malaya was one of the most valuable economic assets in the British Empire. The achievement of self-rule there has been an important step in the gradual evolution of the British Commonwealth from an area of colonialism to one of free association among independent countries.

The Federation of Malaya consists of nine states and the two former British territories of Penang and Malacca on the west coast of the Malay Peninsula. It has an area of about 51,000 square miles and comprises a number of mountain regions and extensive coastal lowlands. The upland topography was in part responsible for the country's historical division into the small Malay states, which during the period of British rule managed to retain considerable local autonomy. The city of Kuala Lumpur, located a short distance inland from the west coast, is the capital of the federation. It is the leading city of the peninsula and is connected by rail and highway to other population centers of the country. Because of the forests and mountains, however, there are many isolated parts of Malaya, the significance of which was evident after World War II, when British and Malayan forces waged an all-out war there against Communist guerrillas. Each of the Malay states has its own local core area, but the only urban center approaching Kuala Lumpur in size is the port of Penang, situated on an island off the northwest coast.

Of the federation's population total of about 7 million, 50 per cent are Malays, 37 per cent are Chinese, and over 10 per cent are Indians. Despite the divided character of the population, there was little racial friction in Malaya before 1942. The Chinese provided most of the labor for the tin mines, were engaged in the shipping industry and the processing of pineapples and rice, and controlled much of Malaya's retail business.

Ethnic and Political Problems. In February, 1942, the Japanese conquered Malaya, and during the years of enemy occupation strong antagonisms developed between the Chinese and the Malays. Chinese resistance fighters operated against the Japanese from the Malayan jungles, while the Malays and the Indians took relatively little part in the underground movements. In their efforts to end Chinese resistance activities, the Japanese resorted to the use of Malay police units against the guerrilla fighters.

When British forces returned to Malaya in 1945, they found that the conflicting wartime roles played by the Chinese and Malays had resulted in widespread bitterness between the two groups. Associated with this friction was the beginning of a Communist movement among the Chinese in Malaya.

Friction between the Chinese and the Malays was increased in 1948, when the various Malay states, Penang, and Malacca were organized as the Federation of Malaya. Within the new country citizenship was so defined as to make a Chinese voting majority impossible. In 1948 Chinese Communist guerrillas, many of them members of the wartime resistance groups, began a campaign of terror throughout Malaya. Operating from jungle bases, they raided isolated settlements, murdered plantation workers, and slashed rubber trees. Although the British dispatched thousands of troops against the guerrillas, nonmilitary measures eventually proved to be more effective. Restrictions on Chinese citizenship in the Malayan federation were eased, and many Chinese farmers, suspected of giving food and supplies to the guerrillas, were moved from isolated areas in or close to the jungle and resettled in other parts of the country. By 1954 the terrorism had largely subsided, and the hard core of Communist fighters were forced to move their base of operations into remote mountain areas along the Thai border. In 1957 the Federation of Malaya achieved its independence and became a member of the British Commonwealth.

The British-Held Territories

Singapore.   Located on Singapore Island (217 square miles) just off the Malayan coast are Singapore city, which has been developed into one of the great commercial centers of the world, and the major British naval base in the Far East. Prior to World War II Singapore was administered as a part of the Straits Settlements (see page 496), but in 1946 it was constituted as an individual crown colony. Three-quarters of its approximately 1,600,000 people are Chinese; among the Chinese there are many who have strong "leftist" political leanings.

In June, 1959, Singapore attained limited autonomy, with the British retaining control of defense, foreign affairs, and internal security. The British also retained the right to regain complete political control (as they did in British Guiana) in the event of widespread riots, such as Singapore experienced from left-wing groups in 1956. Along with autonomy have come increasing economic difficulties. The population is growing at such a rate that without large-scale emigration it would double in the next twenty years. There are few industries in Singapore, and the economic policies of both Malaya and Indonesia have tended to reduce its role as a transshipment port for southeast Asia's products. The British military installations in the city support some 50,000 people, but there are indications that in time these installations may be reduced considerably. It is in order to widen its economic base that the government of Singapore began seriously considering joining Malaya in some form of political union (see below).

British Borneo. British Borneo consists of (1) the crown colony of North Borneo, including the island of Labuan six miles off the coast, (2) Sarawak, a crown colony on the northwest coast adjoining North Borneo, and (3) Brunei, a small protectorate which is split by a projection of Sarawak territory. Brunei, over which the sultan exercises absolute rule, has important oil reserves from which its ruler receives some $40 million a year in royalties. With the exception of this oil, most of the resources of British Borneo are little developed, and nearly half of the total population of the three areas are members of pagan tribes. About one-third of the 900,000 inhabitants of British Borneo are Chinese, the majority concentrated in Sarawak.

In June, 1962, the Philippine government formally claimed sovereignty over British North Borneo. The basis of the Philippine position was that the sultan of Brunei had awarded North Borneo to the sultan of Sulu in 1750 as a reward for military assistance. The Sulu Archipelago forms the southeasternmost part of the Philippine Islands and at its closest point is but thirty miles from North Borneo. In 1878 the sultan of Sulu leased North Borneo to the British North Borneo Company, a private commercial organization. According to the British government, Spain (then in control of the Philippines) renounced all claims to North Borneo in 1885, but the Philippine government rejects this position, pointing out among other things that up until 1936 the North Borneo Company made annual payments to the Sulu sultan. In that year a dispute arose over the successor to the Sulu sultanate and the payments ceased. Ten years later the British government took over control of North Borneo from the North Borneo Company. This dispute, if pursued by the Philippines, could become a significant centrifugal force in the non-Communist island perimeter off the east Asian mainland.

The Malaysian Federation

In May, 1961, a suggestion was made by the prime minister of Malaya for the formation of a Federation of Malaysia, to consist of Malaya, Singapore, and the three territories of British Borneo. The suggestion was prompted in part by the possibilities of the eventual election of a pro-Communist regime in Singapore. In 1957 the ruling People's Action party in Singapore broke with the Communists and Communist sympathizers, and since that time Singapore's moderate anti-Communist prime minister has had only a slender margin of majority. Should the Communists be elected to power in Singapore there would be serious problems both for Malaya itself and for British Borneo.

One of the difficulties envisioned by the Malayans in any proposed union with Singapore and British Borneo is the large Chinese populations. Of Malaya's nearly 7 million people, 37 per cent, or approximately 2.5 million, are Chinese; of Singapore's 1.6 million, 75 per cent, or 1.2 million, are Chinese. In a union of the two areas 3.6 million Malayans would be outnumbered by over 3.7 million Chinese. A way out of this dilemma seems to lie in the inclusion of British Borneo with its 1.3 million people, of whom 27 per cent, or 357,000, are Chinese—giving a total population for the proposed union of 9,700,000, with 4,100,000 being Chinese.[5]

There is already a common currency in Malaya, Singapore, and British Borneo, Malay is a lingua franca throughout the area, and Singapore is the main commercial center for the entire region. The creation of Malaysia would end British colonialism in southeast Asia. One of the principal arguments against such a union is that the three territories of British Borneo have not advanced economically, educationally, and politically to the levels of Malaya and Singapore, and that their peoples would in effect be exchanging British colonialism for that of the Federation of Malaya. There is also the possibility that many of the Chinese of Singapore would seek to emigrate to the relatively empty lands of Sarawak and North Borneo. In September, 1963, the independent Malaysian federation came into being, but without the inclusion of Brunei, whose government decided to remain for the time being at least under British control.

The Republic of Indonesia

The Republic of Indonesia consists of four large islands—Java, Sumatra, a part of Borneo, and Celebes—some fifteen medium-size islands, and hundreds of smaller ones (Figure 98). Although the sea acts as a unifying element for the area, there is great physical, cultural, and economic diversity in Indonesia, with the result that it has been difficult to maintain uniform political control over the region. The distribution and types of population in Indonesia indicate the area's historic role as both passageway and settlement area for migrating peoples.

Nearly two-thirds of Indonesia's 95 million people are found on the island of Java, which comprises less than 10 per cent of the republic's area. There are also important population concentrations on Sumatra, Madura, Bali, southern Borneo, and southern Celebes, but Java has been the political, and to some extent commercial, focus of Indonesia. One of the

---

[5] In a Malay-Singapore union the Chinese would number 45 per cent of the total; if British Borneo were added they would represent 42 per cent. Such arithmetic does not take into account the position of the Malays, who would form 43 per cent of the population if only Singapore were added, but 47 per cent with the inclusion of British Borneo—the difference being made up by the addition of 900,000 non-Chinese from Borneo who the Malayan government seems to assume would join the Malays in opposition to attempted Chinese political dominance. The 900,000 Indians and Pakistani in Malaya and Singapore (representing nearly 10 per cent of the proposed union) might conceivably find themselves eventually wielding a balance of political power.

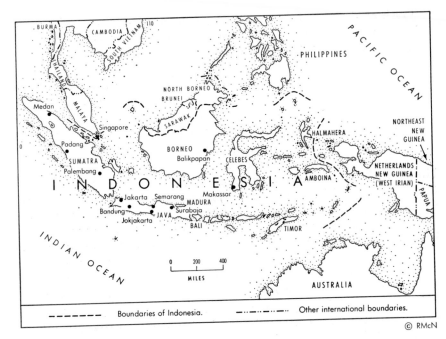

Figure 98. Indonesia.

major problems of the new Indonesian country has been the resentment by peoples of other islands (and by the Sundanese minority on Java itself) against Javanese domination of national affairs.

Cultural diversity stands out in the various languages spoken throughout Indonesia, of which Javanese, Sundanese, and Madurese are the most important. Dutch is still widely used by well-educated Indonesians and Chinese, and the younger generation is learning English in high school. Most of the Chinese speak the dialect of their home districts. A majority of the population is Moslem, but there are about 3 million Christians, a million Buddhists (among the Chinese), and another million Hindus (on Bali and adjacent Lombok), while in the isolated interiors of the islands primitive religions still exist.

The Chinese in Indonesia number just under 2 million and comprise about 3 per cent of the total population. Nearly half the Chinese are concentrated on Java and the nearby island of Madura, but there is a large number engaged in tin mining at Bangka and Billiton, east of Sumatra. Many Chinese merchants are scattered throughout the other islands of Indonesia. Under the Dutch the Chinese were little affected by discrimination, but they suffered during the Japanese occupation of Indonesia and again during the subsequent fighting for independence, when they received protection from neither the Indonesians nor the Dutch. Within the independent State of Indonesia the Chinese are resented for their hold on trade and industry and are the victims of various types of discrimination.

Before World War II Indonesia (then the Netherlands East Indies) was one of the richest colonial holdings in the world, producing cinchona, pepper, rubber, tin, tea, sugar, tobacco, bauxite, and petroleum. Dutch investments in the area totalled over $1 billion, and more than 200,000 Dutch citizens lived in the Netherlands East Indies. Japanese forces seized the area in 1942, and for over three years it remained under enemy control.

The Achievement of Independence. The postwar independence movement in Indonesia began in August, 1945, when Indonesian nationalist leaders (with the approval of the Japanese) proclaimed an independent Republic of Indonesia. British forces, which occupied the Netherlands Indies after Japan's surrender, did little to block the independence drive. By the spring of 1946, when the Dutch resumed control of their dependency, the movement (like that in Indochina) had assumed major proportions, and Dutch forces were soon in open warfare against Indonesian nationalists for control of the area. Realizing the necessity for liberalizing their colonial policy, the Dutch offered the Indonesians partnership in a new Netherlands-Indonesian Union, to consist of the Netherlands on the one hand and the United States of Indonesia (embracing all of the former Netherlands East Indies) on the other. The new political organization, which was to have come into effect in January, 1949, would have been under the sovereignty of the Netherlands crown, with joint control of defense, foreign affairs, and various economic and financial matters. Although both countries signed an agreement in 1946 providing for the establishment of such a union, negotiations on details soon broke down, and fighting again began between Dutch and Indonesian forces. After nearly two and a half years of intermittent warfare, the United States of Indonesia finally came into existence in January, 1950, as a sovereign, independent State. The status of Netherlands New Guinea (West Irian), with a non-Indonesian population of about 700,000, was to be decided later by negotiations, and the area continued to be controlled by the Dutch. The prolonged warfare and bitterness meant that the vague Netherlands-Indonesian Union was reduced to a mere formality, and in 1956 it was completely dissolved. Later in the same year the Indonesian government repudiated the more than $1 billion in debts which had been owed by the former East Indies administration to the Netherlands and which had been assumed by the new Indonesian regime. By 1960 only 10,000 Dutch nationals were still in Indonesia.

Internal Political Problems. The Indonesian republic has had to meet a number of problems that have challenged the internal structure of the country. Among these are the economic dislocation caused by World War

II and the independence struggle, the shortage of trained personnel for governing the large population, and the lack of available capital. Political immaturity is also a handicap in a State with no past history of democracy. The number of conflicting interests is reflected by the existence of some nineteen national political parties.

At the time of Indonesia's independence the country was constituted as a sixteen-state federation in order to permit as much regional autonomy as possible. Later, however, the federal system was abolished, and a unitary government was set up, centered on Java. This move has caused considerable resentment in provincial areas.

Since 1949 the Indonesian government has been challenged by armed resistance in several parts of the country. In various parts of southwestern Java, northern and central Sumatra, and southern Celebes antigovernment guerrilla forces carry on sporadic raids and terrorist acts against the settled areas. In 1948 a Darul Islam movement was started in southwestern Java for the purpose of turning secular Indonesia into a Moslem State. Since that time the movement has spread to Sumatra and Celebes as well. On Amboina in the southern Moluccas (in eastern Indonesia) a Republic of the South Moluccas was proclaimed in 1951, embracing Amboina, Ceram, and others of the once-famous Spice Islands. Many of the natives there are Christians, and they differ from the peoples of western and central Indonesia in race and language. Although the move for a republic was later abandoned, the Indonesian government was faced with armed insurrection in other parts of the archipelago from December, 1956, to September, 1961. One of the principal centers of this five-year activity was south Sumatra, where the rebels for a time established their own government and army.

Indonesia's National Status. The problems of Indonesia well illustrate the functioning of centrifugal and centripetal forces within a nation. The common desire for independence from European colonial control, the relative ease of communication by coastal shipping, the overwhelming predominance of the Moslem religion, and the concentration of population and wealth in the central core area of Java represent major centripetal forces. Against these are ranged the centrifugal elements of geographic diversity, fanatical religious and political organizations, distrust of Java's political power, and a general discontent over prevailing economic conditions. The island of Java normally accounts for exports earning only about one-third of Indonesia's foreign exchange, and one of the primary complaints of some of the other islands is that the funds they receive from the government are in no way proportional to the revenue which their areas earn. One centripetal factor in Indonesia's favor is the absence of nearby States which could exert pressures attracting units of Indonesia away from the capital's control.

In external affairs the Indonesian government has sought to follow a policy of neutrality between major power blocs. Relations with the West have been colored by Indonesia's disputes with the Dutch, particularly over Netherlands New Guinea (see below), but there has also been friction with Communist China over Indonesian restrictions on the activities of its own large Chinese minority. Arms were purchased from the Soviet Union in line with a military build-up for possible invasion of New Guinea. Because of its prolonged economic crises, its internal difficulties, and its obsession with the problem of Dutch control in New Guinea, Indonesia since independence has done relatively little in advancing toward a position of national viability.

West New Guinea (West Irian).   The problem of the former Netherlands New Guinea,[6] unresolved at the time of Indonesia's independence, long plagued Dutch-Indonesian relations. Indonesian nationalists claimed that the new State became heir to all the former Dutch possessions in southeast Asia, and that a majority of the natives in Netherlands New Guinea, if given the chance to express their preference, would choose Indonesian control rather than that of the Netherlands. The Dutch contended that most of the native peoples of Netherlands New Guinea are Papuans with no cultural ties to the peoples of Indonesia; that their level of cultural and political development is still extremely low; and that no significant results could be achieved from a formal plebiscite, even if the details for one could be worked out. The Netherlands has invested considerable sums of money in the development of the area; in 1961 the cost to the Dutch of maintaining New Guinea amounted to $26 million, a sum the Indonesians would be hard pressed to find should they control the area. Petroleum, the one resource of value, reached its peak of production in 1955 (at which time it comprised more than 80 per cent of west New Guinea's exports by value), but since that time production has been falling off. It would appear that without the expenditure of tremendous sums for development west New Guinea would be of little economic value to either the Netherlands or Indonesia.

From the point of view of the local inhabitants it would appear that they might benefit more, at least under existing conditions, from Dutch rather than from Indonesian control, because of Dutch administrative efficiency and the greater availability of capital in the Netherlands. From the point of view of anti-Communist defense moves in the southwest Pacific, Netherlands New Guinea in Dutch hands would be far more preferable than in Indonesian hands. Australia in particular has been concerned over the possibility of Indonesian sovereignty in this area, which

---

[6] The island of New Guinea was divided politically into Netherlands New Guinea in the west; the Territory of New Guinea, a United Nations trusteeship territory under Australian administration, in the northeast; and the Territory of Papua, an Australian possession, in the southeast.

is so vital to Australian defense plans. On the other hand, the Indonesians were unwilling to permit the retention of this colonial toehold by the Dutch, for it represented a potential centrifugal force which might in time lead to a political division of the Indonesian State. Some Indonesians have charged that from Netherlands New Guinea encouragement and material aid were rendered to the insurgents in the nearby south Moluccas, who are seeking an autonomous republic within the Indonesian nation. Actually, much of the Indonesian propaganda about this problem was designed to divert attention from certain unsatisfactory conditions at home.

In October, 1960, the Dutch for the first time suggested the possibility of United Nations control over Netherlands New Guinea, a course which was immediately opposed by the Indonesians. By the following year political groups in New Guinea were claiming the right to be heard in any decisions on their political future and were beginning to press toward ultimate independence, although with the economic problems the area faces it was difficult to see how Netherlands New Guinea could, at this time, develop by itself a successful economic and political structure. Finally, in August, 1962, under the threat of an Indonesian invasion of west New Guinea, the United States and the United Nations together brought the Netherlands to agree to relinquish its sovereignty. Control over west New Guinea would pass to the United Nations, but in May, 1963, Indonesia would gain control of the area, on condition that before the end of 1969 a plebiscite would be held to determine west New Guinea's ultimate status—as an independent State or as a part of Indonesia. Thus the Netherlands is finally removed as a colonial power in Southeast Asia.[7]

BIBLIOGRAPHY

BROEK, JAN O. M. "Diversity and Unity in Southeast Asia," *The Geographical Review,* XXXIV (1944), 175–96.

An outstanding summation of basic geographic elements in Southeast Asia before World War II.

CHRISTIAN, JOHN L. "Anglo-French Rivalry in Southeast Asia: Its Historical Geography and Diplomatic Climate," *The Geographical Review,* XXXI (1941), 272–83.

An interesting combination of geography and history as background elements in this area.

[7] Indonesia's success in ousting the Dutch may in time be followed by pressures against the Portuguese, who control over 7,000 square miles and half a million people on the island of Timor. Since India has already driven the Portuguese from Goa, Indonesia may well be expected to follow suit.

KING, JOHN KERBY. "Rice Politics," *Foreign Affairs,* XXXI (1953), 453–61.

A description of the political implications of rice surpluses and shortages in eastern Asia.

MADDOX, WILLIAM P. "Singapore: Problem Child," *Foreign Affairs,* XL (1962), 479–89.

A survey of Singapore's political and economic problems.

MURPHEY, RHOADS. "Economic Conflicts in South Asia," *Journal of Conflict Resolution,* IV (1960), 83–96.

An excellent regional summary of economic problems.

PAUKER, GUY J. "The Soviet Challenge in Indonesia," *Foreign Affairs,* XL (1962), 612–27.

General account of this problem.

SPENCER, JOSEPH E. *Asia, East by South.* New York: John Wiley & Sons, 1954.

A very good regional text.

UNGER, LEONARD. "The Chinese in Southeast Asia," *The Geographical Review,* XXXIV (1944), 196–218.

A detailed survey of the Chinese minorities in Southeast Asia before World War II.

VAN DER KROEF, J. M. "West New Guinea in the Crucible," *Political Science Quarterly,* LXXV (1960), 519–38.

A careful account of the territorial dispute.

WEST, F. J. "The New Guinea Question: An Australian View," *Foreign Affairs,* XXXIX (1961), 504–12.

A concise summary of the Australians' attitude toward New Guinea.

19

COMMUNIST CHINA

● The political pattern of eastern Asia has been one of frequent conflict and change, particularly since the latter part of the nineteenth century. The geographic diversity and the conflicting power interests in this part of the world have been important aspects of the changing nature of territorial control there. So also has been China's weakness—a situation which only since 1950 has begun to be remedied. The efforts of modern Chinese governments to win and maintain control over the various parts of China's territory are evidenced in the complex history of Far Eastern wars and treaties, particularly since the mid-nineteenth century. Even with the communization of mainland China, the task of uniting the area under Peking's control was not completed; centrifugal forces—in the form of local resistance to Peking and of foreign-controlled enclaves—still remained on the mainland itself, while off the east coast a competing Chinese government retained control of Taiwan (Formosa) and many smaller islands.

Under its Communist regime mainland China has become an area of growing economic strength and nationalistic ambitions, determined to assert its power over peripheral areas—particularly Tibet, Sinkiang, Taiwan, and the offshore islands—and to become the dominant country of eastern Asia. Allied militarily with the U.S.S.R., it forms along with North Korea and North Vietnam the eastern wing of a Eurasian Communist bloc which stretches from the Elbe River to the Pacific, and any major military or political moves which Communist China undertakes involve Soviet interests and possible participation as well.

The Chinese State is potentially one of the great power areas of the world. Among its elements of strength are its population (amounting to nearly one-quarter of the world's total), its great area, its natural resources, and its central location in eastern Asia. Although for centuries China was subjected to foreign pressure and control, the country's position has been greatly strengthened by the recent concentration of administration in the hands of the Chinese Communists and by the changing power pattern in other parts of the Far East since World War II. The result has been the gradual emergence of a strong national unit in an area of traditional division and weakness.

PHYSICAL ELEMENTS

The territory of China consists of several units—China proper (the former eighteen provinces south of the Great Wall), Manchuria, Inner Mongolia, Sinkiang, and Tibet. Outer Mongolia and Tannu Tuva, once units of the Chinese Empire, have been separated from China within recent decades, the former area becoming a separate State and the latter an integral part of the Soviet Union. The total area of China is about 3,745,-000 square miles, of which approximately 35 per cent comprises China proper.

Location

China's location in eastern Asia has in past centuries tended to isolate the country from contacts with other areas. North of Manchuria are the coniferous forests of Siberia, northwest of China proper is the semiarid plateau of Mongolia and the Gobi Desert, to the west is the great mountain complex of Tibet, and to the southwest rugged, forested high plateau and mountain country separates China from the populated areas of southeast Asia. To the east China faces the sea, and it was from the east and southeast that the Europeans came, particularly after 1800, in order to exploit China's market potential. It was also largely by sea that the Japanese attacked China during the 1930's.

Despite the physical barriers which tend to separate China from other countries, the State's vicinal location has been of great importance to its political development. To the east and northeast Korea, Japan, the Ryukyus, and Taiwan have played significant roles in China's changing patterns of control. Both Korea and Taiwan, for example, have been historic areas of conflicting Chinese and Japanese sovereignty; both have been utilized by the Japanese in military operations against China; and since World War II the possibility of Chinese control of these areas has posed a threat to non-Communist Japan. In the north and northwest China borders the Soviet Union, and there, too, a broad belt of conflicting sovereignty has long existed. As in the case of China's eastern frontiers, political control in this central Asian belt has reflected the relative power positions of China and its neighbors. To the south China's territory adjoins that of Indochina, Burma, and the several States of the Indian subcontinent. In the past British and French power in these areas (together with the weakness of China itself) resulted in a relative stabilization of borders. Since World War II European control has ended, while within China itself new ideologies and a new spirit of nationalism have come into being, with the result that Chinese control has gradually been pushed southward across its generally poorly defined southern boundaries into the territories occupied by neighboring States.

Surface Configuration

Only extremely broad generalizations concerning China's topography are possible here (Figure 99). Tibet occupies part of the greatest upland region in the world, a mountain-laced plateau averaging over 10,000 feet in elevation, from which mountain chains extend south and east into China proper. North of Tibet is the arid Tarim basin of southern Sinkiang, with the east-west Tien Shan chain along its northern border. Northeast of the Tien Shan are the deserts and grasslands of Dzungaria (northern Sinkiang) and of Outer and Inner Mongolia. The Great Wall, separating Inner Mongolia from China proper, approximates a climatic as well as an ancient political boundary, for to the south and east of this wall precipitation is generally adequate for agriculture, while in Inner Mongolia it is less abundant and more erratic.

Manchuria consists of a rolling, well-drained lowland about 600 miles north to south and 200–300 miles east to west, surrounded on all sides by rough terrain. This lowland "compartment" is the most important area in China for the production of crop surpluses, primarily because of its larger farm units. South of Manchuria mountains and hills extend eastward from the Tibetan highlands; as they approach the coast the mountains become lower and divide into subranges. Southern China is predominantly hilly with exceedingly rough terrain and only a few areas of level land. Three major rivers—the Hwang Ho (Yellow) in the north, the Yangtze in central China, and the Si (West) in the south—rise in the western highlands and flow south and east to the sea, forming alluvial lowlands in their lower courses. The North China Plain—more than 150,000 square miles in area—is the most extensive of these lowlands.

Surface configuration in China, as in other parts of the world, is important politically because of its effects on population distribution and on transportation routes. Some of the lowland areas have a rural population density of over 2,000 persons per square mile, indicating the intensive land

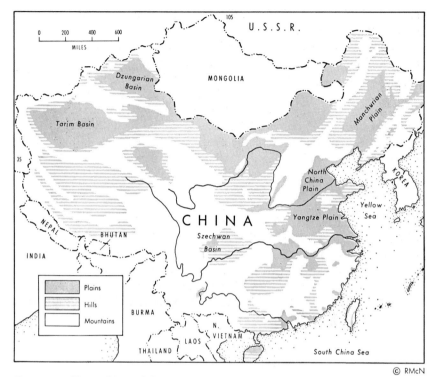

Figure 99. China: Physical Features.

utilization which is carried on there. The hill country, which is typical of much of China proper, has often contained the strongholds of local rebels, thus making difficult the task of uniting the country. The majority of China's population is concentrated near the coast. The Szechwan basin of the upper Yangtze and the Wei Valley, northeast of Szechwan, are also heavily populated; both of these in the past have been important as defense areas.

Climate

China's climate reflects the country's position on the eastern portion of a great land mass. During the summer monsoon eastern China experiences warm, moist winds from the southeast; throughout the rest of the year most of the country is influenced by dry air masses from the Asian interior. Eastern China, including the Manchurian lowland, generally receives adequate precipitation for agriculture, but in the central and western portion of China proper, as well as in most of Tibet, Sinkiang, and Inner and Outer Mongolia, steep slopes, aridity, and cold weather place severe limitations on agriculture. Crop land is estimated to be about 12 per cent of the total area.[1]

Southern China, with its semitropical climate, is predominantly an area of rice cultivation, with tea and silk as secondary products, and the farmers there are generally more prosperous than those in the north. The regional distinctiveness of the south is further evidenced by the importance of fishing along its indented coast, as well as by its contact with other countries because of commercial ties and because most Chinese emigrants have come from this part of the State. Northern China, with its cooler climate and uncertain rainfall, produces wheat, millet, and other grains, as well as cotton and tobacco. Widespread floods and famines are more common there than in the south, and the region is more oriented toward central Asia than toward overseas areas.

Within the framework of this over-all division there are a great number of local variations, such as in the Yangtze basin in central China, the Manchurian plains in the northeast, and the highland areas along China's southern and southwestern borders. In this country of 3¾ million square miles, distance, surface configuration, soils, and other physical elements have posed serious obstacles to political unification under China's central government.

Mineral and Power Resources

Except for coal, mineral and power resources in China are not extensive, considering the country's size and population and its apparent objective of becoming one of the great industrial powers of the world. China ranks third in the world in coal resources, but there is relatively little petroleum, and many of the major sites for hydroelectric power development are located in the western and southwestern mountains, away from the main population centers. Although rich in tin, tungsten, and antimony, China has only moderate amounts of iron ore, copper, bauxite, lead, and zinc. One of the favorable locations for industrialization is southern Manchuria, where deposits of low-grade iron ore are situated close to reserves of coking coal; here again, however, the known reserves of both commodities are not great enough to sustain large-scale industrialization measured in terms of the German Ruhr or the Soviet Ukraine.

Much of China has not been adequately explored for mineral resources, but there are indications that important new reserves will be found. One of the most hopeful developments has been the successful oil drilling in

---

[1] George B. Cressey, *Asia's Land and Peoples* (New York: McGraw-Hill Book Co., Inc., Copyright 1952), p. 89. Used by permission. This figure includes China proper, Tibet, Sinkiang, Inner and Outer Mongolia, and Manchuria.

northern Sinkiang, northern Tibet, and Inner Mongolia. The development of iron ore reserves in Inner Mongolia and the expansion of copper, lead, and zinc production are also predicted by the Peking government and will be important assets to the State in its industrial growth.

POPULATION FEATURES

China has more inhabitants than any other country on earth. The 1962 estimate is 700 million. Birth and death rates are believed to be in the neighborhood of 37 and 17 per thousand, giving an annual population increase of 20 per thousand, or about 14 million persons per year. Some experts, however, feel that the annual population growth is probably closer to 17 million persons per year, indicating a growth rate of about 2½ per cent per year, rather than 2.

China's population is highly concentrated, with three-quarters of the people in about one-sixth of the area. The major areas of settlement are the middle and lower Yangtze Valley, the North China Plain, the Canton delta in the south, the Manchurian plain, and the Szechwan basin of central China. There are also important population concentrations along the southeast China coast. The 1957 census listed fourteen cities of over a million people. Of these Shanghai had nearly 7 million, Peking had close to 5½ million, and Tientsin, in the North China Plain, had over 3 million. Thus there is not one but several core areas in China.

Throughout China there is a single written language, and although over forty dialects exist, probably two-thirds of the population, most of them living in China proper north of the Yangtze, speak Mandarin, the "national language." Most of the Europeans and Japanese have left the country, and the official census listed 94 per cent of the population as "Chinese." Among the minority ethnic groups are the Chinese Moslems, the Tibetans, the Mongolians, and the Koreans; many of these groups have been granted local autonomy, but because of their small numbers in comparison with the Chinese themselves they do not form serious centrifugal elements.

The enormous size of China's population is both an asset and a definite liability to the State's development. If the population can be organized for the service of the State and trained in technical or military skills, it can constitute a strong factor of national strength. In past centuries, however, millions of Chinese have spent their entire lives without adequate food, clothing, and shelter: starvation and disease have long been two great checks to China's population growth. Despite their growing promises of material benefits, the Chinese Communists—like the Nationalists and other governments before them—face a tremendous problem in providing food, clothing, and other necessities of life to hundreds of millions of Chinese.

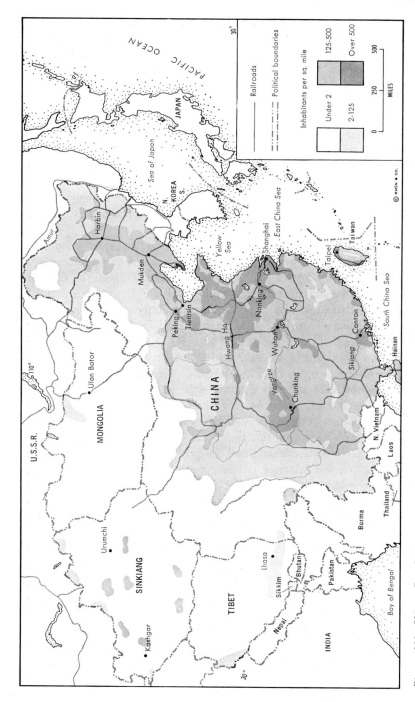

Figure 100. China: Population.

ECONOMIC FEATURES

Two major elements of power in any country are agricultural and industrial production, both dependent in part upon the physical resources of the area. Professor Cressey estimates that the figure of 12 per cent for China's crop land represents "nearly the maximum that is profitable under present economic conditions."[2] Under the Communists various steps are being taken to increase agricultural production: extensive irrigation projects, flood control, redistribution of land, and the training of farmers in modern agricultural techniques. The Yangtze, Hwang Ho, and other rivers are undergoing important flood control development, and efforts have been made to increase substantially the total of irrigated land. The Chinese government has opened up large tracts of semiarid lands to agriculture, although yields there are precarious; otherwise there is little available crop land left to develop, for after centuries of an agricultural economy most of the arable lands are already in cultivation.

One of the basic problems facing the Communists has been the organization of agricultural production. About 40 per cent of the agricultural workers in 1946 were farm owners, 25 per cent were part-owners, and 35 per cent were tenants. Between 1946 and 1949 land was seized and redistributed in the areas occupied by the Communists; by 1952 this redistribution had been completed throughout the country, and the process of collectivization had begun. Most of the cooperatives embraced a few dozen households, and by the end of 1956 close to 100 per cent of the peasant households had been incorporated into cooperatives. In the following years there was a mass transfer of Communist party cadres to the rural areas to organize and direct the farmers, and in 1958 the combination of favorable climate and immense agricultural activity resulted in a record harvest for China. In April of that year the first of the communes was introduced. These were tremendous agricultural units, embracing thousands of households, in which labor was completely organized, the workers generally receiving fixed wages rather than a share of the proceeds. There were public canteens, nurseries, and in some areas, segregated barracks, thus greatly disrupting the traditional Chinese family-unit system. By the end of 1958 an estimated 99 per cent of China's peasant households had been incorporated into the communes, representing a stage of communism far in advance of that prevailing in the Soviet Union and other Communist countries.

In 1958 the Chinese government announced its "great leap forward" program, based upon both agricultural and industrial production. The people were urged to redouble their labor efforts in order that they might

[2] *Ibid.*

in time realize great material benefits. Yet in 1959 parts of China experienced severe drought which prevented realization of the agricultural goals which the government had set forth, and the following year the poor harvest led to a country-wide famine and the need of the Chinese to import grains. Drought again was a factor in the poor harvest of 1961—drought coupled by peasant resistance to exhortations for greater work. By this time much of the commune program had been abandoned, and the government was returning to the "incentive" system which it had followed on the cooperatives.

The successive agricultural failures have represented a very serious problem for the Chinese government, faced as it is with the rapid population rise and the almost total absence of aid from foreign countries. Ideological differences with the Soviet Union have meant a virtual cessation of Soviet goods and credits; indeed, China is obligated to export agricultural products to the U.S.S.R. in payment for past loans. Because of the Western economic embargo China has difficulty in obtaining dollars, pounds, or other forms of "hard" currency with which to purchase grain from Canada, Australia, and other areas of surplus production. In terms of China's overall development plans, such currency should, when available, be used to purchase machinery, rolling stock, petroleum, or other products the country needs in its industrial build-up. Communist China should be a "creditor" rather than a "debtor" nation, since one way to expand influence to underdeveloped countries is to send them foreign aid. Finally, the failure of the government to solve the agricultural crisis has meant a weakening of its prestige in the eyes of the Chinese masses and a reduction in work output, both because of malnutrition and because of lack of enthusiasm and incentive.

The industrialization of China has been hampered by the shortage of capital and trained personnel and by inadequate transportation and power facilities. Before World War II manufacturing in China consisted largely of textiles, food processing, and related industries. Manchuria, then under Japanese control, had the only important iron and steel industry in the area of what is now China. Following World War II the Soviets dismantled much of the industrial facilities in Manchuria and sent them to Russia as war reparations. Consequently, industrialization in this area had to start almost from the beginning after 1945, and it was further handicapped by losses sustained in the subsequent civil war and by the Nationalists' neglect of industrial equipment.

One important shortage in Communist China is investment capital. China in the past was forced to depend to a large extent on foreign capital, but since 1949 the Western powers have not contributed, and relatively little has been advanced by the Soviet Union. Thus, as the Soviet Union did thirty years earlier, China has been forced largely to go it alone in its industrial build-up and has proceeded more slowly than might be the case had it received a substantial share of the billions of dollars of foreign aid distributed to other countries of the world. Yet large-scale industrialization is important to the task of providing employment and a higher standard of living for China's rapidly increasing population. In 1953 China embarked on its first five-year plan, followed by a second ending in 1962. In 1960 China turned out 20 million tons of steel, an increase of 50 per cent over the previous year, and the Chinese planned to turn out nearly 39 million tons by 1965, placing the State third in the world behind the United States and the Soviet Union. By 1962 the agricultural crisis had led to a serious curtailment of the industrial program, however. But with its industrial resources and its population China has the potential of eventually becoming a major industrial country of the world—capable not only of supplying the bulk of its own needs but of producing large quantities of rockets, nuclear weapons, and other armaments as well in order to support its claims to a position of pre-eminence in eastern Asia.

A third facet of China's economy is transportation and trade. As in the Soviet Union, economic growth must depend primarily upon rail transport, since highway transportation is not well developed, and only the Yangtze River, the Si Kiang in the south, and the Sungari River in northern Manchuria are navigable by medium- or large-size ships. The Chinese Communists inherited a fairly extensive rail system in China proper and in Manchuria, although much of the network had been destroyed during the course of the civil war. In addition to repairing this and building new lines to service the eastern areas, the government has embarked on a large-scale program of constructing both railroads and highways to link China proper with the peripheral areas of the country and with neighboring States. A railroad has been built northward between Peking and the Soviet Union through Ulan Bator, the capital of the Mongolian People's Republic (Outer Mongolia), although the gauge is broad to conform with the Soviet rail system, rather than standard, as is used in China. Another line runs from Kweilin in south China to Hanoi in North Vietnam; this road, as well as one from Hanoi to Kunming in China's Yunnan Province, is narrow gauge. A railroad is also under construction in northwest China which will link the Chinese rail system at Lanchow with the Soviet Union's through Urumchi, capital of Sinkiang. Railroads such as these have been extremely important in opening up some of the more remote parts of China to large-scale emigration. A line is under construction across the plateau of Tibet to link Lhasa with Lanchow, and other lines are planned for the Tarim basin of southern Sinkiang. The truck road to Siberia through Sinkiang, built as a supply line during World War II, has been improved, there is a new road from Urumchi through Kashgar to link with the U.S.S.R., and connections between China proper and Tibet have been increased by the construction of two highways from Chinese railheads to Lhasa. Finally, roads are being built close to the southern border of Tibet, one of them passing within the Kashmir province of Ladakh. By building these transportation systems through outlying areas, China is finally beginning to overcome the centrifugal effects which distance and inaccessibility have had on the political and cultural conditions within these areas.

China has historically been an important region for foreign trade. In the nineteenth century the European powers pressed for the opening of China to commerce because of its potential value as a market, as an area for investments, and to a lesser extent as a source for raw materials. In 1950, however, many of the non-Communist States imposed embargoes on the shipments of various commodities to China in retaliation against that country's aggression in North Korea. The country has needed petroleum, rubber, machinery, and transportation equipment, and the difficulties encountered in acquiring these have been another factor delaying China's economic development. Although by 1957 restrictions were gradually being lifted on many of the Western exports to China, the embargoes have been important in the establishment of new trade patterns between China and the states of the Communist bloc.

Despite the poor record of agricultural and industrial outputs in recent years, China has certain international obligations to fulfill. In 1961 the Chinese exported to the Soviet Union $185 million more in goods than it imported in payment for earlier Soviet loans. China shipped 100,000 tons of rice to Cuba in exchange for sugar, largely in order to maintain political and economic influence in that country, and grain shipments to Albania have resulted in China's becoming the principal food supplier there. Yet such exports come at a time when the annual grain production has increased about 6 per cent over an eight-year period, while the population grew by an estimated 100 milliion.

POLITICAL FEATURES

Since the advent of Communist power at the end of 1949, China's administrative structure has been changed several times. The old division of China into eighteen provinces of China proper, Inner and Outer Mongolia, Tibet, Sinkiang, and Manchuria has been abolished. For a time China proper, Inner Mongolia, and Manchuria were grouped together into six administrative areas, within which were thirty-two provinces and thirteen regionally administered cities. The administrative areas were eventually abolished, thereby strengthening Communist control at the provincial level. Provincial boundary adjustments were also made, and by July, 1955, China's internal political system consisted of twenty-five provinces and three centrally administered cities—Peking, Tientsin, and Shanghai (Figure 101). Of the twenty-five provinces, three are autonomous areas (Inner Mongolia,

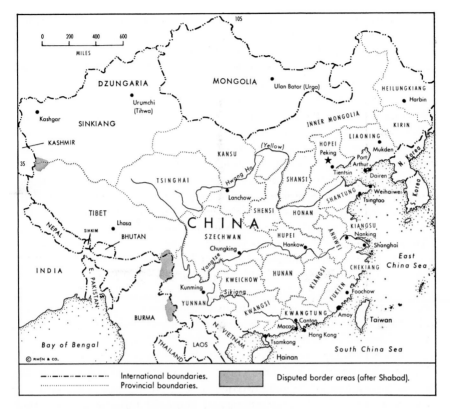

Figure 101. China: Political Divisions. (After Shabad, *China's Changing Map,* Frederick A. Praeger, 1956. Used by permission.)

Sinkiang-Uighur, and Tibet), which are inhabited largely by non-Chinese peoples (Mongols, Uighurs and Kazakhs, and Tibetans, respectively). The Uighur and Kazakh peoples also extend across the border into the Soviet Union as well.

Although the Chinese political structure has certain aspects in common with that of the Soviet Union, there are also important differences. Because of the relatively small non-Chinese minority, the Peking government did not establish its provincial units along the lines of cultural autonomy (except in the case of the three autonomous areas mentioned above), and in the Chinese constitution the provinces, unlike those in the U.S.S.R., are not given the right of secession. The shifting pattern of internal political units is also characteristic of the U.S.S.R., as the Chinese seek to achieve more balanced economic and political functioning. Below the provincial level is the autonomous *chou,* which is somewhat analogous to the Soviet's autonomous oblast, in that it exists for non-Chinese groups whose numbers are not sufficiently great to justify the creation of a more important auton-omous province (autonomous *ch'u*). At a still lower administrative level is the autonomous *hsien*, for small concentrations of minority peoples. The changing political conditions in China are reflected in the shifts in the loca-tion of its capital. From the fifteenth century down to 1928 Peking (mean-ing "northern capital") was the seat of government, but in 1928 the Nationalists shifted the site to Nanking ("southern capital") in the Yangtze Valley, where it was more centrally located with respect to China's popu-lation centers. Ten years later the Japanese captured Nanking, and the capital was moved inland to the Szechwan basin, where it was established at Chungking. Following the end of hostilities it was returned to Nanking, and in 1949 the Communists moved it back to Peking, thus emphasizing the city's traditional position of authority and the reorientation of China away from the Western influences which had once been strong in the lower Yangtze valley.

Of the peripheral mainland areas, China no longer exercises political control over Outer Mongolia, although both Tibet and Sinkiang have been brought within the *de jure* control of Peking. Only British-controlled Hong Kong and Portuguese Macao remain of the former European possessions along the China coast, and the various foreign economic concessions within the Chinese cities have been abolished since World War II.

Since 1949 the Chinese Communist government has been engaged in a large-scale program to unite the various sectors of the country, both within China proper and in the more distant areas. A greatly increased circulatory system, closer political organization, and improved training and education are the methods being employed to strengthen centripetal forces centered on Peking. Particular attention has been given to Manchuria, economically the most valuable of the areas outside China proper. At the same time the establishment of Peking's sovereignty has been impeded by conditions in three areas: (1) Nationalist control of Taiwan and the smaller islands off the China coast, (2) Soviet influence in the Mongolian People's Republic, and (3) the continued existence of European control at Hong Kong and Macao. Of these, the first is by far the most important to the Chinese Communists, since it represents a conspicuous failure on their part to unify all Chinese territory—as it existed after World War II—under Peking's authority.

THE CHANGING PATTERN OF TERRITORIAL CONTROL

The recorded history of China dates back over three thousand years, and over two thousand years ago the State was unified under a single dy-nasty. As a result, the record of China's territorial expansions and contrac-tions, and of political unification and division, is one of the longest and most complicated of any country of the world. In this chapter only the major changes since the late nineteenth century will be considered.

The Period of Territorial Encroachment

During the nineteenth and early twentieth centuries China suffered territorial losses at the hands of the European powers, the Soviet Union, and Japan. The Europeans, who came primarily for commercial profit, won concessions from the Chinese government for the establishment of "treaty ports," amounting to enclaves of foreign territory along China's coast and in certain cities.[3] European countries also received extraterritorial rights, whereby European laws and European court and police systems exercised control over specific areas of China.

During the nineteenth century considerable land along China's north and northwest borders was ceded to Russia, as that country's expanding power began moving into Siberia. Toward the end of the century Russian influence also penetrated Manchuria, but this drive was terminated by Russia's defeat at the hands of Japan in 1905. Following World War I Russian power in Tannu Tuva and Outer Mongolia became more strongly entrenched, and these areas began to move away from the political control of China. In 1921 Tannu Tuva, formerly a part of Outer Mongolia (although differing from Mongolia in that the population was largely Turkic in origin, not Mongol) became a virtual Russian protectorate. In the same year Outer Mongolia itself became the Mongolian People's Republic—nominally a separate independent republic, but in reality another Russian protectorate. The Chinese were never able to counteract these strong centrifugal pulls. In 1950 the Chinese Communist government recognized the independence of Mongolia (something the Chinese Nationalist regime has never done), but Soviet influence in the area remains strong.

The gradual expansion of Japan's control over Chinese territory began in 1895, when Taiwan and the Pescadores passed from China to Japan after the Sino-Japanese War. Ten years later the Japanese acquired Russian leases on territories on the Liaotung Peninsula of southern Manchuria. In 1931 Japan invaded and conquered Manchuria and detached it from China's control. Japanese territorial expansion southward from this region into Jehol province in 1935 was followed in 1937 by the launching of an all-out attempt to conquer China. For eight years Japanese forces occupied areas in eastern China, but they were never able to destroy the Nationalist government in its refuge capital at Chungking, nor to eliminate Chinese military resistance. The eventual liberation of China came in 1945, when

---

[3] In addition to British Hong Kong and Portuguese Macao, which had been acquired early in the nineteenth century, the treaty ports included Kwangchowan (French), now Changkiang, in south China, the New Territories (British), added to Hong Kong colony, and Kiaochow (German) and Weihaiwei (British) on the Shantung Peninsula.

Japan was conquered, largely by United States and British Commonwealth forces operating in the Pacific.

During this era of territorial encroachment China itself was undergoing a series of internal political upheavals, as the old political systems were abandoned and new ideologies were tested. In 1911 the Manchu dynasty, which had been in power for over two and a half centuries, was overthrown. Subsequently, for more than a quarter of a century the administrations of Dr. Sun Yat-sen and (after 1925) Chiang Kai-shek sought to establish the central government's authority over the entire country. In 1926–27 Chiang Kai-shek succeeded in gaining control over much of China, although he was opposed by local war lords, who controlled large stretches of territory, and, after 1927, by the outlawed Chinese Communist Army, which waged intermittent warfare against him. With the Japanese invasion of 1937 the Nationalists were gradually forced back into the interior of the country, from where they continued their attacks against the invaders until Japan was defeated.

The Communist Victory

At the end of World War II Taiwan and the Pescadores were returned by Japan to China, and, with the exception of Hong Kong and Macao, the foreign-held coastal territories gradually passed under Chinese sovereignty. Japanese power was removed from Manchuria, but control over the areas on the Liaotung Peninsula reverted to the Russians. Captured Japanese military equipment in Manchuria was turned over by the Russians to the Chinese Communists, who emerged from the war as a powerful political and military group.

Between 1945 and the end of 1949 there was a series of attempted reconciliations between Nationalist and Communist political leaders in an effort to avert civil war in China, but each group was determined to be the dominant power in the country. By 1947 open warfare was in progress in northern China, and in spite of American military and economic assistance the Nationalists suffered repeated military reverses at the hands of the Communists. The bitter civil war demonstrated the weaknesses of the Nationalist government, particularly the lack of popular support and the widespread graft and inefficiency among its officials. In contrast was the well-disciplined Communist group, with its dedicated followers. Over a two-and-one-half-year period Communist armies gradually won control of northern and central China. By December, 1949, practically all of mainland China was in the hands of the Communists, the People's Republic of China had been proclaimed, and the Nationalist government, with what was left of the national treasury, had fled to the island of Taiwan, where it gathered the remnants of its armies together for a final defense. In 1950 a thirty-year treaty of friendship and mutual aid was signed between China and the Soviet Union, thereby inaugurating a new era in power relationships, not only among the countries of Eurasia, but also of the entire world.

Since the end of 1949 the Chinese Communists have worked to strengthen Peking's authority over Sinkiang and Tibet through diplomatic and military action, as well as by the improvement of transportation facilities to these areas. With the construction of a railroad through Outer Mongolia, the Chinese have sought to counter Soviet pressure in that sector of the former Chinese empire. Late in 1950 the Chinese Communists moved into Korea and drove United Nations forces south of the thirty-eighth parallel; they also increased their supplies to the forces of Ho Chi Minh, fighting the French in neighboring Indochina. In 1951 Chinese forces occupied Tibet and ended the region's semi-independent status. In 1954 the Soviets agreed to relinquish their share of ownership of the Manchurian railroad and to evacuate the base at Port Arthur, so that for the first time in half a century China obtained complete control over Manchuria. As a result of these developments, China has proved itself to be a dynamic and gradually expanding power in eastern Asia—one which has far to go in solving its economic problems, but which has become nevertheless a potent force in the power complex in this part of the world.

PERIPHERAL AREAS OF CHINA

To the west and northwest of China proper are approximately 2 million square miles of territory in which Chinese political control has varied in relation to that of Japan, Russia, Britain, or local groups. This peripheral belt has in the past served to isolate, and often protect, the majority of China's land boundaries, but with the coming of twentieth-century communications these outlying areas have become the scene of power struggles between China and its neighbors. Three areas—Tibet, Sinkiang, and Outer Mongolia—will be considered here as separate units. Manchuria and Inner Mongolia, also lying outside China proper, have been integrated with China to the point where they may no longer be regarded as peripheral. In addition, the former Chinese-controlled territory of Tannu Tuva will be treated here because of its historical associations with China and Outer Mongolia.

Tibet

Tibet lies for the most part at elevations of from 10,000 to 16,000 feet and is one of the most isolated regions of the world. On the south it borders India and the States of Nepal, Bhutan, and Sikkim; on the west it adjoins Kashmir; on the north, Sinkiang; and on the east it borders the provinces of China proper. Its strategic location is enhanced by its control of important passes leading through some of the highest mountain areas of the world into adjoining countries.

Tibet actually consists of several physical regions. Much of the northern and central parts is occupied by the Tibetan (or Chang Tang) Plateau, consisting of basins and low mountain ranges at an average elevation of over 15,000 feet. The region is dry and cold and practically uninhabited. In eastern Tibet are the great canyons formed by the upper courses of the Mekong, Salween, and other rivers of southeast Asia. The obstacles these canyons present to transportation have helped to preserve Tibet's isolated position for many centuries. In southern Tibet is an east-west valley, occupied by the Brahmaputra River (which flows to India) in the eastern portion and by the upper Indus River in the west. This valley forms the populated area of Tibet; here is located Lhasa, the capital and leading city. Although transportation facilities throughout the country are not well developed, the concentration of population in the southern areas has been a centripetal factor.

Few important mineral resources have been discovered within Tibet, and most of the approximately 1.3 million people there have only recently come in contact with twentieth-century economic and political ideas. The construction of new motor roads from China to Tibet's core area and improvements to the route through Sikkim to India have diminished the area's isolation, although attempts to impose the centralized authority of communism upon the traditionally independent Tibetans met with considerable opposition.

Chinese claims to sovereignty in Tibet date back to the early eighteenth century, when China conquered the area. These claims have been complicated, however, by the position of the Dalai Lama, spiritual ruler of the deeply religious Buddhist country, and the priesthood, whose power has been very great. Government has been largely a monopoly of the church, and religious leaders have sought to isolate Tibet from outside influence for as long as possible. The British, operating from India, became interested in establishing Tibet as a buffer area against Russian power to the north in the nineteenth century. After 1914 Britain recognized the area embracing most of the Tibetan highlands as a virtually independent State, with which foreign missions were exchanged and in which British India, with its trade and communication links, had considerable economic and political influence.

Tibet's relative independence lasted until 1951, when Chinese Communist forces occupied the area and announced the establishment of Tibet as an autonomous province of China. Since that time the British policy of maintaining Tibet as a buffer area along India's northern border has been superseded by China's plans to integrate the region as closely as possible within the Chinese State. The 1951 "Agreement on the Peaceful Liberation of Tibet" provided for an autonomous government of the Tibetans, although defense and foreign relations would be handled by Peking. Gradual Chinese encroachments led to a Tibetan outbreak in 1958 which was ruthlessly crushed by the Chinese. The Tibetan government was suspended, thousands of refugees, including the Dalai Lama, fled across the southern border, and Tibet became more strongly integrated into the Chinese State. The continued improvement of circulation facilities within Tibet and between Tibet and China proper, the large numbers of Chinese troops and political officials in the area, and the suppression of any attempts toward asserting Tibetan autonomy indicate that there, in one of the historic buffer areas of the world, Chinese control is becoming firmly entrenched. Among the propaganda claims of the Chinese Communists is the assertion that Tibet should regain sovereignty over Nepal, Bhutan, and Sikkim, which at times in the past have been under its control or protection.

Sinkiang

To the north of Tibet is an area of historic conflict between China and Russia. Sinkiang, separated by distance, mountains, deserts, and ethnic differences from China proper, has been under varying degrees of Chinese control for some 2,000 years. With Soviet development of its central Asian republics close to the Sinkiang borders, powerful centrifugal forces were formed which tended to diminish China's power in this remote sector of the continent.

Sinkiang has an area of about 660,000 square miles and a population of slightly less than 5 million persons, of whom lesss than 10 per cent are Chinese. The majority are Moslems—Uighurs in the south and Kazakhs in Dzungaria to the north. Geographically as well as ethnically, the region is divided into two parts. In the south is the Tarim basin, a desert area surrounded on all sides but the east by mountains. In the foothills surrounding the basin are many oases, of which Kashgar in the west is the most important. The Tarim basin is separated from the Soviet Union by extremely high and difficult mountain regions, while over 1,000 miles of desert and semiarid plateau country lies between the basin and China proper, although across this area stretches the historic Kansu Corridor, containing a chain of oasis settlements which serve as supply points for overland traffic. To the south are the Kunlun Mountains and the Tibetan Plateau.

The Tien Shan, forming both the western and northern borders of the Tarim area, separates it from the basin of Dzungaria. Dzungaria, which is smaller than the Tarim area, also consists of a dry interior and a string of oases in the surrounding foothills. Of these, Urumchi in southern Dzungaria is the largest; it is also the capital for all of Sinkiang. It lies on the truck route which extends eastward to China proper and westward through the low Dzungaria Pass (elevation 1,000 feet) to Siberia. The Turk-Sib branch of Russian's Trans-Siberian Railroad passes within about 100 miles of the Sinkiang border in the neighborhood of this pass, thus making Soviet contacts with Dzungaria relatively easy to maintain.

In the early part of the twentieth century Sinkiang was administered by a local Chinese governor as a practically independent State. The governor's assassination in 1928 opened the way for almost continuous violence and civil war in this area, affording the Soviet Communists an opportunity to extend both economic and political influence into Sinkiang. The Russians were particularly interested in the resources of the area—petroleum, tungsten, tin, gold, and, recently, uranium. Military aid was dispatched to warring groups in Sinkiang, and at times Soviet troops and aircraft took part in local campaigns. While the Chinese government was engaged in politically unifying its own area and in fighting the Japanese, the Soviets increased their efforts to establish power in this region.

During World War II the Soviet government shipped military supplies to the hard-pressed Chinese Nationalist government through Dzungaria. In order to protect the military supply lines, the Russians stationed troops in Dzungaria, enabling them further to influence affairs in that region. In 1944 a revolt was launched by a group of Kazakhs. Supplied by arms and troops from Soviet-controlled Outer Mongolia, they succeeded in destroying the local Chinese Nationalist garrison and establishing temporarily the Republic of East Turkestan, a Soviet puppet regime in western Dzungaria. Following the war tribal revolts broke out, often supported from Outer Mongolia or the U.S.S.R. Moreover, Soviet companies secretly exploited the minerals of western Sinkiang, and efforts by the Nationalist government to work out an agreement with Moscow for the economic development of the region were largely ignored.

The contest between the Soviet Union and China for economic and military control of Sinkiang entered a new phase with the communization of China itself. Both coal and low-grade iron ore have been found to exist there in addition to the petroleum, uranium, and other ores. Sinkiang is now undergoing extensive industrial development, apparently with the aid of Soviet economic and technical assistance. Roads, railroads, and irrigation systems are being constructed, and Sinkiang may eventually become one of the major industrial areas of China, located far from the coast and the dangers of enemy fleets. Such development depends, first, on cooperation from the Soviets in this area and, second, on the migration into Sinkiang of large numbers of Chinese to provide the necessary labor force for both industry and agriculture. Such an influx of Chinese will not only radically alter the ethnic character of Sinkiang, thereby reducing the relative importance of the minorities, it will also strengthen China's hold on the area against any possible future Soviet moves to establish influence there.[4] Thus in Sinkiang, as in Tibet, Communist China has been rapidly welding a historic peripheral area to Peking's control.

Outer Mongolia (The Mongolian People's Republic)

One of the more remote areas of the world is Outer Mongolia, a semiarid plateau region of about 600,000 square miles, located between Siberia and Chinese-controlled Inner Mongolia. Mountains in the northwest separate Outer Mongolia from Tannu Tuva, which up to 1921 was generally considered a province of Outer Mongolia. The Mongolians, numbering less than one million, are distinct in language and culture from both the Russians and the Chinese, and for nearly a century have struggled to maintain independence, or at least autonomy, from China and Russia and to prevent the colonization of their country by either State. Mineral and power resources in Outer Mongolia have not proved to be of much value. The country has primarily a pastoral economy and is extremely undeveloped commercially and politically, with few roads or railroads and only one city —Ulan Bator (formerly Urga), the capital—with over 100,000 persons.

The processes of political control in central Asia are often less clearcut than in most other parts of the world. Many boundaries remain vague and unmarked, and the actual political status of various areas is often difficult, if not impossible, to ascertain. Terms such as "suzerainty," "autonomy," and "sovereignty" have frequently been applied to Outer Mongolia's political status by local political leaders, as well as by the Russians, Chinese, and Japanese, quite often with different interpretations by the respective parties. From 1913 to 1917, for example, the Russians continued to assure China that its sovereignty was recognized over the autonomous area of Outer Mongolia, while at the same time Moscow dealt with Outer Mongolia itself as an independent State. Under such conditions it was impossible to delimit boundaries separating Russian, Chinese, and Outer Mongolian control.

During the nineteenth century Outer Mongolia was technically a part of China, and the Chinese, interested in the area as a buffer against Russia, generally left it alone. Russian activities in southeastern Siberia in the late nineteenth and early twentieth centuries prompted the Chinese to strengthen their hold on Outer Mongolia, however, and they began to settle a considerable number of Chinese in southern Outer Mongolia—a

---

[4] Deteriorating Sino-Soviet relations in the summer of 1963 led to a reopening by the Chinese of the question of their border with the U.S.S.R. By a series of treaties, concluded between 1858 and 1881, the Chinese renounced their claims over large areas of land lying beyond the present boundaries of Sinkiang, Outer Mongolia, and Manchuria. These treaties, the Chinese claim, are not necessarily valid now.

process which greatly antagonized many of the Mongolians. Anti-Chinese riots broke out, and in 1911, at the time of the Chinese Revolution, an independent Outer Mongolian State was proclaimed.

The political maneuverings in this area between 1911 and 1946 illustrate the unstable nature of territorial control in central Asia. In 1912 Russia recognized Outer Mongolia's autonomy and thereby received special economic privileges. Five years later, at the time of its revolution, Russia's power began to wane in Outer Mongolia and was largely replaced by that of the Chinese, but in 1921 a Soviet-styled "people's government" was established at Ulan Bator. Although the U.S.S.R. continued officially to recognize Chinese sovereignty over Outer Mongolia, in 1936, under the pressure of Japanese expansion in Manchuria and Inner Mongolia, the Soviets concluded a treaty of mutual assistance with Outer Mongolia, after which Soviet troops occupied the country. In 1945 Nationalist China agreed to a plebiscite in Outer Mongolia on the question of independence. With Soviet troops occupying the country, a vote was held, resulting in virtually unamimous approval of independence. Not until 1950, however, did China (by this time under a Communist regime) recognize the independence of the Mongolian People's Republic with its Soviet-style form of government.

Since the communization of China the Mongolian People's Republic has been in a position to benefit economically from both of its giant neighbors. Considerable capital from Moscow and Peking has been poured into Mongolia. The agricultural and grazing systems have been collectivized, and industries (particularly food processing, textiles, and building materials) have been expanded, as have irrigation works. Sandwiched between China and the U.S.S.R., its independence of action in foreign affairs is rather difficult to maintain. Its strongest non-Communist contact is with India, although the republic is now a member of the United Nations and has indicated its willingness to establish close diplomatic ties with the United States as well.

Tannu Tuva

In the mountains of what used to be northwestern Outer Mongolia is situated the territory of Tannu Tuva, centered on the upper basin of the Yenisey River, which breaks through the mountains in the northwestern part of the area and flows northward through Siberia to the Arctic Ocean. Much of Tannu Tuva's 64,000 square miles is mountainous. The Sayan Mountains separate the Yenisey basin from Siberia, while the Tannu Ola Mountains form a natural barrier to the south. The strategic advantage of Russian control of this area was recognized as far back as the late seventeenth century. In addition, Tannu Tuva has mineral resources, including gold, coal, asbestos, and copper. Prior to World War I Tannu Tuva was at least nominally a part of the Chinese Empire, and was included within Outer Mongolia. The original inhabitants are largely Turkic rather than Mongol. China's hold on this remote province weakened as Russian expansion increased in south central Siberia in the late nineteenth and early twentieth centuries.

Although Tannu Tuva had close physical ties with Siberia, the Soviets hesitated to incorporate it formally with Russia, for fear of arousing both the Mongolians and the Chinese. Many Russians moved up the Yenisey Valley during the late nineteenth and early twentieth centuries and settled in the area; eventually Russians came to constitute about one-quarter of its 65,000 people. In 1921 a Congress of the People of Tannu Tuva announced the region's independence. China was unable to resist this move effectively, and the "people's government" in Outer Mongolia offered no objections. As a result, Tannu Tuva moved within the Soviet orbit, with a status which might best be termed a protectorate. After Outer Mongolia achieved independence in 1946 Tannu Tuva was formally incorporated within the U.S.S.R. and is now known officially as the Tuvinian Autonomous Soviet Socialist Republic.

Hong Kong and Macao

The two remaining vestiges of European control along the China coast are British-controlled Hong Kong and Portuguese Macao, both of which are located in southern China not far from the port of Canton. At a time when the Chinese Communists are fiercely asserting their anti-Western nationalism, it seems paradoxical that these two enclaves should continue to exist, particularly since Hong Kong has been a place of refuge for anti-Communist Chinese who have fled across its borders since 1949.

Hong Kong. The crown colony of Hong Kong was acquired by the British in 1841, following the Anglo-Chinese War, and was the first European enclave in China (Figure 102). It has an area of 391 square miles and a population of 3,225,000, of which about 10,000 are British. It consists of the island of Hong Kong, on which the city of Victoria is located, and the nearby Kowloon Peninsula, with the city of Kowloon. The inhabitants of these two cities comprise more than nine-tenths of the enclave's population. In addition to the urban sectors, the British-controlled area also includes the mainland territory behind Kowloon as well as a number of coastal islands, which, taken together, comprise the New Territories. The colony includes two airfields and an excellent harbor. It is one of the major free ports of the Far East and handles more of China's overseas trade than any other port along the China coast. Because of Western embargoes placed on exports to Communist China, Hong Kong plays a strategic role in the Chinese economy, for through it come most of the licensed imports from Western countries, as well as much of the unlicensed trade.

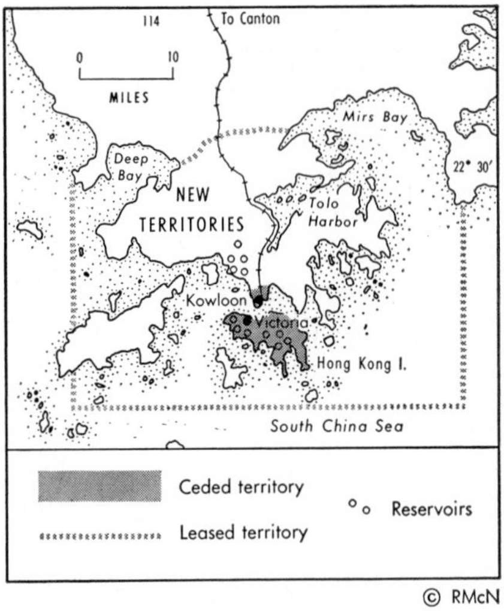

Figure 102. Hong Kong. (After map in *Focus,* IV [Nov., 1953]. Courtesy of *Focus*–American Geographical Society.)

The colony is of economic significance as a retail and wholesale center, but the volume of foreign trade handled there has dropped considerably since 1949. Hong Kong is also important as a listening post for Western States and as a place of safety for refugees from Communist China. With its large population, it is partly dependent upon China for food, and much of its water supply comes from reservoirs in the New Territories, over which Britain's lease expires in 1997.

Hong Kong's continued existence as a British-controlled enclave depends largely upon its future value to China in terms of foreign trade. With a lifting of the Western embargo on trade with China, other ports, particularly Shanghai, might strip Hong Kong of much of its present importance. By imposing a commercial and food blockade on the colony the Chinese could then create serious problems for the Hong Kong authorities. The British, nevertheless, have continued to invest large sums in local industries and public works. Despite the wave of anti-Western nationalism in southern and eastern Asia they give every indication of planning to remain in Hong Kong for a long time to come.

One of the most serious problems in Hong Kong is that of the refugees from Communist China. Over 2 million have fled to the city since 1949, the great majority of them remaining there. The British government is responsible for providing shelter, food, and ultimately employment for these people; in the spring of 1962 the influx of refugees was so great that the British were forced to close the border—the only instance along the rim of the Communist bloc where the non-Communists refuse to accept refugees. Hong Kong appears, however, to have no alternative, unless refugees can be sent in large numbers away from the colony. But what other governments in Asia are willing to accept multitudes of destitute Chinese? The

Taiwan regime has indicated that it would receive refugees, providing some means could be found for transporting them to the island, but no major transfers have actually taken place.

Macao.   Macao, located about sixty miles southwest of Hong Kong, has an area of six square miles and a population of about 200,000, of whom less than 3,000 are Europeans. The Portuguese possession consists of a peninsula and three small islands at the entrance to the Canton River. Macao is far less important commercially than Hong Kong, although it has figured prominently in the illicit trade of embargoed goods into Communist China. It is almost completely dependent on China for food, and thus would be vulnerable to any food blockade the Chinese might impose in order to force the Portuguese from the area. Macao is a relic of bygone European power in the Far East. As was the case with Goa, however, Portugal is unwilling to abandon its colonial possession. But if the Chinese refuse to trade through Macao—thereby ending its economic *raison d'être*—and clamp a food blockade on the enclave, economic measures might succeed in accomplishing what political pressure has been unable to do. There, as in Hong Kong, the pressure of Chinese nationalism may eventually outweigh any actual advantage the enclave has for China, thereby precipitating a move to annex the area.

BIBLIOGRAPHY

CHANG, KUEI-SHENG. "The Changing Railroad Pattern in Mainland China," *The Geographical Review*, LI (1961), 534–49.
Maps and description of China's rail pattern.

"China's Policy Toward Minorities," *The World Today*, XV (1959), 408–17.
A general summary of the political position of China's minorities.

CRESSEY, GEORGE B. *Land of the 500 Million*. New York: McGraw-Hill Book Company, 1955.
A regional geography of China.

FIELD, A. R. "Strategic Development in Sinkiang," *Foreign Affairs*, XXXIX (1961), 312–19.
An excellent summary of events in this area.

GINSBURG, NORTON S. "China's Changing Political Geography," *The Geographical Review*, XLII (1952), 102–18.
Well-documented article, illustrating the internal political structure of China.

GROSS, ERNEST A. "Tibetans Plan for Tomorrow," *Foreign Affairs,* XL (1961), 136–43.
An appraisal of contemporary conditions and future possibilities.

HERMAN, THEODORE. "Group Values Toward the National Space: The Case of China," *The Geographical Review,* XLIX (1959), 164–83.
An excellent study of one aspect of political geography which has seldom been covered.

International Boundary Studies, Washington, Department of State, Office of the Geographer:
"China–Hong Kong Boundary," No. 13, April 5, 1962.
"China–Korea Boundary," No. 17, June 29, 1962.
Detailed maps and descriptions of the boundaries.

JACKSON, W. A. DOUGLAS. *Russo-Chinese Borderlands.* Princeton: D. Van Nostrand Company, 1962.
A brief but valuable account of the peripheral area between China and the U.S.S.R.

KIRBY, E. STUART. "Economic Planning and Policy in Communist China," *International Affairs,* XXXIV (1958), 174–84.
The background of China's "Great Leap Forward."

LATTIMORE, OWEN. "Chinese Colonization in Manchuria," *The Geographical Review,* XXII (1932), 177–96.
Summarizes the nature of pioneer settlement in Manchuria by the Chinese prior to the Japanese invasion of 1931.

ORCHARD, JOHN E. "Industrialization in Japan, China Mainland, and India—Some World Implications," *Annals of the Association of American Geographers,* L (1960), 193–216.
An appraisal of industrialization in eastern Asia.

RUPEN, ROBERT A. "Inside Outer Mongolia," *Foreign Affairs,* XXXVII (1959), 328–34.
A good general account of conditions in this region.

20

JAPAN AND KOREA

● On the eastern margin of the Asiatic land mass are located two areas—one a group of islands and the other a peninsula—whose political development strongly reflects the interaction of continental and maritime powers in the Far East. Japan, a chain of islands off the Asiatic coast, was once the major maritime country of east Asia as well as a dominant force on the Asiatic mainland, but in 1945 it was defeated by military strength which struck from across the Pacific. The peninsular state of Korea, a Japanese colony prior to World War II, was divided politically after the war's end, its northern portion eventually passing within the military and political orbit of China and its southern part coming under the protection of the United States. As a point of conflict between maritime and continenal powers, the Japan-Korea area has come to occupy a strategic position in the over-all border zone between the Communist and non-Communist worlds.

The histories of the two countries have been closely interwoven with one another. The modern period of this interrelationship began in the late nineteenth century, when Japanese power, under the impetus of population growth and industrialization, began to expand outwards to neighboring areas, including Korea. From 1910 to 1945 Korea was a Japanese colony. Since the end of World War II Japan has been used as a supply base for the military occupation of South Korea and for the defense of that area against Communist aggression. In terms of world power alignments, Japan and South Korea have since 1950 represented strongholds of Western ideas in a part of Asia which has otherwise been overrun by communism.

Figure 103. Japan and Korea.

JAPAN

Japan is a striking example of an area in which territorial expansion was motivated primarily by economic pressure. With an area about the size of the state of Montana—and with four-fifths of the land surface covered by mountains—Japan has a population of close to 94 million. Mineral resources are not extensive, and Japan has been hard put to it to earn sufficient foreign credits for the importation of needed commodities. The economic and political repercussions of the country's population-to-resources ratio can help to explain much of Japan's history of aggression since the latter part of the nineteenth century.

The Japanese State consists of four large islands—Hokkaido, Honshu, Shikoku, and Kyushu—as well as hundreds of small ones, with a total area of over 142,000 square miles. The country stretches northeast-south-west off the coasts of southeastern Siberia, Korea, and China north of Shanghai. Prior to 1945 Japan also controlled the Kuril and Ryukyu islands, as well as Taiwan (Formosa), and was thus in a highly strategic position with regard to the Asiatic mainland. The development of a strong navy and merchant fleet, as well as of an effective army, permitted the Japanese to utilize the strategic advantages of the island chain in establishing their power on the Asiatic mainland between 1905 and 1945.

Physical Elements

Location. Japan's maritime and vicinal locations have both been of great importance to the country's capacity to produce food and other raw materials. Although the islands lie off the east coast of Asia and are subject to cold air masses from that area in winter, the central and southern portions benefit throughout much of the year from the moderating influences of surrounding water bodies. Thus on central and northern Hokkaido rice cannot be grown but in much of the State there is double cropping (often rice and barley or wheat), permitting high agricultural production totals.

In order to supplement their national diet, the Japanese have turned to the sea; here again they have profited by vicinal location, for to the north and northeast are some of the richest fishing grounds in the world. Japanese fishing vessels, ranging thousands of miles from their home ports, have often come in conflict with Soviet, Canadian, and American fishermen. Fishing regulations and the resultant disputes of ocean sovereignty have been important to the political geography of the Pacific. Since the end of World War II Japan and the Soviet Union have frequently been at odds over the rights of Japanese fishermen off the Soviet-controlled Kuril Islands.

Under normal conditions Japan produces about three-fourths of its food requirements. Eastern Asia and the island groups to the south of Japan have in the past furnished supplementary sources of food and other raw materials. From the former colonies of Taiwan and Korea between one-fifth and one-fourth of Japan's rice requirements were normally imported in the years before 1945. Sugar and fruit were also obtained from

Taiwan. Coal and iron ore came from Manchukuo,[1] and iron ore was also supplied by Korea and Malaya. China exported raw cotton and raw wool to Japan, and rubber was obtained from Malaya and the Netherlands East Indies.

Vicinal location was also important to Japan's territorial expansion, for with the defeat of Russia in 1905 the major rival to Japan's power in the Far East was removed. China was weakened by internal problems, and the United States and the European powers were too far away and too preoccupied with other developments to offer serious resistance to most of Japan's aggressive moves. The existence of island groups and peninsulas in the eastern Asia–western Pacific area contributed to the gradual expansion of Japanese sovereignty, and the various sea lanes facilitated the maintenance of Japanese control over its far-flung empire.

Surface Configuration and Climate.   The mountainous nature of Japan has already been mentioned. The upland areas offer hydroelectric power potential, a large amount of which has already been developed. Lowland areas occur only in the valleys and coastal plains, and are separated from one another by highlands. This diversity in surface configuration has been reflected in the historical contest between political unity and diversity. During many periods of its history Japan has been split up into small political units; countering these divisive forces, however, have been the centripetal effects of limited size and of the presence of the sea boundaries. Since the late sixteenth century political control in Japan has been consolidated in the central government.

Three lowlands, all located along the southern coast of Honshu, form the principal core areas of the country: the Kwanto Plain, containing the cities of Tokyo and Yokohama; the Kinai Plain, with Osaka, Kyoto, and Kobe; and the Nobi Plain, centered on Nagoya. Since the three are strung out over a distance of less than 300 miles, this concentration of population constitutes a significant unifying element in Japan.

Climatically there is considerable difference between the northern and southern parts of Japan. Heavy snowfalls are characteristic of the western mountain slopes of Hokkaido and northern Honshu, while in southern Japan winters are short and mild. Throughout the entire country precipitation is generally sufficient for agriculture. The relatively mild winters throughout most of Japan permit the use of its seaways for transportation during the entire year.

Natural Resources.   Japan has become the leading industrial power of non-Soviet Asia, despite the fact that it does not possess a rich mineral and power base. Copper, sulphur, gold, and water power are among its principal resources; manganese and chromium are found in small quantities,

---

[1] Between 1932 and 1945 Manchuria, under Japanese control, was officially named Manchukuo. After 1935 it also included the province of Jehol in what had been Inner Mongolia.

and there is low-grade coal and small amounts of petroleum. One of the principal sources of Japan's petroleum was lost, however, when the southern part of Sakhalin Island was ceded to Russia in 1945. Fifteen to 20 per cent of the country's coal needs is normally imported, as well as about 80 per cent of its iron ore.

Agriculturally, Japan suffers mostly from lack of level land. Approximately one-sixth of the State's surface is in agriculture, and the rural densities there, as in parts of China and southeast Asia, are extremely high. Over 60 per cent of Japan is in forests, and both the government and private individuals are active in forest preservation.

Because of the proximity of most population centers to the sea, the indented coast line with numerous harbor sites, and the many small islands which exist within the archipelago, the Japanese have had close contact with the sea. It is of great importance as a source for food and as a means of transportation, both within Japan itself and to overseas areas. An indication of Japan's use of the sea is illustrated by the fact that in 1939 Japan's merchant marine ranked third in the world in tonnage.[2]

Population

The population of Japan has increased rapidly since the end of the country's isolation. In 1868 the population was approximately 33 million. By the early 1930's this figure had doubled, and in 1940 the total was over 73 million. Although the average rate of increase has been dropping since the end of World War I, the country faced a serious problem of population pressure even during the interwar years. Japan's territorial ambitions were often cited as an effort to relieve this population pressure by acquiring new lands for settlement. Large-scale emigration from the Japanese homeland to the colonies did not occur, however; in 1938 approximately 1,665,000 Japanese resided in the colonial territories, or just over 2 per cent of the total national population. The empire was of value as a source for raw materials, markets, and investment opportunities, but it did not serve as a major settlement area for the Japanese.

The annual population increase amounts to over 800,000 per year. Although the birth rate has been gradually declining in recent years, Japan's population pressure has become increasingly serious. Since World War II there has been little emigration to foreign areas, both because of discriminatory immigration laws in many countries and because relatively few Japanese have been interested in leaving the homeland. In terms of national power the large population is an important asset to Japan, since it provides a large supply of cheap labor and since the great majority are sufficiently

---

[2] Wartime losses reduced this tonnage by 88 per cent, and by 1946 the State had dropped to eighth place. Since that time Japan's merchant fleet has gradually been rebuilt.

trained and organized to constitute a pool for military service and for defense industries in time of war.

The people of Japan are closely integrated by language, religion, customs, and national sentiment. In modern times there have been no efforts for political separation of a part of the homeland from Tokyo's control. The geographic unity and compactness of the islands, together with an absence of cultural groups similar to the Japanese on the Asiatic mainland, are factors contributing to this national cohesiveness. The major non-Japanese group in Japan proper are the Koreans, of whom there are over half a million.[3]

Population distribution, of course, is influenced by surface configuration. The principal core areas were mentioned on page 550. Approximately 73 per cent of the population is concentrated on Honshu, and there also are the six cities of over one million population. Tokyo, with a population of over 8 million, is by far the largest city of Japan and has been the national capital for over three and one-half centuries. It is located within the zone of core areas and is well served by transportation lines which connect it with other parts of the nation.

Economic Factors

Japan's industrial development has been based largely upon the fabrication of imported raw materials and the export of finished goods throughout the world. Its textile production was formerly one of the largest in the world, and shipbuilding, metallurgy, and chemicals were also important manufactures. The low-income domestic market was not a particularly large one for the country's finished goods; because of low production costs Japanese products—such as machinery, textiles, pottery, glassware, and toys—were often able to undersell those of their competitors in foreign markets, however. The combination of "trade and the flag" was important in Japan's development, as many of the areas of Japanese political and military activity (for example, Manchuria, China, the Netherlands East Indies) served as export markets and areas for investments. The State has also built up an important structure of heavy industry. In 1959 Japan produced over 16½ million tons of steel, placing it fifth among the countries of the world behind the United States, Russia, West Germany, and Great Britain. Here again imported raw materials have been necessary for this development.

Among the factors of economic power in Japan are the virile, energetic population and the ability of the people to adapt foreign tools and techniques to their own needs. Moreover, the national government has furthered

---

[3] On Hokkaido there are about 1,000 full-blooded Ainus, descendants of the original natives of the islands. These people continue to observe their own language and customs, but because of their small number do not represent an important centrifugal force.

industrial development through various forms of assistance to private organizations. As a result Japan was able to build up its economic strength rapidly in the years before World War II.

Japanese agriculture is characterized by very intensive utilization of the land. As mentioned above, most of Japan's food requirements are normally met by domestic production. The principal food crop is rice, which is produced on about half the cultivated area. Supplementary items include grains, fruits, and vegetables. Silk, tea, and tobacco are important cash crops; Japan is the principal silk exporter of the world. There is only a small livestock industry, but the deficiency in meat is partly compensated by the extensive fishing industry.

Railroads and waterways constitute Japan's chief transportation systems. The rail lines are largely electrified, utilizing the country's hydroelectric power. Highways, on the other hand, are not as well developed, but with newspapers, radio, and other communication media, Japan has an extensive circulatory system.

In foreign commerce Japan, like Britain, has been faced with the necessity of large-scale overseas commercial ties. Inexpensive Japanese manufactured goods flooded the world markets up to the time of World War II and resulted in the imposition of various restrictions on Japanese imports in many countries. Prior to the war Japan ranked fifth among the countries of the world in value of foreign trade (see page 564). Since the war the pattern of Japanese foreign commerce has been changed, due to the loss of the empire and the communization of China. The country also has been troubled by a recurrent unfavorable trade balance, which has been partly met by aid from the United States (see also page 563).

KOREA

Because of its peninsular character, the mountain region separating it from Manchuria, and the cultural homogeneity of its people, Korea forms a distinct geographic unit which throughout much of its history has been subjected to foreign interference and control. The total area is over 85,000 square miles. Because of conflicting international interests, this area has been divided since World War II into the two separate States of North Korea and South Korea, with competing ideologies and with all contacts between them completely severed.

Physical Elements

Location. The Korean Peninsula adjoins Manchuria along its land border, except for a distance of eleven miles in the extreme northeast where it touches the Soviet Union. To the west Korea faces China's Shantung

Peninsula and the Liaotung Peninsula of Manchuria. To the southeast Japan lies less than 100 miles across the Korea Strait. Throughout much of its history Korea has been under varying degrees of Chinese political control. During the twentieth century, however, Japanese and Soviet power—as well as Chinese—have been extended into this area. There, as in other historic buffer regions, independence appears to be possible only in the event of a power stalemate among the nearby countries, or if Korea's sovereignty is guaranteed by some distant State.

Surface Configuration and Climate. Despite the physical and ethnic distinctiveness of the Korean Peninsula, there are many differences between its northern and southern portions. Less than one-fifth of Korea is comprised of lowlands, and most of these are in the south central and southern areas. As in Japan, these lowlands contain important population centers which figure prominently in Korea's economic and political life. A chain of mountains borders Korea's east coast, and elevations drop sharply to the Sea of Japan; thus much of the country's population and economic development are cencentrated in the western portions of the country, facing the Yellow Sea.

Korea's climate reflects the area's transitional location between the Asian mainland and the Pacific. Winters are long and cold in the northern areas and summers short and warm; in contrast, the southern part of the peninsula has hot, humid summers and mild winters. The warmer climate of the south permits double cropping and a wider use of the land, while in parts of North Korea the growing season is too short to permit even one crop of rice.

Natural Resources. Many of Korea's mineral and power resources are concentrated in the north, a factor which facilitated the industrial development of this area by the Japanese prior to World War II. Because of the presence of mountains and of the Yalu River along the Korean-Manchurian border, the area is well supplied with hydroelectric potential. Northern Korea also has coal and iron ore and is an important producer of graphite. Southern Korea is important for its tungsten, and in addition it has small supplies of copper, gold, manganese, and silver. Because of the mountainous character of much of its land, it also has considerable hydroelectric potential, although this has not been as well developed as in the north.

About 20 per cent of Korea is in agriculture, the majority of farms being in the south. As in Japan, the land is intensively cultivated, and the rural density of population is very high. Korea possesses rich forest lands, particularly in the north, but a great proportion of these are in inaccessible locations. Many Koreans have turned to the sea as a supplementary source of food, and disputes have arisen since World War II between the Koreans and the Japanese over areas of fishing rights in the waters between these two countries (see page 564).

Population

The Koreans form a distinct Oriental ethnic group, differing from both the Chinese and Japanese in language and culture. Despite the peninsula's historic cultural unity, internal differences have often been reflected in factional struggles for power. It was in response to internal revolts in the early 1880's that the Korean government turned to China for protection, thereby ending Korea's two and a half centuries of isolation.

Between 1913 and 1950 the population of Korea doubled in size, and the rate of increase is still high. A majority of the people is concentrated in the southern part of Korea. Even before 1945 there were strong regional differences between the people of North Korea, with its predominantly upland rural character, and the people of South Korea, with its greater number of urban areas and densely populated lowland districts.

Of the approximately 34 million people on the Korean Peninsula, about 25 million inhabit South Korea, whose capital is Seoul, the leading city and, until 1945, the capital of all Korea. Seoul is located just south of the thirty-eighth parallel in the principal core area of Korea. Of the other four principal cities, Pyongyang is the capital of North Korea, while Pusan, Taegu, and Inchon are in the south. Before World War II Pyongyang (Heijo) in the western lowlands was the second city of the country, and an industrial and transportation center. Pusan (Fusan) is a port on the southeast coast, facing Japan; Taegu (Taikyu) is a commercial center in southeastern Korea; while Inchon or Chemulpo (Jinsen) is the port for Seoul. Despite the scattered urban areas, Seoul remained the undisputed political and commercial center of Korea until the 1945 partition and the development of Pyongyang as the principal core area of North Korea.

Economy

The political division of Korea is paralleled somewhat by an economic division between north and south. The north was the more industrialized area in prewar Korea, while in the south agriculture predominated. The complementary nature of the two portions of the peninsula resulted in considerable interregional trade. Since 1945, however, trade between the north and the south has ceased.

During their period of occupation the Japanese undertook to develop Korea's agricultural and industrial resources. Agricultural production was increased, and in time rice exports to Japan (representing about 40 per cent of Korea's annual production) came to constitute about 10 per cent of Japan's total consumption. The Japanese constructed several large power installations in the northern part of Korea, as well as steel and textile mills and food processing plants in both the north and the south. The benefits from these developments accrued almost exclusively to the Japanese, who controlled the investments and profited from the finished products. In 1939 trade between Korea and Japan amounted to about 25 per cent of Japan's total foreign and colonial trade. In addition to rice and finished products from Korea, Japan also imported tungsten, graphite, coal, and iron ore. Despite the poverty of the Korean people, the area was a large market for Japanese exports and a source for investments. Thus, of all of Japan's colonies, Korea was the most valuable economically, but because of the ruthless exploitation of its physical and human resources the Koreans developed a profound hatred for the Japanese—a factor of importance in present-day political alignments.

Since the establishment of an iron curtain across the Korean Peninsula there has been little information as to economic development in North Korea. Even before World War II there had been a tendency on the part of the Japanese to strengthen ties between that area and Manchuria; railroads, for example, linked the two regions with one another, and on the Yalu River an important hydroelectric power station was constructed to serve both countries. Since the communization of North Korea its economic ties with the Chinese territory which adjoins it on the north have continued to be strong.

The economic position of South Korea is described on page 562. The country has suffered heavily from the partition of the peninsula and from the war of 1950–53, as well as from the dislocation of its former trade relations with Japan. As a result large-scale assistance from the United States has been necessary in order for it to maintain economic stability.

JAPANESE EXPANSION AND KOREA'S DECLINE

The rapid growth of the Japanese empire between 1871 and World War II is one of the outstanding territorial developments of modern times. Utilizing its large and steadily increasing population, Japan was able to capitalize on the weaknesses and divided policies of other powers and to extend its control over much of the Far East and the western Pacific (Figure 104). The eventual involvement of Japan in a global war as a result of its aggressions brought on the downfall of the Nipponese empire, for although it was the dominant power of eastern Asia, Japan could not stand up against the combined strength of Anglo-America and Europe.

Between the early seventeenth and the late nineteenth centuries both Japan and Korea attempted to isolate themselves from foreign influences. The Tokugawa shoguns in Japan forbade the people to leave the country or to build ships of more than fifty tons, while in Korea the Yi dynasty, in the interests of national protection, followed a somewhat similar course.

In 1853 Commodore Perry and his naval squadron entered the harbor of Tokyo and succeeded in opening up Japan to foreign trade and in securing guarantees for the safety of shipwrecked American sailors who landed on Japanese islands. Thirty-one years later the government of Korea, threatened by internal revolts, received the protection of the Chinese government. Trade agreements were already being concluded between Korea and various foreign powers, and, like Japan, the Koreans gradually emerged from seclusion. Once the isolation was ended, one country became a world power, while the other entered into a period of foreign control and exploitation.

Japanese Empire-Building in the Western Pacific and Yellow Sea Areas

In the early years of its empire-building Japan concentrated on the island areas in the vicinity of the homeland. In 1871 Japan annexed the southern Ryukyus,[4] and four years later the Russians agreed to recognize Japanese sovereignty in the Kuril Islands in exchange for Japanese recognition of Russian control in Sakhalin Island to the north of Japan. The Bonin and Volcano islands, lying to the southeast of Japan, were annexed next, and after victory over China in 1895 the Japanese received Taiwan and the Pescadores. In possession of an island chain stretching through nearly 30 degrees of latitude from the Kamchatka Peninsula to the South China Sea, Japan was in a position after 1895 to turn westward to the Asian mainland.

As a result of its defeat by Japan, China was forced to relinquish its protectorate of Korea, and for a decade Korea struggled to build up its independence in the face of mounting pressure from Japan. Early in the twentieth century Japan instigated a successful war with Russia; by the Treaty of Portsmouth (1905) Russia abandoned its drive for power in Manchuria, ceded to Japan the southern half of Sakhalin Island, and transferred its rights to Kwangtung in the Liaotung Peninsula of southern Manchuria. Thus, because of its location in a part of the world from which other major power centers were considerably removed, Japan was able to establish its position of dominance in the Yellow Sea area. Korea, lying between the Yellow Sea and Japan, became a Japanese protectorate in 1905, and five years later it was annexed as a Japanese colony.

In the three decades following the Treaty of Portsmouth, Japan's two chief antagonists in the Far East—Russia and China—passed through periods of internal disorder, thereby enabling Japan to continue its course

---

[4] The northern Ryukyus (known as the Amami Gunto group) were Japanese-controlled after 1609. The southern Ryukyus, including Okinawa, although retaining a large measure of local autonomy, were a Japanese protectorate—and at the same time paid tribute to China—until 1871, when they were formally annexed by Japan.

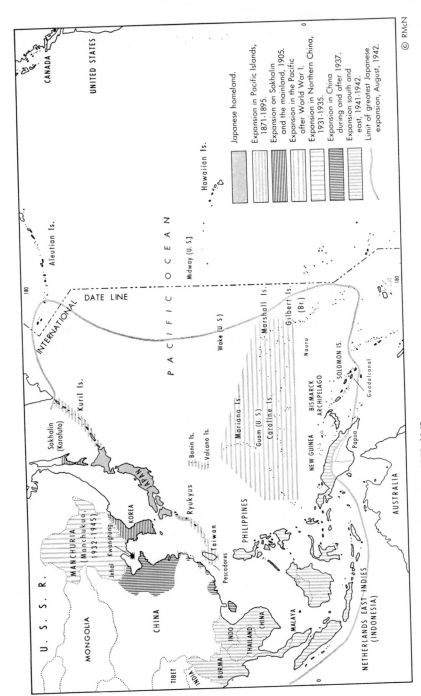

Japanese homeland.

Expansion in Pacific Islands, 1871-1895.

Expansion on Sakhalin and the mainland, 1905.

Expansion in the Pacific after World War I.

Expansion in Northern China, 1931-1935.

Expansion in China during and after 1937.

Expansion south and east, 1941-1942.

Limit of greatest Japanese expansion, August, 1942.

Figure 104. Japan's Territorial Expansion, 1871-1945.

of territorial growth. The Japanese wisely supported the Allies against Germany during World War I and helped to eliminate Germany's growing power in the Far East and the Pacific. Japan subsequently gained control of German territories in the Pacific north of the equator.

Territorial Expansion in China

In 1931 Japan turned again to the Asian mainland and in a short conflict succeeded in conquering Manchuria, with its agricultural, mineral, and power resources and its population of over 35 million. This area in the following years was constituted as the independent country of Manchukuo, but in reality it became a Japanese puppet state. As in Korea, Japanese capital and labor were invested in the development of Manchukuo's resources for Japan's benefit; by the beginning of World War II over 1 million tons each of steel and pig iron were being produced from Japanese-constructed mills in this area. Although Manchuria contains rich agricultural lands, only about 100,000 Japanese farmers emigrated to the area between 1931 and World War II. The Japanese disliked the cold weather of Manchuria and were generally unwilling to compete economically with the farmers there, because the latter accepted lower living standards than the Japanese. Operating from Manchuria, in 1935 the Japanese invaded and occupied the Chinese province of Jehol, thereby extending Japanese territory along the eastern border of Outer Mongolia (see page 535).

An all-out invasion of China proper was launched by Japan in 1937 in a bid for uncontested supremacy in the Far East. The Japanese soon conquered the major population centers of eastern China, but the Chinese government retreated to Chungking, 1,000 miles up the Yangtze River, and from there directed military operations against the invaders. Japan's inability to destroy effective resistance in China represented the first phase in the eventual destruction of the empire. The great size of China, its rugged topography, and the stubborn resistance of its people were obstacles which the Japanese could not overcome. Although by 1941 the military lines in China had become relatively stabilized, the Japanese were continually subjected to a war of attrition carried on by guerrilla forces and by sporadic attacks from military units operating from the Chinese interior.

Conquest in Southern Asia and the Pacific

The final phase of Japan's territorial expansion began in September, 1941, when the country carried out a military occupation of French Indochina. France itself had been conquered by Nazi Germany in the previous year and was in no position to resist this occupation. Three months later the Japanese military leaders launched a supreme effort to achieve Japan's "place in the sun" by eliminating American power from the Pacific and European power from southeast Asia. Japanese forces swept southeast across the Philippines, Indonesia, and areas to the east of southeastern New Guinea. They moved across Thailand, Malaya, and Burma to the borders of India, and within a matter of months in 1941–42 over 135 million people, together with the riches of southeast Asia, were under Japanese control.

In the history of Japan's territorial conquests, particularly after the Pearl Harbor attack of December, 1941, there runs a sort of fatalistic thread, for although the Japanese drew up large-scale plans for their Greater East Asia Co-Prosperity Sphere, embracing both the older empire and the newly won territories, it is hard to imagine the ultimate defeat of the United States, which possessed twice the population of Japan, ten times its industrial production, and a tremendous resource base for waging a long and costly war, should one prove necessary. Those resources of the British Commonwealth which could be spared from the war in Europe were also thrown against Japan, and the threat of Soviet attack was always present as a further strain on Japanese wartime activities. By the time of Germany's surrender in May, 1945, some Japanese officials were actively seeking an armistice. In August of that year Japan capitulated.

THE LOSS OF JAPAN'S EMPIRE AND THE PARTITIONING OF KOREA

The Consequences of Defeat

At the end of World War II Japan's territory was reduced to the former island area from which it had launched its course of expansion in 1871. Actually, the Japan of 1945 was smaller than that of 1871, for then the country controlled the Amami Gunto group of the northern Ryukyus, but after the war even these were taken from it. Russia annexed southern Sakhalin and the Kurils; Manchuria, Taiwan, and the Pescadores were joined to China; Korea was freed from Japanese rule and partitioned into Communist and non-Communist sectors; and the Ryukyus, together with the Bonin-Volcano islands and Marcus Island in the Pacific, passed under the control of the United States. The Japanese mandated islands in the Pacific were eventually constituted as United Nations trusteeship territories under United States administration. The other areas occupied by Japan between 1935 and 1942 were returned to their former status. In September, 1951, a Japanese peace treaty was concluded at San Francisco, confirming the loss of Japan's empire, although the future status of the American-held island groups remained undetermined (see page 566). Thus in a period of seventy-five years Japan's east Asian empire passed through a complete cycle.

Power Struggle in Korea

The division of the Korean Peninsula greatly changed the economic and political structure of that area. It had been agreed by the major Allied powers in 1943 that the country was to receive independence in "due course" after Japan's defeat, although the details had not been worked out. At the time of Japan's surrender Soviet forces rushed across Manchuria and into northern Korea to occupy the area, while United States troops, transported to the area by sea, occupied southern Korea. The dividing line between American and Soviet occupation zones was put at the thirty-eighth parallel, cutting the peninsula in two. In December, 1945, it was decided by the Allied powers that Korea was to be administered under the joint trusteeship of the United States, the U.S.S.R., Britain, and China for a period not to exceed five years, at the end of which time full independence would be granted.

As in the case of other postwar agreements, the Russians refused to compromise on the implementation of the Korean trusteeship. The United States was determined to create in Korea a Western-style (and presumably Western-oriented) democratic government, while the Soviets were equally determined to create a Communist, Soviet-oriented regime. The political impasse was further complicated by the fact that in any unified State the south, with its greater population, would always be able to out-vote the north. While a democratic government was being developed in South Korea, under the leadership of Syngman Rhee, a repatriate from the United States, North Korea became a Communist-dominated State, in which the military forces were built up rapidly under Soviet supervision. United Nations efforts in 1948 to supervise elections for a national government to control all of Korea were blocked by the Soviets, and in August of that year the democratic Republic of Korea was proclaimed at Seoul, with jurisdiction over the area south of the thirty-eighth parallel. Two months later a Communist-dominated People's Democratic Republic was established at Pyongyang, with jurisdiction over North Korea, Soviet troops were withdrawn from North Korea at the end of 1948, and by June, 1949, all American forces had evacuated South Korea, leaving the peninsula divided into a heavily armed Communist State in the north and a weakly defended democratic State in the south.

North Korea forces invaded South Korea without warning on June 25, 1950, in an effort to unify forcibly the peninsula into a Communist State. The United Nations, which had supervised the elections in South Korea two years earlier, voted for prompt retaliatory action, and a United Nations army was organized, largely under United States leadership, to go to the assistance of South Korea. By November the North Koreans had not only been driven back across the thirty-eighth parallel, but in some

areas United Nations forces had reached the Yalu River bordering Manchuria. Communist China then came to the aid of North Korea, and after
seven months of additional warfare the military front was stabilized approximately along the thirty-eighth parallel. In 1953 a Korean armistice agreement provided for the permanent cessation of hostilities, an exchange of
prisoners, and an enforcement of the political and military border along
the cease-fire line in the vicinity of the thirty-eighth parallel (Figure
105). The new dividing line is considerably shorter than was the one along
the thirty-eighth parallel and more militarily defensible for the South
Koreans.

THE ECONOMIC AND POLITICAL PROBLEMS OF SOUTH KOREA AND JAPAN

The economic and political developments within and between Japan
and South Korea are important to the containment of communism in
eastern Asia. Internal disorders in either area, resulting from economic
difficulties, might cause the overthrow of the democratic governments and
their replacement by Communist administrations. Moreover, hostile relations between Japan and South Korea have helped to weaken the solidarity
of the anti-Communist countries in the Far East.

South Korean Economy

The economic difficulties of South Korea result from the partition of
the peninsula, from the tremendous devastation wrought by the 1950–51

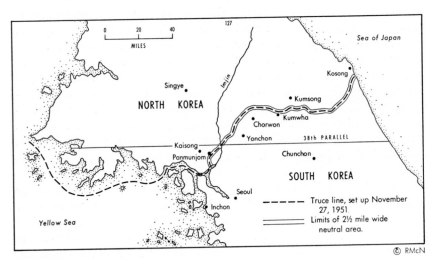

Figure 105. The Truce Line in Korea.

fighting, from the influx of refugees, and from the lack of available capital with which to rebuild the country. With a population of over 25 million and an area of 37,424 square miles, South Korea is one of the most densely populated States of the world. In addition to receiving an estimated 3 million refugees from North Korea, the country experiences an annual population increase of some half a million. Over two-thirds of the population are farmers, most of them extremely poor. Despite the receipt of $4 billion in United States military and economic aid, South Korea's economy has grown very slowly. Nearly half the labor force is employed part time or else unemployed entirely. Although before World War II this was a food-exporting area, the dislocations caused by the Korean conflict and the expanded population of South Korea have led to difficulties in procuring domestic food requirements. The consumer price index increased by 400 per cent between 1953 and 1961. While North Korea, with its considerable industrial potential and its labor shortage, is apparently undergoing relatively rapid economic growth, South Korea has been facing grim economic prospects. There is little hope for large-scale emigration; the government maintains an army of over half a million men as defense against a possible recurrence of invasion from the north. In the long run, however, South Korea's survival may come to depend not so much upon its military strength, but rather on its ability to handle its pressing economic problems and to maintain among its people a faith in the future under an anti-Communist form of government.

Japanese Economy

Japan's economic problem is primarily that of a densely populated State in need of trade partners and a balanced budget. As an indication of its future population growth, estimates for the 1975 figure range from 110 to 135 million (or an average density of 750–900 persons per square mile). Japan's prewar markets, foreign investments, and sources for raw materials are largely gone, and heavy damage was inflicted on the homeland itself in the final months of World War II. The Japanese have worked diligently to restore production and to secure markets for their exports, but the foreign trade deficit has continued to exist. Between 1946 and the end of 1961 the United States granted economic and military aid to Japan totalling over $4 billion.

The economic situation in Japan has certain elements in common with that of Great Britain shortly after World War II. Britain also received aid from the United States, but, in addition, the British inaugurated an austerity program, cutting down imports of consumer items and resorting to strict rationing. This policy was never seriously followed by the Japanese, with the result that imports rose steadily during the postwar years. Since

1952, however, when Japan became again a sovereign State, the nation's economy has soared, with the average growth rate estimated at about 8 per cent per year. In ten years the national income climbed from $14 billion to nearly $33 billion, while the value of foreign trade increased one and a half times. Japan's chronic unemployment, or underemployment, has been sharply reduced, and the State in 1962 had come to rank in fourth or fifth place (with Britain) among the world's industrial powers.

Much of Japan's prosperity depends upon foreign trade. The United States is Japan's foremost trade partner, accounting normally for about one-third of its total by value. In return for American cotton, scrap iron, and machinery the Japanese send such products as textiles and clothing, electrical machinery, and fish. Canada, Australia, the Philippines, West Germany, and Britain are also important in Japanese trade, and government officials have been extremely worried not only by "protectionist" demands in the United States against Japanese imports, but also by the creation and possible expansion of the European Common Market and other proposed economic unions. One potential source of trade is Communist China, but efforts by the Japanese to capitalize on the enormous market there have been largely unsuccessful. The country has received large amounts of foreign aid from the United States. By the terms of the Mutual Defense Assistance Pact of 1954 the United States supplies almost the entire equipment of the Japanese forces, thus relieving Japan of much of the defense costs which most other countries must assume.

Political Problems

In Japan and South Korea the development of anti-Communist policies has been complicated by a growing nationalist spirit in both countries. The Japanese are anxious to realize some benefits from their heavy prewar investments in Korea, a factor which has contributed to ill feeling between Japan and South Korea. On the other hand, South Korea's quarrels with the Japanese over fishing rights have resulted in breakdowns in trade discussions, despite United States appeals to both countries that such disputes weaken their economies and thereby play into the hands of the Communists. Since 1952 Japan has claimed the right to fish within twelve miles of the South Korean coast, while the South Koreans claim that restrictions imposed on Japanese fishing in 1945 (in some cases prohibiting them from coming within 100 miles of Korea) are still in effect (Figure 106). The South Koreans have garrisoned Take (or Tokto) Island in the Sea of Japan between Japan and Korea, a previously uninhabited area of disputed sovereignty, and have interned Japanese ships and crews fishing in the vicinity of Take.

In April, 1960, South Korea's national leader and first President, Dr.

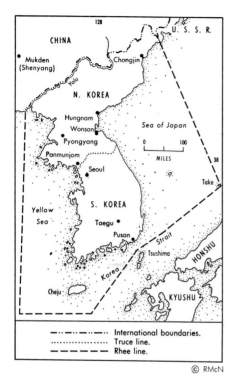

Figure 106. *The Limits of Sovereignty Claimed by South Korea.* The Rhee Line, laid down in January, 1952, delimits the sea areas in which South Korea claims exclusive fishing rights.

Syngman Rhee, resigned his office following considerable rioting and bloodshed. Control of the national government ultimately passed to a military junta which has struggled to bring order and a sense of national cohesion to the troubled country. Lacking both economic viability and the strength alone to defend itself against the Communists from the north, South Korea must depend heavily upon support from the United States, with which it has few interests in common beyond the determination to resist the encroachment of communism. Except for American support, the country is virtually isolated, facing a hostile Asian mainland, an unfriendly Japan, and the northern portion of the peninsula where economic and military growth have apparently well exceeded those of the south.

In Japan many people have become increasingly resentful of their country's role as an American-manned outpost against communism. Having suffered through atomic bombardments, they have little desire to serve as a base for the possible launching of American air attacks against the U.S.S.R. The strength of anti-American feeling was clearly demonstrated by the 1960 outbreaks in Tokyo against revision of the security treaty with the United States. Japan, a powerful industrial State, has been searching for a clear identification of its role on the world scene. Faced with the growing power of communism on the Asian mainland, should the Japanese seek to establish some modus vivendi with China and the Soviet Union, even if this means loosening some of its ties with the United States? Will European economic integration gradually squeeze out Japan—a process which might be further complicated by increasing American and Canadian participation in a west European union? Can Japan unite with the Philippines, Taiwan, and possibly South Korea in some form of "peripheral" anti-Communist bloc, and can closer ties be established with Australia, New Zealand, and the non-Communist countries of southeast Asia? Because of such problems the Japanese are seriously concerned over the course or courses of action which they should follow in the changing world of power relations.

Okinawa and the Ryukyus

Japan and the United States are involved in a territorial dispute concerning the Ryukyu Islands, which extend in an arc 500 miles to the southwest of Japan (Figure 107). The islands have an area of about 1,290 square miles and a population of over 900,000. The Ryukyuans are closely allied to the Japanese in language and physical characteristics and have strong sentimental ties with Japan. Before World War II the standard of living in the Ryukyus was lower than in Japan. The average population density is high, and during the past fifty years thousands of Ryukyuans have emigrated to other Japanese-controlled islands or to Hawaii.

In the spring of 1945, after some of the most costly fighting of the Pacific war, American forces captured Okinawa and began to develop it as a major base for what was to be the final assault on Japan. After Japan's surrender the Ryukyus south of the twenty-ninth parallel were placed under the administration of the United States commander-in-chief in Tokyo. Article 3 of the Japanese Peace Treaty states: "Japan will concur in any proposal of the United States to the United Nations to place under its trusteeship system, with the United States as the sole administering authority . . . the Ryukyu . . . Bonin . . . and Volcano Islands. . . . Pending the making of such a proposal and affirmative action thereof, the United States will have the right to exercise all and any powers of administration . . . over the territory and inhabitants of these islands, including their territorial waters." This paragraph also mentions the former Japanese-controlled Daito Islands, Rosario Island, Parece Vela, and Marcus Island as falling within the same category.

The future status of the Ryukyus, as well as of the Bonin-Volcano group, has remained a subject of controversy between Tokyo and Washington. The United States has constructed a half-billion-dollar air base on Okinawa (sometimes described as the "Gibraltar of the East"), and is natu-

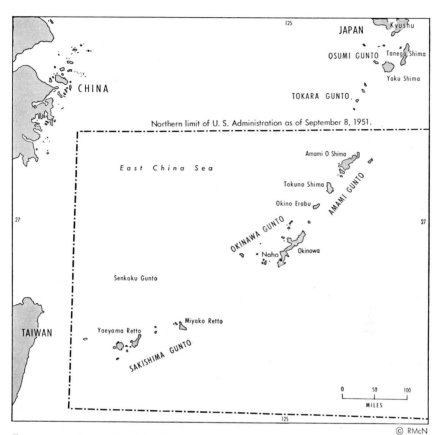

Figure 107. The Ryukyu Islands.

rally reluctant to lose control of the island, even if continued American
sovereignty means that the approximately 400,000 inhabitants are denied
reunion with Japan. In 1953 the United States returned the Amami Gunto
group in the northern Ryukyus, with a population of approximately 200,-
000, to Japanese control, but indicated that for the foreseeable future American control would continue over the remainder of the Ryukyus as well as
the Bonin-Volcano group. Anti-American feeling on Okinawa has been
heightened by the expropriation of agricultural land for military installations.

The United States, long a champion of self-determination, may find its
moral position weakened by continued control in the Ryukyus, for through
their elective body the people have expressed a desire for reunion with
Japan. If the Ryukyus were returned to Japan, agreements could be worked
out between the American and Japanese governments for continued American control over air and radar installations. The Japanese would be in a

Figure 108. The Kuril Islands.

© RMcN

stronger position to demand the return of the Kurils from Russia if America first relinquished control of the Ryukyus. Another possible solution would be the establishment of United Nations trusteeship over the Ryukyus, with the United States as the sole administering power, although many people— including the Ryukyuans themselves—might consider this merely a continuation of the present situation. Finally, all the islands, except for Okinawa, could be returned to Japan. Such a solution would in the end satisfy no one, for Okinawa is by far the most important island in the group in terms of population and the economic value of its sugar exports, and few Ryukyuans would favor the separation of their leading territory from the remainder of the area. In 1957 the American secretary of state officially referred to Japan's "residual sovereignty" over the Ryukyus, and five years later the United States extended a measure of self-government to the islanders by providing, first, that the chief executive of the Ryukyuan government be appointed by the United States high commissioner on the basis of nomination by the local legislature and, second, that the veto power of the high commissioner over bills passed by the legislature be limited to those affecting military security, foreign affairs, and United States property. But the basic desire of the Ryukyuans for "reversion," that is, return to Japanese control, seems to have little chance for fulfillment for some time to come because of the islands' strategic importance to American control in the western Pacific.

The Kuril Islands

A second postwar territorial problem facing the Japanese is that of the Kuril Islands, a chain extending nearly 700 miles northeast from Hokkaido to the Kamchatka Peninsula (Figure 108). The Kurils have a total area of nearly 4,000 square miles and a population of less than 20,000. The inhabitants prior to World War II were entirely Japanese. Over 90 per cent of them inhabited the southern Kurils, within about 200 miles of Hokkaido. The only economic value of the Kurils area is fishing, most of which is done in the northern part of the chain not far from Kamchatka. Shimushir Island in the central Kurils is an excellent site for a naval base. Before and during World War II the Japanese established a number of naval and air bases in the islands, from which they could dominate the southeastern part of the Sea of Okhotsk, as well as strike eastward toward the Aleutians.

The southern part of the Kurils has been Japanese-controlled since the beginning of the nineteenth century, and in 1875 Russian claims to the islands were withdrawn in exchange for control of Sakhalin. They were subsequently administered by the Japanese as part of Japan proper. At the Yalta Conference in 1945 the Soviets demanded possession of the Kurils as a price for their entry into the war against Japan, and to this American officials agreed. After Japan's surrender they were annexed by the U.S.S.R., although the United States has never officially recognized Soviet sovereignty.

Soviet control of the Kurils has had several results. The island chain lies close to the great-circle route from Alaska to Japan, used by American commercial and military aircraft. Several incidents have occurred in which American craft have been attacked by Soviet fighters off the Kuril chain. The southernmost of the islands lies less than ten miles from the Japanese island of Hokkaido. The Soviets are fortifying the Kuril chain and thereby pose a military threat both to northern Japan and to the whole area of the northwestern Pacific. The Japanese inhabitants on the Kurils have passed under Soviet control, and Japanese fishing vessels operating in the area have been seized and their crews interned by the Russians.

The Japanese have requested that the Soviets return to them sovereignty over the Kurils, or at least the southern, most heavily populated

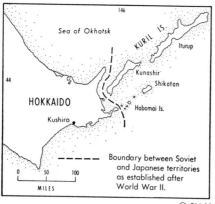

Figure 109. The Hokkaido-Southern Kurils Area. In 1956 the Soviet Union agreed to return Habomai and Shikotan islands to Japan.

part, but the Russians have consistently refused to do this. Control of the Kurils gives the Russians a weapon to hold over Japan in the fishing-rights dispute. It also prevents any hostile screen being imposed across the entrance to the Sea of Okhotsk, and it makes possible Soviet air dominance over the shortest sea and air routes between the United States and Japan. By the terms of the peace treaty concluded between the Soviet Union and Japan in 1956, tiny Habomai and Shikotan islands in the southernmost Kurils were handed back to the Japanese, but the nearby larger islands of Kunashir and Iturup remained under Soviet control (Figure 109).

BIBLIOGRAPHY

BALLANTINE, JOSEPH W. "The Future of the Ryukyus," *Foreign Affairs,* XXXI (1953), 663–75.

A short description of the history and geography of the islands and of alternative solutions to the problem of future control.

FREYMOND, JACQUES. "Supervising Agreements: The Korean Experience," *Foreign Affairs,* XXXVII (1959), 496–504.

Some of the problems involved in carrying out international agreements under Cold War conditions.

HOPPER, BRUCE. "The Perennial Kamchatka Discord," *Foreign Affairs,* XV (1937), 564–68.

A brief history of the fisheries dispute between Japan and Russia up to 1937 and its relation to offshore claims by these countries.

McCUNE, GEORGE. *Korea Today.* Cambridge, Mass.: Harvard University Press, 1950.

The outstanding text on problems in Korea from 1945 to the North Korean invasion.

OKITA, SABURO. "Japan's Economic Prospects," *Foreign Affairs,* XXXIX (1960), 123–32.

A general survey of the problem.

PELZER, KARL J. "Japanese Migration and Colonization," in ISAIAH BOWMAN (ed.), *Limits of Land Settlement.* New York: American Geographical Society, 1937. Pp. 155–95.

A description of Japanese settlement prior to World War II.

REISCHAUER, EDWIN O. *Japan Past and Present.* New York: Alfred A. Knopf, 1953.

A very good survey of Japan by a recognized expert on the area.

TAUEBER, IRENE B. "Japan's Population: Miracle, Model or Case Study?" *Foreign Affairs,* XL (1962), 595–605.

An interesting account of Japan's approach to the problem.

TREWARTHA, GLENN T. *Japan: A Physical, Cultural and Regional Geography.* Madison: University of Wisconsin Press, 1945.

A basic regional geography of the area.

WAGNER, EDWARD W. "Failure in Korea," *Foreign Affairs,* XL (1961), 128–36.

A critical view of Western policies in Korea.

21

CONFLICT IN THE PACIFIC

● The Pacific Ocean, covering just under one-third of the earth's surface, is one of the great regions of power conflict in the modern world. Across its waters the United States faces the Soviet Union and Communist China, while within the vast ocean area are a great number of islands and island groups whose political and economic problems are inexorably bound up with the great power rivalries of the Pacific. During the twentieth century the United States has sought to maintain the Pacific area as one dominated largely by American power. The removal of Japan as a rival power in 1945 was followed by (1) Soviet acquisition of the Kuril Islands, (2) the communization of Mainland China and the withdrawal of the Nationalist government to Taiwan, and (3) the Korean War, resulting in the commitment of American military and economic power in South Korea, and later in South Vietnam and Thailand. As a result American military lines extend across the Pacific to Japan and the Ryukyu Islands, to South Korea, Taiwan and the Formosa Strait, the Philippines, South Vietnam, and Thailand, while the United States also stands behind Commonwealth forces in Australia, New Zealand, Singapore, and British Borneo. Logistics are a very real problem there. The spread of communism on the Asian mainland and the gradual development by the Communist countries of powerful surface, underseas, and air units represents a constant threat to the position of the United States as the predominant military force in the Pacific.

Only a few of the Pacific islands are significant in terms of size, population, or economic value. Many of the smaller islands, however, possess considerable military importance because of their location and have figured prominently in territorial disputes between colonial countries. The resultant political pattern is a complex one, reflecting the existence of the many colonial possessions there, the conflicting interests of countries which border on or lie within the Pacific, and the desires of the island peoples for greater economic and political advancement.

Several of the islands and island groups in the Pacific basin have already been discussed in other chapters. Thus the western island chain, including the Kurils, Japan, and the Ryukyus, will be excluded from the area to be covered in this chapter, as will also Indonesia and the Hawaiian Islands. The rest of the Pacific region will be considered here first as a unit, and then in terms of five areas—Oceania, the Philippines, Taiwan, Australia, and New Zealand—each of which will be treated separately.

ISLANDS AND POWER SPHERES

The eastern and northern portions of the Pacific have relatively few islands, and those which are present are generally small in size (Figure 110). In contrast, the southwestern and western Pacific have a great number and variety of islands, ranging in size from the continental land mass of Australia and the island of New Guinea down to those which comprise less than one acre. The islands of the southwestern Pacific are generally classified in three groups—Micronesia, including the Marshalls, Gilberts, Carolines, and Marianas in the west central Pacific; Melanesia to the south, extending from New Guinea eastward to include the New Hebrides, New Caledonia, and Fiji; and Polynesia, comprising a triangular-shaped area extending from Hawaii south to include Easter Island and west to New Zealand. Australia and the Philippines are not included in these three groups, but some classifications place New Zealand within the limits of Polynesia.

This tripartite division reflects the cultural differences among the island areas, but patterns of political control have not corresponded to those of ethnic characteristics. Most of the colonial powers have territories in two or more of the major divisions (Table 16). This complex distribution has hindered colonial development there, for the territories of a particular country are often separated from one another both by great distances and by island areas belonging to some other power.

Rimming the Pacific, or located within it, are several important countries—the United States, Canada, the Soviet Union, China, Japan, Indonesia, and Australia—as well as such other States as Taiwan, the Philippines, and New Zealand. In addition, British and French interests are represented in colonial territories there. The presence of many islands and peninsulas is important strategically, since certain areas because of their vicinal locations may be highly prized as military or political control centers.

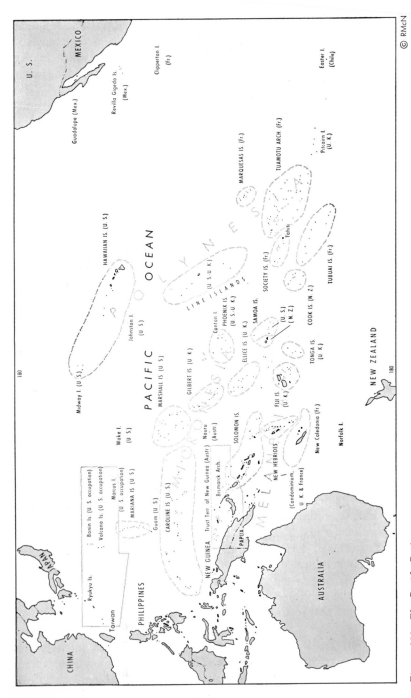

Figure 110. The Pacific Basin.

Historically the Pacific basin has been characterized by the erection of "power spheres," frequently centered on areas such as Guam, Truk, Okinawa, or Oahu. This distribution of power areas is particularly significant in the light of Haushofer's prediction that a future struggle for world power would eventually take place within the Pacific basin.

Most of the islands north of the equator are under United States control. From Hawaii an American supply line extends westward via Midway, Wake, and Guam to United States bases in the Philippines and on Okinawa. This route also serves the United States trusteeship territories of the Mariana, Marshall, and Caroline islands. American power in the northern Pacific is further augmented by the presence of Alaska and the Aleutians near the northernmost point of the great circular-shaped Pacific basin. This power position, however, is limited by Soviet control of Siberia and the Kurils, possible "neutralism" in Japan, and the vulnerability of extended sea and air lanes.

South of the equator Britain, Australia, New Zealand, and France share in the control of most of the islands. Despite the unifying effects of climate and the sea in the southern Pacific, diversity of control has represented an important centrifugal force among the island areas and has served to delay economic and social development (see also page 584). The conflicting forces there are reflected by the political division of island groups, such as the Solomons; by politically divided individual islands, like New Guinea; and by the joint control of an island by two or more powers, as in the case of the New Hebrides (Britain and France).

THE DEVELOPMENT OF THE POLITICAL PATTERN

Six States have played active roles in the contest for control of territory in the Pacific: Spain, Britain, France, Germany, Japan, and the United States. In addition, Australia and New Zealand have received island areas since the start of the twentieth century, Russia owns the Commander (Komandorski) Islands in the northern Pacific, and Chile, Ecuador, Mexico, Colombia, and Costa Rica all control islands off their respective coasts. In the gradual establishment of sovereignty over the land areas in the Pacific, two factors in particular stand out, first, the belated recognition by most countries of the value of the Pacific areas and, second, the eventual development of conflicting power interests in the region.

The Era of Spanish Dominance

The first European explorer to cross the Pacific was Magellan, on an expedition from Spain, who discovered the Philippines in 1521. Forty-four years later the Spanish established a permanent settlement in the

Table 16

ISLANDS AND ISLAND GROUPS OF THE PACIFIC

	Area (sq. mi.)	Population (generally, 1958)
Australia	2,974,581	10,227,000
Possessions		
Papua	90,540	480,000
Territory of New Guinea (trusteeship territory; incl. Northeast New Guinea, Bismark Archipelago, and northern Solomon Islands)	93,000	1,376,000
Nauru (trusteeship territory; joint administration with New Zealand and Great Britain)	8	4,300
Norfolk Island	13	1,000
New Zealand	103,736	2,375,000
Possessions		
Cook Islands	99	18,000
Niue	100	4,800
Tokelau	4	2,000
Philippines	115,600	24,012,000
Western Samoa	1,130	114,000
British Possessions		
Tonga	269	57,000
British Solomon Islands	11,500	115,000
Fiji	7,040	388,000
Gilbert and Ellice Islands (incl. Phoenix and Line isls. and Ocean Island) . .	369	44,000
Pitcairn Island	2	150
New Hebrides (condominium with France)	5,700	56,000
French Possessions		
New Caledonia and dependencies (incl. Isle of Pines, Wallis Archipelago, and Loyalty, Futuna, Huon, Belep, Chesterfield, and Walpole islands) . . .	7,202	72,000
French Oceania (Society Isls. [incl. Tahiti], Marquesas Isls., Tubauai Isls., Clipperton Island)	1,544	75,000
New Hebrides (condominium with Britain)	5,700	56,000
United States Possessions		
Guam	206	67,000
Wake	3	400
Midway	2	400
Johnston	n.a.	50
Howland, Jarvis, Baker	3	n.a.
American Samoa	76	20,000
Canton and Enderbury (condominium with Great Britain)	27	300

Table 16—(Continued)

ISLANDS AND ISLAND GROUPS OF THE PACIFIC

	Area (sq. mi.)	Population (generally, 1958)
United States Possessions (*Continued*)		
Trust Territory of the Pacific Islands (Mariana Isls., Marshall Isls., and Caroline Isls.)	685	76,000
Bonin, Volcano, and Marcus Islands (former Japanese isls. now under U.S. administration)	40	210
Chilean Possessions		
Easter Island	46	600
Juan Fernandez Islands	70	450
San Felix and San Ambrosio Islands . .	2	n.a.
Sala y Gomez Island	n.a.	n.a.
Ecuadorian Possessions		
Galapagos Islands	3,042	1,400
Costa Rican Possessions		
Cocos Island	10	n.a.
Colombian Possessions		
Malpelo Island	n.a.	n.a.
Mexican Possessions		
Revilla Gigedo Islands	320	n.a.
Guadalupe Island	102	20
Soviet Possessions		
Commander (Komandorski) Islands . .	600	n.a.

Source: *The Statesman's Yearbook, 1961–62*, ed. S. H. Steinberg, by permission of St. Martin's Press, Inc., and Macmillan & Co., Ltd.

Philippines, and in the following century they also occupied the Mariana Islands, primarily to serve the sea lanes between Mexico and the Philippine Islands. Although Spain was the first power to win possession in the Pacific, it did little to follow up its early gains. Defeat in the Spanish-American War at the end of the nineteenth century led Spain to sell the Philippines and cede Guam to the United States and to sell the recently acquired Caroline and Mariana islands (excluding Guam) to Germany. Thus by 1900 Spain had disappeared entirely as a Pacific power.

Britain's Territorial Expansion

Britain's early contacts in the Pacific were made largely by pirates. The great era of British exploration and mapping in that area did not come until the voyages of Captain Cook between 1768 and 1780. The first permanent settlement in Australia was made in 1788 and in New Zealand in

1840, but it was only in the mid-nineteenth century that Britain began to annex formally the Pacific islands. By this time the activities of whalers, missionaries, and traders, as well as the prospects of economic gain from such products as sandalwood and copra, had interested several European governments in establishing sovereignty over Pacific island groups. Thus the British soon found themselves in competition with other powers, particularly France and Germany. In 1874 Britain formally annexed Fiji, and eighteen years later the Gilbert and Ellice islands. Other acquisitions followed, practically all of them to the south of the equator.

French Gains in the Southern Pacific

French pirates and adventurers were also exploring this region during the seventeenth and eighteenth centuries. The first formal French annexation was the protectorate over Tahiti in 1842, followed shortly by the acquisition of New Caledonia. As the scramble for territories accelerated during the latter part of the 1800's, French-British rivalry there became increasingly strong. France annexed the remaining Society Islands and the Loyalty group, but disputed sovereignty over the New Hebrides, lying about 1,000 miles east of Australia, led to the establishment in 1887 of dual French-British control over this area.

The Rise and Decline of German Control

Germany came late to the Pacific, as it did also to central and southern Africa. During the 1880's Germany annexed northeast New Guinea, the Bismarck Archipelago, and the northernmost Solomons, and protectorates were established over the Marshall Islands and Nauru Island. At the end of the century Germany purchased from Spain the Caroline and Mariana islands and divided Samoa with the United States.

By 1900 Germany had become an important power in the western Pacific, and the Germans energetically sought to develop the economic wealth of their possessions. Following World War I, however, Germany's Pacific possessions were apportioned out as mandates, Japan receiving the territories north of the equator, while Britain, Australia, and New Zealand divided among themselves those islands which lay to the south of it. Thus Germany, like Spain, was eventually eliminated as a Pacific power.

Japanese Power in the Northern Pacific

A fifth country to establish control in the Pacific was Japan. Prior to World War I the Japanese restricted their territorial interests primarily to the Kuril-Ryukyu-Taiwan chain, after which they turned westward to the

Asiatic mainland, with its large population and potential resources. The only annexations by Japan east of the homeland were the Bonin Islands (1875) and the Volcano group (1891). At the end of World War I, however, Japan's alliance with the Allies against Germany enabled Japan to occupy the German-held Marshall, Caroline, and Mariana island groups.

Between the two world wars the economic development of most of the Pacific islands took precedence over military activities. About 80,000 Japanese emigrated to their mandated territories and built up exports of sugar, processed fish, and copra. In the mandated areas the administering powers were directed not to erect fortifications or military bases or to give military training to the inhabitants. In order to soothe Japanese objections to this provision, the United States agreed to refrain from increasing the fortifications on its own islands west of Hawaii. The Japanese subsequently refused to let foreigners visit their mandated islands, but despite allegations that they violated their mandate obligations and armed Truk and other bases, it has been pointed out[1] that there was no evidence of Japanese defense preparations at least until 1938, three years after Japan left the League of Nations. At the end of World War II defeated Japan was forced to surrender all its holdings in Micronesia as well as its control of Taiwan; however, no permanent disposition of the Bonin-Volcano islands was decided upon (see page 580).

United States Interests in the Pacific

The United States was one of the last powers to acquire territory in the Pacific. Prior to the end of the nineteenth century the country was preoccupied with cheap land within its own boundaries and with its rapidly expanding economy. During the 1850's the United States announced its sovereignty over certain islands along the equator (such as Baker, Howland, and Jarvis) and Johnston Island, southwest of the Hawaiian group, in order to develop their guano deposits. Midway was acquired in 1867 in the interests of whaling ships operating in the mid-Pacific. The major American annexations in the Pacific did not take place, however, until 1898–99, when Hawaii was annexed upon petition of the Hawaiian government, the Philippines and Guam were received from Spain, eastern Samoa was acquired, and sovereignty was established over the previously unclaimed island of Wake. These acquisitions reflected the growing interests of the United States in the Pacific area.

During the period between 1900 and 1941 the United States made relatively few changes in the administration of its Pacific possessions, except for the granting of commonwealth status to the Philippines in 1936

---

[1] Karl J. Pelzer, "Micronesia—A Changing Frontier," *World Politics,* II (1950), 251–67.

as a first step toward independence. At the end of World War II, however, the United States was designated administering power over the trusteeship territories of the Marshall, Caroline, and Mariana islands (again excluding Guam). Most of the Japanese who formerly inhabited these areas have since returned to Japan.

In the charter of the newly formed United Nations several changes were made with respect to the former League mandates, now known as United Nations trusteeship territories. Instead of the old assumption that independence was the ultimate goal for all dependent areas, the charter spoke of "progressive development towards self-government or independence as may be appropriate to the particular circumstances of each territory." This apparent recognition that in some areas independence might not be a practical goal was written into the charter over the protests of ardent "self-determinists," to whom independence was a natural law of political progress.

Another important difference between the United Nations Charter and the former League Covenant with respect to dependent areas was the article which permitted the designation of all or part of a trusteeship territory as a "strategic area," which could be fortified and in which the natives could receive military training. The administering power may at any time temporarily suspend United Nations supervision of a strategic area for security reasons. This privilege, if misused, could establish a dangerous precedent, for no limits are placed on area or length of time involved in the suspension. Since 1947 the United States has maintained fortifications on such trusteeship islands as Saipan and Tinian and has evacuated natives from several of the Marshall Islands in order to conduct atomic experiments in that area.

One territorial problem involving the United States which has remained unsettled is that of the sovereignty over the former Japanese-controlled Bonin and Volcano islands, lying about 600 miles to the southeast of Japan. With their combined population of about 200 and the air and naval base at Iwo Jima, these islands have been administered by the United States since 1945. There would seem to be some logic in designating them as a United Nations strategic trusteeship territory, with the United States as sole administering authority. Such a move was implied in the Japanese Peace Treaty and might place the United States in a better diplomatic position than is at present possible under the conditions of indefinite occupation.

The strategic importance of the Pacific islands has obviously become a factor of great significance to the United States and its allies, frequently outweighing considerations of economic development of the island areas or of the national aspirations of the indigenous peoples. Many of the wartime bases have been abandoned or put on a reserve basis, but in maintaining its supply lines from west coast ports to South Korea, Japan, and the Philippines, the United States continues to man its defense installations, air bases, and repair and supply depots at key points (such as the Guam-Tinian-Saipan complex) in the tremendous area which lies west of Hawaii.

Other Territorial Relationships

Several Latin American states gained possessions in the Pacific during the nineteenth century. In 1837 Ecuador occupied the Galapagos Islands, which straddle the equator some 600 miles west of Ecuador itself. Chile, Costa Rica, and Mexico also acquired sovereignty over various deep-sea islands and island groups lying within about 600 miles of the Latin American coast. In addition, since 1888 Chile has controlled Easter Island, 2,200 miles west of the Chilean mainland.

In the northern Pacific Russian explorers and fishermen were active during the eighteenth and nineteenth centuries, and Russia controlled the Pribilof Islands until 1867, when they were included in the sale of Alaska to the United States. The Russians still maintain sovereignty, however, over the Commander (Komandorski) Islands, which lie 200 miles west of the Aleutians and about 150 miles from the Kamchatka Peninsula.

On July 4, 1946, the Philippines became independent, and within a few months the Philippine government had signed a ninety-nine-year agreement with the United States providing for American use of army, navy, and air bases in the islands (for further details of Philippine independence see page 590). Together with Japan and Okinawa, the Philippines represent the western anchor of the United States Pacific defense network.

OCEANIA

The term Oceania[2] here includes the islands of Micronesia, Melanesia, and Polynesia. It measures about 6,000 miles from north to south and over 7,000 miles from west to east. Within this enormous region the total land area amounts to only about 383,000 square miles, of which the island of New Guinea alone accounts for over 300,000 square miles. Among the other larger islands are New Britain, New Caledonia, New Ireland, Bougainville, and Guadalcanal; they and the rest of those over 1,000 square miles in area lie relatively close to the Australian mainland. These islands are continental in character, in that they are composed of rock types similar to those on continents themselves.

Many of the islands of the Pacific are "deep-sea" or "oceanic," rather than continental. These islands are generally smaller and may be subdivided into two principal types—"high" islands, which are of volcanic origin, and "low" islands, composed of coral. This difference is reflected in amounts of

---

[2] "Oceania" is frequently used to include Australia and New Zealand, but these are considered separately here. The Hawaiian Islands were discussed in Chapter 7.

rainfall, availability of drinking water, and soil types. In the trade-wind belts to the north and south of the equator, the high islands are often able to intercept the rain-bearing winds, so the precipitation falls on the windward side of the island; many of the coral islands, however, receive little precipitation. The volcanic soils of the high islands are frequently of much greater fertility than those of the coral islands.

Population

The total population of Oceania is about 4 million, concentrated largely in Fiji (388,000), and New Guinea (about 2,700,000, including West, formerly Netherlands, New Guinea). There are less than one million persons in the remainder of Oceania.

Most of the nonnative peoples in Oceania are located in the Fijis (about 191,000 Indians). Rates of annual population increase are generally high: Guam, 49 per thousand; Fiji, 33 per thousand; the Cook Islands, 28 per thousand. But dense concentrations occur only in relatively few areas, such as parts of the Gilbert, Ellice, and Tonga groups. On the Ellice Islands, for example, over 4,700 persons live on a total of 9.6 square miles of land. The transfer of native peoples from densely crowded islands to other areas has been a feature of colonial administration in the Pacific. Large amounts of potentially arable land remain unutilized, and even on much of the area now in crops considerably higher yields could be realized with improved farming techniques.

Warren S. Thompson has estimated that there were some three and a half million people in Oceania before the white man arrived, and that contact between the whites and the natives was "a major population catastrophe to most of these people. In addition to the direct attempt to use the natives for plantation work (probably a minor factor), the white man brought whiskey, tuberculosis, syphilis, and clothes, all of which were deadly to people not accustomed to them. But, above all, he broke up the traditional modes of tribal life, and thus robbed the natives of their most precious social heritage."[3] Since 1900 the population of most Pacific islands has been steadily growing through natural increase, although in some areas, particularly in Polynesia, it is probably still declining.

Economy

Large-scale economic development has taken place only in the Fiji islands. Power resources (except some water power) are virtually nonexistent in Oceania, and only in the Fijis is there extensive plantation agricul-

[3] Warren S. Thompson, *Population and Peace in the Pacific* (Chicago: University of Chicago Press, 1946), p. 37.

ture. Sugar, gold, copra, coconut oil, and bananas head the list of Fijian exports. New Caledonia, with its copra and coffee, as well as its nickel and chrome wealth, and New Guinea, with its gold and coconuts, are other exporting regions in Oceania.

Copra and other coconut products, sugar, and bananas are the principal products exported from the other areas of Oceania. Tahiti and Nauru Island also have phosphate, which is valuable as a fertilizer. Average per capita incomes are low throughout the islands, and in most areas there are shortages of funds and trained personnel for schools, hospitals, and other social services. The small areas and populations on most of the islands and the lack of valuable resources have largely been responsible for the shortage of investment capital. In many parts of Oceania, as in Africa, the native culture was supplanted by that of the white man during the nineteenth century, but the net effect has been to create a new way of life in which many of the basic wants cannot be satisfied. Lacking many of the resources of Africa, Oceania faces a difficult economic future in a competitive economic world.

Political Features

Most of the islands of Oceania are colonies, although a few, such as the eastern Solomons, have a protectorate status. The Tonga Islands are an independent kingdom; a unique political situation exists there, for the Tongans, although independent, have voluntarily turned over foreign relations, defense, and finance to the British government for administration. On January 1, 1962, New Zealand ended its trusteeship over Western Samoa, and that area became independent (see below). There are still trusteeship territories divided among the United States, Britain, Australia, and New Zealand. The rise of Australia and New Zealand as important colonial powers in the south Pacific has been occasioned not only by the assignment to them in 1919 of League mandates—now trusteeship territories—but also by the transfer of various British territories to their administration since the start of the twentieth century.

Because of the small and scattered populations and the poor economic potentials throughout most of Oceania, the dependent areas have not been in strong positions to bring pressures on far-off capitals for greater self-rule. Except for the transfer of colonial territories from one nation to another, there have been few changes in the political status of the Oceania islands (except for Western Samoa) since they first became dependent areas. Even though from an economic point of view complete independence may be impractical for many areas, there is room for greater measure of autonomy and of cooperation among the island peoples.

Western Samoa consists of two large islands (Manono and Apolima), two small islands, and several islets. Its total area is 1,130 square miles and the 1962 population was approximately 114,000. The rate of population increase is high (an estimated 60 per cent rise in the coming fifteen years); about 6,000 of the people are Europeans, the rest Samoans. Apia, the capital of Western Samoa, is the only town of any size in the new State. Most of the people are scattered in small villages and continue to live within a traditional social system based on the *aiga*, or extended family group. The village communities are largely self-sufficient in essential commodities. Copra, cocoa, and bananas are the major exports of the country, the bulk of these going to New Zealand. All three commodities are very sensitive to price fluctuations. In 1960–61 Western Samoa experienced considerable economic difficulty when the prices for copra and cocoa dropped substantially and a severe storm caused a decline in the export of bananas.

In Western Samoa may be seen several of the potential problems of independence for the mid-Pacific islands. Although the country can now produce most of its own food (particularly taro, yams, and manioc), the future years may bring both a substantial increase in population and demands by the Samoans for more consumer goods. Lacking minerals or power fuels, Western Samoa will be hard put to it to acquire the necessary capital for imports without large-scale aid from either New Zealand or the United States. Independence for Western Samoa raises the question of the future of Eastern Samoa, a group of islands totaling 76 square miles in area with a 1960 population of 20,000. Parts of the territory have been governed by the United States since 1899; Pago Pago, the capital, has the only good harbor for large vessels in Samoa. The American government has made no preparations for independence in Eastern Samoa; eventually the Samoans there may press for inclusion with Western Samoa—a move which because of Pago Pago's commercial importance, might have a sound economic basis.

Combining certain island groups belonging to the same governing power into a federation is a future possibility, particularly among such groups as the British-controlled Gilbert, Ellice, Fiji, and Solomon Islands. Already a move has been made toward cooperation on the economic and social levels by the creation of a South Pacific Commission, comprising Britain, France, the Netherlands, Australia, New Zealand, and the United States, whose function is to provide a regional basis for the betterment of economic, educational, and health conditions in the islands south of the equator and the Gilbert Islands to the north.

One potential area of conflict is the Fiji Islands, whose population of 388,000 includes 162,000 Fijians and 191,000 Indians. The latter are descendants of indentured laborers brought in between 1879 and 1916 to work on the sugar plantations. The Indians were found to work considerably harder than the Fijians and ultimately came to produce practically the entire sugar crop, the major export commodity of the islands. The Fijians still own most of the arable land, leasing parcels of it to the Indians. In recent years the Indians have been agitating for the right to own land, or to lease it under long-term agreements. They resent the easygoing ways of the Fijians, who are protected by a semiautonomous government department which has jurisdiction over the Fijian population, as well as by considerable economic aid from the British. The Indians, who make up a bare majority of the population, desire economic and political advancement. The Fijians, on the other hand, have little interest in independence, preferring instead that conditions remain as they are. With these complex conditions the Fijis face what may in time become a difficult political future.

It is, of course, impossible to maintain static political conditions indefinitely, even among the scattered peoples of the Pacific. Any isolation which these people possessed in past decades has been shattered by the increase in world-wide communications, the impact of World War II, and postwar efforts for military security. Increased demands for economic and political advancement cannot be ignored, particularly in the light of possible Communist influence among discontented peoples of this strategic non-Communist area. Countries controlling dependent areas in the Pacific will be forced to balance the economic limitations of these regions against the political ambitions of the indigenous peoples, for any land area, no matter how insignificant it may seem, may have strategic importance in this ocean basin.[4]

The Trust Territories of the United States. Since World War II the United States has been faced with the problem of the political and economic future of the islands of the north Pacific which were ceded by Japan and turned over as trusteeship territories to the United Nations. The islands include the Carolines and Marshalls, and all of the Marianas except Guam, which belonged to the United States prior to the war. They spread over 3 million square miles of ocean and measure 4,000 miles from east to west. There are over 2,000 islands and islets, 64 of which are inhabited. The total area is 687 square miles, and the population in 1960 was 75,000. The population increase amounts to close to 4 per cent per year.

The trust islands have generally had little economic advancement since 1945; in fact the average standard of living is probably lower than it was under the Japanese when copra prices were higher. In an effort to avoid "exploitation" of the natives the United States has prohibited private foreign investment, including investment by United States citizens, thus keeping down development of new industries. Fishing, handicrafts, and copra are the economic mainstays of the islands; the United States government pro-

---

[4] The Cook Islands, a group of 15 small islands, hundreds of miles apart, with a population of about 16,000, will receive internal self-rule from New Zealand by 1966. Ultimately, they will become independent or united with nearby islands in a self-governing "Federation of Polynesia."

vides an annual subsidy of approximately $6 million—an extremely small sum, considering the volume of foreign aid sent to other parts of the world. In the spring of 1962 there were reports that the government would open the area to carefully selected American investment, one of the first being a commercial fishery and freezing plant operation.

The trust territories are under the jurisdiction of the United States Department of the Interior, except for the northern Marianas (with the exception of the island of Rota), which are administered by the Department of the Navy. This division of authority has been sharply criticized by the United Nations Trusteeship Council. Although many observers are of the opinion that the trust territory should be treated as a single unit, there are centrifugal forces not only of distance, but also of language (there are nine major indigenous languages) and of island "parochialism." Herold Wiens has written,

> Island loyalties have a restricted range which complicates the task of building an administration staffed by Micronesians and greatly limits the rate of progress toward self-government beyond a local level. . . . What is not yet widely realized among the Micronesians is the necessity for pooled effort by all the islands if the Micronesians are to achieve a more viable economy and the goals that most of them would like to see accomplished for their various communities. On the other hand, it may be that some see as unrealistic the effort to accomplish such goals without the subsidization by the superior resources of a major power and prefer to remain subsidized wards of a trustee power.[5]

The United States government has done little to advance the people of the trust territory toward self-rule. It is felt that the Micronesians must first attain local self-government, after which self-government at higher levels may be achieved. In 1960 an American official testified before the United Nations that it would be five years before an elected territorial legislature could be set up and at least another five years before the territory could fully manage its own affairs. After this, complete independence might then be attained. But in view of events in several of the African territories it is difficult to imagine that the final decision on independence can be delayed until 1970. Since the status of the former Ruanda-Urundi has been settled, northeastern New Guinea and Nauru Island[6] will remain the only other United Nations trusteeship territories.

---

[5] *Pacific Island Bastions of the United States* (Princeton: D. Van Nostrand Company, 1962), pp. 108–9.

[6] The problem of Nauru Island is complicated by the fact that its phosphate deposits (almost the only resource) are facing exhaustion and its infertile soil can scarcely be cultivated. In 1961 the Australian government offered to take in the island's 2,500 inhabitants and resettle them, but political leaders there would prefer that some other Pacific island be turned over to them for settlement.

THE PHILIPPINES

As a young, democratic State at the edge of the turbulent east Asian area, the Philippine Islands have come to represent something of a proving ground for Western political, economic, and social philosophies in the Far East. In many respects the area is a transition zone between East and West in the Pacific. A majority of the Filipinos are descendants of early settlers who came to the islands from Asia; there are significant strains of Chinese and Japanese blood among the Philippine population, although the Malay racial strain predominates throughout the islands. On the other hand, the Philippines are the only preponderantly Christianized country in the Far East; over 80 per cent of the people are Roman Catholic, a predominantly Western religion. Despite economic and cultural ties with other parts of eastern Asia, the Philippines have not been strongly affected by the political forces which have swept across that area in recent decades. The country fought bitterly against Japanese proposals in the 1930's for the creation of an East Asia Co-Prosperity Sphere and was the only colonial area in World War II that throughout the enemy occupation continued unanimously to support the former colonial power. The government concluded a mutual assistance pact with the United States after World War II and took an active part in the defense of South Korea against Communist aggression. As a result, the future stability and progress of the country are of great importance to the contest of ideologies in this part of the world.

Physical Elements

The Republic of the Philippines consists of over 7,000 islands, of which the two major ones (Luzon and Mindanao) are each over 30,000 square miles in area, while nine others each encompass more than 1,000 square miles. The total area of the Philippines is approximately 115,600 square miles.

The strategic location of the Philippines exposes the country to the powerful political forces operating in the Far East. Two hundred and twenty miles to the north of Luzon is Taiwan, a key area in the struggle for the containment of Chinese communism. Approximately 300 miles to the northwest of Luzon is the Chinese mainland, where the new Communist experiment is under way. Vietnam lies to the west, Indonesia to the south, and Japan to the northeast—all of these areas within a thousand miles of the Philippines.

Although there is great diversity of surface configuration on the islands, thereby tending to isolate various groups from one another, the sea, as in Japan and Indonesia, acts as a unifying element. The principal lowland areas are on central Luzon and in parts of Mindanao. Rail and road facilities are not particularly well developed throughout most of the country, and population clusters are generally separated from one another by upland regions. The result has been a tendency for strong divisive forces to develop in various sectors of the country.

The Philippines are well supplied with natural resources, including iron ore, chromite, manganese, gold, and hydroelectric power potential, as well as small amounts of coal. In addition, there is timber and considerable agricultural land amounting to about one-quarter of the total area of the Philippines. The utilization of mineral and power resources, however, has not been extensive in the islands, and as a result the average per capita income has continued to be low.

Population

The total population of the Philippines is approximately 28 million. Most of the Filipinos are united religiously, although not linguistically. About 8 million persons can speak English, and some 300,000 still use Spanish. Among the rest of the population there are 87 native dialects all belonging to the Malay linguistic family, of which 8 are of major importance. In 1946 Tagalog was made the official language of the country, and its use is gradually growing.

The two major minority groups are the Chinese and the Moros. The largely urban pure Chinese number about 300,000, and like other overseas Chinese they maintain a closely knit unity among themselves. They represent a powerful minority in the State because of their widespread business and commercial interests. In addition to this group there are about 1 million Chinese mestizos. A second major minority group are the 300,000 Moros, inhabiting the southern areas, who have resisted attempts by government authorities—Spanish, American, and now native Filipino—to integrate them within the political and economic life of the country. Moslem in faith, they have contributed little to economic and political development in the Philippines, and only within the past few years, through education and resettlement programs, are they beginning to be assimilated.

The settlement pattern is a widely scattered one, with about 35 per cent of the people living on Luzon. Manila, with over a million and a quarter people, is by far the largest city. Quezon City, adjoining Manila on the northeast, has been the official capital since 1948, but most governmental activities are still carried on in Manila. The islands of Cebu, Mindanao, Panay, and Negros also have cities ranging from 40,000 to 100,000 in population, but none of these is a serious contender with Manila for power.

Economic Development

With their various resources, the Philippines possess the basis for a sound economic structure. Although parts of the State have high concentrations of people, the average population density is not great (in contrast with some other areas of eastern Asia), and there are opportunities to increase the production of both foodstuffs for domestic use and cash crops for export. Despite these advantages, however, the economic structure of the country is not yet strong. A small landowning group controls most of the agricultural areas, and much of the commerce and industry is in the hands of the Chinese. As is true in many other areas of changing political status, investments of outside capital (particularly American) were not heavy in the Philippines after the mid-1930's, and as a result the expansion of industries, mining, transportation facilities, and power installations was somewhat curtailed in the years preceding World War II.

About three-quarters of the foreign exchange is earned by the export of agricultural products, particularly copra, abaca, and sugar. Philippine agriculture is generally characterized by low yields per acre; as yet the country does not face the tremendous population pressures existing in China, Taiwan, and other areas. In 1955 the Philippine Congress passed a Land Reform Act designed to break up the large estates and carry out necessary agricultural reforms, but relatively little has been done to enforce the provisions of the law. With low-quality coal and no petroleum the Philippines are hampered in any major industrial build-up. Nevertheless, because of their agriculture, forestry, and fishing potentials and the economic development of the islands in the preindependence years, they are in a better economic position than most of their east Asian neighbors. The average per capita income was third highest in the east Asian area in 1961, surpassed only by Japan and Malaya.

Economic relations between the Philippines and the United States became a matter of concern at the time of Philippine independence, since continued economic instability in the new country might eventually have endangered its democratic form of government. The Philippine Trade Act of 1946 provided for the entry duty-free of Philippine products to the United States for a period of eight years after independence, to be followed by gradually increasing tariffs, until by 1974 the full duty is to be assessed on Philippine imports. In the same year the United States Congress appropriated $520 million for rehabilitation in the Philippines. As further aid to the new country's economy, the United States agreed in 1950 to provide an additional $250 million to be used for such purposes as hydroelectric power development and agrarian reform. If the American policy of assistance to the Philippines during their difficult period of adjustment to independence were applied to other newly created States, it could be of great importance in stabilizing governments based on popular representation.

Political Aspects

The establishment of a commonwealth status for the Philippines in 1936 has already been noted. The Japanese occupied the area at the end of 1941, and for three years the islands were under enemy occupation. After the country was liberated from the Japanese, the Philippines resumed their preparations for independence, and within ten months of Japan's final surrender to the Allies the United States terminated its political control. Although by this action the United States government fulfilled its pledge for a ten-year period of commonwealth status for the area, political and economic development among the Filipinos has been impossible during the war years. The economy of the country had been completely disrupted (total war damage was estimated at about $8 billion), and by mid-1946 the physical destruction and dislocation of production and exports had only begun to be repaired. Subsequently, the Philippines began its independence in the face of major difficulties.

Although no part of the Philippines attempted to secede from Manila's control after World War II, the government faced serious trouble from Communist-led guerrillas, the so-called Hukbalahaps, or Huks, who operated in the mountains of Luzon and on Mindoro Island to the south. Their acts of terrorism hindered economic revival and forced the government to spend a large portion of its revenue in conducting military actions against them. For a time the Huks virtually controlled a number of areas, some of them but a few miles from Manila. Originally the Hukbalahaps had been formed as a guerrilla force against the Japanese, but during the early postwar period they managed to win popular support, particularly among the landless peasants of Luzon, because of their propaganda against outdated laws of land ownership and the depressed level of the Philippine economy. In addition to military action against the Huks, the Philippine government carried out extensive resettlement programs among the landless, moving many thousands of farm families to unused land on the island of Mindanao. Eventually these measures, together with a strengthening of the Philippine economy, succeeded in virtually eliminating the Huk menace.

Since independence the Philippine government has had difficulties with political corruption and mismanagement—practices all too common in new democracies, yet ones which tend to be magnified in a country which is in a sense a "showcase" of democracy in eastern Asia. Such practices also have hindered the economic and social development of the area. Although the United States continues to maintain military bases in the Philippines under the terms of the 1947 ninety-nine-year arrangement, there are strong elements in the country favoring "neutralist" policies for the country. Like Japan and Taiwan, the Philippines form a part of the outer arc of non-Communist, Western-oriented countries facing the Communist mainland of Asia. Thus the ties of the Philippines are with the other countries of this arc, with southeast Asia, and across the Pacific with the United States.

Figure 111. Taiwan and the Offshore Islands.

© RMcN

TAIWAN

The island of Taiwan[7] is a major objective of the expanding power drive of Communist China. It symbolizes the unfulfilled task of extending Peking's control over all Chinese territory, and as such it also represents a rallying point for the opposition to Communist rule, both within and without China itself. Taiwan is also a base for United States air and naval power just off the Chinese coast: in this respect it constitutes a source of danger to the mainland, for the conflict of Chinese and American interests in the Far East has more than once since 1949 led to potentially explosive situations. Finally, Taiwan, like the Philippines, is something of a "showcase" in eastern Asia, inasmuch as a substantial increase in the standard of living there would suggest to other Asiatic peoples the advantages of a Western-oriented political and economic system.

Taiwan has an area of about 13,900 square miles and a population estimated at over 11 million, including over 1 million refugees from China. Over three-quarters of the island is mountainous, and the inaccessibility of some of the upland areas is pointed up by the fact that there are some 100,-000 aborigines who continue to live in an uncivilized state in the mountains. There is a wide variety of minerals, but none exists in large quantities.

---

[7] Since the end of World War II the name Taiwan has been used with increasing frequency, replacing Formosa, the European name also used quite often by the Japanese.

Power resources include a large hydroelectric potential, as well as some coal and a small amount of petroleum.

Taiwan, like southern China, has a moist, subtropical climate, except in the higher parts of the mountains. Approximately one-quarter of the land is arable, and most of this is intensively cultivated. The island has been important for the export of agricultural goods, particularly rice and sugar, as well as fruits, camphor, and tea. Since most of the arable land is already in agriculture, Taiwan faces a difficult future with respect to its food supply, if its population continues to increase. The island has the basis to expand its light industries, providing that foreign capital is made available. The United States since 1949 has advanced well over $1 billion to the area, and as a result there have been important developments in the economic and social structure. Nevertheless, Taiwan, as a separate political unit, has definite limitations to its economic development, while less than 100 miles away China possesses a large potential for expanding its economic strength.

The population of Taiwan is predominantly Chinese, since the island was under Chinese control from the late seventeenth century to 1895, when Japan acquired it. Taipei, in the northern part of the island, is the capital and leading city. Transportation routes through the settled western parts of Taiwan are well developed, and there is little basis for the growth of strong divisive forces there, except possibly between the indigenous Taiwanese population and the Chinese, most of whom came to the island after World War II and maintain political, economic, and military control there. The Japanese developed Taiwan into a major military base, guarding the Chinese coast and posing a threat to the Philippines. Later it became a key area amid the Cold War tensions in the Far East.

In June, 1950, at the time of the North Korean attack on South Korea, the President of the United States ordered the United States Seventh Fleet to the Taiwan Strait to protect the island against Communist invasion, and since that time Taiwan and the Pescadores, which are about 30 miles west of Taiwan in the Strait, have remained under United States protection. The Pescadores are a group of flat, windswept islands which lie 110 miles from Amoy on the Chinese mainland, and which have been fortified to serve as advance bases for the defense of Taiwan. With a population of over 80,000 crowded on less than 78 square miles of land, the islands must depend on Taiwan for over two-thirds of their food supply.

The existence of two Chinese governments, each one committed to the overthrow of the other, represents an extremely unstable political situation, for neither government has been willing to accept an indefinite continuation of the *status quo* in this area. The Nationalists have sought to win the loyalty of the overseas Chinese (including over 2 million in Hong Kong), of the local people on Taiwan, and of anti-Communist groups within China itself. Taiwan's principal hope of providing an alternative to communism would seem to depend on the creation of a truly democratic government (with an end to the abuse of civil liberties) and a sound economic program. Chiang Kai-shek's administration, however, has failed to win anything approaching universal support, because of its pre-1949 autocratic nature and the many holdovers in the present regime and because of the obvious impossibility, without strong American backing, of a Nationalist reconquest of the mainland.

> The essential question for all Chinese, mainland as well as overseas, whose illusions of the "New Democracy" have been shattered by the harsh realities of Communist rule, is whether Formosa holds any promise for the future of their race. It is already apparent that the determining factor will be, not the international legal status of Formosa and its Chinese Nationalist Government, but the opportunity available on the island for ordinary Chinese to express and realize their hopes. The first need of the Chinese today is for an acceptable ideal that offers a demonstrable alternative to their present inadequate experience.[8]

The Offshore Islands

In addition to Taiwan and the Pescadores, the Nationalists also retained control of some thirty-five smaller islands immediately off the China coast, stretching about 300 miles from the Amoy area north to the vicinity of Hangchow, south of Shanghai (Figure 111). Quemoy, guarding the entrance to the port of Amoy, is but five miles from the Chinese mainland and 120 miles from Taiwan, while Matsu, off Foochow, is 105 miles from Taiwan. The offshore islands have served the Nationalists as points of contact with loyalist groups on the mainland and as bases for local attacks on China proper. More important, perhaps, they represent areas under enemy control adjoining the coast of Mainland China.

In 1954 the Communists began heavy shelling of Quemoy Island; this was followed by the conclusion of a mutual security pact between the United States and the Nationalist government pledging American protection of Taiwan and the Pescadores. In 1955 the Nationalists abandoned the Yikian, Tachen, and Nanchi islands to the Communists, but continued to hold Quemoy and Matsu. That same year Congress authorized the President of the United States to use American armed forces "as he deems necessary for the specific purpose of securing and protecting Formosa and the Pescadores," as well as "related positions and territories now in friendly hands." This so-called Formosa Resolution does not mention Quemoy and

---

[8] Albert Ravenholt, "Formosa Today," *Foreign Affairs*, XXX (1952), 622–23. Copyright by the Council on Foreign Relations, Inc.

Matsu specifically, leaving to the discretion of the President whether an attack on these islands would constitute a sufficient threat to Taiwan and the Pescadores to justify the use of force in protecting the offshore islands. The Nationalist Chinese have considerable numbers of troops on the two islands, and the Taiwan Strait is patrolled by units of the American Seventh Fleet against a possible invasion from Communist China toward Formosa or the Pescadores. Thus American power (in cooperation with that of Nationalist China) extends to the very shores of Communist China.

AUSTRALIA

Australia is the world's only politically unified continent. The great distances separating it from Europe resulted in its late settlement by Europeans, and this isolation has contributed to the relatively stable political conditions which have existed there since the entire area became politically organized. With an average population density of only three persons per square mile, however, Australia stands as a tempting prize to the nearby densely crowded countries of southeastern and eastern Asia. The existence of this extremely pronounced population differential is a potential danger to the Australians. In 1942 the Japanese military drive southward was halted in the New Guinea mountains, about 300 miles from the Australian mainland, and in the Solomon Islands and Coral Sea to the northeast.

Physical Elements

The continent consists of three parts: the eastern highlands, the central lowlands, and the western plateau area. There is a narrow, well-watered coastal plain between the eastern highlands and the Pacific, and a coastal plain also lies between the western plateau and the Indian Ocean. The central lowland is a semiarid region, but along the northern coast of the continent there is heavy rainfall because of the monsoon (Figure 112). The western plateau, comprising about half the territory of Australia, is a dry, sparsely inhabited region, except in the northernmost portions and in the southwest, where there is seasonal rainfall around Perth.

Distance and the dry areas separating many of the population centers from one another have represented important centrifugal forces in Australia's development. Not until 1901 were the various early colonies brought together into a federation. Regional differences, particularly between the western and eastern population centers, have since that time continued to be significant.

Australia is well supplied with resources, including gold, coal, iron ore, lead, zinc, silver, and bauxite. Recent discoveries of petroleum reserves suggest that the country may soon become self-sufficient in this resource.

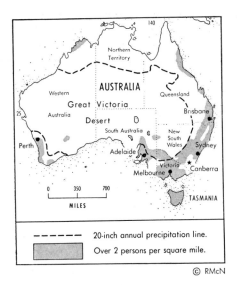

Figure 112. Australia: Precipitation and Population Patterns. Northern Australia, although receiving considerable precipitation, has few inhabitants because of the tropical conditions which exist there.

Although over 85 per cent of the island has an average annual rainfall of less than thirty inches, there is hydroelectric power potential in the eastern highlands, and Australia has a tremendous artesian basin in the northeast which can be used for watering stock. In addition, the Murray and other rivers have been tapped for irrigation. Only about 1 per cent of Australia is in cultivation, but this suffices to provide important agricultural exports.

Population

Australia's population of over 10½ million is overwhelmingly white and English-speaking. The principal minority are the 75,000 aborigines, who live in reserves in the northern part of the continent. The Australians have severely limited the immigration of Orientals, fearing a reduction of the general standard of living. Since the communization of China they have also been apprehensive about the political consequences of a large body of overseas Chinese in Australia. On the other hand, Australia has welcomed the immigration of Europeans, and since World War II over half a million of them (including many displaced persons) have been admitted. Some Australian officials feel that the State could easily accommodate 6 to 8 million more people (Europeans), thereby strengthening the white man's hold on the area. There are major obstacles to such large-scale immigration, however, including the high cost of travelling to Australia and settling there.

Over 60 per cent of Australia's population is concentrated in the two southeastern states of New South Wales and Victoria, in which are located, respectively, Sydney and Melbourne, the two cities of over a million people.

The rivalry between these two urban areas led to the establishment in 1927 of the Australian capital at Canberra in the eastern highlands about midway between them. Brisbane, Adelaide, Perth, and Hobart are the capitals and leading cities of the other four Australian states, and each is an important regional center. Brisbane, Adelaide, and Perth are connected with the two principal core areas and the capital by railroad. Hobart is located on the island of Tasmania, about 100 miles to the south of Australia, and is connected with the mainland by adequate steamship and airline service. Thus, because of the transportation facilities and the relative homogeneity of its population, Australia possesses a strong circulatory system throughout its large area.

Economy

Because of the country's great distance from western Europe and North America, the Australians have worked to develop their own industrial capacity. The State normally produces over 2 million tons of steel a year, as well as a wide variety of manufactured goods. One of the real drawbacks to future industrial expansion lies in the relatively small domestic market.

Australia is more important agriculturally than industrially. Wool is the most valuable export, normally accounting for nearly half the total value of exports. About two-thirds of the country's wheat crop is generally exported. Meats, sugar, and dairy products are also shipped to other countries. Like the United States, Canada, and Argentina, Australia occupies a significant place in the world economic structure as a major exporter of foods. It has been estimated that with more intensive utilization of arable land the continent could increase its production of agricultural goods considerably. A small consumer market has limited economic growth, however. About one-quarter of Australia's exports normally go to Britain; thus the Australians view with concern British moves to become associated with the Common Market, thereby raising British tariffs against the import of Australian goods.

Australia and the Pacific

Australian interests in the southwestern Pacific are represented by its territorial possessions in the area. Australia controls southeast New Guinea (Papua), across the Torres Strait from the Australian mainland, and administers northeast New Guinea (Territory of New Guinea) and the islands to the northeast and east[9] as a United Nations trusteeship territory (Figure 113). In view of the political developments which have taken place in West New Guinea, and with the achievement of independence for most of the

[9] The Bismarck Archipelago (including New Britain, New Ireland, and the Admiralty Islands) and the northernmost Solomon Islands.

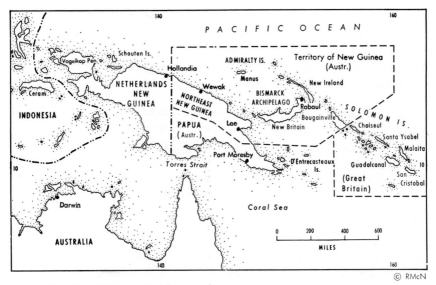

Figure 113. New Guinea and Adjacent Areas.

other trust territories, Australia is faced with problems of the political future of its territories, despite the fact that the great majority of the Papuans there have scarcely emerged from a Stone Age culture. In one area measuring about 10,000 square miles are close to 100,000 "uncontrolled" natives, not as yet visited by white men. Over fifty language groups exist in eastern New Guinea, and the Australians feel it would be folly to think of early independence for this area.

NEW ZEALAND

New Zealand is the farthest removed from Britain of any of the Commonwealth members, yet its ties with Britain are extremely close. Over half of its foreign trade (including 70 per cent of its exports) is normally with Britain, and its government has been a strong supporter of the Commonwealth system and of the bonds uniting New Zealand with the former mother country. One reason for this support is, of course, that there, as in Australia, the great majority of the population is of British origin, and the country must depend in part upon Britain for support in time of war in the Pacific. Perhaps more than any other Commonwealth member, New Zealand is greatly concerned over British moves toward joining the European Common Market.

Physical Elements

New Zealand consists of two large islands (North Island and South Island) as well as several smaller ones. The total area is just over 100,000 square miles. Much of the relief is mountainous, and the population is concentrated largely in the northern and southern lowlands of North Island and in the eastern coastal plain of South Island. The isolation of New Zealand is naturally an important centripetal force which tends to overcome the divisive factors of surface configuration and the existence of two main islands.

New Zealand has few minerals, but there is considerable hydroelectric power potential. Approximately two-thirds of the surface is estimated as suitable for agriculture or grazing. Yet, 60,000 to 65,000 square miles of agricultural land is not enough to permit extensive immigration, and, unlike Australia, New Zealand is not an area for large-scale white settlement.

Population

New Zealand's population totals about 2,400,000. The principal minority group comprises the approximately 140,000 Maoris, descendants of the inhabitants of the islands before the arrival of the Europeans. Relations between the Maoris and the Europeans have in the past been marked by conflict and bitterness. The Maoris resisted the expropriation of their lands for European settlement, and a five-year war was waged during the 1860's between the two groups. At the present time many Maoris continue to pursue their linguistic and cultural traditions, but others have become assimilated into the white man's way of life. The continued poverty of this ethnic group is one of New Zealand's major politico-economic problems.

About two-thirds of the people of New Zealand live on North Island. Auckland in the north central part of North Island is the largest city, followed by Christchurch in the eastern part of South Island. Wellington, the capital and third city, is located in the southern part of North Island, almost midway between the first two cities. Dunedin, the fourth city, is situated in the southern part of South Island. Thus New Zealand has four principal core areas, fairly evenly spaced. The separation of the settlement areas originally caused strong divisive forces, but in recent decades these have largely disappeared with improved means of transportation and communication.

Economy

New Zealand's economy is primarily agricultural; dairy products, meat, and wool form the major items of export. Through the use of refrigerator ships New Zealand is able to send dairy products and fresh meat to Britain and other European markets. New Zealand suffered heavily from the worldwide depression in the 1930's, largely because of its dependence on agricultural exports to western Europe. Unlike conditions in Australia, however, there has been no great effort made to diversify New Zealand's economy and make it less dependent upon world markets. There is some gold, silver, and coal, but because of the shortages of other industrial resources and the small population, the country has not undergone any extensive industrialization. The mild, moist climate which prevails throughout much of New Zealand and the soils which are particularly adaptable to pastures have resulted in the continued emphasis on grazing as a major aspect of the country's economic life. About 850 square miles of good agricultural land are held communally by the Maoris but are not being farmed. Efforts by the New Zealanders to buy the land are complicated by the forms of Maori ownership and by the strong attachment of these people to their land.

New Zealand and the Southern Pacific

The overseas territories of New Zealand consist of the Cook and Tokelau islands in the southern Pacific. None of these islands is of great commercial value. New Zealand also shares with Australia and Britain a trusteeship over the island of Nauru. Like Australia, New Zealand is concerned with the defense of the southwestern Pacific against possible attack from Asia; to this end it is joined in a military alliance with Australia and the United States.

BIBLIOGRAPHY

COULTER, JOHN WESLEY. *The Pacific Dependencies of the United States.* New York: The Macmillan Company, 1957.

A good regional study of the area.

FREEMAN, O. W. (ed.). *Geography of the Pacific.* New York: John Wiley & Sons, 1951.

A basic regional text, with much material on the development and present characteristics of the area's political patterns.

JACOBSON, HAROLD K. "Our 'Colonial' Problem in the Pacific," *Foreign Affairs,* XXXIX (1960), 56–67.

A careful review of the problem of the trust territories.

PELZER, KARL J. "Micronesia—a Changing Frontier," *World Politics,* II (1950), 251–67.

Examines the development of the area under the Japanese, and its role as a United States trust territory.

————. *Population and Land Utilization.* I.P.R. Inquiry Series, *Economic Survey of the Pacific Area,* Part I. New York: Institute of Pacific Relations, 1941.

General survey of economic conditions in the Pacific prior to World War II.

ROBINSON, K. W. "Sixty Years of Federation in Australia," *The Geographical Review,* LI (1961), 1–21.

Centrifugal and centripetal forces in Australia.

SPENCER, JOSEPH E. *Land and People in the Philippines.* Berkeley and Los Angeles: University of California Press, 1952.

A basic regional geography, with particular emphasis on rural problems.

THIAN-HOK, LI. "The China Impasse: a Formosan View," *Foreign Affairs,* XXXVI (1958), 437–49.

The China problem as viewed from Taiwan.

THOMPSON, WARREN S. *Population and Peace in the Pacific.* Chicago: University of Chicago Press, 1946.

A discussion of population problems in both the Pacific and eastern Asia in terms of resource potentials.

WARD, R. GERARD. "The Population of Fiji," *The Geographical Review,* XLIX (1959), 322–42.

Maps and tables of the population structure.

WEIGERT, HANS W. "Haushofer and the Pacific," *Foreign Affairs,* XX (1942), 732–42.

A review of Haushofer's ideas in the light of conditions in the Pacific at the beginning of World War II.

WIENS, HEROLD J. *Pacific Island Bastions of the United States.* Princeton: D. Van Nostrand Company, 1962.

A readable survey of the area.

22

THE CHANGING NATURE OF THE
WORLD POLITICAL PATTERN

● Political geography has been defined as the study of political regions as features of the earth's surface. At one scale of study these regions may be considered in terms of their internal functioning—of political phenomena such as boundaries, capitals, or administrative subdivisions, or of centrifugal and centripetal forces existing within the areas. At another scale they may be analyzed in terms of their external functioning with respect to other political regions. Ultimately, such external studies may lead to a survey of the over-all pattern of political units as they exist on a world basis.

The world political pattern is complex and constantly changing. One of the problems of political geography is how to view this global phenomenon in a meaningful way. First, one must acquire the necessary knowledge of the earth's surface as it actually exists. Second, this knowledge must be organized within the individual's mind so as to be useful for comprehension, evaluation, and decision-making. The individual, in other words, must be able to think not only in terms of the various political units as they exist alone or in combination with one another on the earth's surface, but in terms of their relationship to the whole. In considering the various views of the political world, Stephen Jones has written:

> Every thinking person has thought filters through which he channels the current of communication. One such filter is geographical. . . . Practical men hold global views, though they may not verbalize them, and in the light of their views they make important decisions. The whole direction of a nation's effort may be determined by the global thought filters of its leaders. A global

view is more than just a filing system for information. Necessarily it becomes a system of evaluation. As such it may also be a system of distortion.[1]

The world political pattern is, of course, the result of various conditions rather than a cause. It represents the sum total of the decisions which have been made throughout the world regarding the political organization of space. These decisions in turn come about as a consequence of the interplay of a great variety of forces. Three of these forces affecting contemporary political decisions on the national and international scale are noted here.

1. **The rapid but uneven growth of the world's population.** Between 1960 and 2000 the total population is expected to double. By the latter year two-thirds of the world's people will be in Asia, with China having 1.6 billion and India 1 billion, compared with 370 million for the Soviet Union and 280 million for the United States. Such changes will affect not only the per capita food supply but also the power positions of various areas. With its enormous population and limited resources China, for example, will have to face relatively "empty" areas adjacent to it, such as Burma, Thailand, and Australia, with potentials for the production of considerable surplus food beyond their own people's needs.

2. **Technological advances not only have altered methods of warfare, but also the utilization of resources and the circulation of people, goods, and ideas within and between countries.** If thermonuclear warfare becomes so potentially devastating that it in effect is abandoned as a means for decision-making, then other tactics will be developed, such as "limited" wars, or conquest of countries by subversion. New methods of resource utilization may provide more food and other necessities for the burgeoning population of the world, but they may also lead to rapid depletion of minerals and power fuels and to the misuse of soils, forests, water supplies, and other "renewable" resources. Finally, increased circulation implies increased political instability, as ties with traditionalism are gradually loosened. It also may result in greater proportions of a country's population becoming involved in decision-making processes. Much has been written of the "appeal to the masses"; certainly such "masses" must be taken into account far more than they were even a few decades ago in the adoption of national or international policies.

3. **The ever widening gap between rich and poor countries has strong political implications, particularly since the bulk of the world's population is in the poor countries.** Despite the efforts of the United States and of other "rich" countries to raise the economic levels of "underdeveloped" areas, growing population and (frequently) political instability in many of these areas, coupled with phenomenal rises in the wealth of the richer countries,

---

[1] "Views of the Political World," *The Geographical Review*, XLV (1955), 309–10.

have created a condition which becomes increasingly serious. The level of expectation of the people of poor countries (particularly those people in the urban areas) has risen considerably, due largely to increased circulation of people and ideas, yet many of these countries are actually poorer in terms of per capita wealth than they were at the end of World War II. As their political power grows—both in the United Nations and through individual bargaining with the Great Powers—these countries are moving into position to demand a greater share of the world's wealth, even though they lack the capital or natural resources to acquire such wealth directly. In all three situations cited here it is not unlikely that before long pressures may develop which require extremely radical moves on the part of the richer and more stable countries of the world.

It is against the background of such forces as these that the contemporary world political pattern must be viewed. This pattern has both a space and a time dimension. The space dimension is that of some two hundred national political units, both dependent and independent, spread over the land portions of the globe. Each exists in certain forms of relationship both with the physical and cultural environments within its own confines and with the political regions beyond its borders. Each is unique, yet each has a part to play in the long-range basic trends or processes affecting the world as a whole. Here the time dimension comes in. The world political pattern is never stable. Ideologies change, boundaries shift, empires are created or destroyed. While it is difficult to generalize on such trends, four basic ones were enumerated in the first chapter which might provide clues to an understanding of the time factor in the political pattern:

1. The break-up of empires and establishment of independent States.
2. The expansion of Communist control.
3. The break-up or union of States.
4. The expansion of territorial control into previously unclaimed areas.

These trends or processes are in a sense self-explanatory. Many of the changes which the world political pattern has undergone in recent years could be classified under one or another of the four headings. But, as in the case of the three "forces" listed earlier, we have no way of viewing the over-all pattern meaningfully in terms of its space and time dimensions; all we have are certain ingredients or characteristics of the pattern.

One means of viewing the world political pattern is to divide it into three ideological blocs—Communist, anti-Communist, and neutralist (or noncommitted)—and to examine conditions existing within and between these blocs. Such a division is to some extent an oversimplification of an extremely complex situation; nevertheless, when viewed against the background of the physical and cultural world, it provides at least a system for analysis of the political pattern.

The Communist bloc is a contiguous one, stretching across Eurasia and embracing the Soviet Union, the east European Communist States (including Yugoslavia), Mainland China, the Mongolian People's Republic, North Korea, and North Vietnam. The anti-Communist bloc unites Anglo-America with most of western Europe and includes also Greece, Turkey, Cyprus, Iran, Pakistan, Thailand, Malaya, Australia and New Zealand, Taiwan, the Philippines, and Japan, as well as the colonial possessions of the countries within this bloc. The neutralist bloc includes most of Africa and the Middle East, as well as southern and southeastern Asia. Latin America is difficult to categorize. All of the States except Cuba are aligned with the United States in the Rio Pact, a mutual defense treaty. Yet, except in Panama, Trinidad, and Cuba, the United States operates no military bases in the independent States of this area, and, again with few exceptions, the Latin American States have not been as strong in their reactions to the policies of the Communist bloc as have the members of what is referred to here as the anti-Communist bloc. At the time of this writing, however, the States of Latin America (excluding Cuba) to greater or lesser degrees still support the policy of resistance to expansion of Communist control, and thus should continue to be included within the anti-Communist bloc.

Several points should be noted about this three-way division. The first is that some countries are difficult to label. Are Israel and Ethiopia neutralist or anti-Communist? What of Laos, Nigeria, or Sweden? South Africa, although anti-Communist, closed Britain's naval base at Simonstown several years ago, implying that nationalism is more important to the area than anti-Communism. Countries may also shift blocs rapidly, as in the case of Iraq which, after its 1958 revolution, moved from the anti-Communist to the neutralist group, as did Cuba in 1960.[2] Ireland appears to be moving closer toward the anti-Communist group, Tunisia perhaps away from it. This tripartite division provides at least a yardstick (albeit a rough one) for examining the political world.

Some countries, because of their geographic location, appear "isolated" in terms of their outlooks and policies. In a world of increasing international groupings, such isolated States are becoming something of an anachronism. Israel, Cuba, and the Republic of South Africa are in a sense isolated, as are also Japan, South Korea, South Vietnam, Australia, Finland, and at times Albania. Since "isolation" in this sense is a relative term, the student of political geography might profit from an exercise in selecting and locating on a world map all of the isolated States which he feels exist at the particular time. He might then look for certain character-

---

[2] Cuba might now perhaps be labelled as within the Communist bloc, despite the continued presence of the American base at Guantánamo Bay. Quite a number of countries are obviously "borderline" cases, and any attempts to differentiate these blocs on a world map must to some extent be subjective in nature.

istics which all or most of these States have in common with one another, such as trade problems, tensions with their neighbors, or a sense of militant nationalism. As the new States of Africa "choose sides," as it were, in the ideological struggle, new cases of isolation may well develop.

THE COMMUNIST BLOC

The countries of the Communist bloc are linked together by ideology, although there are basic points of disagreement between Moscow and Peking about the interpretation of this ideology, so far as contemporary conditions are concerned. The smaller Communist countries are linked to the Soviet Union and China by the physical presence of Soviet or Chinese armies within their borders. Fear of attack by the anti-Communists is another centripetal force. Finally, together with ideology, is the belief by many people of the Communist bloc that they are riding the "wave of the future," and that communism will succeed in expanding beyond its own borders to engulf the non-Communist world as well.

Centrifugal forces within the Communist bloc are often difficult to assess. Certainly the uprisings in East Germany in 1953 and in Hungary and in Poland in 1956 were disruptive to Communist unity, as were the uprisings in Tibet in 1958. Tito's "revisionism" has been perhaps the greatest of all centrifugal forces in this bloc; this may in time prove less important than the differences between the U.S.S.R. and China. Despite cooperative efforts in the economic development of Sinkiang and the Mongolian People's Republic (see page 542), the Soviet Union has failed to send massive economic aid to China in its recent years of crisis. Nationalism is apparently a vital force, even within the Communist camp.

One point to note about this bloc is its record of territorial expansion. The second trend, noted on page 603, was expansion of Communist control, a process which has been much in evidence since 1939. The communization of eastern Europe was completed in 1948. Two years later Communist armies invaded South Korea, but were subsequently forced back. In 1954 Communist control in North Vietnam was recognized and was followed by Communist moves in Laos and South Vietnam. Certainly communism has profited from the division of States—notably Germany, Korea, and Vietnam—since portions of these became incorporated within the Communist bloc. Other countries have at times experienced strong pressures from the Communist bloc, among them Afghanistan, Iran, Iraq, Egypt, Guinea, Guatemala, and Cuba. None of these has become Communist-dominated in the sense of East Germany or Hungary, but in the dynamic political world of today communism stands ready to capitalize on discontent and disorganization—in British Guiana, Cyprus, Indonesia, Cuba, or other areas—with or without direct support from the Communist bloc countries.

It is against this possibility of communization that the anti-Communist bloc is organized.

THE ANTI-COMMUNIST BLOC

This bloc stretches nearly two-thirds of the way around the globe from the Sea of Japan eastward across two oceans to the iron curtain dividing Europe. It is largely a Northern Hemisphere phenomenon, with only Australia and New Zealand as militant Southern Hemisphere members. Much of South America also lies south of the equator, although as noted earlier most of the countries of this area tend to place higher priorities on other problems (such as those of economic advancement) than they do to the containment of communism. It is interesting to note that this bloc embraces two ocean basins, that of the north Pacific and of the north Atlantic, indicating the importance of sea and air links to this alliance.

There are three principal centripetal forces which have served to draw together the anti-Communist bloc: (1) fear of the Communist bloc; (2) the foreign aid and alliances of the United States; and (3) existing empire associations. Many governments fear the power potential and the basic objectives of the U.S.S.R. and China, a fear based both upon past Communist aggressions in eastern Europe and in Asia and upon repeated threats by responsible Communist leaders.

United States foreign aid through 1962 totalled nearly $98 billion. Although much of this aid was extended to States of the neutralist bloc, massive amounts were sent to western Europe, Greece, Turkey, South Korea, South Vietnam, and the Philippines. This aid, both military and economic in nature, has been an important force binding these countries to the United States. Militarily the United States is associated with forty-four other countries in various forms of mutual defense pacts, including the Rio Treaty, NATO, the Anzus Treaty (with Australia and New Zealand), SEATO, CENTO (including Turkey, Pakistan, and Iran), and bilateral treaties with Japan, South Korea, and Taiwan. In addition United States units are actively engaged in anti-Communist military operations in South Vietnam.

The centripetal force represented by empire associations is a rapidly dwindling one. The Western colonial empires are basically anti-Communist in nature; with their break-up has come a marked reduction in the extent of the anti-Communist world. Few of the States achieving independence since World War II have joined the anti-Communist bloc. The Philippines, Malaya, Pakistan, and Cyprus are notable exceptions.[3] Along with the break-up of empires has been the division of States, a third basic trend, which in general has been divisive or centrifugal in nature so far as the anti-

---

[3] South Korea and South Vietnam were, in a sense, forced into the anti-Communist camp. Jamaica and Trinidad will probably be included.

Communist bloc is concerned. India, Palestine, and the former French Indochina are the best examples, since in each case partitioning led to international disputes and a weakening of united action against the Communist bloc. Union of States—basically a centripetal force—has been very difficult to achieve, either in this or in the neutralist bloc, although in time some progress may be made either among island groups or among new States, particularly in Africa.

Within the anti-Communist bloc there have been various regional economic groupings, the most important of these being the European Common Market. The Common Market has served to strengthen one segment of the anti-Communist world, although at the same time it also serves as a powerful divisive force. In time, of course, the market may become the nucleus of a great North Atlantic economic bloc, including Britain, the United States, and Canada—a bloc far stronger economically than the Communist bloc. But if Britain and the United States become associated with the Common Market, what of the economic future of other Commonwealth members (particularly Australia and New Zealand) and of such countries as Japan, the Philippines, and Israel?

Cohesion in the anti-Communist world is considerably more difficult to maintain over a period of years than is that in the Communist bloc. Indeed, it may be claimed that a primary objective of Communist foreign policy (particularly in the case of the Soviet Union) is more to disrupt anti-Communist solidarity than it is simply to expand Communist control, as was assumed in the late 1940's and early 1950's. Ties other than those formed by the simple fear of Communist aggression must be developed to bind together the anti-Communist bloc—ties of economic cooperation, of common values and interests, and of common objectives in world development.

THE NEUTRALIST BLOC

This predominantly "Afro-Asian" bloc is composed largely of States which became independent since World War II. Egypt, Saudi Arabia, and Afghanistan have somewhat longer records of self-rule, but by and large the newer States of the world are included here—States which were formed from the empires of anti-Communist countries. Various forces hold these countries to their neutralist position: national pride, dislike of the former mother country; admiration for Communist successes in the Soviet Union (or for the Soviet Union itself); a genuine desire for world peace and with it an aversion to military power blocs.

Many of these countries experience serious problems of economic viability, of internal cohesion, and (in a number of cases) of territorial problems with their neighbors. Thus, to their national governments the specter of Communism is overshadowed by what appear to be more immediate dangers. Obviously the degree of neutrality varies, as from the "Western-oriented" neutralism of Lebanon, to the "anti-Westernism" of Indonesia.

Although within the neutralist bloc there have been efforts at regional groupings (such as the "Casablanca Group," the "Monrovia Group," the Arab League) these have met with relatively little success, and the countries are largely independent of one another in their actions. Various statesmen, such as Nehru, Nasser, Nkrumah, and Tito, have, on occasion, sought to become leaders of the neutralist bloc, but again there has been little success, since there are weaker centripetal forces existing there than in the other two blocs. One advantage to at least some of the neutralists has been the opportunity to receive foreign aid both from the United States and from the Soviet Union, as evidenced by India, Egypt, and Afghanistan.

Perhaps the greatest impact of the neutralist bloc has been felt in the United Nations, where the neutralists are frequently joined in their votes by many of the Latin American States. As the United Nations continues to expand its role as a decision-forming (and, frequently more important, as a decision-enforcing) body, the position of the neutralist bloc will also become increasingly significant. In terms of economic and military power the bloc is still weak and divided, without effective leadership, but these conditions could alter with time, thereby introducing a new and highly significant element into the world power complex.

It was pointed out at the beginning of this chapter that many of the boundaries between the three ideological blocs are ill defined and are periodically changing. The wall in Berlin is a sharp line between the Communists and anti-Communists, the Indian-Chinese border separates Communists from neutralists, while the Indian-Pakistan border has divided neutralists from anti-Communists. Such divisions may be complicated by latent territorial disputes. If Pakistan receives arms from the United States with which to defend itself from the Communists, what will the positions of India and Afghanistan be? If China presses India for border concessions, which country will Pakistan support? Many parts of the world have problems too complex to be viewed in simple black-and-white terms of Communism and anti-Communisn.

Throughout a study of the world political pattern runs the constant theme of international groupings, whether for economic, military, social, or other activities. Some groupings take place within the individual blocs as described here, others across ideological boundaries. The various agencies of the United Nations, the trans-Atlantic OECD (Organization for Economic Cooperation and Development), the Chicago Civil Air Convention—groups such as these point up the need for regional or world-wide cooperation in an era of greatly increased circulation and resource development. While political sovereignty may remain vested in well over a hundred individual governments, with increasing time more and more functions of these governments are being turned over to—or at least coordinated with—supranational organizations.

In an era of rapid change it is often difficult to reconcile traditional concepts of sovereignty with actual existing conditions. Where are today's empires? What roles are boundaries coming to play? What is left of the "free seas" or the "free skies"? Some of the features of nationalism itself are changing—or at least the conditions under which nationalism may operate are changing. Men still think in terms of a world of closed political units; the colors on the world political map may have changed as empires are broken up, but most of the political units are still shown, only now as independent States. But does a map show degrees of *de facto* independence of various States, the boundaries which exist only on paper, the forces tending to draw together or move apart the various regions or countries? Will the map show distribution of population and of resources and levels of economic development? More important, perhaps, will it show patterns of circulation—the movement of men, of goods, and of ideas—and the potential changes which may result from these movements?

What is needed is not simply a static political map of the world to be memorized, but rather what Stephen Jones has called a "composite view" of the world,[4] that is, the world as seen from the standpoint of strategy—the art of using power. Power is needed for the implementation of all political decisons, whether this power be in the form of force (or threat of force), of persuasion, or of some other compelling action. Movement is the essence of strategy; thus we must think not only of "man settling," that is, of population, culture, and the material base of the various parts of the world, but also of "man traveling"—of movement, and the various media through which such movement takes place. In other words, we have here again the space and time dimensions of the political world.

Such a composite view cannot be mapped; it is attainable only after the physical, economic, population, and political maps of the world have been mastered and the changing concepts of sovereignty and of national power are fully understood. "The pursuit of the global view is the geographer's intellectual adventure," Jones has written, but he offers no hope that a realistic and meaningful view can be easily acquired. "On one side is the flood of unfiltered information that rushes endlessly. On the other are the quicksands of oversimplification. To remain still is to be stung by the scholar's conscience."[5] The student of the political world faces a constant challenge of generalizations: to see the whole world as the sum of its many parts, and the parts in the context of the whole.

---

[4] Stephen Jones, "Global Strategic Views," *The Geographical Review*, XLV (1955), 492–509.
[5] *Ibid.*, p. 508.

BIBLIOGRAPHY

Davis, Kingsley. "The Political Impact of New Population Trends," *Foreign Affairs,* XXXVI (1958), 293–302.

Some thought-provoking ideas on population problems.

Laqueur, Walter Z. "The End of the Monolith: World Communism in 1962," *Foreign Affairs,* XL (1962), 360–74.

Centrifugal forces in the Communist bloc.

Spinelli, Alterio. "Atlantic Pact or European Unity," *Foreign Affairs,* XL (1962), 542–53.

Possible trends in future power alignments.

INDEX

(Italicized entries refer to maps.)

PRINTED IN U.S.A.